A Guide to the Sources of United States Military History
Supplement II

A Guide to the Sources of United States Military History: Supplement II

EDITED BY

ROBIN HIGHAM

AND

DONALD J. MROZEK

1986
ARCHON BOOKS

216659

© 1986 Robin Higham and Donald J. Mrozek.

All rights reserved
First published 1986 as an Archon Book,
an imprint of The Shoe String Press, Inc.,
Hamden, Connecticut 06514

Printed in the United States of America

The paper in this book meets the guidelines for
permanence and durability of the Committee on
Production Guidelines for Book Longevity of
the Council on Library Resources.

Library of Congress Cataloging-in-Publication Data
Main entry under title:

A Guide to the sources of United States military
    history. Supplement II.

    Includes bibliographies.
    1. United States—History, Military—Bibliography.
I. Higham, Robin D. S. II. Mrozek, Donald J.
III. Guide to the sources of United States military history.
Z1249.M5G83   1975   Suppl. 2   016.355'00973   85-18688
[E181]
ISBN 0-208-02072-1 (alk. paper)

CONTENTS

EDITORIAL NOTE

The continuing efforts of historians of the American military experience have justified supplements to the original 1975 edition of *A Guide to the Sources of United States Military History*. The outpouring of writings covered in *Supplement I* (1981) to the guide covered works printed from 1973 through 1978. The present volume concentrates on publications released between 1978 and 1983. The essays and material in this volume were received by 1984.

Although some subfields within American military history remain relatively unexploited, the field as a whole has attracted loyal and often prolific researchers. Several supplementary essays in this volume make clear the steady appearance of publications worthy of mention. In others, it is clear that coverage remains so selective as not yet to merit a fresh chapter; we suspect, however, that an influx of new researchers would be welcome. In all, the picture remains one of great activity and considerable promise, tempered with occasional disappointment that worthwhile paths remain untrod.

The majority of the chapters in *Supplement II* have been written by the authors who contributed to the 1981 volume. In several instances, however, new authors have joined the project, covering chapters on the colonial period, the American Revolution, science and technology in the twentieth century, the Department of Defense, and nuclear war and arms control. As the historians retiring from this bibliographic venture have our gratitude, so those joining it have our welcome. In addition, specific coverage of the Coast Guard and the U.S. Army Corps of Engineers has been added. Coverage of military law and of museums as historical resources is scheduled for resumption in 1990.

R. H. and D. M.

Kansas State University

AUTHORS

Dean C. Allard is the senior historian with the U.S. Naval Historical Center in Washington, D.C. He has been associated with that organization since 1956 and currently directs the center's Operational Archives, which maintains research collections on naval operations and strategy since the start of World War II. In addition, the Operational Archives is responsible for research, writing, and publication programs in the field of modern naval history.

Dr. Allard graduated from Dartmouth College in 1955 and holds advanced degrees from Georgetown University and George Washington University. His publications include *The United States Navy and the Vietnam Conflict* (coauthor); *Spencer Fullerton Baird and the U.S. Fish Commission: A Study in the History of American Science*; *U.S. Naval History Sources in the United States* (coeditor); "The Navy, 1941-1973" (in *A Guide to Sources of United States Military History*); "An Era of Transition, 1945-1953" (in *Peace and War: American Naval Policy*); "Anglo-American Naval Differences during World War I" (in *Military Affairs*); and other studies and articles relating to naval and maritime history.

He has served as vice president for the American Military Institute and the North American Society of Oceanic History, and as a director for the American Committee on the History of the Second World War. Dr. Allard also is an adjunct professor at George Washington University, where he currently teaches courses in the field of military history.

Daniel R. Beaver, professor of history at the University of Cincinnati, was educated at Heidelberg College and received his Ph.D. from Northwestern University. A former infantryman, he is the author of *Newton D. Baker* (1966) and of *Some Pathways in Twentieth Century History* (1969).

William R. Braisted, professor of history at the University of Texas at Austin, is a graduate of Stanford and received his Ph.D. from the University of Chicago. A military intelligence analyst for the U.S. Army in World War II, he has since been a Fulbright fellow in Japan. His publications include *The United States Navy in the Pacific, 1897-1909* (1958), and *The United States Navy in the Pacific, 1909-1922* (1971).

James O. Breeden is professor of history at Southern Methodist University. A graduate of the University of Virginia, he obtained his Ph.D. from Tulane University in 1967. He is the author of a number of articles and of *Joseph Jones, MD—Scientist of the Old South* (1974).

Lester H. Brune has been a professor of history at Bradley University since 1969. A graduate of the University of Rochester, he received his Ph.D. in 1959. He is the author of *Origins of American National Security Policy: Sea Power, Air*

Power, and Foreign Policy, 1900 to 1941; and of various articles on air power and war plans between the two wars.

Robert W. Coakley, Deputy Chief Historian, Center for Military History, Department of the Army, Washington, D.C., was graduated from William and Mary and received his Ph.D. from the University of Virginia. He was both a field artilleryman and a military historian in World War II. He is the coauthor of a number of official volumes, including two on global logistics and strategy in World War II, and is also, with Stetson Conn, responsible for the CMH study *The War of the American Revolution: Narrative, Chronology and Bibliography* (1975).

Benjamin Franklin Cooling III was both Assistant Director for Historical Services, U.S. Army Military History Institute, Carlisle Barracks, and member of the faculty, U.S. Army War College. In the Army Reserve, 1956–1963, he graduated from Rutgers University and received his Ph.D. from the University of Pennsylvania. He is past cocompiler of the annual dissertations in *Military Affairs*, past vice president and trustee of the American Military Institute, past Fellow of the Company of Military Historians, and currently Bibliography Committee Chairman for the U.S. Commission on Military History. His publications include *Benjamin Franklin Tracy: Father of the Modern American Fighting Navy (1973); Symbol, Sword, and Shield: Defending Washington during the Civil War* (1975); (editor) *War, Business, and American Society* (1977); (editor) *The New American State Papers: Military Affairs* (1979); and *Gray Steel and Blue Water Navy: Formative Years of America's Military-Industrial Complex, 1881–1917* (1979). He is now with the Office of Air Force History, USAF.

Graham A. Cosmas received his B.A. from Oberlin and his M.S. and Ph.D. from the University of Wisconsin. A member of Phi Beta Kappa, he was selected as a Woodrow Wilson Fellow (1960–1961) and a National Securities Group Fellow (1964–1965). In 1966, he received the Moncado Award of the American Military Institute. He is the author of *An Army for Empire: The United States Army in the Spanish-American War* (1971), and of articles in journals such as *Military Affairs* and the *Wisconsin Journal of History*. He is currently with the Medical History Branch, Histories Division, U.S. Army Center of Military History.

John Morgan Dederer is a graduate council fellow working toward a Ph.D. at the University of Alabama. He has an M.A. from the University of South Florida, and is the author of *Making Bricks Without Straw: Nathanael Greene's Southern Compaigns and Mao Tse-tung's Mobile War*. His studies focus primarily upon American military history.

Richard N. Ellis, professor of history at the University of New Mexico, received his Ph.D. from the University of Colorado in 1967. He has contributed a large number of articles to a variety of periodicals and is the author of *General Pope and the U.S. Indian Policy* (1970); *New Mexico, Past and Present* (1971); and *The Western American Indian: Case Studies in Tribal History* (1972).

Edward C. Ezell, a NASA contractor with the University of Houston, graduated from Butler University, had a Hagley Museum Fellowship, and received his Ph.D. from the Case Institute of Technology. He specializes in arms procurement and has contributed articles to a number of journals in the field. In 1975 he was awarded the AMI's Moncado Prize. He is now the curator of Military/Naval History at the Museum of American History, The Smithsonian, Washington, D.C.

Linda Neuman Ezell has been contributing to the National Aeronautics and Space Administration's historical publications program since 1974. With Edward C. Ezell, she coauthored histories of the Apollo-Soyuz Test Project (1978) and NASA's exploration of the planet Mars (1984). In 1982, she completed the second volume of the NASA Data Book Series "Programs and Projects, 1958-1968," which is being edited for publication. She is currently working on a third volume, which will continue the programs / projects story through 1979, and she is also on the editorial staff of *National Defense* magazine. She took her undergraduate degree at Sangamon State University, Springfield, Illinois, and has done graduate work at the University of Houston at Clear Lake and George Washington University.

Robert T. Finney is Research Professor Emeritus of Military History, Air University. He was a member of the Office of Air Force History, 1944-1958, contributing to the seven-volume *Army Air Forces in World War II* and writing a *History of the Air Corps Tactical School* and many background studies dealing with Air Force affairs, with special emphasis on air force doctrine. From 1959 until retirement in 1976, Mr. Finney was engaged in a program of writing and editing a wide variety of publications for use within Air University.

Dale E. Floyd, formerly with the Naval and Old Army Branch of the National Archives, is a historian with the U.S. Army Corps of Engineers. After study at Ohio University, he pursued graduate work at the University of Dayton. Among his publications is a *World Bibliography of Armed Land Conflict from Waterloo to World War I* (1979).

Robin Higham, professor of history at Kansas State University and editor of both *Military Affairs* and *Aerospace Historian,* has written a number of books and articles and has edited *A Guide to the Sources of British Military History* (1971) and *Bayonets in the Streets* (1969). He is the author of *Air Power: a Concise History* (1973), and of *The Compleat Academic* (1975). He served in the RAFVR, 1943-1947.

Christopher McKee is librarian and Rosenthal Professor of History at Grinnell College. Educated at the University of St. Thomas (Texas) and at the University of Michigan, he has authored *Edward Preble: A Naval Biography, 1761-1807* (1972) and has edited and coedited works for the *American Neptune*. Professor McKee is affiliated with the American Military Institute, the American Historical Association, the American Library Association, and the Organization of American Historians.

Grady McWhiney received his B.S. from Centenary College and his Ph.D. from Columbia. He was chairman of the department of history at the University of

Alabama and is the author of the prize-winning *Braxton Bragg and Confederate Defeat* (1969). Often a visiting professor, he is also the author of *Southerners and Other Americans* (1973); coeditor of *Robert E. Lee's Dispatches to Jefferson Davis* (1957) and of *To Mexico with Taylor and Scott* (1969); and editor of *Grant, Lee, Lincoln and the Radicals* (1964).

Richard H. Marcus, professor of history at the University of Wisconsin-Eau Claire, received his Ph.D. from the University of Colorado. His specialty is the military history of the American colonies, with an emphasis on the militias of the New England colonies. His work has appeared in *Military Affairs*, and in 1969 he recieved the AMI's Moncado Prize.

Donald J. Mrozek, professor of history at Kansas State University, received his undergraduate education at Georgetown University, and took his Ph.D. at Rutgers University. He has published articles on the American military in the twentieth century in such journals as *Military Affairs, The Business History Review*, and various state and regional historical magazines. He is also active in the study of American cultural history.

Timothy K. Nenninger works in the Military Archives Division of the National Archives in Washington, D.C. He took his Ph.D. at the University of Wisconsin, Madison, in 1971, and is the author of *The Leavenworth Schools and the Old Army* (1978). He has also authored articles on military topics that have appeared in a variety of books and journals.

Roger L. Nichols, professor of history at the University of Arizona, graduated from Wisconsin State College, LaCrosse, and received his Ph.D. from the University of Wisconsin. He is the author of *The American Indian: Past and Present* (1971); *The Missouri Expedition, 1818–1820* (1969); *General Henry Atkinson: A Western Military Career* (1965), and some fifty articles.

Truman R. Strobridge is with the Joint Chiefs of Staff (JCS), Historical Division. Previously, he served as the U.S. Coast Guard Historian (1970–1976) and as a historian with the U.S. Army Alaska, the U.S. Army Armament Materiel Readiness Command, the U.S. Marine Corps, the National Archives, and the unified JCS commands in Alaska, Europe, and Pacific. Educated at Michigan State University, University of the Americas, and American University, he has published articles in such scholarly and service journals as *American Neptune, Arizona and the West, Military Review*, and U.S. Naval Institute *Proceedings*, and has written two books— *Western Pacific Operations* (1971) and *Wrecks, Rescues & Investigations* (1978).

Warren A. Trest is senior historian with the USAF Historical Research Center, Maxwell AFB. A Korean War veteran, he joined the air force's historical program in 1962. Having served in a variety of posts, he headed two major command history programs, Air Training Command and U.S. Air Forces in Europe, and was the histories division chief with the Office of Air Force History in Washington, D.C. While a member of the CHECO (Contemporary Historical Examination of Combat Operations) team in Vietnam, 1966–1968, he authored or coauthored fifteen special studies on the employment of air power in Southeast Asia. He also helped establish and direct Project CORONA HARVEST activities within Headquarters Pacific Air Forces. This Air Staff-directed project produced a series of reports evaluating the air force's operations in the Southeast Asian war.

Russell F. Weigley, professor of history at Temple University, graduated from Albright College and received his Ph.D. from the University of Pennsylvania. Editor of *Pennsylvania History,* 1962–67, he is the author of *Quartermaster-General of the Union Army: A Biography of M. C. Meigs* (1959); *Towards an American Army: Military Thought from Washington to Marshall* (1962); *History of the United States Army* (1967); and *The American Way of War* (1973), a multiple book-club selection.

I

INTRODUCTION

Donald J. Mrozek and Robin Higham

Not surprisingly, a variety of factors help to account for the developments in U.S. military history during the past half decade. Among them has been the simple passage of time, which has permitted historians to begin to deal with the massive challenge of recording and assessing the American experience in the Southeast Asian wars cumulatively called "Vietnam." The official historical programs of the U.S. armed forces have begun to produce their standard volumes on Vietnam, having concentrated earlier on such useful but limited tasks as recording the memories and impressions of senior-level participants. Such personal views, rich as sources for future historical research and writing but often reflecting strong bias, are now being succeeded by more comprehensive assessments based on a wealth of documentary evidence. Although the battle against excessive classification of information remains a major one in which historians have had only partial success, the efforts in official history—Air Force search and rescue, the defoliation program, Marine unit operations, and similar matters—are helping to open the way. At the same time, it remains crucial to press for the fullest possible candor in these important resources and to avoid de facto censorship on grounds having little to do with security and much to do with bureaucratic convenience and, in some instances, a measure of political self-protection.

GENERAL HISTORIES. A significant new survey of the American military experience drawing on recent literature and interpretations is Allan R. Millett and Peter Maslowski, *For the Common Defense: A Military History of the United States of America* (82). Another recent survey is Warren W. Hassler, *With Shield and Sword* (79), which echoes the Uptonian charge of American military unpreparedness. First published in 1956, Walter Millis, *Arms and Men* (83), has been reissued and remains a useful mine of ideas about the American military experience. A highly useful set of essays recently published is *The Military in America*, edited by Peter Karsten (80), which provides reprints of outstanding essays on the American military from colonial times to the present.

GENERAL BIBLIOGRAPHIES AND RESEARCH GUIDES. A recent annotated bibliography focusing on the American military experience and including both wars and social and intellectual trends is Jack C. Lane, *America's Military Past: A Guide to Information Sources* (81). Also note the recent appearance of the *Dictionary of American Military Biography* edited by Roger J. Spiller and others (86). Numerous sources of potential use for military historians are included in the emerging series of guides to documents being issued by Chadwyck-Healey. With volumes on state archival materials and on academic and research libraries slated for publication in 1985, the publisher has already released guides on federal records in the National Archives, the presidential libraries, and the Smithsonian Institution Archives, as well as on manuscript holdings in the Library of Congress (84). Also, the sources of bibliographic guidance which have been of use for some time continue to lessen the military historian's burden. Notable are the indexes of significant military history periodicals such as *Military Affairs* and *Aerospace Historian*, and guides such as the *Air University Library Index of Military Periodicals*. These deal, of course, only with their own titles, in the case of the journals, or with works published since the institution itself was founded, as in the case of the Air University Library's *Index*. Nonetheless, these are worthy hard-copy sources. It is difficult to escape the conclusion, however, that in the near future, current bibliographic information related to military history topics will become increasingly available through data services using telephone lines and linked to computers. One would hope that works published before the advent of automated bibliographic retrieval systems will also be made accessible.

GOVERNMENTAL SOURCES. During recent years, several federal governmental sources have begun to issue timely and topical studies in military history and recent military problems. Among the units producing such works are the National Defense University. See, for example, Archie D. Barrett, *Reappraising Defense Organization: An Analysis Based on the Defense Organization Study of 1977–1980* (76), and Alfred H. Paddock, Jr., *U.S. Army Special Warfare: Its Origins* (85). The Air Force's Center for Aerospace Doctrine, Research, and Education (CADRE), located at Maxwell Air Force Base in Alabama, has begun to issue various topical studies aimed at illuminating current military issues by delving into their historical dimensions. Among the early studies appearing are Alan L. Gropman, *Airpower and the Airlift Evacuation of Kham Duc* (78) and Richard W. Stokes, Jr., *Preserving the Lambent Flame: Traditional Values and the USAF Officer Accession Program* (87). But all these are really topics explored in detail by our authors in the chapters which follow.

FOR FURTHER RESEARCH. Writing by civilian authors continues to be exceptionally heavy in matters with a clear relationship to contemporary issues. Thus the literature in nuclear arms and arms control and in the postwar history of the services and the Defense Department establishment seems nearly overwhelming. To some extent, as the most immediate pressures created in American society by the Vietnam War have subsided, there seems to have been something of a decline in efforts to trace the development of U.S. military institutions over the long term and to tie them to general development of civilian social and economic institutions. Even issues which have caused a popular stir, such as those related to new nuclear systems, have been debated to a significant degree in technical terms, although far from solely so. The culmination of this trend, which links fervent advocacy with the coolness of scientific knowledge and technique, may come in the now developing literature on "nuclear winter," a concept whose swift rise to prominence suggests the peculiar linkage in contemporary military issues between scientific principles and insights on the one hand and historical conceptualization on the other.

Although some of the recent writings concerning the Vietnam War have tended to envision it as having been essentially a battle between conventional forces and only trivially an insurgency, experiences of the United States and other countries since 1975 will probably affect the topics deemed worthy of study over the near future. The catastrophic disarray through successive levels of command and execution leading to the fiasco of "Desert One," the abortive U.S. effort to free Americans held hostage in Iran, has invited increasing attention, including book-length studies. The ongoing U.S. involvements in Central America similarly suggest that unconventional conflict is hardly an oddity. Some have begun to suggest that it may become, in fact, the new "standard" form of warfare in coming decades. Such recent, present, and near-future issues may spawn new interest in forerunner experiences in the American military past. Among these might be renewed interest in the U.S. operations against the "insurrectos" and the Moros in the Philippines at the end of the 1890s and in the first two decades of this century. Other such areas where the U.S. had experience with "irregular" warfare could conceivably be of interest. For purposes of the present volume, however, these remain "backburner" issues.

Similarly, it is possible—and it would be highly desirable as well—that military historians might capitalize on the imminent bicentennial of the U.S. Constitution to undertake some fundamental reexamination of the nature of the U.S. military system, of the military ethos in its peculiarly American manifestation, and of the interplay of checks-and-balances on the principle of military responsiveness. The increasingly volatile discussion over the War Powers Act of 1973 suggests that some such consideration of the constitutional underpinnings of the nation's military power would be timely. In addition, the legal confrontation between Gen. William Westmoreland and the CBS television network raises significant constitutional questions about the respective rights, responsibilities, and immunities of those in the media and those in various lines of government service.

Although the future of military history as a legitimate and even prominent branch within the general discipline seems assured, a number of peculiarities persist. The so-called new military history, emphasizing social analysis of the services and various institutional developments over traditional themes such as campaign histories, has had difficulty determining its own relevant, distinctive standards. For example, the study of the organization of the U.S. military system has tended to take for granted an inexorable movement toward a unified and centralized military system, one that may owe more to a Platonic ideal established in organizational theory than to the actual experience of American life. If the "new military history," now no longer so new in any case, made a real contribution in showing how matters other than operational and campaign history legitimately demanded a place in the field, perhaps a new contribution is needed to free researchers and readers from some of the constricting presuppositions that still have exceptional strength. The exact dimensions of such new approaches are yet to be determined, but they might include the development of new logistical services, new institutional balances among the armed forces, changing skills and backgrounds among service personnel, and the impact which new industries have had on US military policy and practice.

BOOKS

75. Abrahamson, James L. *The American Home Front*. Washington, D.C.: National Defense University Press, 1983.
76. Barrett, Archie D. *Reappraising Defense Organization: An Analysis Based on the Defense Organization Study of 1977–1980*. Washington, D.C.: National Defense University Press, 1983.
77. Browning, Robert S., III. *Two if by Sea: The Development of American Coastal Defense Policy*. Westport, Conn.: Greenwood Press, 1983.
78. Gropman, Alan L. *Airpower and the Airlift Evacuation of Kham Duc*. Maxwell Air Force Base, Ala.: Airpower Research Institute, 1979.
79. Hassler, Warren W. *With Shield and Sword: American Military Affairs, Colonial Times to Present*. Ames: Iowa State University Press, 1982.
80. Karsten, Peter, ed. *The Military in America: From the Colonial Era to the Present*. New York: Free Press, 1980.
81. Lane, Jack C. *America's Military Past: A Guide to Information Sources*. Detroit Ill: Gale Research Company, 1980.
82. Millett, Allan R., and Peter Maslowski. *For the Common Defense: A Military History of the United States of America*. New York: Free Press, 1984.
83. Millis, Walter. *Arms and Men, A Study of American Military History*. New Brunswick, N.J.: Rutgers University Press, 1981 [1956].
84. *National Inventory of Documentary Sources in the United States*. Teaneck, N.J.: Chadwyck-Healey, 1983–. Pt. I, *Federal Records, The National Archives, the Presidential Libraries and the Smithsonian Institutuion Archives*, 1983; Pt. II, *Manuscript Division, Library of Congress*, 1984.
85. Paddock, Alfred H., Jr. *U.S. Army Special Warfare: Its Origins*. Washington, D.C.: National Defense University Press, 1982.
86. Spiller, Roger J., et al., eds. *Dictionary of American Military Biography*. Westport, Conn.: Greenwood Press, 1984.
87. Stokes, Richard W., Jr., *Preserving the Lambent Flame: Traditional Values and the USAF Officer Accession Program*. Maxwell Air Force Base, Ala.: Air University Press, 1984.
88. Williams, T. Harry. *The History of American Wars from 1745 to 1918*. New York: Alfred A. Knopf, 1981.

II

EUROPEAN BACKGROUND OF AMERICAN

MILITARY AFFAIRS

Russell F. Weigley

The European background of American military affairs might well be interpreted as encompassing all of European military history, from the ancient world to the present, or at least to the time, about World War II, when the United States ceased to be primarily in military tutelage to Europe. Because being so completely inclusive would obviously require several volumes as large as this guide and its supplements, a principle of limited selection has had to be used. The works cited in the original chapter of the guide and in the first and now in this supplement, have been those concerning aspects of European military history that influenced the United States with reasonable directness, or those of European military thought that appear to have influenced similar American developments.

Sometimes the selectivity applied in the original volume of the guide has come to seem too narrow. The guide ought certainly to have included as part of the European background of American military history the basic works on the international law of war. While the circumstances of conflict against the North American Indians early began to erode European conceptions of the just war and to press Americans toward less limited war, American civil and military leaders were never altogether unmindful of the limits. At times they tried to observe the principles of European international law even in campaigns against the Indians; certainly such a leader as George Washington waged war against European adversaries within the international code of war as he understood it. To remedy at least in part the neglect shown earlier in this guide, translations of the crucial works of Hugo Grotius and Emmerich de Vattel, both of them known to and influential among Americans long before the American Revolution, are now listed (348, 365). So are two major works by modern authors on the history of the limitation of war, James T. Johnson (351) and Michael Walzer (366). The latter especially should be pondered by military historians. If war cannot be eliminated, a return to limitations and to the concept of the just war is an urgent need; military historians ought to grapple with the issues of the limitation of war throughout their work. Walzer offers an elegant dissection of the subject in light of the complexities of modern war.

The rise of the military profession has been a double-edged sword in its impact upon the limitation of war. On the one hand, professional officership has often helped remove war from the mere banditry into which it often descended in the Middle Ages. On the other hand, the claims of military officers to professional

5

status implied a claim to a special expertise, giving the officers increasing grounds for insisting on immunity from detailed civilian direction in the conduct of war. The resultant professional autonomy could open the way to growing circumvention of the code of war based on the plea of a military necessity that only the professional could comprehend. The relationship between military professionalism and the limitation of war requires further study before such generalizations can yield to greater precision. Meanwhile, the study of the rise of the military profession in Europe is important not only in this context but also in exploring the sources of American military professionalism, and several major new considerations of the origins of the profession of officership are listed here. There is a growing tendency among historians to push the origins back to an earlier time than the era of the Prussian reformers during the Napoleonic wars, the era until now usually identified with the birth of the profession.

A seed of professionalism might be found among the mercenary soldiers of Renaissance Italy, discussed by Michael Mallet (355). Certainly Maury D. Feld is persuasive in arguing that salient elements of modern military professionalism emerged among the soliders of the early Dutch Republic (344). J. V. Polisensky, with the collaboration of Frederick Snider, has presented us with an excellent introduction to early modern armies with emphasis on those of the Hapsburgs, which have been neglected in the English-speaking world (357); historians will want to reflect on the extent to which professionalism was emerging in the seventeenth-century Hapsburg forces. Surely the military intellectual Raimondo Montecuccoli represented an early appearance of more than embryonic professionalism in the Hapsburg forces; Thomas M. Barker has provided a review of his career and translated selections from his writings (339). In France, too, the outlines of military professionalism can be discerned in the prerevolutionary armies, as shown by John A. Lynn (353). Side by side with the French professional solider, to be sure, the gentleman-soldier lingered on to the time of the Revolution, as discussed by Samuel F. Scott (362). Another new work, by Jean-Paul Bertrand, surveys the host of changes wrought in the French army by the French Revolution in many areas besides the effects of the Revolution on the professssion of arms (341). The student might well follow up Bertrand's book by turning to Gunther E. Rothenberg's skillfull delineation of *The Art of Warfare in the Age of Napoleon* (360).

On Germany, traditionally but perhaps too exclusively regarded by military historians as the fountainhead of the military profession, Trevor N. Dupuy has contributed a new assessment of the roots and nature of the Prussian and German armies' professional excellence (343), part of the European background of American military affairs if only because of American efforts to emulate the Germans. Even a military historian must suspect that the study of military history may not have been quite so vital an ingredient in German military proficiency as Dupuy suggests, but his exploration of the German *Genius for War* should not be overlooked.

In one of the most important of the books appearing on this supplementary list, André Corvisier includes in his survey of *Armies and Societies in Europe, 1494-1789* (342) a consideration of the rise of a measure of professionalism among enlisted soldiers and particularly, of course, among noncommissioned officers, as well as among the holders of commissions. We have long perceived that a kind of professionalism may have emerged earlier among NCOs than among the commissioned officers for whom membership in the aristocracy was so often a major qualification; Corvisier presents detailed information about the extent to which this proposition was or was not true. His is a stimulating book, never descending into facile generalization.

Another major new work to be added to the guide is William H. McNeill's *The Pursuit of Power: Technology, Armed Force, and Society since A.D. 1000* (354). This book deals with the entire world, not only Europe, and with the relationships of military force to political power at large and to technology in detail. The sweep of its coverage is so wide that it is, perhaps necessarily, episodic and uneven, but it is a work that can fairly be called indispensable to the military historian who seeks to link a specialized field to its larger historical context.

McNeill's emphasis on technology leads him sometimes into the tactical realm, but less often than might be expected. There are, however, several other new works on tactics to be highly commended. Steven Ross, long respected as an authority on the tactics of the French Revolutionary period, has now surveyed eighteenth- and nineteenth-century weapons and tactics over the wider span 1740–1861 (359). An Italian admiral, Giuseppi Fioravanzo, has displayed an impressively comprehensive knowledge of the whole history of naval tactical thought (345).

Military historians have in recent years paid technology more and more of the attention due it, and weapons and tactics are their traditional staples. They have shamefully neglected logistics, which makes all the more remarkable Martin van Creveld's achievement in creating a first-rate summary and interpretation of the history of logistics in modern war, including some direct American experience in addition to the European background (364). Not least, van Creveld demonstrates that the history of logistics need by no means exhibit the dullness often presumed to characterize it.

In Great Britain, the military profession and, except at sea, technological and tactical innovation tended to develop less rapidly than on the European Continent, but British developments obviously have a special importance in the shaping of the American military tradition. Books by John Gillingham (346) and Anthony Goodman (347) on the Wars of the Roses, by Mark A. Kishlansky (352) and Peter Young and Wilfred Emberton (367) on seventeenth-century armies in Britain, and by Tony Hayter (350) on the eighteenth-century British army shed light mainly on the background of American political and cultural attitudes toward the military, rather than on the military profession, weapons, and tactics. Of these five books, Goodman's most emphasizes the military per se and the fighting of battles. Those areas in which Britain sometimes fell behind the Continent nevertheless exhibited British influence on America, and the student should not neglect the study of English weapons and warfare in the medieval and early modern periods by A.V.B. Norman and Don Pottinger (356), Peter E. Russell's article on early British interest and involvement in irregular war (361), and Gwyn Harries-Jenkins's article on the belated rise of British military professionalism (349).

BIBLIOGRAPHY

339. Barker, Thomas M. *The Military Intellectual and Battle: Raimondo Monte-*

cuccoli and the Thirty Years War. Albany: State University of New York Press, 1974.

340. Beeler, John H. "The State of the Art – Recent Scholarship in Late Medieval and Early Modern Military History." *Military Affairs, the Journal of Military History, including Theory and Technology* 47 (October 1983): 141–43.

341. Bertrand, Jean-Paul. *La Revolution armée: Les Soldat-citoyens et la Revolution française.* Paris: Robert Laffont, 1978.

342. Corvisier, André. *Armies and Societies in Europe, 1494–1789.* Tr. Abigail Siddall. Bloomington: Indiana University Press, 1979.

343. Dupuy, Trevor N. *A Genius for War: The German Army and General Staff, 1807–1945.* Englewood Cliffs, N.J.: Prentice-Hall, 1977.

344. Feld, Maury D. "Middle-Class Society and the Rise of Military Professionalism: The Dutch Army, 1589–1609." *Armed Forces and Society: An Interdisciplinary Journal* 1 (Summer 1975), 419–42.

345. Fioravanzo, Giuseppe. *A History of Naval Tactical Thought.* Translated by A. W. Holst. Annapolis Md.: Naval Institute Press, 1979.

346. Gillingham, John. *The Wars of the Roses: Peace and Conflict in Fifteenth Century England.* Baton Rouge: Louisiana State University Press, 1982.

347. Goodman, Anthony. *The Wars of the Roses: Military Activity and English Society, 1452–97.* London: Routledge & Kegan Paul, 1981.

348. Grotius, Hugo. *The Rights of War and Peace.* Translated by A. C. Campbell. New York: H. Walter Dunne, 1901.

349. Harries-Jenkins, Gwyn. "The Development of Professionalism in the Victorian Army." *Armed Forces and Society: An Interdisciplinary Journal,* 1 (Summer 1975): 472–89.

350. Hayter, Tony. *The Army and the Crown in Mid-Georgian England.* Totowa, N.J.: Rowman and Littlefield, 1978.

351. Johnson, James T. *Ideology, Reason, and the Limitation of War: Religious and Secular Concepts, 1200–1740.* Princeton, N.J.: Princeton University Press, 1975.

352. Kishlansky, Mark A. *The Rise of the New Model Army.* Cambridge, England: Cambridge University Press, 1979.

353. Lynn, John A. "The Growth of the French Army during the Seventeenth Century." *Armed Forces and Society: An Interdisciplinary Journal* 6 (Summer 1980): 568–85.

354. McNeill, William H. *The Pursuit of Power: Technology, Armed Force, and Society since* A.D. *1000.* Chicago: University of Chicago Press; London: Basil Blackwell Publisher, 1982.

355. Mallet, Michael. *Mercenaries and Their Masters: Warfare in Renaissance Italy.* Totowa, N.J.: Rowman and Littlefield, 1974.

356. Norman, A.V.B., and Don Pottinger. *English Weapons and Warfare, 449–1660.* Englewood Cliffs, N.J.: Prentice-Hall, 1979.

357. Polisensky, J. V., with the collaboration of Frederick Snider. *War and Societies in Europe, 1618–1648.* Cambridge, England: Cambridge University Press, 1978.

358. Roberts, Adam. "The British Armed Forces and Politics: A Historical Perspective." *Armed Forces and Society: An Interdisciplinary Journal* 3 (Summer 1977): 531–56.

359. Ross, Steven. *From Flintlock to Rifle: Infantry Tactics, 1740–1861*. Rutherford, N.J.: Fairleigh Dickinson University Press, 1979.
360. Rothenberg, Gunther E. *The Art of Warfare in the Age of Napoleon*. Bloomington: Indiana University Press, 1978.
361. Russell, Peter E. "Redcoats in the Wilderness: British Officers and Irregular Warfare in Europe and America, 1740 to 1760." *William and Mary Quarterly* 35 (October 1978), 629–52.
362. Scott, Samuel F. "Gentlemen-Soldiers at the Time of the French Revolution." *Military Affairs, the Journal of Military History, including Theory and Technology* 45 (October 1981): 105-8.
363. Showalter, Dennis E. *German Military History: A Critical Bibliography*. New York: Garland, 1983.
364. van Creveld, Martin. *Supplying War: Logistics from Wallenstein to Patton*. Cambridge, England: Cambridge University Press, 1977.
365. Vattel, Emmerich de. *The Law of Nations*. Tr. Charles G. Fenwick. Washington, D.C.: The Carnegie Institution, 1916.
366. Walzer, Michael. *Just and Unjust Wars: A Moral Argument with Historical Illustrations*. New York: Basic Books, 1977.
367. Young, Peter, and Wilfred Emberton. *The Cavalier Army: Its Organisation and Everyday Life*. London: Allen & Unwin, 1974.

Through inadvertence, a page of manuscript was omitted in the printing of Chapter II of the original volume of this guide, resulting in the disappearance of items 53 through 60 of the intended listings. This opportunity is taken to correct the omission.

53. Chasseloup-Laubat, François, comte de. *Correspondance de deux généraux, sur divers sujets*. Publiée par le citoyen T – –. Paris: Magimel, 1801.
54. Choumara, François Marie Théodore. *Mémoires sur la fortification; ou, Examen raisonné des propriétés et des défauts des fortifications existantes*. 2 vols. and atlas. Paris: Dumaine, 1847.
55. Clausewitz, Karl von. *La Campagne de 1799 en Italie et en Suisse*. Traduit de l'allemand par le Capitaine breveté A. Niessel, 2 vols. Paris: Librairie militaire R. Chapelot, 1906.
56. Clausewitz, Karl von. *On War*. Translated by Col. J. J. Graham. New and rev. ed., with introduction and notes by Col. F. N. Maude. 2d impression. 3 vols. London: K. Paul, Trench, Trübner, 1911. (This English translation first published from the 3rd German edition by K. Trübner, 1873. Not available at the time of the original publication of this *Guide* but now by far the best English translation is Karl von Clausewitz. *On War*, Ed. and tr. Michael Howard and Peter Paret. Introductory essays by Peter Paret, Michael Howard, and Bernard Brodie, with a commentary by Bernard Brodie. Princeton N.J.: Princeton University Press, 1976).
57. Clode, Charles M. *Military Forces of the Crown*. London: John Murray, 1869.
58. Clowes, William Laird. *The Royal Navy: A History: From the Earliest Times to the Present*. 7 vols. Boston: Little, Brown, 1897–1903.
59. Cockle, Maurice, J. D., ed. *A Bibliography of English Military Books up to 1642 and of Contemporary Foreign Works*. With an introductory note

by Charles Oman. London: Simpkin, Marshall, Hamilton, Kent & Co., 1900.

60. Cohorn, Menno, Baron de. *New Method of Fortification.* Translated from the Dutch by Thomas Savery. London: Midwinter, 1705.

III

COLONIAL FORCES, 1607–1776

Richard Marcus

Perhaps it was the bicentennial, perhaps a variety of factors, but the colonial era seems to be enjoying a renaissance involving a reexamination of virtually all aspects of the period, not least among them the military. In particular, the interaction between war, military institutions, and society as a whole continues to stimulate the interest of scholars.

Fred Anderson, in his dissertation, "War and the Bay Colony: Soldiers and Society in Massachusetts during the Seven Years' War, 1754–1763" (430) and two articles (428, 431), drew a remarkable picture of Massachusetts that emphasizes the impact of the war on the lives of common militiamen. Using a similar combination of quantitative and literary sources, plus elements from the archaeological record, the trials and triumphs of ordinary folk were also highlighted in Christopher Moore's *Louisbourg Portraits: Life in an Eighteenth Century Garrison Town* (490). Marcus Rediker's article "Under the Banner of King Death: The Social World of Anglo-American Pirates, 1716–1726" (498) provided a similar examination of a portion of the colonial underclass.

The European ideology which helped to define and create colonial military institutions and the subsequent evolution of these ideological elements under different environmental and social circumstances also drew considerable attention.

Stephen Saunders Webb in *The Governors General: The English Army and the Definition of the Empire* (521) continued to stress the importance of military motivation and the concomitant bureaucracy which implemented it as a key element in the growth of imperial expansion. In a more particularist vein, T. H. Breen's "The Covenanted Militia of Massachusetts Bay: English Background and New World Development" (439) examines the seventeenth-century English militia system and the military structure which the early Bay Colony created in reaction to it. The subsequent ideological evolution of New England militiamen from idealized Christian soldiers to more specialized Indian fighters is covered in John Ferling's "The New England Soldier: A Study in Changing Perceptions" (459). The same author extended his theoretical construct to provide an analysis of the early American way of war in *A Wilderness of Miseries: War and Warriors in Early America* (460).

As usual, studies of New England predominate, but Douglas Leach's 1966 survey of that area (159) has at long last been matched by W. Stitt Robinson's *The Southern Colonial Frontier, 1607–1763* (502). "'Not a Single Soldier in the Province': The Military Establishment of Georgia and the Coming of the American Revolution"

(477), a dissertation by James Johnson, examined military affairs in that colony; and William Shea in an article (507) and a book, *The Virginia Militia in the Seventeenth Century* (508), provided an extended analysis of early military affairs in the Old Dominion. The relationships among labor corvée, militia service, and class structure were examined by Marvin L. Kay and William S. Price, Jr., in "'To Ride the Wood Mare': Road Building and Militia Service in Colonial North Carolina, 1740–1775" (481).

Increased and welcome attention was given to the Spanish South and Southwest. In two articles, "La Defensa de la Luisiana Espanolo en sus Primeros Anos" (453) and "Protecting the 'Barrera': Spain's Defenses in Louisiana, 1763–1779" (454), Gilbert C. Din described the precariousness of the initial situation and the subsequent build-up of Spanish military power. "Lances and Leather Jackets: Presidial Forces in Spanish Alta California, 1769–1821" (485), by John Philip Langellier and Katherine Meyers Peterson, detailed the origins, duties, and rewards of soldiers in another part of the Spanish empire. The multiple problems faced by a specific commander are laid out in "Diary of Pedro Jose de la Fuente, Captain of the Presidio of El Paso del Norte, August–December, 1765" (452), translated and edited by James M. Daniel.

In military matters, as in other respects, the Middle Colonies did not receive the attention they deserved. But in a series of articles (422, 424, 425), of which "New York's Provincial Militia" (423) was the most extensive, Allan C. and Barbara A. Aimone examined different facets of the military structure of early New York. One aspect of the logistical problems inherent in that colony can be found in "Military Victualing in Colonial New York" (486), by Lawrence H. Leder.

The conflict between conscience and military need in Pennsylvania was delineated in Alan Tully's "King George's War and the Quakers: The Defense Crisis of 1732–1742 in Pennsylvania Politics" (514). An attempted solution to the problem, catalyzed by Benjamin Franklin's *Plain Truth*, was briefly described in "Pennsylvania Associators, 1747–1748" (470), by Albert W. Haarman and Eric I. Manders.

Native American military institutions continued to provide rich opportunities for research, with respect to both the pre-European style of war and the new circumstances produced by the impact of European rivalries, tactics, and technology upon ancient traditions. James Axtell and William C. Sturtevant in "The Unkindest Cut, or Who Invented Scalping" (433), and Daniel K. Richter in "War and Culture: The Iroquois Experience" (501), presented balanced reassessments of the "new wisdom" generated during the 1960s. In "The Neglected Side of American Indian War in the Northeast" (455), Leroy V. Eid found the Indian style of war to have been more structured and disciplined than was heretofore thought. Stephen H. Cutcliffe's "Colonial Indian Policy as a Measure of Rising Imperialism: New York and Pennsylvania, 1700–1755" (451) reviewed British attempts to impose structure of a different sort upon the tribes in order to advance imperial interests.

Eid in "The Ojibwa-Iroquois War: The War the Five Nations Did Not Win" (456), and Richard Aquilla in "Down the Warrior's Path: The Causes of the Southern Wars of the Iroquois" (432), analyzed the intricacies of intertribal warfare as practiced by the perennially interesting Iroquois Confederation.

"The 'Barbarous Massacre' Reconsidered: The Powhatan Uprising of 1622 and the Historians" (458), by J. Frederick Fausz, provided an historiographical analysis of that dangerous event in early Virginia history. Using primarily the techniques of literary criticism, Richard Slotkin and James K. Folsom studied accounts left by a variety of Puritan figures to describe an ideological crisis precipitated by the impact of a savage war in *So Dreadful a Judgment: Puritan Response to King Philip's War, 1676-1677* (509). More broadly based analytical tools and a collection of captivity accounts were employed by Alden T. Vaughan and Edward W. Clark in *Puritans among the Indians: Accounts of Captivity and Redemption, 1676-1724* (516) to examine the whole process of Indian-European acculturation.

Intercolonial wars still drew much interest, but effort tended to be centered on causation, planning, and results rather than on actual military operations. Little new work appeared concerning naval affairs, but Carl Eliot Swanson called attention to the impact of privateering during King George's War in his dissertation "Predators and Prizes: Privateering in the British Colonies during the War of 1739-1748" (511) and an associated article (512). His work emphasized the commercial disruption and manpower problems produced by that amateur style of war.

King George's War and the Canadian government's determined effort to restore a centerpiece of that war were reflected in two useful guides, *A Campaign of Amateurs: The Siege of Louisbourg, 1745*, by Raymond F. Baker (434), and *Fortress Louisbourg*, by John Fortier and F. J. Thorpe (462). Taken together with Moore's book, they furnished valuable insights on the problems associated with eighteenth-century warfare and siegecraft.

The strategic fluctuations inherent in the efforts of Great Britain to come to grips with its French enemy in the colonial arena are highlighted by James D. Alsop's "Samuel Vetch's 'Canada Survey D': The Formation of a Colonial Strategy, 1706-1710" (426), T. R. Clayton's "The Duke of New Castle, the Earl of Halifax, and the American Origins of the Seven Years' War" (477), and Steven G. Greiert's "The Board of Trade and the Defense of the Ohio Valley, 1748-1753" (467). All make the point that political factions, conflicting personalities, and war at a distance were not conducive to coherent long-term planning.

The traditional personalities and events still attracted scholarship. Robert Rogers was the subject of a recovered folksong, "A Ballad of Roger's Retreat, 1759," edited by T. D. Basset (439); a set of military principles, "Roger's Rangers: Recon Company 1757," paraphrased by John Cuneo and J. C. Scharfen (450); and an account of a 1758 operation, "The Battle of Snowshoes," provided by Gary Zaboly (525).

The tragedy associated with Edward Braddock's name was reexamined by Elaine G. Breslaw in "A Dismal Tragedy: Drs. Alexander and John Hamilton Comment on Braddock's Defeat" (441), an analysis of letters recently discovered in Scotland, and by "A British Officer's Journal of the Braddock Expedition — Et Cetera" (485), by Paul E. Kopperman and Michael J. Freiling.

Prolonged war and the removal of the French enemy had a powerful effect on the minds of American colonists and provided a key component in the creation of revolutionary sentiment. The argument was reassessed by Jack P. Greene in "The Seven Years' War and the American Revolution: The Causal Relationship Reconsidered" (466). William Penkak's *War, Politics and Revolution in Provincial Massachusetts* (493) and "Warfare and Political Change in Mid-Eighteenth-Century Massachusetts" (494) made the case that the hostility and political dislocation brought about by the war cleared the way for a new peoples' war.

As the title suggests, Lawrence Cress's "Radical Whiggery on the Role of the Military: Ideological Roots of the American Revolutionary Militia" (449) examines certain aspects of seventeenth century British thinking and the subsequent effect of these ideas on the American colonists. These same ideas approached from the perspective of legal history and focused on the issue of a standing army comprise the major emphases of John Philip Reid's *In Defiance of the Law: The Standing Army Controversy, the Two Constitutions, and the Coming of the American Revolution* (500). William E. White's "The Independent Companies of Virginia, 1774-1775" (522) gives some idea of the turmoil produced by the conjunction of these ideas with the evolutionary military formats adopted by the colonies as the revolution approached.

New primary sources include microfilm editions of the papers of Jeffrey Amherst (427) and sections from the British Colonial Office Records (465). The latter centers on the correspondence of the British commanders-in-chief during the French and Indian War and provides insights into high-level British strategic planning and the impact of such planning in the colonies.

Muster lists of colonial soldiers can be found in *Colonial Soldiers of the South, 1732-1774* (446) by Murtie June Clark, and "Genealogical Marylandia: Maryland Muster Rolls, 1757-1758" (489), by Mary K. Meyer. Philip Katcher provided deserter descriptions from the newspapers of Maryland, Virginia, and Pennsylvania (479, 480). The extraordinary uses to which such raw data was, and can be, put can be seen in "A People's Army: Provincial Military Service in Massachusetts during the Seven Years' War," by Fred Anderson (428), and "Migration in Colonial America: Evidence from the Militia Muster Rolls", by Georgia C. Villaflor and Kenneth L. Sokoloff (517). Indeed, such a blending of military history with the new social history may be among the most significant research trends for the future.

Additional directions for research would include studies of the militia focused on the officers and the segments of society from which they came. Little is known of the procedures through which the names of potential officers were selected, placed in nomination, or forwarded to the governors for appointment. Criteria for promotions are also a blank spot. In addition, there were frequently distinct differences between the officers who directed the militia machinery at home and those selected to command elements of the fighting expeditions. Analyses of these military office-holders would give historians another lens through which to examine colonial society.

Attempts to understand colonial military institutions, tactical and logistical systems, training regimes, and operational procedures would profit from studies which compare colony with colony as well as with military organizations developing in Euorpe, particularly in England. Peter E. Russell's "Redcoats in the Wilderness: British Officers and Irregular Warfare in Europe and America, 1740 to 1760" (504) gives some idea of the results which can be derived from such an approach, as does William G. Godfrey's biography of John Bradstreet (464). The companion volume to this series, *A Guide to the Sources of British Military History* (473), provides a useful introduction to some of the materials available for such work.

Colonial military technology also needs additional attention. M. Brown's nicely illustrated *Firearms in Colonial America: The Impact on History and Technology, 1492-1792* (442) points the way. Studies concentrating on naval technology are in particularly short supply and need bolstering. The same can be said for maritime military affairs as a whole.

Historical archaeology is another powerful tool which can provide a particularly useful perspective, not only on technological evolution but on other aspects of colonial military life as well. The Louisbourg example is perhaps the most notable, but articles such as those by the Aimones (425), Robert T. Bray (438), Jay Higginbotham (471), and Joseph L. Peyser (496) indicate a growing recognition of the valuable results which can be obtained from research into pre-revolutionary fortified places.

The five years 1978–1983 saw an extraordinary amount of attention devoted to the military aspects of colonial society. But, as is the way with history, the new work simply brought forth new questions and opened new paths for investigation.

BIBLIOGRAPHY

421. Abbot, W. W., Dorothy Twohig, et al., eds. *The Papers of George Washington. Colonial Series* I: 1748–August 1755, II: August 1755–April 1756. Charlottesville: University Press of Virginia, 1983.

422. Aimone, Alan C. and Barbara A. "New Netherland Defends Itself." *Military Collector and Historian* 32 (1980): 52–57.

423. _____. "New York's Provincial Militia." *Military Collector and Historian* 33 (1981): 52–68.

424. Aimone, Alan C., and Eric I. Manders. "A Note on New York's Independent Companies, 1775–1776." *New York History* 63 (1982): 56–73.

425. Aimone, Alan C. and Barbara A. "Pre-Revolutions Fortified Places of New York." *Periodical: Council on Abandoned Military Posts* (Fall and Winter 1977–1978), 3–32, 22–42.

426. Alsop, James D. "Samuel Vetch's 'Canada Survey D': The Formation of a Colonial Strategy, 1706–1710." *Acadiensis* 12 (1982): 39–58.

427. "The Papers and Correspondence of Sir Jeffrey, 1st Baron Amherst (1717–1797) from the Amherst MSS. in the Kent Archives Office." Microfilm. Sussex: Harvester Microform, 1983.

428. Anderson, Fred. "A People's Army: Provincial Military Service in Massachusetts during the Seven Years' War." *William and Mary Quarterly* 40 (October 1983): 499–527.

429. _____. *Soldiers of the Covenant.* Chapel Hill: University of North Carolina Press, 1984.

430. _____. "War and the Bay Colony: Soldiers and Society in Massachusetts during the Seven Years' War, 1754–1763." Ph.D. diss., Harvard University, 1981.

431. _____. "Why Did Colonial New Englanders Make Bad Soldiers? Contractual Principles and Military Conduct during the Seven Years' War." *William and Mary Quarterly* 38 (1981): 395–417.

432. Aquilla, Richard. "Down the Warrior's Path: The Causes of the Southern Wars of the Iroquois." *American Indian Quarterly* 4 (1978): 211–22.

433. Axtell, James, and William C. Sturtevant. "The Unkindest Cut, or Who Invented Scalping." *William and Mary Quarterly* 37 (1980): 451–72.

434. Baker, Raymond F. *A Campaign of Amateurs: The Siege of Louisbourg, 1745.* Ottawa: Indian and Northern Affairs, National Historical Parks and Sites Branch, 1978.

435. Basset, T. D. Seymour, ed. "A Ballad of Rogers' Retreat, 1759." *Vermont History* 46 (1978): 21–23.

436. Brand, Irene B. "Dunmore's War." *West Virginia History* 40 (1978): 28–46.

437. Brasseaux, Carl A., and Michael J. Leblanc. "France-Indian Diplomacy in the Mississippi Valley 1754–1763: Prelude to Pontiac's Uprising?" *Journal de la Société Américainistes* 68 (1982): 59–71.

438. Bray, Robert T. "Bourgmond's Fort d'Orleans and the Missouri Indians." *Missouri Historical Review* 75 (1980): 1–32.

439. Breen, T. H. "The Covenanted Militia of Massachusetts Bay: English Background and New World Developments." *Puritans and Adventurers*. New York: Oxford University Press, 1980, 25–45.

440. _____. "War, Taxes, and Political Brokers: The Ordeal of Massachusetts Bay, 1675–1692." *Puritans and Adventurers*. New York: Oxford University Press, 1980, 81–105.

441. Breslaw, Elaine G. "A Dismal Tragedy: Drs. Alexander and John Hamilton Comment on Braddock's Defeat." *Maryland Historical Magazine* 75 (1980): 118–44.

442. Brown, M. L. *Firearms in Colonial America: The Impact on History and Technology, 1492–1792*. Washington, D.C.: Smithsonian Institution Press, 1980.

443. Chandler, R. E. "O'Reilly and the Louisiana Militia." *Revue de Louisiane* 6 (1977): 63–68.

444. _____. "Fort St. Gabriel and Fort Bute: A Border Incident of 1768." *Revue de Louisiane* 8 (1979): 174–85.

445. Chaput, Donald. "The Picote de Belestre Family." *Louisiana History* 21 (1980): 67–76.

446. Clark, Murtie June. *Colonial Soldiers of the South, 1732–1774*. Baltimore, Genealogical Publishing Co., 1983.

447. Clayton, T. R. "The Duke of the New Castle, the Earl of Halifax, and the American Origins of the Seven Years' War." *Historical Journal* 24 (1981): 571–603.

448. "The Journal of Captain Samuel Cobb. May 21, 1758–October 29, 1758." *Bulletin of the Fort Ticonderoga Museum* (Summer 1981), 12–31.

449. Cress, Lawrence Delbert. "Radical Whiggery on the Role of the Military: Ideological Roots of the American Revolutionary Militia." *Journal of the History of Ideas* 40 (1979): 43–60.

450. Cuneo, John R., and J. C. Scharfen. "Rogers' Rangers: Recon Company 1757." *Marine Corps Gazette* 45 (1961): 36–41.

451. Cutcliffe, Stephen H. "Colonial Indian Policy as a Measure of Rising Imperialism: New York and Pennsylvania, 1700–1755." *Western Pennsylvania History Magazine* 64 (1981): 237–68.

452. Daniel, James M., tr. and ed. "Diary of Pedro Jose de la Fuente, Captain of the Presidio of El Paso del Norte, August–December, 1765." *South Western Historical Quarterly* 83 (1980): 259–78.

453. Din, Gilbert C. "La Defensa de la Luisiana Espanolo en sus Primeros Anos." *Revista de Historia Militar* 22 (1978): 151–71.

454. _____. "Protecting the 'Barrera': Spain's Defenses in Louisiana, 1763–1779." *Louisiana History* 19 (1978): 183–211.

455. Eid, Leroy V. "The Neglected Side of American Indian War in the Northeast." *Military Review* 61 (1981): 9-21.
456. _____. "The Ojibwa-Iroquois War: The War the Five Nations Did Not Win." *Ethno-history* 26 (1979): 297-324.
457. Ekberg, Carl J. "Terisse de Ternan: Epistoler and Soldier." *Louisiana History* 23 (1982): 400-408.
458. Fausz, J. Frederick. "The 'Barbarous Massacre' Reconsiderd: The Powhatan Uprising of 1622 and the Historians." *Explorations in Ethnic Studies* 1 (1978): 16-36.
459. Ferling, John E. "The New England Soldier: A Study in Changing Perceptions." *American Quarterly* 33 (1981): 26-45.
460. _____. *A Wilderness of Miseries: War and Warriors in Early America.* Westport, Conn.: Greenwood Press, 1980.
461. Foret, Michael J. "The Failure of Administration: The Chickasaw Campaign of 1739-1740." *Louisiana Review* 11 (1982): 49-60.
462. Fortier, John, and F. J. Thorpe. *Fortress of Louisbourg.* Toronto: Oxford University Press, 1979.
463. Geiger, Gregory J. "Journals of Asa Clapp: A Ranger Adventure." *French and Indian War* (Summer 1982), 29-35. Pt. 2 (Fall 1982), 27-33.
464. Godfrey, William G. *Pursuit of Profit and Preferment in Colonial North America: John Bradstreet's Quest.* Atlantic Highlands, N.J.: Humanities Press, 1982.
465. *Great Britain, Colonial Office.* "The French and Indian War." Microfilm, 8 reels. Washington, D.C.: University Publications of America, 1983.
466. Greene, Jack P. "The Seven Years' War and the American Revolution: The Causal Relationship Reconsidered." *Journal of Imperial and Commonwealth History* 8 (1980): 85-105.
467. Greiert, Steven G. "The Board of Trade and the Defense of the Ohio Valley, 1748-1753." *Western Pennsylvania Historical Magazine* 64 (1981): 1-32.
468. Gwyn, Julian. "The Impact of British Military Spending on the Colonial American Money Markets, 1760-1783." *History Papers* (1980), 77-99.
469. Haarman, Albert W. "American Uniforms During the French and Indian War, 1754-1763." *Military Collector and Historian* 32 (1980): 58-66.
470. Haarman, Albert W., and Eric I. Manders. "Pennsylvania Associators, 1747-1748." *Military Collector and Historian* 33 (1981): 100-102.
471. Higginbotham, Jay. *Old Mobile: Fort Louis de la Louisiane, 1702-1711.* Mobile, Ala.: Museum of the City of Mobile, 1977.
472. _____. "Origins of the French-Alabama Conflict, 1703-1704." *Alabama Review* 31 (April 1978): 121-36.
473. Higham, Robin, ed. *A Guide to the Sources of British Military History.* Berkeley: University of California Press, 1971.
474. Horowitz, David. *The First Frontier: The Indian Wars and America's Origins, 1607-1776.* New York: Simon & Schuster, 1979.
475. Hudson, J. P. "The Original Reconnaissance Map for the Battle of Quebec." *British Library Journal* 1 (1975): 22-24.
476. Hutchinson, Thomas. "The Boston Press Gang Riot of 1747." Peter Karsten, ed. *The Military in America: From the Colonial Era to the Present.* New York: Free Press, 1980, 15-17.

477. Johnson, James Michael. "'Not a Single Soldier in the Province': The Military Establishment of Georgia and the Coming of the American Revolution." Ph.D. diss., Duke University, 1980.

478. Jones, Kenneth R. "A 'Full and Particular Account' of the Assault on Charleston in 1706." *South Carolina Historical Magazine* 83 (January 1982): 1-11.

479. Katcher, Philip. "Military Notes and Deserter Descriptions from the *Maryland Gazette* and the *Virginia Gazette*, 1754-1760." *Military Collector and Historian* 33 (1981): 18-20.

480. _____. "Military Notes and Deserter Descriptions from the *Pennsylvania Gazette*, 1755-1758." *Military Collector and Historian* 32 (1980): 66-69.

481. Kay, Marvin L. Michael, and William S. Price, Jr. "'To Ride the Wood Mare': Road Building and Militia Service in Colonial North Carolina, 1740-1775." *North Carolina Historical Review* 57 (1980): 361-409.

482. Kopperman, Paul E. "An Assessment of the Cholmley's Batman and British Journals of Braddock's Campaign." *Western Pennsylvania Historical Magazine* 62 (1979): 197-220.

483. _____. "The British High Command and Soldiers' Wives in America, 1755-1782." *Journal of the Society of Army Historical Research* (Spring 1982), 14-34.

484. Kopperman, Paul E., and Michael J. Freiling. "A British Officer's Journal of the Braddock Expedition—Et Cetera." *Western Pennsylvania Historical Magazine* 64 (July 1981): 269-87.

485. Langellier, John Philip, and Katherine Meyers Peterson. "Lances and Leather Jackets: Presidial Forces in Spanish Alta California, 1769-1821." *Journal of the West* 20 (1981): 3-11.

486. Leder, Lawrence H. "Military Victualing in Colonial New York. *Business Enterprise in Early New York*, 16-54. Joseph R. Frese and Jacob Judd, eds. Tarrytown, N.Y.: Sleepy Hollow Press. 1979.

487. Lehmann, Susan Gibbs. "The Problems of Founding a Viable Colony: The Military in Early French Louisiana." *Proceedings of the French Colonial Historical Society* 6-7 (1980-1981): 27-35.

488. Martin, James Kirby, and Mark Edward Lender. *A Respectable Army: The Military Origins of the Republic, 1763-1789.* Arlington Heights, Ill.: Harlan Davidson, 1982.

489. Meyer, Mary K. "Genealogical Marylandia: Maryland Muster Rolls, 1757-1758." *Maryland History Magazine* 70 (1975): 104-9.

490. Moore, Christopher. *Louisbourg Portraits: Life in an Eighteenth Century Garrison Town.* Toronto: Macmillan, 1982.

491. Neal, Larry. "The Cost of Impressment during the Seven Years' War." *Mariner's Mirror* (February 1978), 45-46.

492. Niven, John, and George Athan Billias. *Connecticut Hero: Israel Putnam.* Hartford: American Revolution Bicentennial Committee of Connecticut, 1977.

493. Penkak, William. *War, Politics and Revolution in Provincial Massachusetts.* Boston: Northeastern University Press, 1981.

494. _____. "Warfare and Political Change in Mid-Eighteenth-Century Massachusetts." *Journal of Imperial and Commonwealth History* 8 (1980): 51-73.

495. "Life of David Perry." *Bulletin of Fort Ticonderoga Museum* (Summer 1981), 4–11.
496. Peyser, Jospeh L. "The Chickasaw War of 1736 and 1740: French Military Drawings and Plans Document of the Struggle for the Lower Mississippi." *Journal of Mississippi History* 44 (1982): 1–25.
497. _____. "The 1730 Fox Fort: A Recently Discovered Map Throws Light on its Size and Location." *Journal of the Illinois Historical Society* 73 (1980): 201–13.
498. Rediker, Marcus. "Under the Banner of King Death: The Social World of Anglo-American Pirates, 1716–1726." *William and Mary Quarterly* 38 (1981): 203–27.
499. Reid, Brian Holden. "A Survey of the Militia in 18th-Century America." *Army Quarterly and Defense Journal* 110 (1980): 48–55.
500. Reid, John Philip. *In Defiance of the Law: The Standing Army Controversy, the Two Constitutions, and the Coming of the American Revolution.* Chapel Hill: University of North Carolina Press, 1981.
501. Richter, Daniel K. "War and Culture: The Iroquois Experience." *William and Mary Quarterly* 40 (October 1983): 528–59.
502. Robinson, W. Stitt. *The Southern Colonial Frontier, 1607–1763.* Albuquerque: University of New Mexico Press, 1979.
503. Roosevelt, George E. "Das Blanie." *French and Indian War* (Fall 1982), 17–23.
504. Russell, Peter E. "Redcoats in the Wilderness: British Officers and Irregular Warfare in Europe and America, 1740 to 1760." *William and Mary Quarterly* 35 (October 1978): 629–52.
505. Saussy, George S. "Hector Vaughn and His Forty Marines: The British 6th Regiment of Marines (49th Foot), Charleston, S.C., 1744." *Military Collector and Historian* 32 (1980): 109–13.
506. Sells, Richard A. *Fort Burd: Redstone's Historic Frontier Fort.* Annadale, Va.: Charles Baptie Studies, 1981.
507. Shea, William L. "The First American Militia." *Military Affairs* 46 (1982): 15–18.
508. _____. *The Virginia Militia in the Seventeenth Century.* Baton Rouge: Louisiana State University Press, 1983.
509. Slotkin, Richard, and James K. Folsom, ed. *So Dreadful a Judgment: Puritan Responses to King Philip's War, 1676–1677.* Middletown, Conn.: Wesleyan University Press, 1978.
510. Smith, Thomas H. *Scoouwa: James Smith's Indian Captivity Narrative.* Columbus: Ohio Historical Society, 1978.
511. Swanson, Carl Eliot. "Predators and Prizes: Privateering in the British Colonies during the War of 1739–1748." Ph.D. diss. University of Western Ontario, 1979.
512. _____. "The Profitability of Privateering: Reflections on British Colonial Privateers during the War of 1739–1748." *American Neptune* 42 (1982): 36–56.
513. Thomas, Peter D. G. "New Light on the Commons Debate of 1763 on the American Army." *William and Mary Quarterly* 38 (1981): 110–12.
514. Tully, Alan. "King George's War and the Quakers: The Defense Crisis of 1732–1742 in Pennsylvania Politics." *Journal of the Lancaster County*

Historical Society 82 (1978): 174–98.

515. Ulle, Robert F. "Pacifists, Paxton, and Politics: Colonial Pennsylvania, 1763–1768." *Pennsylvania Mennonite Heritage* 1 (1978): 18–21.

516. Vaughan, Alden T., and Edward W. Clark, eds. *Puritans among the Indians: Accounts of Captivity and Redemption, 1676–1724.* Cambridge, Mass.: Harvard University Press, 1981.

517. Villaflor, Georgia C., and Kenneth L. Sokoloff. "Migration in Colonial America: Evidence from the Militia Muster Rolls. *Social Science History* 6 (1982): 539–70.

518. _____. "The American Career of Henry Bouquet, 1755–1765." *Swiss American History Society Newsletter* 17 (1981): 13–38.

519. _____. "Rival Candidates for Brigadier General: Jean-Baptiste (John) Bradstreet versus Henry Bouquet." *French and Indian War* (Fall 1982), 39–46.

520. Washaski, Raymond A. "Interrogation of Michael La Chauvignerie, Jr.: A French Officer from Fort Machault." *French and Indian War* (Summer 1982), 24–28, 70.

521. Webb, Stephen Saunders. *The Governors General: The English Army and The Definition of the Empire.* Chapel Hill: University of North Carolina Press, 1981.

522. White, William E. "The Independent Companies of Virginia, 1774–1775." *Virginia Magazine of History and Biography* 86 (1978): 149–62.

523. Williams, Edward G. "A Survey of Bouquet's Road, 1764: Samuel Findley's Field Notes." *Western Pennsylvania Historical Magazine* 66 (April 1983): 129–68.

524. Worral, Arthur J. "Persecution, Politics and War: Roger Williams, Quakers and King Philip's War." *Quaker History* (Fall 1977), 73–86.

525. Zaboly, Gary. "The Battle on Snowshoes." *American History Illustrated* 14 (December 1979): 12–24.

IV

THE AMERICAN REVOLUTION

John Morgan Dederer

From the 1960s through the review of the tall ships in New York harbor, the bicentennial celebration spawned a wealth of military studies of the American Revolution. With so many fine works published, conceivably there was little need for further scholarly inquiry. Instead, the bicentennial introduced a breath of fresh air to the field, sparking a resurgence.

The bicentennial acted as a cathartic, providing historians who study military aspects of the Revolution with a chance to bring scholarly research into the mainstream of military history. These historians (John R. Alden, Don Higginbotham, Hugh F. Rankin, John W. Shy, and Russell F. Weigley, to name but a few) did not see military history as beginning and ending on a battlefield; they perceived, and rightly so, the military side of the Revolution as only one part of the entire Revolutionary experience. One could not study just the military without a firm grasp of the interaction of ideology, politics, and economics, and vice versa. Taking a page from Clausewitz, these scholars recognized that war did not occur in a vacuum, that the study of things military could not be separated from study of the period as a whole. This was especially true in the Revolutionary War, which was, in John Shy's fine words, "a political education conducted by military means." (504)

Another influence on recent military historiography was the Vietnam War. The role of America's military was reappraised, even back to the Revolution. Military spirit was seen by some as a post-World War II phenomenon, but, as John S. Ferling (426) pointed out, Americans long enjoyed a warrior tradition. A martial spirit was not infused suddenly in the "embattled farmers" on Lexington Green in April 1775 only to diffuse itself in 1783; though unprofessional, war and warfare had been thoroughly impressed on Americans from their colonial beginning. Efforts by historians to comprehend the anti-military sentiment that paralleled the bicentennial showed that if a society dictates what its military will be, as ours does, then that service was but a magnified reflection of that nation. By studying the microcosm of the military, historians discovered new ways to examine Revolutionary society. One obvious reason why was that the military maintained relatively excellent records.

Many works cited below reflected this new academic interest. Instead of "drums-and-trumpets" history, the new military history asked social questions: who actually fought the war; who was Whig or Tory and what were their socioeconomic backgrounds; how did the war affect blacks and women; and what was the war's impact on various locales? In short, rather than being a moribund field, the Revolutionary War has become a hotbed of fresh scholarly inquiry in many areas. For works that called for this new approach, see (466, 499, 500, 501, 666). Many journal articles cited below are seminal works illustrating new interpretations, but some were added to show the myriad journals from which a researcher can glean valuable material.

GENERAL AND SOCIAL. Social dynamics motivating people to wage war continued to arouse much study. The ideals people fought for often were compromised by methods actually employed in fighting the war, resulting in something of an ideological schizophrenia, especially among citizens of a democracy. Charles Royster, in *A Revolutionary People at War* (597), explored the American Revolutionary rebellion of a people who had deep, long-held beliefs against a standing army. During the war, George Washington wrote that he appreciated Americans' dislike of a peacetime standing army, but he could not understand their hatred of one in wartime. Royster found that the army became the center of Revolutionary spirit after the war's initial popularity waned. A critique of Royster's book can be found in Martin and Lender's *A Respectable Army* (531).

The Continental private left few written accounts, but Jeremiah Greenman's journal (367) was an exception. A Rhode Islander, Greenman served with Arnold at Quebec, was captured and repatriated, and fought with Washington's army until mustering out in 1782. The composition and background of Gen. William Small-wood's Maryland Regiment was explored by Edward C. Papenfuse and Gregory A. Stiverson (565). Their groundbreaking work developed portraits of Continental recruits heretofore unknown. Howard L. Applegate's unpublished work (339) described a Continental soldier's daily life.

Two major works cutting across the Revolutionary period were by Reginald C. Stuart (640) and Lawrence Delbert Cress (390). Stuart, a Canadian scholar, posited that force was a cultural instrument of national policy, and that Americans of the Revolutionary generation believed that national conflict was inevitable. Stuart's proto-Clausewitzian perspective melded with Cress's study to raise important questions about pre-Revolutionary ideology. Cress exhaustively detailed the standing army / militia debate. Steven J. Rosswurm's dissertation (596) examined the social standing of one unit. Both Richard Buel, Jr.'s (372), and Donald W. White's (670) respective studies of how war affected one state and a small village were fine examples of social-military history. Buel portrayed the socio-economic and political impact of the war on Connecticut, while White chronicled a colonial community caught up in atypical times. Ian R. Christie (385) looked at how Britain survived these troubled years.

Various symposia held honoring the bicentennial gave birth to several collections of essays. Among them was the Library of Congress meeting on leadership (514), especially Don Higginbotham's salient essay on military leadership. In *The Military in America* (487), Mark Edward Lender's "The Social Structure of the New Jersey Brigade: The Continental Line as an American Standing Army," was valuable, as was Larry R. Gerlach's edited collection (443), with articles by Michael Kammen and John W. Shy. Another fine essay was John R. Alden's article in *1776* (370). Horst Dippel's "The American Revolution and the Modern Concept of 'Revolution'" was but one of many comparative studies written (338); and Don Higginbotham's "The Debate Over National Military Institutions" and Piers

Mackesy's "The Redcoat Revived," both in *The American Revolution* (437), were noteworthy. Other collected essays on specific topics will be found below.

As with most studies of women, the role they played in Revolutionary America has long been neglected. The works cited were just the tip of an unexplored iceberg. Mary Beth Norton's *Liberty's Daughters* (556) revealed women's changing responsibilities as they assumed unfamiliar occupations running farms and shops while their husbands and sons were at war. Norton's article in James K. Martin and K. R. Stubas's collected essays (532) dealt with Loyalist women. How women coped with these new roles, with armies and brigands trampling through their communities, and with life during war was described in letters in *This Glorious Cause* (657). Some women elected not to stay at home; Walter H. Blumenthal (359) showed that, just as in the British army, most women who followed the troops were not slatterns but wives seeking to comfort their husbands. Linda Grant De Pauw looked at another group of women, albeit smaller, who did not wish to stay at home nor become camp followers; these women fought in combat (406).

Revolutionary War experiences of black Americans continued to be covered. A new work by Ellen Gibson Wilson (678) told what happened to Loyalist blacks who fled with the British in 1783 (many were relocated to Sierra Leone). Jason M. Guthrie's (454) and William C. Nell's (552) works should still be consulted.

Discipline, desertion, historiography, and veterans' groups received close scrutiny. Harsh by modern standards, Continental army discipline was examined in four works (355, 356, 534). James Howard Edmunson's dissertation showed that at least 25 percent of all American soldiers were AWOL at one time; most went home for harvests or when war moved into their communities, only to return when the crisis passed (415). Two articles (494, 615) illustrated changing interpretations and the care with which published primary sources must be used. Edmund S. Morgan's short book on Washington (540) showed that a fresh approach can still be taken to understanding the well-known commander-in-chief. Some military works read by Washington were documented by Oliver L. Spaulding, Jr. (631), while the postwar organization founded by Washington's officers, the Society of the Cincinnati, was the subject of Minor Myers, Jr. (547). A 1783 tract by South Carolinian Aedanus Burke was critical of the Society (497). Noteworthy on American POWs in the Revolution was Larry Bowman's *Captive Americans* (363). Theodore W. Egly, Jr., followed the First New York Regiment from Quebec to Yorktown (416).

BATTLES AND CAMPAIGNS. The centerpiece of American Revolutionary military study remained its battles and campaigns, yet the influence of bicentennial-era interpretations and social-military history were felt even in these accounts. The only new survey covering both origins and battles of the Revolution was Robert Middlekauf's *A Glorious Cause* (536), excellent on major engagements. Piers Mackesy's portrait of a world at war by 1778 was continued in R. Ernest Dupuy's *The American Revolution: A Global War* (411).

The war in the South received a great deal of attention. Henry Lumpkin (517) and John S. Pancake (563) covered the later years of the Southern campaigns; Lumpkin was more anecdotal, while Pancake was especially good on the battle of Guilford Courthouse. The best work on the pivotal battle of Moore's Creek Bridge was by Hugh F. Rankin (579), while the same author's article on Cowpens (578) remained valuable. Early clashes at Kettle and Brier creeks were described by Ashmore and Olmstead (340). The ethnic background of some Tarheels and their Loyalism was well explored by Duane Myers in *The Highland Scots of North Carolina* (546).

Several collections of essays on the South contained important interpretive articles. A 1976 West Point symposia saw several seminal papers delivered (467). These include Ira D. Gruber on British strategy; Russell F. Weigley on American strategy; John W. Shy's "American Society and Its War for Independence"; and Don Higginbotham's "The American Militia: A Traditional Institution with Revolutionary Responsibilities." The essays edited by Jeffrey J. Crow and Larry E. Tise (392) provided an equally valuable collection, with particularly significant articles by Shy and Clyde R. Ferguson. Shy cogently perceived Britain's Southern strategy as "Americanization" of the war, while Ferguson took a kinder view of Southern militia than contemporary generals. Expanding this theme in an essay in *The Revolutionary War in the South* (468), which superseded Robert C. Pugh's earlier work (577), Ferguson portrayed a militia that did more than augment Continentals on the battlefield; in the South, militia maintained order, patrolled against Indian and Tory raiders, and represented Revolutionary government in the backcountry. On the Indian threat, see (422); and on the turmoil in the South Carolina backcountry, see Robert Weir's essay in (474).

American generals in the South were long considered blunderers (Benjamin Lincoln) or lucky (Nathanael Greene), but John C. Cavanagh ascribed Lincoln's problems to incoherent political leadership (468), while Fletcher Pratt proclaimed Greene, "the Quaker Turenne" (574). Comparisons of American and modern Marxist-Leninist revolutionary military strategy showed that Americans such as Greene waged warfare ahead of their times. For more on this perspective, see Russell F. Weigley's *The Partisan War* (668), chapter II of Weigley's *The American Way of War* (667), and John Morgan Dederer's *Making Bricks without Straw* (403, 404). Papers delivered at a symposium held at the U.S. Air Force Academy are also of interest (651).

Greene's Carolina campaigns received much attention. Besides Lumpkin (517) and Pancake (563), see Michael Conrad's unpublished work (388). Conrad found Greene less than successful because he lost every battle he fought; Dederer (403, 404) took an opposing view. The letters of Charles O'Hara, Lord Cornwallis's second-in-command, portrayed a commander physically and mentally exhausted from chasing Greene (591). Militia general Andrew Pickens' life and war experiences were well described in Clyde R. Ferguson's unpublished dissertation (424), while Thomas E. Templin's biography of Henry "Light-Horse Harry" Lee, also published, was excellent on Lee's guerrilla actions (644). Loyalist partisan activities can be followed in David Fanning's memoirs (423). Other important works dealing with the Carolina campaigns include (444, 450, 506, 519, 520, 543, 606, 669).

The war, however, was not confined to the Carolinas. Works by Samuel Proctor (576), William S. Coker (387), and James A. Servies (614) dealt with the Revolution in Florida, while Martha C. Searcy covered the 1776–1778 campaigns in Florida and Georgia (611). Other Georgia action, including the battle for Savannah, can be found in (475, 482), with Spanish involvement seen in Lewis (512). Ernest Eller's collected essays spanned the seven major invasions of the Chesapeake Bay region—by Lord Dunmore 1775–1776; Sir William Howe, 1777; Generals Mathew and Collier, 1779; General Leslie, 1780; and Benedict Arnold,

General Phillips, and Lord Cornwallis in 1781 (417). St. George Tucker's eyewitness account of the siege of Yorktown (584) was an invaluable source. The Yorktown campaign, both land and sea, was chronicled in Landers (507). Hugh F. Rankin wrote a superb book on war in the Old Dominion (580), while other works on Virginia were helpful (607, 613, 662).

The Northern theater of war also received considerable attention. Always useful were the papers of the Maryland Line (342), especially rifleman Daniel McCurtin's account of the siege of Boston. Newspaperman William M. Dwyer (413) took another look at the Trenton-Princeton campaign, while Richard Ketchum's *The Winter Soldiers* (492) remained one of the better narratives of the war's first two years. The struggle in New Jersey for the hearts and minds of inhabitants had more than Whig-Loyalist overtones. As Adrian C. Leiby pointed out in the classic *Revolutionary War in the Hackensack Valley* (510), the Revolution gave free rein to existing prewar hatreds. In fact, only the bitter violence of 1780–1781 in South Carolina exceeded New Jersey's internecine warfare. Other New Jersey works included Dennis P. Ryan's helpful chronology (602), an exploration of how the Revolution affected one county (645), and William Stryker's five-volume compilation of extracts from contemporary newspapers (639).

The Benedict Arnold-Richard Montgomery Canadian campaign of 1775–1776 can be followed in Hatch (461), and in the journals collected and edited by novelist Kenneth Roberts (587) and Brown and Peckham (369). An interesting new look at Canadians who came south to fight with the Whigs was in Allan S. Everest (421). Britain's deferential postwar treatment of displaced Loyalists contrasted sharply with American neglect of her Canadian allies. A good local history on the importance of Lake Champlain as an invasion route was in (469), while Sir William Howe's explanation to Parliament on why he would rather have been in Philadelphia instead of Saratoga made for interesting reading (476, 539). A good overview of the 1777 campaigns can be found in John Pancake's *The Year of the Hangman* (564), which showed that Washington denuded his army to forward the troops who actually fought and won the battles at Saratoga. Other works related to the Philadelphia area campaigns were in (371, 435, 628, 650), while a good work on Burgoyne's surrendered "Convention Army" was in (515).

Training, raiding, and alliances were written about. Baron von Steuben's contributions to American arms was lauded in (384, 641), while Templin (644) aptly described Henry Lee's raid on Paulus Hook as "audacious." Problems in the Franco-American alliance were explained in Dearden (402), but Lee Kennett, *The French Forces in America* (490), was more detailed on the trials, tribulations, and eventual successes of the allies. British naval mastery of Long Island Sound made Connecticut's extensive shoreline vulnerable to pillaging; (522) showed raids on Fairfield and New London from a British perspective. Other helpful works were (505, 509, 581, 656, 679).

The Washington-Horatio Gates imbroglio, the Conway Cabal, and the Newburgh Conspiracy continued to receive scholarly inquiry. A new biography of Washington's aide Tench Tilghman (617) was anti-Gates, as would be expected. On Newburgh, Bernard Knollenberg applied a lawyer's approach (495) in dealing with the matter, while Richard Kohn (498) implicated Gates, but only circumstantially. Other articles that dealt with the ongoing Newburgh controversy can be found in citations to Don Higginbotham's essay (514). Gates's aide at Newburgh, John Armstrong, who anonymously penned the inflammatory addresses which so infuriated Washington, has had a biography written about him (623). Jonathan Rossie's work (595) dealt primarily with the Gates-Philip Schuyler squabble over command of the Northern front.

The war in the West remains sparsely covered, although significant works have been published. George M. Waller (660) wrote a survey covering the Western war. John D. Barnhart (346, 347) stated that British leader Henry "The Hair-Buyer" Hamilton did not buy scalps, but he acknowledged that Hamilton's callous attitude allowed Western Indians to run wild. Orville J. Jaebker (478) disgreed, and the works of James A. James (479, 480) should be consulted. Jospeh Brant, the Indian leader at the Wyoming Massacre, was defended by Marc Smith (625). The War of Posts waged in the West was well discussed (573, 646, 677). Richard G. Stone, Jr., covered the Kentucky militia of the period (638), Louise P. Kellog documented American difficulties (488), and various punitive expeditions conducted by Whig forces against Indian settlements were detailed (377, 432, 680). Gustav Rozenthal's journal (600) was particularly interesting. A Russian noble who fled to America following a victorious duel, Rozenthal joined the Continental Army at Valley Forge; he served under the name John Rose, and Private "Rose" was promoted to major by war's end. Years later, he was the only member of the Tsar's court to wear the insignia of the Order of the Cincinnati.

LOGISTICS AND SUPPORT. Revolutionary battles, like warfare throughout the ages, often hinged on whether powder horns and soldier's stomachs were or were not filled. Yet, for all the emphasis placed on logistics and lines of communication, these were usually the last areas explored by military historians. Therefore, the publication of Erna Risch's *Supplying Washington's Army* (585), filled a large historical gap, and it should act as a stepping-stone for further inquiry. Two other salient accounts by Harold L. Peterson, one on a Continental solider's kit or equipment (571) and another on Revolutonary artillery (572), were essential research tools.

Prior to Risch's work, most research in logistics had been printed in articles. Edmund Cody Burnett wrote about army grain supplies (373), and John C. Fitzpatrick about army bakers (430), and George D. Griffenhagen discussed the dearth of medical supplies (451). The all-important quest for munitions received the attention of Elizabeth Nuxoll (557), Orlando W. Stephenson (632), and Donald Reynolds (583).

Wars were not cheap even in the eighteenth century. The states's slipshod manner of trying to wage war without paying for it was the subject of E. Wayne Carp's soon-to-be-published dissertation (383). Congressional fiscal problems which led to shortfalls in military supplies were ably documented by Forrest McDonald (523). Congress, however, was quick to set up watchdog committees to see where their miserly appropriations were spent (425). One Congressional remedy to Continental financial problems, printing more money, resulted in difficulties described by Anne Bezanson (357). Besides French aid, Dutch merchants provided some assistance to the colonists (541); most of these supplies were channeled through the island of St. Eustatius (481) until closed by the Royal Navy. See also (649).

Support groups such as engineers and chaplains still need further inquiry. Early chapters in three recently published books surveyed the work of Revolutionary military engineers (486, 566, 659). Joel Tyler Headley's 1864 edition (463) and Frank Moore's 1862 collection (538) were useful on chaplains, but they were obviously dated. The medical corps benefited from recent scholarly activity. Mary C. Gillett's book from the Center for Military History series (446) was a fine overview of the army's medical department. Gillett found that typhus, dysentery, smallpox, and battle wounds kept from 14 to 20 percent of American troops unfit for duty at any one time. The conditions doctors practiced under and the type of medical care afforded Continental soldiers can be found in Richard Blanco (358), Whitfield J. Bell, Jr. (351), James E. Gibson (445), J. Worth Estes (419), and Morris H. Saffron (604), and in the personal remembrances of Albigence Waldo (658). John Jones's "how-to" book, published in 1775, assisted doctors unused to the carnage of war (485).

INTELLIGENCE AND PROPAGANDA. In 1777, George Washington requested a portable printing press for his headquarters to counteract the effects British propaganda had on the local populace. Washington's requisition went unfilled, but the unrelenting war of words for the hearts and minds of Americans that began in 1763 continued through the Revolution. Philip Davidson's *Propaganda and the American Revolution* (398) traced the increasingly vitrioloic pamphlet and newspaper attacks from 1763 into the war. Carl Berger's revised *Broadsides and Bayonets* (354) complemented and extended Davidson's coverage through the war. Arthur M. Schlesinger (609) was also valuable. British pamphlets and selected press accounts filled Adams's *The American Controversy* (333), while Albert Kroger portrayed the war as seen in the German press (502). The absence of libel laws in wartime made the Loyalist newspapers sources of wonderful quotes—Washington was alleged to have thirteen toes, having grown three since independence was declared (610)—but, as Catherine S. Crary pointed out, one Tory editor played a double game (389). Two other works to be consulted: David Murdoch (545), which has facsimile pages from Edmund Burke's *Annual Register*, and Solomon Lutnick's often humorous look at America through the eyes of the British press (518).

Propaganda as a weapon of war was explored in Lyman H. Butterfield's article (378); before the first German stepped ashore on Staten Island, plans were already drawn to woo them to America's side. James T. Flexner uncovered little new about the Arnold-John André affair (431), while the contemporary account by James Rivington remained worth noting (586).

Even though the Revolution was a period when men commonly wore cloaks and carried daggers (of sorts), intelligence operations during the war were relatively untouched. Much of the older works involved diplomatic intelligence gathering, but the military implications were obvious as supplies, communications, and even alliances were compromised. Two articles by Samuel Flagg Bemis (352, 353) were noteworthy as he established that a well organized and highly effective British secret service operated during the Revolution, especially in Europe; see also (401). Headed by spymaster and part-time peace commissioner William Eden (368), British intelligence agents, including some Americans, roamed European capitals disrupting American diplomacy and trade negotiations. As Cecil B. Currey noted in his provocative *Code Number 72* (395), the plans of American commissioners in Paris were known in London even before ships carrying the messages left Brest. Benjamin Franklin's entourage was riddled with British agents, most notably his personal secretary, Dr. Edward Bancroft (537, 484). Julian P.

Boyd suggested that Bancroft "terminated" the duplicitous American commissioner, Silas Deane (364). The machinations of Deane and Caron de Beaumarchais, playwright and secret agent, which saw them net a million *sous* destined for American military supplies, were well described in Stille (636) and Currey (395). The movements of French agents in America were chronicled by Josephine Pachero (561).

BRITISH FORCES. The three groups composing Britain's forces in America—British, Germans, and Loyalist Americans—continued to receive important scholarly attention. A highly regarded example of the marriage of social and military history was Sylvia Frey's *The British Soldier in America* (439). After Frey's work, no longer can British troops stationed in America be considered "scum of the earth", as the Iron Duke described his men. Frey found many recruits enlisting for the duration of the war, not the traditional lifetime contracts; many were not societal dregs but unemployed artisans, victims of economic hard times. This did not alter American's opinions, Frey noted, that the typical British soldier was a "loser."

Marion Balderston and David Syrett compiled letters of British officers in America (343); generals often found their glowing reports undercut by a powerfully connected subaltern's personal letter. Piers Mackesy's meticulously researched vindication of Lord George Sackville at Minden (526) provided an inner glimpse of the mind of the future Lord Germain. The effect fighting in America had on the development of British light infantry was explored by Fuller (441) and Robson (588). H.C.B. Rogers's (592) provided excellent double study of the battles of Camden and Guilford Courthouse from a very British perspective.

William B. Willcox's edited version of *Sir Henry Clinton's Narrative of His Campaigns* (676) remained an essential work on the war. Through Clinton's rarely objective eyes, the campaigns unfolded. Willcox and Frederick Wyatt put Sir Henry "on the couch" in their psychological profile of the anxious British commander-in-chief (683). Three articles by Willcox on British strategy were valuable for their content and because of the disparate journals in which they appeared (673, 674, 675). A careful researcher must be willing to look into even the most unlikely periodicals for information.

Three recent works on German mercenaries reflected primary sources long neglected. Ernest Kipping (493) provided a non-British professional soldier's opinion of the war in America. Johann Ewald was a jaeger officer (422) who set up and commanded anti-partisan units in New Jersey. His approach to counterinsurgency was advanced by the standards of most British thinking of the day. Rodney Atwood combed the German national archives to build his work on *Mercenaries from Hessen-Kassel* (341).

Loyal Americans benefited from several books. Adele Hast (460) examined Loyalism in a selected area of Virginia, combining Loyalist, social, and local history. Robert Demond's work on North Carolina Loyalists (405) captured the horror of war in the South; it was especially good on the raising of Loyalist troops for Moore's Creek Bridge. Robert W. Barnwell's unpublished study (348) remained the best of its kind on south Carolina Loyalists. Robert Calhoon's well-written work encompassed the entire thirteen colonies (379); it will be the new standard. There were other, more localized, Loyalist studies to be consulted (433, 455, 459, 618, 619, 655).

NAVAL AND MARITIME. Naval and maritime aspects of the American Revolution were long ignored, and they continued to be. Most biographies of American naval figures needed updating or complete revision, and there has been little effort to incorporate social, economic, or political history with naval / maritime affairs. From the American side, with few exceptions (412), the war at sea has been forgotten. In short, as David Syrett cogently noted (642), the naval / maritime field was wide open. Syrett took a fresh heading with his *Study of British Transport Organization* (643). Even before France's entrance into the war, Britain's 3,000-mile-long line of communicatin was a hazardous route; this alone made the war of attrition in America prohibitive. Early chapters in *Sea Lanes in War Time*, by Robert Albion and his wife, Jennie Barnes Pope (334), examined this problem.

Several works on the Royal Navy of the time were worth noting. Chapters in Michael Lewis (513) and in Paul Kennedy's naval-economic work (489) were important. Marcus's *Heart of Oak* (528), title of a well-known song, covered His Majesty's Royal Navy from Quiberon Bay through the Napoleonic Wars. John Andrew Tilley (647) and Gerald S. Graham (448) were helpful. The initial and beneficial use of coppered bottoms was described by Maurer Maurer (533).

By 1778, the Royal Navy was spread thin, covering operations and protecting convoys and coastal shipping from Antigua to Land's End to Trincomalee. The French sought to take advantage of this, as can be seen in Claude Manceron (527) and in two works on the ill-fated French invasion of England in 1779 (567, 570). American privateers roamed the Channel and Irish Sea at will (344). John Paul Jones's adventures were chronicled in his published logs (345) and in John E. Walsh's book (661). A work on unfortunate American POWs in Britain and the songs they sang were in *A Sailor's Songbag* (381).

New England's contributions to the Continental Navy and to privateersmen were captured in several works (350, 541, 542). Revolutionary privateersmen as forerunners of today's Naval Reserve was the thrust of Reuben E. Stivers (637). Massachusetts's effort in 1779 that failed and all but knocked her out of the war — the fiasco at Penobscot — was briefly covered (554). Alex Roland's soon-to-be-published study examined American ingenuity in "The Development of Underwater Warfare" (593), while Robert Duncan looked at the early use of American sea mines (410).

Congress, the establishment of the navy, and John Adams's influence were discussed in two unpublished works (337, 535). Congressional orders regarding the navy were compiled by Charles O. Paullin (568), while the new *U.S. Naval History Sources in the United States* (336) promised to benefit researchers. Jonathan Dull argued that French naval strategy benefited the Americans but did little for France (409). Other works to be consulted include William N. Still's short work on the North Carolina state navy (635); Isaac Greenwood's biography of Continental captain John Manley (449); a short work on the USS *Alfred* (521); and Ryan's arrangement of naval officers' letters (601). *Navies of the American Revolution* was a handsome, well-illustrated coffee-table work (575).

BIOGRAPHY. Solid biographies of key Revolutionary military figures continued to be written. Recent work, however, shifted to biographic studies of unit commanders, staff officers, and civilian leaders who worked closely with the military. The leader of an elite legion that fought under Washington and Greene and alongside guerrilla leader Francis Marion, Henry "Light-Horse Harry" Lee has been the subject of two fine biographies. Charles Royster (599) examined the effect that war experience and expectations raised by the Revolution had on the men of Lee's generation. Thomas E. Templin's unpublished biography took a more traditional approach; he carefully traced the life of Robert E. Lee's father from his dashing wartime exploits to his disgraced and lonely death in 1818 (644). Other Virginians with new biographies included: tavern owner and division commander George Weedon (662); Washington's loyal aide Tench Tilghman (322); Thomas Nelson, signer, militia leader, and governor (420); and Benjamin Harrison, father of one president, great-grandfather of another, who served three terms as Virginia governor, 1781–1784 (624).

Other members of Washington's official family have had their reputations salvaged. Timothy Pickering wrote a pamphlet on American tactics, but he failed as quartermaster general; biographer Clarfield portrayed him as more successful in the postwar years (386). Longtime patriot Joseph Reed was falsely accused of treasonous activities after the war; John Roche (589) did much to cleanse his name. An older, very defensive work by Reed's grandson (582) has important correspondence in it. Other works included biographies of Washington's mapmaker (465), and of New York radical, Sons of Liberty leader, and divisional commander Alexander McDougall (524) by a kinsman. Older works on Anthony Wayne (365, 496), Peter Muhlenberg (471, 544), Daniel Morgan (380), William Drayton (396), the colorful, hardfighting William "Lord Stirling" Alexander (408), and Hugh Mercer (665) remained worth consulting.

Naval figures and British military leaders received scant attention. Philip Smith wrote a biography of a New England Continental captain (626; see also 449). Hargrove's *General John Burgoyne* (458) laid much of the blame for Saratoga on Lord Germain. Two works by Supreme Court justices continued to be valuable for historical and political content: William Johnson's biography of Nathanael Greene (483) and John Marshall's *Life of Washington* (530). Andrew Pickens has two biographies (424, 664), while the Southern campaigns and the Maryland line were featured in a work on Colonel John Gunby (453). South Carolina partisan leader Elijah Clark's (sometimes spelled "Clarke") biography has value (462).

SOURCES. Collected writings of major Revolutionary military figures were continually being published or updated, increasing printed primary sources available to researchers. Although original manuscripts always should be consulted if possible, the accessibility of printed and microfilmed personal papers has cut spiraling travel costs for students of the war. For anyone working on almost any military aspect of the Revolution, *The Writings of George Washington* (429) were essential. Superbly edited by John C. Fitzpatrick, this thirty-nine-volume set contains only Washington's outgoing correspondence, so other papers, including those of Jared Sparks (630), still must be used. When completed, a new edition of the Washington papers, edited by W. W. Abbot, will supersede the Fitzpatrick edition, as it will contain both outgoing and incoming letters (331). Other still valuable sources included Peter Force's *American Archives* (434); the *Letter Books* of Admiral George Rodney (590); Lord Cornwallis's letters (594); young John Laurens's papers (621); many volumes from the Historical Manuscript Commission, for example, the *Manuscripts of Mrs. Stopford-Sackville* (470); and the *Papers of the Continental Congress* (653), which can be found on microfilm. John P. Butler compiled a five-volume index (375) to these papers.

Significant additions have been published. John C. Dann mined the Revolutionary War pension applications in *The Revolution Remembered* (397). These heretofore untouched stories of pension claimants added dramatically to our understanding of yesterday's warriors, providing a look at the war from below the command level, as most of these veterans were either junior officers or enlisted men during the war. An important series just completed was Kenneth G. Davies's edition of *Documents of the American Revolution* (399). Culled from the Colonial Office, these volumes focused primarily upon the letters of Lord Dartmouth and Lord Germain to their commanders in the field. Howard H. Peckham's edited selection from the Clements Library collections (569) were noteworthy, especially Robert Mitchell's chapter of Anthony Wayne-Nathanael Greene correspondence. Greene's papers were published in a selected fashion (616), with a full microfilmed series to follow. Another series not yet completed was Paul H. Smith's *Letters to Delegates of Congress* (627), which superseded an earlier set. See also (525).

Much like the Historical Manuscripts Commission, the Navy Records Society of Britain continued to publish important primary works. Of particular note to researchers in the American Revolution were the *Private Papers of John, Earl of Sandwich* (550) in four volumes; Sandwich was the First Lord of the Admiralty, from 1771–1782. The *Letters* (549) of Adm. Samuel Hood covered the years 1780–1782, and they were particularly important on the Battle of the Capes. Hood was less than complimentary toward his commander, Lord Rodney. Also, while fleet signals might only interest the specialist, the *Instructions* (551) of British admirals, their standing orders which supposedly governed all contingencies at sea, made interesting reading for all. See also (548).

Other important sources were published. Gilbert Bodinier listed French officers who fought in America along with their units (361). In another French publication, Olivier compiled a bibliography of works on the Marquis and Marquise de Lafayette (559). For anyone seeking to do primary research in the Library of Congress, John R. Sellers's work (612) was invaluable. *Fighters for Independence* (672) was excellent on local and personally published biographies of common soldiers. A U.S. Army bibliographic aid, compiled by Robert W. Coakley and Stetson Conn (652), was dated but still of some value, as were Fitzpatrick's calendars of Washington's letters (427, 428). Robert K. Wright's published (682) and unpublished (681) works discussed doctrine and organization, but they also provided a lineage of every permanent unit in the Revolution. This will prove to be an essential tool for researchers. And, for certainly a different interpretation, see Leo Okinshevich's bibliography of the Soviet view of American history (558).

SUGGESTIONS FOR FURTHER INVESTIGATION. As mentioned in the introduction, the American Revolution is not a moribund field. Changing interpretations, fresh comparative studies, and a wealth of printed primary materials provided scholars with new vistas to explore in Revolutionary military history. Inquiry into the social history of the Continental soldiers has only scratched the surface; further exploration, unit by unit, state by state, has to be done. Just a few questions such an inquiry might raise include: Did prewar ideology really influence colonial public opinion, or were socioeconomic, religious, and ethnic differences more influential in making the Revolution? How did these elements determine why some men fought as Whigs? as Tories? or not fight at all? Did a Continental trooper, marching in the ice and snow of New Jersey with a tattered copy of *Common Sense* in his rolled blanket, think of himself as an idealistic winter soldier? Or, perhaps did he just wish that Washington would call a halt and hope that Greene had something better to eat than the moldy biscuit he had eaten for breakfast?

The effect of war on the home front and on American manufacturing requires a deeper look. What was the role played by women and blacks in Revolutionary war production? Erna Risch (585) laid the groundwork in logistics, but there remains much work to be done for each theater of war and for each army. How supplies reached the armies is an area little touched upon, as is transport in general.

On the battlefield, there is much room for study. Fresh, intensive examinations of certain campaigns and battles are needed in light of new interpretations and information. Why generals acted in certain ways can possibly explained in light of new causal understanding. This, too, goes for many biographies. Naval biographies are desperate for update and revision, and many corps and divisional commanders and staff officers have yet to be written upon. Areas in need of more research include the war in the West, the Indian campaigns in the South, the Southern backcountry, coastal raids and offshore bombardment in New England, a fresh look at Washington as a strategist, and Loyalist counterinsurgency in the South and in the New York City area.

The support areas need much more work. Engineers, chaplains, and intelligence operatives and operations require scholarly research to put these very important detachments into perspective. And for those with larger visions, a good overall narrative incorporating recent scholarship is always needed.

Above all, it should be remembered that America's Revolutionary War was fought and endured by real men and women; mythology has no business in modern military history. There is a great need to remove halos from Revolutionary leaders and to examine their deeds as the actions of real people, not gods. Conversely, the concept of "embattled farmers" has too long saddled the American military of the day with the term "amateur," as in the amateur Americans fought the professional British. What was true in 1775–1776 was no longer true in 1780–1781; American military leaders learned, and learned quickly, to wage their war in an American fashion. It is time to blow the clouds of glory from the battlefield to see America's Revolution as a war. There is much work to do, many ideas to explore.

BIBLIOGRAPHY

331. Abbot, W. W., ed. *The Papers of George Washington: Colonial Series.* 2 vols. to date. Charlottesville: University Press of Virginia, 1983.
332. Adams, Charles F. *Studies Military and Diplomatic.* New York: Macmillan, 1911.
333. Adams, Thomas R., ed. *The American Controversy: A Bibliographical Study of the British Pamphlets about the American Disputes, 1764–1783.* 2 vols. Providence, R.I.: Brown University Press, 1980.
334. Albion, Robert B., and Jennie Barnes Pope. *Sea Lanes in War Time: The American Experience, 1775–1942.* New York: W. W. Norton, 1942.
335. Alexander, Vern Louis. "Black Opposition to Participation in American Military Engagements From the American Revolution to Vietnam." M.S. thesis, North Texas State University, 1976.

336. Allard, Dean, Martha L. Crowley, and Mary W.Edmison, eds. *U.S. Naval History Sources in the United States.* Washington, D.C.: GPO, 1979.
337. Anderson, William G. "John Adams and the Creation of the American Navy." Ph.D. diss., State University of New York at Stony Brook, 1975.
338. Angermann, Erich, Marie-Luise Frings, and Hermann Wellenreuther, eds. *New Wine in Old Skins: A Comparative View of Socio-Political Structures and Values Affecting the American Revolution.* Stuttgart: Ernest Kett Verlag, 1976.
339. Applegate, Howard L. "Constitutions Like Iron: The Life of the American Revolutionary War Soliders in the Middle Department, 1775–1783." Ph.D. diss., University of Syracuse, 1966.
340. Ashmore, Otis, and Charles Olmstead. "The Battles of Kettle Creek and Brier Creek." *Georgia Historical Quarterly* 10 (1926): 85–125.
341. Atwood, Rodney. *The Hessians: Mercenaries from Hessen-Kassel in the American Revolution.* Cambridge England: Cambridge University Press, 1980.
342. Balch, Thomas, ed. *Papers Relating Chiefly to the Maryland Line during the Revolution.* Philadelphia: Seventy-Six Society, 1857.
343. Balderston, Marion, and David Syrett, eds. *The Lost War: Letters from British Officers during the American Revolution.* New York: Horizon Press, 1975.
344. Barnes, James. *With the Flag in the Channel.* New York: Applegate, 1902.
345. Barnes, John S., ed. *The Log of the* Serapis-Alliance-Ariel*, Under the Command of John Paul Jones,* New York: Naval History Society, 1911.
346. Barnhart, John D. *Henry Hamilton and George Rogers Clark in the American Revolution with the Unpublished Journal of Lieut. Gov. Henry Hamilton* Crawfordsville, Ind.: R. E. Banta, 1951.
347. _____. "A New Evaluation of Henry Hamilton and George Rogers Clark." *Mississippi Valley Historical Review* 37 (1951): 643–52.
348. Barnwell, Robert W., Jr. "Loyalism in South Carolina." Ph.D. diss., Duke University, 1941.
349. Baur, Frederick G. "Notes on the Use of Cavalry in the American Revolution." *Cavalry Journal* 47 (1938): 136–43.
350. Beattie, Donald W., and J. Richard Collin. *Washington's New England Fleet: Beverly's Role in its Origins, 1775–1777.* Salem, Mass. Necom & Gauss, 1969.
351. Bell, Whitfield J., Jr. *John Morgan, Continental Doctor.* Philadelphia: University of Pennsylvania Press, 1965.
352. Bemis, Samuel Flagg. "British Secret Service and the Franco-American Alliance." *American Historical Review* 24 (1924): 475–95.
353. _____. "Secret Intelligence, 1777: Two Documents." *Huntington Library Quarterly* 24 (1961): 223–49.
354. Berger, Carl. *Broadsides and Bayonets: The Propaganda War of the American Revolution.* Rev. ed. San Rafael, Calif.: Presidio Press, 1976.
355. Berlin, Robert Henry. "The Administration of Military Justice in the Continental Army during the American Revolution, 1775–1783." Ph.D. diss., University of California, Santa Barbara, 1976.
356. Bernath, Stuart L. "George Washington and the Genesis of American Military Discipline." *Mid-America* 49 (1967): 83–100.

34 • SOURCES OF U.S. MILITARY HISTORY: SUPPLEMENT II

357. Bezanson, Anne. *Prices and Inflation during the American Revolution, 1770-1790.* Philadelphia: University of Pennsylvania Press, 1951.
358. Blanco, Richard L. *Physician of the American Revolution, Jonathan Potts.* New York: Garland STPM Press, 1979.
359. Blumenthal, Walter H. *Women Camp Followers of the American Revolution.* Philadelphia: G. S. MacManus, 1952.
360. Bodenger, Robert G. "Soldiers' Bonuses: A History of Veterans' Benefits in the United States, 1776-1967." Ph.D. diss., Pennsylvania State University, 1972.
361. Bodinier, Gilbert. *Dictionnaire des officers de l'armée royale qui ont combattu aux Etats-Unis pendant la guerre d'Independence, 1776-1783.* Vincennes: Service Historique de l'Armée de Terre, 1982.
362. Boucher, Jonathon. *Reminiscences of an American Loyalist, 1738-1789.* Boston: Houghton Mifflin, 1925; reprint, 1967.
363. Bowman, Larry. *Captive American Prisoners during the American Revolution.* Athens: Ohio University Press, 1976.
364. Boyd, Julian P. "Silas Deane: Death by a Kindly Teacher of Treason." *William and Mary Quarterly* 16 (1959): 165.87, 319-42, 515-50.
365. Boyd, Thomas A. *Mad Anthony Wayne.* New York: Scribner's Sons, 1929.
366. Boynton, Edward C. *General Orders of General Washington Issued at Newburgh-on-the-Hudson, 1782-1783.* New intro. by Alan C. Aimone. Harrison, N.Y.: Harbor Hill Books, 1973.
367. Bray, Robert C., and Paul E. Bushnell. *The Diary of a Common Solider.* DeKalb: Northern Illinois University Press, 1978.
368. Brown, Alan S. "William Eden and the American Revolution." Ph.D. diss., University of Michigan, 1953.
369. Brown, Lloyd A., and Howard H. Peckham, eds. *Revolutionary War Journals of Henry Dearborn.* Chicago University of Chicago Press, 1939.
370. Browning, John, and Richard Morton, eds. *1776.* Toronto: Hakkent, 1976; Sarasota, Fla., S. Stevens, 1976.
371. Brownlow, Donald G. *A Documentary History of the Battle of Germantown.* Germantown, Pa.: Germantown Historical Society, 1955.
372. Buel, Richard, Jr. *Dear Liberty: Connecticut's Mobilization for Revolutionary War.* Middletown, Conn. Wesleyan University Press, 1980.
373. Burnett, Edmund C. "The Continental Congress and Agricultural Supplies." *Agricultural History* 2 (1928): 111-28.
374. Bush, Martin H. *Revolutionary Enigma: A Reappraisal of General Philip Schuyler of New York.* Port Washington, N.Y.: Friedman, 1969.
375. Butler, John P., comp. *Index: The Papers of the Continental Congress, 1774-1789.* 5 vols. Washington, D.C.: GPO 1978.
376. Butler, Lewis W. G. *The Annals of the King's Royal Rifle Corps.* 5 vols. London: Smith, Elder, 1913-1932.
377. Butterfield, Consul W. *Historical Accounts of the Expedition against Sandusky under Colonel William Crawford in 1782.* Cincinnati, Ohio: Clarke, 1873.
378. Butterfield, Lyman H. "Psychological Warfare in 1776: The Jefferson-Franklin Plan to Cause Hessian Desertions." American Philosophical Society *Proceedings* 94 (1950): 233-41.
379. Calhoon, Robert M. *Loyalists in Revolutionary America.* New York:

Harcourt Brace Jovanovich, 1973.

380. Callahan, North. *Daniel Morgan: Ranger of the Revolution*. New York: Holt, Rinehart & Winston, 1961.

381. Carey, George G., ed. *A Sailor's Songbag: An American Rebel in an English Prison, 1777–1779*. Amherst: University of Massachusetts Press, 1976.

382. Caron, Max. *Admiral de Grasse: One of the Great Forgotten Men*. Boston: Four Seas, 1924.

383. Carp, E. Wayne. "Supplying the Revolution: Continental Administration and American Political Culture, 1775–1783." Ph.D. diss., University of California, Berkeley, 1981.

384. Chase, Philander Dean. "Baron Von Steuben in the War of Independence." Ph.D. diss., Duke University, 1973.

385. Christie, Ian R. *Wars and Revolutions: Britain, 1760–1815*. London: Edward Arnold, 1982.

386. Clarfield, Gerard H. *Timothy Pickering and the American Republic*. Pittsburgh, Pa.: University of Pittsburgh Press, 1980.

387. Coker, William S. *The Siege of Pensacola, 1781, in Maps*. Pensacola, Fla.: Perdido Bay Press, 1981.

388. Conrad, Dennis Michael. "Nathanael Greene and the Southern Campaigns, 1780–1783." Ph.D. diss., Duke University, 1979.

389. Crary, Catherine S. "The Tory and the Spy: The Double Life of James Rivington." *William and Mary Quarterly* 26 (1959): 61–72.

390. Cress, Lawrence Delbert. *Citizens in Arms: The Army and Militia in American Society to the War of 1812*. Chapel Hill: University of North Carolina Press, 1982.

391. _____. "The Standing Army, the Militia, and the New Republic: Changing Attitudes Toward the Military in American Society, 1768–1820." Ph.D. diss., University of Virginia, 1977.

392. Crow, Jeffrey J., and Larry E. Tise, eds. *The Southern Experience in the American Revolution*. Chapel Hill: University of North Carolina Press, 1978.

393. Crane, Ronald I., and F.B. Kaye. *A Census of British Newspapers and Periodicals, 1620–1800*. Chapel Hill: University of North Carolina Press, 1927.

394. Cunliffe, Marcus. *Soldiers and Civilians: The Martial Spirit in America, 1775–1865*. Boston: Little, Brown, 1968.

395. Currey, Cecil B. *Code Number 72: Benjamin Franklin: Patriot or Spy?* Englewood Cliffs, N.J.: Prentice-Hall, 1972.

396. Dabney, William, and Marion Dargen. *William Drayton and the American Revolution*. Albuquerque: University of New Mexico Press, 1962.

397. Dann, John C., ed. *The Revolution Remembered: Eyewitness Accounts of the War for Independence*. Chicago: University of Chicago Press, 1980.

398. Davidson, Philip. *Propaganda and the American Revolution*. Chapel Hill: University of North Carolina Press, 1941.

399. Davies, Kenneth G., ed. *Documents of the American Revolution, 1770–1783* (Colonial Records Series). 24 vols. Dublin: Irish University Press, 1972–1981.

400. Davis, Andrew M. "The Employment of Indian Auxiliaries in the American War." *English Historical Review* 2 (1887): 709–28.

401. Deacon, Richard. *A History of the British Secret Service*. London: Muller, 1969; New York: Taplinger, 1970.
402. Dearden, Paul F. *The Rhode Island Campaign of 1778: Inauspicious Dawn of Alliance*. Providence: Rhode Island Bicentennial Foundation, 1980.
403. Dederer, John Morgan. "Making Bricks without Straw: Nathanael Greene's Southern Campaigns and Mao Tse-tung's Mobile War." *Military Affairs* 47 (October 1983): 115–21.
404. _____. *Making Bricks Without Straw: Nathanael Greene's Southern Campaigns and Mao Tse-tung's Mobile War*. Manhattan, Kans. Sunflower University Press, 1983.
405. Demond, Robert O. *The Loyalists in North Carolina during the Revolution*. Durham, N.C.: Duke University Press, 1940.
406. De Pauw, Linda Grant. "Women in Combat: The Revolutionary War Experience." *Armed Forces and Society* 7 (1981): 209–26.
407. Donkin, Robert. *Military Collections and Remarks*. New York: H. Gaines, 1777.
408. Duer, William Alexander. *The Life of William Alexander, Earl of Stirling*. New York Wiley and Putnam, 1847.
409. Dull, Jonathan Romer. "The French Navy and American Independence: Naval Factors in French Diplomacy and War Strategy, 1774–1780." Ph.D. diss., University of California, Berekley, 1972.
410. Duncan, Robert C. *America's Use of Sea Mines*. White Oak, Md. U.S. Naval Ordnance Laboratory, 1962.
411. Dupuy, R. Ernest, Gay Hammerman, and Grace P. Hayes. *The American Revolution: A Global War*. New York: D. McKay, 1977.
412. Dupuy, Trevor N., and Grace P. Hayes. *The Military History of Revolutionary Naval Battles*. New York: Franklin Watts, 1970.
413. Dwyer, William M. *The Day is Ours! November 1776–January 1777: An Inside View of the Battles of Trenton and Princeton*. New York: Viking Press, 1983.
414. Editors of *Military Affairs*, eds. *Military Analysis of the Revolutionary War: An Anthology*. Millwood, N.Y.: KTO Press, 1977.
415. Edmunson, James Howard. "Desertion in the American Army during the Revolutionary War." Ph.D. diss., Louisiana State University, 1972.
416. Egly, Theodore W., Jr. *History of the First New York Regiment, 1775–1783*. Hampton, N.H.: P. E. Randall, 1981.
417. Eller, Ernest, and E. McNeill, eds. *Chesapeake Bay in the American Revolution*. Centreville, Md.: Tidewater Publishers, 1981.
418. Ellis, John. *Armies in Revolution* New York: Oxford University Press, 1974.
419. Estes, J. Worth. *Hall Jackson and the Purple Foxglove: Medical Practice and Research in Revolutionary America, 1760–1820*. Hanover: University Press of New Hampshire, 1980.
420. Evans, Emory G. *Thomas Nelson and the Revolution in Virginia*. Williamsburg: Virginia Independence Bicentennial Commission, 1978.
421. Everest, Allan S. *Moses Hazen and the Canadian Refugees in the American Revolution*. Syracuse, N.Y.: Syracuse University Press, 1976.
422. Ewald, Johann. *Diary of the American War: A Hessian Journal*. Trans. by Joseph P. Tustin. New Haven, Conn.: Yale University Press, 1979.

423. Fanning, David. *The Narrative of Colonel David Fanning*. New York: Sabine, 1865.
424. Ferguson, Clyde R. "General Andrew Pickens." Ph.D. diss., Duke University, 1960.
425. Ferguson, E. James. "Business, Government, and Congressional Investigation in the Revolution." *William and Mary Quarterly* 16 (1959): 293–318.
426. Ferling, John S. *A Wilderness of Miseries: War and Warriors in Early America*. Westport, Conn. Greenwood Press, 1980.
427. Fitzpatrick, John Co., comp. *Calendar of the Correspondence of George Washington, Commander in Chief of the Continental Army with the Continental Congress*. Washington, D.C.: GPO, 1906.
428. _____. comp. *Calendar of the Correspondence of George Washington, Commander in Chief of the Continental Army with the Officers*. 4 vols. Washington, D.C.: GPO, 1915.
429. Fitzpatrick, John C., ed. *The Writings of George Washington from the Original Manuscripts, 1745–1799*. 39 vols. Washington, D.C.: GPO, 1931–1944.
430. _____. *The Spirit of the Revolution: New Light from Some of the Original Sources of American History*. Boston: Houghton Mifflin, 1924.
431. Flexner, James T. *The Traitor and the Spy*. New York: Harcourt, Brace, 1953.
432. Flick, Alexander C., comp. "New Sources on the Sullivan Campaign in 1779," *New York State Historical Association Journal* 10 (1929): 185–294, 315.
433. _____. *Loyalism in New York during the American Revolution*. New York: Columbia University Press, 1901.
434. Force, Peter, ed. *American Archives*, 9 vols. Washington, D.C.: M. St. Clair & Peter Force, 1837–1853.
435. Ford, Worthington C., ed. *Defenses of Philadelphia in 1777*. Brooklyn, N.Y.: Historical Printing Club, 1897; reprint, New York: Da Capo Press, 1971.
436. Forry, Richard R. "Edward Hand: His Role in the American Revolution." Ph.D. diss., Duke University, 1976.
437. Fowler, William M., Jr., and Wallace Coyle, eds. *The American Revolution: Changing Perspectives*. Boston: Northeastern University Press, 1979.
438. _____. "The Business of War: Boston as a Navy Base, 1776–1783." *American Neptune* 42 (January 1982): 25–35.
439. Frey, Sylvia R. *The British Soldier in America: A Social History of Military Life in the Revolutionary Period*. Austin: University of Texas Press, 1981.
440. _____. "The Common British Solider in the Late Eighteenth Century: A Profile." *Societas* 5 (1975): 117–31.
441. Fuller, J.F.C. *British Light Infantry in the Eighteenth Century*. London: Hutchinson, 1925.
442. Ganyard, Robert L. "Threat from the West: North Carolina and the Cherokee, 1776–1778." *North Carolina Historical Review* 45 (Jan. 1968): 47–66.
443. Gerlach, Larry R., et al, eds. *Legacies of the American Revolution*. Ogden: Utah State University Press, 1978.

444. Gibbes, Robert W., ed. *Documentary History of the American Revolution Consisting of Letters and Papers Relating to the Contest for Liberty, Chiefly in South Carolina in 1776 and 1782*. 3 vols. Columbia S.C.: Banner Steam-Power Press, 1853–1857. Reprint. New York: Arno Press, 1971.

445. Gibson, James E. *Bodo Otto and the Medical Background of the American Revolution*. Baltimore, Md.: C. C. Thomas, 1937.

446. Gillett, Mary C. *The Army Medical Department, 1775–1818*. Washington, D.C.: Center for Military History, 1981.

447. Gordon, Maurice Bear. *Naval and Maritime Medicine During the American Revolution*. Ventnor, N.J.: Ventnor Publishing, 1978.

448. Graham, Gerald S. *Empire of the North Atlantic: The Maritime Struggle for North America*. 2d ed. Toronto: University of Toronto Press, 1950.

449. Greenwood, Isaac J. *Captain John Manley: Second-in-Rank in the United States Navy, 1776–1783*. Boston: Goodspeed, 1915; reprint, 1970.

450. Gregg, Alexander. *History of the Old Cheraws*. Columbia, S.C.: State Company, 1905.

451. Griffenhagen, George D. "Drug Supplies in the American Revolution." United States National Museum *Bulletin* 225 (1961): 110–33.

452. Griffiths, Samuel B., II. *In Defence of the Public Liberty: Britain, America, and the Struggle for Independence from 1760 to the Surrender at Yorktown in 1781*. New York: Doubleday, 1976.

453. Gunby, Andrew. *Colonel John Gunby of the Maryland Continental Line*. Cincinnati, Ohio: R. Clarke, 1902.

454. Guthrie, Jason M. *Camp-Fires of the Afro-American*. Philadelphia: Afro-American Publishing, 1899.

455. Hammond, Otis Grant. *Tories of New Hampshire*. Concord: New Hampshire Historical Society, 1917.

456. Hanson, Thomas. *The Prussian Evolution in Actual Engagement*. Philadelphia: J. Dougls McDougall, 1775.

457. Hargreaves, Reginald. "The Fabulous Ferguson Rifle and Its Brief Career as a Military Arm: The Gun that Died with its Young Designer." *American Rifleman* (August 1971), 33–37.

458. Hargrove, Richard J., Jr. *General John Burgoyne*. Newark: University of Delaware Press, 1983.

459. Harrell, Isaac S. *Loyalism in Virginia*. Durham, N.C.: Duke University Press, 1926.

460. Hast, Adele. *Loyalism in Revolutionary Virginia: The Norfolk Area and the Eastern Shore*. Ann Arbor, Mich. UMI Research Press, 1982.

461. Hatch, Robert McConnell. *Thrust for Canada: The American Attempt on Quebec in 1775–1776*. Boston: Houghton Mifflin, 1979.

462. Hays, Louise F. *Hero of the Hornet's Nest: A Biography of Elijah Clark, 1733–1799*. New York: Hobson Book Press, 1946.

463. Headley, Joel T. *The Chaplains and Clergy of the Revolution*. New York: Charles Scribner's Sons. 1864.

464. Henrich, Joseph G. "The Triumph of Ideology: The Jeffersonians and the Navy, 1779–1803." Ph.D. diss., Duke University, 1972.

465. Heusser, Albert H. *George Washington's Map Maker: A Biography of Robert Erskine*. New Brunswick, N.J.: Rutgers University Press, 1966.

466. Higginbotham, R. Don. "American Historians and the Military History

of the American Revolution." *American Historical Review* 70 (1964): 18–34.

467. _____, ed. *Reconsiderations on the Revolutionary War: Selected Essays from a Symposium at West Point in 1976.* Westport, Conn. Greenwood Press, 1978.

468. Higgins, W. Robert, ed. *The Revolutionary War in the South: Power, Conflict, and Leadership.* Durham, N.C.: Duke University Press, 1979.

469. Hill, Ralph N. *Lake Champlain: Key to Liberty.* Taftsville, N.H.: Countryman Press, 1977.

470. Historical Manuscripts Commission. *Report on the Manuscripts of Mrs. Stopford-Sackville of Drayton House.* 2 vols. London: For H.M. Stationery Office by Mackie, 1904–1910.

471. Hocker, Edward W. *The Fighting Parson of the American Revolution: A Biography of General Peter Muhlenberg, Lutheran Clergyman, Military Chieftain, and Political Leader.* Philadelphia: The author, 1936.

472. Hoffman, Ronald, and Peter Albert, eds. *Arms and Independence: The Military Character of the American Revolution.* Charlottesville: University Press of Virginia for the U.S. Capitol Historical Society, 1983.

473. _____. *Diplomacy and Revolution: The Franco-American Alliance of 1778.* Charlottesville: University Press of Virginia for the U.S. Capitol Historical Society, 1981.

474. Hoffman, Ronald, Thad W. Tate, and Peter Albert, eds. *An UnCivil War: The Southern Backcountry during the American Revolution.* Charlottesville: University Press of Virginia for the U.S. Capitol Historical Society, 1984.

475. Hough, Franklin B., ed. *The Siege of Savannah by the Combined American and French Forces.* Albany, N.Y.: J. Munsell, 1866.

476. Howe, William. *The Narrative of Lt. Gen. Sir William Howe in a Committee of the House of Commons on 29th April 1779.* London: Baldwin, 1780.

477. Jackson, John W. *With the British Army in Philadelphia, 1777–1778.* San Rafael, Calif. Presidio Press, 1979.

478. Jaebker, Orville J. "Henry Hamilton: British Soldier and Colonial Governor." Ph.D. diss., Indiana University, 1954.

479. James, James A., ed. *George Rogers Clark Papers, 1771–1784.* Springfield: Illinois State Historical Library, 1912–1926. Reprinted. 2 vols., New York: AMS Press, 1972.

480. _____. *The Life of George Rogers Clark.* Chicago: University of Chicago Press, 1928.

481. Jameson, John Franklin. "St. Eustatius in the American Revolution." *American Historical Review* 8 (1903): 683–708.

482. Johnson, James M. "'Not a Single Soldier in the Province': The Military Establishment of Georgia, and the Coming of the Revolution." Ph.D. diss. Duke University, 1980.

483. Johnson, William. *Sketches of the Life and Correspondence of Nathanael Greene.* 2 vols. Charleston, S.C.: A. E. Miller, 1822. Reprint. New York: Da Capo, 1973.

484. Johnston, Henry P. "The Secret Service of the Revolution." *Magazine of American History* 8 (1882): 95–105.

485. Jones, John. *Plain Concise Practical Remarks on the Treatment of Wounds and Fractures.* New York: John Holt, 1775.

486. Kanarek, Harold. *The Mid-Atlantic Engineers: A History of the Baltimore Engineers, 1774–1974.* Washington, D.C.: GPO, 1978.
487. Karsten, Peter, ed. *The Military in America: From the Colonial Era to the Present.* New York: Free Press, 1980.
488. Kellog, Louise P., ed. *Frontier Retreat on the Upper Ohio, 1779–1781.* Madison: University of Wisconsin Press, 1917.
489. Kennedy, Paul M. *The Rise and Fall of British Naval Mastery.* London: Allen Lane, 1976.
490. Kennett, Lee. The French Forces in America, 1780–1783. Westport, Conn. Greenwood Press, 1978.
491. Kerr, W. B. *Bermuda and the American Revolution.* Princeton, N.J.: Princeton University Press, 1936.
492. Ketchum, Richard M. *The Winter Soldiers.* New York.: Doubleday, 1973.
493. Kipping, Ernest. *The Hessian View of America, 1776–1783.* Translated by Bernhard A. Uhlendorf. New York: Freneau Press, 1971.
494. Knollenberg, Bernard. "Bunker Hill Revisited: A Study of the Conflict of Historical Evidence." Massachusetts Historical Society *Proceedings* 72 (1959–60): 84–100.
495. _____. *Washington and the Revolution: A Reappraisal: Gates, Conway, and the Continental Congress.* New York: Macmillan, 1940.
496. Knopf, Richard C., ed. *Anthony Wayne, A Name in Arms.* Pittsburgh, Pa.: University of Pittsburgh Press, 1960.
497. Kohn, Richard H., ed. *Anglo-American Anti-Military Tracts, 1697–1830.* New York: Arno Press, 1979.
498. _____. "The Inside History of the Newburgh Conspiracy: America and the Coup d'Etat." *William and Mary Quarterly* 27 (1970): 187–220.
499. _____. "Military History at the Crossroads." *Reviews in American History* 2 (June 1974): 222–26.
500. _____. "The Social History of the American Soldier: A Review and Prospectus for Research." *American Historical Review* 86 (1981): 553–67.
501. _____. "War as Revolution and Social Process." *Reviews in American History* 5 (March 1977): 56–61.
502. Kroger, Albert. *Geburtder USA: German Newspaper Accounts of the American Revolution.* Madison: University of Wisconsin Press, 1962.
503. Krueger, John William. "Troop Life at the Champlain Valley Forts during the American Revolution, 1756 to 1783." Ph.D. diss., State University of New York at Albany, 1981.
504. Kurtz, Stephan, and James H. Hutson, eds. *Essays on the American Revolution.* Chapel Hill: University of North Carolina Press, 1973.
505. Kyte, George W. "A Projected British Attack upon Philadelphia in 1781." *Pennsylvania Magazine of History and Biography* 76 (Oct. 1925): 279–393.
506. _____. "Strategic Blunder: Lord Cornwallis Abandons the Carolinas, 1781." *Historian* 22 (February 1960): 29–144.
507. Landers, Howard L. *The Virginia Compaign and the Blockade and Siege of Yorktown, 1781.* Washington, D.C.: U.S. Army War College, 1931.
508. La Valliére, François. *The Art of War, Containing the Duties of All Military Officers in Actual Service.* Philadelphia: R. Bell, 1776.
509. Lee, Charles. "The Lee Papers." New-York Historical Society *Collections* 4–7 (1872–1875).

510. Leiby, Adrian C. *The Revolutionary War in the Hackensack Valley: The Jersey Dutch and the Neutral Ground, 1775-1783*. New Brunswick, N.J.: Rutgers University Press, 1962.
511. Lender, Mark Edward. "The Enlisted Line: The Continental Soldiers of New Jersey." Ph.D. diss., Rutgers University, 1975.
512. Lewis, James A. "New Spain during the American Revolution, 1779-1783: A Viceroyalty at War." Ph.D. diss., Duke University, 1975.
513. Lewis, Michael. *The Navy of Britain*. London: Allen & Unwin, 1948.
514. Library of Congress. *Library of Congress Symposia on the American Revolution: Leadership in the American Revolution*. Washington, D.C.: Library of Congress, 1974.
515. Lingley, Charles R. "The Treatment of Burgoyne's Troops Under the Saratoga Convention." *Political Science Quarterly* 22 (1907): 440-59.
516. "Christopher Ludwig, Baker-General of the Army of the United States During the Revolutionary War." *Pennsylvania Magazine of History and Biography* 16 (1982): 343-48.
517. Lumpkin, Henry. *From Savannah to Yorktown: The American Revolution in the South*. Columbia: University of South Carolina Press, 1981.
518. Lutnick, Solomon. *The American Revolution and the British Press, 1775-1783*. Columbia: University of Missouri Press, 1967.
519. McCrady, Edward. *The History of South Carolina in the Revolution, 1775-1780*. New York: Macmillan, 1901.
520. _____. *The History of South Carolina in the Revolution, 1780-1783*. New York: Macmillan, 1902.
521. McCusker, John J. Alfred: *The First Continental Flagship, 1775-1778*. Washington, D.C.: Smithsonian Institution Press, 1973.
522. McDevitt, Robert F. *Connecticut Attacked: A British Perspective*. Chester, Conn.: Pequot Press, 1974.
523. McDonald, Forrest. *E Pluribus Unum: The Formation of the American Republic, 1776-1790*. Boston: Houghton Mifflin, 1965.
524. MacDougall, William L. *American Revolutionary: A Biography of General Alexander McDougall*. Westport, Conn.: Greenwood Press, 1977.
525. MacGregor, Morris J., ed. *Blacks in the U.S. Armed Forces: Basic Documents, 1639-1973*. Wilmington, Del.: Scholarly Resources, 1976.
526. Mackesy, Piers. *The Coward of Minden: The Affair of Lord George Sackville*. London: Allen Lane, 1979.
527. Manceron, Claude. *The Wind from America: Necker's Defeat and Victory at Yorktown, 1778-1782*. New York: Alfred A. Knopf, 1978.
528. Marcus, G[odfrey] J. *Heart of Oak: A Survey of British Seapower in the Georgian Era*. New York: Oxford University Press, 1975.
529. Marshall, Douglas W. "The British Military Engineers, 1745-1783: A Study of Organization, Social Origin, and Cartography." Ph.D. diss., University of Michigan, 1976.
530. Marshall, John. *The Life of George Washington: Commander in Chief of the American Forces*. 2 vols. London: R. Phillips, 1805. Reprint New York: AMS Press, 1969.
531. Martin, James Kirby, and Mark Edward Lender. *A Respectable Army: The Military Origins of the Republic, 1763-1789*. Arlington Heights, Ill.: Harlan Davidson, 1982.

532. Martin, James Kirby, and K. R. Stubas, eds. *The American Revolution: Whose Revolution?* Rev. ed. Huntington, N.Y.: R. E. Kriens, 1977.

533. Maurer, Maurer. "Coppered Bottom for the Royal Navy: A Factor in the Maritime War of 1778-1783." *Military Affairs* 14 (1950): 57-61.

534. _____. "Military Justice under General Washington." *Military Affairs* 28 (1964): 8-16.

535. Mevers, Frank Clement, III. "Congress and the Navy: The Establishment and Administration of the American Revolutionary Navy by the Continental Congress, 1775-1784." Ph.D. diss., University of North Carolina at Chapel Hill, 1973.

536. Middlekauf, Robert. *The Glorious Cause: The American Revolution, 1763-1789.* New York: Oxford University Press, 1982.

537. Miller, Margaret A. "The Spy Activities of Doctor Edward Bancroft." *Journal of American History* 22 (1928): 70-77. [Note: Not to be confused with the modern journal of the same time.]

538. Moore, Frank. *The Patriot Preachers of the American Revolution.* New York: C. T. Evans, 1862.

539. Moomaw, William H. "The Denoument of General Howe's Campaign of 1777." *English Historical Review* 79 (July 1964): 498-512.

540. Morgan, Edmund S. *The Genius of George Washington* New York: W. W. Norton, 1981.

541. Morgan, William J. *Captains to the Northward: The New England Captains in the Continental Navy.* Barre, Mass.: Barre Gazette, 1959.

542. Morse, Stanley G. "Yankee Privateersman of 1776" *New England Quarterly* 17 (1944): 71-86.

543. Moultrie, William *Memoirs of the American Revolution.* 2 vols. New York: David Longworth, 1802.

544. Muhlenberg, Henry A. *The Life of Major-General Peter Muhlenberg of the Revolutionary Army.* Philadelphia: Carey and Hart, 1849.

545. Murdoch, David H., ed. *Rebellion in America: A Contemporary British Viewpoint, 1765-1783.* Santa Barbara, Calif.: Clio Press, 1979.

546. Myers, Duane. *The Highland Scots of North Carolina, 1732-1776.* Chapel Hill: University of North Carolina Press, 1961.

547. Myers, Minor, Jr. *Liberty without Anarchy: A History of the Society of the Cincinnatus.* Charlottesville: University Press of Virginia, 1983.

548. Navy Records Society. *Letters and Papers of Charles, Lord Barham, Admiral of the Red Squadron, 1758-1813.* vol. 32. Ed. by John Laughton. London: For the Society, 1907.

549. _____ *Letters Written by Sir Samuel Hood (Viscount Hood) in 1781,-2,-3.* Vol. 3. London: For the Society, 1895.

550. _____. *The Private Papers of John, Earl of Sandwich, First Lord of the Admiralty, 1771-1782.* 4 vols. Vols. 69, 71, 75, 78. London: For the Society, 1932-1938.

551. _____. *Signals and Instructions, 1776-1794.* Vol. 35 Ed. by Julian S. Corbett. London: For the Society, 1908.

552. Nell, William C. *The Colored Patriots of the American Revolution.* Boston: R. F. Wallcut, 1855; reprint, New York: Arno Press, 1968.

553. Nicola, Lewis. *A Treatise of Military Excercises Calculated for the Use of Americans.* Philadelphia: Styner & Cist, 1776.

554. Nielson, Jon M. "Penobscot: From the Jaws of Victory Our Navy's Worst Defeat." *American Neptune* 37 (October 1977): 288–305.
555. Nordholt, Jan Willem Schulte. *The Dutch Republic and American Independence*. Translated by Herbert H. Rowen. Chapel Hill: University of North Carolina Press, 1982.
556. Norton, Mary Beth. *Liberty's Daughters; The Revolutionary Experiences of American Women, 1750–1800*. Boston: Little, Brown, 1980.
557. Nuxoll, Elizabeth Miles. "Congress and the Munitions Merchants: The Secret Committee of Trade during the American Revolution, 1775–1777." Ph.D. diss., City University of New York, 1979.
558. Okinshevich, Leo, comp. *United States History and Historical in Postwar Soviet Writings, 1945–1970*. Santa Barbara, Calif.: Clio Press, 1976.
559. Olivier, Philippe. *Bibliographie des travaux relatif à Gilbert du Motier, Marquis de Lafayette (1757–1834), et á Adrienne de Noailles, Marquise de Lafayette (1759–1807)*. Clermont-Ferrand: The Institut, 1979.
560. Owen, William P., ed. *The Medical Department of the United States Army during the Period of the Revolution*. New York: P. B. Hoeber, 1920.
561. Pachero, Josephine F. "French Secret Agents in America, 1763–1778." Ph.D. diss., University of Chicago, 1950.
562. Paine, Ralph D. *Joshua Barney: A Forgotten Hero of Blue Water*. New York: Century, 1924.
563. Pancake, John S. *This Destructive War: The British Campaign in the Carolinas, 1780–1782*. University: University of Alabama Press, 1985.
564. _____. *1777: The Year of the Hangman*. University: University of Alabama Press, 1976.
565. Papenfuse, Edward C., and Gregory A. Stiverson. "General Smallwood's Recruits: The Peacetime Career of the Revolutionary War Private." *William and Mary Quarterly* 30 (1973): 117–32.
566. Parkman, Aubrey. *Army Engineers in New England: The Military and Civil Works of the Corps of Engineers in New England, 1775–1975*. Washington, D.C.: GPO, 1978.
567. Patterson, A. Temple. *The Other Armada*. Manchester: Manchester University Press, 1960.
568. Paullin, Charles O., ed. *Out-Letters of the Continental Marine Committee and Board of Admiralty, August 1776–September 1780*. New York: Da Vine Press, 1914.
569. Peckham, Howard H., ed. *Sources of American Independence: Selected Manuscripts from the Collections of the William L. Clements Library*. 2 vols. Chicago: University of Chicago Press, 1978.
570. Perugia, P. del *Le tentative d'invasion d'Angleterre en 1779*. Paris: Alcon Presses Université de France, 1939.
571. Peterson, Harold L. *The Book of the Continental Soldier: Being a Complete Account of the Uniforms, Weapons, and Equipment in which He Lived and Fought*. Harrisburg, Pa.: Stackpole Books, 1968.
572. _____. *Round Shot and Rammers*. Harrisburg, Pa.: Stackpole Books, 1969.
573. Pieper, Thomas I. *Fort Laurens, 1778–1779*: The Revolutionary War in Ohio. Kent, Ohio: Kent State Univeristy Press, 1976.
574. Pratt, Fletcher. *Eleven Generals: Studies in American Command*. New

York: Sloane, 1949.

575. Preston, Antony, David Lyon, and John H. Batchelor, eds. *Navies of the American Revolution*. Englewood Cliffs, N.J.: Prentice-Hall, 1975.

576. Proctor, Samuel, ed. *Eighteenth Century Florida and the Revolutionary South*. Gainesville: University Presses of Florida, 1978.

577. Pugh, Robert C. "The Revolutionary Militia in the Southern Campaigns, 1780–1781." *William and Mary Quarterly* 14 (April 957): 154–75.

578. Rankin, Hugh F. "Cowpens, Prelude to Yorktown." *North Carolina Historical Review* 31 (July 1954): 336–69.

579. _____. "The Moore's Creek Campaign, 1776." *North Carolina Historical Review* 30 (1953): 30–56.

580. _____. *The War of the Revolution in Virginia*. Williamsburg: Virginia Independence Bicentennial Commission, 1979.

581. Ranlet, Philip. "British Recruitment of Americans in New York During the American Revolution." *Military Affairs* 48 (January 1984): 26–28.

582. Reed, William B. *Life and Correspondence of Joseph Reed*. 2 vols. Philadelphia: Lindsay and Blakiston, 1847

583. Reynolds, Donald E. "Aummunition Supply in Revolutionary Virginia." *Virginia Magazine of History and Biography* 73 (1965): 56–60.

584. Riley, Edward M. "St. George Tucker's Journal of the Siege of Yorktown, 1781." *William and Mary Quarterly* 5 (July 1948): 375–95.

585. Risch, Erna. *Supplying Washington's Army*. Washington, D.C.: Center of Military History, 1981.

586. Rivington, James. *The Case of Major John André*. New York: James Rivington, 1780.

587. Roberts, Kenneth, ed. *March to Quebec: Journals of the Members of Arnold's Expedition*. New York: Doubleday, 1938.

588. Robson, Eric. "British Light Infantry in the Mid-Eighteenth Century: The Effect of American Conditions." *Army Quarterly* 62 (1950): 209–22.

589. Roche, John F. *Joseph Reed: A Moderate in the American Revolution*. New York: Columbia University Press, 1957.

590. Rodney, George. *Letter Books and Order Books of George, Lord Rodney, Admiral of the White Squadron, 1780–1782*. 2 vols. Charlottesville: University Press of Virginia, 1932.

591. Rogers, George C., Jr. "Letters of Charles O'Hara to the Duke of Grafton." *South Carolina Historical Magazine* 65 (1964): 158–80.

592. Rogers, Hugh C. B. *The British Army of the 18th Century*. New York: Hippocrene, 1977.

593. Roland, Alex Frederick. "A Triumph of Natural Magic: The Development of Underwater Warfare in the Age of Sail, 1571–1865." Ph.D. diss., Duke University, 1975.

594. Ross, Charles, ed. *Correspondence of Charles, First Marquis Cornwallis*. 3 vols. 2d ed. London: John Murray, 1859.

595. Rossie, Johathan G. *The Politics of Command in the American Revolution*. Syracuse, N.Y.: Syracuse University Press, 1975.

596. Rosswurm, Steven J. "Arms, Culture, and Class: The Philadelphia Militia and 'Lower Orders' in the American Revolution, 1765 to 1783." Ph.D. diss., Northern Illinois University, 1979.

597. Royster, Charles William. *A Revolutionary People at War: The Continental*

Army and the American Character, 1775–1783. Chapel Hill: University of North Carolina Press for the Institute of Early American History and Culture, 1979; New York: W. W. Norton, 1981.

598. _____. "The Continental Army in the American Mind: 1775-1783." Ph.D. diss., University of California, Berkeley, 1977.

599. _____. *Light-Horse Harry Lee and the Legacy of the American Revolution.* New York: Alfred A. Knopf, 1981.

600. Rozenthal, Gustav. "Journal of a Volunteer Expedition to Sandusky, From May 24 to June 13, 1782." *Pennsylvania Magazine of History and Biography* 28 (1894): 129–57.

601. Ryan, Dennis P., ed. *A Salute to Courage: The American Revolution as Seen through the Wartime Writings of Officers of the Continental Army and Navy.* New York: Columbia University Press, 1979.

602. _____. *New Jersey in the American Revolution, 1763–1783: A Chronology.* Trenton: New Jersey Historical Commission, 1974.

603. Sabine, William H. *Murder, 1776, and Washington's Policy of Silence.* New York: Theo Gaus' Sons, 1973.

604. Saffron, Morris H. *Surgeon to Washington: Dr. John Cochran.* New York: Columbia University Press, 1977.

605. Salay, David Lewis. "Arming for War: The Production of War Material in Pennsylvania for the American Armies during the Revolution." Ph.D. diss., University of Delaware, 1979.

606. Salley, Alexander, S., Jr., ed. *Documents Relating to the History of South Carolina during the Revolutionary War.* Columbia, S.C.: State Company, 1908.

607. Sanchez-Saavedra, E. M., comp. *A Guide to Virginia Military Organizations in the American Revolution, 1774–1787.* Richmond: Virginia State Library, 1978.

608. Sands, John Ogilby. "Sea Power at Yorktown: The Archeology of the Captive Fleet." Ph.D. diss., George Washington University, 1980.

609. Schlesinger, Arthur M. *Prelude to Independence: The Newspaper War on Britain, 1764–1776.* New York: Knopf, 1958.

610. Scott, Kenneth, ed. *Rivington's New York Newspaper: Excerpts from a Loyalist Press, 1773–1783.* New York: New York Historical Society, 1973.

611. Searcy, Martha Condray. "The Georgia-Florida Campaigns in the American Revolution, 1776, 1777, and 1778." Ph.D. diss., Tulane University, 1979.

612. Sellers, John R., comp. *Manuscript Sources in the Library of Congress for Research on the American Revolution.* Washington, D.C.: Library of Congress, 1975.

613. _____. *The Virginia Continental Line.* Williamsburg: Virginia Independence Bicentennial Commission, 1978.

614. Servies, James A. *The Siege of Pensacola: A Bibliography.* Pensacola, Fla.: John C. Pace Library, 1981.

615. Sheldon, Richard N. "Editing a Historical Manuscript: Jared Sparks, Douglas Southall Freeman, and the Battle of Brandywine." *William and Mary Quarterly* 36 (April 1979): 255–63.

616. Showman, Richard K., ed. *The Papers of General Nathanael Greene.* 3 vols. to date. Chapel Hill: University of North Carolina Press, 1976–.

617. Shreve, L. G. *Tench Tilghman: The Life and Times of Washington's Aide-*

de-Camp. Centreville, Md.: Tidewater Publishers, 1982.

618. Siebert, Wilbur H., ed. *Loyalists in East Florida, 1774–1785*. Deland: Florida State Historical Society, 1929.

619. _____. *Loyalists of Pennsylvania*. Columbus: Ohio State University Press, 1920.

620. Simms, Lynn Lee. "The Military Career of John Lamb." Ph.D. diss., New York University, 1975.

621. Simms, William B., ed. *The Army Correspondence of Colonel John Laurens, in the Year 1777–1778*. New York: Bradford Club, 1867.

622. Skaggs, David Curtis, ed. *The Old Northwest in the American Revolution: An Anthology*. Madison: State Historical Society of Wisconsin, 1977.

623. Skeen, C. Edward. *John Armstrong, Jr., 1758–1843: A Biography*. Syracuse, N.Y.: Syracuse University Press, 1981.

624. Smith, Howard W. *Benjamin Harrison and the American Revolution*. Williamsburg: Virginia Independence Bicentennial Commission, 1978.

625. Smith, Marc. "Joseph Brant: Mohawk Stateman." Ph.D. diss., University of Wisconsin, 1946.

626. Smith, Philip C. F. *Captain Samuel Tucker (1747–1833), Continental Navy*. Salem, Mass.: Essex Institute, 1976.

627. Smith, Paul H., ed. *Letters of Delegates to Congress, 1774–1789*. 9 vols. to date. Washington, D.C.: GPO, 1976–.

628. Smith, Samuel S. *Fight for the Delaware, 1777*. Monmouth Beach, N.J.: Philip Freneau Press, 1970.

629. Sosin, Jack M. "The Use of Indians in the War of the American Revolution: A Reassessment of Responsiblity." *Canadian Historical Review* 46 (1965): 101–21.

630. Sparks, Jared, ed. *Correspondence of the American Revolution, Being Letters of Eminent Men to George Washington*. 4 vols. Boston: Little, Brown, 1853.

631. Spaulding, Oliver L., Jr. "The Military Studies of George Washington." *American Historical Review* 29 (April 1924): 675–80.

632. Stephenson, Orlando W. "The Supply of Gunpowder in 1776." *American Historical Review* 30 (1925): 271–81.

633. Stevens, Benjamin Franklin, ed. *Stevens's Facsimilies of Manuscripts in European Archives Relating to America, 1775–1783*. 25 vols. London: Malby and Sons [microfilm], 1889–1895.

634. Stevenson, Roger. *Military Instructions for Officers Detached in the Field: Containing a Scheme for Forming a Corps of Partisans. Illustrated with Plans of the Manoeuvres Necessary in Carrying on the PETITE GUERRE*. Philadelphia: R. Aitken, 1775.

635. Still, William N., Jr. *North Carolina's Revolutionary Navy*. Zebulon, N.C.: Theo Davis Sons, 1976.

636. Stille, Charles J. "Beaumarchais and the Lost Million." *Pennsylvania Magazine of History and Biography* 2 (1887): 1–36.

637. Stivers, Reuben E. *Privateers and Volunteers: The Men and Women of Our Reserve Naval Forces, 1776–1866*. Annapolis, Md.: Naval Institute Press,

638. Stone, Richard G., Jr. *A Brittle Sword: The Kentucky Militia, 1776–1912*. Lexington: University of Kentucky Press, 1978.

639. Stryker, William S., ed. *Documents Relating to the Revolutionary History of New Jersey: Extracts from American Newspapers*. 5 vols. Trenton, N.J.: J. L. Murphy, 1901–1917.

640. Stuart, Reginald C. *War and American Thought from the Revolution to the Monroe Doctrine*. Kent, Ohio: Kent State University Press, 1982.

641. Sunseri, Alvin R. "Frederick Wilhelm von Steuben and the Re-Education of the American Army: A Lesson in Practicality." *Armor* 74 (1965): 40–47.

642. Syrett, David. "American and British Naval Historians and the American Revolutionary War, 1875–1980." *American Neptune* 52 (July 1982): 179–82.

643. _____. *Shipping and the American War, 1775–83: A Study of British Transport Organization*. London: University of London, Athlone Press, 1970.

644. Templin, Thomas E. "Henry 'Light-Horse Harry' Lee: A Biography." Ph.D. diss., University of Kentucky, 1975.

645. Thayer, Theodore. *Colonial and Revolutionary Morris County*. Morristown, N.J.: Morris County Heritage Commission, 1975.

646. Thwaites, Reuben Gold, and Louise P. Kellog, eds. *Frontier Defenses on the Upper Ohio, 1777–1778*. Madison: University of Wisconsin Press, 1912.

647. Tilley, John Andrew. "The Royal Navy in North America, 1774–1781: A Study in Command." Ph.D. diss., Ohio State University, 1981.

648. Todd, Frederick P. *Soldiers of the American Army, 1775–1954*. Rev. ed. Chicago: H. Regnery, 1954.

649. Toth, Charles, ed. *The American Revolution and the West Indies*. Port Washington: N.Y.: Kennikat, 1975.

650. Trussell, John B. B., Jr. *The Pennsylvania Line: Regimental Organization and Operations, 1776–1783*. Harrisburg: Pennsylvania Historical and Museum Commission, 1977.

651. Underdal, Stanley J., ed. *Proceedings of the 6th Military History Symposium, U.S. Air Force Academy, 1974*. Washington, D.C.: GPO, 1976.

652. U.S. Army. *The War of the American Revolution: Narrative, Chronology, and Bibliography*. Compiled by Robert W. Coakley and Stetson Conn. Washington, D.C.: GPO, 1975.

653. U.S. Continental Congress. *The Papers of the Continental Congress, 1774–1789*. Washington, D.C.: National Archives and Records Service [Microfilm], 1971.

654. Van Alstyne, Richard W. "Great Britain, the War of Independence, and the 'Gathering Storm' in Europe." *Huntington Library Quarterly* 27 (1964): 311–46.

655. Van Tyne, Claude H. *The Loyalists of the American Revolution*. New York: P. Smith, 1902, 1929.

656. Von Eelking, Max. *Memoirs and Letters and Journals of Major General Riedesel during his Residence in America*. Albany, N.Y.: J. Munsell, 1868; Reprint, New York: New York Times/Arno Press, 1969.

657. Wade, H. T., and R. A. Lively *This Glorious Cause: The Adventures of Two Company Officers in Washington's Army*. Princeton, N.J.: Princeton University Press, 1958.

658. Waldo, Albigence. "Diary of Surgeon Albigence Waldo, of the Continental Line." *Pennsylvania Magazine of History and Biography* 21 (1897): 299-323.

659. Walker, Paul K. *Engineers of Independence: A Documentary History of the Army Engineers in the American Revolution, 1775-1783.* Washington, D.C.: Historical Division, Office of the Chief of Engineers, 1982.

660. Waller, George M. *The American Revolution in the West.* Chicago: Nelson-Hall, 1976

661. Walsh, John E. *Night on Fire: The First Complete Account of John Paul Jones' Greatest Battle.* New York: McGraw-Hill, 1978.

662. Ward, Harry H. *Duty, Honor, or Country: General George Weedon and the American Revolution.* Philadelphia: American Philosophical Society, 1979.

663. Ward, Harry, and Harold E. Green, Jr. *Richmond during the Revolution, 1775-1783.* Charlottesville: University Press of Virginia, 1977.

664. Waring, Alice Noble. *The Fighting Elder: Andrew Pickens, 1739-1817.* Columbia: University of South Carolina Press, 1962.

665. Waterman, Joseph M. *With Sword and Lancet: The Life of General Hugh Mercer.* Richmond, Va.: Garret and Massie, 1941.

666. Weigley, Russell F. "Military History: Not Yet Over the Top." *Reviews in American History* 1 (June 1973): 237-44.

667. _____. *The American Way of War: A History of United States Military Strategy and Policy.* New York: Macmillan, 1973; Bloomington: Indiana University Press, 1977.

668. _____. *The Partisan War: The South Carolina Compaign of 1780-1782.* Columbia: University of South Carolina Press, 1970.

669. Weir, Robert M. *Colonial South Carolina: A History.* Millwod, N.Y.: KTO Press, 1983.

670. White, Donald Wallace. *A Village at War: Chatham, New Jersey, and the American Revolution.* Rutherford, N.J.: Fairleigh Dickinson University Press, 1979.

671. White, John Todd. "Standing Armies in Time of War: Republican Theory and Military Practice during the American Revolution." Ph.D. diss., George Washington University, 1978.

672. White, John Todd, and Charles H. Lesser, eds. *Fighters for Independence: A Guide to Sources of Biographical Information on Soldiers and Sailors of the American Revolution.* Chicago: University of Chicago Press, 1977.

673. Willcox, William B. "British Strategy in America, 1778." *Journal of Modern History* 19 (1947): 97-121.

674. _____. "Too Many Cooks: British Planning before Saratoga." *Journal of British Studies* 2 (November 1962): 56-90.

675. _____. "Why Did the British Lose the American Revolution?" *Michigan Alumnus Quarterly Review* 62 (1956): 317-24.

676. _____. ed. *The American Rebellion: Sir Henry Clinton's Narrative of His Campaigns, 1775-1782.* New Haven: Yale University Press, 1954.

677. Williams, Edward G. *Fort Pitt and the Revolution on the Western Frontier.* Pittsburgh: Historical Society of Western Pennsylvania, 1978.

678. Wilson, Ellen Gibson. *The Loyal Blacks.* New York: Capricorn Books, 1976.

679. Wilson, Rufus R., ed. *Memoirs of Major General William Heath*. New York: A. Wessels, 1904. Reprint, Freeport, N.Y.: Books for Libraries Press, 1970.
680. Wright, Albert C., comp. *The Sullivan Expedition of 1779*. Ithaca, N.Y.: A. H. Wright, 1943.
681. Wright, Robert K., Jr. "Organization and Doctrine in the Continental Army, 1774 to 1784." Ph.D. diss., College of William and Mary, 1981.
682. _____. *The Continental Army*. Washington, D.C.: Center of Military History, 1983.
683. Wyatt, Frederick, and William B. Willcox. "Sir Henry Clinton: A Psychological Exploration in History." *William and Mary Quarterly* 16 (January 1959): 2–26.

V

FROM THE REVOLUTION TO THE MEXICAN WAR

Roger L. Nichols

Interest in and scholarly study of the post-Revolutionary War era continues at the same level as reported in the first supplement. For the most part, military historians continue to focus on the topics already mentioned. Nevertheless, some investigators have called for new approaches, and others have begun to accept the challenge. Thus there are more studies which focus on the close interrelationship between politics and the development of military institutions and policies than previously. In addition, there is a renewed interest in the professionalization and bureaucratization of the army during the first six decades of national independence. A few writers have employed some of the statistical techniques popularized by proponents of the so-called New Social History in their studies of military topics and issues. Nearly all of the studies, however, focus on some aspect of long-established lines of study. So what has emerged is a blending of old topics and issues with new approaches and techniques.

GENERAL MILITARY HISTORIES. Works in this category demonstrate the range and variety in contemporary military histories. T. Harry Williams's survey *The History of American Wars from 1745 to 1918* (368) offers a traditional narrative of wars, campaigns, and battles that stretches from the late colonial era through World War I. Although skewed heavily toward the Civil War, it does offer a brief discussion of earlier military actions. In *A Brittle Sword: The Kentucky Militia, 1776–1912* (360), Richard G. Stone, Jr., examines early American reliance on the citizen soldier to perform a multitude of tasks. He considers the militiaman's pre-1815 role in national defense and traces its shift to local police functions by the mid-nineteenth century. The book title portrays his view of militia effectiveness most of the time. Willard B. Robinson's *American Forts: Architectural Form and Function* (355) traces the design and building of American forts from the sixteenth to the nineteenth centuries. In doing so, he considers everything from frontier log stockades to heavy stone coastal defenses.

ESTABLISHING A PEACETIME ARMY, 1783–1812. Studies of this era vary widely in scope and method too. Lawrence D. Cress, *Citizens in Arms: The Army and the Militia in American Society to the War of 1812* (331), delves into the ideas and attitudes Americans expressed toward the military. He suggests that the debate over dependence upon a citizen militia or a standing army resulted from long-standing arguments within Britain which carried over to the United States. The Federalists accepted arguments of the moderate Whigs and favored a regular army controlled by the civilian government, while the Jeffersonians sided with the radical Whigs in wanting to place more dependence on the militia. In *War and American Thought from the Revolution to the Monroe Doctrine* (361), Reginald C. Stuart claims that the era was one of national myth-making about wars. He sees a limited war mentality and the related idea of just wars as being the most significant theories at the time.

A second group of studies considers the close relationship between politics and military decisions and policy. Both John F. and Kathleen Smith Kutolowski (349), and Patrick J. Furlong in his "The Investigation of General Arthur St. Clair 1792-1793" (335), fall into this category. The latter shows that this event went far beyond the question of St. Clair's military competence. Rather, it revolved around the questions of how much discretion frontier commanders should be given and which part of the federal government should be responsible when campaigns failed. "Anthony Wayne: Soldier as Politician" (350), by Paul David Nelson, shows the close relationships between the two professions. Two other studies, by Theodore J. Crackel (330) and Donald Jackson (343), deal with Thomas Jefferson's approach to the army. Crackel shows that despite Jeffersonian rhetoric, army reduction was modest, and that the president used political compatibility as one of the chief criteria for which officers were retained or removed from the army. The article demonstrates that political considerations lay at the base of all the reduction efforts. Looking at the Federalist opposition during the same years, Donald R. Hickey's "Federalist Defense Policy in the Age of Jefferson, 1801-1812" (339) shows that they worked with the Jeffersonians to achieve their military goals.

Continuing interest in growing army professionalization may be seen in two studies of this period. Mary C. Gillett's *The Army Medical Department, 1775-1818* (337) is a relatively narrow administrative study of developments within the medical department. Arthur P. Wade's dissertation "Artillerists and Engineers: The Beginnings of American Seacoast Fortifications, 1794-1815" (365) considers an aspect of army effort which usually gets little attention. Related to the army role in enlarging the scope of the federal government are two items which discuss using soldiers as explorers. Donald Jackson's *Thomas Jefferson and the Stony Mountains: Exploring the West from Monticello* (344), and Phillip D. Thomas's "The United States Army as the Early Patron of Naturalists in the Trans-Mississippi West, 1803-1820" (363), consider Jeffersonian efforts to gain knowledge of the West, and trace federal explorations from Lewis and Clark through the 1820 expedition of Stephen Long.

THE WAR OF 1812. This conflict continues to receive attention from scholars interested in foreign affairs, military campaigning, army-civilian disputes, and the role of Indians in the fighting. The latter topic attracted little attention, perhaps because so much work has already been done on it. Both John Sugden (362), in his "The Southern Indians in the War of 1812: The Closing Phase," and Frank L. Owsley, Jr. (354), in his *Struggle for the Borderlands: The Creek War and the Battle of New Orleans, 1812-1815*, depict the southern Indian fighting within the context of the war against Britain. Sugden claims that Creek anti-American activities resulted from the Indian efforts at cultural and physical survival, rather than from their service as British pawns. Owsley shows Spanish ties to the Creeks but nevertheless considers the Creek War as another part of the larger international conflict.

Actual campaigning serves as focus for several items. A biographical article, "Winfield Scott, the Soldier" (329), by Albert Castel, focuses on his efforts in the north. Allan S. Everest's *The War of 1812 in the Champlain Valley* (332) is a solid study of that important theater. Another, by Leonard H. Scott (357), considers the surrender of Detroit in 1812, while Arthur H. Frazier (334) discusses Fort Dearborn. Much criticism of American campaign and command decisions resulted from this conflict, and in "The Fog and Friction of Frontier War: The Role of Logistics in American Offensive Failure during the War of 1812" (346) Jeffrey Kimball looks at the reasons for the frequent failures. He claims that strategic ignorance, over-reliance on the militia, weak logistical capabilities, economic disorganization, and a strong British and Canadian defense helped defeat American arms for much of the war. Charles E. Walker (366) considers the army engineers' work at the time.

Politics and diplomacy during the war continue to receive attention. Donald R. Hickey (341) shows how Federalist Party members used military preparedness and latent anti-British feelings in their political speeches and campaigns during the year immediately before hostilities began. In "Federalist Party Unity and the War of 1812" (340), he uses voting counts in Congress to show that the Federalists maintained a high degree of party unity on the issues of trade, commerce, and war during the fighting. Clearly the Federalists were not divided and leaderless on these issues, although they lacked the votes in Congress to sustain their views. In his theoretical article "The Laws of War in the 1812 Conflict" (333), Robin F. A. Fabel considers the ideas of both British and American armies about such issues as the treatment of prisoners, uses of flags of truce and surrender, and the rights of private property during the campaigning. He shows how Vattel's principles were often used in discussing these questions. In "The Battle of New Orleans and the Treaty of Ghent" (328), James E. Carr discounts supposed British efforts to undermine the treaty and shows that they wanted to end the conflict according to the treaty agreement.

THE POSTWAR ARMY. As in the discussion of the era preceding the War of 1812, scholars have shown a growing interest in the bureaucratization process through which the army passed. Roger J. Spiller's "Calhoun's Expansible Army: The History of a Military Idea" (359) discusses the foundation upon which postwar reductions and reorganizations of the army took place. In "Professionalization of the U.S. Officer Corps during the Age of Jackson" (358), William B. Skelton continues his studies of army officers during the 1820s and 1830s. Here he focuses on the gradual development of professionalism among the officers. In a study which extends to the Civil War, J. Patrick Hughes discusses the development of the adjutant general's office as the administrative branch of the army (342). Frank N. Schubert's *Vanguard of Expansion: Army Engineers in the Trans-Mississippi West, 1819–1879* (356) does the same thing for this army department. He discusses the corps as apolitical explorers and professionals, showing the administrative evolution of the engineers during those decades. Two other studies, by Marilyn A. Kindred (347) of the officer corps and John B. Garver, Jr. (336), of the army in general, consider issues related to the army's institutional impact upon Western exploration and upon the arts in American society during the nineteenth century.

Studies of individual forts and life at frontier posts continue to appear. Virgil

C. Ney (351) and Bertrand B. Banta, Jr. (326) discuss posts on the Mississippi and Missouri rivers, while Brad Agnew's *Fort Gibson: Terminal on the Trail of Tears* (325) focuses most of its attention on the soldiers' relationship with the nearby Indians. Other studies of Indian-related subjects reflect the continuing interest in campaign history. Among these, Jeffrey Wert's "Old Hickory and the Seminoles" (367) discusses Jackson's 1817 invasion of Florida, while Kenneth L. Valliere offers a careful examination of fraud and other causes of "The Creek War of 1836, a Military History" (364). In "The Arikara Indians and the Missouri River Trade: A Quest for Survival" (352), Roger L. Nichols focuses on the relationship among the troops, the fur traders, and the tribes of the upper Missouri Valley. The same author's "The Black Hawk War in Retrospect" (353) considers that conflict within the context of Midwestern frontier settlement and the national policy of Indian removal.

The careers of individual officers also received continuing attention. Edmund C. Bray and Martha Coleman Bray, in *Joseph N. Nicollet on the Plains and Prairies: The Expeditions of 1838–39 with Journals, Letters, and Notes on the Dakota Indians* (327), provide the only major collection of new primary material to be published in the past few years. The journals demonstrate the continuing use of soldiers as explorers and data gatherers, and the expeditions they discuss introduced young John C. Fremont to frontier exploration. Three other biographical studies point out two parallel trends in the mid-nineteenth century army. George R. Adams's "General William Selby Harney, Frontier Soldier, 1800–1889" (324) traces the career of an untrained officer who learned soldiering on the job. At the same time as many of the officer corps assumed their duties with no formal instruction, the army strove to increase professional competence, particularly through the staff departments. In *Maligned General: The Biography of Thomas Sidney Jesup* (345), Chester L. Kieffer traces Jesup's career, particularly as quartermaster-general for several decades. Although this is a one-sided, laudatory study, it offers some understanding of the continuing efforts to overcome the vast difficulties distance, communication, and a headstrong officer corps posed for the army. Mary C. Gillett's "Thomas Lawson, Second Surgeon General of the U.S. Army: A Character Sketch" (338) focuses chiefly on Lawson's difficult personality. Nevertheless, it shows the growing professionalization, already mentioned elsewhere, taking place in the medical department too.

SUGGESTIONS FOR FURTHER RESEARCH. In the preceding supplement, I pointed out the desirability of more biographical studies and of the need to examine army-militia relations. Whether researchers took this advice or were already working on those topics is not clear, but both tasks have received attention within the past five years. There is a need for more work using techniques borrowed from the New Social History. Studies of the enlisted personnel of the army can certainly be managed, particularly with the growing sophistication of computer-based statistical techniques now available. There may be enough studies of individual army departments and offices such as those of the engineers, the adjutant general, the surgeon general, and the artillery, so that a more comprehensive study of the administrative development of the entire army could be attempted.

Richard H. Kohn's "The Social History of the American Soldier: A Review and Prospectus for Research" (348) offers several excellent suggestions that may be applied to practically all eras of American military history. Certainly demographic and statistical studies of the enlisted men, including who they were, their levels of education, ethnic background, and even country of origin, would all prove valuable. He suggests applying the methods and approach of the *Annales* school of French historiography by considering all phases of military life and the social setting of the era. His third general idea is to study the interrelationships between the military and the rest of American society. Even if we limit our efforts to these, there would appear to be plenty of work left, although the resulting military history may well be startlingly different from the work of veteran practitioners of the craft.

BIBLIOGRAPHY

324. Adams, George R. "General William Selby Harney, Frontier Soldier, 1800–1889." Ph.D. diss., University of Arizona, 1983.
325. Agnew, Brad. *Fort Gibson: Terminal on the Trail of Tears.* Norman: University of Oklahoma Press, 1980.
326. Banta, Bertrand B., Jr. "A History of Jefferson Barracks, 1826–1860." Ph.D. diss., Louisiana State University, 1981.
327. Bray, Edmund C. and Martha Coleman, eds. *Joseph N. Nicollet on the Plains and Prairies: The Expeditions of 1838–39 With Journals, Letters, and Notes on the Dakota Indians.* St. Paul: Minnesota Historical Society Press, 1976.
328. Carr, James E. "The Battle of New Orleans and the Treaty of Ghent." *Diplomatic History* 3 (Summer 1979): 273–81.
329. Castel, Albert. "Winfield Scott, the Soldier." *American History Illustrated* 16 (June 1981): 10–17.
330. Crackel, Theodore J. "Jefferson, Politics, and the Army: An Examination of the Military Peace Establishment Act of 1802." *Journal of the Early Republic* 2 (Spring 1982): 21–38.
331. Cress, Lawrence Delbert. *Citizens in Arms: The Army and the Militia in American Society to the War of 1812.* Chapel Hill: University of North Carolina Press, 1982.
332. Everest, Allan S. *The War of 1812 in the Champlain Valley.* Syracuse, N.Y.: Syracuse University Press, 1981.
333. Fabel, Robin F. A. "The Laws of War in the 1812 Conflict." *Journal of American Studies* 14 (August 1980): 199–218.
334. Frazier, Arthur H. "The Military Frontier: Fort Dearborn." *Chicago History* 9 (Summer 1980): 80–85.
335. Furlong, Patrick J. "The Investigation of General Arthur St. Clair 1792–1793." *Capitol Studies* 5 (Fall 1977): 65–86.
336. Garver, John B., Jr. "The Role of the United States Army in the Colonization of the Trans-Missouri West: Kansas, 1804–1861." Ph.D. diss., Syracuse University, 1981.
337. Gillett, Mary C. *The Army Medical Department, 1775–1818.* Washington, D.C.: Center of Military History, 1981.
338. _____. "Thomas Lawson, Second Surgeon General of the U.S. Army: A Character Sketch." *Prologue* 14 (Spring 1982): 15–24.
339. Hickey, Donald R. "Federalist Defense Policy in the Age of Jefferson,

1801–1812." *Military Affairs* 45 (April 1981): 63–70.
340. _____. "Federalist Party Unity and the War of 1812." *Journal of American Studies* 12 (April 1978): 23–39.
341. _____. "The Federalists and the Coming of the War, 1811–1812." *Indiana Magazine of History* 75 (March 1979): 70–87.
342. Hughes, J. Patrick. "The Adjutant General's Office, 1821–1861: A Study in Administrative History." Ph.D. diss., Ohio State University, 1977.
343. Jackson, Donald. "Jefferson, Meriwether Lewis, and the Reduction of the United States Army." *Proceedings of the American Philosophical Society* 124 (April 1980).
344. _____. *Thomas Jefferson and the Stony Mountains: Exploring the West from Monticello.* Urbana: University of Illinois Press, 1981.
345. Kieffer, Chester L. *Maligned General: The Biography of Thomas Sidney Jesup.* San Rafael, Calif.: Presidio Press, 1979.
346. Kimball, Jeffery. "The Fog and Friction of Frontier War: The Role of Logistics in American Offensive Failure during the War of 1812." *Old Northwest* 5 (Winter 1979–80): 323–43.
347. Kindred, Marilyn A. "The Army Officer Corps and the Arts: Artistic Patronage and Practice in America, 1820–85." Ph.D. diss., University of Kansas, 1981.
348. Kohn, Richard H. "The Social History of the American Soldier: A Review and Prospectus for Research." *American Historical Review* 86 (June 1981): 553–67.
349. Kutolowski, John F. and Kathleen Smith. "Commissions and Canvasses: The Militia and Politics in Western New York, 1800–1845." *New York History* 63 (January 1982): 5–38.
350. Nelson, Paul David. "Anthony Wayne: Soldier as Politician." *Pennsylvania Magazine of History and Biography* 106 (October 1982): 463–82.
351. Ney, Virgil C. "Daily Life at Fort Atkinson on the Missouri 1820–1827." Part I. *Military Review* 57 (January 1977): 36–48; Part II. *Ibid.* (February 1977): 50–66.
352. Nichols, Roger L. "The Arikara Indians and the Missouri River Trade: A Quest for Survival." *Great Plains Quarterly* 2 (Spring 1982): 77–93.
353. _____. "The Black Hawk War in Retrospect." *Wisconsin Magazine of History* 65 (Summer 1982): 239–46.
354. Owsley, Frank L., Jr. *Struggle for the Borderlands: The Creek War and the Battle of New Orleans, 1812–1815.* Gainesville: University of Florida Presses, 1981.
355. Robinson, Willard B. *American Forts: Architectural Form and Function.* Urbana: University of Illinois Press, 1977.
356. Schubert, Frank N. *Vanguard of Expansion: Army Engineers in the Trans-Mississippi West, 1819–1879.* Washington, D.C.: Office of the Chief of Engineers, 1980.
357. Scott, Leonard H. "The Surrender of Detroit." *American History Illustrated* 12 (June 1977): 28–36.
358. Skelton, William B. "Professionalization of the U.S. Officer Corps During the Age of Jackson." *Armed Forces and Society* 1 (Summer 1975): 445–71.
359. Spiller, Roger J. "Calhoun's Expansible Army: The History of a Military Idea." *South Atlantic Quarterly* 79 (Spring 1980): 189–203.

360. Stone, Richard G., Jr. *A Brittle Sword: The Kentucky Militia, 1776–1912.* Lexington: University Press of Kentucky, 1977.
361. Stuart, Reginald C. *War and American Thought from the Revolution to the Monroe Doctrine.* Kent, Ohio: Kent State University Press, 1982.
362. Sugden, John. "The Southern Indians in the War of 1812: The Closing Phase." *Florida Historical Quarterly* 60 (January 1982): 273–312.
363. Thomas, Phillip Drennen. "The United States Army as the Early Patron of Naturalists in the Trans-Mississippi West, 1803–1820." *Chronicles of Oklahoma* 56 (Summer 1978): 171–93.
364. Valliere, Kenneth L. "The Creek War of 1836, a Military History." *Chronicles of Oklahoma* 57 (Winter 1979): 463–85.
365. Wade, Arthur P. "Artillerists and Engineers: The Beginnings of American Seacoast Fortifications, 1794–1815." Ph.D. diss., Kansas State University, 1977.
366. Walker, Charles E. "The Other Good Guys: Army Engineers in the War of 1812." *Military Engineer* 70 (May / June, 1978): 178–83.
367. Wert, Jeffrey. "Old Hickory and the Seminoles." *American History Illustrated* 15 (October 1980): 28–35.
368. Williams, T. Harry. *The History of American Wars from 1745 to 1918.* New York: Alfred A. Knopf, 1981.

VI

THE NAVY IN THE NINETEENTH CENTURY, 1789–1889

Christopher McKee

In *Supplement I* to *A Guide to the Sources of United States Military History*, this historian chronicled and evaluated scholarly publication relating to the U.S. Navy's first century of existence from the appearance of the original guide down to the last quarter of 1979. The present essay picks up the thread of scholarship at the latter point and follows it through the year 1983. It attempts to report, as comprehensively as possible, all books and articles published within that period which appear to make an original contribution to the subject. A number of titles not caught in the net of *Supplement I* or in that of the original guide are here belatedly noted. Once again, for the reasons explained in *Supplement I*, no attempt is made to include unpublished doctoral dissertations.

Four years may be too brief a period to detect accurately major changes of direction in scholarly publication on the nineteenth-century U.S. Navy. That caution duly noted, one trend suspected in *Supplement I* seems to stand out even more in *Supplement II:* mounting interest in the navy's history during the years 1816–1860 and 1866–1889. A number of factors appear to be driving this wave of publication. Heretofore, the periods in question have been largely ignored by historians. A wealth of interesting, virtually untouched topics awaited the original and enterprising scholar, but an extended lag time was seemingly required before writers became widely aware of rich archival resources for the study of these periods that the National Archives began to make available in microfilm editions as long ago as the 1940s and 1950s. Some of the pioneers who first explored the post-1815 years were the biographers of figures usually associated with the more-studied War of 1812 period. As these biographers followed their subjects into the deeply changed world of 1816 and beyond, not only did they investigate and report that latter day's special problems with care and enthusiasm—rather than hurrying to wrap up their subjects' post-1815 lives in cursory fashion—but their writings also served to alert others to the historical riches awaiting them in libraries and archives. Moreover, it is during these years that one finds the navy engaged in its customary peacetime functions—protecting commerce, conducting or assisting diplomatic negotiations, pursuing scientific activities. Here was common ground whereon traditional naval historians could join historians of diplomacy, of commerce, of science and technology, and address shared concerns. Finally—and this is particularly true of the 1866–1889 years—the U.S. Navy's major social and organizational mutations have usually occurred not during major wars but in the years preceding or following these comprehensive hostilities. The historian seeking to discover and understand such changes has had to seek them in what is rather misleadingly labeled the "peacetime" navy.

BIBLIOGRAPHIES AND GENERAL HISTORIES. A lifetime of studying the nineteenth- and twentieth-century U.S. Navy is reflected in Paolo Coletta's *A Bibliography of American Naval History* (388). Coletta's coverage, which embraces English-language books, government documents, dissertations and theses, articles, oral history transcripts, and historical fiction, extends to the end of 1979. However, he attempts but little critical evaluation or annotation of the scholarship so fully listed. Manuscript and archival holdings relevant to the study of American naval history in more than 250 institutions are described in Dean C. Allard and associates' *U.S. Naval History Sources in the United States* (360). This highly useful volume is the first place a scholar should turn to discover what unpublished materials are available for research under consideration.

One of the most important publications to appear during the period covered by this essay is *New American State Papers, Naval Affairs*, edited by K. Jack Bauer (443). Its ten volumes are made up of selections from the official records of the navy, drawn from both manuscript archives and papers previously printed in congressional and departmental publications. Coverage extends from 1794 through 1860, with primary emphasis on the post-1807 years to complement the Navy Department's *Quasi-War* and *Barbary Wars* series (262, 263, 264). *New American State Papers, Naval Affairs* includes no annotation apart from the editor's introduction to each volume and a table giving the provenance of every document. All papers published therein are photocopied from the original printed or manuscript documents, rather than being newly set up in type. Despite this drawback, the results are reasonably legible. A more serious handicap is the absence of any general index, and this lack is compounded by the subject arrangement of the series. Locating a particular document can become a tedious process.

American Secretaries of the Navy (364), a collaborative effort under the leadership of Paolo Coletta, seeks to provide a biographical and historical evaluation of each man's term of office. The 1980 publication date is deceptive. Many of the essays were completed at least ten years earlier, but the project experienced a frustratingly long delay in reaching print. As is often the case in such team ventures, the individual essays vary in quality. To cite one example, the author of the essays on William Jones and Benjamin Crowninshield did not consult the readily available private papers of either man, although both left personal archives which are essential to understanding their secretaryships. An even longer delay in publication was experienced by Robert G. Albion's *Makers of Naval Policy, 1798-1947* (359), a comprehensive history of United States naval administration. The work of a master historian deeply immersed in the subject, *Makers* bristles with keen insights, memorable personalities, and arguable judgments. Albion's original manuscript, written under contract with the Navy Department, was completed in 1950 but never published. Rowena Reed prepared the present edition from the author's imperfect retained copy. Unfortunately, neither here nor elsewhere in print will one find a candid explanation of why the manuscript was suppressed in 1950 — nor, indeed, what has become of the author's original text submitted to the Navy Department.

Navy yards and shore installations have not always been subjects studied in accordance with the highest standards of historical practice. George F. Pearce's *The U.S. Navy in Pensacola: From Sailing Ships to Naval Aviation, 1825-1930*

(446) is one of the better such studies yet written and is based on a wide range of little-read sources. However, the author's research unaccountably missed certain mainline materials, such as the records of the Board of Navy Commissioners at the National Archives, which would be essential to presenting the full story. Those students of the sailing navy of 1797–1840 interested in knowing how a gun drill of a ship's primary armament was supposed to have been conducted – at least if the textbooks are to be believed – will find that exercise admirably detailed in an article by Charles R. Fisher (403), which complements a related piece (311) noted in the previous supplement.

SHIPS: CONSTRUCTION, HISTORY, UNDERWATER ARCHAEOLOGY. Ever since the publication of William Bell Clark's biography of John Barry (51) and Eugene S. Ferguson's life of Thomas Truxtun (77), historians have been well aware of the importance of Southern live oak in naval ship construction. However, Virginia Steele Wood's *Live Oaking: Southern Timber for Tall Ships* (477) is the first comprehensive examination of the harvesting and use of this timber. *Live Oaking* covers both merchant marine as well as naval uses of the timber, is enhanced by superlative graphics, and ranks as a work of the highest stature among recent maritime publications. Live oak timber was used in shipbuilding because it was judged to be a wood of great durability. Charles Haines examines the pre-Civil War navy's official efforts to prolong the life of its wooden ships in "Ship Preservation in the Old Navy" (408); he fails, regrettably, to provide a yardstick of the latest scientific knowledge regarding the causes of rot in wood and the means of its prevention against which to assess the nineteenth-century navy's effort. Maury Baker's promisingly titled "Cost Overrun, an Early Naval Precedent: Building the First U.S. Warships, 1794–98" (367) proves to be based entirely on older, long-familiar printed sources. Rather than providing a fresh look at the problems of expenditure control in the building of the frigates *Constellation, Constitution*, and *United States*, it is chiefly a retelling of a construction history well known to scholars. Baker appears to have made no substantive use of relevant sources published later than 1949 – Ferguson's book on Truxtun (77) is a prime omission – leading one to suppose the essay may have been essentially completed years before its publication date.

Histories of a substantial number of navy ships – some still preserved, others long since broken up – have appeared since 1979. *A Most Fortunate Ship* (436), Tyrone G. Martin's biography of the *Constitution*, is a welcome addition to the literature because it gives as much coverage to the famous frigate's post-1815 years as it does to better-known episodes from the Tripolitan War and the War of 1812. Martin's is, clearly, the best general history of the subject extant. William P. and Ethel L. Bass are engaged in an original and valuable attempt to reconstruct, from narrative and graphic evidence, the many changes of appearance and physical configuration which the *Constitution* has undergone over the years. Their *Constitution, Second Phase 1802–07 – Mediterranean, Tripoli, Malta & More* (370) makes available the first impressive results of this labor of love. Its graphic work is of superlative quality. The latest, and the least impassioned, entry in the ongoing debate over the physical history of the *Constitution*'s sister ship *Constellation*, that is, whether the extant vessel is the ship launched in 1797, may be seen in Evan Randolph's careful survey of relevant documents (449). Those interested in this vexed question of the *Constellation*'s provenance will also want to consult two earlier contributions to the debate (383, 457) not noted in the original guide. Fred W. Hopkins summarizes the history of a less famous vessel, the sloop-of-war *Ontario* (416). She served both as a naval vessel (1813–1856) and as a short-lived civilian schoolship (1857–1867), sponsored by Baltimore's Board of Trade and its Board of School Commissioners, for the training of merchant mariners.

The branch of historical study that appears to be doing the most to stimulate interest in the navy's material and social history is underwater archaeology. A report on the discovery of the Civil War *Monitor* off the North Carolina coast (355) was noted in *Supplement I*. Not listed there, though it should have been, was Edward M. Miller's USS *Monitor: The Ship That Launched a Modern Navy* (439), a first-rate account of the vessel which tells not only the familiar story of her conception, building, and battle history but details the lesser-known loss of the ship in December 1862 and the efforts to discover her final resting place. Once the wreck was found, the question became what should be done with the *Monitor*: Leave her where she lies? Recover significant portions of the remains? Attempt to raise the entire vessel? These and related issues were the agenda of a national conference whose proceedings (440) should make sobering reading for enthusiasts of raising sunken wrecks. Scholars desiring to follow current developments regarding the *Monitor* and the federally-designated Marine Sanctuary where she rests may do so by consulting *Cheesebox* (385), a semiannual newsletter devoted to these developments which the Program in Maritime History and Underwater Archaeology at East Carolina University began issuing in 1982. Edwin C. Bearss's work on another Civil War survivor, *Hardluck Ironclad: The Sinking and Salvage of the Cairo*, was originally issued in 1966 but was not noted in the guide. A revised edition (372), which carries down to 1979 the cautionary tale of the efforts to preserve the remains of the vessel, appeared in 1980. Discovery of the *Monitor* lying on the ocean floor ignited general interest among United States naval historians in the findings of underwater archaeology. This enthusiasm became more intense as reports began to appear in the press of finding, 300 feet below the surface of Lake Ontario, the almost perfectly preserved remains of the War of 1812 schooners *Hamilton* and *Scourge*. The first detailed report on *Hamilton* and *Scourge* was Daniel Nelson's March 1983 *National Geographic* article (442), with its dramatic underwater photographs of the intact ships. Nelson's account, and one by Richard F. Palmer (445), are amplified by Emily Cain in her beautifully illustrated *Ghost Ships: Hamilton and Scourge: Historical Treasures from the War of 1812* (382), which provides a goodly measure of historical background on the two schooners as well. A successful, though historically less rewarding, effort to find the remains of Joshua Barney's War of 1812 light vessels in the silt of Maryland's Patuxent River is reported in Donald G. Shomette and Fred W. Hopkins, "The Search for the Chesapeake Flotilla" (460), and in the illustrated catalog of artifacts recovered from the Barney vessel (417).

Histories of Civil War vessels by Christley (386), Donnelly (395), Heitzmann (410), Reynolds (450), and Smith (463) will be found annotated under that chronological heading.

SOCIAL HISTORY. Only three articles falling directly under this rubric have appeared since 1979, but all three are noteworthy as examples of excellence in historical scholarship. Arthur Gilbert's "Crime as Disorder" (407), a brilliant psychological study of eighteenth-century British naval officers, may seem out of place in a survey of scholarship on the nineteenth-century U.S. Navy, but the present historian would argue that its insights apply equally well to the American corps of seagoing officers in the sailing ship era. As noted in *Supplement I*, the lack of cross-cultural studies of different national navies remains the most blatant gap in naval historiography. Gilbert's work on deviant behavior in the Royal Navy in this article and in his earlier essay, "Buggery in the British Navy, 1700–1861" (406), might constitute an excellent foundation for commencing comparative study of two navies that present numerous similarities – and differences. J. Worth Estes's discovery of the medical archive of Dr. Peter St. Medard has stimulated what promises to be an exceedingly valuable study of health, morbidity, and mortality in the early U.S. Navy. Estes's first findings to reach print may be examined in "Naval Medicine in the Age of Sail: The Voyage of the *New York* 1802–1803" (401). A social profile of one riverine Civil War naval vessel is the subject of David F. Riggs, "Sailors of the USS *Cairo*" (452).

Rich lodes of source material exist in certain manuscript collections, but scholars have written almost nothing about the wives and children of nineteenth-century naval officers, their lives, their problems, and their coping techniques. Here one finds a corps of women, often managing on their own, and creating in the process a full record of how they did it in letters to absent spouses; yet this dimension of womens' and family history is almost wholly uninvestigated. A pioneering effort along these lines is Harold D. Langley's examination of the life of Marian Coote Speiden, the wife of a navy purser, during her husband's extended absence on the United States Exploring Expedition (426). And, although it cannot be classified as a piece of scholarly social history, Sidney E. Lang's account of his father's misadventures on the Asiatic Station of the 1880s, "A Boy at Sea" (424), should also be mentioned under this section. Alfred P. Lang, then a 17-year-old third-class boy serving in the *Enterprise*, deserted from that ship at Melbourne, Australia, in October 1885 to escape harassment for refusing to submit to sodomy, the practice of which he alleged was rife in the *Enterprise* and other ships of the station. Lang subsequently became a lieutenant in the Naval Reserve and still later secured a presidential pardon for his 1885 desertion. One case history does not a monograph on shipboard homosexuality in the nineteenth-century navy make, but this topic will probably continue to attract scholarly interest.

For two other studies with a social history orientation, see work by Dudley (399) and Laas (423), annotated under the Civil War heading.

BIOGRAPHIES. Despite grumbling by publishers that biography of second-rank figures in American history does not sell and the methodological doubts of scholars concerned about the distortions produced by the one-great-man focus, a steady stream of biographical studies continues to roll from the presses. Three book-length biographies falling entirely within the chronological scope of this essay are David F. Long's lives of William Bainbridge (433) and James Biddle (434), and George M. Brooke's *John M. Brooke, Naval Scientist and Educator* (379). The latter two are noteworthy for the emphasis on their subjects' peacetime contributions to diplomacy and science in the years between the War of 1812 and the Civil War. Wallace Hutcheon's *Robert Fulton, Pioneer of Undersea Warfare* (421) is less a biography than a specialized study of a facet of Fulton's varied career. One related and important Fulton study not mentioned in the original *Guide* is Howard I. Chapelle's *Fulton's "Steam Battery": Blockship and Catamaran*

(384). An outstandingly illustrated catalog of Isaac Hull portraits and memorabilia (451) has been issued by the USS *Constitution* Museum, Boston, as a guide to its exhibition of these artifacts which opened in 1983. The catalog includes a short essay on Hull's life by Linda M. Maloney, whose long-anticipated Hull biography is as yet unpublished.

Edward Fitzgerald Beale's claim to historical importance rests on his multiple roles as participant in the land fighting in California during the war with Mexico, as self-appointed herald for the discovery of gold in California, as cross-continental bearer of dispatches – often under conditions of substantial personal danger – as sponsor of the experimental camel herd in the Southwestern deserts, and as federal officeholder in California. However, throughout the early part of this varied career, Beale was successively a midshipman, master, and lieutenant in the navy. After a long period of comparative scholarly neglect, Beale has, in one year, become the subject of two biographies (378, 469). Although both are readable, scholars will prefer the work of Gerald Thompson to that of Carl Briggs and Clyde F. Trudell.

Three article-length biographical sketches concern subjects whose careers were wholly confined to the nineteenth century. For a number of years Harold D. Langley has been investigating the early history of the naval medical corps. He details what is known regarding the life of one of its members in "Edward Field: A Pioneer Practitioner of the Old Navy" (425). Langley's "Respect for Civilian Authority: The Tragic Career of Captain [Samuel] Angus" (427) chronicles the fate of an able officer whose psychological problems, stemming from service-related injuries, led to his dismissal from the navy. Both pieces are works of impeccable scholarship. The eighty-year life of Bernard Henry, which encompassed service both as a naval officer and as a United States consul, has been traced by Ira Rosenwaike (456).

Paolo Coletta's volumes on French Ensor Chadwick (391), Bradley A. Fiske (387), and Bowman Hendry McCalla (389), as well as Margaret Brearley's article on Albert Gleaves Berry (377), all deal with officers the most important portions of whose careers fell after 1889. However, because all four men entered the navy in the middle years of the nineteenth century, the earlier portion of each life story lies well within the chronological scope of the present bibliographical essay. In addition to his book-length biography of McCalla, Coletta has also presented an abbreviated summary of one controversial aspect of his subject's career as an article (390).

Three other articles are not biographical sketches of naval officers but are most appropriately mentioned under the biographical rubric. Rebecca Hoskins's "The Death and Interment of Joshua Barney" (419) contains new material on that famous officer's burial and the monument at his grave. Novelist James Fenimore Cooper's association with the unhappy Wolcott Chauncey is briefly described in Thomas Philbrick, "Cooper's Naval Friend in Paris" (447). One of the nineteenth century's most notorious duelists, Alexander K. McClung, was briefly a navy midshipman before resigning under pressure in 1829. The story of McClung's life has been related by Fred Darkis in an article (393) that relies almost entirely on published sources but is a useful starting place for those wishing to study this disturbed individual in greater depth.

For books and articles that are at least partly biographical in their content but are discussed in other sections of this essay, see Anderson (365), Bartlett (369), Birkner (375), Bishop (376), Brynn and Bishop (380), Coletta (364), Dudley (399),

Forrest (404), Francis (405), Ingersoll (422), Laas (423), Langley (426, 428), Merrill (438), Norberg (444), Plumb (448), and Swartout (466).

FROM THE QUASI-WAR WITH FRANCE THROUGH THE WAR OF 1812. As scholarly interest in the navy of 1816–1860 and 1866–1889 waxes, both the quantity and the overall quality of work on the navy's earliest two decades continues to wane – confirming a trend cautiously noted in *Supplement I.* It would be a mistake to assume that the period is written out, but it will require new methodologies and fresh perspectives, such as those inspiring Worth Estes (401) or Emily Cain (382) or Ira Dye (307), to exploit the subjects as yet untapped. Save for such excellent exceptions, much of the writing on the pre-1815 years remains ensnarled in old, questionable theses and in unimaginative research methods.

Donald Hickey (413) has explored the ideas expressed by members of the Federalist party between their fall from power in 1801 and the War of 1812 on three key issues in national defense – naval expansion, coastal fortification, and maintenance of the standing army. As was the case with earlier, similar studies by Harold and Margaret Sprout (231) and Marshall Smelser (222), Hickey's work does not penetrate behind the facade of Congressional rhetoric to any underlying realities. The originality of the work of Craig Symonds (350, 351) is lacking here. Using similar sources but achieving rather more convincing results, Hickey argues in a companion piece, "The Federalists and the Coming of the War, 1811–1812" (414), that the members of the opposition party might have been willing to go to war with Great Britain in 1812 if the hostilities had taken the form of a limited war on the high seas analogous in character to the earlier quasi-war with France.

For all the ink spilled and emotion vented on the subject, there still exists no adequate treatment of the gunboat flotillas of the Jefferson and Madison presidencies. Spencer C. Tucker, "Mr. Jefferson's Gunboat Navy" (470), is accurate and succinct but adds relatively little to what was already known about the subject. "Jeffersonian Gunboats in the War of 1812," by Dean R. Mayhew (437), is more ambitious than Tucker's essay. It attempts to follow the gunboats' operational history but, in the absence of any organizing themes, becomes a chronological recitation of data; moreover, the article is so riddled with errors of fact and of interpretation that specific points ought not to be trusted without further verification. Frederick C. Leiner, in "The 'Whimsical Phylosophic President' and His Gunboats" (431), is as handicapped by his organizing theory as Mayhew was by the lack of one. For all its impressive citation of recent literature, Leiner's article is simply a restatement of the hoary thesis that President Jefferson was anti-navy and that the gunboat-building program was a prime example both of that animus and of his impractical idealism. One suspects that Leiner's conclusions were substantially formed before he began his research. What is sorely needed is a comprehensive study of the gunboat flotillas which divests itself of prejudice and presupposition before approaching the ample surviving records to ask: What were the expectations which underlay the gunboat construction program? What roles did these craft actually play? Are there useful analogies to light, experimental craft of later eras, such as torpedo boats? Until such a work is written, Howard I. Chapelle (46) remains the best authority on the construction and physical characteristics of the gunboat navy – so long as one ignores his obiter dicta on the policy behind the gunboats, flights of fancy not based on the solid archival research that supported his studies of the vessels themselves.

Some of the very best work on the War of 1812 has been done by Canadian scholars. A well-researched new essay in this strong Canadian tradition is W. A. B. Douglas's study of maritime forces on Lakes Erie and Ontario through the outbreak of the War of 1812 (398). Robin F. A. Fabel (402) has provided a hitherto missing perspective on the war, by land as well as in coastal waters, through measuring British and American conduct of operations against the doctrines of the then most commonly cited authority on international law, Emmerich de Vattel's *The Law of Nations*. With the establishment of a tight British blockade of New England in the latter phases of the War of 1812, Nantucket became an isolated shoal in a British-controlled sea. The island's neutrality agreement with the British naval command and its renunciation of all support to the United States for the duration of the war are the subjects of Reginald Horsman's article "Nantucket's Peace Treaty with England in 1814" (418). An attempt by British naval forces to secure the cooperation of Jean Lafitte in the campaign against New Orleans is a well-known episode in the same conflict. John Sugden provides a somewhat revisionist account of this business, based on manuscript British records, in his article "Jean Lafitte and the British Offer of 1814" (465). Greg Dening, seeking to examine a particular event in the light of larger theory, has applied the concepts of John Keegan's *The Face of Battle* (New York: Viking Press, 1976) to David Porter's battle with the British squadron at Valparaiso in 1814. If the result (394) is less than wholly satisfying, it is probably because Dening relied on existing—but flawed—secondary sources for the combat. He might, for example, have examined muster rolls to provide specific numbers to indicate just how serious the United States casualties really were. *Flotilla: Battle for the Patuxent*, by Donald G. Shomette (459), is an excellent narrative history of Joshua Barney's War of 1812 force and its attempt to defend the waters of the upper Chesapeake against superior British forces. In a related article, Stuart L. Butler (381) has published the dispatches of a civilian observer who tracked British naval movements in the Chesapeake Bay area in the summer of 1813 and in January 1814. Finally, a far-from-complete account of the distribution of prize money to Perry's squadron following the battle of Lake Erie in 1813 may be seen in William M. Howell's "Purser Samuel Hambleton" (420).

Other studies, wholly or partially related to this period of the navy's history but cited in earlier sections of this essay, include Baker (367), Bass (370), Cain (382), Chapelle (384), Estes (401), Fisher (403), Hopkins (417), Hutcheon (421), Langley (425, 427), Long (433, 434), Martin (436), Nelson (442), Palmer (445), Richmond (451), Rosenwaike (456), Shomette and Hopkins (460), and Wood (477).

FROM 1815 TO THE EVE OF THE CIVIL WAR. Although these years are now the focus of substantial scholarly activity, that activity has taken the form of articles and special studies which examine narrowly defined aspects of the period. Lacking is any general history of the navy in this era which provides a framework against which to situate these highly specialized studies. K. Jack Bauer points out some of the issues such a general history might address in "The Navy in an Age of Manifest Destiny: Some Suggestions for Sources and Research" (371).

The U.S. Navy of 1816–1860 was given responsibilities all around the globe, and a means of organizing the flow of specialized scholarly studies is to proceed region by geographical region. One may begin with the navy on its home territory. Lt. Robert B. Randolph's physical attack on President Andrew Jackson (the first such assault in United States history), after the latter had dismissed Randolph from the navy, has been examined by John M. Belohlavek (374). The author places the Randolph incident well in the context of later violence — fatal and nonfatal — against presidents, but his analysis of the lieutenant's difficulties surrounding his official financial transactions would have been stronger if appropriate navy accounting records had been consulted. Activities of a senator who played a powerful role in the shaping of United States naval policy are traced by Harold D. Langley with his customary scholarly thoroughness in "Robert Y. Hayne and the Navy" (428). A portion of the diary of Sailing Master Edward C. Anderson, covering his naval service in Florida, was published in 1977 by W. Stanley Hoole as *Florida Territory in 1844* (365) but was not noted in time for *Supplement I*. This slender volume may be added to the small shelf of naval officers' diaries which should not escape the historian's scrutiny. A letter of Levin M. Powell, a naval officer stationed at Charleston during the nullification crisis of 1832-1833, and a related newspaper article — both edited by Howard H. Wehmann (474) — are perhaps most useful for their illumination of the social life of the officer corps.

As for the navy on the European scene, the extensive and consistently valuable corpus of Samuel F. DuPont manuscripts has been tapped by James M. Merrill in his "Midshipman DuPont and the Cruise of *North Carolina* 1825-1827" (438). Merrill's article quotes extensively from DuPont's letters, which in this instance are notable for their not-always-flattering portrayal of Commodore John Rodgers. Francis X. Holbrook and John Nikol make extensive use of direct quotation from the official dispatches of senior officers in their "Reporting the Sicilian Revolution of 1848-1849" (415). The reader may, however, wish that the authors had provided more historical background for the events being described in the on-the-spot dispatches.

Latin American waters were the scene of much United States naval activity in the years before the Civil War. Raymond Shoemaker has surveyed briefly the diplomatic roles fulfilled by naval officers in Caribbean waters in the years 1815-1830 (458). One such officer, whose diplomatic activity in a fever-ridden climate led directly to his death, was Oliver Hazard Perry. Alexander Monroe's "Chaplain John Hambleton, U.S.N.: A Diplomatic Correspondent" (441) is a partial printing of Hambleton's journal kept during Perry's fatal 1819 mission to Venezuela. This same journal has been published at least twice before (368, 472) — and with better scholarly apparatus. In the instances of the second and third publications, the editors seem to have been unaware that the journal was already available in print. Michael Birkner presents an evenhanded examination of David Porter's notorious 1824 incursion at Puerto Rico (375). His work provides a balance to the understandably pro-Porter account in David Long's biography (131) and sympathetically states Secretary of the Navy Samuel L. Southard's view of the incident. J. Scott Harmon's "The United States Navy and the Suppression of the Illegal Slave Trade, 1830-1850" (409) argues that it was the internal abolition of the slave trade by Brazil and Cuba, rather than the anti-slaver naval patrols, that should be given primary credit for the curtailing of participation by United States vessels in this illegal traffic. The importance of the naval patrols was, Harmon argues, more symbolic than real. Two studies examine United States naval activity on the west coast of South America during the final stages of the Latin-American wars of independence. Ray T. Shurbutt (461) sees it through the eyes of United States diplomats stationed in Chile and Peru, while Linda Maloney (435) reverses direction and looks at the same events — albeit for a shorter time span — from the perspective of one squadron commander, Isaac Hull. Moving farther to the north, John F. Henry's "The Midshipman's Revenge" (411) asks: How did the United States Exploring Expedition under Charles Wilkes come to include two nonexistent islands in its 1841 chart of the San Juans in Puget Sound? This interesting short piece is marred by too much tenuous speculation, as when the author elaborately argues that "Gordon Island" is named for William L. Gordon, an ex-shipmate of Wilkes, although the adjacent quotation from Wilkes should have made it clear that the illusory island was named for Captain Charles Gordon (d. 1816).

Naval commitments in Asiatic waters in the pre-Civil War years have attracted a band of scholars nearly as large as that examining the navy in Latin America. *Commissioners and Commodores*, by Curtis T. Henson (412), is a fine study of the East India Squadron's role in diplomatic relations with China, 1835–1861. Sarah Larson (429) has used the story of the wreck of the whaler *Lagoda* near Japan, the imprisonment of the survivors by the isolation-bent Japanese, and the sailors' eventual rescue by the sloop-of-war *Preble* as a means of illustrating the historical resources awaiting exploitation in the manuscript "Letters Received by the Secretary of the Navy from Commanding Officers of Squadrons," at the U.S. National Archives. Two noteworthy events in the history of the East India Squadron are explored in detail in specialized studies. Merrill L. Bartlett's "Commodore James Biddle and the First Naval Mission to Japan, 1845–1846" (369) should be read in conjunction with the appropriate chapter of David Long's more recent biography of Biddle (434). Long himself employs his mastery of the Chinese sources, of United States diplomatic history, and of the storyteller's art to examine the squadron's 1856 destruction of the Chinese fortifications below Canton (432)—a subject treated more briefly and less sensitively by Hanson. The deft and restrained manner in which power was applied in this particular incident draws high praise from Long.

Biographies of naval officers with extensive material on the 1816–1860 years, discussed in detail under that heading, include Briggs (378), Brooke (379), Langley (427), Long (433), and Thompson (469); see also Langley (426) in the Social History section.

CIVIL WAR. One might suppose that all significant primary sources for the War between the States had long since been published, but good new material does, from time to time, turn up in print. That certainly is how one would classify William N. Still's edition of the diary of Confederate Navy Assistant Paymaster Douglas French Forrest (404), which covers the years 1863–1865 and includes service in CSS *Rappahannock* and during the Confederacy's last stand in Texas. A possibly less important diary of Union Acting Assistant Paymaster Richard French Goodman forms the basis of Robert J. Plumb's "Yankee Paymaster" (448). Plumb quotes at length from the manuscript Goodman diary but does not reveal the whereabouts of the original. The letters of Elizabeth Blair Lee to her husband, U.S. Navy Commander Samuel Phillips Lee, edited by Virginia Jeans Laas (423) and covering the early weeks of 1861, are more significant for her comments on the Washington political and social scene than for material immediately useful to naval historians, but the latter should examine them for a few nuggets scattered here and there. Six letters of Acting Ensign Purnell F. Harrington, USN, describing the Union attack on Mobile Bay in 1864 have also appeared in print (400).

In his *Going South: U.S. Navy Officer Resignations & Dismissals on the Eve of the Civil War* (399), William S. Dudley applies some of the techniques of social and quantitative history to the exodus of U.S. Navy officers of Southern sympathies in the months surrounding the outbreak of war in 1861 and provides the first thorough examination of this subject. A related essay by Ralph W. Donnelly (396) follows, as best its author can, the fate of former officers of the U.S. Revenue Marine Service in the Confederate forces.

Histories of several individual Civil War naval vessels have appeared during the years covered by this essay. The construction of the *Galena*, "the first seagoing ironclad warship to take its place on the rolls of the United States Navy," is the subject of James L. Christley's "Mystic River Builds an Ironclad" (386). Ralph W. Donnelly has followed the fortunes of a former steam ferry, the *George Page*, which served the Confederacy on the upper Potomac during the early stages of the conflict (395). The Union ironclad *Weehawken* is a far better known ship. Her history has been retold by William Ray Heitzmann (410). Myron J. Smith has prepared a lengthy and comprehensive history of the Union gunboat *Carondolet* (463). At this writing there appear to be few copies of this on-demand publication in existence, a situation which may make it a challenge for the would-be reader to lay hands on the volume. Some of the final naval events of the war, on the waters of the James River below Richmond, are the focus of Clark Reynolds's "Yankee Supership? Sortie of *Spuyten Duyvil*" (450), a tale told with all of Reynolds's customary skill.

At the interface of naval and diplomatic history, Gordon H. Warren has examined Captain Charles Wilkes's removal of the Confederate agents James M. Mason and John Slidell from the British mail steamer *Trent* and that incident's impact on Anglo-American relations in his thorough and well-written *Fountain of Discontent* (473). Gideon Welles's angry denial that he sought to build Union naval vessels under contract in Great Britain is the subject of a short study by John David Smith (462). The difficulties of British officials in trying to maintain strict neutrality as the Confederate cruiser *Tallahassee* appeared first in one port and then another during the closing year of the war have been chronicled by Mary Elizabeth Thomas in an admirable 1975 article (468) that went unnoticed in *Supplement I*.

Finally, specialized aspects of the naval war have not escaped attention. R. D. Layman, *To Ascend from a Floating Base: Shipboard Aeronautics and Aviation, 1783-1914* (430), has a good survey of both Union and Confederate water-based balloon efforts. Edwin C. Bearss, "The Ironclads at Fort Donelson" (373), and Maxine Turner, "Naval Operations on the Apalachicola and Chattahoochee Rivers" (471) – extended articles that also should have been noted in *Supplement I* – are fairly conventional Civil War history, emphasizing fact and narrative rather than analysis. The efforts of a Union naval officer (and his wife) to obtain his restoration to active duty and his eligibility for promotion after the Virginia-born veteran had been put on the beach as a consequence of questionable performance on the Great Lakes frontier are the subject of David W. Francis's "The United States Navy and the Johnson's Island Conspiracy: The Case of John C. Carter" (405).

For work dealing with the Civil War navies but discussed elsewhere in this essay, see Bearss (372), Brooke (379), *Cheesebox* (385), Miller (439), Monitor Conference (440), and Riggs (452).

FROM THE CIVIL WAR TO THE NEW NAVY. Long the darkest and most neglected corner of United States naval history, the years between 1866 and 1889 now receive a full share of scholarly attention. And here, more than in earlier periods, that scholarly attention focuses on the upper echelons of the·navy's central leadership. As is the case with several of the other books and articles which will be cited in this section, Jeffery M. Dorwart's *The Office of Naval Intelligence: The Birth of America's First Intelligence Agency, 1865–1918* (397) extends well into the twentieth century. Indeed, the greater part of the volume is concerned with the post-1889 years, but the office's 1882 establishment places it squarely within the scope of the present essay as well. Dorwart's is an excellent piece of scholarship. Its author has a keen grasp of the importance of individuals in shaping history—as well as skill in portraying those personalities. Many of the same officers who played key roles in the Office of Naval Intelligence are also at center stage in Lawrence C. Allin's history of the first two decades of the United States Naval Institute, which association he rightly characterizes as the "Intellectual Forum of the New Navy" (363). In contrast to Dorwart's work, Allin's emphasis is always on ideas and policies—not their interaction with quirky personality. "The First Unification Crisis" (361), also by Allin, concerns itself with the navy's attempt to bring all federal activities relating to the country's merchant marine under the administrative oversight of the Navy Department and that effort's defeat by the civilian shipping community. In yet another article (362), Allin outlines the three major concepts of naval warfare current in the 1880s—war against commerce, war on the high seas, and war on the coast—then discusses in more detail the U.S. Navy's intellectual leadership's brief flirtation with the third concept at the close of the decade. A symbiotic relationship between the navy and the steel industry is the subject of *Gray Steel and Blue Water Navy: The Formative Years of America's Military-Industrial Complex, 1881–1917*, by Benjamin Franklin Cooling (392). However, readers of Cooling's work should also be aware of the fundamental critique of it in *Journal of American History* 67(1980 / 81): 426. The professional life of a civilian scientist employed by the navy in its astronomical effort has been investigated by Arthur L. Norberg in his article "Simon Newcomb's Early Astronomical Career" (444).

Of course, not all the action was in the offices at Washington, D.C., mesmerizing as that world has become to historians of the period. The navy was scattered about the globe, performing a variety of functions to protect American interests. In "An Indicator of Informal Empire: Patterns of U.S. Navy Cruising on Overseas Stations, 1869–1897" (453), Stephen S. Roberts has quantified ship movements to discover if those movements support the hypothesis that the navy was concentrated in places at which the United States was seeking to project "informal empire" through economic penetration. Roberts's findings probably would have been more effectively presented in graphic form rather than fact-ridden and repetitive prose. Not altogether successful efforts to police the United States-Mexican border by stationing a naval vessel on the river that separates the two countries is the little-known subject of Robert L. Robinson's "The U.S. Navy vs. Cattle Rustlers: The USS *Rio Bravo* on the Rio Grande, 1875–1879" (455). Daniel H. Wicks has reported the highly unrealistic arguments used by proponents of an American-built canal across Nicaragua, arguments to the effect that the United States fleet could be based in Lake Nicaragua and thereby be available to operate on either the Atlantic or the Pacific oceans (476). In a more important article (475), Wicks investigates America's 1885 armed intervention in rebellion-torn Panama to restore the authority of the Colombian government and the ways in which high naval officers under the leadership of Capt. John G. Walker subverted the intentions of the civilian secretaries of the Cleveland administration.

Farther afield, William N. Still has filled a major gap in the historical literature with his general history of United States naval activities, 1865–1917, in European and Near-Eastern waters, *American Sea Power in the Old World* (464). One particular incident falling within the scope of Still's comprehensive work – United States naval involvement in the events before and during the 1882 bombardment and occupation of Alexandria, Egypt, by British forces – is examined in detail in an article by Robert L. Robinson (454). Under the title *Cruising in the Old Navy* (422), the Naval Historical Foundation has published the autobiographical recollections of Rear Adm. Royal R. Ingersoll covering the years 1887–1890, when Ingersoll was executive officer of the *Enterprise*. *Cruising in the Old Navy* is only an excerpt from Ingersoll's much longer manuscript autobiography, "The Story of My Life and Times." If this excerpt be a fair sample, the whole deserves publication. Although it is based on readily available printed sources, Ernest Anrade's narrative (366) of the destruction of the German and American squadrons at Samoa by the forces of nature in 1889 is a tale well worth the retelling.

Thanks to the work of two energetic scholars, Donald M. Bishop and Robert Swartout, American naval contacts with nineteenth-century Korea have received an unusual degree of attention. Bishop's "Navy Blue in Old Korea: The Asiatic Squadron and the American Legation, 1882–1897" (294) was noted in *Supplement I*. In "Policy and Personality in Early Korean-American Relations: The Case of George Clayton Foulk" (376), he provides the fullest account to date of the Korean career of the United States naval attaché who was, for much of his tour, the de facto American diplomatic representative to that kingdom. Bishop has also joined Edward Brynn in editing a letter (380) of Foulk's describing an 1884 tour of Ceylon at a time when he was escorting three Korean diplomats home after a visit to the United States. In "Cultural Conflict and Gunboat Diplomacy: The Development of the 1871 Korean-American Incident" (467), Swartout argues that radically different cultural heritages exacerbated the difficulties Americans and Asians experienced in understanding and dealing with one another and thus led to wholly avoidable bloodshed typified in Rear Adm. John Rodgers's 1871 assault on the Korean forts. Finally, Swartout and Fred C. Bohm have published the diary of George W. Woods (466), an American naval officer who visited Korea in 1884. As is often the case with such documents, the journal reveals as much about the prejudices of the author as it does about late-nineteenth-century Korea and its resident diplomatic community.

Research described elsewhere in this essay but relevant to the 1866–1889 years will be found under Brearley (377), Coletta, (387, 389, 390, 391), and Lang (424).

BIBLIOGRAPHY

359. Albion, Robert Greenhalgh. *Makers of Naval Policy, 1798–1947.* Edited by Rowena Reed. Annapolis, Md.: Naval Institute Press, 1980.

360. Allard, Dean C., et al. *U.S. Naval History Sources in the United States.*

Washington, D.C.: Naval History Division, Dept. of the Navy, 1979.
361. Allin, Lawrence Carroll. "The First Unification Crisis: Chandler, Dingley, Folger, and the Bureau of Navigation, 1879–1884." *Military Affairs* 47 (1983): 133–40.
362. _____. "The Navy and *la Guerre de Côte*." *Periodical: Journal of the Council on Abandoned Military Posts* [now the Council on America's Military Past] 11, no. 3 (March 1981): 3–16.
363. _____. *The United States Naval Institute: Intellectual Forum of the New Navy, 1873–1889*. Manhattan, Kans.: MA / AH Publishing, 1978.
364. *American Secretaries of the Navy*. 2 vols. Edited by Paolo E. Coletta. Annapolis, Md.: Naval Institute Press, 1980.
365. Anderson, Edward C. *Florida Territory in 1844: The Diary of Master Edward C. Anderson, United States Navy*. Edited by W. Stanley Hoole. University: University of Alabama Press, 1977.
366. Anrade, Ernest. "The Great Samoan Hurricane of 1899 [i.e., 1889]." *Naval War College Review* 34, no. 1 (January–February 1981): 73–81.
367. Baker, Maury. "Cost Overrun, an Early Naval Precedent: Building the First U.S. Warships, 1794–98." *Maryland Historical Magazine* 72 (1977): 361–72.
368. _____, ed. "The Voyage of the U.S. Schooner *Nonsuch* up the Orinoco: Journal of the Perry Mission of 1819 to South America." *Hispanic American Historical Review* 30 (1950): 480–98.
369. Bartlett, Merrill L. "Commodore James Biddle and the First Naval Mission to Japan, 1845–1846." *American Neptune* 41 (1981): 25–35.
370. Bass, William P. and Ethel L. *Constitution, Second Phase 1802–07–Mediterranean, Tripoli, Malta & More*. Melbourne, Fla.: Shipsresearch, 1981.
371. Bauer, K. Jack. "The Navy in an Age of Manifest Destiny: Some Suggestions for Sources and Research." *Versatile Guardian: Research in Naval History*, edited by Richard A. von Doenhoff, pages 161–75. Washington, D.C.: Howard University Press, 1979.
372. Bearss, Edwin C. *Hardluck Ironclad: The Sinking and Salvage of the Cairo*. Rev. ed. Baton Rouge: Louisiana State University Press, 1980.
373. _____. "The Ironclads at Fort Donelson." Kentucky Historical Society *Register* 74 (1976): 1–9, 73–84, 167–91.
374. Belohlavek, John M. "Assault on the President: The Jackson-Randolph Affair of 1833." *Presidential Studies Quarterly* 12 (1982): 361–68.
375. Birkner, Michael. "The 'Foxardo Affair' Revisited: Porter, Pirates, and the Problem of Civilian Authority in the Early Republic." *American Neptune* 42 (1982): 165–78.
376. Bishop, Donald M. "Policy and Personality in Early Korean-American Relations: The Case of George Clayton Foulk." In *The United States and Korea: American-Korean Relations, 1866–1976*, edited by Andrew C. Nahm, 27–63. Kalamazoo: Center for Korean Studies, Western Michigan University, 1979.
377. Brearley, Margaret M. "Rear-Admiral Albert Gleaves Berry, 1848–1938." *Tennessee Historical Quarterly* 40 (1981): 85–94.
378. Briggs, Carl, and Clyde Francis Trudell. *Quarterdeck & Saddlehorn: The Story of Edward F. Beale, 1822–1893*. Glendale, Calif.: Arthur H. Clark

Co., 1983.
379. Brooke, George M., Jr. *John M. Brooke, Naval Scientist and Educator.* Charlottesville: University Press of Virginia, 1980.
380. Brynn, Edward, and Donald M. Bishop. "An American-Korean Diplomatic Mission in Sri Lanka, 1884." *Ceylon Journal of Historical and Social Studies*, n.s. 6, no. 2 (July–December 1976): 1–18.
381. Butler, Stuart Lee. "Thomas Swann and the British in St. Mary's County." *Maryland Historical Magazine* 73 (1978): 71–78.
382. Cain, Emily. *Ghost Ships: Hamilton and Scourge: Historical Treasures from the War of 1812.* Toronto: Musson, 1983; New York: Beaufort Books, 1983.
383. Chapelle, Howard I., and Leon D. Pollard. *The Constellation Question.* Smithsonian Studies in History and Technology, no. 5. Washington, D.C.: Smithsonian Institution Press, 1970.
384. Chapelle, Howard I. *Fulton's "Steam Battery": Blockship and Catamaran.* Contributions from the Museum of History and Technology, paper 39. Washington, D.C.: Smithsonian Institution Press, 1964.
385. *Cheesebox.* Greenville, N.C.: Program in Maritime History and Underwater Archaeology, Dept. of History, East Carolina University, 1982–. Semiannual.
386. Christley, James L. "Mystic River Builds an Ironclad." *Log of Mystic Seaport* 32 (1980): 129–38.
387. Coletta, Paolo E. *Admiral Bradley A. Fiske and the American Navy.* Lawrence: Regents Press of Kansas, 1979.
388. _____. *A Bibliography of American Naval History.* Annapolis, Md.: Naval Institute Press, 1981.
389. _____. *Bowman Hendry McCalla, a Fighting Sailor.* Washington, D.C.: University Press of America, 1979.
390. _____. "The Court-Martial of Bowman Hendry McCalla." *American Neptune* 40 (1980): 127–34.
391. _____. *French Ensor Chadwick, Scholarly Warrior.* Washington, D.C.: University Press of America, 1980.
392. Cooling, Benjamin Franklin. *Gray Steel and Blue Water Navy: The Formative Years of America's Military-Industrial Complex, 1881–1917.* Hamden, Conn.: Archon Books, 1979.
393. Darkis, Fred, Jr. "Alexander Keith McClung (1811–1855)." *Journal of Mississippi History* 40 (1978): 289–96.
394. Dening, Greg. "The Face of Battle, Valparaiso, 1814." *War & Society* 1 (1983–84): 25–42.
395. Donnelly, Ralph W. "Gadfly on the Potomac, CSS *George Page.*" *American Neptune* 43 (1983): 129–34.
396. _____. "Officers of the Revenue Marine Service in the Confederacy." *American Neptune* 40 (1980): 298–304.
397. Dorwart, Jeffery M. *The Office of Naval Intelligence: The Birth of America's First Intelligence Agency, 1865–1918.* Annapolis, Md.: Naval Institute Press, 1979.
398. Douglas, W. A. B. "The Anatomy of Naval Incompetence: The Provincial Marine in Defence of Upper Canada before 1813." *Ontario History* 71 (1979): 3–25.

399. Dudley, William S. *Going South: U.S. Navy Officer Resignations & Dismissals on the Eve of the Civil War.* Washington, D.C.: Naval Historical Foundation, 1981.

400. Duncan, Richard R., ed. "The Storming of Mobile Bay." *Alabama Historical Quarterly* 40 (1978): 6–19.

401. Estes, J. Worth. "Naval Medicine in the Age of Sail: The Voyage of the *New York*, 1802–1803." *Bulletin of the History of Medicine* 56 (1982): 238–53.

402. Fabel, Robin F. A. "The Laws of War in the 1812 Conflict." *Journal of American Studies* 14 (1980): 199–218.

403. Fisher, Charles R. "Gun Drill in the Sailing Navy, 1797 to 1840." *American Neptune* 41 (1981): 85–92.

404. Forrest, Douglas French. *Odyssey in Gray: A Diary of Confederate Service, 1863–1865.* Edited by William N. Still, Jr. Richmond: Virginia State Library, 1979.

405. Francis, David W. "The United States Navy and the Johnson's Island Conspiracy: The Case of John C. Carter." *Northwest Ohio Quarterly* 52 (1980): 229–43.

406. Gilbert, Arthur N. "Buggery and the British Navy, 1700–1861." *Journal of Social History* 10 (1976 / 77): 72–98.

407. _____. "Crime as Disorder: Criminality and the Symbolic Universe of the 18th Century British Naval Officer." In *Changing Interpretations and New Sources in Naval History*, United States Naval Academy History Symposium (3d: 1977), edited by Robert William Love, Jr., 110–22. New York: Garland, 1980.

408. Haines, Charles. "Ship Preservation in the Old Navy." *American Neptune* 42 (1982): 276–94.

409. Harmon, J. Scott. "The United States Navy and the Suppression of the Illegal Slave Trade, 1830–1850." In *New Aspects of Naval History*, United States Naval Academy History Symposium (4th: 1979), edited by Craig L. Symonds, 211–19. Annapolis, Md.: Naval Institute Press, 1981.

410. Heitzmann, William Ray. "The Ironclad *Weehawken* in the Civil War." *American Neptune* 42 (1982): 193–202.

411. Henry, John Frazier. "The Midshipman's Revenge; or, The Case of the Missing Islands." *Pacific Northwest Quarterly* 73 (1982): 156–64.

412. Henson, Curtis T., Jr. *Commissioners and Commodores: The East India Squadron and American Diplomacy in China.* University: University of Alabama Press, 1982.

413. Hickey, Donald R. "Federalist Defense Policy in the Age of Jefferson, 1801–1812." *Military Affairs* 45 (1981): 63–70.

414. _____. "The Federalists and the Coming of the War, 1811–1812." *Indiana Magazine of History* 75 (1979): 70–88.

415. Holbrook, Francis X., and John Nikol. "Reporting the Sicilian Revolution of 1848–1849." *American Neptune* 43 (1983): 165–76.

416. Hopkins, Fred W. "From Warship to School Ship: The History of USS *Ontario*, America's First Floating School." *American Neptune* 40 (1980): 38–45.

417. Hopkins, Fred W., and Donald G. Shomette. *War on the Patuxent, 1814: A Catalog of Artifacts.* Solomons, Md.: Nautical Archaeological Associates;

Calvert Marine Museum Press, 1981.

418. Horsman, Reginald. "Nantucket's Peace Treaty with England in 1814." *New England Quarterly* 54 (1981): 180-98.

419. Hoskins, Rebecca. "The Death and Interment of Joshua Barney." *Western Pennsylvania Historical Magazine* 65 (1982): 75-78.

420. Howell, William Maher. "Purser Samuel Hambleton." *Inland Seas* 36 (1980): 168-76.

421. Hutcheson, Wallace, Jr. *Robert Fulton, Pioneer of Undersea Warfare.* Annapolis, Md.: Naval Institute Press, 1981.

422. Ingersoll, Royal R. *Cruising in the Old Navy.* Washington, D.C.: Naval Historical Foundation, 1974.

423. Laas, Virginia Jeans, ed. "'On the Qui Vive for the Long Letter': Washington Letters from a Navy Wife, 1861." *Civil War History* 29 (1983): 28-52.

424. Lang, Sidney E. "A Boy at Sea." United States Naval Institute *Proceedings* 107, no. 7 (July 1981): 51-53.

425. Langley, Harold D. "Edward Field: A Pioneer Practitioner of the Old Navy." *Connecticut Medicine* 46 (1982): 667-72.

426. _____. "A Naval Dependent in Washington, 1837-1842: Letters of Marian Coote Speiden." Columbia Historical Society (Washington, D.C.) *Records* 50 (1980): 105-22.

427. _____. "Respect for Civilian Authority: The Tragic Career of Captain Angus." *American Neptune* 40 (1980): 23-37.

428. _____. "Robert Y. Hayne and the Navy." *South Carolina Historical Magazine* 82 (1981): 311-30.

429. Larson, Sarah. "East India Squadron Letters: A Passage of Arms." *Prologue* 13 (1981): 39-48.

430. Layman, R. D. *To Ascend from a Floating Base: Shipboard Aeronautics and Aviation, 1783-1914.* Rutherford, N.J.: Fairleigh Dickinson University Press, 1979.

431. Leiner, Frederick C. "The 'Whimsical Phylosophic President' and His Gunboats." *American Neptune* 43 (1983): 245-66.

432. Long, David F. "A Case for Intervention: Armstrong, Foote, and the Destruction of the Barrier Forts, Canton, China, 1865." In *New Aspects of Naval History*, edited by Craig L. Symonds, 220-37. Annapolis, Md.: Naval Institute Press, 1981.

433. _____. *Ready to Hazard: A Biography of Commodore William Bainbridge, 1774-1833.* Hanover, N.H.: University Press of New England for the University of New Hampshire; Ann Arbor, Mich. University Microfilms, 1981.

434. _____. *Sailor-Diplomat: A Biography of Commodore James Biddle, 1783-1848.* Boston: Northeastern University Press, 1983.

435. Maloney, Linda M. "The U.S. Navy's Pacific Squadron, 1824-1827." In *Changing Interpretations and New Sources in Naval History*, United States Naval Academy History Symposium (3d: 1977), edited by Robert William Love, Jr., 180-91. New York: Garland, 1980.

436. Martin, Tyrone G. *A Most Fortunate Ship: A Narrative History of "Old Ironsides."* Chester, Conn.: Globe Pequot Press, 1980; rev. ed., 1982.

437. Mayhew, Dean R. "Jeffersonian Gunboats in the War of 1812." *American*

Neptune 42 (1982): 101–17.

438. Merrill, James M. "Midshipman DuPont and the Cruise of *North Carolina*, 1825–1827." *American Neptune* 40 (1980): 211–25.

439. Miller, Edward M. *U.S.S.* Monitor: *The Ship That Launched a Modern Navy*. Annapolis, Md.: Leeward Publications, 1978.

440. Monitor Conference (1978: Raleigh N.C.). *The* Monitor, *Its Meaning and Future: Papers from a National Conference, Raleigh, North Carolina, April 2–4, 1978*. Washington, D.C.: Preservation Press, 1978.

441. Monroe, Alexander. "Chaplain John [Needles] Hambleton, U.S.N.: A Diplomatic Correspondent." *Log of Mystic Seaport* 27 (1975): 34–41.

442. Nelson, Daniel A. "*Hamilton & Scourge*: Ghost Ships of the War of 1812." *National Geographic* 163 (1983): 288–313.

443. *New American State Papers, Naval Affairs*. 10 vols. Edited by K. Jack Bauer. Wilmington, Del.: Scholarly Resources, 1981.

444. Norberg, Arthur L. "Simon Newcomb's Early Astronomical Career." *Isis* 69 (1978): 209–25.

445. Palmer, Richard F. "The *General* [sic] *Hamilton* and the *Scourge*: 'One of the Most Exciting Finds of This Century." *Inland Seas* 38 (1982): 252–59.

446. Pearce, George F. *The U.S. Navy in Pensacola: From Sailing Ships to Naval Aviation, 1825–1930*. Pensacola: University Presses of Florida, 1980.

447. Philbrick, Thomas. "Cooper's Naval Friend in Paris." *American Literature* 52 (1980 / 81): 634–38.

448. Plumb, Robert J. "Yankee Paymaster." United States Naval Institute *Proceedings* 103, no. 10 (October 1977): 50–57.

449. Randolph, Evan. "USS *Constellation*, 1797 to 1979." *American Neptune* 39 (1979): 235–55.

450. Reynolds, Clark G. "Yankee Supership? Sortie of *Spuyten Duyvil*." *American Neptune* 42 (1982): 85–100.

451. Richmond, Helen. *Isaac Hull, a Forgotten American Hero*. Boston: USS *Constitution* Museum, 1983.

452. Riggs, David F. "Sailors of the USS *Cairo*: Anatomy of a Gunboat Crew." *Civil War History* 28 (1982): 266–73.

453. Roberts, Stephen S. "An Indicator of Informal Empire: Patterns of U.S. Navy Cruising on Overseas Stations, 1869–1897." In *New Aspects of Naval History*, United States Naval Academy History Symposium (4th: 1979), edited by Craig L. Symonds, 253–67. Annapolis, Md.: Naval Institute Press, 1981.

454. Robinson, Robert L. "Gunboat Diplomacy, 1882: The United States Navy and the Bombardment of Alexandria." *Warship International* 19 (1982): 47–56.

455. _____. "The U.S. Navy vs. Cattle Rustlers: The USS *Rio Bravo* on the Rio Grande, 1875–1879." *Military History of Texas and the Southwest* 15, no. 2 [1979]: 43–52.

456. Rosenwaike, Ira. "Bernard Henry: His Naval and Diplomatic Career." *American Jewish History* 69 (1979 / 80): 488–96.

457. Scarlett, Charles, Jr., et al. "Yankee Race Horse: The USS *Constellation*." *Maryland Historical Magazine* 56 (1961): 15–38.

458. Shoemaker, Raymond L. "Diplomacy from the Quarterdeck: The U.S. Navy in the Caribbean, 1815-1830." In *Changing Interpretations and New Sources in Naval History*, United States Naval Academy History Symposium (3d: 1977), edited by Robert William Love, Jr., 169-79. New York: Garland, 1980.

459. Shomette, Donald G. *Flotilla: Battle for the Patuxent.* Solomons, Md.: Calvert Marine Museum Press, 1981.

460. Shomette, Donald G., and Fred W. Hopkins. "The Search for the Chesapeake Flotilla." *American Neptune* 43 (1983) 5-19.

461. Shurbutt, T. Ray. "Chile, Peru, and the U.S. Pacific Squadron, 1823-1850." In *New Aspects of Naval History*, United States Naval Academy History Symposium (4th: 1979), edited by Craig L. Symonds, 201-10. Annapolis, Md.: Naval Institute Press, 1981.

462. Smith, John David. "Yankee Ironclads at Birkenhead? A Note on Gideon Welles, John Laird and Gustavus V. Fox." *Mariner's Mirror* 67 (1981): 77-82.

463. Smith, Myron J. *The U.S. Gunboat* Carondolet, *1861-1865.* Manhattan, Kans.: MA/AH Publishing, 1982.

464. Still, William N., Jr. *American Sea Power in the Old World: The United States Navy in European and Near Eastern Waters, 1865-1917.* Westport, Conn.: Greenwood Press, 1980.

465. Sugden, John. "Jean Lafitte and the British Offer of 1814." *Louisiana History* 20 (1979): 159-67.

466. Swartout, Robert, Jr., and Fred C. Bohm. "An American Naval Officer in 19th Century Korea: The Journal of George W. Woods." *Journal of Social Sciences and Humanities* (South Korea) 52 (1980): 18-30.

467. Swartout, Robert, Jr. "Cultural Conflict and Gunboat Diplomacy: The Development of the 1871 Korean-American Incident." *Journal of Social Sciences and Humanities* (South Korea) 43 (1976): 117-169.

468. Thomas, Mary Elizabeth. "The CSS *Tallahassee:* A Factor in Anglo-American Relations, 1864-1866." *Civil War History* 21 (1975): 148-59.

469. Thompson, Gerald. *Edward F. Beale & the American West.* Albuquerque: University of New Mexico Press, 1983.

470. Tucker, Spencer C. "Mr. Jefferson's Gunboat Navy." *American Neptune* 43 (1983) 135-41.

471. Turner, Maxine. "Naval Operations on the Apalachicola and Chattahoochee Rivers, 1861-1865." *Alabama Historical Quarterly* 36 (1974): 189-266.

472. Vivian, James F. "The Orinoco River and Angostura, Venezuela, in the Summer of 1819: The Narrative of a Maryland Naval Chaplain." *The Americas* 24 (1967/68): 160-83.

473. Warren, Gordon H. *Fountain of Discontent: The Trent Affair and Freedom of the Seas.* Boston: Northeastern University Press, 1981.

474. Wehmann, Howard H., ed. "Noise, Novelties and Nullifiers: A U.S. Navy Officer's Impressions of the Nullification Controversy." *South Carolina Historical Magazine* 76 (1975): 21-24.

475. Wicks, Daniel H. "Dress Rehearsal: United States Intervention on the Isthmus of Panama, 1885." *Pacific Historical Review* 49 (1980): 581-605.

476. _____. "The Lake Nicaragua Naval Base Scheme." United States Naval Institute *Proceedings* 106, no. 8 (August 1980): 56-60.

477. Wood, Virginia Steele. *Live Oaking: Southern Timber for Tall Ships.* Boston: Northeastern University Press, 1981.

Preparation of an essay such as this would not be possible without the untiring assistance of skilled interlibrary loan specialists. In the present instance the author extends the bouquet of American Beauty roses and his warmest thanks to Ms. Lisa K. Adkins of the Grinnell College Library, for she was amazingly effective in locating and borrowing a substantial number of books and articles on short notice.

VII

SCIENCE AND TECHNOLOGY IN THE NINETEENTH CENTURY

Edward C. Ezell

The application of scientific and technological knowledge to military under-takings is the topic of William H. McNeill's study *The Pursuit of Power: Technology, Armed Force, and Society since A.D. 1000* (538). It is appropriate to open this second update on science and technology in the 19th century, as it applies to the military, with a discussion of McNeill's book. The author attempts to explain the interaction among military technology, the armed forces, and the social and political structures that they defend and which support them. McNeill argues that social structure is significantly shaped by the technology of war, e.g., feudalism resulted from the emergence of the heavy armored cavalry that evolved to defend rural economic units. He examines the appearance of the first military-industrial complex in 19th-century England, a logical consequence of the Industrial Revolution of the 18th century. His narrative will give European and American historians much to examine, debate, and ponder in years to come. His analysis, regardless of one's initial opinion, should provide historians of American military technology with a framework for evaluating those developments in the United States over the last two centuries.

Daniel R. Headrick's *The Tools of Empire: Technology and European Imperialism in the Nineteenth Century* (526) is equally provocative. He concludes that technology gave imperialists the tools of empire and helped motivate them as well. Although Headrick concentrates on Britain's African and Indian frontiers, his discussions of improved naval vessels, the construction of the Suez canal, and the building of frontier railroads, as well as of the appearance of improved military weapons such as the breechloader, could be transformed into discussion of various American adventures from the Western frontier to expansion in the Caribbean and the Pacific. Merritt Roe Smith has tentatively explored the fringes of this frontier in "Military Entrepreneurship" (558), as has M. L. Brown in *Firearms in Colonial America: The Impact on History and Technology, 1492–1792.* (511).

MILITARY ENGINEERING AND EDUCATION. Coastal defense was a topic of considerable political debate and concern in 19th-century America. Since our last edition, several authors have examined this topic more fully. Bergerson, in a two-volume doctoral dissertation, looked at the changing nature of harbor defense in his study of "The Confederate Defense of Mobile, 1861–1865" (507). Weinert and Arthur have demonstrated the evolution of coastal defense thought and technology in their book on Fort Monroe, Virginia (562). Russell S. Gilmore's monograph *Guarding America's Front Door: Harbor Forts in the Defense of New York City* (523) is a sample of what can be done with this subject. Still, there is a need for a study that expands on Lewis's *Seacoast Fortifications of the United States: An Introductory History* (532). Dale Floyd's work at the History Office of the Corps of Engineers may well fill this lacunae. A doctoral dissertation of value in this area is Robert Stanton Browning III, "Shielding the Republic: America's Coastal Defense Policy in the Nineteenth Century" (512). The Greenwood Press continues the reprinting of significant books from the past with their 1971 edition of V.E.K.R. von Scheliha, *A Treatise on Coast Defence* (560).

Janis Langins has added to our understanding of military education with her book *The Ecole Polytechnique (1794–1804): From Encyclopaedic School to Military Instruction* (531). And Evald Rink's *Technical Americana: A Checklist of Technical Publications Printed before 1838* (547) helps define the context in which early American military science and technology evolved.

THE AMERICAN SYSTEM OF INTERCHANGEABLE MANUFACTURE. In March 1978 a symposium was held at the National Museum of American History with the purpose of convening the community of scholars investigating aspects of the evolution of the American System and its social, economic, and political consequences. The results of this gathering were published in *Yankee Enterprise: The Rise of the American System of Manufacturers* (537), edited by Otto Mayr and Robert C. Post. Students of American military history will find most of the essays of interest, but Eugene S. Ferguson's "History and Historiography" (520) should be especially helpful.

MANUFACTURE OF MILITARY SMALL ARMS. Two pairs of books have appeared since the last bibliographic update for both the Springfield "trap door" series of breech-loading rifles (521 and 561) and the Springfield Krag rifles (510 and 534). Together these volumes span the years 1865 to 1903 and thus fill a long-standing gap. Created to meet the needs of the military-rifle-collecting community, these four books have much of interest for the student of the "breech-loading rifle revolution" that transpired at the end of the nineteenth century. Implicit in these studies is the military predeliction for product-improvement of existing designs. Totally new designs must always fight an uphill battle for adoption. This theme, which is addressed in earlier works (158 et al.), is also described in Richard I. Wolf's dissertation "Arms and Innovation: The United States Army and the Repeating Rifle, 1865–1900" and David A. Armstrong's *Bullets and Bureaucrats: The Machine Gun and the United States Army, 1861–1916* (505), a published version of his dissertation (390).

Specific manufacturers and their products have been the subject of recent studies. These include Samuel Colt's London pistol-manufacturing enterprise (551), the Sharps Rifle Company (556), and the repeating firearms of Christopher M. Spencer (535). William O. Achtermeir's *Rhode Island Arms Makers & Gunsmiths, 1643–1883* (503) is valuable for several reasons, but the essay on the "Providence Tool Company (1834–1883)," pp. 28–45 and 77–78, is superb. George A. Hoyem has produced a two-volume study of *The History and Development of Small Arms Ammunition* (529) that covers the development of cartridge ammunition during the last part of the 19th century. For a more general reference to military small arms, H. Michael Madus's *The Warner Collector's Guide to American Longarms* is a must (533). A reference of similar import for the British scene is Herbert J. Woodend's *British Rifles: A Catalogue of the Enfield Pattern Room* (541). An unpublished treasure in the holdings of the Division of Armed Forces History, National Museum of American History, is Andrew H. Russell's "Government Exhibit of Guns and Ammunition at the World's Columbian Exposition, Chicago, Illinois, 1893" (553), which is a typescript annotation of the official catalog. This work is important because many of the guns described are still in the national collections, and because the glass-plate negatives used to illustrate a companion photograph album still survive. Edward C. Ezell's *Handguns of the World: Military Revolvers and Self-loaders from 1870 to 1945* (519) represents an attempt to follow the development of the handgun in a number of countries, examining in the process the impact of tactics and technology on the design of this class of weapons. A two-volume study of the development of the military rifle, by the same author, is in preparation.

NAVAL TECHNOLOGY. Frank J. Anderson has compiled a bibliography on *Submarines, Diving and the Underwater World* (504), and his publisher, the Oxford University Press, has reissued Baxter's *The Introduction of the Ironclad Warship* (31). Baxter's classic has been supplemented by B. F. Cooling's *Gray Steel and Blue Water Navy: The Formative Years of America's Military Industrial Complex, 1881–1917* (514) and Richard D. Glasow's dissertation "Prelude to a Naval Renaissance: Ordnance Innovation in the United States Navy during the 1870s" (524).

SUGGESTIONS FOR FURTHER RESEARCH. Many of the topics in the first two editions of this essay still merit further study. There are still others that come to mind. One is a biography / technical study of the design career of Edward Maynard, whose experiments spanned the period from the introduction of the percussion cap to the standardization of the breech-loading rifle. His business papers and most of his experimental firearms and cartridges are held by the Armed Forces History Division of the National Museum of American History. His personal papers are at the Library of Congress. This would make a neat package for a doctoral dissertation illuminating an interesting and important inventor. A biographical dictionary of U.S. Army ordnance officers in the nineteenth century would be another worthwhile project. For all the work that has been done, much remains to be examined.

BIBLIOGRAPHY

503. Achtermeir, William O. *Rhode Island Arms Makers & Gunsmiths, 1643–1883*. Providence, R.I.: A Man at Arms Publication, 1980.
504. Anderson, Frank J. *Submarines, Diving, and the Underwater World: A Bibliography*. New York: Oxford University Press, 1981.
505. Armstrong, David A. *Bullets and Bureaucrats: The Machine Gun and the United States Army, 1861–1916*. Westport, Conn.: Greenwood Press, 1982.

Revision of (390).

506. Baxter, James P., III. *The Introduction of the Ironclad Warship.* New York: Oxford University Press, 1981. Reissue of (31).

507. Bergerson, Arthur W., Jr. "The Confederate Defense of Mobile, 1861–1865." 2 vols. Ph.D. diss., Louisiana State University and Agricultural and Mechanical College, 1980. University microfilm no. 8103623.

508. Birnie, Rogers. *Gunmaking in the United States.* Washington, D.C.: GPO, 1918. Reprinted from the *Journal of the Military Service Institution,* 1888, this is an essay on the development of heavy ordnance for the U.S. Army.

509. Brooke, George M., Jr. *John M. Brooke: Naval Scientist and Educator.* Charlottesville: University of Virginia Press, 1980.

510. Brophy, William S. *The Krag Rifle.* North Hollywood, Calif.: Beinfeld Publishing, 1980.

511. Brown, M. L. *Firearms in Colonial America: The Impact on History and Technology, 1492–1792.* Washington, D.C.: Smithsonian Institution Press, 1980.

512. Browning, Robert Stanton, III. "Shielding the Republic: American Coastal Defense Policy in the Nineteenth Century." Ph.D. diss., University of Wisconsin, Madison, 1981. University microfilm no. 8115900. Published as *Two If By Sea: The Development of American Coastal Defense Policy.* Westport, Conn.: Greenwood Press, 1983.

513. Byron, David. *Gunmarks: Trademarks, Codemarks, and Proofs from 1870 to the Present.* New York: Crown, 1979.

514. Cooling, Benjamin Franklin, III. *Gray Steel and Blue Water Navy: The Formative Years of America's Military Industrial Complex, 1881–1917.* New York: Oxford University Press, 1981.

515. Dahlgren, John A. B. *Shell and Shell Guns.* Philadelphia: King and Baird, 1856.

516. Di Filippo, Anthony J. "Militarism and Machine Tool Building in America." Ph.D. diss., Temple University, 1981. University microfilm no. 8124561.

517. Dillion, Lester R. *American Artillery in the Mexican War, 1846–1847.* Austin, Tex.: Presidial Press, 1975.

518. Donnelly, Ralph D. "Local Defense in the Confederate Munitions Area." *Military Affairs* 18 (1954): 118–30.

519. Ezell, Edward C. *Handguns of the World: Military Revolvers and Self-loaders from 1870 to 1945.* Harrisburg, Pa.: Stackpole Books, 1981.

520. Ferguson, Eugene S. "History and Historiography," in Mayr and Post (537), 1–23.

521. Frasca, Albert J., and Robert H. Hill. *The .45-70 Springfield.* Northridge, Calif.: Springfield Publishing Co., 1980.

522. Gaier, Claude. *Small Arms Ignition Systems and Ammunition.* Liège, Belgium: Imprimerie Georges Thone, 1969. Translated by F. Norris.

523. Gilmore, Russell S. *Guarding America's Front Door: Harbor Forts in the Defense of New York City.* [Brooklyn, N.Y.]: Fort Hamilton Historical Society, ca. 1983.

524. Glasow, Richard Dwight. "Prelude to a Naval Renaissance: Ordnance Innovation in the United States Navy during the 1870s." Ph.D. diss., University of Delaware, 1978.

525. Graham, Ron, John A. Kopec, and Kenneth Moore. *A Study of the Colt Single-Action Army Revolver*. Dallas, Tex.: Taylor Publishing Co., 1976.
526. Headrick, Daniel R. *The Tools of Empire: Technology and European Imperialism in the Nineteenth Century*. New York: Oxford University Press, 1981.
527. Heer, Eugen, and Johan F. Stockel. *Heer Der Neue Stockel*. Schwabisch Hall, West Germany: Journal-Verlag Schwend GmbH. vol. 1 (1978), vol. 2 (1979), and vol. 3 (1982). This is an international listing of gunsmiths, armsmakers, and edged-weapons makers.
528. Hill, Richard Taylor, and William Edward Anthony. *Confederate Longarms and Pistols: A Pictorial Study*. Charlotte, N.C.: Richard Taylor Hill and William Edward Anthony, 1978.
529. Hoyem, George A. *The History and Development of Small Arms Ammunition*. 2 vols. Tacoma, Wash.: Armory Publications, 1981-1982.
530. Huddleston, Joe D. *Colonial Riflemen in the American Revolution*. York, Pa.: George Shumway Publisher, 1978.
531. Langins, Janis. *The Ecole Polytechnique (1794-1804): From Encyclopaedic School to Military Institution*. New York: Oxford University Press, 1981.
532. Lewis, Emanuel Raymond. *Seacoast Fortifications of the United States: An Introductory History*. Washington, D.C.: Smithsonian Institution Press, 1970.
533. Madus, H. Michael. *The Warner Collector's Guide to American Longarms*. New York: Warner Books, 1981.
534. Mallory, Franklin B., and Ludwig E. Olson. *The Krag Rifle Story*. Silver Spring, Md.: Springfield Research Service, 1979.
535. Marcot, Roy. *Spencer Repeating Firearms*. Dallas, Tex.: Taylor Publishing Co., 1984.
536. Maxwell, Samuel L., Sr. *Lever-Action Magazine Rifles*. Dallas, Tex.: Samuel L. Maxwell, Sr., 1976.
537. Mayr, Otto, and Robert C. Post, eds. *Yankee Enterprise: The Rise of the American System of Manufacturers*. Washington, D.C.: Smithsonian Institution Press, 1981.
538. McNeill, William H. *The Pursuit of Power: Technology, Armed Force, and Society Since A.D. 1000*. Chicago: University of Chicago Press, 1982.
539. Metcalf, 1st Lt. Henry. *The Ordnance Department, U.S. Army at the International Exhibition, 1876*. Washington, D.C.: GPO, 1884.
540. Milner Associates, John. *Historical and Archaeological Survey of Frankford Arsenal*. West Chester, Pa.: John Milner Associates, 1979. Prepared for the Baltimore District of the U.S. Army Corps of Engineers.
541. Ministry of Defence [Herbert J. Woodend]. *British Rifles: A Catalogue of the Enfield Pattern Room* [Museum]. London: Her Majesty's Stationery Office, 1981.
542. Nuxoll, Elizabeth Miles. *Congress and the Munitions Merchants: The Secret Committee of Trade during the American Revolution, 1775-1777*. New York: Oxford University Press, 1981.
543. O'Connell, Charles F., Jr. "The United States Army and the Origins of Modern Management, 1818-1860." Ph.D. diss., Ohio State University, 1982. University microfilm no. 8222143.
544. Parkes, Oscar. *British Battleships, 1860-1950: A History of Design,*

Construction, and Armament. Hamden, Conn.: Archon Books, 1981.

545. Pool, Bernard. *Navy Board Contracts, 1660–1832: Contract Administration under the Navy Board*. London: Longman's, 1966.

546. Porter, Joseph G. "John Gregory Bourke, Victorian Soldier Scientist: The Western Apprenticeship, 1869–1886." Ph.D. diss., University of Texas, Austin, 1980. University microfilm no. 8217955.

547. Rink, Evald. *Technical Americana: A Checklist of Technical Publications Printed before 1831*. New York: Oxford University Press, 1981.

548. Risch, Erna. *Supplying Washington's Army*. Washington, D.C.: Center of Military History, 1981.

549. Roberts, Larry Don. "The Artillery with the Regular Army in the West from 1866 to 1890." Ph.D. diss., Oklahoma State University, 1981. University microfilm no. 8123855.

550. Robinson, Willard B. *American Forts: Architectural Form and Function*. Urbana: University of Illinois Press, 1977.

551. Rosa, Joseph G. *Colonel Colt London: The History of Colt's London Firearms, 1851–1857*. London: Arms & Armour Press, 1976.

552. Rosen, Howard. "The *Système Gribeauval*: A Study in Technological Development and Institutional Change in Eighteenth Century France." Ph.D. diss., University of Chicago, 1981.

553. Russell, Capt. Andrew H. "Government Exhibit of Guns and Ammunition at the World's Columbian Exposition, Chicago, Illinois, 1893." Combination of printed and typescript pages. Washington, D.C.: Division of Armed Forces History, National Museum of American History, Smithsonian Institution.

554. Schaeffer, James A. "The Tactical and Strategic Evolution of Cavalry during the American Civil War." Ph.D. diss., University of Toledo, 1982.

555. Schubert, Frank N. *Vanguard of Expansion: Army Engineers in the Trans-Mississippi West, 1819–1879*. Washington, D.C.: Office of the Chief of Engineers, 1980.

556. Sellers, Frank. *Sharps Firearms*. North Hollywood, Calif.: Beinfeld Publishing, 1978.

557. Shumway, George. *Rifles of Colonial America*. 2 vols. York, Pa.: George Shumway Publisher, 1980.

558. Smith, Merritt Roe. "Military Entrepreneurship," in Mayr and Post (537), 63–102.

559. U.S. Navy. *Report on a Naval Mission to Europe; Especially Devoted to the Material and Construction of Artillery*, by Capt. Edward Simpson. 2 vols. Washington, D.C.: GPO, 1873.

560. von Scheliha, V.E.K.R. *A Treatise on Coast Defence*. Westport, Conn.: Greenwood Press, 1971. Reprint of 1868 edition.

561. Waite, M. D., and B. D. Ernst. *Trapdoor Springfield*. North Hollywood, Calif.: Beinfeld Publishing, 1980.

562. Weinert, Richard P., Jr., and Col. Robert Arthur. *Defender of the Chesapeake: The Story of Fort Monroe*. Annapolis, Md.: Leeward Publications, 1978.

563. Wilkinson, Norman B. "The Pennsylvania Rifle." *American Heritage* 7 (1950): 3–5, 64–66.

564. Wolf, Richard I. "Arms and Innovation: The United States Army and the

Repeating Rifle, 1865–1900." Ph.D. diss., Boston University, 1981. University microfilm no. 8126819.
565. Wright, John W. "The Rifle in the American Revolution." *American Historical Review* 29 (1924): 293–99.
566. York, Neil Longley. *Technology in Revolutionary America, 1760–1790.* New York: Oxford University Press, 1981.

VIII

THE MEXICAN WAR AND THE CIVIL WAR

Grady McWhiney

There are good reasons to consider the sources on the military history of the Mexican War and the Civil War together. In many ways the Mexican War was, as one writer called it, a rehearsal for conflict. It was more than that, of course, and anyone who examines it from such a limited perspective is likely to miss much of importance. On the other hand, it would be equally shortsighted to ignore the continuity between these two wars despite their significant differences. What young Americans saw and did in Mexico from 1846 to 1847 strongly influenced the way they fought each other from 1861 to 1865. Indeed, many of the Union and Confederate officers who led large bodies of men in the Civil War learned much of what they knew about combat in Mexico. A certain continuity is equally as apparent in some of the sources. Many collections of primary material that are useful in studying one war also are valuable in studying the other. This is true not only of certain unpublished papers, but of some published material as well—especially biographies, letters, and memoirs.

POLICY, STRATEGY, AND TACTICS. Two important new works focus on these relatively neglected areas. *How the North Won* (433), by Herman Hattaway and Archer Jones, is an elaborate and valuable treatment of Civil War leadership, organization, logistics, strategy, and tactics. *Attack and Die* (443), by Grady McWhiney and Perry D. Jamieson, analyzes both Mexican War and Civil War strategy and tactics and concludes that "the Confederates bled themselves nearly to death in the first three years of the war by making costly attacks." *Lincoln and the Indians* (447), by David A. Nichols, focuses on the Minnesota Sioux War of 1862 and demonstrates that Lincoln's Indian policy was politically expedient and inhumane. How federal military occupation of the South shaped the formulation of Reconstruction policy, an important but relatively neglected topic, is examined by Peter Maslowski, who concentrates on Nashville (446), and by Joseph G. Dawson III, who deals with wartime military government under Generals Benjamin F. Butler and Nathaniel P. Banks and their conflicts with civilian authorities in Louisiana (426).

BIOGRAPHIES. Recent studies indicate that the desire to reevaluate individuals remains strong, as does the determination not to overlook some of the relatively obscure military commanders. Chester L. Kieffer's *Maligned General* (436), a reassessment of the forty-two-year career of Thomas S. Jesup as the army's quartermaster general, is helpful in understanding the problems of logistics during the Mexican War. Confederate general John Bell Hood is treated critically in an excellent new biography by Richard M. McMurry (442). Gen. Ulysses S. Grant receives revisionist treatment by William S. McFeely (441) in a volume that one reviewer notes is heavily burdened with the author's "tone of moral superiority on the subject of war," and is full of questionable generalizations about both Grant and warfare. Biographies of other Union generals include E.O.C. Ord, whose military career spanned the forty-five years, from 1835 to 1880, and who served under Grant in the West and in the East, by Bernard Cresap (422); John Sedgwick, the stolid corps commander who served in the Army of the Potomac from the Peninsula campaign until his death at Spotsylvania, by Richard Elliot Winslow III (461); and Isaac I. Stevens, a West Point graduate who was on General Scott's staff in Mexico and died leading a charge at Chantilly in 1862, by Kent D. Richards (453). The popularity of ethnic history can be seen in several recent biographies. *Stand Watie* (428), by Kenny A. Franks, is a well-documented account of a Cherokee Indian who became a Confederate general; *Warrior in Two Camps* (416) by William H. Armstrong, is a study of Ely S. Parker, a Seneca chief who was Grant's assistant adjutant general and personal secretary during the Civil War. Hans L. Trefousse has reevaluated Carl Schurz (458), a German politician who served as a Union general; and two Polish refugees who served as Union commanders—Joseph Kargé, a cavalryman, and Wladimir Krzyzanowski, a brigade commander in the German Eleventh Corps—are the heroes of biographies by Francis C. Kajencki (435) and James S. Pula (452). Robert K. Krick's *Lee's Colonels* (437) is a valuable biographical register of 1,954 field-grade officers who served in the Army of Northern Virginia.

CAMPAIGNS AND BATTLES. James Lee McDonough's *Stones River* is the best modern account of the critical 1862–1863 Murfreesboro campaign (439). Edwin C. Bearss has written a carefully researched tactical study not only of Confederate general Nathan B. Forrest at Brice's Cross Roads (419) but of the entire campaign in northern Mississippi from mid-April through August 1864. An expert and readable assessment by Richard J. Sommers of *Richmond Redeemed* (456) deals with strategy, tactics, and generalship during Grant's fifth assault on Petersburg in September and October 1864, with particular emphasis on its opening battles of Chaffin's Bluff and Poplar Spring Church. *Five Tragic Hours: The Battle of Franklin* (440), by James Lee McDonough and Thomas L. Connelly, is by far the best treatment of that Confederate disaster.

SPECIAL STUDIES. Stephen Z. Starr has completed two of a projected three-volume work on the Union cavalry that promises to be definitive (457). *Cry Comanche* (455), by Harold B. Simpson, outlines the activities in Texas from 1855 to 1861 of the Second United States Cavalry—a unit that included several important Civil War soldiers. Kenneth E. Olson's *Music and Musket* (448) is an informative and meticulously detailed account of Civil War bandsmen, with considerably more details on Northern than on Southern musicians. William C. Davis's history of Kentucky's *Orphan Brigade* (424) is an important addition to the literature on individual units. In a work that subjects the letters and diaries of Civil War soldiers to computer analysis, Michael Barton tries to measure the unmeasurable—the character of Civil War soldiers (418). Phillip S. Paludan recounts in *Victims* (449) how Confederate troops executed thirteen Union prisoners in North Carolina in 1863 and the role of Confederate general Henry Heth in this atrocity. *Sherman's Other War* (445), by John F. Marszalek, analyzes Gen. William T. Sherman's guerrilla warfare with newspapermen. The struggle – chiefly a war of words – between Brigham Young and Union general Patrick Edward Connor is the focus of E. B. Long's study of Utah Territory during the Civil War (438). *Texas in the Confederacy* (460), by Bill Windsor, is an encyclopedic listing of Confederate and Union military facilities, naval operations along the Gulf Coast, railroads, and manufacturing, as well as the major Confederate military figures in the state during the war. William C. Davis has edited three volumes of a projected six-volume pictorial history of the Civil War (425) that promised to supersede Miller's old *Photographic History of the Civil War* as the standard source. William A. Frassanito continues, in *Grant and Lee* (429), to chronicle, in 255 contemporary photographs, the final year of the war in the East.

PRINTED PRIMARY SOURCES. *The Papers of Jefferson Davis* (423), now under the editorship of Lynda L. Crist, and *The Papers of Ulysses S. Grant* (432), edited by John Y. Simon, are the two most important editing projects relating to Civil War military history now under way. Four volumes of Davis's papers, through 1852, and ten volumes of Grant's papers, through 31 May 1864, are available. All of these volumes are carefully edited, and indispensable for an understanding of their subjects and the war. New and useful collections of Civil War letters, diaries, and memoirs include a complete and accurate text of the 1880s memoir / novel, *Mary Chesnut's Civil War* (421), that had previously been misrepresented as a diary together with emendations from the original journal kept during the war, all carefully edited and explained by editor C. Vann Woodward; a revealing series of letters by one of the commanders of the famous Stonewall Brigade (450); the diary and recollections of a captain in Granbury's Texas Brigade, describing service in the Army of Tennessee as well as giving opinions of Generals Joseph E. Johnston and John Bell Hood (427); the letters of an Alabamian, which are helpful in understanding conditions and operations around Mobile (459); the diary of a New York volunteer who participated in Gen. Ambrose Burnside's "Mud March," was wounded at Chancellorsville, and later took part in the Atlanta campaign (420); the letters of a Confederate captain in Walker's Texas Division (451); the letters of a Jesuit chaplain of a Louisiana Confederate regiment who served in Lee's army (430); the letters of a pro-Confederate German family, which provide useful information on life in Texas and western Louisiana during the war (431); the diary and letters of an abolitionist and a feminist who became the matron of a Union hospital in Georgetown (454); and the diary of a very proper Charleston lady, who commented on the shelling of Fort Sumter and various wartime activities, as well as on political and military leaders and the depredations of Union soldiers (434). Among the better recently published memoirs are those of Confederate general Arthur M. Manigault, who commanded a brigade in the Army of Tennessee (444), and of Union general William W. Averell, who was removed from command of Union cavalry in the Shenandoah Valley by Gen. Philip Sheridan in 1864 (417).

SUGGESTIONS FOR FURTHER RESEARCH. In earlier editions of this guide, it was suggested that much work remained to be done on the military history of both the Mexican War and the Civil War. That is still true, though fewer obvious gaps remain unfilled. The Mexican War continues to be a relatively neglected field. Besides biographies of such leaders as John A. Quitman and Persifor F. Smith and a fresh study of Winfield Scott, more detailed examinations of operations and tactics would add to our understanding of that conflict. Civil War general Don Carlos Buell deserves a biography, and better studies of Generals Philip H. Sheridan and James Longstreet are needed. Staff studies and analyses of military administration deserve more attention than they have received. A call for more unit histories and accounts of battles and campaigns has been partly answered, but the history of many brigades and regiments, as well as of several significant campaigns and battles in both the Mexican War and the Civil War, need to be written or rewritten. To be worthwhile, such studies should combine exhaustive research in the published and unpublished sources with the techniques of quantification and the insights and concerns of the social and military historian.

BIBLIOGRAPHY

416. Armstrong, William H. *Warrior in Two Camps: Ely S. Parker, Union General and Seneca Chief.* Syracuse, N.Y.: Syracuse University Press, 1978.
417. Averell, William Woods. *Ten Years in the Saddle: The Memoir of William Woods Averell.* Edited by Edward K. Eckert and Nicholas J. Amato. San Raphael, Calif.: Presidio Press, 1978.
418. Barton, Michael. *Goodmen: The Character of Civil War Soldiers.* University Park: Pennsylvania State University Press, 1981.
419. Bearss, Edwin C. *Forrest at Brice's Cross Roads.* Dayton, Ohio: Morningside Bookshop, 1979.
420. Bull, Rice C. *Soldiering: The Civil War Diary of Rice C. Bull, 123rd New York Volunteer Infantry.* Edited by K. Jack Bauer. San Rafael, Calif.: Presidio Press, 1977.
421. Chesnut, Mary B. *Mary Chesnut's Civil War.* Edited by C. Vann Woodward. New Haven, Conn.: Yale University Press, 1981.
422. Cresap, Bernard. *Appomattox Commander: The Story of General E.O.C. Ord.* San Diego: A. S. Barnes, 1981.
423. Davis, Jefferson. *The Papers of Jefferson Davis. Vol. 3, July 1846–December 1848.* Edited by James T. McIntosh. *Vol. 4, 1849–1852.* Edited by Lynda Lasswell Crist. 4 vols. to date. Baton Rouge: Louisiana State University Press, 1971–.
424. Davis, William C. *The Orphan Brigade: The Kentucky Confederates Who Couldn't Go Home.* New York: Doubleday, 1980.
425. _____, ed. *The Image of War, 1861–1865.* 6 vols. to date. New York: Doubleday, 1981–.
426. Dawson, Joseph G., III. *Army Generals and Reconstruction: Louisiana, 1862–1877.* Baton Rouge: Louisiana State University Press, 1982.
427. Foster, Samuel T. *One of Cleburne's Command: The Civil War Reminiscences and Diary of Capt. Samuel T. Foster, Granbury's Texas Brigade, CSA.* Edited by Norman D. Brown. Austin: University of Texas Press, 1980.

428. Franks, Kenny A. *Stand Watie and the Agony of the Cherokee Nation.* Memphis, Tenn.: Memphis State University Press, 1979.
429. Frassanito, William A. *Grant and Lee: The Virginia Campaigns, 1864–1865.* New York: Charles Scribner's Sons, 1983.
430. Gache, Louis-Hippolyte. *A Frenchman, a Chaplain, a Rebel: The War Letters of Pere Louis-Hippolyte Gache, S.J.* Translated and edited by Cornelius M. Buckley, S.J. Chicago: Loyola University Press, 1981.
431. Goyne, Minetta Altgelt, ed. *Lone Star and Double Eagle: Civil War Letters of a German-Texas Family.* Fort Worth: Texas Christian University Press, 1982.
432. Grant, Ulysses S. *The Papers of Ulysses S. Grant.* Edited by John Y. Simon. 10 vols. to date. Carbondale: Southern Illinois University Press, 1967–.
433. Hattaway, Herman, and Archer Jones. *How the North Won: A Military History of the Civil War.* Urbana: University of Illinois Press, 1983.
434. Holmes, Emma. *The Diary of Miss Emma Holmes: 1861–1866.* Edited by John F. Marszalek. Baton Rouge: Louisiana State University Press, 1979.
435. Kajencki, Francis C. *Star on Many a Battlefield: Brevet Brigadier General Joseph Kargé in the American Civil War.* Rutherford, N.J.: Fairleigh Dickinson University Press, 1980.
436. Kieffer, Chester L. *Maligned General: The Biography of Thomas Sidney Jesup.* San Rafael, Calif.: Presidio Press, 1979.
437. Krick, Robert K. *Lee's Colonels: A Biographical Register of the Field Officers of the Army of Northern Virginia.* Dayton, Ohio: Morningside Bookshop, 1979.
438. Long, E. B. *The Saints and the Union: Utah Territory during the Civil War.* Urbana: University of Illinois Press, 1981.
439. McDonough, James Lee. *Stones River—Bloody Winter in Tennessee.* Knoxville: University of Tennessee Press, 1980.
440. McDonough, James Lee, and Thomas L. Connelly. *Five Tragic Hours: The Battle of Franklin.* Knoxville: University of Tennessee Press, 1983.
441. McFeely, William S. *Grant: A Biography.* New York: W. W. Norton, 1981.
442. McMurry, Richard M. *John Bell Hood and the War for Southern Independence.* Lexington: University Press of Kentucky, 1982.
443. McWhiney, Grady, and Perry D. Jamieson. *Attack and Die: Civil War Military Tactics and the Southern Heritage.* University: University of Alabama Press, 1982.
444. Manigault, Arthur M. *A Carolinian Goes to War: The Civil War Narrative of Arthur Middleton Manigault, Brigadier General, C.S.A.* Edited by R. Lockwood Tower. Also *With His Mexican War Narrative,* edited by Warren Ripley and Arthur M. Wilcox. Columbia: University of South Carolina Press, 1983.
445. Marszalek, John F. *Sherman's Other War: The General and the Civil War Press.* Memphis, Tenn.: Memphis State University Press, 1981.
446. Maslowski, Peter. *Treason Must be Made Odious: Military Occupation and Wartime Reconstruction in Nashville, Tennessee, 1862–65.* Millwood, N.Y.: KTO Press, 1978.
447. Nichols, David A. *Lincoln and the Indians: Civil War Policy and Politics.* Columbia: University of Missouri Press, 1978.

448. Olson, Kenneth E. *Music and Musket: Bands and Bandsmen of the American Civil War.* Westport, Conn.: Greenwood Press, 1981.
449. Paludan, Phillip Shaw. *Victims: A True Story of the Civil War.* Knoxville: University of Tennessee Press, 1981.
450. Paxton, Frank. *The Civil War Letters of General Frank "Bull" Paxton, CSA: A Lieutenant of Lee & Jackson.* Edited by John Gallatin Paxton. Hillsboro, Tex.: Hill Junior College Press, 1978.
451. Petty, Elijah P. *Journey to Pleasant Hill: The Civil War Letters of Captain Elijah P. Petty, Walker's Texas Division, CSA.* Edited by Norman D. Brown. San Antonio: Institute of Texas Cultures, 1982.
452. Pula, James S. *For Liberty and Justice: The Life and Times of Wladimir Krzyzanowski.* Chicago: Polish American Congress Charitable Foundation, 1978.
453. Richards, Kent D. *Isaac I. Stevens: Young Man in a Hurry.* Provo, Utah: Brigham Young University Press, 1979.
454. Ropes, Hannah. *Civil War Nurse: The Diary and Letters of Hannah Ropes.* Edited by John R. Brumgardt. Knoxville: University of Tennessee Press, 1980.
455. Simpson, Harold B. *Cry Comanche: The 2nd U.S. Cavalry in Texas, 1955-1861.* Hillsboro, Tex.: Hill Junior College Press, 1979.
456. Sommers, Richard J. *Richmond Redeemed: The Siege at Petersburg.* New York: Doubleday, 1981.
457. Starr, Stephen Z. *The Union Cavalry in the Civil War.* 2 vols. to date. Baton Rouge: Louisiana State University Press, 1979–.
458. Trefousse, Hans L. *Carl Schurz: A Biography.* Knoxville: University of Tennessee Press, 1982.
459. Williams, James M. *From That Terrible Field: Civil War Letters of James M. Williams, Twenty-first Alabama Infantry Volunteers.* Edited by John Kent Folmer. University: University of Alabama Press, 1981.
460. Windsor, Bill. *Texas in the Confederacy: Military Installations, Economy & People.* Hillsboro, Tex.: Hill Junior College Press, 1978.
461. Winslow, Richard Elliot, III. *General John Sedgwick: The Story of a Union Corps Commander.* Novato, Calif.: Presidio Press, 1982.

IX

CIVIL-MILITARY RELATIONS, OPERATIONS AND THE ARMY, 1865–1917

Richard N. Ellis

The period from 1865 to 1971 was a time of transition in American military history. Concomitant with demobilization of the Civil War Union army and subsequent reorganization that further reduced the army in size was involvement in Reconstruction and service in the West. While frontier duty occupied army manpower, the thinking of military leaders focused on the needs of conventional warfare. This was a period of active military thought, much of it influenced by Emory Upton; it was a period of significant changes in weaponry. Blacks served in regular army regiments and entered the officer corps, while reorganization brought the formation of the general staff. It was a period of combat in the Spanish-American War and the Philippines and ultimately of preparation for entry into Word War I. The literature for these years has grown accordingly, with continued emphasis on the frontier army but also with new interest in the domestic functions of the army.

GENERAL WORKS. While there are no new works that deal with all of the major issues for the period from the Civil War to World War I, there are a number of studies that deal with important topics or with a broad time period. *America Arms for a New Century*, by Abrahamson (339), is an important book that deals with the years from roughly 1880 to 1920 and explores the reaction of military officers to change in the United States, both to internal developments and to great power status. Abrahamson argues that reform-minded officers furthered the modernization of America by modifying institutions to keep up with a changing America. In *Bullets and Bureaucrats*, Armstrong (343) analyzes the development of the machine-gun and the factors that delayed its adoption and hindered weapons innovation in general and in *Above the Battle* (376), Leonard seeks to describe how soldiers reacted to battle. The latter should be used in connection with *The American Soldier in Fiction, 1880–1963* (340) by Aichinger.

Useful articles for this period include Moore's study of national security in the army's definition of mission (386); a centennial assessment of Emory Upton, by Bacevich (345); and Gates's provocative analysis of the army's experience with insurgency (363).

Several broader studies also deserve mention. Allan Millett's important history of the Marine Corps (385) has a significant portion on these years, while

Browning's study of coastal-defense policy devotes several chapters to the period (350). Although Patton's (391) study of black officers in the military focuses on 1915-1941, he provides background material and stresses racism in the early twentieth century. Also important is John Mahon's *History of the Militia and the National Guard* (377), which deals with Reconstruction and the birth of the guard, the war with Spain, and subsequent reorganization of the guard. Stone (395) relates the history of the militia and guard in Kentucky to 1912 and argues that most significant improvements were imposed by the Federal Government.

Several biographies also have appeared. In *Brandy Station to Manila Bay*, Don Alberts (341) describes the career of Wesley Merritt, the Civil War veteran who commanded a black regiment on the frontier, was superintendent of West Point, was involved in the Pullman Strike and the Spanish-American War, and was military governor in Manila. Lane (375) covers the career of Leonard Wood in a more critical work than the old biography by Hagedorn, while a portion of Holley's (369) study of John Palmer is on pre-World War I years. House (370) focuses on one aspect of Palmer's career.

FRONTIER ARMY. The sheer volume of publications on the Indian-fighting army indicates the continued interest in that topic by scholars and the general public. Significant works have appeared in the past several years, and while some scholars focus on campaigns against Western tribes, others continue a trend noticeable in the 1970s and concentrate on other subjects, particularly in the areas of social and economic history.

For many years Robert M. Utley has been considered the preeminent figure in the study of the frontier army. Utley (401) adds to that reputation with *The Indian Frontier of the American West, 1846-1890*, a volume in the History of American Frontiers Series. In this exceptionally readable work, Utley places the role of the army in Indian-white warfare in the broader context of Indian policy and of cultural contact and misunderstanding. A master storyteller, Utley demonstrates the ability to deal equally well with major issues, individuals, and events. Utley also edited the diaries and letters of a cavalryman with Custer (402). Another broad study is Dunlay's *Wolves for the Blue Soldiers* (357). While Ellis, Tate, and others have looked at aspects of army utilization of Indian fighters, Dunlay provides a comprehensive study of the topic for the trans-Mississippi West.

Several scholars have looked at army-Indian relations, including Bailey (347) who deals with Alfred Terry, a figure of secondary importance, and his role in the decline of the Sioux. Hoig (368) treats the battle of the Washita, which involved George Custer, while Hutton (372) evaluates the treatment of Custer in film and Hofling (367) offers a psychological biography that focuses on Custer's relationships with superiors and identifies a cyclic pattern of behavior that included periodic self-destructive actions. Greene (364) and Hutton (373) deal with specific campaigns, and Danker (355) describes the Eli Riker interviews on the battle of Wounded Knee. The Riker Collection, with its Indian testimony, is an important body of source material. Altshuler (342) carefully outlines the changing military organization in Arizona, and Sherman's participation in the important 1868 Navajo treaty is evaluated by Kessell (374).

In addition to more traditional approaches to the history of the frontier army, a number of scholars have looked at new topics. Darlis Miller (383) analyses the relationship between civilians and military supply in the Southwest, Sandra

Myres (388) describes the views of army wives on the frontier and Miller Stewart (394) deals with army laundresses in the West. Olch (389) and Wier (404) look at army medicine in the West, and Turcheneske (400) evaluates the scientific work of one officer, John G. Bourke.

A similar pattern of traditional and nontraditional topics emerges in the broader subject of military history in the late nineteenth and early twentieth centuries. In studying the role of army officers in Reconstruction in Louisiana, Dawson (356) concludes that most officers carefully administered the military reconstruction acts and did a remarkable job in administering a hostile state. The failure to carry out Reconstruction and protect blacks, he finds, rested with the president.

The role of the army in dealing with civil disorder has attracted additional attention. Cooper (353, 354) provides something of an overview of military intervention in labor disputes, but he is selective and concentrates on major strikes in 1877 and 1894 and in the Coeur d'Alene area of Idaho. He is critical of the use of the army in strikebreaking but finds that it acted with little violence, although the officer corps was tied to upper and middle-class values and interests and was seen as an enemy by labor. Osur (390) critically describes the role of the Colorado National Guard in civil disturbances, particularly in the mining regions, while Ball (349) evaluates the involvement of New Mexico's territorial militia in law enforcement and Ellis (360) describes the use of the army to suppress suspected draft-resistance among the Goshute Indians on the eve of entry into World War I—even though Indians, as noncitizens, were not required to register for the draft.

Social and economic history also attracted attention, and Miller (382) describes the long-term impact on New Mexico of the California troops who came to that territory during the Civil War and remained to play an important role in the development of the region. While rapid integration of Civil War veterans into the society and economic life of a growing territory might be expected, Emory Upton and Samuel Huntington have argued that the regular army was isolated from American society after that war. This view has been challenged by Gates (362) and Bacevich (346) in a pair of thoughtful studies of the late nineteenth and early twentieth centuries, as well as by the aforementioned work of Cooper (353). A different aspect of social history is Sandos's look at the army, prostitution, and drugs on the Mexican border in 1916–17 (392). Continued research on the history of the Corps of Engineers also resulted in works by Schubert (393), Merritt (380), and Cas (351) that touch on the years 1865–1917.

THE ARMY OVERSEAS. Interest in the Spanish-American War and the so-called little wars, particulary the army's role in the Philippines, continues. Easily the most important book to appear on these subjects is *The War with Spain*, by David Trask (399), a well researched and excellent survey of that conflict. Trask deals with military and political history and with all participants. He challenges the thesis that the army performed badly, demonstrates the importance of the Naval War Board, and argues that McKinley was a serious strategist.

Webb (403) looks at army shipping during the war with Spain. A new study of the conquest of the Philippines by Miller (384) stands in contrast to the earlier work of John Gates and is critical of the army for racism and ruthlessness and for causing the Filipino insurrection. Bacevich (344) and May (379) focus on aspects of the insurrection, while Chaput (352) looks at an enlisted man in the

Philippines and Fritz (361) describes the career of Jacob H. Smith and his activity at Samar. The occupation of Peking is covered by Hunt (371), while Millard (381) looks at logistics during Pershing's punitive expedition into Mexico and Haycock (366) covers the American Legion in the Canadian expeditionary force 1914 to 1917.

BIBLIOGRAPHY

339. Abrahamson, James L. *America Arms for a New Century: The Making of a Great Military Power*. New York: Free Press, 1981.
340. Aichinger, Peter. *The American Soldier in Fiction, 1880–1963: A History of Attitudes toward Warfare and the Military Establishment*. Ames: Iowa State University Press, 1975.
341. Alberts, Don E. *Brandy Station to Manila Bay: A Biography of General Wesley Merritt*. Austin, Tex.: Presidial Press, 1981.
342. Altshuler, Constance W. *Chains of Command: Arizona and the Army, 1856–1875*. Tucson: Arizona Historical Society, 1981.
343. Armstrong, David A. *Bullets and Bureaucrats: The Machine Gun and the United States Army, 1861–1916*. Westport, Conn.: Greenwood Press, 1982.
344. Bacevich, Andrew J., Jr. "Disagreeable Work: Pacifying the Moros, 1903–1906." *Military Review* (1982): 49–61.
345. _____. "Emory Upton: A Centennial Assessment." *Military Review* (1981): 21–28.
346. _____. "Family Matters: American Civilian and Military Elites in the Progressive Era." *Armed Forces and Society* 8 (1982): 405–15.
347. Bailey, John W. *Pacifying the Plains: General Alfred Terry and the Decline of the Sioux, 1866–1890*. Westport, Conn.: Greenwood Press, 1979.
348. Ball, Eve. *Indeh: An Apache Odyssey*. Provo, Utah: Brigham Young University Press, 1980.
349. Ball, Larry D. "Militia Posses: The Territorial Militia in Civil Law Enforcement in New Mexico Territory, 1877–1883." *New Mexico Historical Review* 55 (1980): 47–69.
350. Browning, Robert S. III. *Two if by Sea: The Development of American Coastal Defense Policy*. Westport, Conn.: Greenwood Press, 1983.
351. Cass, Edward C. "Flood Control and the Corps of Engineers in the Missouri Valley, 1902–73." *Nebraska History* 63 (1982): 108–22.
352. Chaput, Donald. "Private William W. Grayson's War in the Philippines, 1899." *Nebraska History* 61 (1980): 355–66.
353. Cooper, Jerry M. *The Army and Civil Disorder: Federal Military Intervention in Labor Disputes, 1877–1900*. Westport, Conn.: Greenwood Press, 1980.
354. _____. "The Army as Strikebreaker in the Railroad Strikes of 1877 and 1894." *Labor History* 18 (1977): 179–96.
355. Danker, Donald F. "The Wounded Knee Interviews of Eli S. Riker." *Nebraska History* 62 (1982): 161–243.
356. Dawson, Joseph G., III. *Army Generals and Reconstruction: Louisiana, 1862–1877*. Baton Rouge: Louisiana State University Press, 1982.
357. Dunlay, Thomas W. *Wolves for the Blue Soldiers: Indian Scouts and*

Auxiliaries with the United States Army, 1860–90. Lincoln: University of Nebraska Press, 1982.

358. _____. "General Crook and the White Man Problem." *Journal of the West* 93 (1979): 3–10.

359. _____. "Indian Allies in the Armies of New Spain and the United States: A Comparative Study." *New Mexico Historical Review* 56 (1981): 239–58.

360. Ellis, Richard N. "Indians at Ibapah in Revolt: Goshutes, the Draft and the Indian Bureau, 1917–1919." *Nevada Historical Society Quarterly* 19 (1976): 162–170.

361. Fritz, David L. "Before the 'Howling Wilderness': The Military Career of Jacob Hurd Smith, 1862–1902." *Military Affairs* 43 (1979): 186–90.

362. Gates, John M. "The Alleged Isolation of U.S. Army Officers in the Late 19th Century." *Parameters* 10 (1980): 32–45.

363. _____. "Indians and Insurrectos: The U.S. Army's Experience with Insurgency." *Parameters* 13 (1983): 59–68.

364. Greene, Jerome A. *Slim Buttes, Eighteen Seventy-Six: An Episode of the Treat Sioux War.* Norman: University of Oklahoma Press, 1982.

365. Hardeman, Nicholas P. "Brick Stronghold of the Border: Fort Assiniboine, 1879–1911." *Montana* 29 (1979): 54–67.

366. Haycock, Ronald G. "The American Legion in the Canadian Expeditionary Force, 1914–1917: A Study in Failure." *Military Affairs* 43 (1979): 115–19.

367. Hofling, Charles K. *Custer and the Little Big Horn: A Psychobiographical Inquiry,* Detroit, Mich.: Wayne State University Press, 1981.

368. Hoig, Stan. *The Battle of the Washita: The Sheridan-Custer Indian Campaign of 1867–69.* Lincoln: University of Nebraska Press, 1979.

369. Holley, I. B., Jr. *General John M. Palmer, Citizen Soldiers, and the Army of a Democracy.* Westport, Conn.: Greenwood Press, 1982.

370. House, Jonathan M. "John McAuley Palmer and the Reserve Component." *Parameters* 12 (1982): 11–18.

371. Hunt, Michael H. "The Forgotten Occupation: Peking, 1900–1901." *Pacific Historical Review* 48 (1979): 501–29.

372. Hutton, Paul A. "The Celluloid Custer." *Red River Valley Historical Review* 4 (1979): 20–43.

373. Hutton, Paul A. "Phil Sheridan's Pyrrhic Victory: The Piegan Massacre, Army Politics, and the Transfer Debate," *Montana* 32 (1982): 32–43.

374. Kessell, John L. "General Sherman and the Navajo Treaty of 1868: A Basic and Expedient Misunderstanding." *Western Historical Quarterly* 12 (1981): 251–72.

375. Lane, Jack. *Armed Progressive: General Leonard Wood.* San Rafael, Calif.: Presidio Press, 1978.

376. Leonard, Thomas C. *Above the Battle: War-Making in America from Appomattox to Versailles.* New York: Oxford University Press, 1978.

377. Mahon, John K. *History of the Militia and the National Guard.* New York: Macmillan, 1983.

378. McClymer, John F. *War and Warfare: Social Engineering in America, 1890–1925.* Westport, Conn. Greenwood Press, 1980.

379. May, Glenn A. "Filipino Resistance to American Occupation: Batangas, 1899–1902." *Pacific Historical Review* 48 (1970): 531–56.

380. Merritt, Raymond H. *Creativity, Conflict and Controversy: A History of*

the *St. Paul District, U.S. Army Corps of Engineers.* Washington, D.C.: GPO, n.d.

381. Millard, George A. "U.S. Army Logistics During the Mexican Punitive Expedition of 1916." *Military Review* 60 (1980): 58-68.

382. Miller, Darlis A. *The California Column in New Mexico.* Albuquerque: University of New Mexico Press, 1982.

383. _____. "Civilians and Military Supply in the Southwest." *Journal of Arizona History* 23 (1982): 115-38.

384. Miller, Stuart C. *"Benevolent Assimilation": The American Conquest of the Philippines, 1899-1903.* New Haven, Conn.: Yale University Press, 1982.

385. Millett, Allan R. *Semper Fidelis: The History of the United States Marine Corps.* New York: Macmillian, 1980.

386. Moore, Jamie W. "National Security in the American Army's Definition of Mission, 1865-1914." *Military Affairs* 46 (1982): 127-31.

387. Moore, John Hammond. "The Norfolk Riot: 16 April 1866." *Virginia Magazine of History and Biography* 90 (1982): 155-64.

388. Myres, Sandra L. "Romance and Reality on the American Frontier: Views of Army Wives." *Western Historical Quarterly* 13 (1982): 409-27.

389. Olch, Peter D. "Medicine in the Indian-Fighting Army, 1866-1890." *Journal of the West* 21 (1982): 32-41.

390. Osur, Alan M. "The Role of the Colorado National Guard In Civil Disturbances." *Military Affairs* 46 (1982): 19-24.

391. Patton, Gerald W. *War and Race: The Black Officer in the American Military, 1915-1941.* Westport, Conn.: Greenwood Press, 1981.

392. Sandos, James A. "Prostitution and Drugs: The United States Army on the Mexican-American Border, 1916-1917." *Pacific Historical Review* 49 (1980): 621-45.

393. Schubert, Frank N. *Vanguard of Expansion: Army Engineers in the Trans-Mississippi West, 1819-1979.* Washington, D.C.: Office of the Corps of Engineers, 1980.

394. Stewart, Miller J. "Army Laundresses: Ladies of the 'Soap Suds Row.'" *Nebraska History* 61 (1980): 421-36.

395. Stone, Richard G., Jr. *A Brittle Sword: The Kentucky Militia, 1776-1912.* Lexington: University Press of Kentucky, 1977.

396. Thompson, Neil B. *Crazy Horse Called Them Walk-a-Heaps: The Origin of the "Old Army."* St. Cloud, Minn.: North Star Press, 1979.

397. Thrapp, Dan L. *Dateline Fort Bowie: Charles Fletcher Lummis Reports on an Apache War.* Norman: Univeristy of Oklahoma Press, 1979.

399. Trask, David F. *The War with Spain in 1898.* New York: Macmillan, 1981.

400. Turcheneske, John A., Jr. "John G. Bourke: Troubled Scientist." *Journal of Arizona History* 20 (1979): 323-44.

401. Utley, Robert M. *The Indian Frontier of the American West, 1846-1890.* Albuquerque: University of New Mexico Press, 1984.

402. _____. ed. *Life in Custer's Cavalry: Diaries and Letters of Albert and Jennie Barnitz, 1867-68.* New Haven, Conn.: Yale University Press, 1977.

403. Webb, William Joe. "The Spanish-American War and United States Army Shipping." *American Neptune* 40 (1980): 167-91.

404. Wier, James A. "19th Century Army Doctors on the Frontier in Nebraska." *Nebraska History* 61 (1980): 192-214.

X

SCIENCE AND TECHNOLOGY
IN THE TWENTIETH CENTURY

Linda Neuman Ezell

In his introduction to this chapter in Supplement I (1981), Carroll W. Pursell, Jr., remarked on the need for more scholarly research in the field of military science and technology in the 20th century, particularly on the impact of war on civilian technology. His call can be repeated today. A quick scan of Dissertation Abstracts or Books Forthcoming reveals that historians are continuing to shy away from the often complex world of military technology and advanced research and development. Titles that examined a single weapon system or took a general look at a broad field could be found, but few authors went beyond telling the story of what happened and when to ask why or to assess what impact the new technology spawned by war had on peacetime society. Studying the use of nuclear weapons — or the threat to use them — was a noticeable exception to this observation (288, 293, 316, 317, 320, 329, 331, 335, 337, 338). Other authors looked at the machines created to deliver such weapons (286, 319, 336).

The most popular subjects of study continue to be military aviation and naval hardware. A thoughtful and detailed account of the turbojet revolution was provided by Edward W. Constant II (299). Paul A. Hanle discussed the beginnings of aerodynamics in America (314). And Richard P. Hallion delved into the world of the test pilot (313). Because the fields of aviation and naval hardware include such a plethora of classes, models, nomenclature, and makes, historians should not ignore popular "All the World's" guides such as those produced by Jane's Publishing Company and others (289, 297, 300, 333). The Naval Institute Press has continued to publish a generous number of books that combine the historical and buff approach to naval history (305, 321, 339, 340).

Other topics that attracted writers included transportation for the army and tracked vehicles (283, 296), radar and acoustics (282, 311, 312, 323, 341), electronic warfare (294, 344), small arms (302, 303, 304, 315), and chemical warfare (306).

The air force, army, navy, and the Corps of Engineers continued to sponsor official histories. Air force historian Jack Ballard considered fixed-wing gunships used in Vietnam (284); the Naval Research Laboratory published David Allison's history of radar (282); J. D. Gerrard-Gough and Albert B. Christman prepared a narrative history of the Naval Weapons Center at China Lake (309); naval aviation from 1910 to 1980 was the subject of a book by Clarke Van Vleet and

William J. Armstrong (346); Corps of Engineers authors led by Alfred M. Beck completed a volume on the Corps in World War II in Europe (285); and Lida Mayo produced a book on the ordnance department as part of the army's World War II series (330).

The users of this bibliography will soon note the inclusion of several journal articles that may be categorized as more journalistic than historical. These articles include useful background information on important military hardware that has been largely ignored by historians or is perhaps too technical to be easily understood by persons outside the field (such as electronic counter-counter-measures, electronic beam warefare, and underwater acoustics). Historians of science and technology who wish to consider the weapons of the post-Vietnam era may wish to use such articles as primers to these complex, dynamic systems.

A highly readable essay on the influence of new technology on military tactics was provided by I. B. Holley, Jr. (322).

Researchers should also consult other chapters in this supplement that consider the 20th century. Studies whose primary emphasis is policy, military tactics, organization, or personnel may also consider the hardware and technology of the period.

BIBLIOGRAPHY

282. Allison, David. *New Eye for the Navy: The Origin of Radar at the Naval Research Laboratory.* Washington, D.C.: GPO, 1981.

283. Baily, Charles M. "Faint Praise: The Development of American Tanks and Tank Destroyers during World War II." Ph.D. diss., Duke University, 1977. University microfilm no. 7815658.

284. Ballard, Jack. *Development and Employment of Fixed-Wing Gunships, 1962–1972.* Washington, D.C.: GPO, 1982. Part of The United States Air Force in Southeast Asia Series.

285. Beck, Alfred, M., et al. *The Corps of Engineers in the War against Germany and Italy.* Washington, D.C.: GPO, 1984.

286. Betts, Richard K., ed. *Cruise Missiles: Technology, Strategy, Politics.* Washington, D.C.: Brookings Institution, 1981.

287. Bilstein, Roger E. *Stages to Saturn: A Technological History of the Apollo / Saturn Launch Vehicles.* Washington, D.C.: GPO, 1980.

288. Borowski, Harry R. "Air Force Atomic Capability from V-J Day to the Berlin Blockade – Potential or Real?" *Military Affairs* 44 (1980): 105–10.

289. Bowers, Peter M. *Curtiss Aircraft, 1907–1947.* London: Putnam, 1979.

290. Bowling, Roland A. "The Negative Influence of Mahan on the Protection of Shipping in Wartime: The Convoy Controversy in the Twentieth Century." Ph.D. diss. University of Maine, 1980.

291. Braybrook, Ray. "Helicopters at Sea," *Navy International* 85 (September 1980): 529–34.

292. _____. "V / STOL Perspectives: 20 Years Back, 20 Years on," *Air International* 18 (February 1980): 71–76.

293. Brown, Anthony C., and Charles B. MacDonald. *The Secret History of the Atomic Bomb.* New York: Dial Press, 1977.

294. Burke, Kelly H. "Electronic Combat: Warfare of the Future." *Armed Forces Journal International* 120 (December 1982): 52–54.
295. Cabot, Lon. "Of Prairie Dogs and Planes." *All Hands* (December 1982): 16–21.
296. Cary, Norman M. *The Use of the Motor Vehicle in the United States Army, 1899–1939*. New York: Oxford University Press, 1981.
297. Chesnau, Roger. *Conway's All The World's Fighting Ships, 1922–1946*. London: Conway Maritime, 1980.
298. Coletta, Paolo E. "The Perils of Invention: Bradley A. Fiske and the Torpedo Plane." *American Neptune* 37 (April 1977): 111–27.
299. Constant, Edward W., II. *The Origins of the Turboject Revolution*. Baltimore, Md.: Johns Hopkins University Press, 1981.
300. Ethell, J. *Mustang: A Documentary History of the P-51*. London: Jane's, 1981.
301. Ezell, Edward C. *ETL* [Engineer Topographical Laboratory] *History Update, 1968–1978*. Ft. Belvoir, Va.: U.S. Army Engineer Topographic Laboratory, 1979.
302. _____. *Handguns of the World: Military Revolvers and Self-Loaders from 1870 to 1945*. Harrisburg, Pa.: Stackpole Books, 1981.
303. _____. *Small Arms of the World*. 12th ed. Harrisburg, Pa.: Stackpole Books, 1983.
304. _____. *Small Arms Today: Latest Reports on the World's Weapons and Ammunition*. Harrisburg, Pa.: Stackpole Books, 1984.
305. Freidman, Norman. *U.S. Aircraft Carriers: An Illustrated Design History*. Annapolis, Md.: Naval Institute Press, 1983.
306. Fries, Amos A., and Clarence J. West. *Chemical Warfare*. New York: McGraw-Hill, 1921.
307. Gaines, Mike. "Maritime Patrol Aircraft." *Navy International* 85 (September 1980): 524–28.
308. Garrett, Jeffrey M. "The Coast Guard's Red Fleet." *United States Naval Institute Proceedings* 106 (December 1981): 101–3.
309. Gerrard-Gough, J. D., and Albert B. Christman. *History of the Naval Weapons Center, China Lake, California*. vol. 2, *The Grand Experiment at Inyokern: Narrative of the Naval Ordnance Test Station during the Immediate Postwar Years*. Washington, D.C.: GPO, 1978.
310. Godson, Susan H. "The Development of Amphibious Warfare in World War II as Reflected in the Campaigns of Admiral John Lesslie Hall, Jr., USN." Ph.D. diss. American University, 1979. University microfilm no. 7917346.
311. Gray, T., and T. G. Thorne. "Modern Doppler Navigation Systems." *Journal of Navigation* 33 (September 1980): 482–98.
312. Hackmann, W. D. "Underwater Acoustics and the Royal Navy, 1893–1930." Annals of Science 36 (1979): 255–78.
313. Hallion, Richard P. *Test Pilots: The Frontiersmen of Flight; An Illustrated History*. New York: Doubleday, 1981.
314. Hanle, Paul A. *Bringing Aerodynamics to America*. Cambridge, Mass.: MIT Press, 1982.
315. Helmer, William J. *The Gun that Made the Twenties Roar*. Highland Park, N.J.: Gun Room Press, 1969.

316. Herken, Gregg. "'A Most Deadly Illusion': The Atomic Secret and American Nuclear Policy, 1945-1950." *Pacific Historical Review* 49 (1980): 51-76.
317. _____. *The Winning Weapon: The Atomic Bomb in the Cold War, 1945-1950.* New York: Alfred A. Knopf, 1980.
318. Hewes, Amy. *Women as Munitions Makers: A Study of Conditions in Bridgeport, Connecticut.* New York: Russell Sage Foundation, 1917.
319. Hewish, Mark. "Satellites Show Their Warlike Force." *New Scientist* 92 (1 Oct. 1981): 36-40.
320. Hewlett, Richard G., and Francis Duncan. *Atomic Shield, 1947-1952.* University Park: Pennsylvania State University Press, 1969.
321. Hodges, Peter. *The Big Gun: Battleship Main Armament, 1860-1945.* Annapolis, Md.: Naval Institute Press, 1981.
322. Holley, I. B., Jr. "Of Saber Charges, Escort Fighters, and Spacecraft." *Air University Review* 34 (September–October 1983): 2-11.
323. Lasky, Marvin. "Review of Undersea Acoustics to 1950." *Journal of the Acoustical Society of America* 61 (1977) 283-97.
324. Lichtman, Sheila T. "Women at Work, 1941-1945: Wartime Employment in the San Francisco Bay Area." Ph.D. diss., University of California, Davis, 1981. University microfilm no. 8211722.
325. Long, Franklin A., and Judith Reppy, eds. *The Genesis of New Weapons: Decision-Making for Military R&D.* Elmsford, N.Y.: Pergamon Press, 1980.
326. Macbain, Merle. "Mines: The Forgotten Weapon." *Sea Power* 23 (May 1980): 30-36.
327. McNeill, William H. *The Pursuit of Power: Technology, Armed Force, and Society since A.D. 1000.* Chicago: University of Chicago Press, 1982.
328. Mahoney, Leo J. "A History of the War Department Scientific Intelligence Mission (ALSOS), 1943-1945." Ph.D. diss. Kent State University, 1981. University microfilm no. 8202163.
329. Mandelbaum, Michael. *The Nuclear Question: The United States and Nuclear Weapons, 1946-1976.* Cambridge, England: Cambridge University Press, 1979.
330. Mayo, Lida. *The Ordnance Department: On Beachhead and Battlefront.* Washington, D.C. GPO, 1968. Part of United States Army in World War II, The Technical Services, Series.
331. Meigs, Montgomery C. "Managing Uncertainty: Vannevar Bush, James B. Conant and the Development of the Atomic Bomb, 1940-1945." Ph.D. diss., University of Wisconsin, 1982. University microfilm no. 8215951.
332. Milliken, Eugene J. "Remembering the C-109." *Journal of the American Aviation Historical Society* 26 (1981); 272-78.
333. Morison, Samuel L., and John S. Rowe. *Warships of the U.S. Navy.* London: Jane's, 1983.
334. Morse, David B. "Eye in the Sky: The Boeing F-13." *Journal of the American Aviation Historical Society* 26 (1981): 150-68.
335. O'Brien, Larry D. "National Security and the New Warfare: Defense Policy, War Planning, and Nuclear Weapons, 1945-1950." Ph.D. diss., Ohio State University, 1981. University microfilm no. 8121837.
336. Ordway, Frederick J., and Mitchell R Sharpe. *The Rocket Team.* New

York: Thomas Y. Crowell, 1979.

337. Panofsky, W.K.H. "Science, Technology and the Arms Buildup—I." *Bulletin of the Atomic Scientist* 37 (June–July 1981): 48–54.

338. _____. "Science, Technology and the Arms Buildup—II." *Bulletin of the Atomic Scientist* 37 (June–July 1981): 55–59.

339. Polmar, Norman, ed. *The Ships and Aircraft of the U.S. Fleet.* Annapolis, Md.: Naval Institute Press, 1981.

340. Polmar, Norman, and Floyd D. Kennedy, Jr. *Military Helicopters of the World: Military Rotary-Wing Aircraft since 1917.* Annapolis, Md.: Naval Institute Press, 1981.

341. Rhodes, Milton. "Radar: Wartime Development—Postwar Application, An / APS-10." *Aerospace Historian* 28 (1981): 231–40.

342. Shapley, Deborah. "Arms Control as a Regulator of Military Technology." *Daedalus* 109 (Winter 1980): 145–57.

343. Strang, Mincher. "The Navy in the Desert." *United States Naval Institute Proceedings* 107 (September 1981): 65–71.

344. Streetly, Martin. *World Electronic Warfare Aircraft.* London: Jane's, 1983.

345. Wettern, Desmond. "Hovercraft and Hydrofoils—The Past 20 Years." *High-Speed Surface Craft* 20 (October–November 1981): 4–9.

346. Van Vleet, Clarke, and William J. Armstrong. *United States Naval Aviation, 1910–1980.* Washington, D.C.: GPO, 1980.

XI

WORLD WAR I AND THE
PEACTIME ARMY, 1917–1941

Daniel R. Beaver

For twenty years an organizational hypothesis has been emerging which places the military within a general stream of American institutional "modernization." That interpretation has now become the conventional wisdom, and general mobilization studies have been integrated into a broader "corporate" interpretation of twentieth-century American history. Several general histories of American military forces have appeared and there has been a flurry of debate between "Uptonians" and "citizen-soldiers" about the National Guard and conscription. Command and leadership has received attention, but real interest has emerged, especially among "solider-scholars," in doctrine and technology. Among the more exciting results of that interest has been the appearance of several critical works on the combat performance of John J. Pershing's AEF. The experience of women at war has become a significant area of published research, and urban historians have discovered links between American cities and the army. The lives and careers of minorities within the military have continued to attract scholarly attention.

BIBLIOGRAPHIES. A.G.S. Enser has published *A Subject Bibliography of the First World War* (344); Philip E. Hager and Desmond Taylor have prepared an excellent annotated bibliography, *The Novels of World War I* (360); and Patricia Rosof, William Zeisel, and Jean B. Quandt have edited a more general survey of some use for American scholars of the war and interwar periods entitled *The Military and Society: Reviews of Recent Research* (414).

GENERAL WORKS. Peter Karsten, *The Military in America from the Colonial Era to the Present* (374), makes conveniently available a number of articles on the war and interwar periods. T. Harry Williams's defense of the citizen-soldier, *The History of American Wars from 1745 to 1918* (438), published posthumously, and Warren W. Hassler, Jr.'s "neo-Uptonian" *With Shield and Sword* (362) are the latest attempts to create some sort of conceptual military framework. Far more significant are the exciting new books which place the army within the broader context of American institutional history. David M. Kennedy's *Over Here: The First World War and American Society* (376) is an able effort to synthesize within a framework of "modernization" numerous aspects of the war effort. Kennedy's book is especially important for its contribution to the literature on industrial mobilization and its provocative analysis of contemporary literary currents. Ellis Hawley's *The Great War and the Search for a Modern Order* (363), Richard L. Watson, Jr.'s, *The Development of National Power: The United States, 1900*–1919 (435), and Stephen Skowronek's *Building a New American State: The Expansion of National Administrative Capacities, 1877–1920* (419) follow similar themes over broader periods of time to arrive at similar conclusions. Thomas A. Bailey's *The Pugnacious Presidents* (304), containing his usual penetrating vignettes on executive leadership, is intended, apparently, to prove that Democratic presidents did not start all America's wars.

NATIONAL POLICY 1917–1941: THE NATION, THE STATES, AND MANPOWER PROCUREMENT. John Mahon's *History of the Militia and National Guard* (393), an institutional history, is especially useful for its excellent bibliography. James J. Hudson's "The Role of the California National Guard during the San Francisco General Strike in 1934" (369) stresses the positive side of the Guard's role in maintaining internal order. The most refreshing new book is I. B. Holley's long-awaited *General John P. Palmer, Citizen Soldier, and the Army of a Democracy* (367). John C. Edwards, *Patriots in Pinstripes* (341), is the story of the National Security League and its impact on American military policy in the first half of the 20th century. John W. Chambers continues his important revisionist work on conscription with "Conscripting for Colossus" (321) and *Draftees for Volunteers* (322). Peter Karsten has edited a contemporary article, "Unle Sam's Little War in the Arkansas Ozarks" (375), that reveals the continued importance of local resistance to central authority in American society. The position is reinforced by Christopher C. Gibbs's "Missouri Farmers and World War I: Resistance to Mobilization" (349), part of his doctoral dissertation, "The Impact of World War I on Missouri" (350). William J. Breen's "Mobilization and Cooperative Federalism: The Connecticut State Council of Defense, 1917–1919" (315) and Nancy R. Derr's "Iowans during World War I: A Study of Change under Stress" (337) reveal the same local resistance to federal power in America in the early twentieth century. The interwar period has also received attention. Robert K. Griffith, Jr., has contributed a book, *Men Wanted for the U.S. Army* (356), and an article, "Quality not Quantity" (357), to the study of the American all-volunteer army during the twenties and thirties. Stephen Wesbrook has added to our understanding of the last years of the peacetime army in "The Bailey Report and Army Morale, 1941: Anatomy of a Crisis" (436).

NATIONAL POLICY, 1917–1941: THE PROBLEM OF COMMAND. Four important studies of the organization and policy of the army before 1920 are James Abrahamson, *America Arms for a New Century: The Making of a Great Military Power* (300); Timothy K. Nenninger, *The Leavenworth Schools and the Old Army* (403); Boyd L. Dastrup's centennial history (336a); and William R. Roberts's recent dissertation, "Loyalty and Expertise" (413). The American wartime command system and its difficulties has been analyzed by Donald Smythe in "The Pershing-March Conflict in World War I" (423) and "Your Authority in France Will be Supreme: The Baker-Pershing Relationship in World War I" (425). The first volume of the papers of George C. Marshall, *The Soldierly Spirit*, edited by Larry Bland and Sharon R. Ritenour (311), covers the First Word War and interwar period. Russell A. Gugeler deals with prewar planning in the late thirties and early forties in "George Marshall and Orlando Ward, 1939–1941" (358). Two recent biographies, Carol Morris Petillo's *Douglas MacArthur, the Philippine Years* (409) and Omar N. Bradley and Clay Blair's *A General's Life: An Autobiography by General of the Army Omar N. Bradley* (313), add new dimensions to the lives of those very complex men.

NATIONAL POLICY 1917–1941: THE PROBLEM OF SUPPLY. World war mobilization has received increasingly sophisticated treatment. The discussion continues about what was really occurring during the teens, twenties, and thirties. Was an "industrial-military complex" developing? Or was it a warfare state and War Department socialism? Or was the whole organizational effort part of an emerging corporate commonwealth? Despite attempts to de-demonize the issues by B. Franklin Cooling, in *Gray Steel and Blue Water Navy* (326), by Robert D. Cuff in "American Mobilization for War, 1917–1945" (330), "We Band of Brothers – Woodrow Wilson's War Managers" (334), and "Herbert Hoover, the Ideology of Voluntarism and War Organization during the Great War" (332), Paul Koistinen's compilation of essays *The Military-Industrial Complex: A Historical Perspective* (379) still exerts great influence. Austin K. Kerr has written two much needed studies, "Decision for Federal Control: Wilson, McAdoo and the Railroads, 1917" (378) and a broader monograph, *American Railroad Politics, 1914–1920: Rates, Wages and Efficiency* (377), that give us much new information from a national perspective on rail utilization. Carl W. Condit's *The Port of New York* (324) is an admirable accompanying piece which reveals the wartime logistical problems encountered by the army. Jordan A. Schwartz, *The Speculator: Bernard M. Baruch in Washington, 1917–1965* (416), makes a little clearer just what that wily opportunist did as chairman of the War Industries Board. John K. Ohl, "General Hugh Johnson and the War Industries Board" (405), tells the story from the army side. The entire October 1978 issue of the *Journal of Forest History* is committed to analyzing the impact of the Great War on the lumber industry. The most significant article published there is James E. Fickle's "Defense Mobilization in the Southern Pine Industry: The Experience of World War I" (346). Valerie Jean Connor articulates what has come to be the conventional wisdom in *The National War Labor Board: Stability, Social Justice and the Voluntary State in World War I* (325). Historians have come to understand, also, that mobilization and supply were not simply American problems in 1917. The war played a role in bringing the entire North Atlantic community into an uneasy but cooperative relationship during the war. Three recent books – Michael J. Hogan, *Informal Entente* (366); Jeffrey J. Safford, *Wilsonian Maritime Diplomacy, 1913–1921* (415); and Carl P. Parrini, *Heir to Empire* (407), study the complications that occurred when the great western powers explored the limits of combined economic warfare for the first time in this century. Although the twenties and thirties have not attracted similar attention, Richard A. Lauderbaugh's dissertation," American Steel Makers and the Coming of the Second World War" (381), is, perhaps, a harbinger of the future.

STRATEGY, DOCTRINE AND TECHNOLOGY, 1917–1941. This is one of the most active areas of investigation in the field, partially because of the army staff colleges' renewed interest in doctrine and weapons, and partially because of increased scholarly interest in technology and society. General works of interest to students of military history are Thomas P. Hughes, *Networks of Power, Electrification in Western Society, 1880–1930* (370), and David F. Noble's groundbreaking *America by Design: Science, Technology and the Rise of Corporate Capitalism* (404). A book applicable to all models of institutional change is Shelford Bidwell and Dominick Graham, *Fire-Power: British Army Weapons and Theories of War, 1904–1945* (310), and those who think this a book about guns are sadly mistaken. John Terraine has attempted to integrate technology, doctrine, and operations during the Great War in *White Heat: The New Warfare, 1914–18* (431). Other attempts to link tactics and technological change include Charles D. McKenna's fine dissertation, "The Forgotten Reform: Field Maneuvers in the Development of the Untied States Army, 1902–1920" (390), and Russell Gilmore's excellent article "Rifles and Soldier Individualism, 1876–1918" (351). James W. Rainey has contributed a long overdue evaluation of American combat performance in 1917–1918 in "Ambivalent Warfare: The Tactical Doctrine of the AEF in World War I" (411), while John B. Wilson has carried doctrinal issues forward into the twenties in "Mobility Versus Firepower: The Post World War I Infantry Division" (439). Barton C. Hacker, "Imagination in Thrall: The Social Psychology of Military Mechanization, 1919–1939" (359), is an imaginative, if controversial, approach to the doctrinal debates of the era. Norman Cary's dissertation, "The Use of the Motor Vehicle in the United States Army, 1899–1939" (320), is a narrative with emphasis on the period before 1930. Daniel R. Beaver's "Politics and Policy" (308) discusses the successful development of standard motor vehicles during the interwar period. Studies of military hardware are Paul S. Dickey III, "The Liberty Engine, 1918–1942" (338); Ronald E. Olson, "The American Schneider" (406); and John W. Mountcastle, "Trial by Fire: U.S. Incendiary Weapons, 1918–1945" (400). A provocative entry into a previously unworked area is Anthony DiFilippo, "Militarism and Machine-Tool Building in America" (339).

THE AMERICAN ARMY AT WAR, 1917–1919. The best new history of the Great War is James L. Stokesbury, *A Short History of World War I* (429), which gives the Americans appropriate space. Others are Correlli Barnett, *The Great War* (306), and Gerd Hardach, *The First World War, 1914*–1918 (361). Gordon Brook-Shepard, *November, 1918* (317), is an attempt to describe the impact of the armistice and its aftermath in all the warring countries. John Terraine, *To Win a War: 1918, The Year of Victory* (430), continues his effort to vindicate Sir Douglas Haig and his associates. On the American effort, Donald Smythe's "St. Mihiel: The Birth of an American Army" (424) is critical of the American effort. James L. Stokesbury is equally critical in his "The Aisne-Marne Offensive" (428). Martin Blumenson has contributed a short piece, "World War I: Proving Ground for World War II" (412), while F. Maitland Cuthbertson, "Pershing's Logistical Nightmare" (336), shows that support in the AEF was not all it should have been. J. Douglas Brown, "In Action with the Rainbow Division, 1918–1919" (319), and the first part of S.L.A. Marshall, *Bringing Up the Rear* (396), add to the company level officer's view of the war. An overlooked part of the postwar role of AEF is examined by Alfred E. Cornebise, *Typhus and Doughboys: The American-Polish Typhus Relief Expedition, 1919–1921* (329). The American interventions in Russia have received renewed attention in Robert Maddox, *The Unknown War with Russia* (392), and John W. Long, "American Intervention in Russia: The North Russian Expedition, 1918-1919" (385). A most important body of literature is appearing on trench life. Most of it applies to the French, British, and Germans, but careful use can help explore the American experience as well. It includes Tony Ashworth, *Trench Warfare, 1914-1918: The Live and Let Live System* (302); Dorothy and Thomas Hoobler, *The Trenches: Fighting on the Western Front in World War I* (368); Alan Lloyd, *The War in the Trenches* (384); and Eric J. Leeds, *No Man's Land: Combat and Identity in World War I* (383).

THE ARMY AND AMERICAN SOCIETY, 1917-1941. Arthur Marwick's *War and Social Change in the Twentieth Century* (397) is still a most appropriate starting point. Barbara J. Steinson has surveyed the impact of the war on women in *American Woman's Activism in World War I* (426) and "Sisters and Soldiers; American Women and the National Service Schools, 1916-1917" (427). The latter is a unique study of privately supported women's "preparedness camps." Maurine Weiner Greenwald's *Women, Work and War: The Impact of World War I on Women Workers in the United States* (353) analyzes their role in the economy. William J. Breen, "Black Women and the Great War: Mobilization and Reform in the South" (314), and Darlene Clark Hine, "The Call that Never Came: Black Women Nurses and World War I" (364), describe the way blacks were denied participation in the war effort. Andrew J. Bacevich, Jr., "Family Matters: American Civilian and Military Elites in the Progressive Era" (303), examines the myth of military isolation in the early twentieth century, and Fred D. Baldwin's "The American Enlisted Man in World War I" (305) is a significant study in social history. Bruce White's "The American Military and the Melting Pot in World War I" (437) has been reprinted in Peter Karsten, *The Military in America* (374). Jack D. Foner, *Blacks and the Military in American History* (347), remains the best study of American black soldiers. William W. Griffin, "Mobilization of Black Militiamen in World War I: Ohio's Ninth Battalion" (355), and Gerald W. Patton, *War and Race: The Black Officers in the American Military, 1915-1941* (408), reveal a continuing pattern of white discrimination. Bernard C. Nalty and Morris J. MacGregor have edited an excellent set of primary sources, *Blacks in the Military: Essential Documents* (402). Two recent books on government control of informal and civil liberty are Stephen Vaughn, *Holding Fast the Inner Lines* (432), the first critical study of the Committee on Public Information in many years; and Paul L. Murphy, *World War I and the Origins of Civil Liberty in the United States* (401), a critical examination of the plight of political minorities in wartime America. Larry W. Ward has examined the use of film for propaganda in *The Motion Picture Goes to War* (434). The German-American ordeal has been retold by Frederick C. Luebke in *Bonds of Loyalty: German Americans and World War I* (389), while Sarah D. Shields discusses conscientious objectors in "The Treatment of Conscientious Objectors during World War I: Mennonites at Camp Funston" (418). Two new studies of pacifism are Leslie Anders, "American Pacifists: The Peculiar Breed' (301), and Eileen M. Eagan, "The Student Peace Movement in the United States, 1930-1941" (340). An article of special interest is Herbert F. Margullies, "The Articles of War, 1920: The History of a Forgotten Reform" (395). A new issue concerns the military and urban life. Roger W. Lotchin has developed the idea of a "metropolitan-military complex" in three articles: "The City and the Sword in Metropolitan California, 1919-1941" (386),

"The City and the Sword: San Francisco and the Rise of the Metropolitan-Military Complex, 1919–1941" (387), and "The Metropolitan-Military Complex in Comparative Perspective" (388). More traditional topics are John Lax and William Pencak, "Creating the American Legion" (382), Michael W. Sherraden, "Military Participation in a Youth Employment Program: The Civilian Conservation Corps" (417), and Frank J. Rader, "The Works Progress Administration and Hawaiian Preparedness, 1935–1940" (410). A very special book on interwar garrison life from a boy's perspective is William Jay Smith, *Army Brat: A Memoir* (421).

LIBRARIES AND ARCHIVES. At the United States Army Military History Institute, at Carlisle Barracks, the World War I project continues to flourish. It includes not only letters and papers of former officers and enlisted people but also standard questionnaires completed by participants which lend themselves admirably to comparative and quantitative studies. Significant oral histories by veterans support the collection. A visit to the MHI is now a necessity for any serious student of American military affairs.

BIBLIOGRAPHY

300. Abrahamson, James L. *American Arms for a New Century: The Making of a Great Military Power*. New York: Free Press, 1981.
301. Anders, Leslie. "American Pacifists: The Peculiar Breed." *Parameters* 10 (September 1981): 46–50.
302. Ashworth, Tony. *Trench Warfare, 1914–1918: The Live and Let Live System*. New York: Holmes & Meier, 1980.
303. Bacevich, Andrew J., Jr. "Family Matters: American Cliques and Military Elites in the Progressive Era." *Armed Forces and Society* 8 (Spring 1982): 405–18.
304. Bailey, Thomas. *The Pugnacious Presidents*. New York: Free Press, 1980.
305. Baldwin, Fred D. "The American Enlisted Man in World War I." Ph.D. diss., Princeton University, 1964.
306. Barnett, Correlli. *The Great War*. New York: Putnam, 1979.
307. Bartlett, C. J. "The U.S. Army and Global Politics, 1917–1927." *Journal of American Studies* 14 (August 1980): 249–52.
308. Beaver, Daniel R. "Politics and Policy: The War Department Motorization and Standardization Program for Wheeled Transport Vehicles, 1920–1940." *Military Affairs* 47 (October 1983): 101–108.
309. Best, Geoffrey. *Humanity in Warfare*. New York: Columbia University Press, 1980.
310. Bidwell, Shelford, and Dominick Graham. *Fire-power: British Army Weapons and Theories of War, 1904–1945*. London: Allen & Unwin, 1982.
311. Bland, Larry, and Sharon R. Ritenour, eds. *The Soldierly Spirit, Dec. 1880–June 1939*. Vol. I of *The Papers of George C. Marshall*. Baltimore, Md.: Johns Hopkins Univeristy Press, 1981.
312. Blumenson, Martin. "World War I: Proving Ground for World War II." *Army* 31 (March 1981): 48–53, 56.
313. Bradley, Omar N., and Clay Blair. *A General's Life: An Autobiograhpy*

by General of the Army Omar N. Bradley. New York: Simon & Schuster, 1983.

314. Breen, William J. "Black Women and the Great War: Mobilization and Reform in the South." *Journal of Southern History* 44 (August 1978): 421–40.

315. _____. "Mobilization and Cooperative Federalism: The Connecticut State Council of Defense, 1917–1919." *Historian* 1 (November 1979): 58–84.

316. _____. "Southern Women in the War: The North Carolina Women's Committee, 1917–1919." *North Carolina Historical Review* 55 (July 1978): 251–53.

317. Brook-Shepherd, Gordon. *November, 1918.* New York: Little, Brown, 1981.

318. Brown, George C., ed. "With the Ambulance Service in France: The Wartime Letters of William Gorham Rice, Jr." *Wisconsin Magazine of History* (3 parts; 64 Summer 1981; 278–293; 65 Autumn 1981, 11–35; 65, Winter 1918–82 103–119).

319. Brown, J. Douglas. "In Action with the Rainbow Division, 1918–19." *Military Review* 58 (January 1981): 35–46.

320. Cary, Norman M., Jr. "The Use of the Motor Vehicle in the United States Army, 1899–1939." Ph.D. diss., University of Georgia, 1980.

321. Chambers, John W. "Conscripting for Colossus: The Progressive Era and the Origins of the Modern Military Draft in the United States in World War I." In Peter Karsten, ed., *The Military in America from the Colonial Era to the Present.* New York: Free Press, 1980.

322. Chambers, John W., ed. *Draftees or Volunteers: A Documentary History of the Debate over Military Conscription in the United States, 1787–1973.* New York: Garland, 1975.

323. Churchill, Allen. *Over Here: An Informal Recreation of the Home Front in World War I.* New York: Dodd, Mead, 1968.

324. Condit, Carl W. *The Port of New York: A History of the Rail and Terminal System from the Grand Central Electrification to the Present.* Chicago: University of Chicago Press, 1981.

325. Connor, Valerie Jean. *The National War Labor Board: Stability, Social Justice and the Voluntary State in World War I.* Chapel Hill: University of North Carolina Press, 1983.

326. Cooling, Benjamin Franklin. *Gray Steel and Blue Water Navy: The Formative Years of America's Military-Industrial Complex.* Hamden, Conn.: Archon Books, 1979.

327. Cornebise, Alfred E. *The Armaroc News: The Daily Newspaper of the American Armed Forces in Germany, 1919–1920.* Carbondale: Southern Illinois University Press, 1981.

328. _____. "'Der Rhein Entlang': The American Occupation Forces in Germany, 1918–1923—A Photo Essay." *Military Affairs* 46 (December 1982): 183–89.

329. _____. *Typhus and Doughboys: The American-Polish Typhus Relief Expedition, 1919–1921.* Newark: University of Delaware Press, 1982.

330. Cuff, Robert D. "American Mobilization for War, 1917–1945: Political Culture vs. Bureaucratic Administration." In *Military History Symposium, Royal Military College of Canada (1980).*

331. _____. "Harry Garfield, the Fuel Administration and the Search for a Cooperative Order." *American Quarterly* 30 (Spring 1978): 39–53.

332. _____. "Herbert Hoover, The Ideology of Voluntarism and War Organization during the Great War." *Journal of American History* 64 (September 1977), 358–72.

333. _____. "The Politics of Labor Administration During World War I." *Labor History* 21 (Fall 1980): 546–59.

334. _____. "We Band of Brothers–Woodrow Wilson's War Managers." *Canadian Review of American Studies* 5 (Fall 1974): 135–48.

335. Cummings, Donald L. "Army ROTC: A Study of the Army's Primary Officer Procurement Program, 1862–1977." Ph.D. diss., University of California, Santa Barbara, 1982.

336. Cuthbertson, F. Maitland. "Pershing's Logistical Nightmare." *Armour* 91 (September–October 1982): 31–34.

336a. Dastrup, Boyd L. *The U.S. Army Command and General Staff College: A centennial history.* Manhattan, Kans.: Sunflower University Press, 1982.

337. Deer, Nancy R. "Iowans during World War I: A Study of Change under Stress." Ph.D. diss., George Washington University, 1979.

338. Dickey, Paul S., III. *The Liberty Engine, 1918–1942. Smithsonian Annals of Flight,* vol. I, no. 3. Washington, D.C.: Smithsonian Institution Press, 1968.

339. DiFilippo, Anthony. "Militarism and Machine Tool Building in America." Ph.D. diss., Temple University, 1981.

340. Eagan, Eileen M. "The Student Peace Movement in the United States, 1930–1941." Ph.D. diss., Temple University, 1979.

341. Edwards, John Carver. *Patriots in Pinstripes: Men of the National Security League.* Washington, D.C.: University Press of America, 1982.

342. Ellis, Edward. *Echoes of Distant Thunder: Life in the United States, 1914–1918.* New York: Coward, McCann and Geoghegan, 1975.

343. Elting, John R. *American Army Life.* New York: Charles Scribner's, Sons, 1982.

344. Enser, A.G.S. *A Subject Bibliography of the First World War.* Boulder, Colo.: Westview Press, 1980.

345. Everett, Susanne. *World War I: An Illustrated History.* Introduction by John Keegan. Chicago: Rand McNally, 1980.

346. Fickle, James E. "Defense Mobilization in the Southern Pine Industry: The Experience of World War I." *Journal of Forest History.* 22 (October 1978): 206–23.

347. Foner, Jack D. *Blacks and the Military in American History: A New Perspective.* New York: Praeger, 1974.

348. Fowles, Brian D. "A History of the Kansas National Guard, 1854–1975." Ph.D. diss., Kansas State University, 1982.

349. Gibbs, Christopher C. "Missouri Farmers and World War I: Resistance to Mobilization." *Bulletin of the Missouri Historical Society* 35 (October 1978): 17–27.

350. _____. "Patriots and Slackers: The Impact of World War I on Missouri." Ph.D. diss., University of Missouri, 1980.

351. Gilmore, Russell. "Rifles and Soldier Individualism, 1876–1918." *Military Affairs* 40 (October 1976): 97–102.

352. Godfrey, Aaron A. *Government Operation of the Railroads, 1918–1920: Its Necessity, Success, and Consequences.* Austin, Tex.: Jenkins Publishing Co., 1979.

353. Greenwald, Maurine Weiner. *Women, War and Work: The Impact of World War I on Women Workers in the United States.* Westport, Conn.: Greenwood Press, 1980.

354. _____. "Women Workers and World War I: The American Railroad Industry, a Case Study." *Journal of Social History* 9 (Winter 1975): 154–77.

355. Griffin, William W. "Mobilization of Black Militiamen in World War I: Ohio's Ninth Battalion." *Historian* 40 (August 1978): 686–703.

356. Griffith, Robert K., Jr. *Men Wanted for the U.S. Army: American Experience with an All Volunteer Army between the Wars.* Westport, Conn.: Greenwood Press, 1982.

357. _____. "Quality not Quantity: The Volunteer Army during the Depression." *Military Affairs* 43 (December 1979): 171–77.

358. Gugeler, Russell A. "George Marshall and Orlando Ward, 1939–1941." *Parameters* 13 (March 1983): 28–42.

359. Hacker, Barton C. "Imagination in Thrall: The Social Psychology of Military Mechanization, 1919–1939." *Parameters* 12 (March 1982): 50–61.

360. Hager, Phillip E., and Desmond Taylor. *The Novels of World War I: An Annotated Bibliography.* New York: Garland, 1981.

361. Hardach, Gerd. *The First World War, 1914–1918.* Berkeley: University of California Press, 1977.

362. Hassler, Warren W., Jr. *With Shield and Sword: American Military Affairs, Colonial Times to the Present.* Ames: Iowa State University Press, 1982.

363. Hawley, Ellis. *The Great War and the Search for a Modern Order: A History of the American People and their Institutions, 1917–1933.* New York: St. Martin's, 1979.

364. Hine, Darlene Clark. "The Call That Never Came: Black Women Nurses and World War I, An Historical Note." *Indiana Military History Journal* 8 (January 1983): 23–27.

365. Hogan, George. "The Infantry Board, 1931." *Infantry* 69 (July / August 1979): 30–33.

366. Hogan, Michael J. *Informal Entente: The Private Structure of Cooperation in Anglo-American Economic Diplomacy, 1918–1928.* Columbia: University of Missouri Press, 1977.

367. Holley, I. B., Jr. *General John M. Palmer, Citizen Soldier, and the Army of a Democracy.* Westport, Conn.: Greenwood Press, 1982.

368. Hoobler, Dorothy and Thomas. *The Trenches: Fighting the Western Front in World War I.* New York: Putnam, 1978.

369. Hudson, James J. "The Role of the California National Guard during the San Francisco General Strike in 1934." *Military Affairs* 46 (April 1982): 76–83.

370. Hughes, Thomas P. *Networks of Power, Electrification in Western Society, 1880–1930.* Baltimore, Md.: Johns Hopkins University Press, 1983.

371. Johnson, Elliot L. "The Military Experiences of General Hugh A. Drum from 1898–1918." Ph.D. diss., University of Wisconsin, 1975.

372. Johnson, Vernon E. *Development of the National War College and Peer Institutions.* Ann Arbor: University of Michigan Microfilms, 1982.

373. Jones, Ralph E., George R. Rarey, and Robert J. Icks. *The Fighting Tanks, 1916-1933*. Thornwood, N.Y.: Carshine House Publishers, 1979.
374. Karsten, Peter, ed. *The Military in America from the Colonial Era to the Present*. New York: Free Press, 1980.
375. _____. "Uncle Sam's Little War in the Arkansas Ozarks." In Peter Karsten, ed., *The Military in America from the Colonial Era to the Present*. New York: Free Press, 1980.
376. Kennedy, David M. *Over Here: The First World War and American Society*. New York: Oxford University Press, 1980.
377. Kerr, K. Austin. *American Railroad Politics, 1914-1920: Rates, Wages and Efficiency*. Pittsburgh, Pa.: University of Pittsburgh Press, 1968.
378. _____. "Decision for Federal Control: Wilson, McAdoo and the Railroads, 1917." *Journal of American History* 54 (December 1967): 550-60.
379. Koistinen, Paul A. C. *The Military-Industrial Complex: A Historical Perspective*. New York: Praeger, 1980.
380. Lael, Richard L., and Linda Killen. "The Pressure of Shortage: Platinum Policy and the Wilson Administration during World War I." *Business History Review* 56 (Winter 1982): 545-58.
381. Lauderbaugh, Richard A. "American Steel Makers and the Coming of the Second World War." Ph.D. diss., Washington University, 1979.
382. Lax, John, and William Pencak. "Creating the American Legion." *South Atlantic Quarterly* 81 (Winter 1981-82): 43-55.
383. Leeds, Eric J. *No Man's Land: Combat and Identity in World War I*. Cambridge, England: Cambridge Univeristy Press, 1982.
384. Lloyd, Alan. *The War in the Trenches*. New York: David McKay, 1976.
385. Long, John W. "American Intervention in Russia: The North Russian Expedition, 1918-1919." *Diplomatic History* 6 (Winter 1982): 45-67.
386. Lotchin, Roger N. "The City and the Sword in Metropolitan California, 1919-1941." *Urbanism Past and Present* 7 (Summer-Autumn 1982): 1-16.
387. _____. "The City and the Sword: San Francisco and the Rise of the Metropolitan-Military Complex, 1919-1941." *Journal of American History* 65 (March 1979): 996-1020.
388. _____. "The Metropolitan-Military Complex in Comparative Perspective: San Francisco, Los Angeles and San Diego, 1919-1941." *Journal of the West* 18 (July 1979): 19-30.
389. Luebke, Frederick C. *Bonds of Loyalty: German Americans and World War I*. DeKalb: University of Northern Illinois Press, 1974.
390. McKenna, Charles D. "The Forgotten Reform: Field Maneuvers in the Development of the United States Army, 1902-1920." Ph.D. diss., Duke University, 1981.
391. Maddox, Robert. "The Saint Mihiel Salient." *American History Illustrated* 16 (April 1981): 42-50.
382. _____. *The Unknown War with Russia: Wilson's Siberian Intervention*. San Rafael, Calif.: Presidio Press, 1977.
393. Mahon, John K. *History of the Militia and the National Guard*. New York: Macmillan, 1983.
394. Malan, Nancy. "'How Ya Gonna Keep Em Down': Women and World War I." *Prologue* 5 (Winter 1973): 208-39.
395. Margullies, Herbert F. "The Articles of War, 1920: The History of a

Forgotten Reform." *Military Affairs* 43 (April 1979): 85-89.
396. Marshall, S.L.A. *Bringing Up the Rear: A Memoir*. Edited by Cate Marshall San Rafael, Calif: Presidio Press, 1979.
397. Marwick, Arthur. *War and Social Change in the Twentieth Century: A Comparative Study of Britain, France, Germany, Russia, and the United States*. New York: St. Martin's, 1974.
398. Millard, George A. "U.S. Army Logistics during the Mexican Punitive Expedition of 1916." *Military Review* 60 (October 1980): 58-68.
399. Moore, Jamie W. "National Security in the American Army's Definition of Mission, 1865-1914." *Military Affairs* 46 (October 1982): 127-31.
400. Mountcastle, John W. "Trial by Fire: U. S. Incendiary Weapons, 1918-1945." Ph.d. diss., Duke University, 1979.
401. Murphy, Paul L. *World War I and the Origins of Civil Liberty in the United States*. New York: W. W. Norton, 1979.
402. Nalty, Bernard C., and Morris J. MacGregor, eds. *Blacks in the Military: Essential Documents* . Wilmington, Del.: Scholarly Resources, 1981.
403. Nenninger, Timothy K. *The Leavenworth Schools and the Old Army: Education, Professionalism and the Officer Corps of the United States Army, 1881-1918*. Westport, Conn.: Greenwood Press, 1978.
404. Noble, David F. *America by Design: Science, Technology and the Rise of Corporate Capitalism*. New York: Oxford University Press, 1979.
405. Ohl, John K. "General Hugh Johnson and the War Industries Board." *Military Review* 55 (May 1975): 35-47.
406. Olson, Ronald E. "The American 'Schneider.'" *Field Artillery Journal* 48 (November-December 1980): 48-49.
407. Parrini, Carl P. *Heir to Empire: United States Economic Diplomacy, 1916-1923*. Pittsburgh, Pa.: University of Pittsburgh Press, 1969.
408. Patton, Gerald W. *War and Race: The Black Officer in the American Military, 1915-1941*. Westport, Conn.: Greenwood Press, 1981.
409. Petillo, Carol Morris. *Douglas MacArthur: The Philippine Years*. Bloomington: University of Indiana Press, 1981.
410. Rader, Frank J. "The Works Progress Administration and Hawaiian Preparedness, 1935-1940." *Military Affairs* 43 (February 1979): 12-17.
411. Rainey, James W. "Ambivalent Warfare: The Tactical Doctrine of the AEF in World War I." *Parameters* 13 (September 1983): 34-46.
412. Rigsley, Edwin. "Winchester Goes to War." *National Defense* 65 (October 1980): 56-57, 86.
413. Roberts, William R. "Loyalty and Expertise: The Transformation of the Nineteenth Century American General Staff and the Creation of the Modern Military Establishment." Ph.D. diss., Johns Hopkins University, 1980.
414. Rosof, Patricia, William Zeisel, and Jean B. Quandt, eds. *The Military and Society: Reviews of Recent Research*. New York: Haworth Press, 1982.
415. Safford, Jeffrey J. *Wilsonian Maritime Diplomacy, 1913-1921*. New Brunswick, N.J.: Rutgers University Press, 1978.
416. Schwartz, Jordan A. *The Speculator: Bernard M. Baruch in Washington, 1917-1965*. Chapel Hill: University of North Carolina Press, 1981.
417. Sherraden, Michael W. "Military Participation in a Youth Employment Program: The Civilian Conservation Corps." *Armed Forces and Society* 7 (Winter 1981): 227-46.

418. Shields, Sarah D. "The Treatment of Conscientious Objectors during World War I: Mennonites at Camp Funston." *Kansas History* 4 (Winter 1981): 255–69.

419. Skowronek, Stephen. *Building a New American State: The Expansion of National Administrative Capacities, 1877–1920.* New York: Cambridge University Press, 1982.

420. Smith, Robert C. "Tank Killers: Between Wars." *Infantry* 71 (March / April 1981): 9.

421. Smith, William Jay. *Army Brat: A Memoir.* New York: Persea Books, 1980.

422. Smythe, Donald. "Honoring the Nation's Dead: General Pershing's Battle Monument Commission." *American History Illustrated* 16 (May 1981): 26–33.

423. _____. "The Pershing-March Conflict in World War I." *Parameters* 11 (December 1981): 53–62.

424. _____. "St. Mihiel: The Birth of an American Army." *Parameters* 13 (June 1983): 47–57.

425. _____. "Your Authority in France Will Be Supreme: The Baker-Pershing Relationship in World War I." *Parameters* 9 (September 1979): 38–45.

426. Steinson, Barbara J. *American Woman's Activism in World War I.* New York: Garland, 1982.

427. _____. "Sisters and Soldiers: American Women and the National Service Schools, 1916–1917." *The Historian* 43 (February 1918): 225–39.

428. Stokesbury, James L. "The Aisne-Marne Offensive." *American History Illustrated* (July 1980): 8–17.

429. _____. *A Short History of World War I.* New York: William Morrow, 1981.

430. Terraine, John. *To Win a War: 1918, the Year of Victory.* New York: Doubleday, 1981.

431. _____. *White Heat: The New Warfare, 1914–18.* London: Sidgwick & Jackson, 1982.

432. Vaughn, Stephen. *Holding Fast the Inner Lines: Democracy, Nationalism and the Committee on Public Information.* Chapel Hill: University of North Carolina Press, 1979.

433. Vaughn, Stephen. "Prologue to *Public Opinion*: Walter Lippman's Work in Military Intelligence." *Prologue* 15 (Fall 1983): 151–63.

434. Ward, Larry W. "The Motion Picture Goes to War: A Political History of the U.S. Government's Film Effort in the World War, 1914–1918." Ph.D. diss., University of Iowa, 1981.

435. Watson, Richard L. Jr. *The Development of National Power: The United States, 1900–1919.* Boston: Houghton Mifflin, 1976.

436. Wesbrook, Stephen. "The Baily Report and Army Morale, 1941: Anatomy of a Crisis." *Military Review* 60 (June 1980): 11–24.

437. White, Bruce. "The American Military and the Melting Pot in World War I. " Peter Karsten, ed., In *The Military in America from the Colonial Era to the Present.* New York: Free Press, 1980.

438. Williams, T. Harry *The History of American Wars from 1745 to 1918.* New York: Alfred A. Knopf, 1981.

439. Wilson, John B. "Mobility Versus Firepower: The Post World War I Infantry Division." *Parameters* 13 (September 1983): 47–52.

XII

MILITARY AND NAVAL MEDICINE

James O. Breeden

Quantitatively, the last five-year period clearly surpassed the previous one in studies pertaining to the history of military and naval medicine. Qualitatively, however, the picture remains largely unchanged. As before, traditional military history, sometimes called military antiquarianism, predominated over the "new military history," or the growing trend to relate the military to society. In light of this state of affairs, the works singled out below, by no means an exhaustive list, were selected to illustrate the current status of the field and to call attention to the most important studies that have appeared since the last update five years ago. In addition, several useful articles that were overlooked earlier have been included.

GENERAL STUDIES. Works of a general nature continue to occupy a prominent place in the literature of military and naval medicine. In the first of a projected multivolume history of the Army Medical Department, Mary C. Gillett (372) recounts, with a minimum of analysis, the department's first four decades, 1775–1818. In spite of this limitation, however, Gillett's undertaking, the first attempt at a comprehensive history of the Army Medical Department in over fifty years, is a most commendable one, and her subsequent volumes are anxiously awaited. In two brief articles (401, 402), Louis J. Polskin traces the evolution of the insignias of the medical departments of the United States armed services. Miller J. Stewart, in a valuable reference work (412), describes in historical perspective the various means used to transport the wounded during the period 1776–1876. Sam Shannon (407) calls to attention the significance of the army pharmacist in military medicine. In like manner, Elizabeth A. Shields's *Highlights in the History of the Army Nurse Corps* (409) serves to remind us of the distinguished and proud record of this indispensable ally of the military physician. James A. Weir, a former commanding general, records the milestones in the history of the Fitzsimons Army Medical Center (420). Useful overviews by David B. Adams (329) and Robert L. Reid (403) place the treatment of abdominal gunshot wounds and hand injuries in historical perspective. John P. Heggers (374) and Charles Ellenbogen (368) briefly but perceptively review the persistent threat of natural biological agents to military health. Rudolph H. Kampmeier (383) superficially surveys the prevalence of one class of these disorders, venereal disease, in the army between 1775 and 1900. Finally, two recent articles (416, 423) pay well-deserved tribute to military medicine's numerous contributions to public health.

THE AMERICAN REVOLUTION. The medical aspects of America's war for independence received scant attention during the last five years, and over half of the studies selected for inclusion in this chapter were written by one scholar, Richard L. Blanco. His biography of Jonathan Potts (338), examination of army hospitals in Pennsylvania (335), and analyses of military medicine in northern New York (337) and the Continental Army (336), while offering little new, contribute to a fuller understanding of medicine and medical practices during this formative period. Blanco's most important finding, and one advanced as a suggestion, is that the campaign to protect the health of soldiers may have hastened the professionalization of American medicine. In a brief piece, noteworthy because of its interdisciplinary nature, Carl Jelenko III and two co-authors (380) survey emergency medical services in the Revolution. George A. Bender and John Parascondola's previously overlooked *American Pharmacy in the Colonial and Revolutionary Periods* (334) is an excellent account of drug therapy during the hostilities. Eric T. Carlso (352) explores in detail the history and significance of Benjamin Rush's wartime classic, *Directions for Preserving the Health of Soldiers.*

FROM THE REVOLUTION TO THE CIVIL WAR. Like the Revolution, military medicine during this long period has attracted little recent attention. Eldon G. Chuinard's *Only One Man Died: The Medical Aspects of the Lewis and Clark Expedition* (358), although containing little not already known, is a well done and welcome addition to the literature of the army and Western exploration. Few studies pertaining to naval medicine were published during the last five years. Two of these deal with the early nineteenth-century navy. In a highly perceptive piece, Christopher McKee (390) persuasively argues for a history of the enlisted man written primarily thorugh his eyes—a history, he contends, that may alter traditional perceptions about the social order and the quality of life in America during the early national period. The second of these studies, that of J. Worth Estes (369), provides important insights into naval medicine through an examination of a journal kept by the surgeon of the *New York*, a thirty-six gun frigate, during a sixteen-month voyage commencing in 1802. Worth's essay is an excellent analysis of the day-to-day practice of the naval physician at sea. Mary C. Gillett (373), in an exhaustively researched and skillfully crafted article that will in all likelihood figure prominently in the next volume of her history of the Army Medical Department, profiles the character of Thomas Lawson, the second surgeon-general of the Army. William M. Straight's narrative account of army medicine during the Seminole Wars, 1818–56 (413), illuminates a little-explored chapter of military medical history. William Beaumont, the frontier army surgeon who through a quirk of fate became internationally known for his physiological experiments on Alexis St. Martin, has been the subject of considerable recent attention. Ronald L. Numbers (393) analyzes Beaumont's experiments in the context of the ethics of human experimentation, concluding that they conformed to the accepted standards of the day. Numbers in conjunction with William J. Orr, Jr. (394), assesses Beaumont's reception at home and abroad, finding that his medical experiments had their greatest contemporary impact in Europe, where a greater premium was placed on medical research. A final work (333) makes available three out-of-print works on Beaumont's life and career. Roger G. Miller's study of the influence of yellow fever on Gen. Winfield Scott's expedition against

Mexico City in 1847 (392) provides an added dimension to this operation. Fear of this dreaded killer, Miller argues, delayed Scott's march on Mexico City, resulting in increased American casualties. Ironically, and largely through accident, yellow fever had little effect on the American army.

THE CIVIL WAR. That this much celebrated conflict dominated military medical scholarship during the last five years should not be surprising. Much of the material that appeared, however, is of little value to the serious scholar. This is especially noticeable in regards to overview studies. Most of these can be dismissed as superficial and based on existing knowledge. A possible exception, and admittedly a minor one, is my examination of the experiences of the largely ignored combat physician (341). Of the half dozen or so articles on Civil War medicine at the state level, only William M. Straight's piece on Florida (414) is deserving of mention. Gordon Dammann's *Pictorial Encyclopedia of Civil War Medical Instruments and Equipment* (363) is a superbly done and valuable reference work. Stanley B. Burns's *Early Medical Photography in America (1830–1883)* (348) contains an excellent chapter on the use of photography for medical purposes during the Civil War. Burns contends that although physicians has used photography in their practice and research as early as the 1840s, the unparalleled volume of pathology available as a result of the war's carnage had an important and lasting effect on the use of photography in medicine. The work is illustrated by numerous photographs, some quite rare. This chapter is more readily available, since the book was privately printed, in periodical form (349). John D. Smith follows up his previous informative analysis of the health of Vermont's Civil War recruits, cited in the first update, with an equally praiseworthy profile of Kentucky's enlistees (410). Two studies, one for the North (388) and the other for the South (389), depict the hazards of camp life. The ledger of one important Confederate hospital (376) and the death roster of another (378) have been made available to scholars for the first time. The edited diaries and letters of Civil War medical figures continue to appear in both periodical (331, 382) and book (345, 362) form. Although such publications generally contain little that is new, they serve to reemphasize the conflict's frightful carnage. Three noteworthy studies analyze the health of prominent Civil War leaders. Gabor S. Boritt and Adam Borit (339) take issue with the contention that Abraham Lincoln suffered from the Marfan syndrome. The case for the opposite view, however, remains more compelling. Dr. Harris D. Riley, Jr.'s, carefully reconstructed health profile of Robert E. Lee (404) reveals that this great Confederate chieftain suffered from poor health, probably the result of the onset of heart disease, beginning in the spring of 1863, a factor that may have impaired his effectiveness as a leader. An English psychologist (375) suggests that Stonewall Jackson's twin personality traits – rigidly controlled emotions in everyday life and reckless abandon on the battlefield – are indicative of a schizoid personality. Among recent popular pieces on Civil War medicine, two – one dealing with surgeon William Fuller's informative essay on malingering (353) and the other with Surgeon Richard Vickery's medical thesis on the duties of the surgeon in action (354) – merit mention. The medical legacy of the Civil War is a largely ignored subject. Two studies address aspects of this topic. David Courtwright (360) assesses the role of the war in late-nineteenth-century opium addiction. He concludes that the hostilities were neither the cause of the problem nor a convenient excuse for it.

Rather, Courtwright argues, the war was but one of several causes that contributed to an increase of opiate addition in the postbellum period. In a seriocomic essay (340), I call attention to the medical "tall tales" that ensued from wartime experiences.

CIVIL WAR TO WORLD WAR I. The chief arenas for military medicine during these years were, at the outset, the American West and, later, the Caribbean basin. Peter D. Olch's survey of army medicine on the Western frontier between 1866 and 1890 (395) is selective in coverage but useful. The same can be said for four (385, 387, 405, 417) recent local studies. Anthony Palmieri III and Daniel J. Hammond (397) discuss drug therapy at a frontier fort. In an excellent interdisciplinary study (424), Anne I. Woosley, an anthropologist, recreates health care at Fort Burgwin, New Mexico, from the diary of Dr. William Wallace Anderson, the post surgeon, and a 1979 archaeology dig. John M. Carroll's reprint of George Otis's *Transport of Sick and Wounded by Pack Animals* (396), which first appeared in 1877, recalls this important treatise to attention. The published diary of Dr. Holmes O. Paulding, the surgeon of the Montana Column that arrived at Little Big Horn after the tragic heroics of George Armstrong Custer, was cited in the last update (267). Thomas R. Bueckner (346) complements this volume with the publication of a number of letters Paulding wrote home from the field. Although Paulding helped treat Maj. Marcus A. Reno's casualties, there is little of value in these letters for the historian of military medicine. The medical consequences of prostitution was a persistent problem for military surgeons. Anne M. Butler (350) examines the army's attempts to deal with prostitution on the Western frontier. The results, she contends, were myopic: on the one hand, military officials vigorously denounced the practice, but on the other, their actions tacitly encouraged it. In two previously overlooked studies that were prepared for popular audiences (418, 419), James A. Weir, a former military physician, discusses the largely antagonistic interfacing of military and Indian medicines.

The medical aspects of America's expansionist outreach have generated far less interest than medicine on the western frontier. James B. Agnew's account of the experiences of a private in the medical corps during the Spanish-American War (330) is both interesting and informative. William B. Bean's biography of Walter Reed (332) is satisfactory but not definitive. Two short pieces (356, 357) deal with the medical problems that had to be overcome in the construction of the Panama Canal. James A. Sandos (406) analyzes Gen. John J. Pershing's unique solution to the problem of prostitution and drugs in the American army on the Mexican border during 1916 to 1917. Ignoring, for pragmatic reasons, conventional thinking on such social evils, Pershing achieved remarkable success through a program of controlled prostitution, tacit approval of gambling, and drug prohibition.

WORLD WAR I AND THE INTERWAR YEARS. The medical history of World War I has suffered from a noticeable neglect during the last five years. Michael Pearlman's background study (398) on Leonard Wood and the prewar University Military Training Program argues that Wood, the foremost spokesman for this undertaking, sought to transform it into a receptacle for a regimen centered on discipline and outdated moralistic medical values. Only two publications (344, 361) on wartime medicine were located. Each deals with the personal experiences of ambulance drivers, contributing further to the already large body of material on this topic. Aspects of postwar military humanitarianism are discussed in three studies. Two of these (359, 371) pertain to the army's typhus expedition to Poland at the close of hostilities. The former is a generally disappointing exercise in traditional military history; the latter, however, is a highly perceptive analytical synthesis of the expedition's well intended but only marginally successful operations. The third study (355) attempts, with mixed results, to recount and analyze Leonard Wood's controversial involvement with the Philippines' Culion leper colony between 1921 and 1927.

WORLD WAR II TO PRESENT. Unlike the First World War, World War II has received considerable recent attention. Lyman A. Brewer III (342), one of its most prominent members, recounts the heroic accomplishments of the Second Auxiliary Surgical Group. Perhaps the most enduring achievement (343) of this organization was its research on the threat of "wet lung" (now known as the Respiratory Distress Syndrome, or RDS) in war casualities. A second significant wartime study (347), this one dealing with pilonidal disease, or "Jeep disease", as it was called at the time, was recently republished. Floyd W. Denny's analysis of the role of the Armed Forces Epidemiological Board in the conquest of atypical (microplasma) pneumonia (366) is an excellent case study of the military's contributions to public health. An analysis of the health records of 303 American prisoners-of-war interned at Osaka, Japan, from December 1942 to April 1945 (365) illuminates a little-researched aspect of World War II military medical history. Larry W. Stephenson (411) reflects on the sustained contribution of the University of Pennsylvania School of Medicine to wartime medicine. This school had been the genesis of Base Hospital No. 20 during World War I. Reactivated as General Hospital No. 20 at the outbreak of World War II, the organization served with distinction in India. A number of noteworthy personal accounts that recount a wide range of wartime medical experiences (364, 379, 399, 422) have also appeared.

No recent studies pertaining to the medical aspects of the Korean War were located. The war in Vietnam, however, is the subject of growing interest. Two volumes (415) of a projected multivolume history of internal medicine in Vietnam have been published to date. Although they suffer from the shortcomings of in-house official history, these studies, dealing with skin diseases and general medicine and infectious diseases, contain much useful information. Peter Dorland's and James Nanney's *Dust Off* (367) documents the activities of air-ambulance crews during the hostilities. George J. Hill (377) evaluates the work of military physicians in the training of the South Vietnamese in general surgery during 1972 and 1973 and finds much to praise. Fred A. Wilcox's *Waiting for an Army to Die* (421) poignantly exposes the tragic health and societal toll of the military's herbicide defoliation program. Robert Shaw (408) analyzes the medical lessons learned during the 1975 Vietnamese evacuation, focusing on their potential value in future disasters.

A wide variety of studies have appeared on recent military medical history. Two brief articles (381, 400) chronicle the history of the societies of army and air force flight surgeons. Robert B. McLean (391) pays tribute to the distinguished career of Leonard D. Heaton, a former surgeon-general and one of the preeminent figures in 20th-century military medicine. In works overlooked previously, Peter A. Flynn (370) makes a convincing case for the continuation of the navy's medical deparment, and Douglas Kolb and E. K. Eric Gunderson (386) report on the findings of a study on alcholism in the navy conducted by the Naval Health Research Center. A team of medical researchers (351) who have carefully monitored the health of military participants in a 1957 nuclear test conclude that there is no conclusive evidence of a link between their participation and the frequency of cancer among them. Finally, in a sobering piece (384), R. H. Kessler speculates on the potential impact of nuclear weapons on military medicine.

SUGGESTIONS FOR FURTHER RESEARCH. As I have pointed out throughout the life of this guide, military and naval medical history is an underdeveloped area in the broader field of military history. Opportunities of every type, ranging from overview studies to period pieces and from seminal developments to key individuals, are available for the taking. And, as also noted previously, source materials, in most instances, do not pose a major problem. The paucity of first-rate health stuides, it strikes me, is largely the result of the hold of traditional military history with its emhasis on battles and leaders. If the new military history endures and grows in favor, perhaps this situation will change. In the meantime, because of the lack of serious attention to health factors, the story of American military history remains incomplete.

BIBLIOGRAPHY

329. Adams, David B. "Abdominal Gunshot Wounds in Warfare: A Historical Review." *Military Medicine* 148 (1983): 15–20.
330. Agnew, James B. "Carromatos and Quinine: Private Logden and the Medical Corps of 1898." *Military Review* 54 (1979): 11–21.
331. Baird, Nancy D. "There is No Sunday in the Army: Civil War Letters of Lunsford D. Yandell, 1861–62." *Filson Club Historical Quarterly* 53 (1979): 317–27.
332. Bean, William B. *Walter Reed: A Biography*. Charlottesville: University Press of Virginia, 1892.
333. Beaumont, William. *The Career of William Beaumont and the Reception of His Discovery*. New York: Arno Press, 1980.
334. Bender, George A., and John Parascondola. *American Pharmacy in the Colonial and Revolutionary Periods*. Madison, Wisc.: American Institute of Pharmacy, 1977.
335. Blanco, Richard L. "Army Hospitals in Pennsylvania during the Revolutionary War." *Pennsylvania History* 48 (1981): 347–68.
336. _____. "Medicine in the Continental Army, 1775–1781." *Bulletin of the New York Academy of Medicine* 57 (1981): 677–704.
337. _____. "Military Medicine in Northern New York, 1776–1777." *New York History* 63 (1982): 39–58.
338. _____. *Physician of the American Revolution, Jonathan Potts*. New York: Garland STPM Press, 1979.
339. Boritt, Gabor S., and Adam Borit. "Lincoln and the Marfan Syndrome: The Medical Diagnosis of a Historical Figure." *Civil War History* 29 (1983): 212–29.
340. Breeden, James O. "'The Case of the Miraculous Bullet' Revisited." *Military Affairs* 45 (1981): 23–26.

341. _____. "The 'Forgotten Man' of the Civil War: The Southern Experience." *Bulletin of the New York Academy of Medicine* 55 (1979): 652–69.

342. Brewer, Lyman A., III. "The Contributions of the Second Auxiliary Surgical Group to Military Surgery during World War II with Special Reference to Thoracic Surgery." *Annals of Surgery* 197 (1983) 318–36.

343. Brewer, Lyman A., III, Benjamin Burbank, and Paul C. Samson. "The 'Wet Lung' in War Casualties." *Annals of Surgery* 123 (1946): 343–62.

344. Brown, George C., ed. "With the Ambulance Service in France: The Wartime Letters of William Gorham Rice, Jr." *Wisconsin Magazine of History* 64 (1981): 278–93; 65 (1981–82): 11–35, 103–19.

345. Brumgardt, John R., ed. *Civil War Nurse: The Diary and Letters of Hannah Ropes*. Knoxville: University of Tennessee Press, 1980.

346. Bueckner, Thomas R., ed. "A Surgeon at the Little Big Horn: The Letters of Dr. Homes O. Paulding." *Montana* 32 (1982): 34–49.

347. Buie, Louis A. "Jeep Disease (Pilonidal Disease of Mechanized Warfare)." *Diseases of the Colon and Rectum* 25 (1982): 384–90. Reprinted from *Southern Medical Journal* 37 (1944): 103–9.

348. Burns, Stanley B. *Early Medical Photography in America (1839–1883)*. New York: The author, 1983.

349. _____. "Early Medical Photography in America (1839–1883); VI. Civil War Medical Photography." *New York State Journal of Medicine* 80 (1980): 1444–69.

350. Butler, Anne M. "Military Myopia: Prostitution on the Frontier." *Prologue* 13 (1981): 232–50.

351. Caldwell, Glyn G., Della Kelley, Matthew Zack, Henry Falk, and Clark W. Heath, Jr. "Mortality and Cancer Frequency among Military Nuclear Test (Smoky) Participants, 1957 through 1979." *Journal of the American Medical Association* 250 (1983): 620–24.

352. Carlson, Eric T. "Benjamin Rush on Revolutionary War Hygiene." *Bulletin of the New York Academy of Medicine* 55 (1979): 614–35.

353. Castel, Albert, ed. "Malingering: "Many...Diseases are ...Feigned.'" *Civil War Times Illustrated* 16 (1977): 29–32.

354. _____. "On the Duties of the Surgeon in Action: Surgeon Richard Vickery." *Civil War Times Illustrated* 17 (1978): 12–23.

355. Chapman, Ronald F. *Leonard Wood and Leprosy in the Philippines: The Culion Leper Colony, 1921–1927*. Washington, D.C.: University Press of America, 1982.

356. Chaves-Carballo, Enrique. "Samuel T. Darling: Studies on Malaria and the Panama Canal." *Bulletin of the History of Medicine* 54 (1980): 95–100.

357. Christie, Amos. "Medical Conquest of the 'Big Ditch.'" *Southern Medical Journal* 71 (1978): 717–23.

358. Chuinard, Eldon G. *Only One Man Died: The Medical Aspects of the Lewis and Clark Expedition*. Glendale, Calif.: Arthur H. Clark, 1979.

359. Cornebise, Alfred E. *Typhus and Doughboys: The American-Polish Typhus Relief Expedition, 1919–1921*. Newark: University of Delaware Press, 1982.

360. Courtwright, David T. "Opiate Addiction as a Consequence of the Civil War." *Civil War History* 24 (1978): 101–11.

361. Cutler, G. Ripley. *Of Battles Long Ago: Memoirs of an American*

Ambulance Driver in World War I. New York: Exposition Press, 1979.

362. Cuttino, George P., ed. *Saddle Bag and Spinning Wheel: Being the Civil War Letters of George W. Peddy, M.D., Surgeon, 56th Georgia Volunteer Regiment, C.S.A., and His Wife, Kate Featherston Peddy*. Macon, Ga.: Mercer University Press, 1981.

363. Dammann, Gordon. *A Pictorial Encyclopedia of Civil War Medical Instruments and Equipment*. Missoula, Mont.: Pictorial Histories Publishing Company, 1983.

364. Davis, Richard A. "A Surgeon at War." *Surgery, Gynecology and Obstetrics* 157 (1983): 147–49.

365. Dean, Larry M., Frank N. Willis, and Robert Obourn. "Health Records of American Prisoners of the Japanese during World War II." *Military Medicine* 145 (1980): 838–41.

366. Denny, Floyd W. "Atypical Pneumonia and the Armed Forces Epidemiological Board." *Journal of Infectious Diseases* 143 (1981): 305–16.

367. Dorland, Peter, and James Nanney. *Dust Off: Army Aeromedical Evacuation in Vietnam*. Washington, D.C.: Center of Military History, 1981.

368. Ellenbogen, Charles. "The Infectious Diseases of War." *Military Medicine* 147 (1982): 185–88.

369. Estes, J. Worth. "Naval Medicine in the Age of Sail: The Voyage of the *New York*, 1802–1803." *Bulletin of the History of Medicine* 56 (1982): 238–53.

370. Flynn, Peter A. "The Influence of Medical Considerations on Modern Naval Warfare." *U.S. Naval Institute Proceedings* 5 (1977): 170–85.

371. Foster, Gaines, M. "Typhus Disaster in the Wake of War: The American-Polish Relief Expedition, 1919–1920." *Bulletin of the History of Medicine* 55 (1981): 221–32.

372. Gillett, Mary C. *The Army Medical Department, 1775–1818*. Washington, D.C.: Center of Military History, 1981.

373. _____. "Thomas Lawson, Second Surgeon-General of the U.S. Army: A Character Sketch." *Prologue* 14 (1982): 14–24.

374. Heggers, John P. "Microbial Invasion—The Major Ally of War." *Military Medicine* 143 (1982): 390–94.

375. Henry, W. D. "Stonewall Jackson—the Soldier Eccentric." *Practitioner* 223 (1979): 580–87.

376. Hewitt, Lawrence L., and Arthur W. Bergeron, Jr., eds. *Post Hospital Ledger: Port Hudson, Louisiana, 1862–1863*. Baton Rouge: Le Comité des Archives de La Louisiane, 1981.

377. Hill, George J. "'Lerne and Gladly Teche'—A View of the Vietnam Medical Education Project." *Military Medicine* 144 (1979): 124–28.

378. Hodge, Robert A., comp. *A Death Roster of the Confederate General Hospital at Culpeper, Virginia*. Fredericksburg, Va.: The Author, 1977.

379. Jacobs, Eugene C. "A Medical Memoir of MacArthur's First Guerrilla Regiment." *Military Medicine* 144 (1979): 402–5.

380. Jelenko, Carl, III, Judith B. Matthews, and John C. Matthews. "Emergency Medicine in Colonial America: Revolutionary War Casualties." *Annals of Emergency Medicine* 11 (1982): 73–76.

381. Johnson, Douglas N., and Hubert F. Bonfili. "The Society of United States Air Force Flight Surgeons." *Aviation, Space, and Environmental Medicine*

50 (1979): 509–12.
382. Jordan, Phillip D. "The Career of Henry M. Farr, Civil War Surgeon." *Annals of Iowa* 44 (1982): 191–211.
383. Kampmeier, Rudolph H. "Venereal Disease in the United States Army: 1775–1900." *Sexually Transmitted Diseases* 9 (1982): 100–103.
384. Kessler, R. H. "Gunpowder Altered the Physician's Wartime Role. Should Nuclear Weapons Change It Again?" *Archives of Internal Medicine* 143 (1983): 784–86.
385. Kennedy, J. W. "Military Medicine on the Arizona Frontier circa 1870–1880." *Arizona Medicine* 39 (1982): 122–29.
386. Kolb, Douglas, and E. K. Eric Gunderson. "Alcoholism in the United States Navy." *Armed Forces and Society* 3 (1977): 183–94.
387. Langellier, John P. "Surgeon in Blue: An Arizona Diary of Dr. William Henry Corbusier." In *Medicine in the West*, edited by James O. Breeden, 65–74. Manhattan, Kans.: Sunflower University Press, 1982.
388. Link, Kenneth. "Potomac Fever: The Hazards of Camp Life." *Vermont History* 51 (1983): 69–88.
389. McInvale, Morton R. "'That Thing of Infamy,' Macon's Camp Oglethorpe during the Civil War." *Georgia Historical Quarterly* 63 (1979):279–91.
390. McKee, Christopher. "Fantasies of Mutiny and Murder: A Suggested PsychoHistory of the Seaman in the United States Navy, 1798–1815." *Armed Forces and Society* 4 (1978): 293–304.
391. McLean, Robert B. "Leonard D. Heaton—Military Surgeon." *Military Medicine* 147 (1982): 722–23, 727.
392. Miller, Roger G. "Yellow Jack at Vera Cruz." *Prologue* 10 (1978): 43–53.
393. Numbers, Ronald L. "William Beaumont and the Ethics of Human Experimentation." *Journal of the History of Biology* 12 (1979): 113–35.
394. Numbers, Ronald L., and William J. Orr, Jr. "William Beaumont's Reception at Home and Abroad." *Isis* 72 (1981): 590–612.
395. Olch, Peter D. "Medicine in the Indian-Fighting Army, 1866–1890." In *Medicine in the West*, edited by James O. Breeden, 32–41. Manhattan, Kans. Sunflower University Press, 1982.
396. Otis, George A. *A Report to the Surgeon General on the Transport of Sick and Wounded by Pack Animals*. 1877. Reprint. Bryan, Tex.: John M. Carroll, 1979.
397. Palmieri, Anthony, III, and Daniel J. Hammond. "Drug Therapy at a Frontier Hospital. Fort Laramie, Wyoming Territory, 1870–1889." *Pharmacy History* 21 (1979): 35–44.
398. Pearlman, Michael. "Leonard Wood, William Muldoon and the Medical Profession: Public Health and University Military Training." *New England Quarterly* 52 (1979): 326–44.
399. Penn, J. "The Reminiscences of a Plastic Surgeon during World War II." *Annals of Plastic Surgery* 1 (1978): 105–15.
400. Pettyjohn, Frank S. "The Society of U.S. Army Flight Surgeons." *Aviation, Space, and Environmental Medicine* 50 (1979): 533–35.
401. Polskin, Louis J. "The Caduceus in Logo Devised for the 1775–1975 Bicentennial of the Army Medical Department." *Military Medicine* 144 (1979): 236–38.
402. _____. "The Forging of the Caduceus from DODONA to DoD: A Tribute

to the Medical Departments of the United States Armed Services." *Military Medicine* 143 (1978): 844–55.

403. Reid, Robert L. "Hand Surgery and the Military: A Historical Overview." *Military Medicine* 144 (1979): 385–88.

404. Riley, Harris D., Jr., M.D. "General Robert E. Lee: His Medical Profile." *Virginia Medical* 105 (1978): 495–500.

405. Roberson, Jere W. "A View from Oklahoma, 1866–1868: The Diary and Letters of Dr. James Reagles, Jr., Assistant Surgeon, U.S. Army." *Red River Historical Quarterly* 3 (1978): 19–46.

406. Sandos, James A. "Prostitution and Drugs: The United States Army on the Mexican-American Border, 1916–1917." *Pacific Historical Review* 49 (1980): 621–45.

407. Shannon, Sam. "The Army Pharmacist: A Historical Review." *Military Medicine* 143 (1978): 542–45.

408. Shaw, Robert. "Health Services in a Disaster: Lessons from the 1975 Vietnamese Evacuation." *Military Medicine* 144 (1979): 307–11.

409. Shields, Elizabeth A., ed. *Highlights in the History of the Army Nurse Corps.* Washington, D.C.: Center of Military History, 1981.

410. Smith, John D. "Kentucky Civil War Recruits: A Medical Profile." *Medical History* 24 (1980): 185–96.

411. Stephenson, Larry W. "Reflections on the Military Involvement of a Medical School." *Surgery, Gynecology, and Obstetrics* 154 (1982): 888–96.

412. Stewart, Miller J. *Moving the Wounded: Litters, Cacolets & Ambulance Wagons, U.S. Army, 1776–1876.* Ft. Collins, Colo.: Old Army Press, 1979.

413. Straight, William M. "Calomel, Quinine and Laudanum: Army Medicine in the Seminole Wars." *Journal of the Florida Medical Association* 65 (1978): 627–43.

414. _____. "Florida Medicine and the War between the States." *Journal of the Florida Medical Association* 67 (1980): 748–60.

415. U.S. Army Medical Department. *Internal Medicine in Vietnam.* Vols. 1, 2. Washington, D.C.: Office of the Surgeon General and Center of Military History, 1977–82.

416. Vester, John W. "The Valiant Physicians." *Military Medicine* 147 (1982): 1041–47.

417. Weir, James A. "19th-Century Army Doctors on the Frontier and in Nebraska." *Nebraska History* 61 (1980): 192–214.

418. Weir, James A. "The Army Doctor and the Indian." *Denver Westerners Roundup* 31 (September 1975): 3–14.

419. _____. "The Army Doctor Looks at Indian Medicine." *Denver Westerners Roundup* 33 (September–October 1977): 12–28.

420. _____. "The History of Fitzsimons Army Medical Center." *Denver Westerners Roundup* 36 (January 1980): 3–14.

421. Wilcox, Fred A. *Waiting for an Army to Die: The Tragedy of Agent Orange.* New York: Vintage Books, 1983.

422. Wolde, Arthur W. *Ambulance No. 11.* New York: Vantage Press, 1982.

423. Woodward, Theodore E. "The Public's Debt to Military Medicine." *Military Medicine* 143 (1981): 168–73.

424. Woosley, Anne I. "Fort Burgwin's Hospital: A Surgeon's Journal and an

Archaeological Dig Reveal the Nature of Frontier Medicine and Healing." *El Palacio* 86 (1980): 3–7, 36–39.

XIII

THE NAVY IN THE EARLY TWENTIETH CENTURY

1890–1941

William R. Braisted

Historians of the navy's battleship age, 1890–1941, have moved from earlier well-beaten paths into previously unexplored areas. There have been notable studies on the navy's linkages with society, naval institutional history, naval technology, and naval diplomacy. To judge from their product, historians seem to have lost some of their enthusiasm for the diplomacy of naval arms limitation. Their most important work has tended to deal with the early years and with the approaches to World War II. Practically ignored in the last five years has been the navy during World War I and the 1920s.

GUIDES AND BIBLIOGRAPHIES. Among the new guides to materials of the period are a fine survey of naval historical manuscript sources, by Dean Allard and his associates in the Naval History Division (609); a guide to the Naval War College archives, by Anthony Nicolosi (572); an introduction to the sources in naval air history, by William J. Armstrong (488); a selected bibliography of printed American naval history materials, by Paolo E. Coletta (499); and an assessment of the naval attaché reports relating to ordnance, by John C. Reilly, Jr. (585).

MICROFORM PUBLICATIONS. Several major microform companies, such as Scholarly Resources and Michael Glazier, have been engaged in extensive reproduction of naval historical materials, including the hearings of the General Board of the Navy, 1917–1950 (531); papers on naval strategic planning, 1891–1945 (594); and the Japanese "magic" intercepts (546, 559). There being no guide to naval historical materials in microform, this type of material can best be identified by consulting the publishers' trade lists or the general guides to microform materials prepared by Meckler Publishing (527, 568).

THE NEW NAVY THROUGH WORLD WAR I. In the area of general surveys, E. B. Potter and his associates have revised and reduced their well-known volume on *Sea Power* (581). James Abrahamson (481) has studied the military and naval reformers during the four decades before World War I in the context of the progressive and other movements in society, and Benjamin Franklin Cooling (506) has examined the relations between the navy and the steel industry before 1917 for evidence of military-industrial linkages. David Trask's superb monograph on the Spanish-American War (602) is likely to remain unrivaled for years to come. Terrell Gottschall's dissertation (524) exposes the imperialist and naval pressures behind German actions during the Spanish-American War. Two volumes by Lewis Gould (525, 526) add substance to President McKinley as a war leader. On the navy during World War I, there are only the articles by Dean Allard on Anglo-American differences (485), and by Vice-Admiral Allen E. Smith (593) on the Sixth Battle Squadron's service with the Grand Fleet.

THE INTERWAR YEARS. Probably the most meaningful exposition on the navy during the interwar years, 1919–1941, may be found in the essays on the chiefs of naval operations edited by Robert W. Love, Jr. (556). Additional light on naval arms limitation is now shed in the articles by Norman Gibbs on Anglo-American relations at the various conferences (522), and by William Trimble on Adm. Hilary P. Jones at the 1927 Geneva Arms Conference (604), as well as in Patrick J. Gallo's brief monograph *Swords and Plowshares* (520). Anticipating his long-planned study of the treaty navy are several articles and in-house papers by Thomas P. Hone on such subjects as the effectiveness of the treaty navy (538); patterns of naval spending, 1921–1941 (539); and naval management during the interwar period (540).

Charles V. Reynold's dissertation on the navy during the New Deal (588) is notable for relating the fleet problems to naval policy; Michael A. West's dissertation on the House Naval Affairs Committee (617) is chiefly concerned with Carl Vinson's chairmanship through passage of the Vinson-Trammell Act of 1934. Pressures mounted by "Uncle Carl" on the reluctant Pres. Franklin D. Roosevelt are the theme of John C. Walter's article (615). Arthur Marder's *Old Friends, New Enemies* (562) is a superb account of the deterioration of Anglo-Japanese naval relations and its significance for the United States Navy, and Paul Haggie's *Britannia at Bay* (527) deals succinctly with the build-up of the Royal navy before World War II. Malcom Muir, Jr. (570), puts a good part of the blame for the failure by the Soviet Union to purchase battleships and other naval armament in the United States during the late thirties on obstruction from American naval men.

THE NAVY'S ROAD TO PEARL HARBOR. Literature on the Pearl Harbor attack and its sequel continues to flow rich and heated. In quick succession, there appeared full studies of Pearl Harbor by Peter Herde (533) and Gordon Prange (582), only to be followed by John Toland's deeply revisionist *Infamy* (601). Similarly revisionist is Bruce Bartlett's brief *Cover Up . . . , 1941–1946* (489). Martin Melosi (565) accepts the revisionist view that there was a cover-up without subscribing to the charge that Franklin D. Roosevelt maneuvered the Japanese attack. Both Melosi (566) and Hans L. Trefousse (603) have also provided convenient summaries of the Pearl Harbor debate. In his *Pacific War* (507) and a subsequent article (508), John Costello has given advance notice of still another Pearl Harbor study under way. Paul Stilwell's *Air Raid: Pearl Harbor* (597) is a lively collection of reflections by persons close to the affair; and Richard Collier's *Road to Pearl Harbor* (503) is a rather episodic account of the year 1941. Pearl Harbor seen from the lower decks of battleships *California* and *Nevada* has been recounted respectively by Theodore Mason (563) and Wallace Exum (513). The Deparment of Defense has contributed to the continuing search by publishing eight volumes of the Japanese "magic" intercepts (606). Japanese perspectives on Pearl Harbor are presented in Agawa Hiroyuki's superb biography of Admiral Yamamoto Isoroku (482) and an item by Tsunoda Jun on Yamamoto's concept of attack (605). About a third of H. P. Willmott's *Empires in the Balance (618)* deals with the rival strategies that brought collision in the Pacific. Significant also are the articles by William Heimdahl and Geraldine Phillips on the recently opened records of the navy's Pearl Harbor liaison office (382); by Mark M. Lowenthal on Admiral Stark's famed "Plan Dog" memorandum (556); and by Fred E. Pollock on the importance to Britain of the Canadian-American naval accord at Ogdensberg (578).

ON DISTANT STATIONS. Although distant stations are commonly associated with the navy during the days of wood and sail, recent books, dissertations, and articles all attest to the navy's continuing role in showing the flag in Asian, Mediterranean, and Middle Eastern waters. Bernard Cole's *Gunboats and Marines* (497) reviews the debates between diplomats and servicemen over the use of the navy and the marines in China during the Nationalist revolution, 1925–1928, in a manner that invites comparison with American involvements elsewhere at other times. William N. Still's account of the navy in European waters from the Civil War to World War I (596) is detailed operational history; Thomas A. Bryson's *Tars, Turks and Tankers* (494) is a somewhat popular review of the navy in Near Eastern waters over 179 years. William J. Hourihan has drawn from his dissertation to produce four very lively articles on the navy in European and Mediterranean waters from the Spanish-American War to 1904 (541, 542, 543, 544). Donald A. Yerxa devotes about equal time to strategy and diplomacy in his dissertation on the navy in the Caribbean, 1914–1919 (619), and Joyce S. Goldberg's dissertation on the "Baltimore Affair" (523) delves into the Chilean as well as the American political ramifications behind the crisis, 1891–1892. There are also substantial recent articles on the navy in Brazil, 1893–1895 (612); the gunboat *Petrel* on the Yangtze during the Spanish-American War (576); and the naval maverick Philo McGiffen's service with Li Hung-Chang's fleet (491).

BIOGRAPHY. William E. Livezey ends the full revision of his well-known analysis of Alfred Thayer Mahan's thought (554) with the conclusion that Mahan has been outdated by technology. Paolo Coletta's biographies of the inventor-reformer Bradley Fiske (498), the scholarly French Ensor Chadwick (501), and the controversial Bowman H. McCalla (500) all contribute an understanding of the manners, mores, and achievements of naval officers during the generation before World War I. Complementing Coletta's work are the collection of Chadwick's writings edited by Doris D. Maguire (560), and the delightfully frank memoirs of *The Old Navy* by Rear Adm. David P. Mannix 3d (561). James R. Leutze's sensitive biography of Adm. Thomas C. Hart (552) similarly conveys feeling for the generation of the world war and interwar years, as do the early chapters in the biographies of admirals Ernest J. King, by Thomas B. Buell (495); Hyman Rickover, by Norman Polmar and Thomas Allen (580); and Chester Nimitz, by Frank A. Driskill and Dede W. Casad (512). Admiral Nimitz's widow, the former Catherine Freeman, has contributed memoirs of her bridal days before World War I (591), and the Naval War College has published a reduced version of the paper on tactics against Orange and Red that Nimitz wrote as a member of the class of 1922–1923 (573). The volume on the chiefs of naval operations edited by Robert Love (555) includes sketches of William S. Benson, Robert E. Coontz, Edward W. Eberle, Charles Frederick Hughes, William V. Pratt, William H. Standley, William D. Leahy, and Harold Stark. Factual biographies of a number of flag officers of the period may also be found in Clark G. Reynolds's *Famous American Admirals* (589).

INSTITUTIONAL, PERSONNEL, EDUCATIONAL, MISCELLANEOUS. Surely one of the most important events in recent naval historiography was the publication, about thirty years late, of Robert G. Albion's *Makers of Naval Policy* (483). Albion's study is probably the most important single contribution to naval institutional history since C. O. Paullin's pioneering work on naval administration seventy years ago. The two volumes edited by Paolo Coletta on the secretaries of the navy (502) are important for what they tell of the office as well as of the men, as are the essays on the chiefs of naval operations edited by Robert Love (555). Lester Brune's *Origins of American National Security Policy* (493) deals especially with the interplay between sea and air power in the early American quest for a national security policy.

In his *Conflict of Duty* (510), Jeffrey Dorwart argues that American naval intelligence officers were torn by their rival commitments to overt and covert intelligence between 1919 and 1945. The volumes by Wilfred J. Holmes (537), Edward Van Der Rhoer (610), and Ronald Lewin (553) on intercept intelligence all include background material on the years before 1941.

The Naval Research Laboratory has published detailed studies by Louis A. Gebbard on naval radio electronics (521) and by David K. Allison on the origin of radar (486) that are also in large part histories of the laboratory itself. Norman Friedman's *Naval Radar* (515), although chiefly concerned with World War II and after, deals briefly with earlier development of radio, radar, and electronic warfare. *Dahlgren*, edited by Kenneth G. McCollum (557), the Naval Weapons Center's official history, also describes the facility as a proving ground and testing center before World War II. Other naval shore activities are represented by a pictorial history of the Mare Island Shipyard, by Sue Lemmon and E.D. Wichels (551); a review of civil-naval relations at Pensacola to 1930, by George F. Pearce (577); Frederick H. Olsen's fine study of the navy as the protector of native Samoans (575); and the dissertation by Bradley M. Reynolds (588) on the decision to establish a naval base at Guantanamo.

About a third of Jack Sweetman's popular illustrated history of the Naval Academy (599) is concerned with the academy during the battleship age. In his *Blue Sword* (613), Michael Vlahos attempts to convey the ethos at the Naval War College during the interwar period. Vlahos has also explored in an important article the contribution by the War College to the early Orange Plans (614), and Michael Doyle (511) has argued that the navy developed its later Orange Plans without overlooking alternate operations, such as cooperation with Britain in the Pacific. The significant but difficult-to-secure articles by J.A.S. Grenville, Holger Herwig, and David Trask on German and American war planning may be found in the volume edited by Paul Kennedy on the *War Plans of the Great Powers, 1880–1914* (549). A symposium at the Air Force Academy in 1980 produced a fine paper by Roger Dingham and comments by other leading authorities on American strategies in East Asia, 1898–1948 (509).

To his earlier work on naval enlisted personnel Frederick S. Harrod has added pioneering articles on blacks in the navy (529, 530). John Maurer's "Fuel and the Battle Fleet" (564) assesses the influence of coal and oil on American naval strategy, 1898–1923. Although not strictly naval history, Allan R. Millett's superb new history of the marines, *Semper Fidelis* (569), should be especially noted for its materials on naval-marine interventions, advanced bases, amphibious warfare, and much more. Raymond G. O'Connor's *War, Diplomacy, and History* (574) reproduces O'Connor's more significant writings that have never appeared in book form.

ON SHIPS AND GUNS. The last five years have witnessed a continued surge of handsome volumes on various classes of American warships. More than picture books, many of these studies are serious inquiries into the reasons behind ship construction and design based upon considerable archival research. The Naval Historical Center has completed the final volumes of its *Dictionary of American Naval Fighting Ships* (608). *American Battleships, 1886–1923*, by John C. Reilly, Jr., and Robert L. Scheina (586), deals professionally with the design and construction of battleships from the *Maine* to the *Mississippi* class. Reilly's *United States Destroyers of World War II* (584), its title notwithstanding, treats in some detail destroyers designed and constructed before the war. Especially significant for their research into the reasoning behind ships' designs and for their line drawings are the studies by Norman Friedman and his associates on battleships (514), aircraft carriers (516), and destroyers (517). Other studies on capital ships include an updating of Siegfried Breyer's well-known work on battleships (492); a compendium on battleships and battlecruisers, by William E. McMahon (558); and an article on American battlecruisers, by Ernest Andrade (487). John D. Alden (484) and Norman Polmar (579) have both written histories of American submarine construction from the beginning. Edwin P. Hoyt's *Submarines at War* (545) is a popular account of the silent service. The massive volumes of *Conway's All the World's Fighting Ships* (504, 505) include separate sections on American warships and on the warships of other leading navies. Two quarterlies, the British *Warship* (616) and the American *Warship International* (620), publish useful articles on American fighting ships. The former is assembled in annual volumes by the Naval Institute. Finally, there should be mentioned recent monographs and articles on the battleships *Pennsylvania* (594) *West Virginia* (595), *Arizona* (519), and *North Carolina* (490), the aircraft carrier *Langley* (600), the heavy cruiser *Houston* (536), and the dynamite gunboat *Vesuvius* (583).

Among the recent works dealing with naval weaponry are a survey of all American naval weapons since 1883, by Norman Friedman (518), and studies on the main armament of battleships, by Peter Hodges (534), and the guns on British and American destroyers of the World War II era, by Hodges and Norman Friedman (535).

NAVAL AIR. Brian Johnson's *Fly Navy* (547) is a comparative account of British, American, Japanese, and German naval air that does not replace the older national histories of naval aviation. George Van Duers (611) has surveyed American naval aviation between the two world wars in a study that, like his earlier contributions, stresses the achievements of naval aviators. John Shiner's important article on the controversy between the navy and the army air force over their respective spheres in coast defense (592) should provoke further inquiry into this neglected subject. Welsey P. Newton's *Perilous Sky* (571) deals wtih the efforts by the navy, the army, and Pan American Airways to protect the security of Latin America, especially Panama. Other additions to naval air history include an exciting account by Dwight Messimer of the first flight from Claifornia to Hawaii (567), Richard Knott's comprehensive history of naval flying boats (550), Louis S. Casey's study of Glenn Curtiss's early experimental years (496), and an updating of Douglas Robinson's history of rigid airships (590).

SUGGESTIONS FOR RESEARCH. Recent work by historians of the navy's battleship age often suggests what has yet to be undertaken. The studies by Abrahamson and Cooling invite further inquiry into the linkages between the navy and diverse segments of American society, even as Dorwart's histories of the Office of Naval Intelligence should promote studies of the navy's offices, bureaus, and corps. The recent writing on Carl Vinson and the House Naval Affairs Committee should stimulate further inquiry into naval-congressional relations, including an appreciation of the neglected long-time member and chairman of the House Naval Affairs Committee, colorful Thomas Smedley Butler. We do not really know how the Office of Naval Operations functioned during its first twenty-five years or how Operations, the War College, and the fleets interacted to produce naval policy. Central to understanding the formulation of naval policy would be thorough analyses of Opnav's powerful War Plans Division and of the navy's budget processes. The writing of state-navy relations should be matched by army-navy studies. To Harrod's volume on enlisted personnel should be added companion works on officers, civilians, blacks, and women, as well as on such amenities as steam heat, food, and health services. Warship enthusiasts might well broaden their sights to include monographs on armor, engines, and ancillary power systems, including electricity on shipboard. Historians have been attracted to the Asiatic Fleet and Special Service Squadron without examining the organization, operations, and doctrines of the more prestigeous fleets. They have also written extensively on naval arms limitation without providing a full account of the arms conferences, 1921–1936, based on multi-archival research. It is surely time to replace Thomas G. Frothingham's antiquated history of the navy in World War I and to update the classic on naval air by Archibald Turnbull and Clifford Lord (326). Pearl Harbor buffs would do well to look beyond the intelligence intercepts and 1941 to study Pearl Harbor *before* 1941, as well as the other naval commitments at Panama, on the West Coast, in Alaska, and elsewhere. Of the naval secretaries, Josephus Daniels remains a wonderfully controversial subject for a good biographer. Forgotten and ignored have been most of the naval leaders of the World War I and interwar years, and yet to be completed is a really comprehensive naval biographical dictionary.

BIBLIOGRAPHY

481. Abrahamson, James L. *America Arms for a New Century: The Making of a Great Military Power.* New York: Free Press, 1981.
482. Agawa, Hiroyuki. *The Reluctant Admiral: Yamamoto and the Imperial*

Navy. Tokyo: Kodansha International, 1979.

483. Albion, Robert G. *The Makers of Naval Policy, 1798-1947.* Annapolis, Md.: Naval Institute Press, 1980.

484. Alden, John D. *The Fleet Submarine in the United States Navy: A Design and Construction History.* Annapolis, Md.: Naval Institute Press, 1979.

485. Allard, Dean C. "Anglo-American Naval Differences during World War I." *Military Affairs* 44 (April 1980): 75-81.

486. Allison, David K. *New Eye for the Navy: The Origin of Radar at the Naval Research Laboratory.* Washington, D.C.: Naval Research Laboratory, 1981.

487. Andrade, Ernest. "The Battle Cruiser in the United States Navy." *Military Affairs* 44 (February 1980): 18-24.

488. Armstrong, William J. "United States Naval Aviation History: A Guide to Sources." *Aerospace Historian* 27 (June 1980): 27-28.

489. Bartlett, Bruce R. *Cover Up: The Politics of Pearl Harbor, 1941-1946.* New Rochelle, N.Y.: Arlington House, 1978.

490. Blee, Ben W. *Battleship North Carolina (BB 55).* Wilmington: North Carolina Battleship Commission, 1982.

491. Bradford, Richard H. "That Prodigal Son: Philo McGiffin and the Chinese Navy." *American Neptune* 38 (July 1978): 157-69.

492. Breyer, Siegfried. *Battleships of the World, 1905-1970.* New York: Mayflower Books, 1980.

493. Brune, Lester H. *The Origins of American National Security Policy: Sea Power, Air Power and Foreign Policy.* Manhattan, Kans. Military Affairs / Aerospace Historian Publishing, 1981.

494. Bryson, Thomas A. *Tars, Turks, and Tankers: The Role of the United States Navy in the Middle East, 1800-1979.* Metuchen, N.J.: Scarecrow Press, 1980.

495. Buell, Thomas B. *Master of the Sea: A Biography of Fleet Admiral Ernest J. King.* Boston: Little, Brown, 1980.

496. Casey, Louis S. *Curtiss, the Hammondsport Era, 1907-*1915. New York: Crown, 1981.

497. Cole, Bernard D. *Gunboats and Marines: The United States Navy in China, 1925-1928.* Newark: University of Delaware Press, 1983.

498. Coletta, Paolo E. *Bradley A. Fiske and the American Navy.* Lawrence: Regents Press of Kansas, 1979.

499. _____. *Bibliography of American Naval History.* Annapolis, Md.: Naval Institute Press, 1981.

500. _____. *Bowman Hendry McCalla, A Fighting Sailor.* Washington, D.C.: University Press of America, 1979.

501. _____. *French Ensor Chadwick: Scholarly Warrior.* Lanham, Md.: University Press of America, 1980.

502. _____, ed. *American Secretaries of the Navy.* 2 vols. Annapolis, Md.: Naval Institute Press, 1980.

503. Collier, Richard The Road to Pearl Harbor, 1941. New York: Atheneum, 1981.

504. *Conway's All the World's Fighting Ships, 1860-1905.* New York: Mayflower Books, 1979.

505. *Conway's All the World's Fighting Ships, 1905-1946.* New York: Mayflower

Books, 1980.
506. Cooling, Benjamin Franklin *Gray Steel and Blue Water Navy: The Formative Years of America's Military Industrial Complex, 1881-1917.* Hamden, Conn.: Archon Books, 1979.
507. Costello, John. *The Pacific War.* New York: Rawson, Wade, 1981.
508. _____. "Remember Pearl Harbor." *U.S. Naval Institute Proceedings* 109 (September 1983): 52-62.
509. Dingman, Roger. "American Policy and Strategy in East Asia, 1898-1950." In *The American Military in the Far East*, edited by Joe C. Dixon, pp. 2-46. Washington, D.C.: Office of U.S. Air Force History, 1980.
510. Dorwart, Jeffrey M. *Conflict of Duty: The U.S. Navy's Intelligence Dilemma, 1919-1945.* Annapolis, Md.: Naval Institute Press, 1983.
511. Doyle, Michael K. "The U.S. Navy and War Plan Orange, 1933-1940." *Naval War College Review* 33 (May-June 1980): 49-83.
512. Driskill, Frank A., and Dede W. Casad. *Chester W. Nimitz: Admiral from the Hills.* Austin, Tex.: Eakins Press, 1983.
513. Exum, Wallace L. *Battleship: Pearl Harbor, 1941.* Virginia Beach, Va.: Donning Company, 1981.
514. Friedman, Norman. *Battleship Design and Development, 1905-1945.* New York: Mayflower Books, 1978.
515. _____. *Naval Radar.* Annapolis, Md.: Naval Institute Press, 1981.
516. _____. *U.S. Aircraft Carriers: An Illustrated Design History.* Annapolis, Md.: Naval Institute Press, 1983.
517. _____. *U.S. Destroyers: An Illustrated Design History.* Annapolis, Md.: Naval Institute Press, 1982.
518. _____. *U.S. Naval Weapons: Every Gun, Missile, Mine and Torpedo Used by the U.S. Navy from 1883 to the Present Day.* Annapolis, Md.: Naval Institute Press, 1982.
519. Friedman, Norman et al. *USS Arizona (BB39).* Annapolis, Md.: Leeward Publications, 1978.
520. Gallo, Patrick J. *Swords and Plowshares: The United States and Disarmament, 1898-1979.* Manhattan, Kans.: Military Affairs / Aerospace Historian Publishing, 1981.
521. Beggard, Louis A. *Evolution of Naval Radio-Electronics and Contributions of the Naval Research Laboratory.* Washington, D.C.: Naval Research Laboratory, 1979.
522. Gibbs, Norman. "Naval Conferences of the Interwar Years: A Study of Anglo-American Relations." *Naval War College Review* 30 (Summer 1977): 50-63.
523. Goldberg, Joyce S. "The *Baltimore* Affair: United States Relations with Chile, 1891-1892." Ph.D. diss. Indiana University, 1981.
524. Gottschall, Terrell D. "Germany and the Spanish-American War: A Case Study of Navalism and Imperialism, 1898." Ph.D. diss., Washington State University, 1981."
525. Gould, Lewis. *The Presidency of William McKinley.* Lawrence: Regents Press of Kansas, 1980.
526. _____. *The Spanish-American War and William McKinley.* Lawrence: University Press of Kansas, 1982.
527. *Guide to Microforms in Print.* 4 vols. Westport, Conn.: Meckler Publishing,

1983.
528. Haggie, Paul. *Britannia at Bay: The Defense of the British Empire, 1931–1941.* New York: Oxford University Press, 1981.
529. Harrod, Frederick S. "Integration of the Navy." *U.S. Naval Institute Proceedings* 105 (October 1979): 40–47.
530. _____. "Jim Crow and the Navy." *U.S. Naval Institute Proceedings* 105 (September 1979): 46–53.
531. Hearings of the General Board of the U.S. Navy, 1917–1950. 16 rolls of microfilm. Wilmington, Del.: Scholarly Resources, 1982.
532. Heimdahl, William, and Geraldine Phillips. "The Navy and Investigating the Pearl Harbor Attack: A Consideration of New Source Material." In *Changing Interpretations and New Sources in Naval History,* edited by Robert W. Love, Jr., 400–412. New York Garland, 1980.
533. Herde, Peter. *Pearl Harbor 7. Dezember 1941.* Darmstadt: Wissenchaftliche Buchgesellschaft, 1980.
534. Hodges, Peter. *The Big Gun: Battleship Main Armament, 1860–1945.* Annapolis, Md.: Naval Institute Press, 1981.
535. Hodges, Peter, and Norman Friedman. *Destroyer Weapons in World War 2.* Annapolis, Md.: Naval Institute Press, 1979.
536. Holbrook, Heber A. *U.S.S. Houston: The Last Flagship of the Asiatic Fleet.* Dixon, Calif: Pacific Ship and Shore, 1981.
537. Holmes, Wilfred J. *Double-Edged Secrets: U.S. Naval Intelligence Operations in the Pacific during World War II.* Annapolis, Md.: Naval Institute Press, 1979.
538. Hone, Thomas C. "The Effectiveness of the 'Washington Treaty' Navy." *Naval War College Review* 32 (November–December 1979): 35–59.
539. _____. "Spending Patterns of the United States Navy, 1921–1941." *Armed Forces and Society* (Spring 1982), 443–62.
540. Hone, Thomas C., and Mark David Mandeles, "Managerial Style in the Interwar Navy: A Reappraisal." *Naval War College Review* 33 (September 1980): 88–101.
541. Hourihan, William J. "The Best Ambassador: Rear Admiral Cotton and the Cruise of the European Squadron, 1903." *Naval War College Review* 32 (June–July 1979): 63–72.
542. _____. "The Big Stick in Turkey: American Diplomacy and Naval Operations against the Ottoman Empire, 1903–1904." *Naval War College Review* 34 (September–October 1981): 93–109.
543. _____. "The Fleet That Never Was: Commodore John Crittenden Watson and the Eastern Squadron." *American Neptune* 41 (April 1981): 93–109.
544. _____. "Marlinspike Diplomacy: The Navy in the Mediterranean, 1904." *U.S. Naval Institute Proceedings* 105 (January 1979): 42–51.
545. Hoyt, Edwin P. *Submarines at War: The History of the Silent Service.* New York Stein & Day, 1983.
546. "Intercepted Japanese Messages: The Documents of Magic." [1938–1942]. Wilmington, Del: Michael Glazier, [1979?] [microfilm].
547. Johnson, Brian. *Fly Navy: The History of Naval Aviation.* New York: William Morrow, 1981.
548. Jones, Lloyd S. *U.S. Naval Fighters.* Fallbrook, Calif.: Aero Publishers, 1977.

549. Kennedy, Paul M., ed. *The War Plans of the Great Powers, 1880-1914.* London: Allen & Unwin, 1979.

550. Knott, Richard C. *The American Flying-Boat.* Annapolis, Md.: Naval Institute Press, 1979.

551. Lemmon, Sue, and E. D. Wichols. *Sidewheelers to Nuclear Power: A Pictorial Essay Covering 123 Years of the Mare Island Shipyard.* Annapolis, Md.: Leeward Publications, 1977.

552. Leutze, James R. *A Different Kind of Victory: A Biography of Admiral Thomas C. Hart.* Annapolis, Md.: Naval Institute Press, 1981.

553. Lewin, Ronald *The American Magic: Codes, Ciphers and the Defeat of Japan.* New York: Farrar, Straus & Giroux, 1982.

554. Livezey, William E. *Mahan on Sea Power.* Norman: University of Oklahoma Press, 1982.

555. Love, Robert W., Jr, ed. *The Chiefs of Naval Operations.* Annapolis, Md.: Naval Institute Press, 1980.

556. Lowenthal, Mark M. "The Stark Memorandum and the American Security Process, 1940." In *Changing Interpretations and New Sources in Naval History,* edited by Robert W. Love, Jr., 352-61. New York: Garland, 1980.

557. McCollum, Kenneth G., ed. *Dahlgren.* Dahlgren, Va.: Naval Surface Weapons Center, 1977.

558. McMahon, William E. *Dreadnought Battleships and Battle Cruisers.* Washington, D.C.: University Press of America, 1978.

559. "The Magic Documents: Summaries and Transcripts of Top Secret Diplomatic Communications of Japan, 1938-1945." 14 rolls of microfilm. Washington, D.C.: University Publications of America, 1979.

560. Maguire, Doris D., ed. *French Ensor Chadwick: Selected Letters and Papers.* Washington, D.C.: University Press of America, 1981.

561. Mannix, Daniel P., 3d. *The Old Navy: Rear Admiral Daniel P. Mannix 3d.* Annapolis, Md.: Naval Institute Press, 1983.

562. Marder, Arthur J. *Old Friends, New Enemies: The Royal and the Imperial Japanese Navy.* New York: Oxford University Press, 1981.

563. Mason, Theodore. *Battleship Sailor.* Annapolis, Md.: Naval Institute Press, 1982.

564. Maurer, John H. "Fuel and the Battle Fleet: Coal, Oil, and American Naval Strategy, 1898-1925." *Naval War College Review* 34 (November–December 1981): 60-77.

565. Melosi, Martin V. *The Shadow of Pearl Harbor.* College Station: Texas A & M University Press, 1977.

566. _____. "The Triumph of Revisionisms: The Pearl Harbor Controversy, 1941-1982." *The Public Historian* 5 (Spring 1983): 87-91.

567. Messimer, Dwight R. *No Margin for Error: The U.S. Navy's Trans-Pacific Flight of 1925.* Annapolis, Md.: Naval Institute Press, 1981.

568. *The Micropublishers' Trade List Annual.* Westport, Conn.: Meckler Publishing.

569. Millett, Allan R. *Semper Fidelis: The History of the United States Marine Corps.* New York: Macmillan, 1980.

570. Muir, Malcom, Jr. "American Warship Construction for Stalin's Navy prior to World War II: A Study in Paralysis Policy." *Diplomatic History* 5 (Fall 1981): 337-51.

571. Newton, Wesley P. *The Perilous Sky: U.S. Aviation Diplomacy in Latin America, 1919–1931.* Coral Gables, Fla.: University of Miami Press, 1978.

572. Nicolosi, Anthony S. *A Guide to Research Source Materials in the Naval War College Historical Collections.* Newport, R.I.: Naval War College Press 1981.

573. Nimitz, Comdr. Chester W. "Naval Tactics." *Naval War College Review* 35 (November–December 1982): 8–13.

574. O'Connor, Raymond G. *War, Diplomacy, and History: Papers and Reviews.* Washington, D.C.: University Press of America, 1979.

575. Olsen, Frederick H. "The Navy and the White Man's Burden: Naval Administration in Samoa." Ph.D. diss., Washington University at St. Louis, 1976.

576. Paulson, George E. "*Petrel* Shows the Flag." *American Neptune* 40 (April 1980): 100–107.

577. Pearce, George F. *The United States Navy at Pensacola, from Sailing Ships to Naval Aviation, 1825–1930.* Pensacola: A University of West Florida Book / University Presses of Florida, 1980.

578. Pollock, Fred E. "Roosevelt, the Ogdensberg Agreement, and the British Fleet: All Done with Mirrors." *Diplomatic History* 5 (Summer 1981): 203–19.

579. Polmar, Norman. *The American Submarine.* Annapolis, Md.: Nautical & Aviation Publishing Company, 1981.

580. Polmar, Norman, and Thomas B. Allen. *Rickover.* New York: Simon & Schuster, 1982.

581. Potter, E. B., ed. *Sea Power: A Naval History.* Annapolis, Md.: Naval Institute Press, 1981.

582. Prange, Gordon. *At Dawn We Slept: The Untold Story of Pearl Harbor.* New York: McGraw-Hill, 1981.

583. Quinby, Edwin J. "Uncle Jack's *Vesuvius*: The Dynamite Gunboat of the Spanish-American War." *Shipmate* 44 (July–August 1981): 22–24.

584. Reilly, John C., Jr. *United States Destroyers of World War II.* Poole, England: Blandford Press, 1983.

585. _____. "U.S. Naval Intelligence and the Ordnance Revolution, 1900–1930." In *Changing Interpretations and New Sources in Naval History,* editd by Robert W. Love, Jr., 325–39. New York: Garland, 1980.

586. Reilly, John C., Jr., and Robert L. Scheina. *American Battleships, 1886–1923.* Annapolis, Md.: Naval Institute Press, 1980.

587. Reynolds, Bradley M. "Guantanamo Bay, Cuba: The History of an American Naval Base and Its Relation to the Formulation of United States Foreign Policy and Military Strategy toward the Caribbean, 1895–1910." Ph.D. diss. University of Southern California, 1982.

588. Reynolds, Charles, V., Jr. "America and a Two-Ocean Navy, 1933–1941." Ph.D. diss., Boston University, 1978.

589. Reynolds, Clark G. *Famous American Admirals.* New York: Van Nostrand, 1978.

590. Robinson, Douglas H., and Charles H. Keller. *"Up Ship!" U.S. Navy Rigid Airships, 1919–1935.* Annapolis, Md.: Naval Institute Press, 1982.

591. Ryan, Paul B., ed. "A Yankee Bride in the Old Navy: Catherine Freeman Nimitz Looks Back to the Days before World War I." *American Neptune*

38 (January 1978): 5–14.

592. Shiner, John F. "The Air Corps, the Navy, and Coast Defense, 1919–1941." *Military Affairs* 45 (October 1981): 113–20.

593. Smith, Vice Admiral Allen E. "The Sixth Battle Squadron: A Reminiscence." *American Neptune* 40 (January 1980): 50–62.

594. Smith, Myron J. *Keystone Battlewagon: USS Pennsylvania.* Charleston, W.Va.: Pictorial Histories Publishing Company, 1983.

595. Smith, Myron J. *The Mountain State Battleship: USS* West Virginia. Richwood: West Virginia Press Club, 1981.

596. Still, William N., Jr. *American Sea Power in the Old World: The United State Navy in European and Near Eastern Waters, 1865–1917.* Westport, Conn.: Greenwood Press, 1980.

597. Stilwell, Paul. *Air Raid: Pearl Harbor: Recollections of a Day of Infamy.* Annapolis, Md.: Naval Institute Press, 1982.

598. "Strategic Planning in the U.S. Navy: Its Evolution and Execution, 1891–1945." 16 rolls of microfilm. Wilmington, Del.: Scholarly Resources, 1977.

599. Sweetman, Jack. *The U.S. Naval Academy: An Illustrated History.* Annapolis, Md.: Naval Institute Press, 1979.

600. Tate, Rear Admiral Jackson. "We Rode the Covered Wagon." *U.S. Naval Institute Proceedings* 104 (October 1978): 62–69.

601. Toland, John. *Infamy: Pearl Harbor and Its Aftermath.* New York: Doubleday, 1982.

602. Trask, David F. *The War with Spain in 1898.* New York: Macmillan, 1981.

603. Trefousse, Hans L. *Pearl Harbor: The Continuing Controversy.* Maliban, Fla.: Robert E. Krieger Publishing Company, 1982.

604. Trimble, William F. "Admiral Hilary P. Jones and the 1927 Naval Conference." *Military Affairs* 43 (February 1979): 1–4.

605. Tsunoda, Jun and Admiral Uchida Kazutomi. "The Pearl Harbor Attack: Admiral Yamamoto's Fundamental Concept with Reference to Paul S. Dull's *A Battle History of the Imperial Japanese Navy (1941–1945)."* *Naval War College Review* 31 (Fall 1978): 83–88.

606. U.S. Department of Defense. *The "Magic" Background of Pearl Harbor.* 8 vols. Washington, D.C.: GPO, 1978.

607. U.S. Deputy Chief of Naval Operations (Air Warfare) and the Commander, Naval Air Systems Command. *United States Naval Aviation, 1910–1980.* Washington, D.C. GPO 1981.

608. U.S. Naval Historical Center. *Dictionary of American Naval Fighting Ships.* 8 vols. Washington, D.C.: GPO, 1959–1981.

609. U.S. Naval History Division. *U.S. Naval History Sources in the United States.* Washington, D.C.: GPO, 1979.

610. Van Der Rhoer, Edward. *Deadly Magic: A Personal Account of Communication Intelligence in World War II in the Pacific.* New York: Charles Scribner's Sons, 1978.

611. Van Duers, George. "Navy Wings between the Wars: A Narrative." Microfilm. Copyright 1981. On deposit at the Navy Department Library, Washington, D.C.

612. Vivian, James F. "United States Policy during the Brazilian Naval Revolt, 1893–1894: The Case for American Neutrality." *American Neptune* 41

(October 1981): 245–61.
613. Vlahos, Michael. *The Blue Sword: The Naval War College and the American Mission, 1919–1941*. Newport, R.I.: Naval War College Press, 1980.
614. Vlahos, Michael. "The Naval War College and the Origins of War Planning against Japan." *Naval War College Review* 33 (July–August 1980): 23–41.
615. Walter, John C. "Congressman Carl Vinson and Franklin D. Roosevelt: Naval Preparedness and the Coming of World War II, 1939–1940." *Georgia Historical Quarterly* 615 (Fall 1980): 294–305."
616. *Warship*. 6 vols. to 1982. Annapolis, Md.: Naval Institute Press, 1977–.
617. West, Michael A. "Laying the Legislative Foundation: The House Naval Affairs Committee and the Construction of the Treaty Navy, 1926–1934." Ph.D. diss. Ohio State University, 1980.
618. Willmott, H. P. *Empires in the Balance: Japanese and Allied Pacific Strategy to April 1942*. Annapolis, Md.: Naval Institute Press, 1982.
619. Yerxa, Donald Allan. "The United States Navy in the Caribbean Sea, 1914–1941." Ph.D. diss. University of Maine, 1982.
620. *Warship International*. 1964(?)–.

XIV

THE UNITED STATES ARMY IN WORLD WAR II

Robert W. Coakley

The U.S. Army in World War II has again attracted its share of attention during the past five years, perhaps somewhat more than during the previous five, as the Vietnam War has passed from center stage. The last six of the eighty volumes scheduled in the U.S. Army in World War II Series, however, have not appeared. And there have been no major additions to the bibliographies or the guides to the manuscript sources in the various repositories cited in the original guide and the last supplement. Major works have been concentrated in four main areas — the Pearl Harbor attack; the strategy and conduct of the war in Europe; biographies of both major and minor figures; and the intelligence aspects of the war, particularly the impact of ULTRA and MAGIC.

REFERENCE WORKS. James L. Stokesbury's *Short History of World War II* (348) and Robert Goralski's *World War II Almanac* (326) are useful references for the framework within which the Army operated. George Forty's edition of *U.S. Army Handbooks, 1939–1945* (324) is similarly useful for detail. At this point it is also worth noting that selected records of the Joint Chiefs of Staff during World War II are available from University Publications of America (351).

THE PEARL HARBOR ATTACK AND THE WAR IN THE PACIFIC. Gordon Prange's detailed and precise examination of the Pearl Harbor attack from both American and Japanese vantage points, *At Dawn We Slept* (345), has finally been published posthumously. Prange adds much detail to existing knowledge of the affair but does not challenge the exisiting consensus that it was blunders, not conspiracy, that produced the American debacle in Hawaii. John Toland (350), on the other hand, has revived the old charges of conspiracy against Roosevelt and the American high command. He is supported, from a somewhat different angle, by the British author John Costello in the opening chapters of his *Pacific War* (312). Neither has won much acceptance in the scholarly community, where Prange's work is regarded as a more nearly blanced treatment. Costello's volume is better as a general history of the Pacific war. Other works on the opening phases of the Pacific war, more specialized in nature, include Eric Morris's *Corregidor* (339), a sort of episodic oral history of the whole Philippine campaign, and Mallonée's diary of events on Bataan (337).

BIOGRAPHY AND MEMOIRS. Stephen Ambrose has completed his one-volume biography of Eisenhower (302) covering both the war and the presidential years. Clay Blair, Jr., working with interviews and the papers, of Omar N. Bradley, has put together what is said to be an "autobiography" of the general (307). The controversial Britisher David Irving has stressed the sensational in dealing with *The War between the Generals* (332), British and American, during the European campaign. Farago has supplemented his earlier biography with a piece on Patton's last days (320). Leonard Mosely has provided a popular and laudatory biography of George C. Marshall (340). Petillo's *MacArthur: The Philippine Years* (341a) is less an account of the general's military achievements than an effort at a psychological portrait. Two lesser figures in the European war, P. Wood and Troy Middleton, are treated by Hanson Baldwin (304) and Frank Price (346), respectively. The wife of the noted military commentator and historian S.L.A. Marshall has arranged his memoirs for publication in *Bringing up the Rear* (338).

OPERATIONS IN THE WAR AGAINST GERMANY. The most significiant work in this area is certainly Weigley's *Eisenhower's Lieutenants* (354), a critical account of the conduct of the campaign in northwest Europe by the American generals. Also critical at a different level are works by Walter S. Dunn, in the United States (315), and John Grigg, in England (327), arguing in some detail that the Allied invasion of Europe could have been successfully executed in 1943. David Reynolds (347) and John Eisenhower (318) treat respectively of the creation of the Anglo-American alliance and its stresses and strains in the European war. John Keegan, of *Face of Battle* fame, provides an interesting comparative analysis of the various Allied armies who participated in the Normandy campaign and the drive to the Seine (334). Allen Wilt, in an account of the campaign in southern France (355), fills in part a void that still exists in the U.S. Army in World War II Series. Forty (323) and Phillips (344) have published valuable combat history of specific organizations, the former of Patton's Third Army and the latter of the 28th Infantry Division. Works on operations in the Mediterranean theater have been more narrative than critical. They include Yarborough on the first combat parachute mission in North Africa (356), Vernay on Anzio (353), Trevelyan on the battle for Rome (349), Pielkalkicwicz on Cassino (343), and Forty, again, on the Fifth U.S. Army (322). Col. William O. Darby and William Baumer have collaborated to produce an interesting account of one of the more heroic units of the war, Darby's Rangers (314).

INTELLIGENCE. The exploitation of materials released on the ULTRA secret has not yet proceeded to the point where either the remarkable achievement at Bletchley Park or the role of intelligence generally in determing the course of World War II can be completely assayed. Some experts at the international conference in 1979 on ULTRA, described by David Kahn in an article in *Military Affairs* (333), reached the conclusion that "no quantification was possible because the value of ULTRA varied, depending on the time and place in which it was used." Alexander Cochran, surveying developments three years later, has a roughly similar conclusion (311), and argues that even in evaluating particular battles and campaigns, the assessment has not proceeded far. The most positive contributions to greater understanding in the last five years have been Hinsley's second volume in the official British history of intelligence in World War II (330), and Ralph Bennett's *ULTRA in the West* (306), an effort to assess ULTRA's value in the campaign in northwest Europe. Bennett summarized some of his conclusions in an essay in a collection edited by Walter Laqueur (335). Garlinski (325) and Calvocoressi (308) have also produced individual insights. Treatment of other sources of intelligence in the European war is to be found in Ambrose's book on Eisenhower's use of spies (301), and Cruikshank's summary of the use of deception (313). Turning to intelligence in the war in the Pacific, Ronald Lewin's account of the role of the MAGIC interceptions in the defeat of Japan (336) is a counterpart to his earlier work on ULTRA in the European war (274). In the course of the work, Lewin advances effective arguments against the conspiracy theories of Toland (350) and Costello (312). Clark, in a biography of William Friedman, the man who broke PURPLE (309), and Cochran, in a finding aid for the MAGIC summaries (310), provide additional material on the breaking of the Japanese code. Holmes's account of naval intelligence operations in the Pacific (331) also has its value for the student of army intelligence operations.

THE AMERICAN SOLDIER. A concomitant to the revisionism with regard to strategy and tactics in the European War (315, 327, 354) has been the appearance of literature questioning the comparative fighting ability of the American soldier vis-á-vis his German opponent. Trevor Dupuy, in a series of studies (316, 317), has used computer analysis ostensibly to demonstrate a measure of American inferiority. Martin van Creveld in a comparative study of fighting power (352), also heavily mathematical, reached similar conclusions. John Ellis is less analytical or critical in a study of fighting men of all nations in World War II (319). Marc Hillel, writing on the life and morals of GIs in Europe in a book available only in French, is quite iconoclastic, painting a lurid picture of soldier behavior in cities and towns behind the lines both in England and on the Continent (329). Mary Motley's *Invisible Soldiers* (341) contains personal narratives of black soldiers, confirming the poor treatment of blacks that Hillel also emphasizes.

SPECIAL TOPICS. Pielkalkicwicz (342) and Hickey (328) have contributed general histories of cavalry and airborne troops, respectively. And Charles M. Baily, in *With Faint Praise* (303), has written a detailed analysis of research and development, procurement, and deployment of tanks and tank destroyers in World War II, concluding that the failure to match the German Panzers on the battlefield was the result of built-in delays in the development and deployment process, not of General MacNair's failure to appreciate the need for a better tank. Ralph B. Baldwin one of scientists involved, has contributed a similar study on the development of the VT proximity fuze and its use in combat (305), one of the major technology breakthroughs of the war.

SUGGESTIONS FOR FURTHER RESEARCH. Certainly the area of intelligence deserves further study despite the efforts of the last ten years. And there is also room for many more studies of the development and deployment of specific weapons systems and individual weapons such as those of Baily (303) and Baldwin (305) cited above. Indeed, the whole area of logistics has been relatively neglected in the last ten years in favor of more glamorous topics such as battle history, generalship, and intelligence. There should be some careful analysis of the "logistical pusillanimity" that van Creveld charged the Allied planners with in the European campaign (294), a charge that Weigley echoes (354). Similarly, on the personnel side, there is still room for many studies of the American soldier to confirm, deny, or modify the contentions of Dupuy (316, 317), van Creveld (352), and Hillel (329). Weigley has also raised many questions about the doctrine and training of the U.S. Army in the Second World War that should encourage further investigation.

BIBLIOGRAPHY

301. Ambrose, Stephen E. *Ike's Spies: Eisenhower and the Espionage Establishment.* New York: Doubleday, 1981.
302. _____. *Eisenhower: Soldier, General of the Army, President Elect.* New York: Simon & Schuster, 1983.
303. Baily, Charles M. *Faint Praise: American Tanks and Tank Destroyers during World War II.* Hamden, Conn.: Archon Books, 1983.
304. Baldwin, Hanson W. *Tiger Jack.* Fort Collins, Colo: Old Army Press, 1980.
305. Baldwin, Ralph B. *The Deadly Fuze: Secret Weapon of World War II.* San Rafael, Calif: Presidio Press, 1980.
306. Bennett, Ralph. *ULTRA in the West: The Normandy Campaign of 1944–45.* New York: Charles Scribner's Sons, 1979.
307. Bradley, Gen. Omar N., and Clay Blair, Jr. *A General's Life: An Autobiography.* New York: Simon & Schuster, 1983.
308. Calvocoressi, Peter. *Top Secret ULTRA.* London: Cassell, 1980.
309. Clark, Ronald. *The Man Who Broke Purple.* Boston: Little, Brown, 1977.
310. Cochran, Alexander S., Jr. *The MAGIC Summaries. A Chronological Finding Aid.* New York: Garland, 1982.
311. _____. "'Magic,' 'Ultra,' and the Second World War: Literature, Sources, and Outlook." *Military Affairs* 46 (April 1982): 88–92.
312. Costello, John. *The Pacific War.* New York: Rawson, Wade, 1981.
313. Cruikshank, Charles. *Deception in World War II.* New York: Oxford University Press, 1980.
314. Darby, William O., and William H. Baumer. *Darby's Rangers: We Led the Way.* San Rafael, Calif.: Presidio Press, 1980.
315. Dunn, Walter Scott. *Second Front Now, 1943.* University: University of Alabama Press, 1980.
316. Dupuy, Trevor N. *Nurnberg, Prediction, and War.* Indianapolis, Ind.: Bobbs-Merrill, 1979.
317. _____. *A Genius for War: The German Army and General Staff, 1807–1945.* Englewood Cliffs: N.J.: Prentice-Hall, 1977.
318. Eisenhower, John S. D. *Allies: Pearl Harbor to D-Day.* New York: Doubleday, 1982.
319. Ellis, John. *The Sharp End: The Fighting Man in World War II.* New York: Charles Scribner's Sons, 1982.
320. Farago, Lladislas. *The Last Days of Patton.* New York: McGraw-Hill, 1981.
321. Foot, M.R., and J. M. Langley. *MI Nine: Escape and Evasion, 1939–1945.* Boston, Little, Brown, 1980.

322. Forty, George. *The Fifth Army at War*. New York: Charles Scribner's Sons, 1980.

323. _____. *Patton's Third Army at War*. New York: Charles Scribner's Sons, 1979.

324. _____. *U.S. Army Handbooks, 1939–1945*. New York: Charles Scribner's Sons, 1980.

325. Garlinski, Joseph. *The Engima War: The Inside Story of the German Enigma Codes and How the Allies Broke Them*. New York: Charles Scribner's Sons, 1979.

326. Goralski, Robert. *World War II Almanac, 1931–1945: A Political and Military Record*. New York: Putnam, 1981.

327. Grigg, John. *Nineteen Forty-Three: The Victory that Never Was*. New York: Hill and Wang, 1980.

328. Hickey, Michael. *Out of the Sky: A History of Airborne Warfare*. New York: Charles Scribner's Sons, 1980.

329. Hillel, Marc. *Vie et Moeurs des G.I.'s en Europe, 1942–1947*. France: Ballard, 1981.

330. Hinsley, F. H., with E. E. Thomas, C. F. G. Ranson, and R. C. Knight. *British Intelligence in the Second World War*. Vol. 2. New York: Cambridge University Press, 1981.

331. Holmes, Willard J. *Double-Edged Secrets: U.S. Naval Intelligence Operations in the Pacific during World War II*. Annapolis, Md.: Naval Institute Press, 1979.

332. Irving, David. *The War between the Generals*. New York: Congdon & Lattés, 1981.

333. Kahn, David. "The International Conference on ULTRA." *Military Affairs* 43 (April 1979): 97–98.

334. Keegan, John. *Six Armies in Normandy: From D-Day to the Liberation of Paris, June 6th–August 25th, 1944*. New York: Viking Press, 1982.

335. Laqueur, Walter, ed. *The Second World War: Essays in Military and Political History*. London: Sage, 1982.

336. Lewin, Ronald. *The American MAGIC: Codes, Ciphers, and the Defeat of Japan*. New York: Viking Press, 1982.

337. Mallonée, Richard C., II. ed. *The Naked Flagpole: Battle for Bataan; from the Diary of Richard C. Mallonée*. San Rafael, Calif.: Presidio Press, 1980.

338. Marshall, S.L.A. *Bringing up the Rear, A Memoir*. Edited by Cate Marshall. San Rafael, Calif.: Presidio Press, 1980.

339. Morris, Eric. *Corregidor: The End of the Line*. New York: Stein & Day, 1982.

340. Mosely, Leonard. *Marshall: Hero for Our Time*. New York: Hearst Books, 1982.

341. Motley, Mary Parish. *The Invisible Soldiers: The Experience of the Black Soldier, World War II*. Detroit, Mich.: Wayne State Univeristy Press, 1975.

341a. Petillo, Carol M. *Douglas MacArthur: The Philippine Years*. Bloomington: Indiana University Press, 1981.

342. Pielkalkicwicz, Janusz. *The Cavàlry of World War II*. New York: Stein & Day, 1980.

343. _____. *The Battle for Cassino*. Indianapolis, Ind.: Bobbs-Merrill, 1980.

344. Phillips, Robert F. *To Save Bastogne*. New York: Stein & Day, 1983.

345. Prange, Gordon W. *At Dawn We Slept: The Untold Story of Pearl Harbor*. New York: McGraw-Hill, 1981.
346. Price, Frank James. *Troy H. Middleton: A Biography*. Baton Rouge: Louisiana State University Press, 1974.
347. Reynolds, David. *The Creation of the Anglo-American Alliance, 1937-1941*. Chapel Hill: University of North Carolina Press, 1982.
348. Stokesbury, James L. *A Short History of World War II*. New York: William Morrow, 1981.
349. Trevelyan, Raleigh. *Rome '44: The Battle for the Eternal City*. New York: Viking Press, 1982.
350. Toland, John. *Infamy: Pearl Harbor and its Aftermath*. New York: Doubleday, 1982.
351. United States Joint Chiefs of Staff. *Records of the Joint Chiefs of Staff*. Part I, *1942-45*. Available on microfilm from University Publications of America, Inc., 44 No. Market St., Frederick, Md. 21701.
352. van Creveld, Martin. *Fighting Power: German and U.S. Army Performances, 1939-1945*. Westport, Conn.: Greenwood Press, 1982.
353. Vernay, Peter. *Anzio, 1944: An Unexpected Fury*. North Pomfret, Vt.: Batsford, 1980.
354. Weigley, Russell F. *Eisenhower's Lieutenants: The Campaign in France and Germany, 1944-1945*. Bloomington: Indiana University Press, 1981.
355. Wilt, Alan F. *The French Riviera Campaign of August 1944*. Carbondale: Southern Illinois University Press, 1981.
356. Yarborough, William Pelham. *Bail Out over North Africa; America's First Combat Parachute Missions, 1942*. Williamsport, N.J.: Phillips Publications, 1981.

XV

THE U.S. ARMY AIR CORPS

AND

THE UNITED STATES AIR FORCE, 1909–1983

Robert T. Finney

The history of the United States Air Force and its predecessors – Air Service, Air Corps, and Army Air Forces – continues to appear piecemeal. There is no lack of interest in air force history. Articles, monographs, serious history and not-so-serious history flow out copiously. With few exceptions, however, publications cover limited aspects of air force affairs: specific operations, particular types of missions or operations, individual aircraft descriptions and operations, memoirs of the pilots who flew the aircraft, and unit histories dominate the field. The larger task of presenting a comprehensive, analytical history of the air force remains to be undertaken. Recent official historical studies deal primarily with the Southeast Asia conflict. Popular accounts continue to focus on the army air forces' operations and aircraft of World War II. It appears that an increasing number of air force veterans have determined that their individual experiences during the war are worth a permanent record. These memoirs of individual exploits or unit histories by participants do, indeed, provide the professional military historian with a body of sources in researching the realities of aerial warfare and, on occasion, with a point of view on the success or failure of the air war not found in official records. They will aid the professional military historian in the preparation of scholarly appraisals and analyses of causes and effects, results, lessons learned, and philosophies of the employment of air power.

OFFICIAL HISTORIES AND GOVERNMENT DOCUMENTS. The major efforts of the Office of Air Force History recently have turned toward supplementing Berger's *The United States Air Force in Southeast Asia, 1961–1973* (319) with a series of studies dealing with specific aspects of the U.S. Air Force involvement in that conflict. Something of an introduction to the USAF's participation is Futrell and Blumenson's *The United States Air Force in Southeast Asia: The Advisory Years to 1965* (418). The study in its published version is, in essence, a summarization of aspects of air force involvement in Indochina from 1945 to February 1965; it suffers from probably over-cautious and over-zealous security editing. Other volumes deal with more specific operational details. These include Ballard's detailed coverage of the evolution of fixed-wing gunship operations (388);

Buckingham's comprehensive investigation of the air force's evolving doctrine, policy, equipment, and operations relating to the spraying of herbicides in the conflict (398); and Tilford's story of air force efforts to recover aircrews downed in combat (467). Especially noteworthy in this series is Bowers's treatment of tactical airlift aviation from the early years of United States involvement to the withdrawal of the U.S. Air Force from Vietnam (394). A highly technical and often overlooked aspect of the Southeast Asia war is the subject of Hopkin's study of tanker operations (428).

Two publications, one of them particularly fascinating, reflect personal reminiscences of World War II. The first is Gaston's intimate look at the men and work involved in producing AWPD-1 (419); although it adds little to older versions, it presents a personal insight into the planning process and evaluation of the personalities involved. Of greater interest and value to future historians is Kohn and Harahan's interview with four distinguished and experienced air leaders who flew, fought, and commanded tactical air forces in combat (433); although their discussion focuses on air superiority, their comments become far-ranging, inevitably touching on a number of related topics—aircraft development and the early lack of appreciation for the necessity for air superiority, for example. The volume is made especially useful as a result of the editors' careful annotation, designed to keep the interviews in proper perspective. *Air Superiority* is a volume in a projected series designated Project Warrior that calls for the "continuing study of military history combat leadership, the principles of war, and particularly, the application of air power"; at the same time it is a part of an oral history series.

Oral history is becoming increasingly popular as a means of preserving a vast array of invaluable information. The Air Force Oral History Program is proving to be a valuable vehicle for obtaining personal historical data from a broad cross-section of air force personalities who do not have the time, talent, or inclination to write. An indispensable tool for military historians, then, is the United States Air Force Historical Research Center (a redesignation of the Albert F. Simpson Historical Research Center) *Oral History Catalog* (469), which lists all oral history interviews in the center's collection; its subject index gives it an added advantage.

Kohn and Harahan's *Air Superiority* volume (433) also touches briefly on air force operations in Korea. Of more importance, of course, for a detailed and comprehensive look at the Korean War is Futrell's *The United States Air Force in Korea, 1950–1953* (417). Published originally in 1961 by Duell and reprinted in 1971 by Arno, the volume was reissued in 1983 by the Office of Air Force History as a revised edition, although the revision amounts to little more than the addition of a fresh preface and an occasional change in a statistical figure and reidentification in an illustration caption.

Other studies are under way. Futrell's important doctrinal history (333) is being updated through 1983; present plans call for the update to appear in two volumes. Another work scheduled for early publication is John F. Shiner's investigation of the air corps and Foulois in the mid-1930s (460). Shiner presents the view, among others, that the army general staff took a more enlightened approach to air power in the mid-thirties than military historians have been prone to give it.

Military historians will want to keep advised of studies being prepared by the components of Air University's Center for Aerospace Doctrine, Research and Education (CADRE). Created in January 1983, CADRE is designed to develop doctrine, concepts, and strategy relating to air power, present and future. To this end, it is in the process of publishing a number of important studies dealing with various aspects of air force affairs. Its contributions so far are exemplified by Murray (444) on the defeat of the *Luftwaffe*; Seiler (459) on strategic nuclear force requirements; and Orr (466) on command, control, communications, and intelligence. Studies under way include the impact of air power on the ground war in Vietnam, space doctrine, and foundations of American air doctrine (in which the author selects certain aspects of air doctrine and applies a set of rather stringent criteria against them in an effort to determine their validity, thus differing from Futrell's chronological history of air doctrine). The results of CADRE research and writing are edited, produced, and published by the Air University Press, a directorate within CADRE. Air University Press also publishes twice yearly (on 1 January and 1 July) a *Research Abstract*, which gives concise and accurate descriptions of each CADRE book and report currently available. For convenience, release information is entered for each entry: "Public release" indicates the book or report is cleared for release to the general public; "FOUO" indicates the publication is "For Official Use Only" by U.S. government organizations. Copies of the *Abstract* can be obtained through the Air University Press, CADRE, Maxwell Air Base, Alabama 36112. Each issue of the *Abstract* explains the procedures for obtaining CADRE publications.

A primary source for the serious student of military history is found in the hearings and reports of Congressional committees, especially the House and Senate committees on appropriations and on the armed services. For the period 1970–1982 a ready source for relevant government documents is the Congressional Information Service, CIS / Annual (325). For more current information, the CIS monthly Index and Abstract are available. CIS also publishes a comprehensive guide and index to the statistical publications of the United States Government in two volumes, under the titles *American Statistics Index* and *American Statistics Index Abstracts*. The best guide to earlier Government publications remains the *Monthly Catalogue for United States Government Publications* (285).

The United States Air Force Historical Research Center has produced a number of publications that might be classed as ready references. Two are by Ravenstein (449, 450); *Organization of the Air Force* traces the evolution of early organizations into the present USAF field structure (a revised edition is scheduled for inclusion in the Warrior series); *A Guide to Air Force Lineage and Honors* explains the terms used and methods employed in establishing the lineage and honors of air force units. Mueller's study gives a detailed account of a hundred USAF bases located throughout the United States (443); this soft-covered first volume is to be followed by a more detailed hardcover edition from the Office of Air Force History. A second volume treating overseas bases is projected. Ravenstein's treatment of combat wings (453), scheduled for early publication, follows in general the pattern of Maurer's volumes on combat units and combat wings (189, 190), both of which have been reprinted by the Office of Air Force History.

GENERAL HISTORIES. A single, scholarly, definitive history of the United States Air Force has yet to appear. There are, however, a number of works which present the history of specific aspects of the air force's evolution. By all odds, the most significant recent contribution to the growing body of special studies are Copp's two volumes (404, 405). They together form something of a biography of "a few great captains" (notably Arnold, Andrews, Eaker, Spaatz, and others) and a history of the air arm from the beginning of American air power through the testing and application of air power theories in the European theater of World War II. Borowski (393) presents, essentially, a history of the impact of atomic weapons on the postwar air force. Bell (389) offers an unusual and interesting aspect of air force history in explaining the importance of, and the methods used in selecting, colors for air force units.

A number of general works add to an understanding of and help place in proper perspective U.S. Air Force history. Nevin and the editors of Time-Life Books (445) present an excellent overview of military aviation from World War I to just before World War II, giving short biographies of major personalities, including General Mitchell. Kennett's *History of Strategic Bombing* (432) should be consulted in evaluating and understanding U.S. Air Force history.

EARLY DAYS AND WORLD WAR I. Despite such aids and guides to scholarly research as Maurer's four volumes (362), Smith's *Bibliography* (382), and the National Archives guide (369), scholars have shied away from the beginning of the air force and the air experience of World War I as proper subjects for investigation. One valuable addition to the history of the period, made available to the public, is Flammer's scholarly account of the Lafayette Escadrille (414), a doctoral dissertation which has now been published.

BETWEEN THE WARS. Almost as badly neglected as World War I is the period between the wars. Yet it is one of the most significant periods in the history of the air force. It was the period when airmen who were to become the leaders of the army air forces in World War II were forging out of their fertile imaginations, in the absence of experience or suitable equipment, a remarkable air-power doctrine of warfare. Copp's *A Few Great Captains* (404) and Shiner's volume on Foulois (460) are major efforts toward filling the void of scholarly studies.

WORLD WAR II. World War II is the dominant theme of a host of popular writers on air warfare. Nothing new in the form of official history of the army air forces in that war has emerged, but personal and popular accounts abound. Literature of this nature has become voluminous. Scholars would be hard pressed to investigate every memoir and unit history available. Yet, although these publications do not bear the stamp of "official history," most of them present opinions on such topics as characteristics of aircraft flown, comparisons of Allied aircraft with hostile, abilities of senior commanders, morale, and air-to-air combat. Thus, taken together, they make a significant contribution toward the total history of the AAF's participation in the war. Scholars will want, at the very least, to sample the mass of published material coming primarily from participants.

In addition to the published memoirs, there must exist an endless number still in the hands of veterans of every phase of air force activity. For the most part these are, and will remain, unavailable to scholars. Fortunately, a number of organizations have sprung up, dedicated to the task of preserving and augmenting the war record of specific air force units. For example, the Eighth Air Force Historical Society, with a permanent headquarters in Hollywood, Florida, publishes a *Quarterly* and has collected a surprising amount of material on the Eighth. The China-Burma-India Hump Pilots' Association produces a yearbook which alternates materials from reunions with the developing story of the airlift to China in World War II. The Flying Tigers of the Fourteenth Air Force Association also publishes a journal. In addition to these formal organizations, individual units, especially combat units, have reunions, out of which occasionally appear a magazine or journal containing noteworthy historical information. An indispensable reference to scholars in locating these sources is the index to *Aerospace Historian*.

Two popular works cover the air war in general. Thomas Siefring (461) has produced a volume that purports to be a history of the air force in World War II, but it actually concentrates on the Eighth Air Force and contains factual errors. Jablonski and the editors of Time-Life Books (430) have come out with a surprisingly good coverage of America's air war—surprising in that the book is not merely a photographic album but also a good, brief narrative of air operations.

Myron Smith's incomplete *Air War Chronology* (462) is amazingly detailed. Chaz Bowyer (396) devotes a large portion of his book to AAF gunners.

Ken Rust (454, 455, 456, 457) has continued to produce brief but generally accurate and well-researched operational histories of the overseas air forces. His works are, however, popular operational accounts, and deal only in passing with thorny problems facing commanders and the impact of high-level decisions.

The largest and most famous of the AAF overseas air forces was the Eighth Air Force, based in England. It is understandable that the exploits of the Eighth and its numerous units would become the subject for a continuing flow of works, which range widely in scope and quality. A few are truly outstanding. Roger Freeman (415) has added to his *Mighty Eighth* a detailed operational diary of the more than a thousand missions flown by the Eighth's units, while John Woolnough (474, 475) has edited two excellent photographic studies.

Specific aspects of the Eighth's history are the subject of two exceptional books. Rostow (453) adds a new dimension to the study of the still controversial decision of 25 March 1944 to attack marshalling yards rather than other strategic targets in preparation for Overlord. Ethell and Price (413) present an encyclopedic report on the first massive Eighth Air Force raid on Berlin. Werrell (471) has provided an invaluable guide to scholarly research on the Eighth with his *Bibliography*.

Individual units of the Eighth have come in for their share of attention. The Fourth Fighter Group, which was created from the three Eagle Squadrons, Americans flying with the RAF, has been the most popular subject. The best for an overall historical account of the group, as well as an insight into its operations, are Haugland (422, 423) and Hall (421). Fry and Ethell (416) have condensed a day-to-day operational diary. One of the better unit histories is Woolnough's story of the 466th Bombardment Group (476).

Gen. Philip Ardery's *Bomber Pilot* (387) is a particularly valuable addition to the history of the Eighth; historians researching the famous Ploesti raid and "Big Week" operations of the Eighth will want to consult Ardery. Bledsoe (391) has also made a welcome contribution, but his study lacks the depth of Ardery's coverage. McCrary and Scherman (436) make a unique addition; although only recently published, the manuscript for their book was actually written during the war and recaptures for the researcher something of the attitudes and language of the war era. Stafford (465) provides a useful service in cataloging Eighth Air Force aces by fighter group. One of the shortcomings of military historians has been their preoccupation with bomber and fighter operations to the sacrifice of other types of air force activities. Ivie (429) helps to fill a void with his study of aerial reconnaissance.

In contrast to the attention paid to the air war in Europe, the air effort in other theaters has been seriously neglected. Don Woerpel (473) adds to the history of the air war in the Mediterranean by placing the 79th Fighter Group's operations in the perspective of ground operations and command decisions. Only two general works on the air war in the Pacific have appeared recently, and one of them, Sunderman (466), is a reissue of the original (250). The other, by Mondey and Nalls (441), has selective coverage. Of two studies of B-29 operations against Japan, Herbert's (424) is autobiographical as seen by a tailgunner, while Birdsall (390) is the fuller story, including a view of the Twentieth Air Force.

A number of unit histories shed new light on the Pacific air war. Burkett (399) gives a better overall view of bomber operations than Cleveland (402). Lambert (434) provides an above-average history of a fighter group. Boeman's *Memoir* of a B-24 pilot in the southwest Pacific (392) is exceptional in that it reports in detail the author's experience of a "pilot error" takeoff accident and the resulting psychological impact of the crash.

The China-Burma-India theater is often virtually overlooked. Recent accounts of the air war in China in particular almost invariably combine something of the history of the Fourteenth Air Force and its units with tributes to the Fourteenth's commander, Gen. Claire L. Chennault. For example, Cornelius and Short's volume (406) is part biography of General Chennault and part history of the 23rd Fighter Group. Likewise, the China-Burma-India Hump Pilots' Association pays a tribute to Chennault and includes an immense amount of historical detail in its study of China's aerial lifeline, the Hump. Another fascinating story of fighter pilots—and, incidentally, of Chennault—is found in Luther Kissick's account (432) of the 74th Fighter Squadron. Two pictorial records of the Fourteenth Air Force are presented by Rosholt (452) and Pistole (447); both are worth looking into when researching Fourteenth Air Force history.

AFTER WORLD WAR II. Official histories have turned almost exclusively to the post-World War II period, as noted above. Probably because of classification problems, veterans and popular writers have not been attracted to the more recent period of air force history. Lou Drendel (408) has come up with a pictorial record of the air war in Southeast Asia. An intriguing treatment of the Southeast Asia war, revealing some of the frustrations and questioning attitudes of the fighting men in Vietnam, is found in Drury's *My Secret War* (409). Scholars doing research on the Vietnam war will be rewarded by turning to Myron Smith's *Bibliography* (463).

BIOGRAPHIES AND AUTOBIOGRAPHIES. Military historians continue to note the paucity of biographies or autobiographies of air force leaders, especially of senior officers. There has not been a rash of such publications, but something of a beginning has been made. Copp's two volumes (404, 405) must be considered, at least in part, biographical studies of the principles of his texts. Moreover, Shiner's work (460) could be classified as a biography of General Foulois. The most significant recent straight biography is Coffey's story of Gen. H. H. Arnold (403). Puryear (448) has produced a readable but far from definitive biography of Gen. George S. Brown. General Chennault has received some attention in Cornelius and Short's *Air War in China* (406), which is partially a biography; a more penetrating view of Chennault is found in the commemorative issue of the Flying Tigers of the Fourteenth Air Force Association's *Pictorial* magazine (451). Historians seeking information on Chennault can also be helped by the guide to his papers in the Hoover Institution on War, Revolution and Peace (427).

PILOTS AND PLANES. Interest remains amazingly high in the origin, development, characteristics, and employment of aircraft, and in the exploits of the men who flew them. Several publishing houses are doing a series on aircraft, each different in some detail or approach. Charles Scribner's Sons, for example, has an *At War* series which includes Anderton on the B-29 (386), Joe Christy and Jeff Ethell on the P-40 and P-38 (400, 401), Hess on the A-20 (425), Scutts on the F-105 (458), and Mikesh on the B-57 (440), and others. Although these studies vary somewhat in quality, in general they detail the development of the aircraft and include a brief operational history of each. Aero Publishers has a "Detail and Scale" series; Lloyd and Moore (435) do not emphasize the history of the B-17 but focus on the physical details. Squadron / Signal Publications' In Action series may be mistitled, as each volume traces the evolution of each model of the aircraft and gives only passing attention to an outstanding operation or two. Included in the series is, for example, McDowell on the P-39 and B-25 (437, 438), the latter including a brief account of the Doolittle raid. Larry Davis's *Gunships: A Pictorial History of Spooky* (407) is also in this series. Some of the other best descriptions and, in some cases, brief discussions of combat usage are Jeff Ethell's story of the F-15 (410), which includes an in-depth consideration of theories and concepts in fighter aviation, and his superior work on the P-51 (411). Also notable are Mendenhall on the B-25 and B-26 (439); Bowman on the B-24 (395), including a brief account of its operations in all theaters; Boyne on the B-52 (397); Johnson on the B-17 (431); and Wooldridge on the P-80 (477), one of the Smithsonian's famous aircraft in the National Air and Space Museum.

Those interested in pilots' stories should turn to Moore (442), Ardery (387), and Drury (409). Higham, Siddall, and Williams (426) continue their excellent series covering accurate and authentic reports by air force pilots who knew exactly what it is, or was like, to fly each aircraft included.

Two general references on air force aircraft are available. Waters (472) includes both a description and a brief operational record of every aircraft used by the United States Air Force. Gunston (420) falls short of his usual thorough job in presenting the fighters of the fifties. Walker and the editors of Time-Life Books (470) include discussions of the emergence of USAF jets.

SUGGESTIONS FOR FURTHER RESEARCH. In spite of the steady stream of books, pamphlets, journals, and articles that continue to appear treating various aspects of the United States Air Force and its predecessors, much more serious, scholarly, analytical study remains to be done in a wide variety of fields. Except for the work being done by professionals within the air force and an occasional doctoral dissertation, historical accounts generally deal with the more glamorous activities of the air force. Little has been done to record the contribution to the air force mission made by service elements, or to assess the relationship between service activities and flying operations in peace and war. All of the emphasis on bomber and fighter operations needs to be supplemented with studies of other types of aerial activities, such as night flying, troop carrier operations, reconnaissance, and training. The period from the close of World War II until the beginning of U.S. involvement in Southeast Asia has received little attention. Yet during this period the United States Air Force came into being and faced the formidable task of preparing its own rules and regulations. Biographies of air force senior officials are available, however, in a number of depositories, such as the United States Air Force Historical Research Center, the Air Force Academy, and the National Archives. The publication of selected annotated papers of important air force figures would be an invaluable service to researchers.

Another totally different area of air force history that bears investigating is that of air force-community relations. What has been the impact of the air force and its predecessors on local communities when a base or other air force installation is established in an area? The effect of the air force on the industrial base needs to be explored. Why and how the air force chooses a site for an air base or other installation needs to be explained. Finally, there really is no end to the broad range of problems, solved and unsolved, that the air force and its predecessors have faced in the past almost eighty years that should attract the serious military historian.

BIBLIOGRAPHY

386. Anderton, David A. *B-29 Superfortress at War*. New York: Charles Scribner's Sons, 1978.

387. Ardery, Gen. Philip. *Bomber Pilot: A Memoir of World War II*. Lexington: University Press of Kentucky, 1978.

388. Ballard, Jack S. *Development and Employment of Fixed-Wing Gunships*. Washington, D.C.: GPO, 1982.

389. Bell, Dana. *Air Force Colors*, Vols. 1 , 2. Carrollton, Tex.: Squadron / Signal Publications, 1979–1980.

390. Birdsall, Steve. *Saga of the Superfortress: The Dramatic Story of the B-29 and the Twentieth Air Force*. New York: Doubleday, 1980.

391. Bledsoe, Marvin. *Thunderbolt: Memoirs of a World War II Fighter Pilot*. New York: Van Nostrand, 1982.

392. Boeman, John. *Morotai—A Memoir of War*. New York: Doubleday, 1981.

393. Borowski, Harry R. *A Hollow Threat: Strategic Air Power and Containment before Korea*. Westport, Conn.: Greenwood Press, 1982.

394. Bowers, Roy L. *The Air Force in Southeast Asia: Tactical Airlift*. Washington, D.C.: GPO, 1983.

395. Bowman, Martin. *The B-24 Liberator*. New York: Rand McNally, 1980.

396. Boyer, Chaz. *Guns in the Sky: The Air Gunners of World War II*. New York: Charles Scribner's Sons, 1979.

397. Boyne, Walter J. *Boeing B-52: A Documentary History*. New York: Franklin Watts, 1979.

398. Buckingham, William A. *Operation Ranch Hand: The Air Force and Herbicides in Southeast Asia, 1961–1971*. Washington, D.C.: GPO, 1982.

399. Burkett, Prentiss. *The Unofficial History of the 499th Bomb Group (VH)*. Temple City, Calif.: Historical Aviation Album, 1981.

400. Christy, Joe, and Jeffrey L. Ethell. *P-40 Hawks at War*. New York: Charles Scribner's Sons, 1980.

401. _____. *P-38 Lightning at War*. New York: Charles Scribner's Sons, 1978.

402. Cleveland, W. M., ed. *Grey Geese Calling: A History of the 11th Bombardment Group (H) in the Pacific, 1940-1945.* Askow, Minn.: American Publishing Company, 1981.

403. Coffey, Thomas M. *HAP: The Story of the U.S. Air Force and the Man Who Built It: General Henry H. "Hap" Arnold.* New York: Viking Press, 1982.

404. Copp, DeWitt S. *A Few Great Captains: The Men and Events that Shaped the Development of U.S. Air Power.* New York: Doubleday, 1980.

405. _____. *Forged in Fire: Strategy and Decisions in the Air War over Europe.* New York: Doubleday, 1982.

406. Cornelius, Wanda, and Thayne Short. *Ding Hao: America's Air War in China, 1937-1945.* Gretna, La.: Pelican Publishing Company, 1980.

407. Davis, Larry. *Gunships: A Pictorial History of Spooky.* Carrollton, Tex.: Squadron / Signal Publications, 1982.

408. Drendel, Lou. *Air War over Southeast Asia: A Pictorial Record.* Carrollton, Tex.: Squadron / Signal Publications, 1982.

409. Drury, Richard S. *My Secret War.* Fallbrook, Calif.: Aero Publishers, 1979.

410. Ethell, Jeffrey L. *F-15 Eagle.* Osceola, Wis.: Specialty Press, 1981.

411. _____. *Mustang: A Documentary History of the P-51.* New York: Jane's Publishing Co., 1981.

412. Ethell, Jeffrey L., and Joe Christy. *B-52 Stratofortress*, New York: Charles Scribner's Sons, 1981.

413. Ethell, Jeffrey L., and Alfred Price. *Target Berlin: Mission 250, 6 March 1944.* New York: Jane's, 1981.

414. Flammer, Philip M. *The Vivid Air: The Lafayette Escadrille.* Athens: University of Georgia Press, 1981.

415. Freeman, Roger A. *Mighty Eighth War Diary.* New York: Jane's, 1981.

416. Fry, Garry L., and Jeffrey L. Ethell. *Escort to Berlin: The Fourth USAF Fighter Group in World War II.* New York: Arco Publishing, 1980.

417. Futrell, Robert Frank. *The United States Air Force in Korea, 1950-1953.* Rev. ed. Washington, D.C.: GPO, 1983.

418. Futrell, Robert Frank, and Martin Blumenson. *The United States Air Force in Southeast Asia: The Advisory Years to 1965.* Washington, D.C.: GPO, 1981.

419. Gaston, James C. *Planning the American Air War: Four Men and Nine Days in 1941: An Inside Narrative.* Washington, D.C.: National Defense University Press, 1982.

420. Gunston, Bill. *Fighters in the Fifties.* Osceola, Wis.: Specialty Press, 1982.

421. Hall, Grover, C., Jr. *1000 Destroyed.* Fallbrook, Calif.: Aero Publishers, 1978.

422. Haugland, Vern. *The Eagle Squadron: Yanks in the RAF, 1940-1942.* New York: Ziff-Davis, 1979.

423. _____. *The Eagles' War: The Saga of the Eagle Squadron Pilots, 1940-1945.* New York: Jason Aronson, 1982.

424. Herbert, Kevin. *The B-29s Against Japan.* Manhattan, Kans.: Sunflower University Press, 1983.

425. Hess, William. *A-20 Havoc at War.* New York: Charles Scribner's Sor , 1980.

426. Higham, Robin, and Carol Williams, eds. *Flying Combat Aircraft of the USAAF and USAF.* Vol. 3. Manhattan, Kans.: Sunflower University Press,

1981.

427. Hoover Institution on War, Revolution, and Peace. *General Claire Lee Chennault: A Guide to His Papers in the Hoover Institution Archives.* Stanford, Calif.: Hoover Institution Press, 1983.

428. Hopkins, Charles K. *SAC Tanker Operations in the Southeast Asia War.* Offutt Air Force Base, Nebr.: Headquarters, SAC / HO, 1979.

429. Ivie, Thomas G. *Aerial Reconnaissance: The 10th Photo Group in World War II.* Fallbrook, Calif.: Aero Publishers, 1981.

430. Jablonski, Edward, and the editors of Time-Life Books. *America in the Air War.* Alexandria, Va.: Time-Life Books, 1982.

431. Johnson, Frederick A., ed. *Winged Majesty: The Boeing B-17 Flying Fortress in War and Peace.* Tacoma, Wash.: Bomber Books, 1980.

432. Kennett, Lee. *A History of Strategic Bombing.* New York: Charles Scribner's Sons, 1982.

432a. Kissick, Luther C., Jr. *Guerrilla One: The 74th Fighter Squadron behind Enemy Lines in China, 1942–45.* Manhattan, Kans.: Sunflower University Press, 1983.

433. Kohn, Richard, and Joseph P. Harahan, eds. *Air Superiority in World War II and Korea: An Interview with Gen. James Ferguson, Gen. Robert M. Lee, Gen. William Momyer, and Lt. Gen. Elwood R. Quesada.* USAF Warrior Studies. Washington, D.C.: Office of Air Force History, 1983.

434. Lambert, John W. *The Long Campaign: The History of the 15th Fighter Group in World War II.* Manhattan, Kans.: Sunflower University Press, 1982.

435. Lloyd, Alwyn T., and Terry D. Moore. *B-17 Flying Fortress: Production Versions in Detail and Scale.* Fallbrook, Calif.: Aero Publishers, 1981.

436. McCrary, John R., and David E. Scherman. *First of Many.* Glendale, Calif.: Aviation Books, 1981.

437. McDowell, Ernest R. *B-25 Mitchell in Action.* Carrollton, Tex.: Squadron / Signal Publications, 1979.

438. _____. *Airacobra in Action.* Carrollton, Tex.: Squadron / Signal Publications, 1980.

439. Mendenhall, Charles A. *The Deadly Duo: The B-25 and B-26 in World War II.* Osceola, Wis.: Specialty Press, 1981.

440. Mikesh, Robert C. *B-57 Canberra at War, 1964–1972.* New York: Charles Scribner's Sons, 1980.

441. Mondey, David, and Lewis Nalls. *USAAF at War in the Pacific.* New York: Charles Scribner's Sons, 1980.

442. Moore, Carl H. *Flying the B-26 Marauder over Europe.* Blue Ridge Summit, Pa.: Modern Aviation Series, Tab Books, 1980.

443. Mueller, Robert. *Air Force Bases.* Vol. 1, *Active Air Force Bases within the United States of America.* Maxwell Air Force Base, Ala.: United States Air Force Historical Research Center, 1982.

444. Murray, Williamson. *Strategy for Defeat: The Luftwaffe, 1933–1945.* Maxwell Air Force Base, Ala.: Center for Aerospace Doctrine, Research, and Education, 1983.

445. Nevin, David, and the editors of Time-Life Books. *Architects of Air Power.* Alexandria, Va.: Time-Life Books, 1981.

446. Orr, Maj. George E. *Combat Operations C³I: Fundamentals and Inter-*

actions. Maxwell Air Force Base, Ala.: Center for Aerospace Doctrine, Research, and Education, 1983.

447. Pistole, Larry M. *The Pictorial History of the Flying Tigers.* Orange, Va.: Moss Publications, 1981.

448. Puryear, Edgar F., Jr. *George S. Brown, General, U.S. Air Force: Destined for Stars.* San Rafael, Calif.: Presido Press, 1983.

449. Ravenstein, Charles A. *Organization of the Air Force.* Maxwell Air Force Base, Ala.: United States Air Force Historical Research Center, 1982.

450. _____. *A Guide to Air Force Lineage and Honors.* Maxwell Air Force Base, Ala.: United States Air Force Historical Research Center, 1983.

451. Rosholt, Malcolm L. *Claire L. Chennault: A Tribute.* Silver Bay, Mich.: Flying Tigers of the 14th Air Force Association, 1983.

452. _____. *Days of the Ching Pao.* Amherst, Wis.: Palmer Publications, 1978.

453. Rostow, W. W. *Pre-Invasion Bombing Strategy: General Eisenhower's Decision of March 25, 1944.* Austin: University of Texas Press, 1981.

454. Rust, Kenn C. *Seventh Air Force Story.* Temple City, Calif.: Historical Aviation Album, 1979.

455. _____. *Twentieth Air Force Story.* Temple City, Calif.: Historical Aviation Album, 1979.

456. _____. *Tenth Air Force Story.* Temple City, Calif.: Historical Aviation Album, 1980.

457. Rust, Kenn C., and Dana Bell. *Thirteenth Air Force Story.* Temple City, Calif.: Historical Aviation Album, 1982.

458. Scutts, J. C. *F-105 Thunderchief at War.* New York: Charles Scribner's Sons, 1981.

459. Seiler, Capt. George J. *Strategic Nuclear Force Requirements and Issues.* Maxwell Air Force Base, Ala.: Center for Aerospace Doctrine, Research, and Education, 1983.

460. Shiner, John F. *The Army Air Arm in Transition: General Benjamin D. Foulois and the Army Air Corps, 1931-1935.* Washington, D.C.: Office of Air Force History, 1984.

461. Siefring, Sgt. Thomas. *U.S. Air Force in World War II.* London: Hamlyn, 1979.

462. Smith, Myron J., Jr. *Air War Chronology, 1939-1945.* Vol. 3, *1943 Interim Year, Part I, January-April.* Manhattan, Kans.: Military Affairs / Aerospace Historian Publishing, 1979.

463. Smith, Myron J., Jr. *Air War in Southeast Asia, 1961-1973: An Annotated Bibliography and 16mm Film Guide.* Metuchen, N.J.: Scarecrow Press, 1979.

464. Staff of *After The Battle* magazine. *Airfields of the Eighth, Then and Now.* Text by Roger Freeman. London: Battle Prints International, 1979.

465. Stafford, Gene B. *Aces of the Eighth.* Carrollton, Tex.: Squadron / Signal Publications, 1978.

466. Sunderman, James F., ed. *World War II in the Air: The Pacific.* New York: Van Nostrand, 1981.

467. Tilford, Earl H., Jr. *Search and Rescue in Southeast Asia, 1961-1975.* Washington, D.C.: Office of Air Force History, 1980.

468. Toliver, Raymond F., and Trevor J. Constable. *Fighter Aces of the U.S.A.* Fallbrook, Calif.: Aero Publishers, 1979.

469. United States Air Force Historical Research Center. *U.S. Air Force Oral History Catalog.* Maxwell Air Force Base, Ala.: United States Air Force Historical Research Center, 1982. (Published originally as an Albert F. Simpson Historical Research Center publication.)

470. Walker, Bryce, and editors of Time-Life Books. *Fighting Jets.* Alexandria, Va.: Time-Life Books, 1983.

471. Werrell, Kenneth P. *Eighth Air Force Bibliography: An Extended Essay and Listing of Published and Unpublished Materials.* Edited by Robin Higham. Manhattan, Kans.: Military Affairs / Aerospace Historian Publishing, 1981.

472. Waters, Andrew W. *All the U.S. Air Force Planes, 1907–1983.* New York: Hippocrene Books, 1983.

473. Woerpel, Don. *A Hostile Sky: The Mediterranean Air War of the 79th Fighter Group.* Marshall, Wis.: The Andon Press, 1977.

474. Woolnough, John H. *The Eighth Air Force Yearbook.* Hollywood, Fla.: 8th Air Force News, 1981.

475. _____. *The Eighth Air Force Album: The Story of the Mighty Eighth Air Force in World War II.* San Angelo, Tex.: 1978.

476. _____. *Attlebridge Diaries: The History of the 466th Bombardment Group (Heavy).* Hollywood, Fla.: 8th Air Force News, 1979.

477. Wooldridge, E. T., Jr. *The P-80 Shooting Star: Evolution of a Jet Fighter.* Washington, D.C.: Smithsonian Institution Press, 1979.

XVI

THE DEPARTMENT OF DEFENSE,

DEFENSE POLICY, AND DIPLOMACY SINCE 1945

Lester H. Brune

Between 1978 and 1983, the literature on American national security and foreign policies has been influenced by the renewal of cold war confrontational policies and by the declassification of additional materials on the era from 1945 to 1963.

President Richard Nixon's detente policies deteriorated under Presidents Gerald Ford and Jimmy Carter, the latter renewing cold war confrontation after the Soviet Union intervened in Afghanistan in December 1979. President Ronald Reagan further froze relations with Moscow, claiming the Soviets used detente to gain a "definite margin of superiority" in nuclear weapons and beginning a huge build-up of America's nuclear and conventional forces throughout the period from 1978 to 1983. American spokesmen who advocated detente and traditional deterrent policies conducted paper debates with proponents of confronting Moscow and attaining a nuclear war-fighting capability. Publications about nuclear war increased. According to the *New York Times* Information Bank, nuclear war was cited in 278 articles in 1978 and 1,612 articles during 1982, the number rising each year.

During the past five years, research has also been influenced by the availability of new documents at the National Archives and various presidential libraries. This has resulted especially in more detailed studies on the early post-World War II years of cold war and in a continued reevaluation of the Eisenhower and Kennedy administrations, evaluations generally favorable to Dwight Eisenhower but critical of John F. Kennedy.

Because *Supplement I* of this guide gave extensive coverage to printed congressional materials, the present chapter cites only those congressional materials especially pertinent to this past five years. Research for this chapter included all significant material available before 31 December 1983.

GENERAL SOURCES; BIBLIOGRAPHIC GUIDES. The most important diplomatic reference source to appear in forty years was editor Richard D. Burns's *Guide to American Foreign Relations since 1700* (1671). A team effort by members of the Society for Historians of American Foreign Relations, this is the first guide on U.S. diplomatic history since the publication of the Samuel R. Bemis and Grace Griffin volume in 1935.

Three specialized bibliographies worth consulting are John Newman's *Vietnam*

War Literature (1680); the Dwight D. Eisenhower Library's list of periodical and dissertation materials on that president's term of office (1674); and Arkin's guide to military and strategic debates of the 1970s (1670).

Seven periodical articles provide important commentaries about sources on specific topics. Two of these articles deal with the reevaluation of the Eisenhower presidency; McAuliffe's (1679) and Schlesinger's (1682). The status of cold war "post-revisionist" interpretations is described by Gaddis (1676) with commentaries by other scholars of the cold war.

In other historiographical review articles, Dunn discusses 23 POW chronicles of the Vietnam War (1673); Perez surveys the literature of America's Caribbean policy to 1980 (1681). Hilsman describes 11 volumes dealing with U.S. intelligence operations (1678); and Travgott inventories holdings on area studies and international relations available from the Inter-University Consortium for Political and Social Research (1684).

Two reference works of some value were printed recently. John Findling's *Dictionary of American Diplomatic History* (1675) covers 1,000 entries, a number which is insufficient to assist any but undergraduate students; Haines and Walker's *American Foreign Relations, A Historiographical Review* (1677) contains a series of sixteen articles on various topics of U.S. diplomacy.

Two special reference works may be valuable to scholars in certain specialties. Robert A. Divine (1440) surveys the literature on various typics of Lyndon Johnson's political era and describes unpublished sources at the Johnson Library. For researchers on Third World topics, the *Current History Encyclopedia of Developing Nations* (1683) may prove helpful.

In addition to the resource materials described in *Supplement I* of this guide (pp. 116–17), two new search aids are of great assistance to scholars. One is the Dialog Information Services, a computer line providing annotated bibliographical references that many university libraries make available. The second is the catalog of doctoral dissertations available from University Microfilm's International. To place your name on their mailing list, write to UMI, 300 N. Zeeb Road, P.O. Box 1764, Ann Arbor, Michigan 48106.

MANUSCRIPTS AND DOCUMENTS. Two developments occurred recently regarding the papers of Richard Nixon. First, the Laguna Niguel, California, regional branch of the National Archives announced the opening of two sets of Nixon's pre-presidential papers: general correspondence, 1953 to 1961; and material on Nixon's eight foreign trips between 1953 and 1959. Secondly, as of this writing, plans are to locate Nixon's presidential library at San Clemente.

The Gerald R. Ford Library now publishes a newsletter for researchers. For research information or to receive the newsletter, scholars should write to The Director, Gerald R. Ford Library, 1000 Beal Avenue, Ann Arbor, Michigan 48109.

Researchers may now benefit from the publication of microfiche or microfilm collections. University Publications of America (UPA) has issued microfilms of documents such as Joint Chief of Staff records, Confidential U.S. Diplomatic Post Reports, CIA Research Reports, National Security Council Documents, and Transcripts and Files of the Paris Peace Talks on Vietnam, 1969–1973. For complete information on UPA publications, write to 44 North Market Street, Frederick, Maryland 21701.

Scholarly Resources has micro-published documents such as the State-War-Navy-Air Force Coordinating Committee, 1944–1949; U.S. Correspondence with the British Foreign Office, 1930–1948; and a microfiche program on the origins of the cold war. They have also prepared various British Public Record Office materials and have guides to archives in Germany, France, and Italy. For details, write to SR, 104 Greenhill Avenue, Wilmington, Delaware 19805.

The John F. Kennedy Library has begun transcribing and declassifying recordings of meetings in the Oval Office during Kennedy's presidency. The pace of the work is slow, and the archivist expects to release an average of three recording hours per year. In October 1983, the library released transcripts of the 16 October 1962 session of the Executive Committee convened for the Cuban missile crisis. For details of this process, write Research Archivist, John F. Kennedy Library, Columbia Point, Boston, Massachusetts 02125.

The National Archives microfilms contain records for sale to researchers and libraries. Recent microfilm records included in their program have included the secretary of state's staff committee, 1945–7; the State Department's policy planning staff papers, 1947–1950; and the Marshall-Lovett memos to Truman. To obtain a list of available documents for sale, write to the Sales Manager, National Archives, Washington, D.C. 20408.

Since 1978, the State Department's Historical Office has published volumes of documents for 1951 and, by 27 December 1983, six of the sixteen volumes covering the years 1952 through 1954. Among the more recently published volumes are those on Indochina, 1952–1954, and the Geneva Conference of 1954. Also issued in December 1983 was volume 4, *The American Republics* (1664), as well as public statements and documents on the Arab-Israeli peace process, 1967–1983 (1667).

Two recent articles provide critical appraisals of the published *Foreign Relations* documents series. One, by Slany (1609), discusses recent scholarly efforts to improve the dissemination of documents, including a report of the Advisory Committee on Historical Diplomatic Documentation. The second, by Lees and Treadway (1528), is concerned about the shortcomings of the series and the public's need to have information earlier than is now possible under the government's present process.

A variety of other published documents are also valuable for researchers. Robert Ferrell has edited for publication the diaries of Eisenhower (1453) and of his press secretary James Hagerty for 1954–1955 (1477). Other published documents include Porter's *Vietnam* documents (1581) and Herring's secret negotiating volumes of the Pentagon papers (1483).

Among the important congressional publications are the continued issuance of the series *Executive Sessions of the Senate Foreign Relations Committee*. The most recent volume at the time of writing is that of the 88th Congress for 1960 (1667). Keeping abreast of the quantity of Congressional publications is often difficult. In addition to the *Annual* and *Monthly Index* of the Congressional Information Service (CIS), scholars should check the quarterly issues of *Foreign Affairs*, where Janet Rigney edits a list of source materials.

AUTOBIOGRAPHICAL AND BIOGRAPHICAL MATERIALS. Recent years have produced fewer biographical than historic studies on the Truman era. Donovan's second volume on Truman's presidency (1444) has made this the best available study of the president. Hadsel and Bland (1477) have issued the first volume of the papers of George Marshall, and another five volumes remain to be published. While scholars await further volumes on Marshall by Forrest Pogue, Mosley (1554) has written a sympathetic biography with little new data but many anecdotes. Brown's study of William Donovan (1405) emphasizes the early escapades of the OSS and its founder but gives no attention to organizational or performance ratings for the OSS. Jurika has edited and condensed Admiral Radford's 2,000 pages of memoirs into one volume (1505). Radford was a leading figure in the post-1945 adjustment of the navy's strategic role to the nuclear age. Jurika's edition stresses the official record, offering few insights into Radford's personal role during these controversial years.

Studies about Douglas MacArthur continue to deflate the general's activities. Smith's account of MacArthur in Korea is excessively critical (1612) and should be used in combination with recent studies on the Korean War. Petillo (1575) explores the general's career by using psycho-history, a method still disputed by professional historians. Finally, a small, interesting memoir which scholars may miss is Melby's account (1549) as a member of the 1950 joint State-Defense Department mission to Vietnam.

President Eisenhower continues to receive favorable assessments of his presidency. Included in this category are books by Lee (1527), on his public career, and Greenstein (1474), on his leadership style, and an article by Nelson (1559) on his relations with the NSC. Cook's study (1429) praises Eisenhower's desire to avoid nuclear war but raises questions about his use of intelligence activity for political and psychological purposes. Rostow's account (1589) of Eisenhower's 11 March 1953 decisions indicate that the president's desire to accept Premier Malenkov's overtures to thaw the cold war was delayed by Secretary of State John Foster Dulles and other Republicans. More light on the Eisenhower-Dulles relationship may be shed when Pruessen publishes the second volume on Dulles. The first biographical volume, completed in 1982 (1583), covered his career to 1952.

Through 1983, records classification generally limited scholars from thoroughly assessing the Kennedy-Johnson administrations. Richard Walton's 1972 account, which criticized most of Kennedy's foreign policies, has been balanced by the two more favorable volumes by Parmet (1569). Nevertheless, several research articles have detracted further from Kennedy's image. While Beck's description of Cuba in the 1960 campaign (1437) favors Kennedy more than Nixon, Noer's study (1437) indicates that Kennedy was less humanitarian toward Africa in the Volta River project than even Walton conceded. Deterrent analysts also continue to demonstrate that the Cuban missile crisis was not Kennedy's "finest hour." Both Bernstein (1394) and Scherer (1597) have further evidence of Kennedy's faults in 1962.

On Johnson, Caro's first (1415) of three volumes on the president's early career describe his ambitious designs. Humphreys gives information on the Tuesday lunches, where Johnson was alleged to have informally established policy (1437). Cohen's volume on Dean Rusk as Secretary of State (1426) emphasizes his "loyal servant" role for Kennedy and Johnson. Finally, George Ball's memoirs (1388) cover a lengthy public career and are of special value on the Kennedy-Johnson years.

For the period from 1969 to 1980, memoirs of participants dominate the publication lists since 1978. Kissinger's lengthy two-volume memoirs (1521) are especially interesting for information on global leaders during the period. Scholars should read a fascinating review of Kissinger's memoirs by a British historian, Michael Howard (1491). Participants in the Carter administration, whose memoirs are useful to diplomatic and national security scholars, are those of Carter himself (1416), Vance (1646), Brzezinski (1407), and Hamilton Jordan (1504). LaFeber has written an insightful review of the Carter, Vance, and Brzezinski volumes (1525). Secretary of Defense Brown's recent book (1404) is only partly based on his 1977–1981 experiences, being designed as a serious, moderate discussion of the relationship between foreign and defense policies.

For the Reagan administration, the one valuable biographical book to appear thus far is Brownstein and Easton's sketches of personalities appointed by Reagan, including some who had already been replaced (1406).

A number of books worth consulting concern men whose work spans many presidential years. The memoirs of John Fairbank (1450), Charles Yost (1655), and John Kenneth Galbraith (1460) provide valuable insights into U.S. policy since 1945. Likewise, scholars should be familiar with Steel's biography of Walter Lippman (1617), and Polmar and Allen's account of the versatile Admiral Rickover (1580).

NATIONAL SECURITY POLICY. America's proper national security strategy became a major issue between 1978 and 1984. Proponents of a limited, controlled nuclear war-fighting option challenged and, with Ronald Reagan's election as president, replaced the strategic group advocating the assured-destruction, retaliatory stance which had prevailed since 1969. Sanders (1593) and Prados (1582) describe how the Team B Experts outside the Ford and Carter administrations obtained leaked intelligence data to criticize the CIA's and the National Intelligence Estimate's (NIE) analysis of the Soviet defense build-up and the Kremlin's strategic preparations for an alleged first strike at U.S. ICBMs. Led by members such as Richard Pipes, Colin Gray, Paul Nitze, and Albert Wohlstetter, and helped by the publicity campaign of the Committee on the Present Danger, Team B influenced the Republican Party's 1980 platform, which called for achieving an American military and technological superiority over the USSR. Subsequent to his election, Reagan appointed many leaders of the Committee for the Present Danger to high policy positions in the State and Defense departments. In addition, Team B's campaign successfully prevented the Senate's ratification of SALT II in 1979, and probably led Carter to adopt the hard-line approach toward Soviet relations which ended detente in 1980. The deterioration of American-Soviet relations, combined with the nuclear war-fighting options attributed to the military theorists of both superpowers, heightened cold war tensions to the pre-1962 level, causing the *Bulletin of the Atomic Scientists* to move its doomsday clock to three minutes to twelve in December 1983.

Team B's two major assumptions were that the Soviet Union was constructing a superior ICBM force, and that they planned to use it either to win major diplomatic victories or as a first-strike counterforce to destroy America's ICBMs. This would force the U.S. to surrender or escalate the nuclear war to population-destroying dimensions. The U.S., they argued, must establish both a land-based strategic option prepared for a counterforce nuclear victory, and large conventional forces designed to fight a protracted war which could delay use of the nuclear options. A publication of the Committee on the Present Danger (1448) describes these concepts succinctly. More details about the evolving Soviet superiority are presented by Douglas and Hoeber (1446), Gouré and Deane (1470), Lockwood (1533), and Cline (1423). Several authors emphasize that the U.S. must have a superior first-strike option such as they believe the Soviets have. An article by Builder (1410) urges the U.S. to have a first-strike force in terms the author had expressed in a 1978 Rand Corporation study for the air force. Studies advocating a U.S. victory in a limited nuclear war are by Gray (1471) and Keith Payne (1571). Gray and Payne also co-wrote "Victory is Possible" for *Foreign Policy* in 1980 (1472).

Team B's concepts have many opponents among advocates of deterrent-retaliation policy and the nuclear freeze movement. Snow's volume presents ideas of both sides in this dispute (1614). Jervis (1502) contends that even if the Soviets had nuclear equivalency or superiority, they could not insure success in pursuing successful international objectives. Several writers deny that the USSR will have a superior nuclear force or that its political leaders plan to fight a counterforce nuclear war. Among these are Arnett (1384), Brodie (1403), Cockburn (1424), Howard (1492), and Christopher Jones (1503). Samuel Payne (1572) and Trofimenko (1637) argue that the U.S. retained nuclear superiority under SALT I because of its lead in MIRV technology in 1973. Because SALT I did not limit the application of MIRV to launchers, the Soviets developed new ICBMs with MIRV capability. This permitted the USSR to move toward parity with America in nuclear warheads, a development which alarmed the Carter Administration as well as Team B and led to plans for the MX land-based missile.

Between 1977 and 1983, the development and basing of the MX symbolized American concern for the Soviet's SS-18s with ten MIRV warheads and greater accuracy. The MX was not considered necessary by Scoville (1602), Adams and Gold (1376), and Carter's CIA director Stansfield Turner (1644). Nevertheless, the Carter administration developed the MX, planning to link it to existing retaliatory strategy by basing MXs in a large mobile racetrack in several Western states. This system and other mobile-basing modes caused problems which are discussed in articles by Ball (1385) and Snow (1613), and by a 1980 Defense Department study on basing options (1663). Other Congressional publications gave official views on MX program costs (1658) and basing options (1659, 1660). Hoover's book on the MX controversy (1487) is an excellent summary of the debate and includes bibliographic references on the conflicting views.

Team B's nuclear war-fighting option also enlivened the issue of civil defense. Leon Gouré's 1976 book, *War Survival in Soviet Strategy*, claimed Russia's civil defense plans would allow sufficient survival in a limited nuclear war to enable the Soviets to win. Thus, Gouré argued, the U.S. needed an improved civil defense, especially to insure the survival of the nation's communications, command, and control system (C3). Later, intelligence-gathering devices were added to this survival package (C3I). Although written in a popular, journalistic style, Robert Scheer's *With Enough Shovels* (1595) described Gouré's views and those of T. K. Jones, who became Reagan's deputy undersecretary of defense specializing in nuclear defense methods. Scheer's book is especially valuable for its appendix of transcribed interviews with Reagan, Vice-President Bush, Vance, McNamara, and others.

In a *Worldview* article, Paul Nitze and Richard Barnet debated the pros and cons of civil defense (1560). Katz (1514) contended that there would not be much life remaining after a nuclear war. Both Ball (1386) and the U.S. Office of Technical Assessment in 1979 (1668) described nuclear destruction which made such wars a Pyrrhic lose-lose situation, neither side being able to win, as Gray and Payne contended they could.

Many additional scholars joined the debate between advocates of a retaliatory and a war-fighting strategy. Included in these studies are anti-nuclear war arguments by Schell (1596), Zuckerman (1656), and Lifton and Falk (1532); advocates of the need for strong (or superior) U.S. nuclear and conventional forces such as Huntington (1494) and Nitze (1561); and moderates who emphasize deterrence and seek a middle position, such as George (1465), Carnesale and the Harvard Study Group (1414), Wieselter (1651), Robert Tucker (1641), and Blechman's edition of the Aspen Group's views (1398).

As some scholars noted, regardless of which nuclear strategy is accepted, the most critical issue is U.S.-Soviet relations. Emphasizing that the Russians could not be trusted in negotiations, Team B members disliked detente, asserting that Soviet acquisition of a superior land-based strategic force would result in a "window of vulnerability" for the U.S. by 1984 or 1985. Sullivan's account of Soviet deceptions under SALT I (1627) indicated the judgments of this group. To the contrary, Ulam's study, *Dangerous Relations (1645)*, described the consequences of the cold-war tension arising from such attitudes in the Reagan administration. By 1980, the options of detente or cold war confrontation were juxtaposed in the volume edited by Neal (1557), in which several writers emphasized the need for continuing detente, and by Conquest's gloomy picture of dangers threatening the U.S. as a result of detente policies (1428). As Kegley and Wittkopf indicated (1516), the only clear policy the Reagan administration held by 1982 was the anti-communist notion that Russia was an "evil empire."

Most scholars did not, however, accept President Reagan's 1982 statement that the USSR is an "evil empire." The Soviet experts whose views appear in the volumes edited by Byrnes (1411) and Bertram (1395) anticipated only prudent changes in Soviet policy during the 1980s. The Kremlin's leaders are conservative, responding carefully to both domestic economic and foreign political problems, according to analysts such as Bialer (1396), Stephen Kaplan (1510), and Becker (1392).

By the end of 1983, keeping aware of recent developments in the national security debate became difficult. On 11 April 1983, the Reagan-appointed Scowcroft Commission on the MX reported (1603) in favor of building the MX in existing but hardened silos, a decision which appeared to be more a political than a security-minded judgment. The commission also implied that there had never been a "window of vulnerability" such as President Reagan previously described. Nevertheless, the report resulted in the continued development of the MX and did not affect Reagan's determination to base the cruise and Pershing II missiles in Europe in November 1983. The most balanced summary of the situation by early 1984 was Leslie Gelb's *New York Times Magazine* article (1464).

The debate about a nuclear war-fighting option also affected U.S. strategy regarding theater nuclear weapons based, or proposed to be based, in Europe. The end of U.S.-Soviet detente relations and the talk of limited nuclear war altered the considerations that had differentiated between intermediate and strategic nuclear weapons, at least in the view of many Europeans. As a result, prior decisions to base cruise and Pershing II missiles in Europe seemed less attractive by 1982.

The connection between strategic and theater weapons became apparent in a series of articles in *Foreign Affairs* during 1982 (1454). In these, Kenney and Panofsky described the conflicting strategies of retaliatory assured destruction

(MAD) and limited nuclear war fighting (NUTS); Bertram, Hoffman, Rogers, and others discussed the new problems in the Atlantic Alliance; and scholars from various nations argued for and against an American declaration that it would *not* be the first to use nuclear weapons.

By 1983, American-NATO relations included both political and national security issues, resulting in a host of studies concerning the strategy and status of the Atlantic Alliance. Three groups of U.S. and European experts who studied the situation reached some similarly important conclusions, including the assessment that NATO and Warsaw Pact conventional forces approached parity in fighting capacity, and that NATO's reliance on nuclear weapons could gradually be reduced. These three studies were those of a European Security Study group (1624); an Atlantic Council Group (1591); and a special group of experts convened specifically to consider the no-first-use doctrine in Europe, edited by Steinbruner and Sigal (1619). Mearsheimer (1548) reached a similar conclusion on Europe's conventional forces, while Tucker and Wrigley (1642) edited a series of six expert reports which emphasized the critical nature of the U.S.-West German relationship. Mako (1537) and Schwartz (1600) surveyed the past history of the U.S. role in Europe, Mako emphasizing the role of American ground forces since the 1940s and Schwartz focusing on American efforts since the 1950s to couple its nuclear forces with NATO's conventional ones in defending Europe.

Other studies on NATO strategy are Nitze and Sullivan's work for the Atlantic Council on *Securing the Seas* (1562); and two official documents: a staff report for the House Foreign Affairs Committee (1662), and the same body's hearings on NATO's future (1661).

While the debate on national security strategy has highlighted recent years, several studies have dealt with the history of U.S. strategic policies since World War II. The best of these is Gaddis' piece (1459) on U.S. containment strategies and his essay on "The Rise, Fall and Future of Detente" (1458). Freedman surveys 35 years of nuclear strategy, being especially insightful on the ideas of the 1950s and 1960s (1456). Kaplan (1507) covers similar material but devotes his attention to the writers who originated nuclear strategic theory, men such as Bernard Brodie and Herman Kahn. Mandelbaum published two complementary books in 1979 and 1981. The first dealt with U.S. policy from 1946 to 1976, giving its greatest attention to the Kennedy-McNamara era (1539); the second, which was more original and provocative, raised basic questions about the nuclear age in terms of historic concepts of war going back to Thucydides (1538).

Since 1978, two new periodicals devoted to strategy are the *Journal of Strategic Studies* (1685) and *World Policy Journal* (1681).

DEFENSE ORGANIZATION AND INTELLIGENCE OPERATIONS. The debate about national security strategy turned the attention of scholars away from their mid-1970s emphasis on the structure of the defense and intelligence organizations. Historical studies of the relationship between the secretary of defense and the military chiefs indicated the evolving importance of the Defense Department and its secretary as equaling or exceeding the role of the State Department and its secretary in national security affairs.

Douglas Kinnard's study of the evolving importance of the secretary of defense (1518) provided a theme which other studies concurred in and amplified. This theme is that under Truman, the Defense Department established a shaky foundation from which its vital role grew. Eisenhower enhanced the department's status even though he acted, in effect, as his own secretary of defense, a concept which Geelhoed's volume on Charles Wilson and Eisenhower confirms (1462). During Secretary McNamara's tenure, the Joint Chiefs' influence declined, but the department's status, and the secretary's, increased as its managerial operations improved. Although Palmer's study emphasizes McNamara's budgeting process relative to Vietnam (1567), his conclusions suit Kinnard's analysis. Finally, Korb's 1979 study of the growing influence of the military in the policies of the secretary of defense (1523) also matches Kinnard's theme, which concluded with James Schlesinger's term as secretary of defense.

The official documents connected with the Department of Defense between 1944 and 1978 were published in 1979 (1657). Although the editors let the documents speak for themselves, scholars familiar with the studies mentioned in the paragraph above will discern the interservice rivalries and the services' early fears that the secretary of defense would be too powerful. Gradually, however, defense necessities led Congress to legislate greater authority for the defense secretary over the service secretaries.

In contrast to the studies dealing with the broader evolution of the Defense Department, recent research has focused on the early years of America's intelligence organizations. Four studies deal with the origins of the OSS and CIA. Troy (1638) and A. C. Brown (1405) emphasize Donovan's role in the OSS / CIA relationship. Bradley Smith (1610) has written an excellent, brief general history of the OSS, using British and American records, while R. Harris Smith (1611) describes the ties of the OSS to the East Coast American foreign policy establishment. The studies of Cook (1429) and Ambrose (1378) on President Eisenhower's intelligence program added essential dimensions to the history of those operations. Both authors tend to criticize Eisenhower for giving less importance to gathering intelligence data than to maintaining covert and psychological activity in the cold war.

After 1981, the Reagan administration revised rules on intelligence operations designed to again secure the CIA from public scrutiny. Few voices objected to the new guidelines. But one notably critical article was written by former CIA director Turner and Thibault (1643).

DEFENSE PROBLEMS. Even before the Reagan administration began its huge defense build-up in 1981, defense costs and the military-industrial complex had been major issues. Koistinen surveyed this problem from the American Revolutionary War through World War II (1522). His theme was that defense expenditures require policy priorities; therefore, costs involve the need for clear foreign policy decisions. Koistinen's conception became the basis upon which critics such as DeGrasse (1433) claimed the Reagan administration erred. Critics claimed that "posture statements" such as those issued by Secretary of Defense Weinberger in 1982 (1669) lacked direction by assuming everything in the world had to be defended. Adams's study (1375) had a different cost concern, that of the type of contract system the Pentagon uses. Unlike many books on defense contracts, Adams presented both advantages and disadvantages of the system.

Three recent studies raised questions about the responsiveness of American industry to a military emergency, concluding that it is not prepared to respond. Gansler (1461), Pfaltzgraff and Ra'anan (1576), and a group of experts in Olvey, et al. (1565), reached the similar conclusions that American industry is not geared to respond to a national emergency and few plans envision such preparations. The military draft issue was revived between 1978 and 1983 because some national defense observers argued that the all-volunteer force was proving to be unsatisfactory. A 1982 report of the Atlantic Council advocated the resumption of the draft (1468). In contrast, both Moskos (1553) and the American Assembly Conference papers, edited by Scowcroft (1604), concluded that the draft was unnecessary. Two volumes discuss the various aspects of the draft: a series of readings covering historical and current materials edited by Anderson and Honegger (1380); and eight articles edited by Sarkesian (1594), which include the important question of the combat effectiveness of volunteer forces.

Several studies consider and make recommendations on improving military training programs. Buck and Korb (1408) edited ten essays on military leadership, dealing with topics such as organization theory, the psychology and ethics of leadership, and future challenges to leaders. Ten essays edited by Janowitz and Westbrook (1500) comment on education of the military, focusing on the question of "indoctrination" or "civic training." Stromberg, Wakin, and Callahan (1625) consider the role of teaching ethics to the military, including the morality of war. This last volume includes a solid bibliography on ethics in military affairs.

Arms sales as global policy is comprehensively analyzed by Pierre (1577). Dorfer (1445) and Sorley (1615) published less extensive studies regarding the value of U.S. arms sales. Dorfer deals with the successful sale of the F-16 to Belgium, Norway, Denmark, and the Netherlands in 1971. Sorley describes Nixon's policy of having arms sales serve U.S. foreign policy interests, concluding, in contrast to previous studies, that this was a "wise" program. (For a contrasting view, see Gervasi, *Supplement I* of this guide, p. 139.)

Although most studies of weapons development concentrate on one or two weapons, Fallows deals generally with the technical and bureaucratic deficiencies of preparing defense, emphasizing the difficulties encountered with the M-16 rifle and the F-16 aircraft (1451). Dagleish and Schweikart describe the evolution of the Trident submarine (1432). Huisken explains how the cruise missile was discarded during the 1950s but resurrected to meet the political needs of the 1970s SALT negotiations (1493). A broader perspective toward weapons acquisition is described in a series of essays edited by Long and Reppy (1534), which follow the weapons process from conception to operation and include one essay on the divergent process used by the Soviet Union.

Studies by Canan (1413) and Karas (1511) deal with space weapons. Canan describes the Pentagon's plans for space battle stations to knock out Soviet anti-satellite weapons, but he also deals with less futuristic weapons such as the MX, the Trident sub, and the Stealth bomber. Karas depicts the possible use of space weapons, at the same time expressing his belief that Reagan's space proposals not only endanger U.S.-Soviet space agreements but cannot create the defense system the president envisions.

The question of the Soviet use of chemical-biological weapons was raised during the early 1980s. Seagrave (1605) described the evidence for the Soviet use of these products in Southeast Asia and Afghanistan and advocated a limited U.S. program for chemical weapons. An Australian sociologist, Grant Evans, made a detailed study of American claims that the Soviets used poisons, "yellow rain," in Laos, refuting the State Department's charges (1449). Evans's study indicates that mycotaxicosis was a natural health hazard derived from fungus growing in Southeast Asia.

DIPLOMATIC PRACTICE: PAST AND PRESENT. Historical studies of the cold war's origins now have a post-revisionist synthesis in which the United States and the Soviet Union share varying degrees of blame for the breakdown of cooperation after 1945. Gaddis's historiographical essay describes the synthesis as it materialized by 1983 (1676). Gaddis has also contributed a study of 30 years of containment policy (1459) and an essay on the rise and fall of detente during the 1970s (1458). Four notable books also cover 30 years of cold war and detente and tend to reflect this synthesis: Caldwell's policy analysis (1412); Kenneth Thompson's effort to relate theories of the cold war to particular events (1633); Wettig's moderately critical attitude toward U.S. policy (1649); and Kennan's collection of essays spanning three decades of nuclear problems (1517).

The present cold war synthesis has been enhanced by two studies which emphasize Moscow's responsibility for creating postwar tensions. Mastny deals with the World War II years but demonstrates Stalin's policy of expanding Russia's security interests (1543). Taubman indicates that Soviet policy to 1953 served their political interests (1631).

Specialized studies of the Truman years have also showed the dual U.S.-Soviet role in the origins of the cold war. Hammond's edition of the recollections of ten American participants in the early cold war affirms that U.S. policy adjusted to a genuine Soviet threat (1479). Mark has edited, with commentary, the diary which Truman kept at the Potsdam Conference (1542), as well as Chester Bohlen's "realistic" 1945 memorandum indicating that Soviet activity in Eastern Europe went beyond the acceptable limits of Russia's security needs (1541). Both Messer (1550) and Ward (1647) describe Secretary of State Byrnes's role during 1945–1946, Messer stressing the relationship between Truman and Byrnes, which affected foreign policy, and Ward investigating Byrnes's unsuccessful search for a policy between harsh anticommercial rhetoric and conciliation of the USSR.

Two interesting accounts of divergent groups by DeSantis (1434) and Doenecke (1442) illustrate how U.S. cold war anti-communism developed by 1949. DeSantis studies the diverse views of U.S. Foreign Service officers who increasingly spoke to the communist threat. Doenecke explains how pre-1941 isolationists evolved an international perspective circumscribed by ardent anti-communist opinions.

The difficulty of devising foreign policies to fit atomic force and the inability of U.S. policymakers to think in terms of both force capability and foreign policies are perceived by combining the information in studies by Borowski (1401) and Herken (1481). Borowski's thesis is that the Strategic Air Command did not have a credible deterrent capacity between 1945 and 1950. Simple possession of a few atomic bombs and the planes to deliver them would have been insufficient if the U.S. had been challenged. Herken's excellent study examines how Truman's advisors hoped to monopolize atomic weapons for, according to General Graves's mistaken estimate, at least twenty years. Consequently, these men avoided postwar proposals for international control of such weapons because they planned to retain the nuclear advantage for American use in international politics.

Two other specialized studies in the Truman era deserve mention: Ballard's description of American demobilization between 1945 and 1948 (1389); and Shlaim's analysis of the decision-making process related to the Berlin blockade (1607).

Although the documentary resources necessary for improved evaluations of the years after 1953 have barely begun to become available, several studies about the period to 1968 have illuminated Soviet-American relations. Divine's works on the test-ban discussions begun under Eisenhower (1438) and, more generally, of Eisenhower's Cold War policies (1439) reflect the recent reevaluations of that president's status. Kaufman's investigation of Eisenhower's foreign economic policy describes a seldom-studied area of cold war relations (1515). Desmond Ball investigates the missile-gap controversy to its conclusion, explaining how politics forced Kennedy to pursue a strategic missile build-up even after he learned that his prior criticisms of Eisenhower's policy were incorrect (1387). This is a piece of political theater repeated in terms of Reagan's "window-of-vulnerability" myth between 1979 and 1983. Catudal's volume on Kennedy during the Berlin Wall crisis confirms prior estimates of JFK's cautious policy toward the Russians in 1961 (1418). Finally, Stern investigates how the lack of bipartisan relations with Congress handicapped Nixon's detente policies from the outset (1622).

Between 1978 and 1983, commentators found a new topic to analyze: the rise of detente from 1963 to 1975 and its demise between 1976 and 1981. Ulam's account of U.S.-Soviet relations during this period contains that author's usual insightful description of complex issues (1645). Two contrasting studies of the detente era illustrate the polemical attitudes on the issue. Pipes, who became President Reagan's expert on the USSR, published a collection of essays expressing his view that Moscow gained and the U.S. lost as a result of detente (1578). Jonathan Steele, a left-wing British journalist, opposes Pipes's "worst-case" attitude of Soviet behavior with a "best-case" opinion of Soviet intentions as entirely peace-oriented (1618). Those desiring a balanced account should read the nine essays on foreign policy issues of the 1970s edited by Gray and Michalak (1473). Evaluations must now consider Hersh's harsh criticism of Kissinger's role in detente (1484).

America's relations with its European allies has become a perennial subject for study and commentary. Ireland (1497) and Lawrence Kaplan (1508) examine the period of NATO's origins in the 1940s. Ireland finds that U.S. policymakers originally desired to rebuild Western European nations to form their own power balance. Gradually, however, the U.S. became entangled in Europe's politics as the dominant partner. Kaplan describes the U.S. bureaucratic relationship between the State and Defense departments where conflict sometimes hindered assistance programs to Europe. Kaplan also has edited a volume of twelve papers presented by experts at the Conference Center for NATO Studies in 1980. They describe the problems and plans of the 30-year NATO relationship (1509).

Between 1978 and 1983, the issue of basing new U.S. missiles in NATO countries caused further concern about NATO's future. Grosser's account of NATO's first thirty years is a Eurocentric interpretation of the difficulties of the alliance (1476). Tucker and Wrigley edited papers by three Americans and three Europeans which consider NATO problems, emphasizing the important relationship of West Germany and the U.S. and suggesting methods to improve the alliance (1642).

Four recent studies examine British-American relations between 1945 and 1949. These relations in Greece before and after the Truman Doctrine are investigated by Alexander (1317) and Wittner (1652). Alexander used British documents to conclude that Great Britain wanted a friendly, democratic Greek nation, protecting its security until the U.S. took over in 1947. Giving much attention to the internal developments in Greece, Wittner finds that the Anglo-American support of the Greek monarchy unjustly associated Greek democratic groups with left-wing communism, making Greece an early example of U.S. support for right-wing leaders and oversimplifying the relationship between moderate and socialist revolutionaries. Because Wittner is also critical of the Soviet Union's interference in Greece, his study fits the synthesis category of cold war interpretations.

Hathaway (1480) and Terry Anderson (1381) deal with separate topics of the U.S.-British relationship. Hathaway focuses on the period when Britain pulled out of Palestine and Israel became an independent nation, strongly backed by Washington. Anderson explains the broad shift of U.S. policy from mediating between British-Soviet problems to adopting an essentially British idea of the containment of Soviet influence in Europe and the Mediterranean.

Four studies explore problems of U.S. relations in Central Europe. Shlaim studies the decision-making process during the Berlin blockade (1607). Catudal has two books which examine problems of Berlin; Kennedy's cautious policy when the Berlin Wall was erected in 1961 (1418); and the detente relation which resulted in the quadripartite agreement on Berlin in 1971 (1417). Stent has an important study of the economic relationships between West Germany and the Soviet Union from 1955 to 1980 (1621). Finally, the Polish-American relationship from 1945 to 1947 is described by Lukas (1535). Providing much valuable information on a variety of problems in this relationship, Lukas concludes the U.S. did little to prevent Russian hegemony in Eastern Europe, but he fails to consider exactly what the U.S. could have effectively done to counteract it.

Two recent studies consider the triangular relationship involving the U.S., Japan, and the Atlantic Alliance. Barnet describes the creation of this power relationship, emphasizing the persistent problems which could lead to its demise (1390). A more optimistic analysis of the trilateral group is reported by the Joint Atlantic Alliance-Tokyo Institute group of experts who met in 1981 (1501). Future developments of the trilateral group may now be followed in *Trialogue*, the quarterly journal of the Trilateral Commission which began publication in 1980 (1686).

Since 1978, historical accounts of American relations with East Asia have focused on the period from 1945 to 1952. The most challenging but least conclusive of these is the report of a 1978 conference of experts on East Asia, edited by Borg and Heinrichs (1400). Among the topics covered at the conference were the perimeter strategy revived in 1949 and whether or not the Truman administration lost its chance to affirm good relations with Mao Tse-tung in 1949. In contrast to some historians of U.S. diplomacy who emphasize the "last chance" theory, Asian historians at the conference tended to doubt that Mao Tse-tung's terms for recognition could have been accepted by any American president at that time.

One advocate of the "last chance" idea is Nancy Tucker (1640), whose study emphasizes that most American groups dealing with China policy favored recognition in 1949; the Truman administration did not act because low priority was attributed to that problem. Scholars dealing with this issue will want to read the recent opinions of two diplomatic participants in the events of 1949–1950, Philip D. Sprouse and O. Edmund Clubb, which Warren Cohen comments on and *Diplomatic History* reprints (1425).

Buhite (1409) and Chern (1420) examine different aspects of the Chinese recognition question. Buhite deals with broad aspects of U.S. policy from 1945 to 1950, contending that Washington policymakers could not decide on East Asia's strategic value and, consequently, were uncertain about the correct policy. Chern finds the origins of America's domestic political dispute on East Asia evolving from

Hurley's mission of 1945 and reaching such heated controversy that Truman could not recognize the communists in 1949.

Stueck (1626) and Blum (1399) investigate other East Asia consequences connected to the China policy. Examining the U.S.-China-Korean relationship, Steuck concludes that Truman's policy of restraint in China led to recklessness in Korea in 1950 because Truman and Secretary Acheson had to demonstrate American credibility. Blum researches the U.S.-China-Southeast Asia connection, reaching a conclusion similar to Stueck but substituting Southeast Asia for Korea.

While Stueck relates America's Korean policy to the China card, Cumings (1431), Dobbs (1441), and Matray (1544) treat the Korean issue largely as a separate question. Both Cumings, whose study is the first of two planned volumes, and Dobbs deal with U.S. reactions to internal political developments in Korea, emphasizing how Washington followed a counterrevolutionary course as part of its anti-communist policy. Cumings is especially valuable for material on Korea's internal situation. Matray has published several articles dealing with the Washington decisions made about Korea. One example of his work is an article on the decision to divide Korea.

Two other recent books on Korea should be noted. Cumings has edited a series of essays on U.S.-Korean relations, one of which surveys the sources on the topic available at the National Archives (1430). Goulden's account of the Korean War is concerned primarily with the consequences of MacArthur's insubordination (1469).

Historical studies of post-1945 American-Japanese relations have been relatively few. Yoshitsu (1654) and Shiels (1606) write about opposite eras of U.S.-Japanese history. The San Francisco Treaty of 1951 and its negotiation process is described by Yoshitsu. Shiels examines the difficulties that had developed in the Tokyo-Washington alliance by 1970. Two other volumes provide a valuable analysis of contemporary Japanese-American relations. Destler and Sato prepared a study explaining how the two nations worked out their problems in the early 1970s as a guide to working them out again in the 1980s (1435). Tsurutani explains Japan's important role in the late 20th century and argues that Tokyo must assume greater responsibility for its actions relative to its status (1639).

Since 1978, general accounts of America's involvement in Vietnam have begun to appear. The most balanced study is Herring's *America's Longest War* (1482), although by 1983 parts of the volume have become outdated by the appearance of declassified material and new research. Gelb and Betts analyze the Washington decisions on Vietnam, arguing that in the context of the containment policy which predominated to 1968, the American involvement worked by delaying the communist take-over for 20 years (1463). Lewy's study became controversial because he examined difficult issues such as whether U.S. bombings were so terrifying (they were not, he says), and why U.S. army officers did *not* adopt General Abram's changes in General Westmoreland's attrition strategy (1531). Two books have resulted from separate television programs on the conflict: Maclear's, based on a Canadian series (1536); and Karnow's, which was the textbook for a 13-part U.S. television program (1512).

Specialized studies on Vietnam have covered a variety of topics. A former U.S. intelligence officer, Patti, mourns the American failure to support Ho Chi Minh in 1945, a decision whose consequences are known but whose counterfactual results never will be (1570). Berman (1393) and Thies (1632) examine President

Johnson's decisions in 1965 and the results of those decisions, Berman focusing on July 1965, when America assumed control of the ground war, and Thies demonstrating the limits of coercive diplomacy which could not obtain Hanoi's surrender. Summers (1629) and "Cincinnatus" (1421) make critiques of U.S. military strategy in Vietnam. Summers's study is the more important, concluding that clarity of political and military objectives are essential. "Cincinnatus," the pseudonym for Cecil B. Currey, writes a passionate, perhaps exaggerated, criticism of the U.S. army's breakdown. This volume may have become better known because of the initial mystery surrounding its author.

Five books investigate the 1973 truce and the fall of Saigon. Goodman uses many nonattributable interviews as the basis for a study of the negotiating process leading to the 1973 truce (1467). Isaacs writes a journalistic description of the conflict from January 1973 to April 1975, when Saigon fell (1498). Hosmer summarizes the views of 27 former South Vietnamese officials who criticize their own behavior but attribute most of the blame for their plight to the role of the U.S. in their country (1488). Haley composes a case study of Congressional responsibility for the disaster in Cambodia and South Vietnam, arguing that some blame resulted from the president's assumption that congressional silence meant consent, because Nixon seldom consulted directly with leaders of Congress (1478).

Two additional studies about Southeast Asia should be noted. Papp's unusual study examines the diverse attitudes toward the Vietnam conflict emanating from Moscow, Peking, and Washington (1568). Futrell and Blumenson narrate the evolution of the U.S. Air Force's involvement in Vietnam from an early advisory-training status to operations and combat in 1962. An official history, this study avoids controversial but essential political questions, such as: Did the Air Force know its precise objectives in Vietnam, or simply follow orders? (1457).

Concerning U.S.-Middle Eastern policy, the two best general accounts are by Tillman (1636) and the *Congressional Quarterly* (1427). Tillman's study of the issues of the 1970s emphasizes the Arab-Israeli problem, assuming that the problems of the Northern Tier and Persian Gulf states are peripheral. The *Congressional Quarterly* provides an excellent basic discussion on Middle Eastern problems and has useful maps, chronologies, and texts of documents.

Kuniholm (1524), Irvine Anderson (1379), and Miller (1551) investigate the origins of America's interest in Middle East oil resources and consequent big power politics in that region. Kuniholm believes the Truman Doctrine extended further into the Middle East through Greece and Turkey, inaugurating cold war tensions in that region as well as in Europe. Anderson explains how U.S. policymakers became aware of the nation's need for Saudi Arabian oil during World War II, and how the State Department assisted private U.S. business interests in replacing British hegemony in the area. While Anderson gives primary attention to the relations between the State Department and Aramco, Miller offers a more traditional diplomatic history of the U.S. contacts with Saudi Arabia.

Two studies of U.S. policy surrounding the 1956 Suez crisis contribute further to the positive evaluations of Eisenhower's presidency. Myers describes American relations with Eqypt from 1952 to 1958, years when the British left Suez, President Nasser inspired Arab nationalism, and Soviet interests expanded in the Middle East (1555). Neff deals more particularly with the Suez crisis, providing a fairly coherent description of the complex issues raised at the United Nations as well as in Washington, London, and Paris (1558).

No satisfactory study of the Camp David agreements between Egypt and Israel has yet appeared. Friedlander's account of the discussions between Sadat and Begin from 1977 to 1979 emphasizes the domestic political influences on the two leaders (1454). Undoubtedly, the continued difficulty in obtaining any agreement on the West Bank settlements makes commentators hesitant to reach conclusions about the final effect of President Carter's achievement at Camp David.

In contrast to the dearth of material about Camp David, the fall of the shah of Iran in January 1980 inspired numerous descriptions of American-Iranian relations. Rabin has an excellent general account of U.S. policy toward Iran from 1905 to 1980 (1585). Saikal's study is best in its coverage of the period from 1953 to 1970, following the overthrow of Mosadegh's nationalist government (1592). Stempel gives an insider's view of the shah's final years in power (1620), while Hoveyda, a brother of a former Iranian prime minister, writes a good personal account of the shah (1490).

Students may become acquainted with four recent studies on Soviet policy and U.S. security interests in the Middle East by reading Dekmejian's review article (1672). As the author notes, events in the Middle East have happened so quickly from 1979 to 1984 that any attempt at current commentaries on that region quickly becomes obsolete.

Since 1978, four noteworthy studies have dealt with U.S. policy in Africa. Lemarchand edited a series of essays which were generally critical of American policy in South Africa (1530). Jackson surveys various cases of U.S. involvement in Africa such as the Congo in 1960 and Angola in the 1970s, concluding that Washington preferred to react to African problems in cold war terms rather than understand the difficulties facing the African people (1499). In a more detailed study of U.S. policy in the Congo under Eisenhower and Kennedy, Kalb reached similar conclusions in one of the best researched studies available on the U.S. and Africa (1506). Ottaway investigates Soviet and American influence in the Horn of Africa, demonstrating that neither power has achieved an effective role in that region (1566).

The Third World's problems and their relation to the cold war are discussed in seven recent volumes. Three of these describe the Soviet Union's policies in less-developed nations. Laqueur (1526) and Donaldson (1443) each edit essays by different experts which indicate the shortsighted policies of both Moscow and Washington in the Third World. Hosmer and Wolfe compose a general survey of Soviet activity in the Third World, including in their study a valuable list of bibliographic references (1489).

Rothstein offers tough-minded insights into understanding American policy prospects in the Third World (1590). Stavrianos surveys the historic economic problems of the Third World since 1945 (1616). Olson, a retired foreign service officer, describes the north-south negotiations conducted during the 1970s (1564). Finally, the report of the North-South Commission headed by West German politician Willy Brandt provides a sympathetic tone in assessing the financial and economic problems of the southern nations, which the northern nations must resolve (1402).

Although Latin America should be of central importance to the United States, high-level independent policy conferences on this region are infrequent. Nevertheless, individual scholars investigate the Americas and explain their concern that Americans give only peripheral attention to understanding their near neighbors. Pearce (1573) and Perkins (1574) have written contrasting evaluations of America's Caribbean policies. Pearce is critical of past U.S. interventions in Caribbean-Central American nations; Perkins's official-style study emphasizes that the U.S. usually restrains its use of power in the area. A third general study of Latin America, by Blaiser (1397), describes Soviet policy in Latin America. Blaiser, like most experts on Moscow's behavior in the Western Hemisphere, concludes that excepting its strong support for Cuban communism, the Soviet leaders are generally cautious in trying to exert influence in Latin America.

Since 1978, other notable studies on Latin American-U.S. relations have covered a scattering of topics. Immerman's account of the 1954 overthrow of Jacobo Arbenz in Guatemala concludes that Eisenhower waited as long as possible to avoid American action, depicting the president in the favorable light of recent Eisenhower studies (1495). A more popular account of the Guatemalan coup of 1954, written by Stephen Schlesinger and Stephen Kinzer, borrows heavily from Immerman's doctoral dissertation (1588). Rabe surveys the generally good relations between the U.S. and Venezuela from 1919 to 1976, relations which did not sour even when Venezuela joined OPEC in raising oil prices (1584). Sigmund's study of Salvador Allende should be noted because it examines the internal economic and political problems of Chile which, the author contends, were most critical in causing Pinochet's 1973 coup (1608).

In the early 1980s, Nicaragua and El Salvador became the focal points of American policy. A French commentator, Weber, sympathetically describes the Sandanista revolution in Nicaragua (1648). Gettleman has edited an excellent series of documents and essays on El Salvador which is useful in understanding that nation's crisis (1466). Armstrong and Shenk's volume on El Salvador (1383) is pro-revolutionary, describing the host of economic and political difficulties facing peasants in that country. A contrary anti-revolutionary view of Central American struggles is presented in two articles by Kirkpatrick (1519, 1520). As Reagan's principal advisor on Latin America, Kirkpatrick's views are essential to comprehending the president's attitudes.

The issuance in January 1984 of the Report of the President's Commission on Central America, chaired by Henry Kissinger (1587), spawned two significant volumes which differed from the commission's findings. One, edited by Diskin, displays the radical opposition's belief that the report failed to understand the economic and social conditions in Central America (1436). The second, edited by Leikin and sponsored by the Carnegie Endowment for International Peace, is moderate in tone but equally condemning of the commission's unsatisfactory handling of prior American interventions and its support of right-wing regimes in Central America (1529).

RESEARCH RECOMMENDED. The usual detailed analyses of the Eisenhower and Kennedy years should appear as the documentary materials become generally available to scholars. It is hoped that these will include studies on a neglected question: Were diplomatic officers schooled in the military imperatives of their duties in a fashion similar to the military officer's concern for political affairs after 1945? The diplomatic "mind" required a reorientation—did it take place? Within the Defense Department, studies are needed on the relation of the service secretaries and their staffs to the secretary of defense and the NSC. Relating the developments of the "action" level of the armed forces to the shift from NSC-68 to the "new look" and later, under Kennedy, to "flexible response" should provide valuable insights about translating high-level policy into practice. Included in this issue is the practical requirement of carrying out Eisenhower's bugetary restraints on the services.

BIBLIOGRAPHY

ARTICLES AND BOOKS

1375. Adams, Gordon. *The Iron Triangle: The Politics of Defense Contracts.* New York: Council on Economic Priorities, 1981.

1376. Adams, Gordon, and David Gold. "Derail the MX." *Nation* 29 (10 November 1979): 461–62.

1377. Alexander, G. M. *The Prelude to the Truman Doctrine: British Policy in Greece, 1944–1947.* New York: Clarendon Press / Oxford, 1983.

1378. Ambrose, Stephen E. *Ike's Spies: Eisenhower and the Espionage Establishment.* New York: Doubleday, 1981.

1379. Anderson, Irvine H. *Armaco, The United States and Saudi Arabia: A Study of the Dynamics of Foreign Oil Policy, 1933–1950.* Princeton, N.J.: Princeton University Press, 1981.

1380. Anderson, Martin, and Barbara Honegger, eds. *The Military Draft: Selected Readings on Conscription.* Stanford, Calif.: Hoover Institution Press, 1982.

1381. Anderson, Terry H. *The United States, Great Britain, and the Cold War, 1944–1947.* Columbia: University of Missouri, 1981.

1382. Arbatov, Georgi, and William Oltmans. *The Soviet Viewpoint.* New York: Dodd, Mead, 1983.

1383. Armstrong, Robert, and Janet Shenk. *El Salvador: The Face of Revolution.* Boston: South End Press, 1983.

1384. Arnett, Robert L. "Soviet Military Doctrine: Views on Nuclear War." *Arms Control Today* 8 (October 1978): 1–3.

1385. Ball, Desmond. "The MX Basing Decision." *Survival* 22 (March / April, 1980): 58–65.

1386. _____. "Can Nuclear War Be Controlled?" *Adelphi Papers*, International Institute for Strategic Studies, Fall, 1981.

1387. _____. *Politics and Force Levels: The Strategic Missile Program of the Kennedy Administration.* Berkeley: University of California Press, 1981.

1388. Ball, George W. *The Past Has Another Pattern: Memoirs.* New York: W. W. Norton, 1982.

1389. Ballard, Jack Stokes. *The Shock of Peace: Military and Economic Demobilization After World War II.* Washington, D.C.: University Press of America, 1983.

1390. Barnet, Richard J. *The Alliance: America, Europe, Japan, Makers of the Postwar World.* New York: Simon & Schuster, 1983.

1391. Barrett, Laurence I. *Gambling with History: Reagan in the White House.* New York: Doubleday, 1983.

1392. Becker, Abraham S. *The Burden of Soviet Defense: A Polictical-Economic Essay.* Santa Monica, Calif.: Rand Corporation Report #R-2752-AF, 1981.

1393. Berman, Larry. *Planning a Tragedy: The Americanization of the War in Vietnam*. New York: W. W. Norton, 1982.
1394. Bernstein, Barton J. "The Cuban Missile Crisis: Trading the Jupiters in Turkey?" *Political Science Quarterly* 95 (1980). 87–125.
1395. Bertram, Christopher, ed. *Prospects of Soviet Power in the 1980s*. Hamden, Conn.: Archon Books, 1980.
1396. Bialer, Seweryn. *Stalin's Successors: Leadership, Stability, and Change in the Soviet Union*. New York: Cambridge University Press, 1980.
1397. Blaiser, Cole. *The Giant's Rival: The USSR in Latin America*. Pittsburgh, Pa.: University of Pittsburgh, Press, 1983.
1398. Blechman, Barry M., ed. *Rethinking the U.S. Strategic Posture*. Cambridge, Mass.: Ballinger, 1982.
1399. Blum, Robert M. *Drawing the Line: The Origin of the American Containment Policy in East Asia*. New York: W. W. Norton, 1982.
1400. Borg, Dorothy, and Waldo Heinrichs, eds. *Uncertain Years: Chinese-American Relations, 1947–1950*. New York: Columbia University Press, 1980.
1401. Borowski, Harry R. *A Hollow Threat: Strategic Air Power and Containment before Korea*. Westport, Conn.: Greenwood Press, 1982.
1402. Brandt Commission. *Common Crisis, North-South: Co-operation for World Recovery*. Cambridge, Mass.: MIT Press, 1983.
1403. Brodie, Bernard. "Development of Nuclear Strategy." *International Security* 2 (Spring 1978): 65–83.
1404. Brown, Harold. *Thinking about National Security: Defense and Foreign Policy in a Dangerous World*. Baltimore, Md.: Johns Hopkins University, Press, 1983.
1405. Brown, Anthony Cave. *The Last Hero: Wild Bill Donovan*. New York: Times Books, 1983.
1406. Brownstein, Ronald, and Nina Easton. *Reagan's Ruling Class: Portraits of the President's Top One Hundred Officials*. New York: Pantheon Books, 1983.
1407. Brzezinski, Zbigniew. *Power and Principle: Memoirs of the National Security Adviser, 1977–1981*. New York: Farrar, Straus & Giroux, 1983.
1408. Buck, James H., and Lawrence Korb, eds. *Military Leadership*. Beverly Hills, Calif.: Sage, 1981.
1409. Buhite, Russell D. *Soviet-American Relations in Asia, 1945–1954*. Norman: University of Oklahoma Press, 1981.
1410. Builder, Carl H. "Why Not First Strike Counterforce Capabilities." *Strategic Review* 7 (Spring 1979): 32–39.
1411. Byrnes, Robert F., ed. *After Brezhnev: Sources of Soviet Conduct in the 1980s*. Bloomington: Indiana University, 1983.
1412. Caldwell, Dan. *American-Soviet Relations: From 1947 to the Nixon-Kissinger Grand Design*. Westport, Conn.: Greenwood Press, 1981.
1413. Canan, James. *War in Space*. New York: Harper & Row, 1982.
1414. Carnesale, Arthur, and the Harvard Nuclear Study Group. *Living with Nuclear Weapons*. New York: Bantam Books, 1983.
1415. Caro, Robert A. *The Years of Lyndon Johnson. Vol. 1, The Path to Power*. New York: Alfred A. Knopf, 1982.
1416. Carter, Jimmy. *Keeping Faith: Memoirs of a President*. New York: Bantam

174 • SOURCES OF U.S. MILITARY HISTORY: SUPPLEMENT II

Books, 1982.
1417. Catudal, Honoré M. J. *The Diplomacy of the Quadripartite Agreement on Berlin: A New Era in East-West Politics*. Berlin: Berlin-Verlag, 1978.
1418. _____. *Kennedy and the Berlin Wall Crisis: A Case Study in U.S. Decision Making*. Berlin: Berlin-Verlag, 1980.
1419. Center for Defense Information. "Preparing for Nuclear War: President Reagan's Program." *The Defense Monitor*. Vol. 10, no. 8, 1982.
1420. Chern, Kenneth S. *Dilemma in China: America's Policy Debate, 1945*. Hamden, Conn.: Archon Books, 1980.
1421. "Cincinnatus" [Cecil B. Currey]. *Self-Destruction: The Disintegration and Decay of the United States Army in the Vietnam Era*. New York: W. W. Norton, 1981.
1422. Clark, Ian. *Limited Nuclear War: Political Theory and War*. Princeton, N.J.: Princeton University Press, 1982.
1423. Cline, Ray S. *World Power Trends and the U.S. Foreign Policy for the 1980s*. Boulder, Colo.: Westview Press, 1980.
1424. Cockburn, Andrew. *The Threat: Inside the Soviet Military Machine*. New York: Random House, 1983.
1425. Cohen, Warren I. "Ambassador Philip D. Sprouse on the Question of Recognition..." and "Consul General O. Edmund Clubb on the 'Inevitability' of Conflict..." *Diplomatic History* 2 (1978). 213–17, and 5 (1981). 165–68.
1426. Cohen, Warren I. *Dean Rusk*. Totowa, N.J.: Cooper Square, 1980.
1427. Congressional Quarterly. *The Middle East*. 5th Ed. Washington, D.C., 1981.
1428. Conquest, Robert. *Present Danger: Towards a Foreign Policy*. Stanford, Calif.: Hoover Institution Press, 1979.
1429. Cook, Blanche Wiesen. *The Declassified Eisenhower: A Divided Legacy*. New York: Doubleday, 1981.
1430. Cumings, Bruce, ed. *Child of Conflict: The Korean-American Relationship, 1943–53*. Seattle: Washington University Press, 1983.
1431. _____. *The Origins of the Korean War*. Princeton, N.J.: Princeton University Press, 1981.
1432. Dagleish, D. Douglas, and Larry Schweikart. *Trident*. Carbondale: Southern Illinois University Press, 1982.
1433. DeGrasse, Robert, Paul Murphy, and William Ragen, *The Costs and Consequences of Reagan's Military Build-Up*. New York: Council on Economic Priorities, 1982.
1434. DeSantis, Hugh. *The Diplomacy of Silence: The American Foreign Service, the Soviet Union, and the Cold War, 1933–1947*. Chicago: University of Chicago Press, 1980.
1435. Destler, I. M., and Hideo Sato, eds. *Coping with U.S.-Japanese Conflicts*. Lexington, Mass.: Lexington Books, 1982.
1436. Diskin, Martin, ed. *Trouble in our Backyard: Central America and the United States in the Eighties*. New York: Pantheon Books, 1984.
1437. *Diplomatic History* 8 (Winter 1984). Walter LaFeber, "From Confusion to Cold War: The Memoirs of the Carter Administration," 1–12; Kent M. Beck, "Necessary Lies, Hidden Truths: Cuba in the 1960 Campaign," 37–59; Thomas J. Noer, "The New Frontier and African Neutralism:

Kennedy, Nkrumah, and the Volta River Project," 61–79; David C. Humphreys, "Tuesday Lunch at the White House: A Preliminary Asessment," 81–101.

1438. Divine, Robert A. *Blowing on the Wind: The Nuclear Test Ban Debate, 1954–1960*. New York: Oxford University Press, 1978.

1439. _____. *Eisenhower and the Cold War*. New York: Oxford University Press, 1981.

1440. _____. *Exploring the Johnson Years*. Austin: University of Texas Press, 1981.

1441. Dobbs, Charles M. *The Unwanted Symbol: American Foreign Policy, the Cold War, and Korea, 1945–1950*. Kent, Ohio: Kent State University Press, 1981.

1442. Doenecke, Justus D. *Not to the Swift: The Old Isolationists in the Cold War Era*. Lewisburg, Pa.: Bucknell University, 1979.

1443. Donaldson, Robert H., ed. *The Soviet Union in the Third World: Successes and Failures*. Boulder, Colo.: Westview Press, 1981.

1444. Donovan, Robert J. *Tumultuous Years: The Presidency of Harry S. Truman, 1949–1953*. New York: W. W. Norton, 1982.

1445. Dorfer, Ingemar. *Arms Deal: The Selling of the F-16*. New York: Praeger, 1982.

1446. Douglas, J., and A. Hoeber. *Soviet Strategy of Nuclear War*. Stanford, Calif.: Hoover Institution Press, 1979.

1447. Douglas, Roy. *From War to Cold War, 1942–48*. New York: St. Martin's, 1981.

1448. An *Evaluation of U.S. and Soviet Strategic Capability through the Mid-1980s*. Washington, D.C.: Committee on the Present Danger, 1978.

1449. Evans, Grant. *The Yellow Rainmakers*. New York: Verso / Schocken, 1983.

1450. Fairbank, John K. *Chinabound: A Fifty-Year Memoir*. New York: Harper & Row, 1982.

1451. Fallows, James. *National Defense*. New York: Random House, 1981.

1452. Ferrell, Robert H., ed. *The Eisenhower Diaries*. New York: W. W. Norton, 1981.

1453. Ferrell, Robert H., ed. *The Diary of James C. Hagerty: Eisenhower in Mid-course, 1954–1955*. Bloomington: Indiana University Press, 1983.

1454. *Foreign Affairs*, vol. 60 (1981–1982). Kenny Spurgeon, and Wolfgang Panofsky, "MAD vs. NUTS: The Mutual Hostage Relationship of the Superpowers," 287–304; Stanley Hoffman, "NATO and Nuclear Weapons," 327–46; McGeorge Bundy et al., "Nuclear Weapons and the Atlantic Alliance," 753–68; Stanley Kober et al., "The Debate over No First Use," 71–80.

1455. Friedlander, Melvin A. *Sadat and Begin: The Domestic Politics of Peacemaking*. Boulder, Colo.: Westview Press, 1983.

1456. Freedman, Lawrence. *The Evolution of Nuclear Strategy*. New York: St. Martin's, 1981.

1457. Futrell, Robert F., and Martin Blumenson. *The United States Air Force in Southeast Asia: The Advisory Years to 1965*. Washington, D.C.: Office of Air Force History, 1981.

1458. Gaddis, John Lewis. "The Rise, Fall and Future of Detente." *Foreign Affairs*

62 (Winter 1938–84). 354–77.

1459. _____. *Strategies of Containment: A Critical Appraisal of Postwar American National Security Policy*. New York: Oxford University Press, 1982.

1460. Galbraith, John Kenneth. *A Life in Our Times: Memoirs*. Boston: Houghton Mifflin, 1981.

1461. Gansler, Jacques S. *The Defense Industry*. Cambridge, Mass.: MIT Press, 1980.

1462. Geelhoed, E. Bruce. *Charles E. Wilson and Controversy at the Pentagon, 1953 to 1957*. Detroit, Mich.: Wayne State University Press, 1979.

1463. Gelb, Leslie, and Richard K. Betts. *The Irony of Vietnam: The System Worked*. Washington, D.C.: Brookings Institution, 1979.

1464. Gelb, Leslie. "Is the Nuclear Threat Manageable?" *New York Times Magazine* (4 March 1984), 26–36 ff.

1465. George, Alexander. *Managing U.S.-Soviet Rivalry: Problems of Crisis Prevention*. Boulder, Colo.: Westview Press, 1983.

1466. Gettleman, Marvin E., et al *El Salvador-Central America in the New Cold War*. New York: Evergreen / Grove, 1982.

1467. Goodman, Allan E. *The Lost Peace: America's Search for a Negotiated Settlement of the Vietnam War*. Stanford, Calif. Hoover Institution Press, 1978.

1468. Goodpaster, Andrew J., Lloyd H. Elliott, and J. Allen Hovey, Jr. *Toward a Consensus on Military Service*. Elmsford, N.Y.: Pergamon Press, 1982.

1469. Goulden, Joseph C. *Korea, The Untold Story of the War*. New York: Times Books, 1982.

1470. Gouré, Leon, and Michelle Deane. "The Soviet Strategic View". *Strategic Review 8* (Fall 1980): 79–97.

1471. Gray, Colin S. *The MX ICBM and National Security*. New York: Praeger, 1981.

1472. Gray, Colin S., and Keith Payne. "Victory is Possible." *Foreign Policy* 39 (Summer 1980): 14–27.

1473. Gray, Robert C., and Stanley J. Michalak, Jr., eds. *American Foreign Policy since Detente*. New York: Harper & Row, 1983.

1474. Greenstein, Fred I. *The Hidden-Hand Presidency: Eisenhower as Leader*. New York: Basic Books, 1982.

1475. Griffith, Robert. "Why They Like Ike." *Reviews in American History*, 7 (1979): 577–83.

1476. Grosser, Alfred. *The Western Alliance: European-American Relations since 1945*. Translated by Michael Shaw. New York: Continuum, 1980.

1477. Hadsel, Fred L. and Larry Bland, eds. *The Papers of General George Catlett Marshall*. Vol. I, 1880–1939. Baltimore, Md.: Johns Hopkins University Press, 1981.

1478. Haley, P. Edward. *Congress and the Fall of South Vietnam and Cambodia*. East Brunswick, N.J.: Fairleigh Dickinson University Press, 1982.

1479. Hammond, Thomas T., ed. *Witnesses to the Origins of the Cold War*. Seattle: University of Washington Press, 1982.

1480. Hathaway, Robert M. *Ambiguous Partnership: Britain and America, 1944–1947*. New York: Columbia University, 1981.

1481. Herken, Gregg F., *The Winning Weapon: The Atomic Bomb in the Cold*

War, 1945–1975. New York: Alfred A. Knopf,1981.

1482. Herring, George. *America's Longest War: The United States and Vietnam, 1950–1975.* New York: John Wiley and Sons, 1979.

1483. Herring, George C., ed., *The Secret Diplomacy of the Vietnam War: The Negotiating Volumes of the Pentagon Papers.* Austin: University of Texas Press, 1983.

1484. Hersh, Seymour M. *The Price of Power: Kissinger in the Nixon White House.* New York: Summit Books, 1983.

1485. Hoffman, Stanley. *Duties Beyond Borders: On the Limits and Possibilities of Ethical International Politics.* Syracuse, N.J.: Syracuse University Press, 1981.

1486. Hoffman, Stanley. *Primary or World Order: American Foreign Policy since the Cold War.* New York: McGraw-Hill 1978.

1487. Hoover, Robert A. *The MX Controversy: A Guide to Issues and References.* Claremont, Calif.: Regina Books, 1982.

1488. Hosmer, Stephen T., Konrad Keller, and Brain M. Jenkins. *The Fall of South Vietnam.* New York: Crane, Russak, 1980.

1489. Hosmer, Stephen T., and Thomas W. Wolfe. *Soviet Policy and Practice toward Third World Conflicts.* Lexington, Mass.: Lexington Books 1983

1490. Hoveyda, Fereydown. *The Fall of the Shah.* Translated by Roger Liddell. New York: Wyndham Books, 1980.

1491. Howard, Michael. "Conducting the Concert of Powers." Review of Kissinger's *The White House Years. Times Literary Supplement,* 20 December 1979, 147–49. Reprinted in *Armed Forces and Society, vol. 6.*

1492. Howard , Michael. "On Fighting a Nuclear War." *International Security* 5 (Spring 1981): 3–17.

1493. Huisken, Ronald. *The Origin of the Strategic Cruise Missile.* New York: Praeger, 1981.

1494. Huntington, Samuel P., ed. *The Strategic Imperative: New Policies for American Security.* Cambridge, Mass.: Ballinger (for the Harvard Center for International Affairs), 1982.

1495. Immerman, Richard H. *The CIA in Guatemala: The Foreign Policy of Intervention.* Austin: University of Texas Press, 1982.

1496. Immerman, Richard H. "Eisenhower and Dulles: Who Made the Decisions?" *Political Psychology* 1 (Autumn 1979): 21–38.

1497. Ireland, Timothy P. *Creating the Entangling Alliance: The Origins of the North Atlantic Treaty Organization.* Westport, Conn.: Greenwood Press, 1981.

1498. Isaacs, Arnold R. *Without Honor: Defeat in Vietnam and Cambodia.* Baltimore, Md.: Johns Hopkins University Press, 1983.

1499. Jackson, Henry F. *From the Congo to Soweto: U.S. Foreign Policy toward Africa since 1960.* New York: William Morrow, 1982.

1500. Janowitz, Morris, and Stephen D. Westbrook, eds. *The Political Education of Soldiers.* Beverly Hills, Calif.: Sage, 1982.

1501. Joint Working Group, Atlantic Council of the U.S. and Research Institute for Peace and Security, Tokyo. *The `Common Security Interests of Japan, The United States and NATO.* Cambridge, Mass.: Ballinger, 1981.

1502. Jervis, Robert. "Why Nuclear Superiority Doesn't Matter". *Political Science Quarterly* 94 (Winter 1979–80): 614–34.

1503. Jones, Christopher D. "Soviet Military Doctrine: The Political Dimension." *Arms Control Today* 8 (October 1978): 1, 4–5.

1504. Jordan, Hamilton. *Crisis: The Last Year of the Carter Presidency*. New York: Putnam, 1982.

1505. Jurika, Stephen Jr., ed. *From Pearl Harbor to Vietnam: The Memoirs of Admiral Arthur W. Radford*. Stanford, Calif.: Hoover Institution Press, 1980.

1506. Kalb, Madeleine G. *The Congo Cables: The Cold War in Africa From Eisenhower to Kennedy*. New York: Macmillan, 1982.

1507. Kaplan, Red. *The Wizards of Armageddon*. New York: Simon & Schuster, 1983.

1508. Kaplan, Lawrence S. *A Community of Interests: NATO and the Military Assistance Program, 1948–1951*. Washington, D.C.: Office of Secretary of Defense, 1980.

1509. Kaplan, Lawrence S., and Robert W. Clawson, eds. *NATO After Thirty Years*. Wilmington, Del.: Scholarly Resources, 1980.

1510. Kaplan, Stephen et al. *Diplomacy of Power: Soviet Armed Forces as a Political Instrument*. Washington, D.C.: Brookings Institution, 1981.

1511. Karas, Thomas. *The New High Ground: Systems and Weapons of Space Age War*. New York: Simon & Schuster, 1982.

1512. Karnow, Stanley. *Vietnam—A History*. New York: Viking Press, 1983.

1513. Kattenburg, Paul M. *The Vietnam Trauma in American Foreign Policy, 1945–75*. New Brunswick, N.J.: Transaction Books, 1980.

1514. Katz, Arthur M. *Life after Nuclear War*. Cambridge, Mass.: Ballinger, 1981.

1515. Kaufman, Burton I. *Trade and Aid: Eisenhower's Foreign Economic Policy, 1953–1961*. Baltimore, Md.: Johns Hopkins University Press, 1982.

1516. Kegley, Charles W., and E. Wittkopf. "Reagan Administration's World View." *Orbis* 26 (Spring 1982). 223–44.

1517. Kennan, George F. *The Nuclear Delusion: Soviet-American Relations in the Atomic Age*. New York: Pantheon Books, 1982.

1518. Kinnard, Douglas. *The Secretary of Defense*. Lexington: Kentucky University Press, 1981.

1519. Kirkpatrick, Jeanne. "Dictatorships and Double Standards." *Commentary* 68 (November 1979): 34–45.

1520. _____. "U.S. Security and Latin America." *Commentary* 71 (January 1981): Vol. 1, 29–40.

1521. Kissinger, Henry. *The White House Years*, and vol. 2, *Years of Upheaval*. Boston: Little, Brown, 1979–1982.

1522. Koistinen, Paul A. C. *The Military-Industrial Complex: A Historical Perspective*. New York: Praeger, 1980.

1523. Korb, Lawrence J. *The Fall and Rise of the Pentagon: American Defense Policies in the 1970s*. Westport, Conn.: Greenwood Press, 1979.

1524. Kuniholm, Bruce. *The Origins of the Cold War in the Near East: Great Power Conflict and Diplomacy in Iran, Turkey, and Greece*. Princeton, N.J.: Princeton University Press, 1980.

1525. LaFeber, Walter. "From Confusion to Cold War: The Memoirs of the Carter Administration." *Diplomatic History* 8 (Winter 1984): 1–12.

1526. Laqueur, Walter, ed. *The Pattern of Soviet Conduct in the Third World*.

New York: Praeger, 1983.
1527. Lee, R. Alton. *Dwight D. Eisenhower: Soldier and Statesman.* Chicago: Nelson-Hall, 1981.
1528. Lees, Lorraine M., and Sandra Gioia Treadway. "Review Essay: A Future for Our Diplomatic Past? A Critical Appraisal of the Foreign Relations Series." *Journal of American History* 70 (December 1983): 621–29.
1529. Leiken, Robert S., ed. *Central America: Anatomy of Conflict.* New York: Pergamon Press, 1984.
1530. Lemarchand, Rene, ed. *American Policy in Southern Africa: The Stakes and the Stance.* 2d ed. Washington, D.C.: University Press of America, 1981.
1531. Lewy, Guenter. *America in Vietnam.* New York: Oxford University Press, 1978.
1532. Lifton, Robert Jay, and Richard Falk. *Indefensible Weapons.* New York: Basic Books, 1982.
1533. Lockwood, Jonathan Samuel. *The Soviet View of U.S. Strategic Doctrine.* New Brunswick, N.J.: Transaction Books (for the National Strategy Information Center), 1983.
1534. Long, Franklin A., and Judith Reppy, eds. *The Genesis of New Weapons: Decision Making for Military R & D.* Elmsford, N.Y.: Pergamon Press, 1980.
1535. Lukas, Richard C. *Bitter Legacy: Polish–American Relations in the Wake of World War II.* Lexington: University Press of Kentucky, 1982.
1536. Maclear, Michael. *The Ten Thousand Day War: Vietnam: 1945–1975.* New York: St. Martin's, 1981.
1537. Mako, William P. *U.S. Ground Forces and the Defense of Central Europe.* Washington, D.C.: Brookings, Institution, 1983.
1538. Mandelbaum, Michael. *The Nuclear Revolution: International Politics Before and After Hiroshima.* New York: Cambridge University Press, 1981.
1539. _____. *The Nuclear Question: The United States and Nuclear Weapons, 1946–1976.* Cambridge, Mass.: Cambridge University Press, 1979.
1540. Margiotta, Franklin D., James Brown, and Michael J. Collins, eds. *Changing U.S. Military Manpower Realities.* Boulder, Colo.: Westview Press, 1983.
1541. Mark, Edward, ed. "Charles E. Bohlen and the Acceptable Limits of Soviet Hegemony in Eastern Europe: A Memorandum of 18 October, 1945." *Diplomatic History* 3 (Spring 1979): 201–13.
1542. _____. "Today Has Been a Historical One: Harry S. Truman's Diary of the Potsdam Conference." *Diplomatic History* 4 (Summer 1980). 317–26.
1543. Mastny, Vojtech. *Russia's Road to the Cold War: Diplomacy, Warfare, and the Politics of Communism, 1941–1945.* New York: Columbia University Press, 1979.
1544. Matray, James I. "Captive of the Cold War: The Decision to Divide Korea at the 38th Parallel." *Pacific Historical Review* 50 (May 1981): 145–68.
1545. May, Gary. *China Scapegoat: The Diplomatic Ordeal of John Carter Vincent.* Washington, D.C.: New Republic Books, 1979.
1546. McMahon, Robert J. *Colonialism and Cold War: The United States and the Struggle for Indonesian Independence, 1945–49.* Ithaca, N.Y.: Cornell University Press, 1981.

1547. McWhinney, Edward. *Conflict and Compromise: International Law and World Order in a Revolutionary Age.* New York: Holmes and Meier, 1981.

1548. Mearsheimer, John J. *Conventional Deterrence.* Ithaca, N.Y.: Cornell University Press, 1983.

1549. Melby, John F. "Vietnam--1950." *Diplomatic History* 6 (Winter 1982): 97–109.

1550. Messer, Robert L. *The End of an Alliance: James F. Byrnes, Roosevelt, Truman, and the Origins of the Cold War.* Chapel Hill: University of North Carolina Press, 1982

1551. Miller, Aaron David. *Search for Security: Saudi-Arabian Oil and American Foreign Policy, 1939-1949.* Chapel Hill: University of North Carolina, 1980.

1552. Mooney, Peter J. *The Soviet Superpower: The Soviet Union, 1945-1980.* Exeter, N.H.: Heinemann Books, 1982.

1553. Moskos, Charles C. "Making the All-Volunteer Force Work: A National Service Approach." *Foreign Affairs* 60 (Fall 1981): 17–34.

1554. Mosley, Leonard. *Marshall: Hero for Our Times.* New York: Hearst Books, 1982.

1555. Myers, Ramon H., ed. *A U.S. Foreign Policy for Asia: The 1980s and Beyond.* Stanford, Calif.: Hoover Institution Press, 1982.

1556. Nunda, Ved P., James R. Scaritt, and George W. Shepherd, Jr., eds. *Global Human Rights: Public Policies, Comparative Measures, and NGO Strategies.* Boulder, Colo.: Westview Press, 1981

1557. Neal, Fred Warner, ed. *Detente or Debacle: Common Sense in U.S.-Soviet Relations.* New York: W. W. Norton, 1979.

1158. Neff, Donald. *Warriors at Suez: Eisenhower Takes America into the Middle East.* New York: Linden Press / Simon & Schuster, 1981.

1559. Nelson, Anna Kasten. "The 'Top of Policy Hill': President Eisenhower and the National Security Council." *Diplomatic History* 7 (Fall 1983): 307–26.

1560. Nitze, Paul, and Richard J. Barnet. "Civil Defense...the New Debate." *Worldview* 22 (January / February 1979): 40–48.

1561. Nitze, Paul H. "Strategy in the Decade of the 1980s." *Foreign Affairs*, 59 (1980): 82–101.

1562. Nitze, Paul H., Leonard Sullivan, Jr., and Atlantic Council Working Group on Securing the Seas. *Securing the Seas: The Soviet Naval Challenge and Western Alliance Options.* Boulder, Colo.: Westview Press, 1979.

1563. O'Brien, William V. *The Conduct of Just and Limited War.* New York: Praeger, 1981.

1564. Olson, Robert K. *U.S. Foreign Policy and the New International Economic Order: Negotiating Global Problems, 1974-1981.* Boulder, Colo.: Westview Press, 1981.

1565. Olvey, Less D., Henry A. Leonard, and Bruce E. Arlinghaus, eds. *Industrial Capacity and Defense Planning.* Lexington, Mass.: Lexington Books, 1983.

1566. Ottaway, Marina. *Soviet and American Influence in the Horn of Africa.* New York: Praeger, 1982.

1567. Palmer, Gregory. *The McNamara Strategy and The Vietnam War: Program Budgeting in the Pentagon, 1960-1968.* Wesport, Conn.: Greenwood Press, 1978.

1568. Papp, Daniel S. *Vietnam: The View from Moscow, Peking, Washington.* Jefferson, N.C.: McFarland, 1981.
1569. Parmet, Herbert S. *Jack: The Struggles of John F. Kennedy*, and *JFK: the Presidency of John F. Kennedy.* 2 vols. New York: Dial Press, 1980, 1983.
1570. Patti, Archimedes L. A. *Why Viet Nam?: Prelude to America's Albatross.* Berkeley: University of California Press, 1980.
1571. Payne, Keith. *Nuclear Deterrence in the U.S.-Soviet Relations.* Boulder, Colo.: Westview Press, 1982.
1572. Payne, Samuel, Jr. *The Soviet Union and SALT.* Cambridge, Mass.: MIT Press, 1981.
1573. Pearce, Jenny. *Under the Eagle: U.S. Intervention in Central America and the Caribbean.* Boston: South End Press, 1982.
1574. Perkins, Whitney T. *Constraint of Empire: The United States and Caribbean Interventions. Westport, Conn.: Greenwood Press, 1981.*
1575. Petillo, Carol Morris. *Douglas MacArthur: The Philippine Years.* Bloomington: Indiana University Press, 1981.
1576. Pfaltzgraff, Robert L., Jr., and Uri Ra'anan, eds. *U.S. Defense Mobilization Infrastructure.* Hamden, Conn.: Archon Books, 1983.
1577. Pierre, Andrew J. *The Global Politics of Arms Sales.* Princeton, N.J.: Princeton University Press, 1982.
1578. Pipes, Richard. *U.S.-Soviet Relations in the Era of Detente: A Tragedy of Errors.* Boulder, Colo.: Westview Press, 1981.
1579. Podhoretz, Norman. *Why We Were in Vietnam.* New York: Simon & Schuster, 1982.
1580. Polmar, Norman, and Thomas B. Allen. *Rickover: Controversy and Genius.* New York: Simon & Schuster, 1982.
1581. Porter, Gareth, ed. *Vietnam: A History in Documents.* 2 vols. Stanfordville, N.Y.: 1979.
1582. Prados, John. *The Soviet Estimate.* New York: Dial Press, 1982.
1583. Pruessen, Ronald W. *John Foster Dulles: The Road to Power.* New York: Free Press, 1982.
1584. Rabe, Stephen G. *The Road to OPEC: United States Relations with Venezuela, 1919–1976.* Austin: University of Texas Press, 1982.
1585. Rabin, Barry. *Paved with Good Intentions: The American Experience and Iran.* New York: Oxford University Press, 1980.
1586. Record, Jeffrey. *The Rapid Deployment Force and U.S. Military Intervention in the Persian Gulf.* Cambridge, Mass.: Institute for Foreign Policy Analysis, 1981.
1587. *The Report of the President's National Bipartisan Commission on Central America.* New York: Macmillan, 1984.
1588. Rosenberg, David Alan. "American Atomic Strategy and the Hydrogen Bomb Decision". *Journal of American History* 66 (1979): 62–87.
1589. Rostow, Walt Whitman. *Europe after Stalin: Eisenhower's Three Decisions of March 11, 1953.* Austin: University of Texas Press, 1982.
1590. Rothstein, Robert L. *The Third World and U.S. Foreign Policy.* Boulder, Colo.: Westview Press, 1981.
1591. Rush, Kenneth, Brent Scowcroft, Joseph J. Wolf, and the Atlantic Council Group. *Strengthening Deterrence: NATO and the Credibility of Western Defense in the 1980s.* Cambridge, Mass.: Ballinger, 1982.

1592. Saikal, Amin. *The Rise and Fall of the Shah*. Princeton, N.J.: Princeton University Press, 1980.
1593. Sanders, Jerry W. *Peddlers of Crisis: The Committee on the Present Danger and the Politics of Containment*. Boston: South End Press, 1983.
1594. Sarkesian, Sam C., ed. *Combat Effectiveness: Cohesion, Stress and the Volunteer Military*. Beverly Hills, Calif.: Sage, 1980.
1595. Scheer, Robert. *With Enough Shovels: Reagan, Bush and Nuclear War*. New York: Random House, 1982.
1596. Schell, Jonathan. *The Fate of the Earth*. New York: Alfred A. Knopf, 1982.
1597. Scherer, John L. "Reinterpreting Soviet Behavior during the Cuban Missile Crisis. *World Affairs*" 144 (Fall 1981): 110–25.
1598. Schlesinger, Stephen, and Stephen Kinzer. *Bitter Fruit: The Untold Story of the American Coup in Guatemala*. New York: Doubleday, 1982.
1599. Schwab, George, ed. *United States Foreign Policy at the Crossroads*. Westport, Conn.: Greenwood Press, 1982.
1600. Schwartz, David N. *NATO's Nuclear Dilemmas*. Washington, D.C.: Brookings Institution, 1983.
1601. Schweigler, Gebhardt. *Von Kissinger zu Carter*. Munich: Oldenbourg, 1982.
1602. Scoville, Herbert, Jr. *MX: Prescription for Disaster*. Cambridge, Mass.: MIT Press, 1981.
1603. Scowcroft Commission Report excerpts. *New York Times* (12 April 1982), I, 1 and 6; II, 18 and 19.
1604. Scowcroft, Brent, ed. *Military Service in the United States*. Englewood Cliffs, N.J.: Prentice-Hall, 1982.
1605. Seagrave, Sterling. *Yellow Rain: A Journey through the Terror of Chemical Warfare*. New York: M. Evans, 1981.
1606. Shiels, Frederick L. *Tokyo and Washington: Dilemmas of a Mature Alliance*. Lexington, Mass.: D. C. Heath, 1980.
1607. Shlaim, Avi. *The United States and the Berlin Blockade, 1948-1949*. Berkeley: University of California Press, 1983.
1608. Sigmund, Paul, E. *The Overthrow of Allende and the Politics of Chile, 1964-1976*. Pittsburgh, Pa.: University of Pittsburgh Press, 1977.
1609. Slany, William Z. "History of the Foreign Relations Series" and "Report on the Advisory Committee on Historical Diplomatic Documentation," in *Newsletter* Society of Historians of America Foreign Relations, 12 (March 1981): 10–30.
1610. Smith, Bradley F. *The Shadow Warriors: O.S.S. and the Origins of the C.I.A.* New York: Basic Books, 1983.
1611. Smith, R. Harris. *O.S.S.: The Secret History of America's First Central Intelligence Agency*. Berkeley: University of California Press, 1980.
1612. Smith, Robert. *MacArthur in Korea: The Naked Emperor*. New York: Simon & Schuster, 1982.
1613. Snow, Donald. "The MX-Basing Mode Muddle." *Air University Review* 31 (July / August 1980): 11–25.
1614. Snow, Donald M. *Nuclear Strategy in a Dynamic World: American Policy in the 1980s*. Birmingham: University of Alabama Press, 1980.
1615. Sorley, Lewis. *Arms Transfers under Nixon*. Lexington: University of Kentucky Press, 1983.

1616. Stravrianos, L. S. *Global Riff: The Third World Comes of Age.* New York: Morrow, 1981.
1617. Steel, Ronald. *Walter Lippmann and the American Century.* New York: Vintage Books, 1981.
1618. Steele, Jonathan. *Soviet Power: The Kremlin's Foreign Policy—Brezhnev to Andropov.* New York: Simon & Schuster, 1983.
1619. Steinbruner, John D., and Leon V. Sigal, eds. *Alliance Security: NATO and the No-First-Use Question.* Washington, D.C.: Brookings Institution 1983.
1620. Stempel, John D. *Inside the Iranian Revolution.* Bloomington: Indiana University Press, 1981.
1621. Stent, Angela. *From Embargo to Ostpolitik: The Political Economy of West German-Soviet Relations, 1955–1980.* New York: Cambridge University Press, 1982.
1622. Stern, Paula. *Water's Edge: Domestic Politics and the Making of American Foreign Policy.* Westport, Conn.: Greenwood Press, 1979.
1623. Stoler, Mark A. "From Continentalism to Globalism: General Stanley D. Embick, the Joint Strategic Survey Committee, and the Military View of American National Policy During the Second World War." *Diplomatic History* 6 (Summer 1982): 303–21.
1624. *Strengthening Conventional Deterrence in Europe: Proposals for the 1980s.* Report of the European Security Study. New York: St. Martin's, 1983.
1625. Stromberg, Peter L., Malham Wakin, and Daniel Callahan. *The Teaching of Ethics in the Military.* Hastings-on-Hudson, N.Y.: Institute of Society, Ethics and the Life Sciences / The Hastings Center, 1983.
1626. Stueck, William Whitney, Jr. *The Road of Confrontation: American Policy toward China and Korea, 1947–1950.* Chapel Hill: University of North Carolina Press, 1981.
1627. Sullivan, David S. "The Legacy of SALT I: Soviet Deception and U.S. Retreat." *Strategic Review* 7 (Winter 1979): 26–41.
1628. Sullivan, Marianna P. *France's Vietnam Policy: A Study in French American Relations.* Westport, Conn.: Greenwood Press, 1978.
1629. Summers, Harry G. *On Strategy: A Critical Analysis of the Vietnam War.* San Rafael: Presidio Press, 1982.
1630. Swanson, Bruce. *Eighth Voyage of the Dragon: A History of China's Quest for Seapower.* Annapolis, Md.: Naval Institute Press, 1982.
1631. Taubman, William. *Stalin's American Policy: From Entente to Detente to Cold War.* New York: W. W. Norton, 1982.
1632. Thies, Wallace J. *When Governments Collide: Coercion and Diplomacy in the Vietnam Conflict, 1964–1968.* Berkeley: University of California Press, 1980.
1633. Thompson, Kenneth W. *Cold War Theories. Vol. 1, World Polarization, 1943–1953.* Baton Rouge: Louisiana State University Press, 1981.
1634. Thompson, W. Scott, ed. *National Security in the 1980s: From Weakness to Strength.* San Francisco, Calif: Institute for Contemporary Studies, 1980.
1635. Thorson, Stuart J., and Donald A. Sylvan. "Counterfactuals and the Cuban Missile Crisis." *International Studies Quarterly* 26 (December 1982): 539–71.
1636. Tillman, Seth P. *The United States in the Middle East.* Bloomington: Indiana

University Press, 1982.
1637. Trofimenko, Henry A. "Counterforce; Illusion of a Panacea." *International Security* 5 (Spring 1981): 28–48.
1638. Troy, Thomas F. *Donovan and the CIA: A History of the Establishment of the Central Intelligence Agency*. Washington, D.C.: University Publications of America, 1981.
1639. Tsurutani, Taketsugu. *Japanese Policy and East Asian Security*. New York: Praeger, 1981.
1640. Tucker, Nancy Bernkopf. *Patterns in the Dust: Chinese-American Relations and the Recognition Controversy, 1949–1950*. New York: Columbia University Press, 1983.
1641. Tucker, Robert W. *The Purposes of American Power: An Essay on National Security*. New York: Praeger, 1981.
1642. Tucker, Robert W., and Linda Wrigley, eds. *The Atlantic Alliance and its Critics*. New York: Praeger, 1983.
1643. Turner, Stansfield, and George Thibault. "Intelligence: The Right Rules." *Foreign Policy* 48 (Fall 1982): 122–38.
1644. Turner, Stansfield. "Why We Shouldn't Build the MX." *New York Times Magazine* (29 March 1981), 15–17 ff.
1645. Ulam, Adam B. *Dangerous Relations: The Soviet Union in World Politics, 1970–1982*. New York: Oxford University Press, 1983.
1646. Vance, Cyrus. *Hard Choices: Critical Years in America's Foreign Policy*. New York: Simon & Schuster, 1983.
1647. Ward, Patricia Dawson. *The Threat of Peace: James F. Byrnes and the Council of Foreign Ministers, 1945–1946*. Kent, Ohio: Kent State University Press, 1979.
1648. Weber, Henri. *Nicaragua: The Sandinist Revolution*. London: NLB, 1982.
1649. Wettig, Gerhard. *Konflikt und Kooperation zwischen Ost und West*. Bonn: Osany Verlag, 1981.
1650. Wich, Richard. *Sino-Soviet Crisis Politics: A Study of Political Change and Communication*. Cambridge, Mass.: Harvard University Press, 1980.
1651. Wieselter, Leon. *Nuclear War, Nuclear Peace*. New York: Holt, Rinehart, 1983.
1652. Wittner, Lawrence S. *American Intervention in Greece, 1943–1949*. New York: Columbia University Press, 1982.
1653. Wyden, Peter. *Bay of Pigs: The Untold Story*. New York: Simon & Schuster, 1979.
1654. Yoshitsu, Michael M. *Japan and the San Francisco Peace Settlement*. New York: Columbia University Press, 1983.
1655. Yost, Charles. *History and Memory*. New York: W. W. Norton, 1980.
1656. Zuckermann, Solly. *Nuclear Illusion and Reality*. New York: Viking, 1982.

GOVERNMENT MATERIALS

1657. Cole, Alice C., Alfred Boldberg, Samuel A. Tucker, and Rudolph A. Winnacker. *The Department of Defense: Documents on Establishment and Organization, 1944–1978*. Washington, D.C.: Office of Secretary of Defense, 1979.
1658. U.S., Comptroller General. *The MX Weapon System: A Program with Cost and Schedule Uncertainties*. Washington, D.C.: GPO, 1980.

1659. U.S., Congressional Budget Office. *The U.S. Sea-Based Strategic Force: Cost of Trident Submarine and Missile Programs and Alternatives.* Washington, D.C.: GPO, 1980.
1660. U.S. Congress, Congressional Research Service. *MX Interncontinental Ballistic Missile Program.* Washington, D.C.: GPO, 1981.
1661. U.S. Congress, House Committee on Foreign Affairs. *NATO's Future Role.* Hearings, Subcommittee on Europe and the Middle East, Committee on Foreign Affairs, House, 20 May–9 June, 1982. Washington, D.C.: GPO, 1982.
1662. U.S. Congress, House. *Northern European Security Issues.* Report of a Staff Study Mission to Five NATO Countries and Sweden, 29 November–14 December, 1982, to the Committee on Foreign Affairs, House. Washington, D.C.: GPO, 1983.
1663. U.S. Congress, Senate. *Executive Sessions of the Senate Foreign Relations Committee* (Historical Series), vol. 12, 86th Congress, 1960. Washington: DC.: GPO, 1982.
1664. U.S. Congress, Senate. *Modernization of the U.S. Strategic Deterrent.* Hearings, Committee on Armed Services, Senate, 5 October–5 November 1981. Washington, D.C.: GPO, 1982.
1665. U.S. Department of Defense. *ICBM Basing Options: A Summary of Major Studies to Define a Survivable Basing Concept for ICBMs.* Washington D.C.: Office of the Deputy Under-Secretary of Defense for Research and Engineering (Strategic and Space Systems), 1980.
1666. U.S. Department of State. *Foreign Relations of the United States.* Issued 1979 to 1983: seven volumes for *1951*; six volumes for *1952* through *1954.* Washington, D.C.: GPO, 1979–1983.
1667. U.S. Department of State. *The Quest for Peace: Principal United States Public Statements and Documents relating to the Arab-Israeli Peace process, 1967–1983.* Washingotn, D.C.: GPO, 1983.
1668. U.S. Office of Technical Assessment. *The Effects of Nuclear War.* Washington, D.C.: GPO, 1979.
1669. Weinberger, Caspar W. *Annual Report to the Congress.* Washington, D.C.: GPO [Stock no. 008-000-99361-1), February 1982.

BIBLIOGRAPHIES AND REFERENCE MATERIALS

1670. Arkin, William M. *Research Guide to Current Military and Strategic Affairs.* Washington, D.C.: Institute for Policy Studies, 1981.
1671. Burns, Richard D., 3d. *Guide to American Foreign Relations since 1700.* Santa Barbara, Calif.: Clio Press, 1983.
1672. Dekmejian, Richard H. "In Defense of the Middle East." *Armed Forces and Society* 9 (Fall 1982): 149–56.
1673. Dunn, Joe. "The Power Chronicle: A Bibliographic Review." *Armed Forces and Society* 9 (Spring 1983): 495–514.
1674. *Dwight D. Eisenhower: A Selected Bibliography of Periodical and Dissertation Literature.* Compiled by Eisenhower, Library, Abilene, Kan., 1981.
1675. Findling, John E. *Dictionary of American Diplomatic History.* Westport, Conn.: Greenwood Press, 1980.
1676. Gaddis, John Lewis. "The Emerging Post-Revisionist Synthesis on the

Origins of the Cold War," and "Responses" to John Lewis Gaddis by Lloyd C. Gardner, Lawrence S. Kaplan, Warren F. Kimball, and Bruce R. Kuniholm. *Diplomatic History* 7 (Summer 1983): 171–204.

1667. Haines, Gerald K., and J. Samuel Walker, eds. *American Foreign Relations: A Historiographical Review*. Westport, Conn.: Greenwood Press, 1981.

1678. Hilsman Roger. "On Intelligence." *Armed Forces and Society* 8 (Fall 1981): 129–43.

1679. McAuliffe, Mary S. "Eisenhower, the President." *Journal of American History* 68 (December 1981): 625–32.

1680. Newman, John. *Vietnam War Literature: An Annotated Biliography of Imaginative Works about Americans Fighting in Vietnam*. Metuchen, N.J.: Scarecrow Press, 1982

1681. Perez, Louis A. "Intervention, Hegemony, and Dependency: The United States in the Circum-Caribbean, 1898–1980." *Pacific Historical Review 51 (May 1982): 165*–94.

1682. Schlesinger, Arthur, Jr. "The Ike Age Revisited." *Reviews in American History 11 (March 1983): 1*–11.

1683. Thompson, Carl L., Mary M. Anderberg, and John B. Antell, eds. *The Current History Encyclopedia of Developing Nations*. New York: McGraw-Hill, 1982.

1684. Travgott, Santa. "Resources for the Study of International Relations *International Studies Newsletter*. vol. 9. no. 2 (February / March 1982): 1, 9–19.

PERIODICALS

1685. *Journal of Strategic Studies*. Three times a year beginning in May 1978, published by Frank Cass and Company, London, England.

1686. *Trialogue*. Quarterly magazine of North American-European-Japanese Affairs, published by the Trilateral Commission, New York.

1687. *World Policy Journal*. Quarterly journal beginning November 1983, published by World Policy Institute, New York.

XVII

THE ARMY, 1945–1983

Benjamin Franklin Cooling III

Election of Ronald Reagan to the presidency in November 1980 returned a chief executive to the White House who was more than willing to employ military force as an instrument of national policy. As of publication, his record of success has been mixed. A "pop-top" action in Grenada has been offset by an unsuccessful peacekeeping deployment in Lebanon. Nonetheless, he had succeeded in reversing the trend of frustration and feeling of insufficiency left over from Vietnam and the Carter years of reconstruction. Where that left the U.S. army remained unclear. Writings since 1978 about the oldest of the services have not been reassuring. Perhaps the trough period presently engulfing the army resembles traditional peacetime reevaluation and inward reform, which usually takes place beyond the gaze of media, scribes, and trumpets of battle. Possibly, it means that the U.S. Army can no longer be written about meaningfully in isolation from her sister services and the whole matrix of integrated U.S. national defense.

Issues continuing to confront the army in the early 1980s include the same problems of readiness, manning, technology, and deployment that have connoted the whole American military experience since 1945. If manning questions no longer involve selective service, they do involve a downturn in recruiting, and the recognition by the chairman of the Joint Chiefs of Staff, Army General John W. Vesey, Jr., that women in the armed services have had more of an effect on the military than nuclear weapons. If nuclear tactical doctrine vies with the controversial M-1 Abrams tank for technocrats, if formation of a "light division", despite its unproven viability in the history of American arms, suggests any army role in any Reagan interventionism, and if critics of armed service organization are once more crying for reform—possibly integration—then these are familiar refrains in recent American military history. "Bureaucrats vs. fighters," "come as you are war" vs. industrial base sustainability, and questions of command and control and White House direction of military operations all loom as issues for researchers of the future concerned with military affairs of the present. They cut across pure service lines and are part of a fundamental phenomenon of our times, captured by British General Sir John Hackett when he noted that the purpose of armies today is less to emerge as the victor than to participate in the containment of the conflict before it spreads to something worse.*

Be this as it may, the writing of recent army history does not seem to be at an ebb. We simply lack a comprehensive, incisive analysis of the U.S. Army

*Gen. Sir John Hackett. *The Profession of Arms* (New York: Macmillan, 1983), 173.

since the advent of the atomic bomb radically altered human affairs. In some ways it seems doubtful that such a volume would serve other than parochial interests – the army is part of a team, and should be treated as such. For the past few years the best material to appear has reflected this theme, as witnessed by those citations which follow. But even within the narrow focus on the army itself, Vietnam has been the all-encompassing preoccupation, it would seem. Most of the work has been critical. Whether or not such post hoc analysis had led to the policy decisions leading to more mobile, lighter, more responsive army forces for use in contingency employment – rather than the two static front missions involving NATO and Korea – this must remain speculative. In any event, while writing about Vietnam continues at a prolific rate, it may be that the U.S. Army has now emerged from that trauma, its officer corps has stopped continual and painful examination of its entrails to discover where it failed, and the public at large has jettisoned its distaste for military fatigue clothes and soldiers marching in parades. Perhaps the period of reconstruction is over, and a return to the post-Korean War era of deterrence has begun. What seems unlikely, in any case, is a recessional to the days of massive retaliation, "battle groups," and limited war advocates like Maxwell Taylor and James Gavin.

Historical analysis itself seems stronger now in army circles than at any time since 1940. Active use of the discipline in classrooms, continuing employment of it in a policy sense by staff officers, and, most certainly, abundant cosmetic reference by nearly every general officer appearing in both public and military circles – all suggest a revival of Clioism, which helped train pre-nuclear age soldiers in defense matters. Similar observations about the private sector – professional historians and popular writers – also indicate an abiding renewal of fascination with military affairs. It is hoped that from all this will emerge readable, useful, capable products benefiting mankind in its search for peaceful solutions in a highly tottery world. Such hope will not be realized, it would seem, from continuing mesmerization with war games, obsession with heroics in battle, or poorly conceived articles and books pandering to the passing fancies of a generation which owes no term of national service to the state. For the moment, at least, the all-volunteer U.S. Army has lost its chance to make this contribution to the psyche of its nation. Whether or not the professional man-at-arms wearing army green today is up to his charge of defending democracy, peace, and the American constitution, he is providing us with a fascinating chapter in the ongoing saga of the nation's oldest armed service as it moves onward in its third century of existence.

PROBLEMS WITH THE SOURCES. Certain "givens" attend any research in official aspects of the recent American past. Research on the U.S. Army proves no exception. The fact that military history since 1945 is generally joint (i.e., services integrated) and often combined (i.e., internationally integrated) in nature compounds the problem. Then too, archival research continues to be plagued by arcane security classifications, overly protective and bureaucratic archivists or records managers, and institutional inertia in providing proper organization and finding aids for their material. The volume of paper associated with modern military institutions as arms of a government dwarfs available staff and budgets as a whole. Thus, great patience and perseverance must accompany any search of military records, combined wth a willingness to resort to the freedom-of-information procedure in dire cases. The National Archives and Records Service, as well as federal records centers around the country, the U.S. Army's institutional archives where they exist (or command history offices in their absence), and the U.S. Army Center of Military History, in Washington (and the subordinate U.S. Army Military History Institute, at Carlisle Barracks, Pennsylvania) continue to provide the starting points for use of written and oral records and audio and visual materials. They are all staffed by earnest historians, archivists, and librarians who will help with the search.

Unfortunately, lack of a comprehensive guide to archival sources for the U.S. Army's past plagues the effort. It remains a serious flaw in that service's own fine historical publication program. Too often the service history offices fail to realize that such a tool warrants expenditure of time and money. Nevertheless, consult Jessup and Coakley (614), Lane (628), and perhaps the Thum sisters (699); enjoy Conn (555) on how the army got into the history business in the first place; and then venture forth to explore the unknown. Rest assured, every year more records and materials (official and unofficial) on the army's recent past will become available to the public. Above all, do not succumb to the Lorelei corps of bureaucrats enveloped by rules and regulations ostensibly designed to protect the national treasure from its citizens under the guise of "national security information." There are ways around such an impasse, as suggested by William M. Arkin's guide (524), for example.

POLICY AND STRATEGY. The U.S. Army can only be properly understood in today's world as part of a changing American defense policy in an evolving highly sensitive world environment. Thus, readers might begin with Collins (553), Etzold (570), Fallows (571), Jenkins (613), and Holloway et al. (603). These works provide a proper matrix of both civilian and military professional views on national security issues. The army's involvement with nuclear matters might be gauged via Rose (669) and Talbott (694). Cordier (556) and Johnson (616) probe the inseparability of joint operations and rapid deployment of military force. Hunt and Schultz (609) suggest the value of applied history and unconventional warfare. Arlinghaus (525), Barnett (530), Cornell (557), Edmonds (567), Howe (607), and Sorley (687) must be used for the land warfare aspects of arms transfer problems. Karas (619) and Kaplan (618) discuss more obtuse questions of the high frontier of space-age warfare, as well as strategic thinkers of our times respectively—both of which naturally involve land warfare questions. Picture book devotees will enjoy Dornan (563), while Pfaltzgraff and Ra'anan (658), as well as Olvey et al. (650), update the ageless military fascination with mobilization problems (manpower and industrial).

MANAGEMENT, ORGANIZATION, AND DOCTRINE. Here again, general questions are explored by Barrett (531), as well as by Yarmolinsky and Foster (719). But for the army side, always try to begin with any available volumes of the Department of the Army's annual *Historical Summary*, currently being compiled in the Center of Military History by Carl Cocke (550). Geelhoed (576) probes a particular timeframe for defense organization and management while Holmes (602) looks at basic training; Hoyt (608) discusses the airborne phenomenon; Bergerson (534) ponders the politics of army aviation; Mahon (638) especially chapters 14-18, discusses the National Guard; and Romjue (668) dissects a narrow slice of tactical organization changes. Of course, the army aspects of the Joint Chiefs of Staff and unification should be analyzed through available published volumes, originally done at that organization's historical office (554, 676, 677). One of the best ways to track doctrinal issues and changes remains through Congressional hearings, field regulations and manuals, or other such "authority" material. The Combat Studies Institute, at Fort Leavenworth, may also be a good place to check on this point.

OPERATIONS. The occasional combat operation over the past forty years continues to provide a better proportion of material for the student of recent military affairs than peacetime "housekeeping" chores. Begin with Koenig (626), or even Hackett (587), and on operational considerations in combined operations see Hixson and Cooling (600). While Hackett is hypothetical, his work is really the product of corporate minds in NATO military circles and suggests some dimensions of modern projected conflict in that sector. Specific peacetime incidents worthy of notice may be approached through Spiller (689) for Lebanon, 1958, and Kirkbridge (624) on the tree-pruning incident in Korea, 1976. On the Korean War or "police action," see Goulden (583), Hamel (589), Langley (629), and Smith (686), while Waitley bridges Korea and Vietnam (715). And thus we come to the ill-fated American Crusade in Southeast Asia.

Controversies surrounding the United States and Southeast Asia will not abate in our lifetime. Writing and thinking on the subject continues at a fever pitch – although the citizenry may well have lost interest by now. See the sharp essays in the November–December 1983 issue of *Transaction / Society* (702). Lost in the welter of exchanges about a Vietnam memorial in Washington, the matter of just who "won" or "lost" Southeast Asia, the continuing plight of veterans from that conflict, and other subissues are the actual performances of men in battle in that war. Again, however, *the U.S. Army cannot be studied in isolation*. For background of diplomacy, politics, and military affairs, see Baral (529), Berman (535), Charlton and Moncrief (548), Papp (654), Palmer (653), Patti (655), Podhoretz (660), Shawcross (680), Sivaram (682), Summers (693) and Thies (697). Overall accounts of the war should be explored through Amter (521), Anderson (522), Bonds (540), Esper (569), Gelb and Betts (577), Herring (594), Karnow (620), Maclear (637), O'Ballance (648), and Porter (662), while Sharp (679) provides added options, and Dawkins (560) suggests another side to the army's approach to the experience in Southeast Asia, and the potential of doctoral dissertations as sources.

Combat and personal accounts of the carnage are beginning to surface in ever-increasing numbers. They range from memoirs to the "official" history studies finally emerging from the U.S. Army's Center of Military History – all of which sweep across the panorama of men and events. Narratives of specific actions or specific topics produced commercially include Henderson (593) on combat motivation; Herrington (595) and Trullinger (703) on war in the villages; Katcher and Chappell (621) for coverage of arms, equipment, and uniforms; Pisor (659) on Khe Sanh; Smith (684) for the Special Forces; and Stanton (690) on an order of battle for the war. Personal narratives include Baker (528), Downs (564), Goldman and Fuller (581) – which also takes the soldiers over into post-Vietnam life, as does Mason (641) – while Reich (664) on the American division, and Santoli (674) round out some of the current crop of memoirs. For the "official" history side, see the Center of Military History's "Indochina Monographs", including Hinh (598) on Lam Son, Vietnamization, and the cease-fire (599); Lung (635) on the general offensives of 1968–1969; Tho (698) on Cambodia; Truong on the Easter offensive of 1972 (705) and allied interoperability (704); Vien (713) on the U.S. adviser, and Vongsavanh (714) on activities in Laos. Obviously, these studies have enabled Southeast Asian military participants to preserve their side of the story. For the American army side, see two pieces in the general officer "Vietnam Studies" series: Myer (645) on division-level communications, and Starry (691) on mounted combat. Ognibene et al. (649), as well as Dorland and Nanney (562), have contributed works on the medical activities in Southeast Asia. Probably the more publicized army histories will be Scoville (678) on pacification, and the long-awaited Spector (688) volume on the advisory years, 1940–1961.

To truly understand the U.S. Army and Southeast Asia is also to involve the media coverage of the war, as well as the legacy of the conflict for country, institutions, and citizenry. At times, the soldiers have castigated press, politicians, and the general public at home more than the enemy for the failed mission—thus contributing yet another note of sourness to the whole affair. This unpopular crusade can be traced in Braestrup (542), Chandler (547), Keylin and Boiangiu (623), and Goulden (583). The controversial downfall of South Vietnam as an independent nation should be studied via Dillard (561), Nosmer et al. (606), Isaacs (612), Le Gro (631), and Vien (712). The bitter legacy of this war for soldiers and public alike in America can be followed through Capps (545), Card (546), Griffen and Marciano (586), Horne (605), Egendoff et al. (568), Figley (572, 573), Linedecker (632), Klein (625), and the Senate Veterans Affairs Committee (707). Above all, see the famous "Cincinnatus" commentary (549) on the disintegration and decay of the U.S. Army in the period.

CIVIL-MILITARY RELATIONS. Controversial events in Korea, Vietnam, Grenada, and elsewhere in this period have obscured other dimensions of the U.S. Army and society, both at home and abroad. The Corps of Engineers series on Corps activities in national development at home continues apace with Alperin (520), Brown (543) Buker (544), Cotton (558), Drescher (565), Hagwood (588), Merritt (642), and Mills (643). Pew (657) discusses FORSCOM handling of Vietnamese refugees. Foster (574) has investigated army medical disaster relief, while Keveles (622) views military justice in U.S. Army Europe. The question of domestic atomic experiments in the 1950s as they impacted on the soldiers should be approached in Rosenberg (670), as well as in Uhl and Ensign (706). Tent (696) and Skrjabina (683) examine American occupation in Germany, while Perry (656) treats the similar experience in Japan.

MANPOWER AND STAFFING. The advent of all-volunteer military forces for the United States once again has stimulated analysis by scholars and pundits. See Backman et al. (527) and Binkin and Kyriakopoulos (538) on manning problems generally; Anderson (523) and Tarr (695) about selective service reform; and a Defense Department publication (711) concerning the core issue of military compensation. The thorny issue of minority manning can be explored with Young (720) as a good starting point. Move on to blacks via Binkin and Eitelberg (537), Goff et al. (579), Hope (604), MacGregor (636), and Nalty and MacGregor (646), and then to women via Goldman (580), Holm (601), Department of the Army

(710), Rogan (667), Rustad (672), Todd (701), and Wood (718). For a variety of other topics, see Crocker (559) on the latest of the venerable *Army Officer's Guide*; Gabriel (575) with respect to military ethics; and Lovell (634) on the service academies. Ingraham (610) looks at military life, as does a short Fort Carson study (611).

ARMS AND BRANCHES. Relatively little serious work is being done on this segment of recent army history. Still, see Harris (591) on a Puerto Rican infantry regiment; Walthall (716) on the 25th Division; Simpson (681) on special forces; Dunstin (566) on armor; and Hickey (596), Hoyt (608), and Weeks (717) on a part view of the airborne units.

WEAPONS, TECHNOLOGY, LOGISTICS. Renewed interest in the cost and process of weapons acquisition has led to a variety of works relevant to students of American land warfare in this period. From a think-piece by one former army official in the acquisition process, Norman Augustine (526), to more general — and often critical analyses such as Kaldor (626), Koenig (635), Long and Reppy (642), Rasor (672), Robertson (675), Schevitz (684), and Tobias et al. (709), questions about the military-industrial complex seem alive and well. Yet if they are no more productive of positive result than those of the 1960s, they do enable researchers to probe hardware dimensions of recent army history. In addition, a plethora of topic-oriented guides and some serious studies of particular weapons can also be found. For example, Goad and Halsey on ammunition (587), RUSI and *Brassey's* on weapons technology (680), Gordon on electronic warfare (591), Harris and Paxman on CBR (599), Owen on infantry weapons (660), Zaloga and Loop on armor (730), the Stockholm Peace Research Institute on anti-personnel weaponry (701), and Hatcher (601) and Saffer and Kelly (682) on nuclear tests all illustrate sufficient literature to satisfy a variety of researchers. Smith and Chappell (694) give cursory coverage to uniforms, while an unsung U.S. Army Military Traffic Management Command report (718) concerning the railroad system and military logistics suggests the great need for more accessible materials on procurement and supply.

MEN AND EVENTS. History is supposedly the story of man — a fact often lost in the shuffle of studies in contemporary military affairs — and some biographies and works on leadership can be consulted for this period. Collins (551) on leadership qualities, or even Greenstein (585) and Neff (647) concerning former soldier Dwight D. Eisenhower as president, offer engaging views of a military element in rediscovered leadership versus management discussions endemic to our times. Composite views of army chiefs of staff and secretaries of war have emerged in two works by William G. Bell (532, 533). Well-known generals of the period can be approached via Biggs on Gavin (536), Blumenson on Clark (539), Blair on Bradley (541), Mosley on Marshall (644), and J. Lawton Collins on himself (552). S.L.A. Marshall's widow has edited materials relevant to this dedicated soldier and student of contemporary military affairs (640). Roberts (665) as well as Hill and Craig (597), give us memoirs of lesser lights who remain important for general understanding of military experiences during the cold war era.

SUGGESTIONS FOR FURTHER RESEARCH. Frankly, the suggestions in previous editions of this essay still obtain. None of the areas noted have reached anything approaching saturation. U.S. Army Center of Military History publications anticipated in the near future include the study of the army and the atomic bomb project, and Vietnam series volumes will include a pictoral history, communications in Southeast Asia, and the 1965–1967 buildup from the Department of Army perspective. Perhaps more troublesome, however, is not the question of topics but rather of methodology. A premier question now confronts the profession: Does the old-style, massive, one-service military history really offer the proper perspective on subjects of recent American military experience? What seems more necessary are (1) joint or unified volumes of institutional and operational history involving the armed forces, and (2) shorter, hard-hitting – possibly multi-authored – anthologies, offering case studies of subjects relevant to the needs of both the armed services themselves and the public at large. This topical approach could well surmount policy, organizational, and technological as well as operational issues, thereby making history once more a useful adjunct of the military story rather than a mere chronicle, a "heritage" service, or a popular pastime. Both official government history programs of the U.S. Army and private researchers in modern army affairs would do well to ponder the implications of such suggestions. Topics abound – but direction and focus stand at a crossroads.

BIBLIOGRAPHY

520. Alperin, Lynn. M. *Custodians of the Coast; History of the United States Army Engineers at Galveston*. Galveston, Tex.: U.S. Army Corps of Engineers District Office, 1977.

521. Amter, Joseph A. *Vietnam Verdict: A Citizens History*. New York: Continuum, 1982.

522. Anderson, Charles R. *Vietnam: The Other War*. San Rafael, Calif: Presidio Press, 1982.

523. Anderson, Martin, ed. *Registration and the Draft*. Stanford, Calif: Hoover Institution Press, 1982.

524. Arkin, William M. *Research Guide to Current Military and Strategic Affairs*. Washington, D.C.: Institute for Policy Studies, 1981.

525. Arlinghaus, Bruce E., ed. *Arms for Africa: Military Assistance and Foreign Policy in the Developing World*. Lexington, Mass.: Lexington Books, 1983.

526. Augustine, Norman P. *Augustine's Laws and Major System Development Programs*. New York: American Institute of Aeronautics and Astronautics, 1982.

527. Bachman, Jerald D., John D. Blair, and David R. Segal. *The All-Volunteer Force: A Study in the Military*. Ann Arbor: University of Michigan Press, 1977.

528. Baker, Mark. *Nam; The Vietnam War in the Words of the Men and Women Who Fought There*. New York: William Morrow, 1981.

529. Baral, Jaya Krishna. *The Pentagon and the Making of U.S. Foreign Policy; A Case Study of Vietnam, 1960–1968*. Atlantic Highlands, N.J.: Humanities Press, 1978.

530. Barnett, A. Doak. *U.S. Arms Sales: The China-Taiwan Tangle*.

Washington, D.C.: Brookings Institution, 1982.
531. Barrett, Archie D. *Reappraising Defense Organization: An Analysis Based on the Defense Organization Study of 1977–1980.* Washington, D.C.: National Defense University Press, 1983.
532. Bell, William Gardiner. *Commanding Generals and Chiefs of Staff 1775–1983; Portraits and Biographical Sketches of the U.S. Army's Senior Officers.* Washington, D.C.: Department of the Army, 1983.
533. _____. *Secretaries of War and Secretaries of the Army; Portraits and Biographical Sketches.* Washington, D.C.: Army Center of Military History, 1981.
534. Bergerson, Frederick. *The Army Gets an Air Force: Tactics of Insurgent Bureaucratic Politics.* Baltimore, Md.: Johns Hopkins University Press, 1980.
535. Berman, Larry. *Planning a Tragedy: The Americanization of the War in Vietnam.* New York: W. W. Norton, 1982.
536. Biggs, Bradley. *Gavin.* Hamden, Conn.: Archon Books, 1980.
537. Binkin, Martin, Mark J. Eitelberg, et al. *Blacks and the Military.* Washington, D.C.: Brookings Institution, 1982.
538. Binkin, Martin, and Irene Kyriakopoulos. *Youth or Experience? Manning the Modern Military.* Washington, D.C.: Brookings Institution, 1979.
539. Blumenson, Martin. *Mark Clark.* New York: Congdon and Weed, 1984.
540. Bonds, Ray. *The Vietnam War.* New York: Crown, 1979.
541. Bradley, Omar, and Clay Blair. *A General's Life: An Autobiography.* New York Simon & Schuster, 1983.
542. Braestrup, Peter. *Big Story: How the American Press and Television Reported and Interpreted the Crisis of Tet 1968 in Vietnam and Washington.* New York: Doubleday, 1978. Reprint. New Haven, Conn.: Yale University Press, 1983.
543. Brown, D. Clayton. *Rivers, Rockets and Readiness: Army Engineers in the Sunbelt; A History of the Fort Worth District, U.S. Army Corps of Engineers, 1950–1975.* Fort Worth, Tex.: U.S. Army Corps of Engineers District Office, 1979.
544. Buker, George E. *Sun, Sand and Water: A History of the Jacksonville District U.S. Army Corps of Engineers, 1821–1975.* Jacksonville, Fla.: U.S. Army Corps of Engineers District Office, n.d.
545. Capps, Walter H. *The Unfinished War: Vietnam and the American Conscience.* Boston: Beacon Press, 1982.
546. Card, Josephina. *Lives after Vietnam: The Personal Impact of Military Service.* Lexington, Mass.: Lexington Books, 1983.
547. Chandler, Robert W. *War of Ideas: The U.S. Propaganda Campaign in Vietnam.* Boulder, Colo.: Westview Press, 1981.
548. Charlton, Michael, and Anthony Moncrieff. *Many Reasons Why: The American Involvement in Vietnam.* New York: Hill and Wang, 1978.
549. "Cincinnatus" [Cecil B. Curry]. *Self-Destruction: The Disintegration and Decay of the United States Army during the Vietnam Era.* New York: W. W. Norton, 1981.
550. Cocke, Carl, comp. *Department of the Army Historical Summary, FY 1980.* Washington, D.C.: Department of the Army, 1983.
551. Collins, Arthur S., Jr. *Common Sense Training: A Working Philosophy*

for Leaders. San Rafael, Calif.: Presidio Press, 1978.

552. Collins, J. Lawton. *"Lightning Joe": An Autiobiography*. Baton Rouge: Louisiana State University Press, 1979.

553. Collins, John M. *U.S. Defense Planning: A Critique*. Boulder, Colo.: Westview Press, 1982.

554. Condit, Kenneth W. *The Joint Chiefs of Staff and National Policy, 1947–1949* Vol. 2, The History of the Joint Chiefs of Staff. Wilmington, Del.: Michael Glazier, 1979.

555. Conn, Stetson, *Historical Work in the United States Army, 1862–1954*. Washington, D.C.: Center of Military History, 1980.

556. Cordier, Sherwood S. *U.S. Military Power and Rapid Deployment Requirements in the 1980s*. Boulder, Colo.: Westview Press, 1983.

557. Cornell, Alexander H. *International Collaboration in Weapons and Equipment Development and Production by the NATO Allies: Ten Years Later and Beyond*. Hingham, Mass.: Kluswer Boton, 1981.

558. Cotton, Gordon A. *A History of the Waterways Experiment Station, 1929–1979*. Vicksburgh, Miss.: U.S. Army Waterways Experiment Station, Corps of Engineers, 1979.

559. Crocker, Lawrence P. *The Army Officers Guide*. Harrisburg, Pa.: Stackpole Books, 1983.

560. Dawkins, Peter Miller. *The United States Army and the "Other" War in Vietnam: A Study of the Complexity of Implementing Organizational Change*. Ann Arbor, Mich.: University Microfilms, 1980.

561. Dillard, Walter Scott. *Sixty Days to Peace: Implementing the Paris Peace Accords, Vietnam, 1973*. Washington, D.C.: National Defense University Press, 1982.

562. Dorland, Peter, and James Nanney. *Dust Off: Army Aeromedical Evacuation in Vietnam*. Washington, D.C.: Center of Military History, 1982.

563. Dornan, James E. *The U.S. War Machine: An Illustrated Encyclopedia of American Military Equipment and Strategy*. New York: Crown, 1983.

564. Downs, Frederick. *Aftermath: Return from the Killing Zone*. New York: W. W. Nortin, 1983.

565. Drescher, Nuala. *Engineers for the Public Good: A History of the Buffalo District U.S. Army Corps of Engineers*. Buffalo, N.Y.: U.S. Army Corps of Engineers District Office, 1982.

566. Dunstin, Simon. *Vietnam Track: Armor in Battle, 1945–1975*. London: Osprey, 1982.

567. Edmonds, Martin. *International Arms Procurement: New Directions*. Elmsford, N.Y.: Pergamon Press, 1981.

568. Egendoff, Arthur, et al. *Legacies of Vietnam: Comparative Adjustment of Veterans and their Peers* [U.S. Congress, 97th, 1st session, House Committee on Veterans Affairs].

569. Esper, George, and the Associated Press. *The Eyewitness History of the Vietnam War, 1961–1975*. New York: Ballatine Books, 1983.

570. Etzold, Thomas H. *Defense or Delusion? America's Military in the 1980s*. New York: Harper & Row, 1982.

571. Fallows, James. *National Defense*. New York: Random House, 1979.

572. Figley, Charles R., and Seymour Leventman, eds. *Strangers at Home: Vietnam since the War*. New York: Praeger, 1980.

573. Figley, Charles R. ed. *Stress Disorders among Vietnam Veterans*. New York: Brunner Mazel, 1978.
574. Foster, Gaines, *The Demands of Humanity: Army Medical Disaster Relief*. Washington, D.C.: Center of Military History, 1983.
575. Gabriel, Richard A. *To Serve with Honor: A Treatise in Military Ethics and the Way of the Soldier*. Westport, Conn.: Greenwood Press, 1982.
576. Geelhoed, Edward Bruce. *Charles E. Wilson and Controversy at the Pentagon, 1953–1957*. Detroit, Mich.: Wayne State University Press, 1979.
577. Gelb, Leslie H., with Richard K. Betts. *The Irony of Vietnam: The System Worked*. Washington, D.C.: Brookings Institution, 1979.
578. Goad, K.J.W., and D.H.J. Halsey. *Ammunition (Including Grenades and Mines)* Vol. 3, Brassey's Battlefield Weapons Systems and Technology. London: Brassey's, 1980.
579. Goff, Stanley, Robert Sanders, and Clark Smith. *Brothers: Black Soldiers in the Nam*. San Rafael, Calif.: Presidio Press, 1982.
580. Goldman, Nancy Loring, ed. *Female Soldiers – Combatants or Noncombatants*. Westport, Conn.: Greenwood Press, 1982.
581. Goldman, Peter, and Tony Fuller. *Charlie Company: What Vietnam Did to Us*. New York: William Morrow, 1982.
582. Gordon, Don E. *Electronic Warfare: Element of Strategy and Multiplier of Combat Power*. Elsmford, N.Y.: Pergamon Press, 1981.
583. Goulden, Joseph C. *Korea: The Untold Story of the War*. New York: Times Books, 1982.
584. _____. *Truth is the First Casualty; The Gulf of Tonkin Affair – Illusion and Reality*. Chicago: Adler, 1969.
585. Greenstein, Fred I. *The Hidden-Hand Presidency: Eisenhower as Leader*. New York: Basic Books, 1982.
586. Griffen, William L., and John Marciano. *Teaching the Vietnam War: A Critical Examination of School Texts and an Interpretive Comparative History Utilizing the Pentagon Papers and other Documents*. Montclair, N.J.: Allenheld, Osman, 1979.
587. Hackett, Sir John. *The Third World War: The Untold Story*. New York: Macmillan, 1982.
588. Hagwood, Joseph Jeremiah. *Engineers at the Golden Gate*. San Francisco, Calif.: U.S. Army Corps of Engineers District Office, 1981.
589. Hammel, Eric. *Chosin: Heroic Ordeal of the Korean War*. New York: Vanguard, 1981.
590. Harris, Robert, and Jeremy Paxman. *A Higher Form of Killing: The Secret Story of Chemical and Biological Warfare*. New York: Hill and Wang, 1982.
591. Harris, W. W. *Puerto Rico's Fighting 65th U.S. Infantry: From San Juan to Chorwan*. San Rafael, Calif.: Presidio Press, 1980.
592. Hatcher, John Henry. *Trip Report of Field Search for Exercise Desert Rock Documentation Conducted by Representatives of the Adjutant General, 18 June 1978 to 14 July 1978*. Washington, D.C.: Office of the Adjutant General, 1978.
593. Henderson, William Darryl. *Why the Vietcong Fought: A Study of Motivation and Control in a Modern Army in Combat*. Westport, Conn.: Greenwood Press, 1979.

594. Herring, George C. *America's Longest War: The United States and Vietnam*. New York: John Wiley and Sons, 1979.

595. Herrington, Stuart A. *Silence Was a Weapon: The Vietnam War in the Villages*. San Rafael, Calif.: Presidio Press, 1982.

596. Hickey, Michael. *Out of the Sky: A History of Airborne Warfare*. New York: Charles Scribner's Sons, 1979.

597. Hill, Robert M., and Elizabeth Craig. *In the Wake of War: Memoirs of an Alabama Military Government Officer in World War II Italy*. University: University of Alabama Press, 1982.

598. Hinh, Nguyen Duy. *Lam Son 719*. Indochina Monographs. Washington, D.C.: Center of Military History, 1979.

599. _____. *Vietnamization and the Cease-Fire*. Indochina Monographs. Washington, D. C.: Center of Military History, 1980.

600. Hixson, John, and Benjamin Franklin Cooling. *Combined Operations in Peace and War*. Carlisle Barracks, Pa.: U.S. Army Military History Institute, 1982.

601. Holm, Jeanne. *Women in the Military: An Unfinished Revolution*. San Rafael, Calif.: Presidio Press, 1982.

602. Holmes, Burnham. *Basic Training: A Portrait of Today's Army*. New York: Four Winds Press, 1979.

603. Holloway, Bruce K., et al. *Grand Strategy for the 1980s*. Washington, D.C.: American Enterprise Institute for Public Policy Research, 1978.

604. Hope, Richard O. *Racial Strife in the U.S. Military: Toward the Elimination of Discrimination*. New York: Praeger, 1979.

605. Horne A. D., ed. *The Wounded Generation: America After Vietnam*. Englewood Cliffs, N.J.: Prentice-Hall, 1981.

606. Hosmer, Stephen J., et al. *The Fall of South Vietnam: Statements by Vietnamese Military and Civilian Leaders*. New York: Crane, Russak, 1980.

607. Howe, Russell W. *Weapons: The International Game of Arms, Money and Diplomacy*. New York: Doubleday, 1980.

608. Hoyt, Edwin. *Airborne: The History of American Parachute Forces*. New York: Stein & Day, 1979.

609. Hunt, Richard A., and Richard H. Schultz, Jr. eds. *Lessons From an Unconventional War: Reassessing U.S. Strategies for Future Conflicts*. Elmsford, NY: Pergamon Press, 1982.

610. Ingraham, Larry H. *The Boys in the Barracks: Observations on American Military Life*. Philadelphia: Institute for the Study of Human Issues, 1983.

611. *Ironhorse Footprints: A Unique "History" of Fort Carson from January 1971 to June 1972*. Fort Carson, Col.: PIO Office, 1973.

612. Isaacs, Arnold R. *Without Honor: Defeat in Vietnam and Cambodia*. Baltimore, Md.: John Hopkins University Press, 1983.

613. Jenkins, Brian Michael. *New Modes of Conflict*. Santa Monica, Calif.: Rand, 1983.

614. Jessup, John E., and Robert W. Coakley. *A Guide to the Study and Use of Military History*. Washington, D.C. Center of Military Mistory, 1979.

615. Johnson, Leland R. *The Headwaters District: A History of the Pittsburgh District, U.S. Army Corps of Engineers*. Pittsburgh, Pa.: U.S. Corps of Engineers District Office, 1979.

616. Johnson, Maxwell Orme. *The Military as an Instrument of U.S. Policy in Southwest Asia: The Rapid Deployment Joint Task Force, 1979–1982.* Boulder, Colo.: Westview Press, 1983.

617. Kaldor, Mary. *The Baroque Arsenal.* New York: Hill and Wang, 1981.

618. Kaplan, Fred. *The Wizards of Armageddon.* New York: Simon & Schuster, 1983.

619. Karas, Thomas. *The New High Ground: Strategies and Weapons of Space-Age War.* New York: Simon & Schuster, 1983.

620. Karnow, Stanley. *Vietnam: A History.* New York: Viking Press, 1983.

621. Katcher, Philip, and Mike Chappell. *Armies of the Vietnam War, 1962–1975.* Men-at-Arms Series. London: Osprey, 1980.

622. Keveles, Gary N. *Bargained Justice in the Military: A Study of Practices and Outcomes in the U.S. Army, Europe.* Ann Arbor, Mich.: University Microfilms, 1982.

623. Keylin, Arlene, and Suri Boiangiu. *Front Page Vietnam As Reported by The New York Times.* New York: Arno, 1979.

624. Kirkbridge, Wayne A. *Timber: The Story of Operation Paul Bunyan.* New York: Vantage 1980.

625. Klein, Robert. *Wounded Men, Broken Promises.* New York: Macmillan, 1981.

626. Koenig, W. J. *Americans at War: From the Colonial Wars to Vietnam.* New York: Putnam's 1980.

627. _____. *Weapons of World War III.* London: Bison Books, 1981.

628. Lane, Jack C. *America's Military Past: A Guide to Information Sources.* Detroit, Mich.: Gale Research, 1980.

629. Langley, Michael. *Inchon Landing: MacArthur's Last Triumph.* New York: Times Books, 1979.

630. Larson, John W. *Those Army Engineers: A History of the Chicago District U.S. Army Corps of Engineers.* Chicago: U.S. Corps of Engineers District Office, 1980.

631. Le Gro, William E. *Vietnam From Cease-Fire to Capitulation.* Washington, D.C.: Center of Military History, 1981.

632. Linedecker, Clifford. *Kerry: Agent Orange and an American Family.* New York: St. Martin's, 1982.

633. Long, Franklin A., and Judith Reppy. *The Genesis of New Weapons: Decision Making for Military R&D.* Elmsford, N.Y.: Pergamon Press, 1980.

634. Lovell, John P. *Neither Athens Nor Sparta? The American Service Academies in Transition.* Bloomington: Indiana University Press, 1979.

635. Lung, Hoang Ngoc. *The General Offensives of 1968–69.* Indochina Monographs. Washington, D.C.: Center of Military History, 1981.

636. MacGregor, Morris. *Integration in the Armed Forces, 1945–1965.* Washington, D.C.: GPO, 1981.

637. Maclear, Michael. *The Ten Thousand Day War, Vietnam: 1945–1975.* New York: St. Martin's, 1981.

638. Mahon, John K. *History of the Militia and the National Guard.* New York: Macmillan, 1983.

639. Mantell, David Mark. *True Americanism: Green Berets and War Resisters.* New York: Teachers College Press, 1975.

640. Marshall, S.L.A. *Bringing Up the Rear: A Memoir*. Edited by Cate Marshall. San Rafael, Calif.: Presidio Press, 1979.
641. Mason, Robert. *Chickenhawk*. New York: Viking Press, 1983.
642. Merritt, Raymond H. *Creativity, Conflict and Controversy: A History of the St. Paul District, U.S. Army Corps of Engineers*. Washington, D.C.: GPO, 1979.
643. Mills, Gary B. *Of Men and Rivers: The Story of the Vicksburg District*. Vicksburg, Miss.: U.S. Corps of Engineers District Office, 1978.
644. Mosley, Leonard. *Marshall: Hero for Our Times*. New York: Hearst Books, 1982.
645. Myer, Charles R. *Division-Level Communications 1962–1973*. Vietnam Studies. Washington, D.C.: Department of the Army, 1982.
646. Nalty, Bernard C. and Morris J. MacGregor, eds. *Blacks in the Military; Essential Documents*. Wilmington, Del.: Scholarly Resources, 1981.
647. Neff, Donald. *Warriors at Suez: Eisenhower Takes America into the Middle East*. New York: Linden Press, 1981.
648. O'Ballance, Edgar. *The Wars in Vietnam 1954–1980*. New York: Hippocrene, 1981.
649. Ognibene, Andre J., et al. *Internal Medicine in Vietnam: Medicine and Infections*. Medical Department in Vietnam Series. Washington, D.C.: Center of Military History, 1982.
650. Olivey, Lee D., Henry A. Leonard, and Bruce E. Arlinghaus, eds. *Industrial Capacity and Defense Planning: Sustained Conflict and Surge Capability in the 1980s*. Lexington, Mass.: Lexington Books, 1983.
651. Owen, J.I.H. *Brassey's Infantry Weapons of the World, 1950–1975*, also *1979*. London: Brassey's 1978, 1979.
652. Paddock, Alfred H. *U.S. Army Special Warfare: Its Origins in Psychological and Unconventional Warfare, 1941–1952*. Washington, D.C.: National Defense University, 1982.
653. Palmer, Gregory. *The McNamara Strategy and the Vietnam War: Program Budgeting in the Pentagon, 1960–1968*. Westport, Conn.: Greenwood, 1978.
654. Papp, Daniel S. *Vietnam: The View From Moscow, Peking, Washington*. Jefferson N.C.: McFarland, 1981.
655. Patti, Archimedes L. A. *Why Viet Nam? Prelude to America's Albatross*. Berkeley: University of California Press, 1980.
656. Perry, John Curtis. *Beneath the Eagle's Wings; Americans in Occupied Japan*. New York: Dodd, Mead, 1980.
657. Pew, Frank W. *The Role of the U.S. Army Forces Command in Project New Arrivals: Reception and Care of Refugees from Vietnam*. Fort McPherson, Ga.: U.S. Army Forces Command Historical Office, 1981.
658. Pfaltzgraff, Robert L., and Uri Ra'anan, eds. *U.S. Defense Mobilization Infrastructure: Problems and Priorities*. Hamden, Conn.: Shoe String Press, 1983.
659. Pisor, Robert. *The End of the Line: The Siege of Khe Sanh*. New York: W. W. Norton, 1982.
660. Podhoretz, Norman. *Why We Were in Vietnam*. New York: Simon & Schuster, 1982.
661. Ponton, Jean, et al. *Operation Hardtack II, 1958*. Washington, D.C.:

Defense Nuclear Agency, 1982.

662. Porter, Gareth, ed. *Vietnam: The Definitive Documentation of Human Decisions.* Pine Plains, N.Y.: Earl M. Coleman Enterprises, 1979.

663. Rasor, Dina, ed. *More Bucks, Less Bang: How the Pentagon Buys Ineffective Weapons.* Washington D.C.: Fund for Constitutional Government, 1983.

664. Reich, Dale E. *Good Soldiers Don't Go to Heaven.* Whitewater, Wis.: Garden of Eden Press, 1979.

665. Roberts, Cecil E. *A Soldier From Texas.* Fort Worth, Tex.: Branch-Smith, 1978.

666. Robertson, Jack W. *Selling To The Federal Government.* New York: McGraw-Hill, 1979.

667. Rogan, Helen. *Mixed Company: Women in the Modern Army.* New York: Putnam, 1981.

668. Romjue, John L. *A History of Army 86: Vol. 2, The Development of the Light Division, the Corps, and Echelons above Corps, (November 1979–December 1980).* Fort Monroe, Va.: Historical Office, Training and Doctrine Command, 1981.

669. Rose, John P. *The Evolution of U.S. Army Nuclear Doctrine, 1945–1980.* Boulder, Colo.: Westview Press, 1980.

670. Rosenberg, Howard L. *Atomic Soldiers: American Victims of Nuclear Experiments.* Boston: Beacon Press, 1980.

671. RUSI and Brassey's, *Weapons Technology: A Survey of Current Developments in Weapons Systems.* London: Brassey's, 1980.

672. Rustad, Michael L. *Women in Khaki: The American Enlisted Woman.* New York: Praeger, 1982.

673. Saffer, Thomas H., and Orville E. Kelly. *Countdown Zero.* New York: Putnam, 1982.

674. Santoli, Al. *Everything We Had: An Oral History of the Vietnam War By Thirty-three American Soldiers Who Fought It.* New York: Random House, 1981.

675. Schevitz, Jeffrey M. *The Weaponsmakers: Personal and Professional Crisis during the Vietnam War.* Cambridge, Mass.: Schenkman, 1979.

676. Schnabel, James F. *The Joint Chiefs of Staff and National Policy, 1945–1947.* vol. 2. The History of the Joint Chiefs of Staff. Wilmington, Del.: Michael Glazier, 1979.

677. Schnabel, James F. and Robert J. Watson, *The Korean War, Parts I and II.* Vol. 3. The History of the Joint Chiefs of Staff. Wilmington, Del.: Michael Glazier, 1979.

678. Scoville, Thomas W. *Reorganizing For Pacification Support.* Washington, D.C.: GPO, 1981.

679. Sharp, Ulysses S. Grant. *Strategy for Defeat: Vietnam in Retrospect.* San Rafael, Calif.: Presidio Press, 1979.

680. Shawcross, William. *Side-Show: Kissinger, Nixon and the Destruction of Cambodia.* New York: Pocket Books, 1979.

681. Simpson, Charles M., III. *Inside the Green Berets: The First Thirty Years.* Novato, Calif.: Presidio Press, 1983.

682. Sivaram, M. *The Vietnam War: Why?* Rutland, Vt.: Charles E. Tuttle, 1966.

683. Skrajabina, Elena. *The Allies on the Rhine, 1945-1950*. Translated and edited by Norman Luxemburg. Carbondale: Southern Illinois University Press, 1980.

684. Smith, Cecil B., Jr., comp. *Special Forces in Southeast Asia: U.S. Special Forces, Vietnamese Special Forces, Irregular Forces*. Erin, Tenn.: ARV-CAT, 1979.

685. Smith, Digby, and Michael Chappell. *Army Uniforms since 1945*. Poole, England: Blandford Press, 1980.

686. Smith, Robert. *MacArthur in Korea: The Naked Emperor*. New York: Simon & Schuster, 1982.

687. Sorley, Lewis. *Arms Transfers under Nixon: A Policy Analysis*. Lexington: Universty Press of Kentucky, 1983.

688. Spector, Ronald. *Advice and Support; The Early Years 1940-1961*. U.S. Army in Vietnam Series. Washington, D.C.: GPO, 1983.

689. Spiller, Roger I. *"Not War But Like War": The American Intervention in Lebanon*. Leavenworth Papers no. 3. Fort Leavenworth, Kans.: U.S. Army Command and General Staff College, Combat Studies Institute, 1981.

690. Stanton, Shelby L. *Vietnam Order of Battle. U.S. Army and Allied Ground Forces in Vietnam*. Washington, D.C.: U.S. News Books, 1981.

691. Starry, Donn A. *Mounted Combat in Vietnam*. Vietnam Studies. Washington, D.C.: GPO. 1979.

692. Stockholm International Peace Research Institute. *Anti-Personnel Weapons*. New York: Crane, Russak, 1978.

693. Summers, Harry G., Jr. *On Strategy: The Vietnam War in Context*. Carlisle Barracks, Pa.: Strategic Studies Institute, U.S. Army War College, 1981.

694. Talbott, Strobe. *Endgame: The Inside Story of Salt II*. New York: Harper & Row, 1979.

695. Tarr, Curtis W. *By the Numbers: The Reform of the Selective Service System*. 1970. 1972. Washington, D.C.: National Defense University Press, 1981.

696. Tent, James F. *Mission on the Rhine: Re-education and Denazification in American-Occupied Germany*. Chicago: University of Chicago Press, 1982.

697. Thies, Wallace J. *When Governments Collide: Coercion and Diplomacy in the Vietnam Conflict, 1964-1968*. Berkeley: University of California Press, 1980.

698. Tho, Tran Dinh. *The Cambodian Incursion*. Indochina Mongraphs. Washington, D.C.: Center of Military History, 1979.

699. Thum, Marcella and Gladys. *Exploring Military America*. New York: Atheneum, 1982.

700. Tobias, Sheila et al. *What Kinds of Guns Are They Buying for Your Butter? A Beginner's Guide to Defense Weaponry and Military Spending*. New York: William Morrow, 1982.

701. Todd, James Paul. *An Analysis of Predictor Variables for Completion of Women Soldiers' Initial Training in Non-traditional Service Areas of the United States Army*. Ann Arbor, Mich.: University Microfilms, 1981.

702. *Transaction/Society*, vol. 21, no. 1 (November-December 1983). "Controversies: Vietnam as Unending Trauma." Harry G. Summers, "Defense Without Purpose"; Gareth Porter, "Distorting History"; Thomas

J. Bellows, "Lessons Yet to be Learned"; Franz Michael, "Ideological Guerrillas"; Robert A. Scalapino, "The Open Society at War."

703. Trullinger, James Walker. *Village at War: An Account of Revolution in Vietnam*. New York: Longman's, 1980.

704. Truong, Ngo Quang. *R.V.N.A.F. and U.S. Operational Cooperation and Coordination*. Indochina Monographs. Washington, D.C.: Center of Military History, 1980.

705. _____. *The Easter Offensive of 1972*. Indochina Monographs. Washington, D.C.: Center of Military History, 1980.

706. Uhl, Michael, and Tod Ensign. *GI Guinea Pigs; How the Pentagon Exposed Our Troops to Dangers More Deadly than War; Agent Orange and Atomic Radiation*. Chicago: Playboy Press, 1980.

707. U.S. Congress, 96th, 2d Session. Senate Committee Print Number 29. Submitted by Veterans Administration to Committee on Veterans Affairs. *Myths and Realities: A Study of Attitudes Toward Vietnam Era Veterans*. Washington: D.C.: GPO, 1980.

708. U.S. Department of the Army. *1982 Weapons Systems, United States Army*. Washington, D.C.: GPO, 1983.

709. _____, Military Traffic Management Command. *STRAGNET Condition Report; A Study of Rail Lines Important to National Defense. For Armed Services Committees of the Congress, June 1981*. Washington, D.C.: Department of Defense, 1981.

710. _____, Office, Deputy Chief of Staff for Operations. *Women in the Army: Policy Review*. Washington, D.C.: Department of the Army, 1982.

711. U.S. Department of Defense, Office of the Secretary of Defense. *Military Compensation Background Papers: Compensation Elements and Related Manpower Cost Items: Their Purposes and Legislative Backgrounds*. Washington, D.C.: Department of Defense, 1982.

712. Vien, Cao Van. *The Final Collapse*. Washington, D.C.: Center of Military History, 1983.

713. Vien, Cao Van, et al. *The U.S. Adviser*. Indochina Monographs. Washington, D.C.: Center of Military History, 1980.

714. Vongsavanh, Soutchay. *RLG Military Operations and Activities in the Laotian Panhandle*. Indochina Monographs. Washington, D.C.: Center of Military History, 1981.

715. Waitley, Douglas. *America at War: Korea and Vietnam*. Encino, Calif.: Glencoe, 1980.

716. Walthall, Melvin C. *Lightning Forward; A History of the 25th Infantry Division (Tropic Lightning), 1941–1978*. N.P.: By the Association, 1980.

717. Weeks, John. *The Airborne Soldier*. Poole, England: Blandford Press, 1982.

718. Wood, Sara Loeb. *Let the Army Make a Man of You: A Cultural and Situational Analysis of Women Entering Combat Support Occupations*. Ann Arbor, Mich.: University Microfilms, 1982.

719. Yarmolinksy, Adam, and Gregory, D. Foster. *Paradoxes of Power: The Military Establishment in the Eighties*. Bloomington: Indiana University Press, 1983.

720. Young, Warren L. *Minorities and the Military; A Cross-National Study in World Perspective*. Westport, Conn.: Greenwood Press, 1982.

721. Zaloga, Steven J., and James W. Loop. *Modern American Armor: Combat Vehicles of the United States Army Today*. London: Arms and Armor Press, 1982.

XVIII

THE NAVY, 1941–1983

Dean C. Allard

In the five years since 1978, a surprisingly large number of volumes have appeared that deal with the United States Navy's history over the last four decades. As would be expected, only a relatively small number of these works are solid, scholarly contributions bearing directly on the naval service. Other titles consist of memoirs, popularized accounts, or volumes in which the navy is referred to in a somewhat peripheral sense. Nevertheless, this total body of literature indicates a widespread interest on the part of professional and nonprofessional historians that is highly welcome.

REFERENCE WORKS. The prolific Myron J. Smith, Jr., continues to contribute basic bibliographies that facilitate intellectual control over the extensive literature in the field of modern naval history. Of particular importance is his comprehensive guide to English-language sources dealing with the navy and the Coast Guard from 1946 to 1983 (733). In addition, the navy is represented in Smith's bibliography of air warfare during the Vietnam conflict (732). Another comprehensive bibliography which identifies works dealing with all aspects of the navy's role in Vietnam was compiled by Edward J. Marolda and G. Wesley Pryce III (677).

In addition, Charles Schultz's meticulous bibliography of periodical literature dealing with the navy and the merchant marine deserves notice. The most recent volume in this continuing series, published in 1982, has a cumulative index covering titles appearing between 1970 and 1979 (728). Paolo E. Coletta's *Bibliography of American Naval History* includes periodical as well as book literature covering all aspects of the navy's past and is useful for scholars interested in the modern navy (577).

A new guide to naval manuscripts and archives, located in approximately 250 American repositories, was prepared by Dean C. Allard, Martha L. Crawley, and Mary W. Edmison (545). Another finding aid for unpublished material is the U.S. Naval Institute's catalog to its oral histories of senior naval officers (760). Approximately 130 volumes of transcripts have appeared to date in that distinguished series of reminiscences on the modern navy.

Two outstanding biographical reference works also have become available. These are the two-volume *American Secretaries of the Navy*, edited by Paolo E. Coletta, Robert G. Albion, and K. Jack Bauer, containing scholarly essays on all secretaries serving through 1972 (576); and a similar collaborative volume, recounting the contributions of those officers who served as chief of naval operations, edited by Robert W. Love, Jr. (668). David Mason's *Who's Who in World War II* (678) offers short biographies of American as well as foreign figures, including leaders of the U.S. Navy.

The Naval History Division's *Dictionary of American Naval Fighting Ships*, which contains historical and technical data on all of the navy's vessels, was completed in 1981 (359). This essential eight-volume series will be updated on a continuing basis. Another basic reference, an official chronology of U.S. naval aviation, was revised in 1981 (756). Three other notable contributions, all of which relate to World War II, are Jurgen Rohwer's compilation of the successes of Axis submarines (716), Arthur R. Moore's dictionary of U.S. merchant ship sinkings (687), and Frank J. Olynyk's list of naval air aces (695). Rohwer's volume is a revision of his 1968 work and the definitive source on its subject. Moore and Olynyk also undertook extensive research in preparing their valuable and original reference works. Olynyk can be supplemented by a more general biographical volume by Raymond F. Toliver and Trevor L. Constable that offers an account of the most important naval and non-naval aviation aces of World War II (751).

Due to the keen interest by many general readers in the characteristics of naval ships and weapons, numerous works continue to appear on this subject. Often, these volumes also recount the operational experience of these systems and include references to the institutional framework in which they were developed. Among these contributions are John Alden's perceptive design history of the navy's fleet submarines (544); Eric Brown's description of U.S. and British aircraft (566); Thomas S. Burns's journalistic survey of the development of U.S. and Soviet submarine and antisubmarine warfare technology since World War II (570); Peter Elliott's discussion of Allied minesweeping in World War II (599); a series of contributions by Norman Friedman and his co-authors that discuss naval radar, carriers, and destroyers (611, 612, 613, 630); an account by Gregory Hartman, one of the navy's notable mine experts, on the design and use of sea mines (626); Frank D. Johnson's volume on PT boats (642); a description of the American flying boat by Richard C. Knott (651); Norman Polmar's study of American submarines (702); Rosario Rausa's narrative of the Douglas Skyraider aircraft during its decades of service in the navy (711); John C. Reilly's description of U.S. destroyers (713); a catalog of the Coast Guard's vessels and craft, prepared by Robert L. Scheina (727); Stefan Terzibaschitsch's studies of U.S. aircraft carriers and escort carriers during World War II (744, 745); and, finally, a series of well-written technical and operational volumes, by Barrett Tillman, covering the Hellcat, Crusader, and Wildcat aircraft (747, 748, 749). U.S. naval historians also will be interested in Eberhard Rossler's definitive account of the German U-boat (723), which posed such a formidable threat to the United States and her allies during the war. All of these volumes provide useful insight into the essential material aspects of naval warfare. Other titles that concentrate on broader aspects of science and technology, including associated policy and administrative developments, are discussed later in this essay.

PERIODICALS AND CONFERENCE PROCEEDINGS. In addition to the journals mentioned in earlier essays, *Aerospace Historian* (541), *International Security* (638), and *Warship* (763) contain articles in the field of modern naval history. The naval history symposia, sponsored by the Naval Academy since 1973, also offer papers on U.S. and foreign naval topics. Published proceedings for the 1977 and 1979 conferences have appeared in recent years (667, 743). Another notable biennial conference is the Air Force Academy's Military History Symposium, at which naval historians often speak. Naval papers appear in the proceedings of the 1978 and 1980 conferences (595, 637). A recent conference on the history of the Royal Canadian Navy, which often has operated jointly with the U.S. Navy, also was held. The contributions at that meeting appear in a volume edited by James Boutilier (560). Finally, *The Yankee Mariner and Seapower* (553), the record of a multidisciplinary conference held at the University of Southern California in 1981, contains useful essays on the evolution of American naval strategy and current naval affairs.

WORLD WAR II OPERATIONS, STRATEGY, AND POLICY. Among the broad surveys that include general coverage on World War II are E. B. Potter's 1981 revision of *Sea Power: A Naval History* (704), which discusses that conflict from both an Allied and an enemy perspective. This volume has long been used as a basic text at the Naval Academy. Another comprehensive work is Allan Millett's new history of the Marine Corps (684). It offers a challenging interpretation of that sea service, including its interaction with the U.S. Navy. Robert Albion's *Makers of Naval Policy*, a draft manuscript dating from 1950, was recently published in its original form (543). Fortunately, its author also collaborated with Robert G. Connery in 1962 in preparing a revised and updated version of most of the material in the manuscript that dealt with World War II and the immediate postwar years. Modern naval historians probably will prefer to use this latter work, which appeared under the title *Forrestal and the Navy* (6). Another overall title is a thoughtful essay assessing the navy's overall role in World War II by John D. H. Kane, Jr., the current director of naval history (644).

Several biographical and autobiographical works also provide a general foundation for understanding the worldwide naval conflict that ended in 1945. One of these is Thomas Buell's biography of Fleet Adm. Ernest J. King (569), who served as the navy's senior officer throughout America's involvement in the conflict. Although Buell does not offer a fundamental revision of the accepted view of King's outlook and contributions, his work is the first modern assessment of this important figure. It is supplemented by a lengthy essay on the admiral's strategic thinking by Robert W. Love, Jr. (668), and a collection of memoranda, following off-the-record press conferences with Admiral King and other military leaders in Washington, prepared by the journalist Glen Perry (699). Perry's notes offer unusual insight into the thinking of these officers. The secretary of the navy during the first part of the war, Frank Knox, is a subject of a recent dissertation by Steven M. Mark (676). In addition, Donald Vining has edited a collection of personal diaries maintained primarily by enlisted and junior officer personnel, eight of whom served with the navy (761). Although these individuals were far removed from the high-level policy arena in Washington, their accounts provide excellent insight into the face of war at sea.

The formation of the Anglo-American alliance during the 1937–1941 era, which is of essential importance in understanding the grand strategy of World War II, is studied in a solid monograph by David Reynolds (714). Reynolds made considerable use of U.S. naval sources in preparing his study. As is true for other authors who have explored this subject, including Leutze (469), Louis (474), and

Thorne (523), he concludes that competition, as well as cooperation, characterized British-American relations. Another useful study of the political-military aspects of the world conflict is Anthony Gray's dissertation on American naval policy in Latin America (620). Gray's work extends through the World War II and immediate postwar years.

Further general titles include a cooperative work on the U.S. merchant marine, edited by Robert Kilmarx, covering the maritime aspects of World War II (649), and Richard Compton-Hall's analysis of the role of Allied and enemy submarines in the war at sea (580). Reference also should be made to David MacIsaac's monograph on the U.S. strategic bombing survey (674), which includes a discussion of the importance of strategic bombing, in comparison to maritime and land warfare, in the defeat of Germany and Japan.

ATLANTIC THEATER. Although general syntheses of this aspect of the war have not appeared, a number of more specialized sources can be noted. The U.S. Navy's role in the undeclared war in the Atlantic prior to December 1941 is addressed by the diplomatic historian Thomas A. Bailey and naval officer Paul B. Ryan (551). Another useful volume on the 1939–1941 period publishes Joseph H. Wellings's contemporary observations of the British fleet (764). Admiral Wellings was an assistant naval attaché in the United Kingdom who maintained a diary and files of his official reports.

After a long period of relative neglect, American authors appear to be developing greater interest in the important role of the U.S. Navy in projecting Allied power ashore in the European theater. Recent writings in this field include Alan Wilt's study of the southern France landings (767) and Susan H. Godson's biography of John L. Hall, who was a major American amphibious commander in European waters (618). Both of these volumes are fine works of scholarship, based upon extensive research in original sources. In addition, British writers continue to contribute important writings on this subject. W. G. F. Jackson's account of the differing outlooks of British and American leaders on the invasion of Western Europe culminates in a description of the Normandy landings (639). An important tactic in most of the major amphibious campaigns was the use of strategic and tactical deception, which is the subject of a study by Charles G. Cruickshank (587). One American practitioner of deception was the actor Douglas Fairbanks, Jr., who served as U.S. Naval Reserve officer in the Atlantic. His wartime exploits are included in an older biography by Brian Connell (581).

As has been true for some time, the greatest number of volumes on this region concentrate on the battle of the Atlantic, which revolved around the Allied effort to maintain the security of trans-Atlantic sea lanes against the assault by German U-boats. Two general discussions appear, one in Roland Bowling's dissertation, which argues that Americans were reluctant to employ oceanic convoys due to Mahan's teachings of the overriding importance of actions between major naval fleets (562), and the other in Peter Kemp's incisive account of the British and American antisubmarine campaign (647). The significant role of communications intelligence in submarine and antisubmarine warfare continues to be addressed. Recent writings in this area include a collaborative work edited by the German historians Jurgen Rohwer and Eberhard Jackel (717), and an article by Kenneth Knowles, an American naval officer who played a major role in distributing the communications intelligence product to U.S. forces (653). Several valuable contributions also have appeared on the Canadian Navy's role in the battle of the Atlantic. An excellent essay by W.G.D. Lund discusses the successful effort of that force to assume tactical control from the United States in the antisubmarine campaign in the northwest Atlantic (671). Operational accounts or memoirs of the Canadian Navy appear in works by Milner (685), Lamb (658), and Lawrence (660). A vivid book regarding the grounding and loss of two U.S. naval ships operating in Canadian coastal waters early in 1942, including the heroic rescue attempts by citizens of the area, is offered by Cassie Brown (565). The experiences of individual ships engaged in the Atlantic war also are reflected in a memoir by Joseph A. Donahue, who was a bluejacket in the destroyer *Niblack* (596); in William T. Y'Blood's account of the important contributions made by American escort carriers in the antisubmarine campaign (772); and in the personal diaries collected by Donald Vining (761). An imaginative, if not entirely successful, volume by Edward W. Chester assesses the military, political, and economic significance of six American naval bases in the western Atlantic that were established primarily to support the campaign against German submarines (575).

The attempts of the Axis to use sea-lines of communication for their own logistic purposes involved the operations of a number of surface and submarine blockade runners. Two overall accounts of these vessels and the increasingly successful attacks made on them by Allied forces have been published by Martin Brice (564) and August Muggenthaler (691).

PACIFIC THEATER. One of the major contributions of recent years is Grace Hayes's meticulous and comprehensive history of the role of the Joint Chiefs of Staff in the war against Japan (627). Although completed in 1953, this manuscript long was unavailable due to its security classification. The volume is based upon thorough research in JCS and naval records and may be considered the most complete and perceptive account of the predominantly maritime strategy of the Pacific war that has been produced to date.

Students of Pacific strategy also can turn to the previously cited works on Admiral King by Buell (569) and Love (668), and to a new biography, by Hiroyuki Agawa, of Admiral Yamamoto, the dominant leader in the Imperial Japanese Navy during the early part of the war (542). Further Japanese perspective is offered by the valuable monographs written by former officers of that nation's navy and army after 1945 (159). A number of these accounts have become more accessible due to their publication in a series edited by Donald Detwiler (590). Overviews from a U.S. point of view appear in John Costello's competent survey of the Pacific campaigns (583) and in works by Ronald Lewin (664) and W. J. Holmes (633) that stress the role of communications intelligence in shaping American efforts to defeat Japan. A more specialized contribution is Michael Schaller's monograph on the nation's wartime policy in China (726). Schaller includes references to the naval aspects of these political-military developments.

The fortieth anniversary of the attack on Pearl Harbor led to renewed interest in that always fascinating topic and the appearance of several well-publicized histories. In this author's opinion, the most solid of these contributions is Gordon Prange's long-awaited volume (706). Based upon decades of research in Japanese and U.S. sources, Prange prepared a comprehensive and judicious account that explores virtually all of the events surrounding Japan's assault at Pearl Harbor. The published version, a condensation of Prange's much larger manuscript,

THE NAVY, 1941-1983 · 209

appeared shortly after the author's death. This work is of particular interest due to its rejection of the allegation that President Roosevelt, aware of the imminence of the Japanese attack, conspired with other senior officers in Washington to deny vital intelligence to the commanders at Hawaii in order to assure U.S. entry into World War II. However, Prange was unable to study the large volume of new documents resulting from the U.S. decryption of Japanese communications that began to be released in the United States in the late 1970s. This omission is one of the principal arguments used by John Toland and John Costello in attacking Prange's scholarship. Toland's views appear in *Infamy* (750), a volume that uses newly released intelligence files and testimony from some participants to argue that Roosevelt was well aware of the Japanese task force that reached Hawaiian waters on 7 December, 1941. Costello's overall account of the Pacific war (583), and a more recent article (584), draw upon Japanese communications intelligence and U.S. and British materials. At times, this British journalist appears to suggest that evidence may some day be released which will lend support to the Pearl Harbor conspiracy theory. Nevertheless, based upon the documentation that now is available, Costello reaches conclusions regarding the responsibilities of the president and other Washington officials that are similar to those advanced by Gordon Prange.

In addition to these works, students of the Pearl Harbor attack may consult the writings on U.S. communications intelligence programs by Ronald Lewin (664) and Ruth Harris (625). Both of these authors suggest that ineptitude in the evaluation of Japanese radio intercepts—rather than conspiracy—clouded the intelligence picture available to U.S. leaders in December 1941. The same conclusion was reached a number of years ago in Roberta Wohlstetter's classic monograph (388), despite the limited intelligence documentation that was then available. Today's authors can consult extentive collections of these records in the National Archives, or turn to a published eight-volume compilation of the major series of intercepted Japanese communications issued by the Department of Defense in 1977 (755).

Other useful titles on Pearl Harbor include a compendium of eyewitness accounts of the Japanese raid, edited by Paul Stillwell (738), and the memoir of Theodore Mason, who was a bluejacket on board one of the battleships that received the brunt of the Japanese attack (679). The political controversy that ensued in the United States regarding the responsibility of American officials is traced in a judicious monograph by Bruce Bartlett (554). Bartlett carries this story through the Congressional investigations of 1946.

Works on the origins of the Japanese-American war that go beyond a Pearl Harbor perspective include James Leutze's illuminating biography of Admiral Hart, the commander of the U.S. Asiatic Fleet (663); books by three British writers— Richard Collier (579), David Reynolds (714), and H. P. Willmott (766)—that trace the broad political and strategic outlooks of the United States, Great Britain, and Japan; and a collaborative volume by Japanese diplomatic and military historians, edited by James Morley (689).

The first seven months of the Pacific war, culminating in the classic defeat of Japan at the battle of Midway, is another active topic. The strategic plans of the Japanese are depicted in Agawa's biography of Admiral Yamamoto (542), an original contribution by John J. Stephan that assesses the ambitions of the Japanese to seize Hawaii (736), and two volumes by H. P. Willmott comparing

U.S. and Japanese grand strategy in the early part of the conflict (765, 766). The strategic thinking of U.S. leaders in the immediate aftermath of Pearl Harbor is skillfully depicted in Lloyd Graybar's article on the abortive attempt to relieve the garrison on Wake Island with a naval expeditionary force (621). On the operational level, John Lundstrom's account of U.S. carrier aircraft tactics and doctrine through the battle of Midway is of particular importance (672). As is true of his earlier work on early Pacific strategy, Lundstrom demonstrates that thorough research in original resources can yield fresh insights into a war that has been the subject of so much historical attention.

One of the most dramatic chapters in the Pacific conflict was the doomed effort of the allied forces of the United States, Great Britain, and Holland to defend the southwest Pacific. James Leutze's outstanding biography of Admiral Hart, who became the Allied naval commander in the area, is a welcome addition to the literature on this campaign (663). Among other contributions, Leutze's book includes a lucid discussion of the problems inherent in coalition warfare against an overwhelming enemy. In addition, Walter Winslow has written an operational account of the U.S. Navy in the Asiatic defense campaign that contains a great deal of human interest coverage (768). Dwight Messimer recounts the loss of USS *Langley* and *Pecos* in the Dutch East Indies (682). Another operational contribution is Timothy Hall's detailed account of the Japanese raid on Darwin, Australia, in February 1942 that had remarkable similarities to the earlier attack on Pearl Harbor (623).

The battle of Midway, which marked the end of the first stage of the Pacific campaigns, is one of the best-covered actions in the entire war. It has been addressed anew in Lundstrom's revealing tactical volume (672), and in books by George Gay (615) and Gordon Prange (707). Gay, a fortunate survivor of one of the U.S. torpedo squadrons that pressed home the American attack on Japan's carriers, gives his firsthand impressions of the action. As was true for his Pearl Harbor study, Prange's work was published posthumously with the assistance of two of his associates. This volume offers a solid but unoriginal synthesis of the battle as a whole. An intriguing aftermath of Midway was the preliminary legal action taken by U.S. officials against the *Chicago Tribune* for its alleged security breach in publishing an article implying that Japanese naval communications were being decrypted. Two revealing articles, by Frank (608) and Goren (619), recount this episode and the eventual decision to abandon litigation lest it lend further publicity to the weakness of Japanese cryptographic systems.

Following Midway, the next major campaign was the invasion of Guadalcanal. A memoir by Herbert Merillat, a combat historian with the Marine landing force, offers a superb firsthand account that also includes perceptive comments on the problems faced by naval strategists (680). The prolific author Edwin P. Hoyt (635) and Robert E. Lee (661) also offer overviews of the Guadalcanal campaign. Hoyt's book is based, in part, upon the Japanese official history of World War II, which remains to be translated into English. Logistical aspects of operations in the South Pacific are covered in an account of the important support base at Efate, New Hebrides, by Ritchie Garrison (614).

In 1944, the battles of the Philippine Sea and Leyte Gulf completed the elimination of the Japanese navy as a formidable threat. The first of these actions is described by William Y'Blood (773), and the second, in a rather thin account, by Adrian Stewart (737). The U.S. Navy's experience at Leyte also is depicted in Edwin Hoyt's history of *Gambier Bay*, one of the escort carriers lost in the Samar phase of that action (636). During later operations in support of the reoccupation of the Philippines, Admiral Halsey's Third Fleet received heavy damage from a typhoon. The commanding officer of one of the destroyers that faced the furies of this storm, C. Raymond Calhoun, has written a forthright, professional account that faults the navy's meterologists and ship designers for the losses suffered on that occasion (572).

Finally, the invasion of Okinawa and the ordeal of the naval forces supporting this prolonged campaign are covered in several useful volumes. Of particular note is a revealing account of the Japanese kamikaze corps by Dennis and Peggy Warner (762). With the assistance of a Japanese collaborator, the Warners delve deeply into the Japanese psychology that led to this suicide campaign. They also offer the most definitive account to date of the operational results of the Japanese efforts, which reached the peak of their effectiveness off Okinawa. During this same campaign, a suicide mission was attempted by the super-battleship *Yamato* against the overwhelming strength of the U.S. This disastrous sortie is described by the journalist Russell Spurr (734). An equally valiant ship was the U.S. destroyer *Laffey*, which was hit repeatedly by kamikaze aircraft in the Okinawa area. Her ordeal and remarkable survival are described in graphic detail by the ship's commanding officer, F. Julian Becton (555). In addition, the experiences of Admiral John L. Hall, one of the major amphibious commanders in the Ryukyus, are depicted in Susan Godson's biography (618). The navy's role ashore also is covered in William P. Simpson's reminiscence of the naval advanced base at Okinawa, which is another useful reminder of the importance of logistics in modern war (730).

The major role of naval aviation in the vast Pacific Ocean is another subject that continues to fascinate American readers. At least three general accounts of the navy's carriers that give primary attention to the Pacific have appeared in recent years from the pens of Peter Kilduff (648), John Lindley (666), and Wilbur H. Morrison (690). In addition, a veteran naval aviator, Richard C. Knott, discusses the employment of the lumbering flying boat in offensive operations (651), and Klaus P. Lindemann describes the ruinous raid made by American carrier aircraft against Japanese shipping at Truk in February 1944 (665). Lindemann, who is an experienced diver, also offers intriguing detail on the current status of the hulks of the ships sunk in that attack. Finally, two memoirs have appeared in recent years that throw light on the naval aviator's war. One of these is by Arthur Radford, who writes from the perspective of a successful carrier task-group commander (709). The other is John Monsarrat's well-written reminiscence of his experiences as a reserve officer serving on board the carrier *Langley* (686).

In addition to the works mentioned above, historians of the Pacific war will benefit from a recent biography of Admiral Nimitz, the theater commander, by Frank A. Driskill and Dede W. Cesad (598). This volume stresses the admiral's personal characteristics. Memoir literature on the American-Japanese war appears in Donald Vining's compilation of personal diaries (761), Art Bell's reminiscence of the operations of one of the small patrol craft that played an important if unheralded role in the conflict (556), and Hughston Lowder's account of his experiences as a member of submarine *Batfish*'s crew (670).

OPERATIONS, POLICY, AND STRATEGY, 1945–1983. The appearance

of Paul B. Ryan's general survey of the navy in the postwar decades, which is based primarily upon published sources of the Naval Institute's valuable oral history collection, indicates the extent of the literature now available for his era (724). Jan S. Breemer also has produced a synthesis of the period that is less comprehensive than Ryan's but contains a useful assessment of the navy as of 1983 (563). In addition, overall coverage appears in the studies of individual secretaries of the navy edited by Coletta, Albion, and Bauer (576), and the essays assessing the contributions of postwar chiefs of naval operations edited by Love (668). In revising his overall text of world naval history, Professor Potter paid particular attention to strengthening that book's coverage for the years after World War II (704).

Students of naval history also can consult accounts of some of the major institutions with which the navy was associated. The formulation of national policy by the Joint Chiefs of Staff, between 1945 and 1952, is covered in a series of detailed, official histories by James F. Schnabel, Kenneth W. Condit, Robert J. Watson, and Walter S. Poole (757). Another volume in the JCS series covers that organization's role in formulating U.S. policy in Southeast Asia, especially during the period of the French-Viet Minh War of 1946-1954 (758). An unofficial survey of the first 25 years of the Joint Chiefs has been written by Lawrence Korb (655). The navy's interaction with other key national security organizations is reflected in Douglas Kinnard's books on the secretary of defense (650) and Allan Millett's new, institutional history of the Marine Corps (684).

Several writers have concentrated attention upon the naval and military aspects of the short-of-war international crises involving the United States since 1945. An important contribution in this category is a study by Barry M. Blechman and Stephen S. Kaplan (558). Basing their work upon extensive research in original sources, Blechman and Kaplan offer a general theoretical framework of the role of military forces in recent international affairs and offer useful case studies of several specific incidents of the 1950s and 1960s. Further, James Cable has issued a revised and updated version of his well-known study, *Gunboat Diplomacy*, which covers all of the world's major navies (571); Edward A. Smith's dissertation provides insight into confrontations involving the major naval powers between 1946 and 1973 (731); and Bradford Dismukes and James McConnell have studied the expanding deployment of the Soviet navy and the U.S. Navy's reactions to Russian seapower in the 1960s and 1970s (593). A useful study by Harkavy discusses the overseas basing and naval deployment patterns of the great powers, especially in the post-1945 years (624). The role of the U.S. Navy and other agencies in the development of the nation's nuclear deterrent also has commanded considerable attention. Naval participation in this process especially can be traced in the scholarly writings by David Rosenberg (719, 721, 722), and a more popular work by Fred M. Kaplan (645).

Among other specialized contributions, it is possible to cite a number of solid works addressing the formative period between the end of World War II and the initiation of the Korean War in 1950. A dissertation by Edward J. Sheehy (729) and an honors paper by Naval Academy midshipman Dennis M. Pricolo (708) throw additional light on the origins of the Navy's Sixth Fleet in the Mediterranean. Also useful in this connection is David J. Alvarez's study of U.S.-Turkish relations through 1946 (549). More limited reference to naval aspects appear in Lawrence S. Wittner's monograph on U.S. policy during the Greek civil war (769). Due especially to the growing importance of the Middle East's oil supplies in world affairs, that region also became of growing significance to the United States. Three monographs discussing the development of American oil policy, primarily in the decade of the 1940s, have been written by Irvine H. Anderson (550), David A. Miller (683), and Michael B. Stoff (739). Each of these refers to the role of U.S. naval policymakers. A survey of the navy's operations in the Middle East between 1800 and 1979 has been contributed by Thomas A. Bryson (568).

Turning to the Pacific basin, Roger Dingman's thoughtful discussion of American strategy in that region in the half century prior to the Korean War deserves special notice (591). He also has written an imaginative case study of the U.S. decision to retain a major naval base at Yokosuka, Japan, as an indicator of the development of national policy during the early cold war era (592). The Yokosuka base is addressed more directly in a book by Benton W. Decker, who was the first U.S. commander of that facility (588). Another Naval Academy honors paper, by Samuel J. Cox, traces the institutional history of the U.S. Seventh Fleet, which operated in the western Pacific during the immediate post-World War II period (586). In the meantime, the efforts by U.S. naval advisors based ashore in Nationalist China to improve the navy of that nation is recounted in Bruce Swanson's overall account of Chinese naval affairs (741).

Naval policy and operations in other parts of the world are described in Lisle Rose's study of the Navy's Antarctic expedition of 1946–1947 (718), and a fine article by John Major traces the waning strategic importance of the Panama Canal in the years prior to the Korean War (675). Another excellent article, also based upon extensive original research, is Lloyd Graybar's account of the nuclear tests at Bikini in 1946 (622). Graybar argues that this operation needs to be understood within the context of the navy's efforts to maintain its important role in the nation's defense, especially in the face of competition by the U.S. Air Force. During the same period, an intriguing view of the navy through the eyes of the army is offered by the papers of General Eisenhower, who served as that service's chief of staff between 1945 and 1948 (574).

The issue of defense organization became a dominant concern in the immediate postwar years. Admiral Radford, a central figure representing the navy's interests in this period, covers his activities in a recently published memoir (709). Paolo Coletta's monograph on the navy and unification during the 1947–1953 period (578), and David A. Rosenberg's article on the interaction between naval air doctrine and the service's outlook on unification (720), also are useful. The special problems of the Marine Corps in the face of reorganization proposals are assessed in a book by Gordon W. Keiser (646). Finally, another marine officer, Victor H. Krulak, has written an overall critique of the impact of modern defense organization on military readiness and efficiency (657). General Krulak's book covers the general situation since the end of World War II, including the period between 1945 and 1949 when the foundations were laid for this organizational structure.

The Korean War has received relatively little attention in recent literature. However, William W. Stueck has used naval, as well as diplomatic and military documentation, in his assessment of the origins of that conflict (740). A valuable source document on another policy aspect, the Korean Armistice Conference, is the diary maintained by Admiral Joy at this prolonged proceeding (643). In the operational sphere, John Bovey's article on the role of Canadian destroyers in Korean waters (561), and a popular recounting of the famed Inchon Landings, by Michael Langley (659), merit attention.

In their current reappraisal of the presidency of Dwight D. Eisenhower, American historians tend to emphasize that leader's caution and self-restraint in using military force as an instrument of national policy. Robert Divine's study, *Eisenhower and the Cold War*, which includes frequent reference to the navy, is one title in this category (594). A valuable source document on all aspects of Eisenhower's career is his private diary, which recently was published under the editorship of Robert Ferrell (604). Case studies of some of the major international incidents in which the navy was involved include John Prados's account of the possible use of American air power in 1954 to defend the French outpost at Dien Bien Phu (705). Since Prados is critical of Admiral Radford's role, historians will want to compare his book with Radford's memoirs (709). The Suez crisis of 1956 is the subject of a useful account by the journalist Donald Neff (693), while the Lebanon landings of 1958 are studied as one of Blechman and Kaplan's case studies on the use of armed force in crisis situations (558).

International crises during the Kennedy and Johnson presidencies also have attracted attention. Following the abortive invasion of Cuba at the Bay of Pigs in 1961, a presidential investigative committee was organized that included, as one of its members, Admiral Arleigh A. Burke, the chief of naval operations. The testimony taken by that body and its final report recently were declassified and published (696). Naval deployments during the crisis in Laos in 1962 and involving the Dominican Republic three years later are studied by Blechman and Kaplan (558). Later in the decade, the Israeli attack against USS *Liberty* during the 1967 Arab-Israeli war is described by one of the survivors of that ship, James Ennes (601). Ennes vehemently denies the Israeli claim that this assault was accidental. A British journalist, Anthony Pearson, reaches the same conclusion in his popular work on the *Liberty* incident (697).

The Vietnam War continues to be covered in an extensive literature. Among the general titles on this conflict is a competent account of the navy's air war by Peter B. Merksy and Norman Polmar (681); a popular, illustrated history, covering both the naval and military aspects of Vietnam, edited by Ray Bonds (559); and a compilation of oral history interviews, prepared by Al Santoli (725). Of the 33 contributions in the Santoli volume, nine are by naval personnel. Several other memoirs are valuable in depicting the navy's experience in Vietnam. These include the forthright autobiography by Adm. Elmo Zumwalt, who served as commander, naval forces Vietnam, from 1968 to 1970 and then for the next four years as chief of naval operations (540); a reminiscence by Rosario Rausa, whose career in naval aviation included service in Vietnam (710); Dieter Dengler's account of his captivity and escape from enemy forces in Southeast Asia (589); and the memoir of another naval aviator, James Mulligan, recounting the seven years that he spent as a prisoner of war (692). Other contributions include Denis Fairfax's overall history of Australian naval operations in Vietnamese waters (603), a political and strategic assessment by James Thompson of the air campaign undertaken by the U.S. Navy and Air Force in North Vietnam from 1965 to 1968 (746), and an article by Oscar P. Fitzgerald discussing the role of U.S. naval advisors in Vietnam prior to 1965 (607).

Several titles also have appeared on naval operations in the post-Vietnam period. Admiral Zumwalt's memoir provides a starting point for this era (540), especially since he stresses his efforts to modernize the navy to meet the growing threat of the Soviet fleet. A 1975 crisis in Asia, following the Cambodian capture of the merchant ship *Mayaguez*, led to a strong reaction by a U.S. naval and Marine Corps force. Richard Head and his co-authors have produced a study on this subject that stresses the presidential decision process in a time of crisis (628). Later in the 1970s, the attention of U.S. strategists increasingly turned to the Indian Ocean. A useful study explaining the increasing role of the U.S. Navy in that region has been written by Alvin J. Cottrell and his associates (585). In addition, a basic source document has become available regarding the unsuccessful U.S. attempt in 1980 to rescue the American hostages taken in the aftermath of the Iranian Revolution. This joint operation, which largely was launched from a naval force in the Indian Ocean, was reviewed in a critical report prepared by a Joint Chiefs of Staff review group headed by Adm. James L. Holloway III, a former chief of naval operations (759).

OTHER ASPECTS OF NAVAL HISTORY. The interest by naval and military historians in social, economic, institutional, scientific, and technical topics parallels the popularity of these subjects within the general historical community. Among the notable titles in this category is Morris MacGregor's scholarly account of the integration of black personnel into the nation's military services prior to 1965 (673). MacGregor may be supplemented by Robert Pearson's journalistic study of the 1944 mutiny and subsequent trial of black seamen assigned to the Port Chicago, California, ammunition depot (698), and pamphlet by H. L. Bergsma recounting the careers of the navy's first black chaplains (557). An overall history of military and naval women has been contributed by the retired air force general Jeanne Holm (632). Other titles bearing directly on the navy include a memoir by Marie Alsmeyer, an enlisted WAVE in World War II (548); Helen Fitzgerald's thesis on the development of the navy's nurse corps between 1934 and 1968 (606); and a reminiscence by Phyllis T. Wright, the wife of a prominent flag officer (771). Miriam Frank's book on the contribution of civilian women workers in World War II refers to the feminine work forces of naval-oriented industries (609).

The social and economic impact of the navy upon surrounding communities also has been addressed. Gwenfread Allen's history of Hawaii during World War II, which is the standard account, includes the interaction between the military services and the citizens of those islands (546). In addition, John Stephan discusses the attitudes of the Japanese-American community in Hawaii to the ascendancy of Imperial Japan during the early part of the conflict (736). John Hammond Moore has assessed the large presence of American armed forces in Australia during the same period (688). Within the United States, the economic influence of the aviation industry in the state of Pennsylvania, including manufacturing facilities serving the navy, is discussed in a worthwhile study by William Trimble (753). A general analysis of the relationships between defense industries and the American armed services is offered in Paul Koistinen's monograph on the military-industrial complex (654).

Legal, educational, and cultural aspects of the navy have drawn the attention of other recent authors. Their contributions include Philip R. Piccigallo's account of the post-1945 war crimes trials in the Pacific, including those undertaken by the navy in the Marianas (700). Another fine work, by Ann L. Hollick, discusses the interaction between U.S. foreign policy and the law of the sea since 1935 (631). Hollick includes the naval implications of this subject. A special aspect of the maritime legal system is the extensive use by U.S. shipowners of foreign flags of convenience for the registration of their vessels. This practice and its national security implications are covered in a monograph by Rodney Carlisle (573). As for naval educational programs, Jack Sweetman has written a new history of the Naval Academy (742), while the evolution and current status of all of the service academies are addressed in a valuable, comparative study by John P. Lovell (669). A privately printed work on the navy's V-12 officer training program of World War II has been written by Raymond F. Howes, who helped to manage that effort (634). Howes provides insight into a program that heretofore has received little attention in the literature. Finally, reference can be made to a short biography of the marine artist Anton Fischer, written by his daughter (605). During part of World War II, Fischer served as a combat artist with the Coast Guard.

Several basic studies of naval institutions have appeared in recent years. One of these is Marc Pinsel's account of the Naval Oceanographic Office, which recently celebrated its 150th anniversary (701). The long history of the naval shipyard at Mare Island, California, is described by Sue Lemmon and E. D. Wichels (662), while the U.S. naval base at Yokosuka, Japan, is the subject of a reminiscence by Benton Decker (588). The navy's civil administration of Samoa through 1949 is covered in a dissertation by Frederick Olsen, who concludes that the navy was generally enlightened in handling its governmental responsibilities (694). More specialized titles include Kroll's short account of naval chaplains assigned to the Coast Guard (656), and two pamphlets by Stanley Jersey that discuss some of the naval and military postal systems in the Pacific during World War II (640, 641).

In addition to the previously cited works on World War II communications intelligence, a number of recent titles discuss the institutional aspects of America's intelligence services. A scholarly volume by Thomas Troy exploring the establishment and evolution of the Office of Strategic Services during World War II, is of interest because of the Navy's relationships with that organization (754). Another solid contribution is Roy Stanley's study of photographic intelligence techniques and commands in the same period, which includes some coverage of naval activities (735). Students of naval intelligence also will be interested in a colorful memoir by Kemp Tolley, who served as an assistant naval attaché in the Soviet Union during the war (752). A more controversial title is Jeffrey Dorwart's history of the Office of Naval Intelligence, which extends through 1945 (597). Dorwart reflects a deep suspicion toward intelligence organizations in general. In his highly selective narrative, he stresses ONI's domestic security progams and cites instances of practices in this field that would be not condoned today. Dorwart largely ignores ONI's primary effort, which was the collection and evaluation of information on foreign navies. An older book by the naval intelligence operative Willis George describes a number of surreptitious entries in the United States during World War II in connection with the investigation of possible enemy agents. It was publishd in 1946 (617).

As has been true for a number of years, there is much interest in the scientific and technical programs of the American armed forces. Of direct relevance is David Allison's soundly researched institutional and scientific history of the development of radar at the Naval Research Laboratory in the years prior to America's entry into World War II (547); Ralph Baldwin's administrative and technical study of the development of the proximity fuze, an effort largely sponsored by the navy

(552); Berend Bruins's excellent dissertation discussing the technical, policy, and strategic aspects of the navy's cruise missile program between 1940 and 1958 (567); a volume by Kent C. Redmond and Thomas M. Smith recounting the development of the first practical, general-purpose, digital computer at MIT, which was another outgrowth of the navy's research and development activities in World War II (712); and a memoir by Edward H. Heinemann, who designed some of the most successful combat aircraft in the navy's inventory (629). Admiral Rickover, the famed leader of the nuclear navy, is the subject of a generally critical biography by Norman Polmar and Thomas B. Allen (703). Louis Gebhard's study of the evolution of naval radio and electronic systems at the Naval Research Laboratory (616) is a good addition to a field that was explored earlier by Linwood Howeth (146). Another important work in this area is David L. Wood's collection of source materials on the major radio and visual communications systems used at sea (770). In the biological field, two pertinent volumes are Forrest Wood's popular account of the navy's experimentation with porpoises and sea lions (539), and Douglas H. Robinson's overall history of aviation medicine, which draws, in part, upon the navy's experience (715).

In addition, there is a group of volumes concerning other scientific or technical institutions and programs with which the navy was associated. Among these is a fine history of the National Science Foundation's formative years, written by J. Merton England (600). The NSF was in many respects an outgrowth of the Office of Naval Research. Naval connections also are demonstrated in a comprehensive discussion edited by M. D. Fagen of the work of the Bell Telephone Laboratories, which was one of the navy's prime contractors (602), and more indirectly in Edward Constant's monograph of the international origins of the turbojet aviation engine (582).

SUGGESTIONS FOR FURTHER RESEARCH. Considering the numerous works cited in this chapter, it is obvious that modern naval history does not suffer from a lack of attention. Further, a number of topics suggested in previous editions of this guide now have been explored. Nevertheless, a number of topics continue to deserve study.

Examples from the World War II era would include discussions of the evolution of tactics in specific categories of warfare, comparable to the studies of carrier aviation by Clark G. Reynolds (262) and John Lundstrom (672). An analytical volume on the critical role of the navy's logistical forces ashore and afloat also is needed. One region that has not been assessed in detail is the South Atlantic. The fleet maintained by the navy off South America had considerable operational and diplomatic significance. Although most of the major leaders of the war have been covered in biographies, or are the subject of projects currently under way, a number of other figures could be studied with profit. Among them are H. Kent Hewitt, Julius A. Furer, Alan G. Kirk, or Dudley W. Knox, all of whom left sizable collections of personal papers. In the social, economic, and institutional fields, it is regrettable that there still is no specialized monograph on naval women. Considering the memoirs by enlisted and junior officer personnel that are starting to appear in considerable number, as well as the availability of other sources, it also should be possible to undertake social histories of the navy from their perspective. Current interest in intelligence programs suggests the need for a comprehensive and balanced history of the Office of Naval Intelligence. Another organization that could be studied is the Bureau of Naval Personnel, including its far-reaching programs in recruiting, education, and training. Finally, the navy's relations with the press is one dimension of the service's interface with external groups that has not been explored in sufficient detail.

Naval records generally are available for the first decade of the post-World War II era. Hence, some of the topics referred to above could be extended into this period. Considering the great interest in American foreign policy, monographs bearing directly on the navy's international outlook and policies would be particularly useful. One of these might be a volume on the postwar evolution of Anglo-American naval relations, a subject that has been studied profitably for earlier eras.

Beyond the mid-1950s, historians will need to draw heavily upon the published literature or the collection of oral histories being developed by the U.S. Naval Institute. There are topics, however, that can be developed from these sources. Examples include studies of the navy's institutional and personnel reforms during the 1970s, or assessments of the navy's relationships with the Congress. An overall account of the navy's operations during the Vietnam War also remains to be written. In this case, published materials could be supplemented by the basic operational records that now are accessible in the navy's archives.

The author wishes to thank the staff of the Navy Department Library for their generous assistance in providing the materials cited in this chapter, and expresses his appreciation to Mrs. Jane Huie, who skillfully typed a difficult manuscript.

BIBLIOGRAPHY

(CITATIONS CONTINUED FROM SUPPLEMENT I)

539. Wood Forrest G. *Marine Mammals and Man: The Navy's Porpoises and Sea Lions*. Washington D.C.: Robert B. Luce, 1973.
540. Zumwalt, Elmo G., Jr. *On Watch: A Memoir*. New York: Quadrangle Books, 1976.

(NEW CITATIONS)

541. *Aerospace Historian*. Manhattan, Kans.: Air Force Historical Foundation, 1954–.
542. Agawa, Hiroyuki. *The Reluctant Admiral: Yamamoto and the Imperial Navy*. Tokyo: Kodansha International, 1979.
543. Albion, Robert G. *Makers of Naval Policy, 1798–1947*. Annapolis, Md.: Naval Institute Press, 1980.
544. Alden, John D. *The Fleet Submarine in the U.S. Navy: A Design and Construction History*. Annapolis, Md.: Naval Institute Press, 1979.
545. Allard, Dean C., Martha L. Crawley, and Mary W. Edminson, eds. *U.S. Naval History Sources in the United States*. Washington, D.C.: GPO, 1979.
546. Allen, Gwenfread. *Hawaii's War Years, 1941–1945*. Westport, Conn.: Greenwood Press, 1971.
547. Allison, David Kite. *New Eye for the Navy: The Origin of Radar at the Naval Research Laboratory*. Washington, D.C.: Naval Research

Laboratory, 1981.

548. Alsmeyer, Marie Bennett. *The Way of the Waves: Women in the Navy.* Conway, Ark.: Hamba Books, 1981.

549. Alvarez, David J. *Bureaucracy and Cold War Diplomacy: The United States and Turkey, 1943-1946.* Thessaloniki, Greece: Institute for Balkan Studies, 1980.

550. Anderson, Irvine H. *Aramco, the United States, and Saudi Arabia: A Study in the Dynamics of Foreign Oil Policy, 1933-1950.* Princeton, N.J.: Princeton University Press, 1981.

551. Bailey, Thomas A., and Paul B. Ryan. *Hilter vs. Roosevelt: The Undeclared Naval War.* New York: Free Press, 1979.

552. Baldwin, Ralph B. *The Deadly Fuze: The Secret Weapon of World War II.* San Rafael, Calif.: Presidio Press, 1980.

553. Bartell, Joyce J., ed. *The Yankee Mariner and Seapower: America's Challenge of Ocean Space.* Los Angeles: University of Southern California Press, 1982.

554. Bartlett, Bruce R. *Cover-up: The Politics of Pearl Harbor, 1941-1946.* New Rochelle, N.Y.: Arlington House, 1978.

555. Becton, F. Julian. *The Ship That Would Not Die.* Englewood Cliffs, N.J.: Prentice-Hall, 1980.

556. Bell, Art. *Peter Charlie: The Cruise of the PC 477.* Woodland Hills, Calif.: Courtroom Compendiums, 1982.

557. Bergsma, H. L. *The Pioneers: A Monograph on the First Two Black Chaplains in the Chaplain Corps of the United States Navy.* Washington, D.C.: GPO, 1981.

558. Blechman, Barry M., and Stephen S. Kaplan. *Force Without War: U.S. Armed Forces as a Political Instrument.* Washington, D.C.: Brookings Institution, 1978.

559. Bonds, Ray, ed. *The Vietnam War: The Illustrated History of the Conflict in Southeast Asia.* New York: Crown, 1979.

560. Boutilier, James A., ed. *The RCN in Retrospect, 1910-1968.* Vancouver: University of British Columbia Press, 1982.

561. Bovey, John. "The Destroyers' War in Korea, 1952-53." In *The RCN in Retrospect, 1910-1968,* edited by James A. Boutilier. Vancouver: University of British Columbia Press, 1982.

562. Bowling, Roland A. "The Negative Influence of Mahan on the Protection of Shipping in Wartime: The Convoy Controversy in the Twentieth Century." Ph.D. diss., University of Maine, 1980.

563. Breemer, Jan S. *U.S. Naval Developments.* Annapolis, Md.: Nautical and Aviation Publishing Company of America, 1983.

564. Brice, Martin. *Axis Blockade Runners on World War II.* Annapolis, Md.: Naval Institute Press, 1981.

565. Brown, Cassie. *Standing into Danger: A Dramatic Story of Shipwreck and Rescue.* New York: Doubleday, 1979.

566. Brown, Eric. *Wings of the Navy: Flying Allied Carrier Aircraft of World War II.* London: Jane's 1980.

567. Bruins, Berend D. "U.S. Naval Bombardment Missiles, 1940-1958: A Study in the Weapons Innovation Process." Ph.D. diss., Columbia University, 1981.

568. Bryson, Thomas A. *Tars, Turks and Tankers: The Role of the United States Navy in the Middle East, 1800–1979.* Metuchen, N.J.: Scarecrow Press, 1980.

569. Buell, Thomas B. *Master of Sea Power: A Biography of Fleet Admiral Ernest J. King.* Boston: Little, Brown, 1980.

570. Burns, Thomas S. *The Secret War for the Ocean Depths: Soviet-American Rivalry for Mastery of the Seas.* New York: Rawson Associates Publishers, 1978.

571. Cable, James. *Gunboat Diplomacy, 1919–1979: Political Applications of Limited Naval Force.* New York: St. Martin's, 1981.

572. Calhoun, C. Raymond. *Typhoon: The Other Enemy: The Third Fleet and the Pacific Storm of December 1944.* Annapolis, Md.: Naval Institute Press, 1981.

573. Carlisle, Rodney P. *Sovereignty for Sale: The Origins and Evolution of Panamanian and Liberian Flags of Convenience.* Annapolis, Md.: Naval Institute Press, 1981.

574. Chandler, Alfred D., and Louis Galambos, eds. *The Papers of Dwight David Eisenhower.* Baltimore, Md.: Johns Hopkins University Press, 1970–.

575. Chester, Edward W. *The United States and Six Atlantic Outposts: The Military and Economic Considerations.* Port Washington, N.Y.: Kennikat Press, 1980.

576. Coletta, Paolo E., Robert G. Albion, and K. Jack Bauer, eds. *American Secretaries of the Navy.* 2 vols. Annapolis, Md.: Naval Institute Press, 1980.

577. Coletta, Paolo E. *A Bibliography of American Naval History.* Annapolis, Md.: Naval Institute Press, 1981.

578. _____. *The United States Navy and Defense Unification, 1947–1953.* Newark: University of Delaware Press, 1981.

579. Collier, Richard. *The Road to Pearl Harbor.* New York: Atheneum, 1981.

580. Compton-Hall, Richard. *The Underwater War, 1939–1945.* New York: Sterling Publishing, 1982.

581. Connell, Brian. *Knight Errant: A Biography of Douglas Fairbanks, Jr.* London: Hodder & Stoughton, 1955.

582. Constant, Edward W., II. *The Origins of the Turbojet Revolution.* Baltimore, Md.: Johns Hopkins University Press, 1980.

583. Costello, John. *The Pacific War.* New York: Rawson, Wade, 1981.

584. _____. "Remember Pearl Harbor." *U.S. Naval Institute Proceedings* (September 1983), 53–62.

585. Cottrell, Alvin, J., and associates. *Sea Power and Strategy in the Indian Ocean.* Beverly Hills, Calif.: Sage, 1981.

586. Cox, Samuel J. "U.S. Naval Strategy and Foreign Policy in China, 1945–1950." A Trident Scholar Project Report. Annapolis, Md.: U.S. Naval Academy, 1980.

587. Cruickshank, Charles G. *Deception in World War II.* New York: Oxford University Press, 1979.

588. Decker, Benton W. *Return of the Black Ships.* New York: Vantage, 1978.

589. Dengler, Dieter. *Escape From Laos.* San Rafael, Calif.: Presidio Press, 1979.

590. Detwiler, Donald S., ed. *War in Asia and the Pacific, 1937–1949*. 15 vols. New York: Garland, 1980.

591. Dingman, Roger. "American Policy and Strategy in East Asia, 1898–1950: The Creation of a Commitment." In *The American Military and the Far East*, Joe C. Dixon, ed. Washington, D.C.: Office of U.S. Air Force History, 1980.

592. _____. "The U.S. Navy and the Cold War: The Japan Case." In *New Aspects of Naval History*, edited by Craig L. Symonds. Annapolis, Md.: Naval Institute Press, 1981.

593. Dismukes, Bradford, and James McConnell. *Soviet Naval Policy*. New York: Pergamon Press, 1979.

594. Divine, Robert A. *Eisenhower and the Cold War*. New York: Oxford University Press, 1981.

595. Dixon, Joe C., ed. *The American Military and the Far East*. Washington, D.C.: Office of U.S. Air Force History, 1980.

596. Donahue, Joseph A. *Tin Cans and Other Ships*. North Quincy, Mass.: Christopher Publishing House, 1979.

597. Dorwart, Jeffrey M. *Conflict of Duty: The U.S. Navy's Intelligence Dilemma, 1919–1945*. Annapolis, Md.: Naval Institute Press, 1983.

598. Driskill, Frank A., and Dede W. Cesad. *Chester W. Nimitz: Admiral of the Hills*. Austin, Tex.: Eakin Press, 1983.

599. Elliott, Peter. *Allied Minesweeping in World War II*. Annapolis, Md.: Naval Institute Press, 1979.

600. England, J. Merton. *A Patron of Pure Science: The National Science Foundation's Formative Years, 1945–1957*. Washington, D.C.: National Science Foundation, 1982.

601. Ennes, James M., Jr. *Assault on the* Liberty*: The True Story of the Israeli Attack on an American Intelligence Ship*. New York: Random House, 1979.

602. Fagen, M. D., ed. *A History of Engineering and Science in the Bell System: National Service in War and Peace (1925–1975)*. New York: Bell Telephone Laboratories, 1978.

603. Fairfax, Denis. *Navy in Vietnam: A Record of the Royal Australian Navy in the Vietnam War, 1965–1972*. Canberra: Australian Government Publishing Service, 1980.

604. Ferrell, Robert H., ed. *The Eisenhower Diaries*. New York: W. W. Norton, 1981.

605. Fischer, Katrina Sigsbee. *Anton Otto Fischer, Marine Artist: His Life and Work*. Brighton, England: Teredo Books, 1977.

606. Fitzgerald, Helen M. "A History of the United States Navy Nurse Corps from 1934 to the Present." M.S. thesis, The Ohio State University, 1968.

607. Fitzgerald, Oscar P. "U.S. Naval Forces in the Vietnam War: The Advisory Mission, 1961–1965." In *Changing Interpretations and New Sources in Naval History*, edited by Robert W. Love, Jr. New York: Garland, 1980.

608. Frank, Larry J. "The United States Navy v. the *Chicago Tribune*." *The Historian* (February 1980), 284–303.

609. Frank, Miriam. *The Life and Times of Rosie the Riveter: The Story of Three Million Working Women during War II*. Emeryville, Calif.: Clarity Educational Productions, 1982.

610. Friedman, Norman. *Carrier Air Power*. Annapolis, Md.: Naval Institute

Press, 1981.

611. _____. *Naval Radar*. Annapolis, Md.: Naval Institute Press, 1981.

612. _____. *U.S. Aircraft Carriers: An Illustrated Design History*. Annapolis, Md., Naval Institute Press, 1983.

613. _____. *U.S. Destroyers: An Illustrated Design History*. Annapolis, Md.: Naval Institute Press, 1982.

614. Garrison, Ritchie. *Task Force 9156 and III Island Command: A Story of a South Pacific Advanced Base during World War II, Efate, New Hebrides*. Waban, Mass.: Privately printed, 1983.

615. Gay, George, *Sole Survivor: The Battle of Midway and Its Effect on His Life*. Naples, Fla.: Naples Ad / Graphics Services, 1979.

616. Gebhard, Louis A. *Evolution of Naval Radio-Electronics and Contributions of the Naval Research Laboratory*. Washington, D.C.: GPO, 1979.

617. George, Willis. *Surreptitious Entry*. New York: Appleton-Century, 1946.

618. Godson, Susan H. *Viking of Assault: Admiral John Lesslie Hall, Jr., and Amphibious Warfare*. Washington, D.C.: University Press of America, 1982.

619. Goren, Dina. "Communication Intelligence and the Freedom of the Press: The *Chicago Tribune*'s Battle of Midway Dispatch and the Breaking of the Japanese Naval Code." *Journal of Contemporary History* (October 1981), 663–90.

620. Gray Anthony W., Jr. "The Evolution of U.S. Naval Policy in Latin America." Ph.D. diss. American University, 1982.

621. Graybar, Lloyd J. "American Pacific Strategy after Pearl Harbor: The Relief of Wake Island." *Prologue* (Fall 1980), 134–50.

622. _____. "Bikini Revisited." *Military Affairs* (October 1980), 118–23.

623. Hall, Timothy. *Darwin 1942: Australia's Darkest Hour*. Sydney, Australia: Methuen, 1980.

624. Harkavy, Robert E. *Great Power Competition for Overseas Bases: The Geopolitics of Access Diplomacy*. New York: Pergamon Press, 1982.

625. Harris, Ruth P. "The 'Magic' Leak of 1941 and Japanese-Amerian Relations." *Pacific Historical Review* (February 1981), 77–96.

626. Hartman, Gregory K. *Weapons that Wait*. Annapolis, Md.: Naval Institute Press, 1979.

627. Hayes, Grace P. *The History of the Joint Chiefs of Staff in World War II: The War against Japan*. Annapolis, Md.: Naval Institute Press, 1982.

628. Head, Richard G., Frisco W. Short, and Robert C. McFarlane. *Crisis Resolution: Presidential Decision-Making in the* Mayaguez *and Korean Confrontations*. Boulder, Colo.: Westview Press, 1978.

629. Heinemann, Edward H. *Ed Heinemann: Combat Aircraft Designer*. Annapolis, Md.: Naval Institute Press, 1980.

630. Hodges, Peter, and Norman Friedman. *Destroyer Weapons of World War II*. Annapolis, Md.: Naval Institute Press, 1979.

631. Hollick, Ann L. *U.S. Foreign Policy and the Law of the Sea*. Princeton, N.J.: Princeton University Press, 1981.

632. Holm, Jeanne. *Women in the Military: An Unfinished Revolution*. San Rafael, Calif.: Presidio Press, 1982.

633. Holmes, W. J. "Naval Intelligence in the War Against Japan, 1941–1945: The View from Pearl Harbor." In *New Aspects of Naval History*, edited

by Craig L. Symonds. Annapolis, Md.: Naval Institute Press, 1981.
634. Howes, Raymond F. *The Navy Goes to College*. Riverside, Calif.: Privately printed, 1974.
635. Hoyt, Edwin P. *Guadalcanal*. New York: Stein & Day, 1982.
636. Hoyt, Edwin P. *The Men of Gambier Bay*. Middlebury, Vt.: P. S. Eriksson, 1979.
637. Hurley, Alfred F., and Robert C. Erhart, eds. *Air Power and Warfare: Proceedings of the 8th Military History Symposium, United States Air Force Academy*. Washington, D.C.: GPO, 1979.
638. *International Security*. Cambridge, Mass.: 1976-.
639. Jackson, W.G. F. *Overlord, Normandy, 1944*. Newark: University of Delaware Press, 1979.
640. Jersey, Stanley C. *Postal History of the United States and Japanese Military Forces in the Gilbert and Ellice Islands, World War II*. Leicester, England: Hemmings and Capey, 1978.
641. _____. *Postal History of United States Forces in British Solomon Islands Protectorate during World War II*. State College, Pa.: American Philatelic Society, 1968.
642. Johnson, Frank D. *United States P.T. Boats of World War II*. Poole, England: Blandford Press, 1980.
643. Joy, C. Turner. *Negotiating while Fighting: The Diary of Admiral C. Turner Joy and the Korean Armistice Conference*. Edited by Allan E. Goodman. Stanford, Calif: Hoover Institution Press, 1978.
644. Kane, John D. H., Jr. "The Second World War and its Naval Operations in Perspective." *Indiana Military History Journal* (January 1981), 6-11.
645. Kaplan, Fred M. *The Wizards of Armageddon*. New York: Simon & Schuster, 1983.
646. Keiser, Gordon W. *The U.S. Marine Corps and Defense Unification, 1944-1947*. Washington, D.C.: National Defense University Press, 1982.
647. Kemp, Peter. *Decision at Sea: The Convoy Escorts*. New York: Dutton, 1978.
648. Kilduff, Peter. *U.S. Carriers at War*. Harrisburg, Pa.: Stackpole Books, 1981.
649. Kilmarx, Robert A., ed. *America's Maritime Legacy: A History of the U.S. Merchant Marine and Shipbuilding Industry since Colonial Times*. Boulder, Colo.: Westview Press, 1979.
650. Kinnard, Douglas. *The Secretary of Defense*. Lexington: University of Kentucky Press, 1980.
651. Knott, Richard C. *The American Flying-Boat: An Illustrated History*. Annapolis, Md.: Naval Institute Press, 1979.
652. _____. *Black Cat Raiders of WW II*. Annapolis, Md.: Nautical and Aviation Publishing Company of America, 1981.
653. Knowles, Kenneth A. "ULTRA and the Battle of the Atlantic: The American View." In *Changing Interpretations and New Sources in Naval History*, edited by Robert W. Love, Jr. New York: Garland, 1980.
654. Koistinen, Paul A. C. *The Military-Industrial Complex: A Historical Perspective*. New York: Praeger, 1980.
655. Korb, Lawrence J. *The Joint Chiefs of Staff: The First Twenty-Five Years*. Bloomington: University of Indiana Press, 1976.

656. Kroll, C. Douglas. *A History of Navy Chaplains Serving with the U.S. Coast Guard*. Washington, D.C.: GPO, 1983.

657. Krulak, Victor H. *Organization for National Security: A Study*. Washington, D.C.: United States Strategic Institute, 1983.

658. Lamb, James B. *The Corvette Navy: True Stories from Canada's Atlantic War*. Toronto: Macmillan, 1978.

659. Langley, Michael. *Inchon Landing: MacArthur's Last Triumph*. New York: Times Books, 1979.

660. Lawrence, Hal. *A Bloody War: One Man's Memories of the Candian Navy, 1939–1945*. Toronto: Macmillan, 1979.

661. Lee, Robert Edward. *Victory at Guadalcanal*. San Rafael, Calif.: Presidio Press, 1981.

662. Lemmon, Sue, and E. D. Wichels. *Sidewheelers to Nuclear Power: A Pictorial History Covering 123 Years at the Mare Island Naval Shipyard*. Annapolis, Md.: Leeward Publications, 1977.

663. Leutze, James R. *A Different Kind of Victory: A Biography of Admiral Thomas C. Hart*. Annapolis, Md.: Naval Institute Press, 1981.

664. Lewin, Ronald. *The American Magic: Codes, Ciphers, and the Defeat of Japan*. New York: Farrar, Strauss & Giroux, 1982.

665. Lindemann, Klaus P. *Hailstorm over Truk Lagoon*. Hong Kong: Maruzen Investment, 1982.

666. Lindley, John M. *Carrier Victory: The Air War in the Pacific*. New York: Dutton, 1978.

667. Love, Robert W., Jr., ed. *Changing Interpretations and New Sources in Naval History: Paper from the Third United States Naval Academy History Symposium*. New York: Garland, 1980.

668. _____. *The Chiefs of Naval Operations*. Annapolis, Md.: Naval Institute Press, 1980.

669. Lovell, John P. *Neither Athens nor Sparta? The American Service Academies in Transition*. Bloomington: Indiana University Press, 1979.

670. Lowder, Hughston E., with Jack Scott. *Batfish: The Champion "Submarine Killer" Submarine of World War II*. Englewood Cliffs, N.J.: Prentice-Hall, 1980.

671. Lund, W.G.D. "The Royal Canadian Navy's Quest for Autonomy in the North West Atlantic." In *The RCN in Retrospect, 1910–1968*, edited by James A. Boutilier. Vancouver: University of British Columbia Press, 1982.

672. Lundstrom, John B. *The First Team*. Annapolis, Md.: Naval Institute Press, 1984.

673. MacGregor, Morris J., Jr. *Integration of the Armed Forces, 1940–1965*. Washington, D.C.: Center of Military History, 1981.

674. MacIsaac, David. *Strategic Bombing in World War II: The Story of the United States Strategic Bombing Survey*. New York: Garland, 1976.

675. Major, John. "Wasting Asset: The U.S. Re-Assement of the Panama Canal, 1945–1949." *Journal of Strategic Studies* (September 1980), 123–46.

676. Mark, Steven M. "An American Interventionist: Frank Knox and United States Foreign Relations." Ph.D. diss., University of Maryland, 1977.

677. Marolda, Edward, J., and G. Wesley Pryce III. *A Select Bibliography of the United States Navy and the Vietnam Conflict*. Washington, D.C.: Naval Historical Center, 1982.

678. Mason, David. *Who's Who in World War II.* Boston: Little, Brown, 1978.
679. Mason, Theodore C. *Battleship Sailor.* Annapolis, Md.: Naval Institute Press, 1982.
680. Merillat, Herbert C. *Guadalcanal Remembered.* New York: Dodd, Mead, 1982.
681. Mersky, Peter B., and Norman Polmar. *The Naval Air War in Vietnam.* Annapolis, Md.: Nautical and Aviation Publishing Company of America, 1981.
682. Messimer, Dwight R. *Pawns of War: The Loss of the USS* Langley *and the USS* Pecos. Annapolis, Md.: Naval Institute Press, 1982.
683. Miller, David Aaron. *Search for Security: Saudi Arabian Oil and American Foreign Policy, 1939–1949.* Chapel Hill: University of North Carolina Press, 1980.
684. Millett, Allan Reed. *Semper Fidelis: The History of the United States Marine Corps.* New York: Macmillan, 1980.
685. Milner, Marc. "Royal Candian Navy Participation in the Battle of the Atlantic Crisis of 1943." In *The RCN in Retrospect, 1910–1968* edited by James A. Boutilier. Vancouver: University of British Columbia Press, 1982.
686. Monsarrat, John. *Angel on the Yardarm: Memoir of a Naval Officer in World War II.* N.p.: Privately printed, 1982.
687. Moore, Arthur R. *A Careless Word——A Needless Sinking.* Hallowell, Maine: Granite Hill, 1983.
688. Moore, John Hammond. *Over-Sexed, Over-Paid, and Over Here: Americans in Australia, 1941–1945.* St. Lucia, Australia: University of Queensland Press, 1981.
689. Morely, James William, ed. *The Fateful Choice: Japan's Advance into Southeast Asia, 1939–1941.* New York: Columbia University Press, 1980.
690. Morrison, Wilbur H. *Above and Beyond, 1941–1945.* New York: St. Martin's Press, 1983.
691. Muggenthaler, August K. *German Raiders of World War II.* Englewood Cliffs, N.J.: Prentice-Hall, 1977.
692. Mulligan, Jaems A. *The Hanoi Commitment.* Virginia Beach, Va.: RIF Marketing, 1981.
693. Neff, Donald. *Warriors at Suez.* New York: Linden Press, 1981.
694. Olsen, Frederick H. "The Navy and the White Man's Burden: Naval Administration of Samoa." Ph.D. diss., Washington University, 1976.
695. Olynyk, Frank J. *USN Credits for the Destruction of Enemy Aircraft in Air-to-Air Combat, World War II.* N.p.: The Author, 1982.
696. *Operation Zapata: The "Ultrasensitive" Report and Testimony of the Board of Inquiry into the Bay of Pigs.* Washington, D.C.: University Publications of America, 1981.
697. Pearson, Anthony. *Conspiracy of Silence.* London: Quartet Books, 1978.
698. Pearson, Robert E. *No Share of Glory.* Pacific Palisades, Calif.: Challenge, 1964.
699. Perry, Glen C. H. *"Dear Bart": Washington View of World War II.* Westport, Conn.: Greenwood Press, 1982.
700. Piccigallo, Philip R. *The Japanese on Trial: Allied War Crimes Operations in the East, 1945–1951.* Austin: University of Texas Press, 1979.
701. Pinsel, Marc I. *150 Years of Service on the Seas: A Pictorial History of*

the U.S. Naval Oceonographic Office from 1830 to 1980. Washington, D.C.: GPO, 1981.

702. Polmar, Norman. *The American Submarine*. Annapolis, Md.: Nautical and Aviation Publising Company of America, 1981.

703. Polmar, Norman, and Thomas B. Allen. *Rickover: Controversy and Genius*. New York: Simon & Schuster, 1982.

704. Potter, E. B., ed. *Sea Power: A Naval History*. 2d edition. Annaplis, Md.: Naval Institute Press, 1981.

705. Prados, John. *The Sky Would Fall: Operation Vulture: The U.S. Bombing Mission in Indochina, 1954*. New York: Dial Press, 1983.

706. Prange, Gordon W., in collaboration with Donald M. Goldstein and Katherine V. Dillon. *At Dawn We Slept: The Untold Story of Pearl Harbor*. New York: McGraw-Hill, 1981.

707. Prange, Gordon W., Donald M. Goldstein, and Katherine V. Dillon. *Miracle at Midway*. New York: McGraw-Hill, 1982.

708. Pricolo, Dennis Mitchell. "Naval Presence and Cold War Foreign Policy: A Study of the Decision to Station the 6th Fleet in the Mediterranean, 1945-1958." A Trident Scholar Project Report. Annapolis, Md.: U.S. Naval Academy, 1978.

709. Radford, Arthur W. *From Pearl Harbor to Vietnam: The Memoirs of Admiral Arthur W. Radford*. Edited by Stephen Jurika. Stanford, Calif.: Hoover Institution Press, 1980.

710. Rausa, Rosario. *Gold Wings, Blue Sea: A Naval Aviator's Story*. Annapolis, Md.: Naval Institute Press, 1981.

711. _____*Skyraider: The Douglas A-1 "Flying Dump Truck."* Annapolis, Md.: Nautical and Aviation Publishing Company of America, 1982.

712. Redmond, Kent C., and Thomas M. Smith. *Project Whirlwind: The History of a Pioneer Compter*. Bedford, Mass.: Digital, 1980.

713. Reilly, John C., Jr. *United States Navy Destroyers of World War II*. Poole, England: Blandford Press, 1983.

714. Reynolds, David. *The Creation of the Anglo-American Alliance, 1937-1941: A Study in Competitive Co-Operation*. Chapel Hill: University of North Carolina Press, 1982.

715. Robinson, Douglas H. *The Dangerous Sky: A History of Aviation Medicine*. Seattle: University of Washington Press, 1973.

716. Rohwer, Jurgen. *Axis Submarine Successes, 1939-1945*. Annapolis, Md.: Naval Institute Press, 1983.

717. Rohwer, Jurgen, and Eberhard Jackel eds. *Die Funkaufklarung and ihre Rolle im Zweiten Weltkrieg*. Stuttgart: Motorbuch Verlag, 1979.

718. Rose, Lisle A. *Assault on Eternity: Richard E. Byrd and the Exploration of Antarctica, 1946-47*. Annapolis, Md.: Naval Institute Press, 1980.

719. Rosenberg, David A. "American Atomic Strategy and the Hydrogen Bomb Decision.' *Journal of American History* (June 1979), 62-87.

720. _____. "American Postwar Air Doctrine and Organization: The Navy Experience." In *Air Power and Warfare: Proceedings of the 8th Military History Symposium, United States Air Force Academy*, edited by Alfred F. Hurley and Robert C. Erhart. Washington, D.C.: GPO 1979.

721. _____. "The Origins of Overkill: Nuclear Weapons and American Strategy, 1945-1960." *International Security* (Spring 1983), 3-71.

722. _____. "Toward Armageddon: The Foundations of United States Nuclear Strategy, 1945-1961." Ph.D. diss., University of Chicago, 1983.

723. Rossler, Eberhard. *The U-boat: The Evolution and Technical History of German Submarines.* Annapolis, Md.: Naval Institute Press, 1981.

724. Ryan, Paul B. *First Line of Defense: The U.S. Navy Since 1945.* Stanford, Calif.: Hoover Institution Press, 1981.

725. Santoli, Al. *Everything We Had: An Oral History of the Vietnam War by Thirty-Three American Soldiers Who Fought It.* New York: Random House, 1981.

726. Schaller, Michael. *The U.S. Crusade in China, 1938-1945.* New York: Columbia University Press, 1979.

727. Scheina, Robert L. *U.S. Coast Guard Cutters and Craft of World War II.* Annapolis, Md.: Naval Institute Press, 1982.

728. Schultz, Charles R. *Bibliography of Maritime and Naval History: Periodical Articles Published 1978-1979 with Cumulative Indexes for 1970-1979.* College Station: Texas A & M University, 1982.

729. Sheehy, Edward John. "The United States Navy in the Mediterranean, 1945-1947." Ph.D. Diss. George Washington University, 1983.

730. Simpson, William P. *Island "X": Okinawa.* West Hanover, Mass.: Christopher Publishing House, 1981.

731. Smith, Edward Allen, Jr. "Naval Confrontation: The Intersuperpower Use of Naval Suasion in Times of Crisis." Ph.D. diss., American University, 1979.

732. Smith, Myron J., Jr. *Air War Southeast Asia, 1961-1973: An Annotated Bibliography and 16mm Film Guide.* Metuchen, N.J.: Scarecrow Press, 1979.

733. _____. *The United States Navy and the United States Coast Guard, 1946-1983: A Guide to English Language Sources and 16mm Films.* Jefferson, N.C.: McFarland, 1984.

734. Spurr, Russell. *A Glorious Way to Die: The Kamikaze Mission of the Battleship Yamato, April 1945.* New York: Newmarket Press, 1981.

735. Stanley, Roy M., II. *World War II Photo Intelligence.* New York: Charles Scribner's Sons, 1981.

736. Stephen John J. *Hawaii under the Rising Sun: Japan's Plans for Conquest after Pearl Harbor.* Honolulu: University of Hawaii Press, 1984.

737. Stewart, Adrian. *The Battle of Leyte Gulf.* New York: Charles Scribner's Sons, 1979.

738. Stillwell, Paul, ed. *Air Raid: Pearl Harbor.* Annapolis, Md.: Naval Institute Press, 1981.

739. Stoff, Michael B. *Oil, Water, and American Security.* New Haven, Conn.: Yale University Press, 1980.

740. Stueck, William Whitney, Jr. *The Road to Confrontation: American Policy Toward China and Korea, 1947-1950.* Chapel Hill: University of North Carlina Press, 1981.

741. Swanson, Bruce. *Eighth Voyage of the Dragon.* Annapolis, Md.: Naval Institute Press, 1982.

742. Sweetman, Jack. *The U.S. Naval Academy: An Illustrated History.* Annapolis, Md.: Naval Institute Press, 1979.

743. Symonds, Craig L., ed. *New Aspects of Naval History.* Annapolis, Md.:

Naval Institute Press, 1981.

744. Terzibaschitsch, Stefan. *Aircraft Carriers of the U.S. Navy.* New York: Mayflower Books, 1980.

745. _____. *Escort Carriers and Aviation Support Ships of the U.S. Navy.* Annapolis, Md.: Naval Institute Press, 1981.

746. Thompson, James Clay. *Rolling Thunder: Understanding Policy and Program Failure.* Chapel Hill: University of North Carolina Press, 1980.

747. Tillman, Barrett. *Hellcat: The F6F in World War II.* Annapolis, Md.: Naval Institute Press, 1979.

748. _____. *MiG Master: The Story of the F-8 Crusader.* Annapolis, Md.: Nautical and Aviation Publishing Company of America, 1981.

749. _____. *The Wildcat in World War II.* Annapolis, Md.: Nautical and Aviation Publishing Company of America, 1983.

750. Toland, John. *Infamy: Pearl Harbor and Its Aftermath.* New York: Doubleday, 1982.

751. Toliver, Raymond F., and Trevor J. Constable. *Fighter Aces of the U.S.A.* Fallbrook, Calif.: Aero Publishers, 1979.

752. Tolley, Kemp. *Caviar and Commissars: The Experiences of a U.S. Naval Officer in Stalin's Russia.* Annapolis, Md.: Naval Institute Press, 1983.

753. Trimble, William F. *High Frontier: A History of Aeronautics in Pennsylvania.* Pittsburgh, Pa.: University of Pittsburgh Press, 1982.

754. Troy, Thomas F. *Donovan and the CIA: A History of the Establishment of the Central Intelligence Agency.* Washington, D.C.: University Publications of America, 1981.

755. U.S. Department of Defense. *The "Magic" Background of Pearl Harbor.* 8 vols. Washington, D.C.: GPO, 1977.

756. U.S. Deputy Chief of Naval Operations (Air Warfare) and Commander, Naval Air Systems Command. *United States Naval Aviation, 1910–1980.* Washington, D.C.: GPO, 1981.

757. U.S. Joint Chiefs of Staff. *The History of the Joint Chiefs of Staff, 1945–1952.* 4 vols. Wilmington, Del.: Michael Glazier, 1979–1980.

758. _____. *The Joint Chiefs of Staff and the War in Vietnam.* Wilmington, Del: Michael Glazier, 1982.

759. _____, Special Operations Review Group. *Rescue Mission Report.* Washington, D.C.: Joint Chiefs of Staff, 1980.

760. U.S. Naval Institute, Oral History Collection. *Catalog of Transcripts.* Annapolis, Md.: Naval Institute Press, 1983.

761. Vining, Donald, Ed. *American Diaries of World War II.* New York: Pepys Press, 1982.

762. Warner, Dennis and Peggy, with Sado Seno. *The Sacred Warriors: Japan's Suicide Legions.* New York: Van Nostrand, 1982.

763. *Warship: A Quarterly Journal of Warship History.* Greenwich, England, 1977–.

764. Wellings Joseph H. *On His Majesty's Service: Observations of the British Home Fleet from the Diary, Reports, and Letters of Joseph H. Wellings.* Edited by John Hattendorf. Newport, R.I.: Naval War College Press, 1983.

765. Willmott, H. P. *The Barrier and the Javelin: Japanese and Allied Pacific Strategies February to June 1942.* Annapolis, Md.: Naval Institute Press, 1983.

766. _____*Empires in the Balance: Japanese and Allied Pacific Strategies to April 1942*. Annapolis, Md.: Naval Institute Press, 1982.

767. Wilt, Alan F. *The French Riviera Campaign of August 1944*. Carbondale: Southern Illinois University Press, 1981.

768. Winslow, W. G. *The Fleet the Gods Forgot: The United States Asiatic Fleet in World War II*. Annapolis, Md.: Naval Institute Press, 1982.

769. Wittner, Lawrence S. *American Intervention in Greece, 1943–1949*. New York: Columbia University Press, 1982.

770. Woods, David L., ed. *Signaling and Communications At Sea*. 2 vols. New York: Arno Press, 1980.

771. Wright, Phyllis Thompson. *A Navy Wife's Log*. Washington, D.C.: Andromeda Books, 1978.

772. Y'Blood, William T. *Hunter-Killer: U.S. Escort Carriers in the Battle of the Atlantic*. Annapolis, Md.: Naval Institute Press, 1983.

773. _____. *Red Sun Setting: The Battle of the Philippine Sea*. Annapolis, Md.: Naval Institute Press, 1981.

XIX

THE UNITED STATES MARINE CORPS

Graham A. Cosmas

Since publication of the previous edition of the guide, new works on Marine Corps history have been sporadic in appearance and uneven in coverage. Authors continue to concentrate a disproportionate amount of effort on rehashing the operational history of World War II campaigns. Much writing about the Marine Corps is still polemical, sensational, autobiographical, or a combination of those. Nevertheless, signficant new scholarly and popular works slowly accumulate. They enlarge upon the details of some aspects of Marine Corps history and view old stories from new perspectives.

GENERAL HISTORIES. While no major new general history of the Marine Corps has appeared since Millett (192), several works bear on the overall development of marines and amphibious warfare. Merrill L. Bartlett, in his anthology *Assault from the Sea*, (376), surveys amphibious warfare from ancient times to the Falklands Campaign. Dennis E. Showalter (460) reviews the evolution of the United States Marine Corps as an "elite" military organization. The Marine Corps Historical Center has begun revising and expanding its histories of marine regiments, beginning with James Santelli's work (458) on the 7th Marines. The Center also is producing short histories of marine aircraft squadrons, the first three of which are now in print (446, 456, 457).

JOURNALS. *Fortitudine* (407), the house organ of the Marine Corps historical program, besides reporting current activities at the Washington, D.C. Museum and research center, discusses new documentary and oral history acquisitions and publishers articles on obsure points of Marine Corps history.

BIBLIOGRAPHIES AND PRIMARY SOURCES. The most recent edition of Allard's guide to naval history sources (372) is of value to anyone researching Marine Corps topics, as is Allan Millett's brief summary in *Fortitudine* (440) of the essay on sources in his definitive 1980 history of the Corps. A revised and expanded edition (409) of the Marine Corps Historical Center's oral history catalog is available. Anne C. Venzon has prepared an analysis of the papers of Maj. Gen. Smedley D. Butler (469).

BEGINNINGS, 1775-1783. With the end of the bicentennial, the stream of publications on the Revolutionary War beginnings of the Marine Corps, never large, has dried up entirely. However, Alfred J. Marini, in an important essay in comparative history (430), discusses seventeenth- and eighteenth-century British and American legislative debates on the creation of marine forces; he finds common elements in the tactics and achievements of marines and their supporters in both countries. Dealing more directly with the Revolutionary War, Ralph Donnelly (398) discusses the operations of Virginia state marines in the Ohio Valley in 1782.

REBIRTH AND GROWTH, 1798–1781. A thorough account of the reestablishment of the Corps in 1798 and its development during the first half of the nineteenth century is still awaited, although the Marine Corps Historical Center has under way a volume on marines in the "frigate navy." Alexander (370) covers an episode involving Marines in the 1812–1813 American invasion of east Florida during the second war with Great Britain. Laurie Kittle (425) summarizes the career of Lucy Brewer, the notorious "female marine" of the USS *Constitution*. Ralph Donnelly (399) discusses officer selection in the "Old Corps." Equen B. Meader, in two articles (434, 435), deals with aspects of the marines' role in the war with Mexico.

For the Civil War, basic facts about United States Marine officers who resigned to join the Confederacy can be found in William S. Dudley's *Going South* (402). Rowena Reed places marine operations in a broader context in her study (452) of Union amphibious strategy.

MARINES IN THE NEW NAVY, 1880–1917. The halting reorientation of the marines from their nineteenth-century functions as ships' policemen and fighting-top sharpshooters toward their twentieth-century role as an amphibious / expeditionary force in readiness is receiving increasing attention from historians. Jack Shulimson (461) shows how the marine intervention in Panama in 1885 was an early preview of later expeditionary operations. John J. Reber (451) traces the evolution of marine relations with the fleet from the 1880s through the 1930s. Jack Shulimson and Graham A. Cosmas (463) recount the story of Pres. Theodore Roosevelt's ill-fated 1909 effort to remove marine guards from capital ships and relate this controversy to the larger question of the marines' missions in the new battleship navy. The same two authors (391) describe the marines' first major amphibious exercise, at Culebra, in 1914.

EXPEDITIONARY SERVICE IN THE AGE OF IMPERIALISM. Shulimson (461) describes one of the earliest large-scale marine deployments, the Panama intervention of 1885. Significant articles by Reber (450), Reynolds (454), and Coletta (388) deal with aspects of the marine landing at Guantanamo in 1898. Reber sees the battalion at Guantanamo as the forerunnr of today's Fleet Marine Force; Reynolds argues that the marine operation significantly affected the course of the campaign for Santiago; and Coletta emphasizes navy-marine cooperation. Alexander (371) reviews the 1914 landing at Vera Cruz as an early example of marine rapid deployment in a crisis. The late Robert D. Heinl refines and expands his interpretation of the marine occupation of Haiti in a *Marine Corps Gazette* article (416), and in his sweeping history of that republic, *Written in Blood* (417). A. P. Nastri (444) recounts the development of marine artillery during the expeditionary years.

MARINES IN WORLD WAR I. No major new studies of marine participation in World War I have appeared since the publication of the last volume of this guide, but several works review events or fill in details. Robert H. Williams, in a series of articles (472), recounts the operations of the 4th Marine Brigade in France. Gordon T. West (470) tells how the marine memorial in Belleau Wood was built. Merrill L. Bartlett (378) analyzes the controversial series of events leading to the removal of the marines' astute World War I commandant, Maj. Gen. George Barnett.

BETWEEN THE WARS, 1919-1941. The interwar period, during which marines did expeditionary service in China and Nicaragua, organized the Fleet Marine Force, and developed the basic principles of modern amphibious assault tactics, has received considerable scholarly attention. Bernard D. Cole (387) reviews navy and marine activities in China during the 1920s; and Benis M. Frank (410) looks back at the "glory days" of the 4th Marines in Shanghai. Jim Boyce (382) describes a combat patrol against Sandino during the marines' last "banana war" in Nicaragua. James B. Agnew (369), Richard S. Moore (443), and John J. Reber (451) all discuss aspects of the intellectual and institutional origins of marine amphibious doctrine. George F. Hoffman (418) fills in some of the details of the origins of the amphibian tractor. Taking a comparative approach, Kenneth L. Clifford (386) traces the development of the amphibious warfare in both Britain and the United States in the interwar years. Two *Marine Corps Gazette* articles illuminate marine officer selection and training in these formative years of the modern corps. Robert H. Williams, in "Those Controversial Boards" (473), discusses reduction of the marine officer corps after World War I. Louis Metzger (439) contributes a personal memoir of life at the Basic School in 1939.

The corps had more than its share of eccentric, colorful characters in this period, among them Earl Hancock Ellis, the erratic genius of Pacific war strategic planning, and Smedley D. Butler, hell-for-leather colonial adventurer and late-in-life pacifist and isolationist. Dirk A. Ballendorf (375), after exhaustive research, recreates the details of the mysterious spy mission on which Ellis lost his life and concludes that Ellis perished from the effects of alcohol rather than Japanese villainy. Butler also was aware of the problem of liquor and during Prohibition tried to do something about it, as James W. Hammond recounts in "Butler's Bouts with 'Illegal Substances'" (415). Robert H. Williams, a Marine veteran of the period, has written a book of reminiscences (474) of life in the interwar "Old Corps."

MARINES IN WORLD WAR II. World War II continues to generate more writing about marines, and by marines and former marines, than any other single period. John Costello, in *The Pacific War* (392), offers an important new overview of the gigantic conflict in which marines figured so prominently and performed so heroically. United States and British marine operations can be compared in Ian Dear's *Marines at War* (395). The marines' island battles and campaigns continue to receive attention in scholarly and popular books and articles. Earl A. Junghans (423) recounts the fate of the captured defenders of Wake. Eric M. Hammel (414) recreates the first battle of the Matanikau, on Guadalcanal, while Herbert G. Merillat (437) reveals the impact of ULTRA on that campaign. In two books, Edwin P. Hoyt (419, 420) recounts operations in the Gilberts and the Marianas. Richard Wheeler, in *Iwo* (471), retells the story of that bloody struggle.

A number of marine veterans of the Pacific have produced reminiscences of their service, some in an effort, late in life, to come to grips with traumatic memories of combat. William Manchester, in *Goodby, Darkness* (429), revisits many of the islands for which marines fought, relives his own battles, and in the process tries to exorcise some of his own demons. Eugene B. Sledge (465) tells what it was like to fight as a rifleman at Pelelieu and Okinawa. Henry Berry, in *Semper Fi, Mac* (380) collects the war recollections of a number of marines. Other marines recall Guadalcanal (383, 436), Makin (447), and Tarawa (412); and a former navy medical officer describes his work as a battalion surgeon on Iwo Jima (428). Two Marine generals Pedro Del Valle (386) and Louis Metzger (438), recount their experiences in the World War II corps. Memoirs and biographies (400, 421, 422) of some pioneer black marines of World War II have also begun to appear.

Two notable marine aviators have received new attention: "Pappy" Boyington, in an article by Robert L. Schram (459) questioning the reliability of accounts of that ace's last dogfight; and Sen. Joseph R. McCarthy, whose war services as "Tail Gunner Joe" is described by Thomas C. Reeves (453). Finally, Charles M. Dobbs (397) takes another look at the marines' occupation of North China at the end of the war.

THE COLD WAR, 1945–1983. The post-World War II political battles over service unification and roles and missions, in which marines took an important part, are discussed in books by Paolo Coletta (389) and Gordon Keiser (424). Franklin D. Mitchell (442) tells the story of Pres. Harry S. Truman's well-publicized 1950 "insult" to the corps. In *The Great Santini* (390), a work of fiction, Pat Conroy evokes the family and professional life of a cold war era marine aviator. As Middle East and Caribbean crises occur, marines continue to make their own history. James M. Mead (433) describes marine peacekeeping operaitons in Lebanon during the months before the terrorist bombing of the Beirut headquarters. The Marine Corps Historical Center is collecting documents and oral histories of the Lebanon involvement. Benis Frank (408) discusses these efforts. The Historical Center is preparing monographs on marine operations in both Lebanon and Grenada. Allan Millett (441) provides a convenient overview of Marine Corps development in the post-Vietnam era.

THE KOREAN CONFLICT, 1950–1953. Recent writing on marine operations in Korea centers on the two most dramatic engagements in which the corps participated; the Inchon landing and the withdrawal from the Chosin Reservoir. Bruce R. Pirnie (448) reassesses the risks involved in the controversial Inchon invasion. Eric M. Hammel (413) retells the story of the epic march to the sea, making much use of veterans' reminiscences. James Doyle and Arthur Mayer (401) discuss activities at the Marines' destination, the port of Hungnam. The preparation of marines for their Korean ordeals is discussed in a novel by Edwin McDowell (432) dealing with Parris Island recruit training and its abuses.

VIETNAM AND SOUTHEAST ASIA, 1954–1975. The Marines' official histories of the Southeast Asian war slowly move toward publication. Jack

Shulimson's account (462) of marine activities during 1966 is now in print, with other volumes in the chronological series soon to follow. The Marine Corps Historical Center's new squadron histories (446, 456, 457), and its updated regimental histories, such as Santelli's (458) on the 7th Marines, contain much material on operations in Vietnam. Other recent books and articles deal with particular operations. Robert Pisor, in *The End of the Line* (449), uses both official and unofficial sources to recreate the siege of Khe Sanh. Johnnie Clark (385) describes his experiences in the marines' 1968 battle for Hué. E. W. Besch (381) and Richard Rothwell (455) discuss aspects of the 1972 North Vietnamese Easter Offensive. Ray W. Stubbe, in *AARUGHA!* (468), gives detailed treatment to the exploits of marine force reconnaissance units. Charles R. Anderson's *Vietnam: The Other War* (373) is a participant's account of rear-area life and activities at Da Nang.

MARINE AVIATION, 1912–1975. A significant development is the commencement by the Marine Corps Historical Center of a new series of marine aircraft squadron histories, three of which (446, 456, 457) are now in print. Bruce J. Matheson (431) traces the history of the F4U Corsair in the Marine Corps. The careers of three colorful marine fliers—two historical and one fictional—are treated by Schram (459), Reeves (453), and Conroy (390).

INSTITUTIONAL ASPECTS OF THE MARINE CORPS. A number of nonoperational aspects of the Marine Corps have received significant new treatment. Martin Gordon (411) combines political, economic, and military history in his discussion of the establishment of the San Diego marine base. Charles Fleming (406) and Billy Arthur (374) deal respectively with the growth of Quantico and Camp Lejeune. William Smith (466) recreates life in the old "Marine Barracks" at navy yards. Ralph Donnelly (399), Louis Metzger (439), and Robert Williams (473) discuss aspects of marine officer selection and training. Victor H. Krulak (426) examines the history of marine recruit training, and Edwin McDowell, in fictional form (432), points up its abuses during the 1950s. The evolution of specialized marine units is traced in Nastri's study (444) of artillery and Stubbe's (468) of force reconnaissance.

The incorporation of blacks into the Marine Corps is generating a growing literature. To see the marine experience in context, one should begin with Morris MacGregor's definitive official study (427) of integration in the armed services between 1940 and 1965. Northrup and others (445) analyze statistically present-day navy and marine employment of blacks. Bill Downey (400), James E. Johnson (421), and Jesse J. Johnson (422) tell the integration story as experienced by some of the first black marines.

With the recent spate of attacks on and seizures of American embassies, the role of marines as embassy guards has received increased media and popular attention. Danny J. Crawford, in two articles (393, 394), traces the long history of Marine Corps-State Department cooperation. Rocky Sickmann, a marine held hostage in the embassy in Teheran, provides a personal account (464) of his lengthy captivity.

BIOGRAPHY AND AUTOBIOGRAPHY. Full-length biographies of prominent marines continue to be few and far between. Much of what biographical material has appeared since the last edition of the guide deals with the familiar group of prominent marines, such as John A. Lejeune (377), Earl Ellis (375), and Smedley Butler (384, 415). William S. Dudley's *Going South* (402) contains material on Civil War era marine officers. Two retired marine generals, Pedro del Valle (396) and Robert H. Williams (474), have published autobiographies. Jessie J. Johnson (422) tells the life stories of two black marines whose service extended from the segregated World War II corps through the era of integration. Two other World War II black marines, Bill Downey (400) and James E. Johnson (421), have written autobiographies.

UNIFORMS, TRADITIONS AND LORE. John Stacey (467) tells the story of the Marine Corps campaign hat. Merrill Bartlett (379) traces the history of Mess Night and tells how to conduct such an event. H. G. Duncan has produced three books (403, 404, 405) filled with those occasionally factual tales which marines call "sea stories."

RESEARCH OPPORTUNITIES. For the most part, the research fields listed in this chapter of the previous edition of the guide remain wide open. Except for the efforts of official Marine Corps historians, most writing about the corps continues to concentrate on operational histories and autobiographical narratives of World War II. The development of the marine officer corps, recruit training, logistics, aviation, congressional and public relations – indeed, almost every non-operational, non-World II aspect of the corps – await in-depth study.

BIBLIOGRAPHY

369. Agnew, James B. "From Where Did Our Amphibious Doctrine Come?" *Marine Corps Gazette*, (August 1979), 52–59.
370. Alexander, J. H. "The Ambush of Captain John Williams, USMC: Failure of the East Florida Invasion, 1812–1813." *Florida Historical Quarterly* (January 1978), 280–96.
371. Alexander, J. J. "Roots of Deployment – Vera Cruz, 1914." *Marine Corps Gazette* (November 1982), 71–79.
372. Allard, Dean C., L. Martha Crawley, and Mary W. Edmison, eds. *U.S. Naval History Sources in the United States*. Washington, D.C.: GPO, 1979.
373. Anderson, Charles R. *Vietnam: The Other War*. San Rafael, Calif.: Presidio Press, 1982.
374. Arthur, Billy. "Camp Lejeune – The Early Days." *Leatherneck* (November 1982), 28–31, 69.
375. Ballendorf, Dirk A. "Earl Hancock Ellis: The Man and His Mission." *United States Naval Institute Proceedings* (November 1983), 53–60.
376. Bartlett, Merrill L., ed. *Assault from the Sea: Essays on the History of Amphibious Warfare*. Annapolis, Md.: Naval Institute Press, 1983.
377. Bartlett, Merrill L. "Lejeune as a Midshipman." *Marine Corps Gazette* (May 1982), 73–79.
378. _____. "Ouster of a Commandant." *United States Naval Institute Proceedings* (November 1980), 60–65.

379. _____. "Reflections on a New Tradition: The Marine Corps Mess Night." *Marine Corps Gazette*. (June 1979), 33–40.

380. Berry, Henry. *Semper Fi, Mac: Living Memories of the U.S. Marines in World War II*. New York: Arbor House, 1982.

381. Besch, E. W. "Amphibious Operation at Vinh." *Marine Corps Gazette* (December 1982), 54–60.

382. Boyce, Jim. "Combat Patrol: Nicaragua," *Leatherneck* (October 1982), 40–43.

383. Caporale, Louis G. "Remembering Guadalcanal." *Marine Corps Gazette* (August 1982), 13–16.

384. Carr, Stephen M. "Smedley Butler: Hero or Demagogue?" *American History Illustrated* (April 1980), 30–38.

385. Clark, Johnnie M. "Battle for Truoi Bridge: A Young Man's First Combat in Vietnam." *American Legion* (January 1982), 22–23, 58–64.

386. Clifford, Kenneth L. *Amphibious Warfare Development in Britain and America from 1920–1940*. Laurens, N.Y.: Edgewood, 1983.

387. Cole, Bernard D. *Gunboats and Marines: The United States Navy in China, 1925–1928*. Newark: University of Delaware Press, 1983.

388. Coletta, Paolo E. "Bowman McCalla at Guantanamo: A Link in the Chain of Navy-Marine Corps Cooperation." *Shipmate* (June 1978), 25–28.

389. _____. *The United States Navy and Defense Unification, 1947–1953*. Newark: University of Delaware Press, 1983.

390. Conroy, Pat. *The Great Santini*. Boston: Houghton Mifflin, 1976.

391. Cosmas, Graham A., and Jack Shulimson. "The Culebra Maneuver and the Formation of the U.S. Marine Corps's Advance Base Force, 1913–1914" in Bartlett, *Assault from the Sea* (376), 121–32.

392. Costello, John. *The Pacific War*. New York: Rawson, Wade, 1981.

393. Crawford, Danny J. "Marines and the State Department: 'In Every Clime and Place.'" *Fortitudine* (Winter, 1979–1980), 10–16.

394. _____. "Two Centuries of Teamwork: U.S. Marines and the Foreign Service. *Shipmate* (November 1980), 23–27.

395. Dear, Ian. *Marines at War*. London: Ian Allen, 1982.

396. del Valle-Barca Munoz, Pedro A. J. *Semper Fidelis: An Autobiography*. Hawthorne, Calif.: The Christian Book Club of America, 1976.

397. Dobbs, Charles M. "American Marines in North China, 1945–1946." *South Atlantic Quarterly* (Summer 1977), 318–31.

398. Donnelly, Ralph W. "George Rogers Clark's Row Galley Miami: Virginia Marines in the Ohio Valley, 1782." *Virginia Cavalcade* (Winter 1978), 114–17.

399. _____. "Officer Selection in the 'Old Corps." *Marine Corps Gazette* (November 1982), 81–87.

400. Downey, Bill. *Uncle Sam Must Be Losing the War*. San Francisco: Strawberry Hill Press, 1982.

401. Doyle, James H., and Arthur J. Mayer. "December 1950 at Hungnam." *United States Naval Institute Proceedings* (April 1979), 44–55.

402. Dudley, William S. *Going South: U.S. Navy Officer Resignations and Dismissals on the Eve of the Civil War*. Washington, D.C.: Naval Historical Foundation, 1981.

403. Duncan, H.G., and W. T. Moore. *Green Side Out: Marine Corps Sea*

Stories. Clearwater, Fla.: D & S Publishers, 1980.

404. Duncan, H. G. *Run in Circles*. West Palm Beach, Fla.: Gayle Publishers, 1983.

405. _____. *Brown Side Out*. West Palm Beach, Fla.: Gayle Publishers, 1983.

406. Fleming, Charles A. *Quantico: Crossroads of the Marine Corps*. Washington, D.C.: History and Museums Division, HQMC, 1978.

407. *Fortitudine*. Washington, D.C.: 1970-.

408. Frank, Benis M. "Lebanon Oral Histories Added to Collection," *Fortitudine* (Spring 1983), 10–11.

409. _____. *Marine Corps Oral History Collection Catalog*. Rev. ed. Washington, D.C.: History and Museums Division, HQMC, 1979.

410. _____. "Shanghai's 4th Marines: The Glory Days of the Old Corps." *Shipmate* (November 1979), 13–18.

411. Gordon, Martin K. "The Marines Have Landed and San Diego Is Well in Hand: Local Politics and Marine Corps Base Development." *Journal of the West* (October 1981), 43–50.

412. Haley, J. Frederick. "Reconnaissance at Tarawa Atoll." *Marine Corps Gazette* (November 1980), 51–55.

413. Hammel, Eric M. *Chosin: Heroic Ordeal of the Korean War*. New York: Vanguard, 1981.

414. _____. "Guadalcanal: First Battle of the Matanikau." *Marine Corps Gazette* (August 1982), 48–54.

415. Hammond, James W. "Butler's Bouts with 'Illegal Substances.'" *Marine Corps Gazette* (February 1982), 51–57.

416. Heinl, Robert D. "The American Occupation of Haiti." *Marine Corps Gazette* (November 1978), 28–41.

417. Heinl, Robert D. and Nancy Gordon. *Written in Blood: The Story of the Haitian People, 1492-1971*. Boston: Houghton Mifflin, 1978.

418. Hoffman, George F. "A Self-Made Automotive Engineer Finally Convinced the Military that an LVT Existed in the 1920s." *Marine Corps Gazette* (September 1977), 42–50.

419. Hoyt, Edwin P. *Storm over the Gilberts: War in the Central Pacific*. New York: Van Nostrand, 1978.

420. _____. *To the Marianas: War in the Central Pacific, 1944*. New York: Van Nostrand, 1980.

421. Johnson, James E. *Beyond Defeat*. New York: Doubleday-Galilee, 1978.

422. Johnson, Jesse J. *Roots of Two Black Marine Sergeants Majors: Sergeant Majors Edgar R. Huff and Gilbert H. "Hashmark" Johnson*. Hampton, Va.: Ebony Publishing Co. and Hampton Institute, 1978.

423. Junghans, Earl A. "Wake's POWs." *United States Naval Institute Proceedings* (February 1983), 43–50.

424. Keiser, Gordon W. *The U.S. Marine Corps and Defense Unification, 1944-1947: The Politics of Survival*. Washington, D.C.: National Defense University Press, 1982.

425. Kittle, Laurie L. "Female Marine aboard the *Constitution*." *Marine Corps Gazette* (February 1980), 53–56.

426. Krulak, Victor H. "'This Precious Few...': The Evolution of Marine Recruit Training." *Marine Corps Gazette* (April 1982), 48–55.

427. MacGregor, Morris J., Jr. *Integration of the Armed Forces, 1940-1965*.

Washington, D.C.: Center of Military History, 1981.

428. MacKinnon, Donald A. "Battalion Surgeon on Iwo Jima." *Marine Corps Gazette* (February 1982), 28–37.

429. Manchester, William R. *Goodbye, Darkness: A Memoir of the Pacific.* Boston: Little, Brown, 1980.

430. Marini, Alfred J. "Political Perceptions of the Marine Forces: Great Britain, 1699–1739 and the United States, 1798–1804." *Military Affairs* (December 1980), 171–75.

431. Matheson, Bruce J. "The Corsair and Its Contributions." *Marine Corps Gazette* (May 1981), 59–63.

432. McDowell, Edwin. *To Keep Our Honor Clean.* New York: Vanguard, 1980.

433. Mead, James M. "Lebanon Revisited." *Marine Corps Gazette* (September 1983), 64–73.

434. Meader, Equen B. "A Marine in California: Archibald Gillespie in the Mexican War, West." *Shipmate* (November 1982), 29–31, 36.

435. _____. "Birth of the Amphibian: Navy-Marine Operations in the Mexican Gulf, 1846–1848." *Shipmate* (November 1981), 28–31.

436. Merillat, Herbert G. *Guadalcanal Remembered.* New York: Dodd, Mead, 1982.

437. _____. "The 'Ultra' Weapon at Guadalcanal." *Marine Corps Gazette* (September 1982), 44–49.

438. Metzger, Louis. "Duty beyond the Seas." *Marine Corps Gazette* (January 1982), 28–37.

439. _____. "The Basic School – 1939." *Marine Corps Gazette* (November 1981), 72–77.

440. Millett, Allan R. "Research Sources for Marine Corps History." *Fortitudine* (Spring 1981), 10–12.

441. _____. "The U.S. Marine Corps: Adaptation in the Post-Vietnam Era." *Armed Forces and Society* (Spring 1983), 363–92.

442. Mitchell, Franklin D. "An Act of Presidential Indiscretion: Harry S. Truman, Congressman McDonough and the Marine Corps Incident of 1950." *Presidential Studies Quarterly* (Fall 1981), 565–75.

443. Moore, Richard S. "Ideas and Direction: Building Amphibious Doctrine." *Marine Corps Gazette* (November 1982), 49–58.

444. Nastri, A. P. "USMC Artillery, 1900–1941." *Field Artillery Journal* (July–August 1977), 32–36.

445. Northrup, Herbert R., et al. *Black and Other Minority Participation in the All-Volunteer Navy and Marine Corps.* Philadelphia: The Wharton School, University of Pennsylvania Press, 1979.

446. Parker, Gary W. *A History of Marine Observation Squadron Six.* Washington, D.C.: History and Museums Division, HQMC, 1982.

447. Peatross, O. F. "The Makin Raid." *Marine Corps Gazette* (November 1979), 96–103.

448. Pirnie, Bruce R. "Inchon Landing: How Great Was the Risk?" *Joint Perspectives* (Summer 1982), 86–97.

449. Pisor, Robert. *The End of the Line: The Siege of Khe Sanh.* New York: W. W. Norton, 1982.

450. Reber, John J. "Huntington's Battalion Was the Forerunner of Today's

FMF." *Marine Corps Gazette* (November 1979), 73–78.

451. _____. "The Fleet and the Marines." *United States Naval Institute Proceedings* (November 1982), 66–73.

452. Reed, Rowena. *Combined Operations in the Civil War*. Annapolis, Md.: Naval Institute Press, 1978.

453. Reeves, Thomas C. "Tail Gunner Joe: Joseph R. McCarthy and the Marine Corps." *Wisconsin Magazine of History* (Summer 1979), 300–313.

454. Reynolds, Bradley, M. "Guantanamo Bay: A Doubly Important Advanced Base." *Marine Corps Gazette* (November 1982), 62–68.

455. Rothwell, Richard B. "Leadership and Tactical Reflections on the Battle for Quang Tri." *Marine Corps Gazette* (September 1979), 34–42.

456. Sambito, William J. *History of Marine Attack Squadron 311*. Washington, D.C.: History and Museums Division, HQMC, 1978.

457. *History of Marine Fighter Attack Squadron 232*. Washington, D.C.: History and Museums Division, HQMC, 1978.

458. Santelli, James S. *A Brief History of the 7th Marines*. Washington, D.C.: History and Museums Division, HQMC, 1980.

459. Schram, Robert T. "The Great Hoax: Pappy Boyington's Last Dogfight." *Shipmate* (November 1982), 35–36.

460. Showalter, Dennis E. "Evolution of the U.S. Marine Corps as a Military Elite." *Marine Corps Gazette* (November 1979), 44–58.

461. Shulimson, Jack, "U.S. Marines in Panama, 1885." in Bartlett, *Assault from the Sea* (376), 107–120.

462. _____ *U.S. Marines in Vietnam: An Expanding War, 1966*. Washington, D.C.: History and Museums Division, HQMC, 1982.

463. Shulimson, Jack, and Graham A. Cosmas. "Teddy Roosevelt and the Corps' Sea-Going Mission." *Marine Corps Gazette* (November 1981), 54–61.

464. Sickmann, Rocky. *Iranian Hostage: A Personal Diary*. Topeka, Kans.: The Crawford Press, 1982.

465. Sledge, Eugene B. *With the Old Breed at Peleliu and Okinawa*. San Rafael, Calif.: Presidio Press, 1981.

466. Smith, William R. "Marine Barracks: Essence of the 'Old Corps'". *Marine Corps Gazette* (November 1980), 90–95.

467. Stacey, John. "The U.S.M.C. Campaign Hat." *Military Images* (November / December 1980), 10–13.

468. Stubbe, Ray W. *AARUGHA! Report to the Director, Historical Division, Headquarters, Marine Corps, on the History of Specialized and Force-Level Reconnaissance Activities and Units of the United States Marine Corps, 1900–1974*. Manuscript. Washington, D.C.: History and Museums Division, HQMC, 1981.

469. Venzon, Anne C. "The Papers of General Smedley Darlington Butler, USMC, 1915–1918." Ph.D. diss., Princeton University, 1982.

470. West, Gordon T. "How the Marine Monument in Belleau Wood Got Built." *Marine Corps Gazette* (November 1978), 77–78.

471. Wheeler, Richard. *Iwo*. New York: Lippincott and Crowell, 1980.

472. Williams, Robert H. "The 4th Marine Brigade." *Marine Corps Gazette* (November 1980),58–68; (December 1980), 59–64; (January 1981), 63–68; (February 1981), 56–60.

473. _____. "Those Controversial Boards." *Marine Corps Gazette* (November

1982), 91–96.

474. _____. *The Old Corps—A Portrait of the U.S. Marine Corps between the Wars*. Annapolis, Md.: Naval Institute Press, 1982.

XX

NUCLEAR WAR AND ARMS CONTROL

Warren A. Trest

For a generation and more, the awesome threat of awaking the nuclear phoenix has drawn the world's foremost thinkers into dialogues on nuclear strategy, proliferation, and arms control. Born amid the ashes of Hiroshima and Nagasaki, the strategic arms race between the superpowers began in earnest after the Soviet Union exploded an atomic device in 1949, leading ultimately to the global proliferation of nuclear weapons technology and to international forums on the control of nuclear arsenals. The curricular literature of the 1950s is sprinkled with persuasive rationale for bigger and better weaponry, both strategic and conventional, and equally convincing anti-nuclear arguments by doomsday prophets. The antithetical theses undoubtedly helped shape President Kennedy's precedential strategy of continuing to build the nation's military might, while pursuing an active arms-control policy with the Soviet Union. The resultant signing of the partial nuclear test-ban treaty on 8 August 1963 was a watershed in postwar U.S.-Soviet diplomatic relations. It set the stage for strategic arms limitation talks under four successive U.S. presidents, resulting in the 1972 SALT I agreements and the 1979 Salt II treaty. President Carter postponed SALT II ratification indefinitely after the Soviets invaded Afghanistan in December 1979. With the treaty unratified, strategic arms reduction talks were begun in June 1982 by the Reagan administration.

The controversy surrounding the arms-control talks has helped shape the party platforms and foreign policies for two decades of American presidents. It has further influenced the make-up of defense budgets and the development of strategic arms programs. While successive administrations have fathered efforts in strategic arms development, their policies have not always been consistent. They have always been controversial, providing nectar for the inquisitive minds of historians. The strategic arms talks have received the bulk of literary attention, with journals dedicated to their cause, but the nation's nuclear strategy and posture have not gone unnoticed. Under Presidents Carter and Reagan, the emphasis in strategic weapons development has been on the B-1 bomber, the neutron bomb, the cruise missile, and the MX intercontinental ballistic missile programs. Historical research into these programs has been less than exhaustive.

The cult of writers and the copious body of literature growing out of nuclear proliferation has mushroomed in recent years. Given the era's contemporaneity, the bulk of the literary effort has fallen naturally to the talented pens of strategists, political scientists, and foreign policy experts. However, the relatively few historians who have focused on the era are first-rate, and most are credited with major contributions. A surprising number of the interdisciplinary books and articles, many of which rely at least in part on historical references, are also valuable as relevant sources in military history. The comprehensive essay published in *Supplement I* to the guide (Chapter XXI) listed more than 400 bibliographic items, with a substantial portion comprising political, strategical, or doctrinal analyses as opposed to purely historical interpretation. This follow-on survey begins in 1979 and takes the research through 1983. In addition to selecting the legitimate historical writings for the period, an effort has been made to sort through and catalog other references containing partial historical analyses or those showing reasonable promise as source materials. The previous essay contained an excellent listing of journals and other periodicals. This list has not changed sufficiently to warrant repeating it in this survey.

NUCLEAR POLICY. Following the recent declassification of many previously inaccessible official documents, historians have begun to shed new light on U.S. atomic policy and capabilities during the critical Truman years. Gregg Herken's *The Winning Weapon: The Atomic Bomb in the Cold War, 1945–1950* (463) stands out among such works, as does Harry R. Borowski's *A Hollow Threat: Strategic Air Power and Containment before Korea* (415), which challenges the myth of U.S. nuclear preparedness in the postwar years. Borowski explores the same theme in a *Military Review* article, entitled "Air Force Atomic Capability from V-J Day to the Berlin Blockade – Potential or Real?" (416). Two other articles treating this period are Stephen M. Millett's "The Capabilities of the American Nuclear Deterrent, 1945–1950" (495), in *Aerospace Historian*, and David Alan Rosenberg's "U.S. Nuclear Stockpile, 1945 to 1950" (516), in the *Bulletin of the Atomic Scientists*. Of great interest to historians concerned with the formative years is *The Cult of the Atom: The Secret Papers of the Atomic Energy Commission* (443), by Daniel Ford. A readable account of the birth of the nuclear era is found in James W. Kunetka's *City of Fire: Los Alamos and the Birth of the Atomic Age, 1943–1945* (476). In *The Bomb* (481), Sidney Lens traces the atomic bomb's development and explores the evolution of the nuclear arms race to the present day.

The nuclear policies of other U.S. presidents are also examined. The Kennedy era has received special attention. Desmond Ball's *Politics and Force Levels: The Strategic Missile Program of the Kennedy Administration* (408) addresses the mythical "missile gap" and the major strategic build-up under Kennedy. A compelling account of the Kennedy-Khrushchev "war of nerves" is given in David Detzer's *The Brink: Cuban Missile Crisis, 1962* (432). Two other studies of U.S.-Soviet relations under Kennedy are Bernard J. Firestone's *The Quest for Nuclear Stability: John F. Kennedy and the Soviet Union* (442), and Glenn Seaborg's *Kennedy, Khrushchev and the Test Ban* (526). Treatment of nuclear policy under more recent administrations is furnished in Desmond Ball's *Developments in U.S. Strategic Nuclear Policy under the Carter Administration* (407), and Robert Scheer's *With Enough Shovels: Reagan, Bush and Nuclear War* (522). Theodore Draper also addresses contemporary historical issues in his book *Present History: On Nuclear War, Detente and Other Controversies* (436). Works which provide good, general, historical analyses of nuclear issues are Carl Jacobsen's *The Nuclear Era: Its History; Its Implications* (467), and Michael Mandelbaum's *The Nuclear Question: The United States and Nuclear Weapons, 1946–1976* (484).

Mandelbaum's book examines nuclear progression within the context of Clausewitz and Bernard Brodie. He has also published a book of essays on the impact of nuclear weapons on international politics, entitled *The Nuclear Revolution: International Politics Before and After Hiroshima* (485).

STRATEGY AND DOCTRINE. The study of U.S. nuclear strategy and doctrine continues to appeal to a variety of scholars. Two solid histories of strategic ideas exist in Lawrence Freedman's *The Evolution of Nuclear Strategy* (445) and in editor Laurence Martin's volume *Strategic Thought in the Nuclear Age* (487). U.S. nuclear doctrine since World War II is surveyed in Aaron Friedberg's article in *The Journal of Strategic Studies* (447). *The Nuclear Delusion: Soviet-American Relations in the Atomic Age* (472) preserves a collection of essays, speeches, and policy statements by George F. Kennan, architect of the U.S. strategy of containment. Articles by Robert S. McNamara (489), Donald Rumsfeld (520), and Stanley Sienkiewicz (529) give added insight into contemporary strategic issues. The roles played by Bernard Brodie (558) and Secretary of Defense Brown (430) in the development of strategy are the subject of other articles. Alan Platt addresses the role of Congress is shaping U.S. nuclear strategy in *The U.S. Senate and Strategic Arms Policy, 1969–1977* (504) and *Congress and Arms Control* (505). Service concepts and doctrine are given special treatment in *The Evolution of U.S. Army Nuclear Doctrine, 1945–1980* (515), by John Rose; *Navies and Arms Control* (512), by George Quester; and *Air Power in the Nuclear Age* (406), by M. J. Armitage and R. A. Mason. Tactical and theater nuclear doctrine are discussed in articles in *Military Review* (405, 418), *Air University Review* (414), and *Naval War College Review* (502). An excellent survey of theater doctrine is presented in Jerry M. Sollinger's *Improving U.S. Theater Nuclear Doctrine: A Critical Analysis* (535). The controversial first-strike strategy is covered in works by Robert C. Aldridge (404), Jack H. Nunn (499), and Douglas Terman (540). Nuclear planning is dissected in *S.I.O.P.: The Secret U.S. Plan for Nuclear War* (511), by Peter Pringle and William Arkin. Carl Bracken's *The Command and Control of Nuclear Forces* (417) addresses another complex issue in the nuclear equation.

Other studies in the development of strategic doctrine are Donald W. Snow's *Nuclear Strategy in a Dynamic World: American Policy in the 1980s* (532), and Stewart Menaul's *Changing Concepts of Nuclear War* (490). *Strategic Nuclear Forces Requirements and Issues* (527), by George Seiler, and *Nuclear War in the 1980s?* (423), by Christopher Chant and Ian Hogg, are relevant. For additional articles on strategic issues, see *Orbis* (434), *Comparative Strategy* (444, 457), *Foreign Affairs* (450), and *Air University Review* (488, 494, 533). The Atlantic Alliance receives special attention in books by Paul Bauteux (421, 422), John Keliher (471), and David Schwartz (524), and in a volume edited by John Steinbruner and Leon Sigal (537). Articles on NATO nuclear issues are in *Foreign Affairs* (419, 64) and *NATO Review* (498). Soviet nuclear strategy and doctrine are addressed in works by Joseph Douglass and Amoretta M. Hoeber (435), Avigdor Haselkorn (461), and Mark Miller (493).

NUCLEAR WEAPONS. Solly Zuckerman's *Nuclear Illusion and Reality* (561) provides a history of the evolution of nuclear weapons and their use. General reference works on nuclear weapons exist in the multi-authored *Nuclear Weapons*

Databook, Vol. 1: *U.S. Nuclear Force and Capabilities* (426); James N. Constant's two-volume *Fundamentals of Strategic Weapons: Offense and Defense Systems* (429); the MIT faculty's *The Nuclear Almanac* (488); Norman Polmar's revised edition of *Strategic Weapons: An Introduction* (506); and Kosta Tsipis's *Arsenal: Understanding Weapons in the Nuclear Age* (541). Richard K. Betts wrote *Cruise Missiles and U.S. Policy* (412) and edited *Cruise Missiles: Technology, Strategy, Politics* (413). Ronald Huisken's *The Origin of the Strategic Cruise Missile (465)* and Charles A. Sorrell's *U.S. Cruise Missile Programs: Development, Deployment,and Implications for Arms Control* (536) examine the unique development and the acquisition process for the strategic missile. The controversial MX is the subject of books by John Edwards (440), Colin Gray (458, 459), and Herbert Scoville, Jr. (525), and articles in *Air University Review* (475, 534). The neutron bomb is the subject of two books, Sam Cohen's *The Truth about the Neutron Bomb: The Inventor of the Bomb Speaks Out* (428) and Sherri L. Wasserman's *The Neutron Bomb Controversy: A Study in Alliance Politics* (557). Articles on nuclear weapons and arsenals are in *Bulletin of the Atomic Scientists* (409), *Foreign Service Journal* (427), and *Air University Review* (474). Secretary-General Kurt Waldheim updates the United Nations report on nuclear weapons (556).

PROLIFERATION AND ARMS CONTROL. For general historical treatment of arms control, see Patrick Gallo's *Swords and Plowshares: The United States and Disarmament, 1898-1979* (451); Jozef Goldblat's *Agreements for Arms Control: A Critical Survey* (453); Mohamed Shaker's *The Nuclear Non-Proliferation Treaty: Origin and Implementation, 1959-1979* (528); Robin Ranger's *Arms and Politics, 1958-1978* (513); and Thomas Wolfe's *The SALT Experience* (559). Other general references are *SALT Handbook* (477), by Roger Labrie, and *Negotiating Security: An Arms Control Reader* (473), edited by William H. Kincade and Jeffrey D. Porro. Updated editions of the texts and history of arms-control negotiations (542) (543) by the U.S. Arms Control and Disarmament Agency are also essential references. The agency itself is the subject of Duncan Clarke's *Politics and Arms Control: The Role and Effectiveness of the U.S. Arms Control and Disarmament Agency* (425). Nuclear arms proliferation issues are addressed in books by Lewis A. Dunn (438, 439) and Edward J. Markey (486), and in an article by Stanley Sienkiewicz in *Comparative Strategy* (530). A number of scholars have examined the SALT negotiations: John H. Barton and Imai Ryukichi (410); Jacquelyn K. Davis, Patrick J. Friel, and Robert L. Pfaltzgraff, Jr. (431); Daniel O. Graham (456); John Lehman and Seymour Weiss (480); Stewart Menaul (491); Christer Jonsson (469); Paul Nitze (497); W.K.H. Panofsky (501); William C. Potter (508); Gerard Smith (531); and Strobe Talbott (539). There are relevant government publications (545, 549, 553, 554, 555); See also (544, 547, 550). Other arms control studies are written or edited by Richard Burt (420); William Epstein and Bernard T. Feld (441); Alan Geyer (452); Ralph Goldman (454); Warren Heckrotte and George C. Smith (462); Alan Neidle (496); Edward C. Luck (483); Eugene Rostow (517); Bruce Russett (521), and Joseph A. Yager (560).

RESEARCH NEEDED. Within the profusion, there are gaps in the study of nuclear force as a continuum of U.S. military history. Much of the available literature, while lofty, is slanted or one-dimensional in scope and focus. Taken as a whole, it becomes an asymmetrical treatment of fragments, rather than a full and balanced study of the subject as a unified historical theme. Yet there remains ample room for historians to specialize. The historical assessment of all aspects of nuclear weapons technology, both offensive and defensive, is in demand. Planning for the nuclear role as, say, nuclear propulsion in space exploration and conquest is a fertile field. Historians need to examine all the peaks and valleys of military nuclear doctrine and strategy, as well as the nooks and crannies of arms-control negotiations. Biographies of the nuclear lions are still wanting. The greatest challenge, however, is always embodied in the greatest need. The world awaits the grand, comprehensive historical assessment of the nuclear era thus far, one that binds together the fibers of nuclear arms evolution and control to judge their influence on military history, one that places all the bits and pieces in unified perspective to show us exactly where we have been in relation to where we are going. The definitive history begs to be written.

BIBLIOGRAPHY

403. Adelman, Jonathan R. "American Strategic Nuclear Modernization and the Soviet Succession Struggle." *Air University Review* (November–December 1983): 15–29.

404. Aldridge, Robert C. *First Strike! The Pentagon's Strategy for Nuclear War*. Boston: South End Press, 1983.

405. Andrews, Maj. Andrew E. "Toward a Tactical Nuclear Doctrine." *Military Review* (October 1980): 13–19.

406. Armitage, M. J., and R. A. Mason. *Air Power in the Nuclear Age*. Urbana: University of Illinois Press, 1983.

407. Ball, Desmond. *Developments in U.S. Strategic Nuclear Policy under the Carter Administration*. Los Angeles: University of California Press, 1980.

408. Ball, Desmond. *Politics and Force Levels: The Strategic Missile Program of the Kennedy Administration*. Berkeley: University of California Press, 1981.

409. Barnaby, Frank. "World Arsenals in 1981." *Bulletin of the Atomic Scientists* (August–September 1981): 16–20.

410. Barton, John H., and Imai Ryukichi. *Arms Control II: A New Approach to International Security*. Cambridge, Mass.: Oelgeschlager, Gunn & Hain, 1981.

411. Beres, Louis Rene. *Apocalypse: Nuclear Catastrophe in World Politics*. Chicago: University of Chicago Press, 1980.

412. Betts, Richard K. *Cruise Missiles and U.S. Policy*. Washington, D.C.: Brookings Institution, 1982.

413. _____. ed. *Cruise Missiles: Technology, Strategy, Politics*. Washington, D.C.: Brookings Institution, 1981.

414. Borawski, John. "Theater Nuclear Arms Control and Forward-Based Systems." *Air University Review* (May–June 1982): 11–19.

415. Borowski, Harry R. *A Hollow Threat: Strategic Air Power and Containment before Korea*. Westport, Conn.: Greenwood Press, 1982.

416. _____. "Air Force Atomic Capability from V-J Day to the Berlin Blockade – Potential or Real?" *Military Review* (October 1980): 105–110.

417. Bracken, Paul. *The Command and Control of Nuclear Forces.* New Haven, Conn.: Yale University Press, 1983.

418. Brown, Maj. William D. "Whatever Happened to...Tactical Nuclear Warfare." *Military Review* (January 1980): 46–53.

419. Bundy, McGeorge, George F. Kennan, Robert S. McNamara, and Gerard Smith. "Nuclear Weapons and the Atlantic Alliance." *Foreign Affairs* (Spring 1982): 753–68.

420. Burt, Richard, ed. *Arms Control and Defense Postures in the 1980s.* Boulder, Colo.: Westview Press, 1982.

421. Buteux, Paul. *Strategy, Doctrine, and the Politics of Alliance: Theater Nuclear Force Modernization in NATO.* Boulder, Colo.: Westview Press, 1983.

422. Buteux, Paul. *The Politics of Nuclear Consultation in NATO, 1965-1980.* New York: Cambridge University Press, 1983.

423. Chant, Christopher, and Ian Hogg. *Nuclear War in the 1980s?.* New York: Harper & Row, 1981.

424. Clark, Ian. *Limited Nuclear War: Political Theory and War Conventions.* Princeton, N.J.: Princeton University Press, 1982.

425. Clarke, Duncan L. *Politics of Arms Control: The Role and Effectiveness of the U.S. Arms Control and Disarmament Agency.* New York: Free Press, 1979.

426. Cochran, Thomas R., William M. Arkin, and Milton M. Hoenig. *Nuclear Weapons Databook.* Vol. 1: *U.S. Nuclear Forces and Capabilities.* Cambridge, Mass.: Ballinger, 1983.

427. Cohen, Sam. "Accepting Nuclear Weapons." *Foreign Service Journal* (September 1983): 18–21.

428. _____. *The Truth about the Neutron Bomb: The Inventor of the Bomb Speaks Out.* New York: William Morrow, 1983.

429. Constant, James N. *Fundamentals of Strategic Weapons: Offense and Defense Systems.* 2 vols. Hingham, Mass.: Kluwer Boston, 1981.

430. Cordesman, Anthony H. "Measuring the Strategic Balance; Secretary of Defense Brown as an American Oracle." *Comparative Strategy* 3, no. 3 (1982): 187–218.

431. Davis, Jacquelyn K., Patrick J. Friel, and Robert L. Pfaltzgraff, Jr. *SALT II and U.S.-Soviet Strategic Forces.* Cambridge, Mass.: Institute for Foreign Policy Analysis, 1979.

432. Detzer, David. *The Brink: Cuban Missile Crisis, 1962.* New York: T. Y. Crowell, 1979.

433. Devolpi, A., G. E. March, T. A. Postol, and G. S. Stanford. *Born Secret: The H-Bomb, the Progressive Case and National Security.* Elmsford, N.Y.: Pergamon Press, 1981.

434. Douglass, Joseph D., Jr. "Strategic Planning and Nuclear Insecurity." *Orbis* (Fall 1983): 667–94.

435. Douglass, Joseph D., Jr., and Amoretta M. Hoeber. *Soviet Strategy for Nuclear War.* Stanford, Calif.: Hoover Institution Press, 1979.

436. Draper, Theodore. *Present History: On Nuclear War, Detente and Other Controversies.* New York: Random House, 1983.

437. Drell, Sidney D. *Facing the Threat of Nuclear Weapons*. Seattle: University of Washington Press, 1983.
438. Dunn, Lewis A. *Controlling the Bomb: Nuclear Proliferation in the 1980s*. New Haven, Conn.: Yale University Press, 1982.
439. _____. "U.S. Strategic Force Requirements in a Nuclear-Proliferated World." *Air University Review* (July–August, 1980): 26–33.
440. Ewards, John. *Super Weapon: The Making of MX*. New York: W. W. Norton, 1982.
441. Epstein, William, and Bernard T. Feld, eds. *New Directions in Disarmament*. New York: Praeger, 1981.
442. Firestone, Bernard J. *The Quest for Nuclear Stability: John F. Kennedy and the Soviet Union*. Westport, Conn.: Greenwood Press, 1982.
443. Ford, Daniel. *The Cult of the Atom: The Secret Papers of the Atomic Energy Commission*. New York: Simon & Schuster, 1982.
444. Foster, Richard B. "From Assured Destruction to Assured Survival." *Comparative Strategy* 2, no. 1 (1980): 53–74.
445. Freedman, Lawrence. *The Evolution of Nuclear Strategy*. New York: St. Martin's, 1982.
446. Frei, Daniel. *Risks of Unintentional Nuclear War*. Totowa, N.Y.: Allanheld, Osmun, 1983.
447. Friedberg, Aaron L. "A History of the U.S. Strategic 'Doctrine'—1945 to 1980." *The Journal of Strategic Studies* (December 1980): 39–71.
448. Fritz, Col. Nicholas H. "Clausewitz and U.S. Nuclear Weapons Policy." *Air University Review* (November–December 1982): 18–28.
449. Fritzel, Roger N. *Nuclear Testing and National Security*. Washington, D.C.: National Defense University Press, 1981.
450. Frye, Alton. "Strategic Build-Down: A Context for Restraint." *Foreign Affairs* (Winter 1983 / 1984): 293–317.
451. Gallo, Patrick J. *Swords and Plowshares: The United States and Disarmament, 1898–1979*. Manhattan, Kans.: Military Affairs / Aerospace Historian Publishing, 1980.
452. Geyer Alan. *The Idea of Disarmament!* Elgin, Ill.: Brethren Press, 1982.
453. Goldblat, Jozef. *Agreements for Arms Control: A Critical Survey*. Cambridge, Mass.: Oelgeschlager, Gunn & Hain, 1982.
454. Goldman, Ralph M. *Arms Control and Peacekeeping: Feeling Safe in this World*. New York: Random House, 1981.
455. Goodchild, Peter. *J. Robert Oppenheimer: Shatterer of Worlds*. Boston; Houghton Mifflin, 1980.
456. Graham, Daniel O. *Shall America Be Defended? SALT II and Beyond*. New Rochelle, N.Y.: Arlington House, 1979.
457. Gray, Colin S. "Strategic Forces and SALT: A Question of Strategy." *Comparative Strategy* 2 no. 2 (1980): 113–28.
458. _____. *Strategy and the MX*. Washington, D.C.: Heritage Foundation, 1980.
459. _____. *The MX ICBM & National Security*. New York: Praeger, 1981.
460. Griffiths, Franklin, and John C. Polyani, eds. *The Dangers of Nuclear War*. Toronto: University of Toronto Press, 1979.
461. Haselkorn, Avigdor. *The Evolution of Soviet Nuclear Strategy, 1965–1975*. New York: Crane, Russak, 1978.

462. Heckrotte, Warren, and George C. Smith, eds. *Arms Control in Transition*: *Proceedings of the Livermore Arms Control Conference*. Boulder, Colo.: Westview Press, 1983.

463. Herken, Gregg. *The Winning Weapon: The Atomic Bomb in the Cold War, 1945–1950*. New York: Alfred A. Knopf, 1980.

464. Hoffman, Stanley. "NATO and Nuclear Weapons: Reasons and Unreason." *Foreign Affairs* (Winter 1981 / 1982): 327–46.

465. Huisken, Ronald. *The Origin of the Strategic Cruise Missile*. New York: Praeger, 1981.

466. Hyde, H. Montgomery. *The Atom Bomb Spies*. New York: Atheneum, 1980.

467. Jacobsen, Carl G. *The Nuclear Era: Its History; Its Implications*. Cambridge, Mass.: Oelgeschlager, Gunn & Hain, 1982.

468. Jenson, 1st Lt. John W. "Nuclear Strategy: Differences in Soviet and American Thinking." *Air University Review* (March–April 1979): 2–17.

469. Jonsson, Christer. *Soviet Bargaining Behavior: The Nuclear Test Ban Case*. New York: Columbia University Press, 1979.

470. Keeney, Spurgeon M., Jr., and Wolfgang K. H. Panofsky. "MAD vs NUTS: The Mutual Hostage Relationship of the Superpowers." *Foreign Affairs* (Winter 1981 / 1982): 287–304.

471. Keliher, John G. *The Negotiations on Mutual and Balanced Force Reductions: The Search for Arms Control in Central Europe*. Elmsford, N.Y.: Pergamon Press, 1980.

472. Kennan, George F. *The Nuclear Delusion: Soviet-American Relations in the Atomic Age*. New York: Pantheon Books, 1983.

473. Kincade, William H., and Jeffrey D. Porro, eds. *Negotiating Security: An Arms Control Reader*. Washington, D.C.: Carnegie Endowment for International Peace, 1979.

474. Kohout, Lt. Col. John J., III. " A Post B-1 Look at the Manned Strategic Bomber." *Air University Review* (July–August 1979): 27–51.

475. Korb, Lawrence J. "The Case for the MX." *Air University Review* (July–August 1980): 2–10.

476. Kunetka, James W. *City of Fire: Los Alamos and the Birth of the Atomic Age, 1943–1945*. Englewood Cliffs, N.J.: Prentice-Hall, 1978.

477. Labrie, Roger. *SALT Handbook*. Washington, D.C.: The American Enterprise Institute for Public Policy Research, 1979.

478. Lambeth, Benjamin S., and Kevin N. Lewis. "Economic Targeting Nuclear War: U.S. and Soviet Approaches." *Orbis* (Spring 1983): 127–49.

479. Lefever, Ernest W. *Nuclear Arms in the Third World: U.S. Policy Dilemma*. Washington, D.C.: Brookings Institution, 1979.

480. Lehman, John, and Seymour Weiss. *Beyond the SALT II Failure*. New York: Praeger, 1981.

481. Lens, Sidney. *The Bomb*. New York: Dutton, 1982.

482. Lifton, Robert J., and Richard Falk. *Indefensible Weapons: The Political And Psychological Case against Nuclearism*. New York: Basic Books, 1982.

483. Luck, Edward C., ed. *Arms Control: The Multilateral Alternative*. New York: New York University Press, 1983.

484. Mandelbaum, Michael. *The Nuclear Question: The United States and*

Nuclear Weapons, 1946–1976. New York: Cambridge University Press, 1979.

485. _____. *The Nuclear Revolution: International Politics Before and After Hiroshima.* New York: Cambridge University Press, 1981.

486. Markey, Edward J., with Douglas C. Waller. *Nuclear Peril: The Politics of Proliferation.* Cambridge, Mass.: Ballinger, 1982.

487. Martin, Laurence, ed. *Strategic Thought in the Nuclear Age.* Baltimore, Md.: Johns Hopkins University Press, 1979.

488. Massachusetts Institute of Technology Faculty, eds. *The Nuclear Almanac* Cambridge, Mass.: Addison-Wesley, 1981.

489. McNamara, Robert S. "The Military Role of Nuclear Weapons: Perceptions and Misperceptions." *Foreign Affairs* (Fall 1983): 59–80.

490. Menaul, Stewart. *Changing Concepts of Nuclear War.* London: Institute for the Study of Conflict, 1980.

491. _____. *SALT II: The Eurostrategic Imbalance.* London: Institute for the Study of Conflict, 1979.

492. Millar T. B. *The East-West Strategic Balance.* Winchester, Mass.: Allen & Unwin, 1981.

493. Miller, Mark. *Soviet Strategic Power and Doctrine: The Quest for Superiority.* Washington, D.C.: Advanced International Studies Institute, 1982.

494. Millett, Stephen M. "Soviet Perceptions of Nuclear Strategy and Implications for U.S. Deterrence." *Air University Review* (March–April 1982): 50–61.

495. _____. "The Capabilities of the American Nuclear Deterrent, 1945–1950." *Aerospace Historian* (Spring/March 1980): 27–32.

496. Neidle, Alan F., ed. *Nuclear Negotiations: Reassessing Arms Control Goals in U.S.-Soviet Relations.* Austin: University of Texas Press, 1982.

497. Nitze, Paul. "SALT II and American Strategic Considerations." *Comparative Strategy* 2, no. 1 (1980): 9–34.

498. Nott, John. "Nuclear Weapons and Preventing War." *NATO Review* (June 1981): 24–26.

499. Nunn, Jack H. *The Soviet First Strike Threat: The U.S. Perspective.* New York: Praeger, 1982.

500. Olive, Marsha McGraw, and Jeffrey D. Porro. *Nuclear Weapons in Europe: Modernization and Limitation.* Lexington, Mass.: Lexington Books, 1983.

501. Panofsky, W.K.H. *Arms Control and SALT II.* Seattle: University of Washington Press, 1979.

502. Parker, Lt. Cmdr. T. Wood. "Theater Nuclear Warfare and the U.S. Navy." *Naval War College Review* (January-February 1982): 3–16.

503. Payne, Keith B. *Nuclear Deterrence in U.S.-Soviet Relations.* Boulder, Colo.: Westview Press, 1982.

504. Platt, Alan. *The U.S. Senate and Strategic Arms Policy, 1969–1977.* Boulder, Colo.: Westview Press, 1978.

505. Platt, Alan, and Lawrence D. Weiler, eds. *Congress and Arms Control.* Boulder, Colo.: Westview Press, 1978.

506. Polmar, Norman. *Strategic Weapons: An Introduction.* Rev. ed. New York: Crane, Russak, 1982.

507. Potter, William C. *Nuclear Power and Nonproliferation: An*

Interdisciplinary Perspective. Cambridge, Mass.: Oelgeschlager, Gunn & Hian, 1982.

508. Potter, William C., ed. *Verification and SALT: The Challenge of Strategic Deception*. Boulder, Colo.: Westview Press, 1980.

509. Pringle, Peter. "On the Hill: Nuclear Unsafeguards." *New Republic* (December 23, 1981): 11–13.

510. Pringle, Peter, and James Spigelman. *The Nuclear Barons*. New York: Holt, Rinehart & Winston, 1981.

511. Pringle, Peter, and William Arkin. *S.I.O.P.: The Secret U.S. Plan for Nuclear War*. New York: W. W. Norton, 1983.

512. Quester, George H., ed. *Navies and Arms Control*. New York: Praeger, 1980.

513. Ranger, Robin. *Arms and Politics, 1958–1978*. Toronto: Macmillan, 1979.

514. Rogers, Paul, Malcolm Dando, and Peter ven de Dungen. *As Lambs to the Slaughter: The Facts About Nuclear War*. London: Arrow Books, 1981.

515. Rose, John P. *The Evolution of U.S. Army Nuclear Doctrine, 1945–1980* Boulder Colo.: Westview Press, 1980.

516. Rosenberg, David Alan. "U.S. Nuclear Stockpile, 1945 to 1950," *Bulletin of the Atomic Scientists* (May 1982): 25–30.

517. Rostow, Eugene V. "America's Blueprint for Controlling Nuclear Weapons." *Department of State Bulletin* (August 1981): 59–64.

518. Rotblat, Joseph. *Nuclear Radiation in Warfare*. Cambridge, Mass.: Oelgeschlager, Gunn & Hain, 1981.

519. _____, ed. *Scientists: The Arms Race and Disarmament*. London: Taylor and Francis, 1982.

520. Rumsfeld, Donald. "America Must Respond." *Comparative Strategy* 2 no. 1 (1980): 35–52.

521. Russett, Bruce. *The Prisoners of Insecurity: Nuclear Deterrence, the Arms Race, and Arms Control*. San Francisco: W. H. Freeman, 1983.

522. Scheer, Robert. *With Enough Shovels: Reagan, Bush and Nuclear War*. New York: Random House, 1982.

523. Schell, Jonathan. *The Fate of the Earth*. New York: Alfred A. Knopf, 1982.

524. Schwartz, David N. *NATO's Nuclear Dilemmas*. Washington, D.C.: Brookings Institution, 1983.

525. Scoville, Herbert, Jr. *MX: Prescription for Disaster*. Cambridge, Mass.: MIT Press, 1981.

526. Seaborg, Glenn T. *Kennedy, Khrushchev and the Test Ban*. Berkeley: University of California Press, 1981.

527. Seiler, George J. *Strategic Nuclear Forces Requirements and Issues*. Maxwell AFB, Ala: Air University Press, 1983.

528. Shaker, Mohamed I. *The Nuclear Non-Proliferation Treaty: Origin and Implementation, 1959–1979*. New York: Oceana Publications, 1980.

529. Sienkiewicz, Stanley. "Foreign Policy and Theater Nuclear Force Planning." *Journal of Strategic Studies* (May 1979): 17–33.

530. _____. "National Security and Nuclear Proliferation." *Comparative Strategy* 3, no. 1 (1981): 25–43.

531. Smith, Gerard. *Doubletalk: The Story of SALT I*. New York: Doubleday, 1981.

532. Snow, Donald M. *Nuclear Strategy in a Dynamic World: American Policy*

in the 1980s. Tuscaloosa: University of Alabama Press, 1981.

533. _____. "Strategic Implications of Enhanced Radiation Weapons: A Preliminary Analysis." *Air University Review* (July-August 1979): 2-15.

534. Snow, Donald M. "The MX-Basing Mode Muddle: Issues and Alternatives." *Air University Review* (July-August 1980): 11-25.

535. Sollinger, Jerry M. *Improving U.S. Theater Nuclear Doctrine: A Critical Analysis.* Washington, D.C.: National Defense University Press, 1983.

536. Sorrells, Charles A. *U.S. Cruise Missile Programs: Development, Deployment and Implications for Arms Control.* New York: McGraw-Hill, 1983.

537. Steinbruner, John D., and Leon V. Sigal, eds. *Alliance Security: NATO and the No-First-Use Question.* Washington, D.C.: Brookings Institution, 1983.

538. Strauch, Ralph. *Strategic Warning and General War: A Look at the Conceptual Issues.* Santa Monica, Calif.: RAND Corporation, 1979.

539. Talbott, Strobe. *Endgame: The Inside Story of SALT II.* New York: Harper & Row, 1979.

540. Terman, Douglas. *First Strike.* New York: Charles Scribner's Sons, 1979.

541. Tsipis, Kosta. *Arsenal: Understanding Weapons in the Nuclear Age.* New York: Simon & Schuster, 1983.

542. U.S. Arms Control and Disarmament Agency. *Arms Control and Disarmaments: Texts and History of Negotiations: 1980 Edition.* Washington, D.C.: GPO, 1980.

543. _____. *Arms Control and Disarmaments: Texts and History of Negotiations: 1982 Edition.* Washington, D.C.: GPO, 1982.

544. _____. *World Military Expenditures and Arms Transfers, 1970-1979.* Washington, D.C.: GPO, 1982.

545. U.S. Congress. *Strategic Arms Limitation Talks, Hearings and Briefings.* 95th Cong. Washington D.C.: GPO, 1979.

546. _____. Office of Technology Assessment. *MX Missile Basing Summary.* Washington, D.C.: GPO, 1981.

547. _____. Office of Technology Assessment. *Nuclear Proliferation and Safeguards: Summary.* Washington, D.C.: GPO, 1982.

548. _____. Office of Technology Assessment. *The Effects of Nuclear War.* Washington, D.C.: GPO, 1979.

549. _____. Senate. Committee on Armed Services. *Military Implications of the Treaty on the Limitation of Strategic Offensive Arms and Protocol Thereto (SALT II Treaty).* 96th Cong., 1st Sess. Washington, D.C.: GPO, 1979.

550. _____. Senate. Committee on Foreign Relations. *Arms Control Implications of Current National Defense Programs, Hearings.* 96th Cong., 1st Sess. Washington, D.C.: GPO, 1980.

551. _____. Senate. Committee on Foreign Relations. *Interim Report on Nuclear Weapons in Europe.* Washington, D.C.: GPO, 1981.

552. _____. Senate. Committee on Foreign Relations. *Nuclear War Strategy, Hearings.* 96th Cong., 2d Sess. Washington, D.C.: GPO, 1981.

553. _____. Senate. Committee on Foreign Relations. *The SALT II Treaty, Hearings.* 95th Cong., 1st Sess. Washington, D.C.: GPO, 1980.

554. _____. Senate. Committee on Foreign Relations. *The SALT II Treaty,*

Hearings and Report. 96th Cong., 1st Sess. Washington, D.C.: GPO, 1979.

555. U.S. Department of State. *SALT II Agreement*: *Vienna, June 18, 1979*. Washington, D.C.: GPO. 1979.

556. Waldheim, Kurt. *Nuclear Weapons*: *Report of the Secretary-General, United Nations*. Brookline, Mass.: Autumn Press, 1981.

557. Wasserman, Sherri L. *The Neutron Bomb Controversy: A Study in Alliance Politics*. New York: Praeger, 1983.

558. Wildrick, Capt. Craig D. "Bernard Brodie: Pioneer of the Strategy of Deterrence." *Military Review* (October 1983): 39–45.

559. Wolfe, Thomas W. *The SALT Experience*. Cambridge, Mass.: Ballinger, 1979.

560. Yager, Joseph A., ed. *Nonproliferation and U.S. Foreign Policy*. Washington, D.C.: Brookings Institution, 1980.

561. Zuckerman, Solly. *Nuclear Illusion and Reality*. New York: Viking Press, 1982.

XXI

U.S. GOVERNMENT DOCUMENTATION

Timothy K. Nenninger

Since the publication of the first essay on government records relating to U.S. military history in *Supplement I* of this guide, the custodians of federal military records have accessioned new materials; prepared additional guides, finding aids, and other pertinent publications; and, in a few cases, reorganized.

THE NATIONAL ARCHIVES. Organization. A major reorganization of the Military Archives Division, in 1982, has significantly affected the distribution and allocation of military records at the National Archives. The newly created Military Service Branch is now responsible for all the records in the National Archives building relating to individual military personnel. Not only does this include the Revolutionary War and 19th-century compiled military service records and pension files so heavily used by genealogists, but also records relating to decorations and awards, casualties (including those for Vietnam), and disciplinary actions. Two other branches have responsibility for the remaining military records in the National Archives Building. The Navy and Old Army Branch has custody of army and army air forces records through 1941 and all navy records in the building (which includes some as recent as 1951). The modern military headquarters branch is responsible for post-1941 army, air force, Defense Department, and Joint Chiefs of Staff records in the main archives building. Military records at the Washington National Records Center (Suitland, Maryland), previously serviced by the now abolished General Archives Division, are in the charge of the Modern Military Field Branch of the Military Archives Division. Among their holdings are World War II and postwar operations, theater, and occupation records; some technical, logistic, and support service records of both the army and the navy; and the principal army intelligence files from 1941 to 1963. The Military Archives Division is beginning to shift records among its four component units in an effort to make a clearer, more rational distribution of records particularly between Suitland and the main building. Eventually a pre-1947 / post-1947 split is envisaged.

Recent Acquisitions. A principal function of the National Archives is to appraise the records of the U.S. government in order to identify the small percentage that are permanently valuable and to accession (that is, to bring them under its legal and physical control) those permanent records. Military records from the World War II period to the 1960s are the current focus of appraisal and accessioning efforts. Although the branches of the Military Archives Division are not the only custodial units accessioning military and related records, they are the principal ones.

Virtually all of the recent accessions of the Navy and Old Army Branch involved navy records from World War II and the immediate postwar years. The most significant were the records of Headquarters, Commander-in-Chief U.S. Fleet (COMINCH) 1942–1945, and the central security-classified files of the secretary of the navy / chief of naval operations, 1940–1951. Information in these two groups of records (aggregating about 2,000 shelf feet) covers the range of planning, operations, technology, logistics, intelligence, and foreign affairs from before Pearl Harbor to the Korean War. The Branch also accessioned over 1,000 feet of the navy's Bureau of Aeronautics records from 1943 to 1947, an active period for naval aviation and a time of rapid technological change. These records represent the first increment of a larger effort to appraise and accession important navy bureau records down to the 1960s, when the department abolished the old bureau system.

The Modern Military Headquarters Branch has accessioned central files of the Joint Chiefs of Staff to 1960, of the army staff into the 1960s, and of the secretary of defense to the mid-1950s. Portions of the OSD and army staff records have been declassified and opened to about 1953, while most of the JCS files, with some exceptions, are declassified. The branch has also accessioned manuscript histories produced by army historians for the Center of Military History and its predecessor organizations. Most of these monographs relate to World War II organization or operations and served as background studies for the historians writing the "Green series." Some offer broader coverage, chronologically and topically, such as an organizational history of the field army, a history of the army from 1914 to 1923, a study on the officer efficiency report system, and analyses of gas warfare in World War I done by the Chemical Corps in the 1950s. Annual historical reports and histories of postwar army field and headquarters comands are also in this accession. Finally, the National Security Agency has retired to the Modern Military Headquarters Branch copies (usually electrostatic copies, not original documents) of translations of World War II German and Japanese radio message intercepts, American communications intelligence summaries, and histories of communications intelligence organizations and activities. The histories range from experience reports of the ULTRA representatives with field commands through a study on the use and dissemination of ULTRA in the southwest Pacific area to an analysis of radio intelligence in the campaign against the U-boats. The volume of these NSA materials is substantial, with the listing of the current holdings amounting to over thirty pages. Additional acquisitions, adding further to our knowledge of this "last secret of World War II," are anticipated.

Recent accessions of the Modern Military Field branch have included records of some overseas and continental army units and commands from the 1940s to the 1960s, missing aircrew reports from World War II and Korea, and the army's intelligence document collection (the "ID File") to 1963. Because of recently enacted, more stringent declassification procedures, especially for series of intelligence records, little of the "ID File" past 1947 is available for research.

The Library and Printed Archives Branch has custody of publications of the U.S. government dating back to the early 19th century. The heart of their holdings is the record set of Superintendent of Documents publications formerly in the custody of the Government Printing Office. The collection contains publications of the Navy Department, 1828-1947; of the War Department, 1833-1947; of the National Military Establishment, 1947-1949; and of the Defense Department, 1949-. Publications outside the Superintendent of Documents system are also among the branch's holdings, notably pilot handbooks and erection and maintenance manuals for naval aircraft from the 1930s to the 1960s. Military documents in the custody of the library and printed archives branch include annual reports, field manuals, technical manuals, tables of organization and equipment, and assorted memorandums, circulars, and pamphlets. They represent the means by which the military has attempted to communicate with other parts of the executive branch and with the legislature, and the vehicles utilized to promulgate policy, doctrine, regulations, and information within the services.

In recent years the Cartographic and Architectural Branch has expanded its interests and acquisitions beyond maps to such records as early-19th-century topographical engineer notebooks containing data on potential canal routes in the Northwest Territory to prewar drawings of coastal defense installations in the Canal Zone, Hawaii, and the Philippines, and to aerial photography from World War II and Vietnam. The largest series of aerial photographs is approximately 800,000 prints of captured German material, with coverage from the British Isles to the Urals for the years 1939 to 1945. A much smaller group of Japanese aerial photographs, about 35,000 images, provides coverage of China and the southwest Pacific. The branch also has over 100,000 prints of wartime American military and naval photo-reconnaissance sorties in Europe and the Pacific. A small amount of Vietnam-era aerial photographs has been accessioned, with more yet to come.

The Machine-Readable Branch of the National Archives is responsible for appraising and accessioning permanently valuable federal records created in media designed for electronic computer processing. Their holdings include at least two bodies of records of interest to military historians. The largest, some fifty machine-readable data files, relate to five major aspects of the Vietnam war—the government and population of South Vietnam, including information on military readiness, hamlet security, and rural development; ground operations, including data on effectiveness of friendly forces, enemy and friendly casualties, and enemy organization and operations; air operations, with data on sortie objectives, ordnance expended, strike results, and casualties; naval operations, particularly information related to the effectiveness of the blockade of the Vietnamese coastline and naval gunfire support for ground operations; and the Allied incursion into Cambodia, with information on enemy base areas and the efforts to neutralize them. The second major body of military records in the branch is a set of 200 attitudinal studies covering more than 500,000 army personnel during World War II. Compiled by the war department general staff, the studies were the basis for the two-volume social science classic *The American Soldier*, produced by Samuel A. Stouffer and his associates shortly after the war. In 1977, the army contracted the Roper Center to key-to-tape the nearly 300,000 surviving individual records from the surveys. The National Archives has accessioned these tapes, which contain data on soldiers' attitudes to job assignments, medical care, food, leisure-time activities, race relations, training, war aims, and personal postwar plans, among other topics.

Recent Publications. The National Archives produces a variety of finding aids to assist researchers in using the records in its custody. Finding aids range from introductory pamphlets for microfilm publications describing in detail records of only a single series, to inventories covering all series of an entire record group and specialized guides encompassing records in many record groups that relate to a broad subject. In the past, the archives has also held scholarly conferences and subsequently published their proceedings. Some of the conference volumes, including the three most recent, on women's history (94), black history (92), and naval history (93), contain useful information about organization, content, and possible uses of the military records in the National Archives.

Papers in the women's history volume discuss the role of women in the American Revolution, World War I, and World War II. These papers, although not explicitly research guides, do illustrate many sources for information on women and the military among records of the National Archives. Two of the essays in the black history volume, one on black servicemen and the other on the army and Reconstruction in Texas, further demonstrate the depth and breadth of information to be found in military records. This volume also relates the experiences of several eminent writers and historians in doing research in archival institutions – useful descriptions of how to prepare, what to expect, and how to use finding aids and reference archivists. Essays in the naval history volume describe the organization, content, and problems of managing naval records at the National Archives and the Operational Archives of the Naval Historical Center. In addition, the volume contains essays on sources and potential research topics relating to the navy in the American Revolution, the age of manifest destiny, the Spanish-American War, and World War I. An especially interesting paper deals with the use of archival sources to assist in the search for and eventual discovery of the remains of the USS *Monitor*.

Three subject guides that have recently appeared on American Indians (97), Alaskan history (95), and genealogical research (96) – contain considerable information relating to military records in the National Archives. The Indian guide summarizes the type of information likely to be found in particular bodies of records, but also gives numerous specific examples. Especially illustrative are the descriptions of several hundred large consolidated 19th-century War Department correspondence files on the army and the American Indian. Other entries describe records relating to Indians in the military service, from 19th-century army scouts to infantrymen with the AEF in World War I. The American military has had a long involvement in Alaska, from its earliest occupation to its exploration and its important strategic position in the mid-20th century. Thus it is not surprising that one entire chapter of the Alaska guide deals with records on military and naval activities. More interesting, however, are the descriptions of the records of such agencies as the Bureau of the Budget, General Accounting Office, Interior Department, and Treasury Department, which indicate the military's involvement in such areas as national parks, climate, water resources, and petroleum. Because records on military service are a principal source for genealogical research in the National Archives, the genealogical guide can be a useful tool for military historians. The guide describes, often with reproductions of selected documents, the type of information to be found in particular categories of military records, such as enlistment papers, pension files, and casualty and cemeterial reports. But, in addition, it covers records relating to military units, military posts, civilian employees of the military, military dependents, and Americans (military and civilian) living abroad. Although explicitly for the amateur genealogist interested in information about a particular individual, the descriptions of many of the categories of files implicitly suggest other types of research, particularly quantitative studies.

OTHER INSTITUTIONS. Several other federal archival and research institutions have recently produced important finding aids and guides describing military records. Archivists at the Naval History Division compiled a guide to naval history sources throughout the United States (98). The guide lists archival and manuscript collections held in private, federal, and other public institutions, including state archives and historical societies, elements of the U.S. Navy, and the regional branches of the National Archives. Private papers of naval officers and other government officials, official records of naval units, and papers of companies and other organizations involved in naval affairs are listed, including those in the Operational Archives of the Naval History Division itself. The Naval Historical Collection of the Naval War College, whose holdings cover the period from the 18th century to the present, has begun to publish descriptions of its records. Since 1980 it has produced registers to five of its manuscript collections. On a more general level, the Woodrow Wilson International Center for Scholars has prepared a number of guides to archives, libraries, museums, and other organizations that have scholarly resources relating to particular fields of study. Most of the guides published thus far relate to foreign areas— Africa (99), Central and Eastern Europe (100), East Asia (101), Latin America and the Caribbean (103), the Middle East (104), Russia and the Soviet Union (105), and South Asia (106), although one is on audiovisual collections (102). All of the area guides contain some information about records in the National Archives and elsewhere that relate to American military involvement overseas. Similarly, the audiovisual guide covers military still and motion-picture collections, although some of the organizational administrative information is dated because in 1980 the Defense Department established the Defense Audiovisual Agency (DAVA).

Among other functions, DAVA consolidated under one administrative entity several still and motion-picture depositories containing archival materials that previously had been administered by the separate services. The principal military photographic and motion picture archives are now divided between the National Archives and DAVA, with the split between the two organizations varying from service to service. With some exceptions, DAVA has army still pictures from the mid-1930s to the present, Marine Corps and air force still pictures from the World War II and later period, and navy photographs from January 1958 on; the National Archives has the earlier material. For motion pictures, again with some exceptions, DAVA has army, navy, and Marine Corps films from the 1960s and most of the post-World War II air force films, with the National Archives having earlier dated footage.

CONCLUSIONS. The custodians of federal records relating to U.S. military history continue to publish finding aids describing their holdings, thus making them more usable for scholars. New records continue to be accessioned, including many still from the period of World War II. Declassification and release of records already accessioned continues, although with the enactment of recent regulations (specifically, Executive Order 12356 of 22 June 1982) the rate of declassification has slowed from that of the previous decade.

SOME USEFUL ADDRESSES
(organizations mentioned in this essay)

National Archives
Washington, D.C. 20408

Naval History Division
Washington Navy Yard
Washington, D.C. 20374

Naval Historical Collection
U.S. Naval War College
Newport, R.I. 02840

Woodrow Wilson International Center for Scholars
Smithsonian Institution
Washington, D.C. 20560

Motion Picture Activity
Defense Audiovisual Agency
Norton Air Force Base, Calif. 92409

Still Picture Activity
Defense Audiovisual Agency
Building 219, Washington Navy Yard
Washington, D.C. 20374

BIBLIOGRAPHY

92. Conference on Federal Archives as Sources for Research on Afro-Americans, Washington, D.C., 1973. *National Archives Conferences* Vol. 12, *Afro-American History: Sources for Research.* Edited by Robert L. Clarke. Washington, D.C.: Howard University Press, 1981.

93. Conference on Naval History Washington, D.C., 1974 *National Archives Conferences* Vol. 14, *Versatile Guardian: Research in Naval History.* Edited by Richard A. von Doenhoff. Washington, D.C.: Howard University Press, 1979.

94. Conference on Women's History, Washington, D.C., 1976. *National Archives Conferences.* Vol. 16, *Clio Was a Woman: Studies in the History of American Women.* Edited by Mabel E. Deutrich and Virginia C. Purdy. Washington, D.C.: Howard University Press, 1980.

95. Ulibari, George S., ed. *Documenting Alaskan History: Guide to Federal Archives Relating to Alaska.* Fairbanks: University of Alaska Press, 1982.

96. U.S. National Archives. *Guide to Genealogical Research in the National Archives.* Washington, D.C.: National Archives and Records Service, 1982.

97. _____. *Guide to Records in the National Archives of the United States Relating to American Indians.* Compiled by Edward E. Hill. Washington, D.C.: National Archives and Records Service, 1981.

98. U.S. Naval History Division. *U.S. Naval History Sources in the United States.* Compiled by Dean C. Allard, Martha L. Crawley, and Mary W. Edmison. Washington, D.C.: Naval History Division, 1979.

99. Woodrow Wilson International Center for Scholars. *Scholars' Guide to Washington, D.C. for African Studies*. Compiled by Purnima Mehta Bhatt. Washington, D.C.: Smithsonian Institution Press, 1980.

100. _____. *Scholars' Guide to Washington, D.C. for Central and East European Studies*. compiled by Kenneth J. Dillon. Washington, D.C.: Smithsonian Institution Press, 1980.

100. _____. *Scholars' Guide to Washington, D.C., for East Asian Studies*. Compiled by Hong N. Kim. Washington, D.C.: Smithsonian Institution Press, 1979.

102. _____. *Scholars' Guide to Washington, D.C.: Film and Video Collections*. Compiled by Bonnie G. Rowan. Washington, D.C.: Smithsonian Institution Press, 1980.

103. _____. *Scholars' Guide to Washington, D.C., for Latin American and Caribbean Studies*. Compiled by Michael Grow. Washington, D.C.: Smithsonian Institution Press, 1979.

104. _____. *Scholars' Guide to Washington, D.C., for Middle Eastern Studies*. Compiled by Steven R. Dorr. Washington, D.C.: Smithsonian Institution Press, 1981.

105. _____. *Scholars' Guide to Washington, D.C., for Russian / Soviet Studies*. Compiled by Steven A. Grant. Washington, D.C.: Smithsonian Institution Press, 1977.

106. _____. *Scholars' Guide to Washington, D.C., for South Asian Studies*. Compiled by Enayetur Rahim. Washington, D.C.: Smithsonian Institution Press, 1981.

XXII

THE COAST GUARD, 1790–1983

Truman R. Strobridge

BOTH A MILITARY AND HUMANITARIAN SERVICE AT ALL TIMES. The U.S. Coast Guard is by law an armed force at all times, but, unlike the other military services, it is also a humanitarian service. This duality of two seemingly contradictory missions in a single service not only shapes the U.S. Coast Guard's character in a unique fashion but also continues to confuse the average American down to the present day.

Title 14 of the United States Code, Section 1 (14 USC 1), states that the U.S. Coast Guard "shall be a military service and a branch of the armed forces of the United States at all times... in the Department of Transportation, except when operating as a service in the Navy," while Section 2 states that the service "shall maintain a state of readiness to function as a specialized service in the Navy in time of war." This military heritage of the service dates back to a twofold origin: (1) 1797, when the lack of a standing U.S. Navy during the quasi-war with France forced the U.S. Congress to authorize the president to use revenue cutters for naval defense; and (2) 1799, when the U.S. Congress authorized the president to direct the revenue cutters to operate with the U.S. Navy under the direction of the secretary of the navy.

The same 14 USC 2 also charges the U.S. Coast Guard to "develop, establish, maintain, and operate... rescue facilities for the promotion of safety on, under, and over the high seas and waters subject to the jurisdiction of the United States." This humanitarian heritage of the service can be traced back to a fourfold origin: (1) 1785, when the Massachusetts Humane Society was organized to save people from drowning; (2) 1799, when revenue cutters were dispatched to render assistance to vessels in distress; (3) 1831, when the first winter cruises of the revenue cutters were ordered routinely to provide aid during the gale season; and (4) 1847, when the U.S. Congress authorized funds for the establishment of the first shoreside rescue stations along the eastern coast.

Its most famous heroes, for instance, are not those naval commanders who destroy enemy vessels in bloody sea battles to win fame and honor, but instead those daring ship and small-boat skippers who risk their lives under hazardous conditions to rescue others from the perils of the sea and other natural disasters. Two immediately spring to mind: Joshua James, the celebrated lifesaver who continued rescuing the shipwrecked until he died, at age 75, stepping out of a lifeboat; and 1st Lt. D.H. Jarvis, whose dogsled expedition from the cutter *Bear* drove a herd of reindeer over 1,500 miles to feed ninety-seven starving whalers trapped by Arctic ice in 1897–98 at Cape Barrow, Alaska.

Yet the present-day U.S. Coast Guard has even more functions, for the heritages and missions of at least five federal agencies have been gradually absorbed over the years. Its predecessors – with origins in the separate colonial states and the various federal departments – underwent reorganizations, renaming, and shuffling from one department to another, with missions being added and taken away, until all became amalgamated into the U.S. Coast Guard.

These tangled, twisted, interlocking organizational roots of the service and its predecessors truly pose a maritime Gordian knot. Yet, only by unraveling it can the serious researcher hope to locate the pertinent documentation needed to trace the multifaceted heritage of this most confusing military service.

In an attempt to explain this complex administrative evolution, this chapter deals with the U.S. Coast Guard's predecessors in terms of their major missions. For those preferring a graph depicting this convoluted process, one can be found on p. 1 of the 1982 edition of the official *Coast Guard History* (193).

SURVEY HISTORIES. Although Stephen H. Evans's *The United States Coast Guard, 1790–1915* (43) remains the best overall study of the antecedents of the U.S. Coast Guard, the equally sound, thoroughly researched, and fully documented history by Irving H. King, *George Washington's Coast Guard: Origins Of The U.S. Revenue Cutter Service, 1789–1801* (98), can be used for the early years. The earliest known study, *Early History of the United States Revenue Marine Service (or United States Revenue Cutter Service), 1789–1849* (165), written by Capt. Cdt. Horatio Davis Smith, USRCS (Ret.), who served from 1867 to 1909, includes numerous lengthy quotations from early documents and remains useful.

The full sweep of U.S. Coast Guard history can be found in the more popular accounts too, such as Howard V. L. Bloomfield's *The Compact History of the United States Coast Guard* (14), a lively but light treatment. Capt. Walter C. Capron gives an accurate picture in his *The U.S. Coast Guard* (22) because of his intimate knowledge, especially in his own fields of expertise. Gene Gurney's *The United States Coast Guard: A Pictorial History* (60) is noteworthy for his selection of superb illustrations and photographs, some quite rare. A sound, well-rounded narrative account, interspersed with excellent photographs, especially of the modern-day missions and duties, is *This Is the Coast Guard* (83), by H.R. Kaplan, a former feature writer in the service's public affairs division, and Lt. Cdr. James F. Hunt. Both the official 1958 and 1982 editions of *Coast Guard History* (192, 193) should be perused, since their coverage is drastically different.

Other overall treatments abound. Of varying quality and exactitude, they often emphasize one mission – usually law enforcement, combat, or search-and-rescue – to the neglect of the others. Among these are Karl Baarslag's *Coast Guard to the Rescue* (4); Kensil Bell's *"Always Ready!": The Story of the United States Coast Guard* (8); Riley Brown's *The Story of the Coast Guard: Men, Wind, and Sea* (18); Evan J. David's *Our Coast Guard: High Adventure with the Watchers of our Shores* (36); and Evor Samuel Kerr's *The United States Coast Guard: Its Ships, Duties, Stations* (95).

Regional coverages are found in T. Michael O'Brien's *Guardians of the Eighth Sea: A History of the U.S. Coast Guard on the Great Lakes* (128) and George Richard Reynolds's *The United States Coast Guard in the Northwest, 1854–1900* (148). Many little-known events are contained in the official *Some Unusual Incidents in Coast Guard History* (208).

Several shorter works deal with a specific mission, cover unique aspects or reminiscences of the service, or comprise a concise history. F. R. Eldridge's *"They Have to Go Out"*: *An Historical Sketch of the U.S. Coast Guard* (41) is a brief, accurate history. Two Newcomen Addresses provide unique glimpses of lesser-known aspects of the Service: Harvey Fletcher Johnson's *The United States Coast Guard – Some Adventures* (79), and James Pine's *The Sea and Its Lore* (134). The official *Deeds of Valor from the Annals of the U.S. Coast Guard* (196) contains accounts of heroism, daring, intrepidity, and devotion to duty, both in peace and war, throughout the history of the service since 1790.

A distinct paucity of works on the minorities prevails, outside of a few scattered magazine articles located in the official 1982 bibliography (211). Linda Townsend and Dupree Davenport's *The History of Blacks in the Coast Guard from 1970* (180) is extremely valuable because of its lack of competitors. Morris J. MacGregor's painstakingly researched and lucidly written *Integration of the Armed Forces 1940–1965* (106) contains valuable data relating to the U.S. Coast Guard, particularly during World War II. Bernard C. Nalty and Morris J. MacGregor's *Blacks in the Military* (120) documents how the U.S. Cost Guard, operating under the same guidelines as the U.S. Navy, developed perhaps the most advanced racial policy of the entire military establishment during World War II, with black officers commanding mixed crews and black enlisted men serving in a variety of specialities. Robert E. Greene's *Black Defenders of America, 1775–1973* (57) was first to reveal that Cap. M. A. Healy, a legendary figure in Alaska and the most senior officer in the U.S. Revenue Cutter Service, was a black. Mary C. Lyne and Kay Arthur's *Three Years Behind the Mast* (104), mentioned elsewhere, tells the story of the SPARS in World War II.

ADMINISTRATION AND ORGANIZATION. Thorough examinations of the services and bureaus as they existed when the books were published are Lloyd M. Short's *The Bureau of Navigation* (159) and *Steamboat-Inspection Service* (160); Darrell Hevenor Smith and Fred Wilbur Powell's *The Coast Guard* (162); and George Weiss's *The Lighthouse Service* (250). All are subtitled *Its History, Activities and Organizations* and give the following: (1) history of the establishment and development of the service or bureau; (2) its functions by detailing specific activities; (3) its organization; (4) the character of its plant; (5) a compilation of laws and regulations governing its operations; (6) financial statements showing its appropriations, expenditures, and other data for a period of years; and (7) a bibliography of the sources of information, official and private, bearing on the services or bureau and their operations.

A recent, comprehensive study of the management of the U.S. Coast Guard is Louis K. Bragaw's *Managing a Federal Agency*: *The Hidden Stimulus* (16). The author argues that a powerful hidden stimulus in federal agencies acts as an analogue to the private profit stimulus in promoting effectiveness, efficiency, and innovation. In its mildest form, that stimulus is the threat of a budget cut, and in its severe form, the threat of outright liquidation of the agency. The service is examined historically, organizationally, and managerially in light of this thesis.

Robert Mayo's *The Treasury Department and Its Various Fiscal Bureaus* (110) and *A Synopsis of the Commercial and Revenue System of the United States* (109) significantly discuss both the U.S. Revenue Cutter and the U.S. Lighthouse services as they existed in 1847. The *Brief Sketch of the Naval History of the*

United States Coast Guard with Citations of Various Statutes defining its Military Status from 1790 to 1922 (17) demonstrates the early development and continuous military character of the service. W. F. Willoughby's 1923 study, *The Reorganization of the Administrative Branch of the National Government* (258), contains a discussion of the Institute for Government Research's proposal for the reorganization of the Treasury Department by abolishing the U.S. Coast Guard, and the transfer of the revenue cutter branch to the Navy Department and the life-saving branch to the Commerce Department and its consolidation there with the Bureau of Lighthouses. James E. Beck's *Our Wonderland of Bureaucracy* (7), a critical view of the ever-larger federal government and its destructive effect on the Constitution, contains numerous mentions of the U.S. Coast Guard. The Coast Guard is cited throughout Julius Augustus Furer's *Administration of the Navy Department in World War II* (52).

Three government-sponsored studies, the first in 1948, the second in 1962, and the third in 1982, provide in-depth examinations. *Study of United States Coast Guard* (39), by the Ebasco Services Incorporated, reviews the functions, policies, operations, and procedures of the U.S. Coast Guard with a view toward promoting the efficiency of the service in carrying out its duties and responsibilities to bring to the public the greatest degree of service at the lowest possible cost. The U.S. Treasury's *Study of Roles and Missions of the U.S. Coast Guard* (237) contains reports on the following missions; ocean stations, law enforcement, search and rescue, aids to navigation, military readiness, merchant marine safety, reserve training, port security, ice breaking, and oceanography. The U.S. Coast Guard's 1982 *Roles and Mission Study Report* (205) provides the most up-to-date survey.

The verbatim text of the various laws pertinent to the topics mentioned in their titles are contained in the U.S. Lighthouse Board's *Laws relating to the Acquisition of Title to Land required for Lighthouse Purposes, Cession of Jurisdiction, and Protection of Buoys, Beacons, Etc.* (226), and *Laws of the United States relating to the Establishment, Support, and Management of the Lighthouse, Lightvessels, Monuments, Beacons, Spindles, Buoys, and Public Piers of the United States, from August 7, 1789, to March 3, 1855* (225).

BIBLIOGRAPHIES AND REFERENCE WORKS. Although Robert Greenhalgh Albion's *Naval & Maritime History: An Annotated Bibliography* (2) contains much U.S. Coast Guard-related material, including separate sections on coast guard, lighthouses, and lightships, only the U.S. Coast Guard itself has compiled bibliographies devoted solely to its own activities. The best official ones are those in 1950 (212), 1972 (176), and 1982 (211). Magazine articles, extremely important sources since so few overall or specialized histories of the service's multifaceted activities exist, are listed in the 1950 and 1982 bibliographies, as well as in Dennis L. Noble's bibliography on the U.S. Lifesaving Service (126), and in the annotated bibliography appended to Lt. Eugene N. Tulich's historical monograph on the Vietnam conflict (181).

Brief histories that usually contain the characteristics of the more prominent – as well as a few obscure – vessels are on file in the Public Affairs Division (G-BPA), U.S. Coast Guard Headquarters, Washington, D.C. 20593, which also maintains brief biographies of the senior officers. Many of the service's cutters are in the Naval History Division's *Dictionary of American Naval Fighting Ships* (228). Other publications on naval ships listed elsewhere, such as *Jane's Fighting Ships*, also include U.S. Coast Guard cutters.

AIDS TO NAVIGATION AND THE OLD LIGHTHOUSE SERVICE, 1789–1939. In 1716, the first lighthouse was erected on Little Brewster Island, in Boston Harbor. The thirteen American colonies handled their own aids to navigation, establishing and placing lights to satisfy local needs without regard to others on the coast. No sooner had the federal government been formed, however, than Congress realized that lighthouses were a national concern. By an act of 7 August 1789, Congress accepted title and jurisdiction over all lighthouses then in operation, as well as under construction, and placed the authority and responsibility for their maintenance in the secretary of the treasury. For years, the lighthouse establishment was organized rather loosely, with either the secretary of the treasury himself or a senior departmental official personally administering their day-to-day operations.

Then, on 9 October 1852, Congress created the nine-membered Lighthouse Board to take over and administer the lighthouse establishment. From 14 February 1903 until 4 March 1913, it was located in the Department of Commerce and Labor, and thereafter in the Commerce Department. Meanwhile, in 1910, Congress abolished the Lighthouse Board and established the Bureau of Lighthouses, which was transferred to the U.S. Coast Guard on 7 July 1939.

This evolution from the first lighthouse, in 1716, to the system of 47,600 aids to navigation of all classes maintained by the U.S. Coast Guard today along 47,000 miles of coast, lakes, and rivers is best described in Francis Ross Holland's thoroughly researched and lucidly written *America's Lighthouses: Their Illustrated History since 1716* (66). It is the best treatment in existence not only of the individual lights but of the development of the administrative systems needed to manage them and the utilization of technology over the centuries to provide better illumination devices, as well as the structures and lightships to house them and the men and women to man them. For a date-by-date recounting of this gradual evolution, see Truman R. Strobridge's *Chronology of Aids to Navigation and the Old Lighthouse Service, 1716–1739* (174).

Another authoritative survey of all aids to navigation, their beginnings and development both in America and abroad, and the history of the evolution of the U.S. Lighthouse Service from colonial days to 1917 is George R. Putnam's *Lighthouses and Lightships of the United States* (138). He was the service's first superintendent. An excellent survey of the service in 1899 is Arnold Burges Johnson's *The Modern Lighthouse Service* (78), which covers all aspects, including lighthouse construction, lightships, buoys, river lights, illuminating apparatus and illuminants, fog signals, personnel and their duties, etc. John S. Conway's *The United States Lighthouse Service, 1923* (33) contains an extremely detailed description of the service.

Other broad studies, although of varying quality and reliability, exist. Among them are Hans Christian Adamson's *Keepers of the Lights* (1); Robert Carse's *Keepers of the Lights: A History of American Lighthouses* (24); Francis A. Collins's *Sentinels along our Coast* (32); John J. Floherty's *Sentries of the Sea* (46); Edward Rowe Snow's *Famous Lighthouses of America* (166); Frederick A. Talbot's *Lightships and Lighthouses* (177); and the official *Historically Famous Lighthouses* (197).

Regional coverages are contained in Peter D. Bachelder's *Lighthouses of Casco Bay* (5); David L. Cipra's *Lighthouses & Lightships of the Northern Gulf of Mexico* (29); Robert De Gast's *The Lighthouses of the Chesapeake* (37); James A. Gibbs's *Sentinels of the North Pacific: The Story of Pacific Coast Lighthouses and Lightships* (53) and *West Coast Lighthouses: A Pictorial History of the Guiding Lights of the Sea* (55); Ruth R. Glunt's *Lighthouses and Legends of the Hudson* (56); Dennis L. Noble and T. Michael O'Brien's *Sentinels of the Rocks* (125); Office of Statewide Cultural Programs' *Aids to Navigation in Alaskan History* (131); Ralph and Janette Shanks's *Lighthouses and Lifeboats on the Redwood Coast* (156) and *Lighthouses of San Francisco Bay* (157); Edward Rowe Snow's *Famous New England Lighthouses* (167); Malcolm F. Willoughby's *Lighthouses of New England* (256); and Dudley Whitney's *The Lighthouse* (253), the last providing superb artistic photographs of East Coast American and Canadian lighthouses.

Numerous histories of individual lighthouses have been written, many of excellent quality. The following ones are representative: Jack E. Boucher's *Atlantic City's Historic Absecon Lighthouse* (15); James A. Gibbs's *Tillamook Light* (54); Francis Ross Holland's *A History of the Bodie Island Light Station* (67); and Edward Rowe Snow's *The Story of Minot's Light* (169).

The most authoritative and complete source on the individual aids to navigation are the various editions of the *Light List* (199), published by the U.S. Coast Guard and its predecessors over the years. They not only identify an aid to navigation as being a structure, vessel or buoy, but also give its name, official number, character, and period of light, its location by both latitude and longitude and distances from prominent local geographical features, and its candlepower, apparatus, illuminant, light characteristics, year established, year rebuilt, etc.

The life, duties, hardships, and deprivations of the lighthouse keepers, known as "wickies," are depicted in Gordon P. Manning's *Life in the Colchester Reef Lighthouse* (107) and Robert Thayer Sterling's *Lighthouses of the Maine Coast and the Men Who Keep Them* (171). Several magazine articles cited in the official 1972 bibliography (176) also recount, and give a flavor of, the everyday life of the vanished wickies.

LAW ENFORCEMENT AND THE OLD REVENUE CUTTER SERVICE, 1790–1915. On 4 August 1790, the official birthday of the service, Congress authorized the construction and support of ten boats for the protection of customs revenue and the commissioning of forty officers to man them. The formative early years have been surveyed in a scholarly manner by King's *George Washington's Coast Guard* (98), already mentioned. His thesis is that the essential character of the service had been formed by 1801. Not only had these early revenue cutters acquired a military nature during the quasi-war with France, but also they had assumed most of the other responsibilities that later became traditionally service ones, such as aiding mariners in distress, putting out and maintaining aids to navigation, assisting the operations of the nation's lighthouses, charting America's coastal waters, etc.

In the beginning, the cutter force lacked an official name, being referred to in both government documents and the press more often as the "system of cutters" and "Revenue Service." In April 1843, the secretary of the treasury established a Revenue-Marine Bureau, which centralized control but by 1854 the service was once again merely a "system of cutters," essentially under sectional (Collectors of the Ports), rather than national, control. Congress first referred to the service as a named organization in a law passed in 1863, in which the term "Revenue-Cutter Service" received official sanction. Then, in 1871, the secretary of the treasury reestablished the Revenue-Marine Bureau and assigned it the duty of administering both the cutters and the lifesaving stations. On 3 March 1875, Congress formally established the Revenue-Marine Division, giving a permanence to a centralized, or headquarters, organization. By an act of 31 July 1894, Congress required that the head of the division be a captain of the Revenue Cutter Service. Of the survey histories, Capt. Cdt. Horatio Smith (165) still remains worthwhile until 1849, while Capt. Stephen Evans (43) best explains the organizational development, although Kaplan and Hunt (83) provide a more lively treatment by concentrating on the senior officers and departmental officials.

Being a product of evolution, and developing as the United States itself developed, the U.S. Coast Guard accumulated various additional missions, roles, duties, and tasks over years. At times, this growth was gradual, without any obvious or well-defined reason. All too often, however, some spectacular marine disaster, such as the sinking of the *Titanic*, or the enactment of a new law, such as the Volstead (Prohibition) Act, proved to be the catalyst of a change or extension of the service's missions. Even a transfer to another agency or department could thrust new responsibilities on the service. In 1967, for instance, after its transfer to the Department of Transportation, the U.S. Coast Guard suddenly found itself responsible for the administration of bridges over navigable waters of the United States, even possessing bridge construction permit approval. This evolution is usually dealt with in the survey histories, but better treatments can be found in the various service monographs (159, 160, 162, 250) and the three roles-and-missions studies (39, 205, 237).

As early as 1794, for instance, the revenue cutters were charged with preventing the importing of new slaves from Africa. They captured numerous slave ships and freed almost five hundred slaves before the Civil War ended. In 1799 came the responsibility for aiding in the administration of quarantine regulations and laws. When Pres. Thomas Jefferson declared the highly unpopular total embargo of imports in 1808, the revenue cutters became charged with closing all the nation's ports. They first began enforcing the immigration laws in 1862.

As early as 1822, they became involved in protecting the ecology. Congress had created a timber reserve for the fleet and authorized the president to use whatever forces were necessary to prevent the cutting of live oaks on the public lands, but only the shallow-draft revenue cutters proved equal to the task.

With the purchase of Alaska in 1867, the ecological responsibilities of the service were greatly expanded. Armed with a host of new marine police powers, the officers and crews of the revenue cutters fought brave but lonely battles as the only representatives of law and order on the northern frontier. They prevented the fur seals of the Pribilof Islands from being hunted to extinction, patrolled the fishing banks, transported judges, doctors, and teachers to isolated settlements, saved natives from starvation on several occasions, rescued shipwrecked mariners, participated in numerous explorations, and made soundings, charts, and hydrographic observations. The sources covering these activities and many others are treated in the "Polar, Arctic, and Ice Operations" section (below).

Periodically, meanwhile, the U.S. Navy threatened to take over the service. As Leonard D. White, who analyzes these attempts in his *The Republican Era*:

1869-1901 (251), summarized it neatly: "The Treasury had possession, the Navy coveted ownership." Although disenchanted with the decentralized system of the service in the early 1840s, Congress remained convinced that "sound policy requires that the Revenue Service and the Naval Service should be kept distinct." By the early 1880s, the U.S. Navy saw the service as a convenient place to employ surplus Annapolis graduates, but Congress disagreed. The 1889 attempt was also defeated, although this time the secretary of the treasury reversed the position of his predecessors and approved the transfer. The effort was renewed in 1892, but without success.

Yet a drastic transformation lay just over the horizon, for America had matured by the time it entered the 20th century, and governmental machinery had to be revamped to keep pace. A flood of new duties had involved the U.S. Revenue Cutter Service in many new areas. The Refuge Act of 1899 first addressed the growing problem of clean water and pollution. The Motorboat Act of 1910 prescribed minimal safety standards, causing the revenue cutters to stop motorboats and check for such items as lifejackets. The sinking of the luxury liner *Titanic* in 1912 resulted in the establishment of the International Ice Patrol, as described in the official publication of the same title (198). In 1914, the revenue cutters assumed the task of protecting the sponge industries in the Gulf of Mexico. Finally, in an attempt to make the government more efficient, Congress joined the U.S. Revenue Cutter and Lifesaving Services to create the U.S. Coast Guard, "which shall constitute a part of the military forces of the United States".

SEARCH AND RESCUE AND THE OLD LIFESAVING SERVICE, 1847– 1915. Traditionally tracing its origins back to the organization of the Massachusetts Humane Society in 1785, the U.S. Lifesaving Service had its first federal origins in 1847, when Congress appropriated funds for providing assistance from shore to the shipwrecked. The following year witnessed lifesaving stations being set up in New Jersey. Additional ones were authorized in 1854. Even though federal funds paid for the construction of the stations and for their boats, equipment, and provisions, volunteers manned them.

In 1871, these volunteers became paid professionals when the U.S. Lifesaving Service was created and placed under the Revenue Marine Bureau of the Treasury Department. Organized into twelve, later thirteen, districts, the service was headed by a general superintendent, who had an assistant and his superintendents of construction, while the Revenue Marine, later Cutter, Service provided the inspectors of the lifesaving stations. In 1915, the U.S. Lifesaving Service and the U.S. Revenue Cutter Service merged together to form the U.S. Coast Guard.

These origins of the present-day search and rescue mission, too often clouded by myths and legendary heroes, are competently explained in Cmdr. Robert F. Bennett's labor of love, *Surfboats, Rockets, and Carronades* (10), which depicts the early history and volunteer rescue efforts of the U.S. Lifesaving Service from 1848 to 1871. M. M. de Wolfe Howe's *The Humane Society of the Commonwealth of Massachusetts: An Historical Review, 1786–1916* (72) is a history of the life-saving association that preceded the U.S. Lifesaving Service. The first superintendent, Sumner I. Kimball, presents an accurate picture of the service, its organization, methods, way of life, etc., in his *Organization and Methods of the U.S. Lifesaving Service* (97). A collection of heroic rescues based on official records is presented by William D. O'Connor, assistant general superintendent of the U.S. Lifesaving Service, in his *Heroes of the Storm* (129).

Cmdr. Robert F. Bennett's historical monograph, *The Lifesaving Service at Sandy Hook, 1854–1915* (9), gives a detailed history of this station in New Jersey. J. W. Dalton's *The Life Savers of Cape Cod* (35) provides biographies, duties, manner of living, and the achievements of the lifesavers. Some glimpses of duty at a lifesaving station is contained in the Rev. W. H. Law's *The Life Savers in the Great Lakes* (99). Another look at a Great Lakes lifesaving station can be found in Myron H. Vent's *South Manitoba Island: From Pioneer Settlement to Park* (239).

Because heroic rescues, storms, shipwrecks, and disasters hold a strong fascination for the general public, the years have witnessed a long succession of books with colorful titles centered around dramatic rescues and dashing skippers. The following are representative: Eric Berry's *You Have to Go Out!: The Story of the U.S. Coast Guard* (12); Allen Chaffee's *Heroes of the Shoals* (26); John J. Floherty's *Search and Rescue at Sea* (45) and *Sons of the Hurricane* (47); Glen Perry's *Watchmen of the Sea* (132); Edward Rowe Snow's *Great Gales and Dire Disasters* (168); and John D. Whiting's *Storm Fighters: True Stories of the Coast Guard* (252).

Over the years, several studies have dealt with lifesaving equipment. The earliest one is *Francis' Metallic Life-Boat Company* (50), which describes in detail Joseph Francis's lifeboats and lifecars and how to use them. R. B. Forbes's *Life-Boats, Projectiles, and Other Means for Saving Life* (49) contains material on both English and American equipment and the methods concerning lifeboats and lifesaving apparatus. *Report of a Special Committee of the Philadelphia Board Of Trade in Relation to the Life-Saving Stations Upon the Coast* (133) is the official 1860 report on the investigations into the nature and efficiency of the apparatus of the lifesaving stations on the coasts of New Jersey and Long Island. David Alexander Lyle, the inventor of the line-throwing gun named after him, made his *Report on Life-Saving Ordnance and Appurtenances* (103) in 1878. Theodorus B. M. Mason's *The Preservation of Life at Sea* (108) discusses the various lifesaving techniques and apparatus in use in 1879. James L. Pond's *History of Lifesaving Appliances* (137) is really a biography of Joseph Francis, born 12 March 1801, who devoted his life to the study, creation, and manufacture of lifesaving appliances. J. P. Barnett's *The Lifesaving Guns of David Lyle* (6) covers the entire range of line-passing, from heavy lines to guns, then gives the variations of the different types of lifesaving guns.

Some books devoted primarily to shipwrecks contain pertinent and substantial coverage of lifesaving actitivites. H. R. Kaplan and A. L. Lonsdale's *Voyager Beware* (82) is a collection of thirteen true stories of rescues and adventures at sea during the past century in which the U.S. Coast Guard or Lifesaving Service played a prominent part. Others are William Ratigan's *Great Lakes Shipwrecks & Survivals* (144); Jeannette Edwards Rattary's *Perils of the Port of New York (145) and Ship Ashore!: A Record of Maritime Disasters off Montauk and Easter Long Island, 1640–1955* (146; Birse Shepard's *Lore of the Wreckers* (158); and David Stick's *Graveyard of the Atlantic: Shipwrecks of the North Carolina Coast (172).*

COMMERCIAL VESSEL SAFETY AND THE OLD STEAMBOAT INSPECTION SERVICE, 1838–1932; BUREAU OF NAVIGATION 1872–1932;

BUREAU OF NAVIGATION AND STEAMBOAT INSPECTION, 1932–1936; AND BUREAU OF MARINE INSPECTION AND NAVIGATION, 1936–1942. Although dating from an act of Congress on 7 July 1838 for "better securing of the lives on board vessels propelled in whole or in part by steam," the U.S. Steamboat Inspection Service was not formally established until years later. This act authorized a federal inspector, appointed by a federal judge at each port of entry, to examine machinery and hulls for safety, make sure only skilled men were employed around the steam engines, and check that the steamers carried lifeboats, pumps, and fire hoses. It was an in-port organization of the Treasury Department.

On 30 August 1852, the Steamboat Act formally established the U.S. Steamboat Service. It existed as a separate service until 1932, when it merged with the Bureau of Navigation to form the Bureau of Navigation and Steamboat Inspection. Despite its almost century-long existence, the only source on its history—outside of its *Annual Reports* (234), the survey histories, and archival documents—is Lloyd M. Short's *Steamboat-Inspection Service* (160).

The origins of the U.S. Bureau of Navigation date back to 1872, when Congress recognized federal responsibility for the safety and well-being of seamen by authorizing shipping commissioners to supervise relationships between merchant seamen and their employers. Twelve years later, on 5 July 1884, Congress created the U.S. Bureau of Navigation, which absorbed the shipping commissioners. This new organization in the Treasury Department was charged with supervising the collection of tonnage dues, regulating the hiring and discharge of seamen, documenting vessels, and administering the details of the laws of navigation. Its *Annual Reports* (185) and Lloyd M. Short's *The Bureau of Navigation* (159) still remain the only sources for information on this federal agency, outside of the survey histories and archival records.

On 14 February 1903, Congress established the new Department of Commerce and Labor and transferred the U.S. Steamboat Inspection Service and the U.S. Bureau of Navigation to it. When Congress separated the department into the Commerce and Labor departments on 4 March 1913, both remained with Commerce.

The two were combined on 30 June 1932 into a new bureau, the U.S. Bureau of Navigation and Steamboat Inspection. Its name was changed to the U.S. Bureau of Marine Inspection and Navigation on 27 May 1936. This bureau was temporarily transferred to the U.S. Coast Guard as a wartime measure on 1 March 1942, becoming permanent on 16 July 1946. An excellent source for information on this federal agency, as well as on its two predecessors, is the official historical monograph *Marine Inspection* (194:XIII). Others are its *Annual Reports* (184, 185), the survey histories, and archival sources.

U.S. COAST GUARD, 1915–1983. The 1915 reorganization creating the U.S. Coast Guard combined two of the service's most important mission areas—law enforcement, and search and rescue—and established the multimission operations that are integral to today's U.S. Coast Guard. The absorption of the U.S. Lighthouse Service in 1939 and the U.S. Bureau of Marine Inspection and Navigation in 1942 completed the multifaceted character of the Service.

When the United States entered World War I shortly thereafter, the entire newly created military service passed into the naval establishment as provided by law and directed by Executive Order 2587 on 7 April 1917 and began operating as part of the U.S. Navy. Not until 28 August 1919, long after the armistice, did the U.S. Navy reluctantly permit its return to the Treasury Department, having failed in yet another attempt to make the temporary acquisition a permanent one.

The imposition of Prohibition immediately following the war catapulted the U.S. Coast Guard into national prominence, a position it has never since lost. In effect, Prohibition proved to be an ironic refutation of the time-tested unofficial motto of the service: "In obscurity lies security."

The standard work on the service's battle with the rum runners is Malcolm F. Willoughy's *Rum War at Sea* (257). It relates how the U.S. Coast Guard met the challenge by building the *Secretary* class of fairly large, fast cutters and small, swift patrol boats, refitting U.S. Navy destroyers, expanding its air fleet, and improving its security and intelligence forces. Harold Waters's firsthand accounts, *Patrol Boat 999,* with Aubrey Wisberg (244) and *Smugglers of Spirits* (245), furnish an indispensable enlisted man's viewpoint of the transformation the service underwent during this expansion.

A view from the other side of the battle is given in Jack Randell's *I'm Alone* (140), the memoirs of a Canadian rum runner whose ship was sunk by gunfire from U.S. Coast Guard cutters after a chase lasting from 20 to 22 March 1929. Robert Carse's *Rum Row* (25) and Henry Lee's *How Dry We Were: Prohibition Revisited* (100) both treat the service's activities in their discussions of the "noble experiment."

In the operations of the refitted destroyers and new large cutters against illegal smugglers, the service and its personnel learned lessons which were of immeasurable value in World War II. Peter H. Spectre's *Auxiliary Patrols* (170) describes the comprehensive regatta and safety program of the U.S. Coast Guard Auxiliary, founded in 1939, while the official historical monograph *Auxiliary* (194: XIX) deals with its World War II activities. The ocean stations—mid-ocean sites, manned by cutters, established in 1940 to provide weather reports and serve as emergency rescue sites for aircraft—also proved useful, being greatly expanded during the war, as recounted in the official *Weathermen of the Sea: Ocean Station Vessels* (217) and the historical monograph *Weather Patrol* (194:VII). In early 1941, ten cutters—250 feet long and well fitted for escort-of-convoy—were transferred to Great Britain as part of President Roosevelt's destroyers-for-bases deal. The official *Accomplishments of Ten Coast Guard Cutters Transferred to the United Kingdom* (187) records much statistical information about them, as well as their histories.

Following the war, the U.S. Coast Guard's responsibilities shifted largely to aiding navigation and safety at sea, as covered by Capron's *U.S. Coast Guard* (22), a survey history, and John M. Water's firsthand account, *Rescue at Sea* (247), respectively. Law enforcement once again assumed increased significance by the early 1960s. After Castro's takeover in Cuba, the service established its Cuban Patrol, consisting of cutters and aircraft, to solve the many problems posed by the flow of refugees—peaking in 1965 and then abating—across the Straits of Florida to Key West and freedom. By the early 1970s, drug interception received an increasing emphasis that has continued. Both narrative and pictorial descriptions of these trends are contained in the survey histories (60, 83). Three official publications in the late 1970s deal with the service's ships, planes, and stations (206), its missions and objectives (215), and its participation in international affairs (201).

The 1970s also witnessed one of the most publicized and least honor-reflecting episodes in U.S. Coast Guard history—the defection aboard the cutter *Vigilant* of Simas Kudirka, a Soviet radio operator of Lithuanian extraction. Algis Ruksensas's *Day of Shame: The Truth about the Murderous Happenings aboard the Cutter* Vigilant *during the Russian-American Confrontation off Martha's Vineyard* (152) provides one version of this incident, which resulted in the *Vigilant*'s skipper being immediately removed from command, and his superiors—a captain and an admiral—forced to resign to avoid court-martials.

Technological improvements over the last decade have allowed the U.S. Coast Guard to discontinue the ocean stations, reduce the number of buoy tenders, and eliminate all but one lightship station. The additional regulatory responsibilities have caused a shift of personnel from law enforcement and search and rescue on the high seas to regulatory duties, such as commercial vessel safety and marine environmental protection. This shift of emphasis has resulted in a decrease in the number of cutters from 339, in 1969, to 248, and aircraft from 174 to 154. These service adjustments to changed conditions are discussed in detail in the official 1982 roles and missions study (205), which also attempts to predict future requirements. The American Enterprise Institute's *Conversation with Admiral John B. Hayes* (3) discusses not only the commandant's views on the present-day U.S. Coast Guard but also what the future probably holds for the service. A more indepth analysis of the service, its problems, and prospects is the 1982 study (221) by the Congressional Reference Service of the Library of Congress.

CUTTERS. The construction of the first ten cutters by local builders and manning by officers and seamen from the disbanded Continental Navy and merchant marine has been painstakingly reconstructed by Florence Kern in ten separate booklets (85-94). Although not a trained historian, she has haunted the libraries and archives along the eastern coast for years, even traveling to London to do research, and her fascination with and love of these early cutters shines through on every page.

Despite the lost and destroyed plans of the sailing cutters because the service lacked a construction bureau until long after steamers appeared, Howard I. Chapelle's *The History of American Sailing Ships* (27) makes a significant contribution toward filling this void. Whenever possible, it gives the cutters' plans and designers and, when plans are not available, makes some shrewd professional assumptions as to dimensions and characteristics.

Once the service began designing and building its own cutters, more of the plans and details about the cutters managed to survive. A list of the available historic ship's plans, along with instructions on how to order copies of them, is available from the Public Affairs Division (G-PBA), U.S. Coast Guard Headquarters, Washington, D.C. 20593. Pictures and descriptions of selected U.S. Coast Guard oceanographic ships, past, present, and proposed, can be found in Stewart B. Nelson's *Oceanographic Ships Fore and Aft* (123).

A comprehensive record of the major movements of the service's vessels, excluding such smaller ones as surfboats and 75-foot patrol boats, is the official *Records of Movements, Vessels of the United States Coast Guard, 1790-December 31, 1933* (204). It is a particularly valuable research tool, since the wealth of information, historical data, statistics, and little-known facts in this massive work is not readily available elsewhere. The individual vessel record usually contains assignments, special missions, other movements, when and where and from whom obtained, cost, who built her, when and where built, dimensions and characteristics of the vessel, and reason why eventually struck from the rolls. In some cases pertinent documents, such as letters and reports, are reproduced in whole or part. Separate listings give the vessels participating in wars and expeditions, their commanding officers and, usually, the names of all the officers involved aboard them.

Without a doubt, the most famous cutter is the *Bear*. Launched in a Scottish shipyard in 1873, she was a sealer and a U.S. Navy vessel in the Greely Relief Expedition before beginning her long association with the U.S. Revenue Cutter Service and Alaska in 1885. She was a museum ship in Oakland, Claifornia, with Adm. Richard E. Byrd and the U.S. Navy in his second Antarctic expedition, and with the U.S. Coast Guard again for World War II service with the Greenland Patrol. Later, she was sold to a private company in Halifax, Nova Scotia, and eventually lost at sea on 19 March 1963.

Five books have been written about her: William Bixby's *Track of the* Bear (13); Polly Burrough's *The Great Ice Ship* Bear: *Eighty-Nine Years in Polar Seas* (19); Robert H. Rankin and H. R. Kaplan's *Immortal* Bear: *The Stoutest Polar Ship* (141); Stella F. Rapaport's *The* Bear: *Ship of Many Lives* (143), a juvenile history; and Frank Wead's *Gales, Ice, and Men*: *A Biography of the Steam Barkentine* Bear (248). M. A. Ranson and Eloise Katherine's *Sea of the* Bear: *Journal of a Voyage to Alaska and the Arctic, 1921* (142) is a narrative account of the author's experiences as a young seaman aboard the *Bear* in 1921 on Bering Sea patrol, based on a diary he kept.

Another cutter of worldwide fame is the square-rigged bark *Eagle* (ex-*Horst Wessel* of the World War II German Navy), used by the U.S. Coast Guard Academy to train cadets. Besides giving a short history of the service and earlier *Eagles*, William I. Norton's *Eagle Ventures* (127) describes the acquiring of the *Eagle*, and her refitting, commissioning, maiden voyage, and current activities. A firsthand account by a U.S. Coast Guard officer of the first voyage of the training bark *Eagle* under the American flag following World War II is Gordon McGowan's *The Skipper and the* Eagle (106). Over 200 photographs of the training bark's annual cruise in 1954 to Europe fill the pages of Alan Villiers's *Sailing* Eagle: *The Story of the Coast Guard's Square-Rigger* (240).

CUTTERS IN COMBAT. From their origin in 1790 until 1798, when the U.S. Navy was created, the revenue cutters remained the only national maritime force. By an act of 2 March 1799, Congress authorized the president to direct the revenue cutters to operate with the U.S. Navy under the direction of the secretary of the navy. Ever since, the service has fought side by side with the U.S. Navy in every one of the nation's wars at sea. Traditionally, the U.S. Coast Guard augments the U.S. Navy with men and cutters and performs special missions for which its peacetime experiences had developed unique skills.

Outside of archival sources, the earlier wartime duties of the cutters receive only scant or passing mention in the secondary sources, although the official reports, such as the U.S. Navy's *Annual Reports* (229), do record their exploits. Only a few works devote themselves solely to the deeds of the cutters. Fortunately, the transformation of the first revenue cutters into both a maritime and naval service during the quasi-war with France has been superbly told in detail by Irving H. King in *George Washington's Coast Guard* (98). The revenue cutters took eighteen prizes unaided, and assisted in the capture of two others during that undeclared war.

For coverage of deeds of the cutters during the next three wars, despite their gallant service, only the survey histories exist. In fact, the cutter *Jefferson* defeated HMS *Patriot* and brought her in as the first capture of the War of 1812. In all, sixteen cutters took fourteen prizes. Next, the cutters fought a savage riverine war (1836–1839) with the Seminole Indians. They attacked war bands, blockaded rivers, carried dispatches, rescued fleeing settlers, transported troops, and landed men and artillery to defend the threatened forts as well as shore parties to hunt the Indians among the swamps and jungle trails of Florida. During the Mexican War (1846–1848), eleven cutters, five of them steam-propelled, cooperated with the U.S. Army and Navy, even playing a significant role in the amphibious operations at the mouth of the Alvarado River.

The cutter *Harriet Lane* fired the first naval shot of the Civil War at Fort Sumter. Truman R. Strobridge's *The United States Coast Guard and the Civil War* (175) presents a brief survey, as well as an account of the oddest-looking and most valuable cutter, the semi-submersible ironclad *Naugatuck*. Besides the survey histories, the *Official Records* (230, 238) contain some documents pertaining to the naval and land operations that mention the deeds of the cutters and their crews.

In the Spanish-American War, eight cutters fought in Admiral Sampson's fleet in the Caribbean and one in Admiral Dewey's fleet in the battle of Manila Bay, and four cooperated with the U.S. Navy on the Pacific coast. The cutter *Hudson* performed so nobly during the battle of Cardenas that Congress authorized gold and silver medals issued to the officers and bronze ones to the crews, the only such medals awarded during the war. The official *The United States Revenue Cutter Service in the War with Spain, 1898* (232) is comprised primarily of the official records of the commanding officers submitted to the secretary of the treasury.

When Congress declared war against Germany on 6 April 1917, the newly created U.S. Coast Guard was immediately transferred to the U.S. Navy. Cutters based at Gibraltar performed convoy escort duty between there and the British Isles, as well as in the Mediterranean. Others operated in the vicinity of Azores, off Nova Scotia, in the Caribbean, and along the American coasts. One disappeared with a loud explosion and one hundred eleven U.S. Coast Guardsmen, probably from a German torpedo. These deaths, combined with those elsewhere, added up to 2.2 percent of the service's strength, the highest fatality rate of all the American military services. For World War I service, two official publications exist: *Operations of the Coast Guard in Time of War* (200) and *U.S. Coast Guard Roll of Honor, April 6, 1917–November 30, 1918* (216).

Amidst the global combat of World War II, the U.S. Coast Guard truly came of age, winning acceptance by her sister services and the public alike. The following section discusses the sources recording the numerous roles and missions of the U.S. Coast Guard both at home and in combat.

During the Korean War, the U.S. Coast Guard did not become part of the U.S. Navy but merely performed a supporting role. Besides assuring port security and proper ammunition loading, it maintained an ocean station in the western Pacific to provide improved meterological services. Also, fifteen officers and men traveled to Seoul and showed the Koreans how to organize their own coast guard. Of the survey histories, perhaps Kaplan and Hunt's *This Is the Coast Guard* (83) best describes this supporting role.

A brief description of the activities of U.S. Coast Guard activities, such as cutters, explosive loading, port security, aids to navigation, etc., can be found in H. R. Kaplan's *Coast Guard in Vietnam* (81). A more substantial history, gleaned from the operational and administrative reports submitted by the various cutters, field units, and their commanders, is Lt. Eugene N. Tulich's *The United States Coast Guard in South East Asia during the Vietnam Conflict* (181), which treats all activities, even humanitarianism.

WORLD WAR II. When President Roosevelt proclaimed a national emergency on 8 September 1939, the strength of the U. S. Coast Guard stood at 11,384 military personnel. During the following two years of emergency, the U.S. Coast Guard actively participated in the operations in the Atlantic, because the U.S. Navy lacked enough ships for its increased activities, such as neutrality patrol. Besides convoy escort duties, the U.S. Coast Guard's Greenland patrol also engaged in charting and mapping unexplored fjords, locating suitable sites for sea bases, airfields and weather and radio stations, supplying them after establishment, rescuing people and vessels in distress, and locating foreign military installations.

On 1 November 1941, when events pointed unmistakably toward war, President Roosevelt issued Executive Order 8929, transferring the entire U.S. Coast Guard to the service and jurisdiction of the secretary of the navy and directing it to operate as part of the U.S. Navy. An earlier executive order, on 16 August 1941, had already transferred all U.S. Coast Guard operations in Hawaii to the U.S. Navy. Not until January 1946 did Executive Order 9666 return the U.S. Coast Guard to the Treasury Department.

When war came on 7 December 1941, the strength of the U.S. Coast Guard was 25,000 military personnel, 168 named vessels over 100 feet in length, numerous smaller ones, 39 lightships, and about 50 planes, mostly amphibians and observation scout planes. By mid-1945, the needs of wartime had increased the strength of the U.S. Coast Guard to over 171,000 military personnel with 80,476 at sea, 51,173 temporary reservists (44,307 of whom served part-time without pay, primarily in port security duties), 802 vessels of 65 feet or over, a large number of smaller craft (7,960 at the peak on 1 January 1943), and about 70 aircraft. In addition, the worldwide nautical nature of the war caused the United States to draw heavily upon skilled seamanship of the experienced U.S. Coast Guardsmen, for U.S. Coast Guardsmen totally manned 351 navy ships and close to 288 army vessels.

U.S. Coast Guardsmen participated in every major amphibious landing and sank twelve German U-boats, also having numerous assists, in bitter antisubmarine warfare. At the close of 1943, for example, 406 U.S. Coast Guard and U.S. Coast Guard-manned ships were activly engaged in antisubmarine or convoy escort duty. The U.S. Coast Guardsmen also brought their more traditional activities and skills, such as search and rescue, marine safety, port security, high explosive handling, and aids to navigation in the form of buoy tenders and long-range navigation (LORAN), to the far-flung battles and campaigns of the worldwide struggle.

The standard work on this multifaceted service in wartime is Cmdr. Malcolm F. Willoughby's *The U.S. Coast Guard in World War II* (258). It is primarily based on the more authoritative and detailed, although practically unknown, U.S. Coast Guard's *The Coast Guard at War* (194). Each of its thirty monographs covers a separate phase of the service's special activities during wartime. Complete sets exist in the holdings of the Library of Congress (264), National Archives (268), U.S. Coast Guard Academy Library (266), and the libraries of the U.S. Navy (269) and Transportation (265) departments. One may find among these monographs, but not in all of them, such items as appendixes, bibliographies, chronologies, statistical data, charts, graphs, verbatim eyewitness accounts of combat and disasters, lists of awards, campaigns, persons, cutters, installations, etc. They give an excellent and well-balanced historical coverage for all phases of wartime operations, even treating such activities as communications engineering, finance, intelligence, port security, public relations, medical, etc. All have the same format and ample illustrations.

Two other broad surveys are Reg Ingraham's *First Fleet: The Story of the U.S. Coast Guard at War* (76), and Arch A. Mercey and Lee Grove's *Sea, Surf, and Hell: The Coast Guard in World War II* (113). The official *United States Coast Guard Combat and Overseas Operations* (214) briefly retells the service's wartime operations, such as convoy duty, Arctic combat, amphibious assaults, ocean stations, and overseas activities dealing with the safety of merchant-vessel seamen.

Several wartime activities have been treated separately. Three official studies are *Bering Sea Patrol* (190), *Captains of the Ports* (191) and *Sinking of the Hamilton* (207). Lt. Malcolm F. Willoughby's *The Coast Guard's TRS: First Naval District* (254) is a history of a temporary reserve organization. Another TR unit history is Lt. John F. Gummere's *The History of the Philadelphia Regiment, Volunteer Port Security Force* (58). Chief Gunner's Mate John H. Fenton's *The Battle of Boston Harbor: A Wartime History of Flotilla 1-412, Winthrop, Massachusetts* (44) is a history of a U.S. Coast Guard auxiliary unit. William B. Mellor's *Sank Same* (111) is the story of the volunteer members of the U.S. Coast Guard Auxiliary during the battle against German submarines in the Atlantic.

Robert L. Scheina's *U.S. Coast Guard Cutters & Craft of World War II* (155) presents key dates, characteristics, and an operational sketch for each of the U.S. Coast Guard's more than 400 cutters and 4,000 craft that served from 1939 to 1945. Those ships, manned by U.S. Coast Guardsmen but administratively controlled by another government agency, such as the 351 U.S. Navy ones, are listed in appendixes. Roland W. Charles's *Troopships of World War II* (28) contains photographs, descriptions, salient facts, and brief histories of 288 troopships, many of which were U.S. Coast Guard-manned. Theodore Roscoe's *United States Destroyer Operations in World War II* (152) is worth consulting, for U.S. Coast Guardsmen fought and died individually on the U.S. Navy destroyers and fully manned 30 of the destroyer-escorts.

The dangers, hardships, and sacrifices of convoy escort duty are dramatically told in John M. Waters's *Bloody Winter* (246). Written by a participating U.S. Coast Guard officer, this history covers the six months of savage fighting from December 1942 to May 1943 that climaxed the battle of the Atlantic and drove the U-boat wolf packs from the shipping lanes. Two pamphlets that started out as magazine articles are Charles Rawlings's *We Saw the Battle of the Atlantic* (147) and William Walton's *Scratch One Hearse* (241). Felix Riesenberg's *Sea War: The Story of the U.S. Merchant Marine in World War II* (150) is worth consulting, since the multifaceted activities of the U.S. Coast Guard are intertwined throughout this history, as they are in Samuel Eliot Morison's 15-volume *History of United States Naval Operations in World War II* (115), the standard operational account.

Both icebreakers and cutters performed admirably in Arctic waters during the hostilities. In fact, two months before Pearl Harbor, the icebreaker *Northland* took into "protective custody" the Norwegian trawler *Boskoe* and captured three German radiomen ashore in Greenland, thus giving the honor of the first naval capture of the war to the U.S. Coast Guard. The official historical monographs *Alaska* (194.III) and *Greenland Patrol* (194.II) relate the other accomplishments in accurate detail and are amply illustrated with pertinent and dramatic photographs.

Four novels by former U.S. Coast Guardsmen can also be profitably read for the flavor of World War II service. They are Weldon Hill's *Onionhead* (63), which was made into a movie starring Andy Griffith; Carl Jonas's *Beachhead on the Wind* (80); and Sloan Wilson's *Ice Brothers* (60) and *Voyage to Somewhere* (261).

POLAR, ARCTIC, AND ICE OPERATIONS. Today, only the U.S. Coast Guard possesses icebreakers, for the U.S. Navy divested itself of this capability for a temporary advantage – perhaps now regretted – in 1965 during the Vietnam conflict. Since 1936, the U.S. Coast Guard has been providing domestic icebreaking assistance. Much earlier, the purchase of Alaska in 1867 resulted in the revenue cutter *Lincoln* steaming north to perform its service's traditional role of enforcing the law in the newly acquired possession. Ever since, the histories of Alaska and the U.S. Coast Guard have been intimately linked together. No sooner had the polar ice pack been encountered than the first vessels specially designed to operate under these hazardous conditions began appearing on the rolls of the service.

Five official reports record this duty in the northern waters. Besides being the official narrative report of Capt. C. L. Hooper, USRM, of a cruise in 1880 to the Bering Sea and the Arctic Ocean, and of necessity containing many details on the difficulties of operating a ship, equipment, and men in northern areas, *Report of the Cruise of the U.S. Revenue-Steamer* Thomas Corwin, *in the Arctic Ocean* (70) contains much anthropological, ethnological, sociological, etc., information about Alaska and the nearby islands. His report the following year (71) contains similar information.

Capt. M. A. Healy, USRM, recently discovered to have a black heritage, submitted two reports, *Report of the Cruise of the Revenue Marine Steamer* Corwin *in the Arctic Ocean in the Year 1884* (61) and *1885* (62). Included are the results of some original explorations and observations, made by the officers of the *Corwin*, especially the first exploration of the banks of the Kowak River, in 1884, and the Noatak River, in 1885. They also describe the revenue steamer's operations for the protection of the seal fisheries and sea-otter hunting grounds and notes on the birds and fishes observed, as well as the flora and fauna encountered.

The *Report of the Operations of the U.S. Revenue Steamer* Nunivak *on the Yukon River Station, Alaska, 1899-1901* (21), by 1st Lt. J. C. Cantwell, RCS, is the official report of a U.S. Revenue Cutter Service vessel dispatched primarily to enforce customs and navigation laws among the gold prospectors on the Yukon. This document also contains the account of a reconnaissance of the Koyukuk River by 2d Lt. R. H. Camden, RCS, and the account of a reconnaissance of the Dall River-Koyukuk Trail by 3d Lt. Eugene Blake, RCS, as well as the report of the medical officer, Surgeon James T. White, RCS.

Expeditions by two U.S. Coast Guard cutters to the Davis Strait, Baffin Bay, and the Labrador Sea have produced three official reports. The 1928 one on the *Marion* Expedition (149), written by Noble G. Ricketts and Parker D. Trask, contains a narrative account of the cruise of the *Marion* into the Davis Strait and Baffin Bay in 1928 to carry out scientific investigations connected with the International Ice Patrol, a report and discussion of the sounding work accomplished, and a description and discussion of the bottom samples obtained at some of the places where wire soundings were made.

An accompanying, comprehensive exposition of Arctic ice and its state, behavior, and distribution to the western North Atlantic (164) is by Edward H. ("Iceberg") Smith, a U.S. Coast Guard officer who was a world-renowned iceberg expert as well as the leader of the *Marion* Expedition, which completed a current and ice survey of the entire waters of Davis Straits from Newfoundland northward to the 70th parallel of latitude during the summer of 1928. An oceanographic report (163), by Edward H. Smith, Floyd M. Soule, and Olav Mosby, is based on the observations of the *Marion* Expedition dispatched in the summer of 1928 to carry out an oceanographic survey of the waters between Greenland and the North American continent, with special reference to a study of ice conditions, amplified by the cruise of the U.S. Coast Guard cutter *General Greene* to the Labrador Sea in 1931 and again in 1933-1935.

The *Report of the Cruise of the U.S. Revenue Cutter* Bear *and the Overland Expedition for the Relief of the Whalers in the Arctic Ocean, from November 27, 1897, to September 13, 1898* (236) contains the official reports, amply illustrated with photographs, of the participating officers of the *Bear* in the Overland Expedition to save the starving crews of eight vessels of the whaling fleet caught by the ice in the vicinity of Point Barrow, Alaska, by driving a herd of reindeer overland for some 1,500 miles. The Naval Historical Foundation's *The Incredible Alaska Overland Rescue* (122) is a much shorter version of the same fantastic exploit.

The role played by the U.S. Revenue Cutter Service, its cutters, and especially Capt. M. A. Healy in the introduction of domestic reindeer into Alaska is told by Sheldon Jackson, general agent of education, in his official report (77). John Muir, a scientist and expert on glaciers, recorded his observations and impressions aborad a U.S. Revenue Cutter Service cutter in 1881 in his *Cruise of the* Corwin (117), as she sailed among the islands of the Bering Sea and the Arctic Ocean and visited the frozen shores of northeastern Siberia and northwestern Alaska in search of the missing steamer, *Jeannette*, under the command of Lt. Cmdr. George W. De Long, USN.

An authentic picture of a typical months-long cruise of a cutter on Bering Sea patrol in the 1930s is presented in Max Miller's firsthand account, *Fog and Men on Bering Sea* (113). Emery Huntoon's *Intercept and Board* (75) is a more contemporary account. The author dramatically—and no doubt freely exercising poetic license—tells the tale of the last Alaskan patrol of the U.S. Coast Guard cutter *Wachusett*. Nevertheless, it is still a typically accurate chronicle of both the day-to-day routine aboard a cruising high-endurance cutter and the procedures of intercepting, boarding, and seizing. And it does give not only a realistic picture of an operational mission but also an inner glimpse into the lives and attitudes of the men performing this mission.

Richard Petrow, a former U.S. Coast Guardsman, gives a firsthand account of the 1965 oceanographic mission of the U.S. Coast Guard icebreaker *Northwind* in his *Across the Top of Russia* (132), as well as an explanation of why this attempt to make the Northeast Passage failed.

AVIATION. The role of the crew of the Kill Devil Hills Lifesaving Station in the Wright brother's first flight is the subject of the article "The U.S. Coast Guard: Midwife at the Birth of the Airplane," by Bernard C. Nalty and Truman R. Strobridge in *Aerospace Historian* (120). Their article "The OL-5 and the Beginning of Coast Guard Aviation," in *Journal of the American Aviation Historical Society* (121), deals with the acquisition and operation of the first aircraft built for the specialized needs of the service. The story of U.S. Coast Guard aviation from the opening of the first air station in 1920, at Morehead City, North Carolina, the exploits of the seaplanes during the 1920s and 1930s, World War II activities, and the arrival of the helicopter is covered by the official monograph *Aviation* (194:XXI).

The official *Story of Coast Guard Aviation* (209) extends the coverage of the developments to 1964. The best overall single source on the origin, early activities, and gradual evolution of aviation within the U.S. Coast Guard to the present is the official *Air Search and Rescue: 63 Years of Aerial Lifesaving* (188).

Surprisingly, substantial historical data is hidden in the official *Record of Movements, Vessels of the United States Coast Guard, 1790–December 31, 1933* (204). It gives a brief history of the service's air arm and its equipment, as well as a definitive list of the airplanes assigned from 1925 to 23 April 1935, their U.S. Coast Guard number, type, date accepted, assignment, and more detailed data, such as manufacturer, cost, speed, cruising radius, gasoline capacity, and consumption, etc.

MEMOIRS, BIOGRAPHIES, AND FIRSTHAND ACCOUNTS. Harold Waters's *Adventure Unlimited: My Twenty Years of Experience in the United States Coast Guard* (242) contains the reminiscences of a man who enlisted in the early 1920s, worked his way up through the ranks to become an officer, and served throughout World War II. In *Patrol Boat 999* (244) and *Smugglers of Spirits* (245), he describes his enlisted days aboard the cutters attempting to prevent the smuggling of liquor, narcotics, and illegal aliens during the Prohibition era and gives an insight into the service of those days, its duties, and its colorful characters. His *Christ over the Seven Seas* (243) is worth reading for its delightful true stories, some based on his own experiences in the service.

Ice Patrol duty in the 1920s is described in Leo Shubow's *Iceberg Dead Ahead!* (161), the recollections of a rabbi who served as a yeoman in the U.S. Coast Guard. Other early 20th-century experiences are recalled in Capt. Carl Rydell's *On Pacific Frontiers: A Story of Life at Sea and in the Outlying Possessions of the United States* (153); George R. Putnam's *Sentinel of the Coasts: The Log of a Lighthouse Engineer* (139); and Lt. Cmdr. M. A. Ranson, USCG (Ret.), and Eloise Katherine Engle's *Sea of the Bear: Journal of a Voyage to Alaska and the Arctic, 1921* (142). The reminiscences of the author's Antarctic experiences, beginning as a dog driver with the Byrd Expedition of 1928–1930 and ending as a U.S. Coast Guard Officer, are contained in Lt Cmdr. Jack Bursey's *Antarctic Night: One Man's Story of 28,224 Hours at the Bottom of the World* (20).

Capt. S. Samuels's *From the Forecastle to the Cabin* (154) is the only 19th-century memoir, although Capt. Benjamin J. Willard's *Captain Ben's Book* (254) does contain a firsthand account of the recapture of the revenue cutter *Caleb Cushing* during the Civil War, and Walter Wyman's *A Cruise on the U.S. Practice Ship* S. P. Chase (263) is an eyewitness account by a doctor of the annual training cruise for cadets in 1881.

John M. Waters, as a combat officer, ship captain, or rescue aircraft commander, participated in the search and rescue operations he describes in *Rescue at Sea* (247). In *Ice is Where You Find It* (178), Capt. Charles W. Thomas, USCG, relates his experiences on the Greenland Patrol during World War II, as well as the Antarctic Expedition of 1946–1947 and the Bering Sea Patrol in 1948.

Sloan Wilson's autobiography, *What Shall We Wear to This Party? The Man in The Gray Flannel Suit Twenty Years Before & After* (262), depicts his World War II service as a U.S. Coast Guard officer. Beginning as an ensign on the cutter *Tampa*, escorting merchant vessels from Nova Scotia to airbases in Greenland, he next becomes the commanding officer of the *Nogak*, an American trawler converted to a cutter, supplying weather and LORAN stations in Greenland, and then of a 180-foot supply ship (FS-158) and a small gasoline tanker (Y-14), sailing back and forth in the southwest Pacific in support of the amphibious forces.

Arthur Pocock's *Red Flannels and Green Ice* (135) also gives a firsthand account of wartime duty on the Greenland Patrol, touching upon humorous incidents from time to time. In *To Sea in Haste* (23), Roland T. Carr recalls his experiences on antisubmarine and convoy duty in the Carribean aboard the USS *Haste*, a former Canadian corvette transferred to the U.S. Navy and manned by U.S. Coast Guardsmen. Lieutenants Mary C. Lyne and Kay Arthur's *Three Years behind the Mast* (104) is unique, although chatty in style, for its numerous firsthand accounts of women in the U.S. Coast Guard Reserves (Women), known as SPARS, during World War II.

As for biographies, only John B. Ehrhardt's *Joseph Francis (1801–1893): Shipbuilder: Father of the U.S. Life-Saving Service* (40); Florence Kern's *Captain William Cooke Pease: U.S. Coast Guard Pioneer* (84); Sumner I. Kimball's *Joshua James: Life-Saver* (96), and James L. Pond's *Joseph Francis* (136) exist. Joseph Henry Hughes's *The Making of a Coast Guard Officer: A Covenant with Honor* (73) is a memorial biography of the author's son, who graduated from the U.S. Coast Guard Academy on 5 June 1963 and died 22 days later from injuries received in an automobile accident. It contains numerous reproductions of the sons's letters while a cadet, indicating his impressions of the academy over the four-year course.

Dennis L. Noble's *Recollections of Vice Admiral Stika* (125) presents an intriguing personal view not only of service on the Bering Sea Patrol, in the U.S. Revenue Cutter Service, but also in the U.S. Coast Guard. Vice Admiral Stika, a graduate of the U.S. Revenue Cutter Service's School of Instruction, served during his long career in a cross-section of the service's traditional duties both ashore and afloat in the Atlantic, Caribbean, Pacific, and Alaska, won a Navy Cross during World War I, battled the rum runners, supervised many improvements in lifesaving ordnance (including the Lyle gun), had charge of a large training center and port security of a major post during World War II, and retired as Commander, Western Area.

Nell Wise Wechter's *The Mighty Midgetts of Chicamacomic* (249) tells the story of the Midgett family of North Carolina, which has had members in the U.S. Coast Guard since the days of the early U.S. Lifesaving Service.

Much biographical data can be located in the various editions of the service's

Register of Officers and Cadets (202) and *Register of Reserve Officers* (203). Brief biographies of the more senior officers are available from the Public Affairs Division (G-PBA), U.S. Coast Guard Headquarters, Washington, D.C. 20593, which also has copies of the oral histories of senior service officers, including commandants.

U.S. COAST GUARD ACADEMY. The need for professionally trained officers to man the revenue cutters eventually led to Congress authorizing a two-year cadet training program in 1876. The nine survivors out of the nineteen youthful applicants—the first class of cadets—reported in May 1877 to the schooner *Dobbins*, which had been fitted out as a schoolship.

For several decades, the School of Instruction remained a two-year apprenticeship, supplemented by tutoring in technical subjects, all conducted primarily at sea. Between 1890 and 1895, it was closed, because of the surplus of naval officers left over from the graduating classes of the U.S. Naval Academy, at Annapolis. Not until 1900 were permanent quarters ashore established at Arundel Cove, near Baltimore, Maryland, and moved in 1910 to Fort Trumbull at New London, Connecticut. With the creation of the U.S. Coast Guard, in 1915, the School of Instruction became transformed overnight into the service's academy.

Several books have been devoted solely to this academy. The standard works are Irving Crump's *Our United States Coast Guard Academy* (34) and Riley Hughes's *Our Coast Guard Academy: A History and Guide* (74). Both are designed to acquaint people, especially cadets and potential cadets, with the U.S. Coast Guard Academy, its mission, history, how it operates, the life of a cadet, and the problems he faces, all interspersed with numerous accounts of the more inspirational exploits of the service.

Two other works (30, 42) tell the story primarily through pictures. The most contemporary coverage is Gene Gurney and Brian Sheehan's *Educational Guide to U.S. Service & Maritime Academies* (59). The only scholarly treatment appears in John P. Lovell's *Neither Athens nor Sparta? The American Service Academies in Transition* (102).

PERIODICALS. Although not solely or even mainly devoted to U.S. Coast Guard history, the U.S. Coast Guard Academy Alumni Association *Bulletin* (218) contains a virtual treasure trove of historical articles, some of excellent quality, followed closely by the defunct *U.S. Coast Guard Magazine* 1927–1957 (219). From time to time, the U.S. Coast Guard *Engineers' Digest* (195), although published, like the *Bulletin*, to stimulate professional thought, also publishes historical articles. Other naval-oriented journals, such as the the U.S. Naval Institute *Proceedings* (137), occasionally have superb articles on the U.S. Coast Guard and its precedessors.

All are useful primary sources for 20th-century activities, trends, controversies, and social insights of the service. The U.S. Coast Guard Academy Library (266) has a card index to the entire run of the *U.S. Coast Guard Magazine* and prepares annual indices for the *Bulletin*, while the *Engineers's Digest* prepares its own annual indices.

PUBLISHED DOCUMENTS. Several published documentary works are mentioned elsewhere in this chapter. Bernard C. Nalty, Dennis L. Noble, and

Truman R. Strobridge's *Wrecks, Rescues & Investigation* (119) contains selected documents tracing the evolution of the U.S. Coast Guard and its predecessors and their missions since establishment in 1790.

Invaluable are the *Annual Reports*. Because of the complexities of the service's organizational heritage, the following ones for the years given are pertinent to avoid any chronological gaps: Department of the Treasury, 1789-1967 (235); U.S. Revenue Marine Service, 1844-1891 (233); U.S. Lighthouse Board, 1852-1909 (224); U.S. Steamboat Inspection Service, 1852-1931 (234); U.S. Lifesaving Service, 1877-1914 (223); Bureau of Navigation, 1884-1931 (185); U.S. Revenue Cutter Service, 1892-1914 (231); Bureau of Lighthouses, 1910-1939 (182); U.S. Coast Guard, 1915- (189); Bureau of Navigation and Steamboat Inspection, 1932-1935 (186); Bureau of Marine Inspection and Navigation, 1936-1942 (184); and Department of Transportation, 1967- (222). The U.S. Navy's *Annual Report* (229) should also be consulted for any war years.

Over the years, congressional committee hearings have regularly dealt with not only testimony from the senior officers and officials of the service and its predecessors concerning appropriations, but also other substantial issues, such as the proposed reorganizations, possible transfers to the U.S. Navy or other governmental agencies, handling of major maritime disasters, changes to roles and missions, etc.

Although a few official Marine Board of Investigation reports (for example, *Marine Casualty Report: SS* Frosta *(Norwegian)*, *M/V* George Prince *Collision in the Mississippi River on 20 October 1976 with Loss of Life* or *Marine Casualty Report: USCGC* Cuyahoga, *M/V* Santa Cruz II *(Argentinean): Collision in Chesapeake Bay on 20 October 1978 with Subsequent Sinking of USCGS* Cuyahoga *with Loss of Life*) find their way in to the Department of Transportation Library (265) or the U.S. Navy Department Library (269), most don't. The best way to obtain a copy of the official findings of a marine disaster is to contact Casualty Review Branch (G-MMI-1 / 14), Marine Investigation Division, U.S. Coast Guard Headquarters, 2100 Second Street, S.W., Washington, D.C. 20593.

For aids to navigation, two other governmental publications are indispensable. The U.S. Lighthouse Establishment's *Compilation of Public Documents and Extracts from Reports and Papers relating to Lighthouses, Lightvessels, and Illuminating Apparatus, and to Beacons, Buoys and Fog Signals, 1789 to 1871* (227) is a comprehensive research tool containing the text, often pages long, of laws, reports, papers, letters, etc. The *Light List* (199), described in more detail elsewhere, gives the location and characteristics of each aid to navigation.

ARCHIVES, LIBRARIES, AND A MUSEUM. The primary and virtually indispensable archival depository for serious research into the history of the service and its predecessors is the National Archives, 8th Street and Pennsylvania Avenue, N.W., Washington, D.C. 20408. Fortunately, Forrest R. Holdcamper's *Preliminary Inventory of the Records of the United States Coast Guard (Record Group 26)* (65) describes the more than 10,000 cubic feet of the service's records hierarchically by creating unit, i.e., U.S. Guard and the Lifesaving, Lighthouse, and Revenue Cutter Services. His *Preliminary Inventory of the Field Records of the Lighthouse Service (Record Group 26)* (64) describes another 430 cubic feet of records not covered in his earlier work.

The Records of the Bureau of Marine Inspection and Navigation (Record Group

41), whose voluminous records date back to 1774, include those of the Bureau of Navigation and the Steamboat Inspection Service. One must remember that they also cover the merchant-vessel documentation function that was not transferred to the U.S. Coast Guard until 4 February 1967.

The Manuscript Division, Room 101, James Madison Memorial Building, Library of Congress, Washington, D.C. 20540 (267), contains a few private collections of former service officers, such as the diary of Capt. William C. Pease (15 January–24 July 1854) and the papers of Capt. Charles F. Shoemaker, 1879–1918. These may be consulted by any person engaged in serious research who presents proper identification (preferably identification bearing the applicant's photograph), completes the Manuscript Division's registration form, and agrees to the library's rules for use of rare materials.

The only other important archival collection is located at the U.S. Coast Guard Academy Library. Besides the personal papers of some twenty officers of the service, most of them of this century, its holdings include a small number of original manuscript documents relating to the establishment of the service and its operation during the 19th century. About two dozen rough logs of vessels on the Bering Sea Patrol are on file. Microfilm of the plans of lighthouses and light stations are part of the archival holdings, as well as films of the letters to and from the Treasury Department and the collectors of customs. A collection of photographs, primarily of cutters, are also on file. Related to the archival function is the library's collection of books and serials on the U.S. Coast Guard, the Lighthouse Service, and the Lifesaving Service.

Permission to use the archival material is granted by the Librarian, U.S. Coast Guard Academy, New London, Connecticut 06320. Prior permission is needed for access to the archival materials.

The only official U.S. Coast Guard Museum (270) is also located at the U.S. Coast Guard Academy, with the librarian doubling as the curator. Plans are afoot to house the collection – already overflowing its alloted space – in a new museum building to mark the 200th birthday of the service in 1990.

The Department of Transportation Library, 400 Seventh Street, S.W., Washington, D.C. 20590, also contains much specialized material pertaining to the Coast Guard. Although this library is open to any citizen with proper identification, a letter of inquiry stating the specific area of research interest is a wise prerequisite to a visit to any government library, both to assure that no clearance is needed and to determine the availability of material and hours of operations.

RESEARCH NEEDED. Despite what has been published, the field of U.S. Coast Guard history remains for all practical purposes an open, fertile field for a serious researcher. Not only is an overall scholarly treatment desperately needed, but the service's predecessors, major leaders, dramatic personalities, multi-faceted activities, combat service in every significant engagement since the quasi-war with France, and peacetime experiences over close to two centuries deserve to be covered. These histories lie buried in the official records and elsewhere, like minefields ready to be detonated by an enterprising scholar not blinded to the service's unique heritage by the overwhelming predominance of her powerful attention-gathering sister services. Perhaps she is the "runt of the litter," as Jack Anderson used to refer to her before an indignant U.S. Coast Guard officer bitterly complained, but still her contributions—certainly without doubt in the realm of humanitarian service—remain worthy of professional historical attention.

Not one single commandant, let alone a host of deserving U.S. Coast Guardsmen of lesser rank, has yet found a biographer. Many worthy cutters, lifesaving stations, lighthouses, and shore installations still need their deeds told. An administrative history would fill a long-neglected and deeply felt void. The service's significant contributions in such fields as exploration, oceanography, navigation, law enforcement, and illumination await thorough documentation. In fact, the U.S. Coast Guard's role and place in United States history has yet to be adequately described.

BIBLIOGRAPHY

1. Adamson, Hans Christian. *Keepers of the Lights*. New York: Greenberg, 1955.
2. Albion, Robert Greenhalgh. *Naval & Maritime History: An Annotated Bibliography*. Mystic, Conn.: The Marine Historical Association, 1972.
3. American Enterprise Institute. *A Conversation with Admiral John B. Hayes: Cost Effectiveness in the Coast Guard*. Washington, D.C.: American Enterprise Institute for Public Policy Research, 26 January 1981.
4. Baarslag, Karl. *Coast Guard to the Rescue*. New York: Farrar & Rinehart, 1937.
5. Bachelder, Peter D. *Lighthouses of Casco Bay*. Portland, Maine: Breakwater Press, 1975.
6. Barnett, J. P. *The Lifesaving Guns of David Lyle*. South Bend, Ind.: South Bend Replicas, printed by Town and Country Press, Plymouth, Ind. 1976.
7. Beck, James B. *Our Wonderland of Bureaucracy: A Study of the Growth of Bureaucracy in the Federal Government, and its Destructive Effect upon the Constitution*. New York: Macmillan, 1932.
8. Bell, Kensil. *"Always Ready!": The Story of the United States Coast Guard*. New York: Dodd, Mead, 1943.
9. Bennett, Cmdr. Robert F., USCG. *The Lifesaving Service at Sandy Hook Station, 1854-1915*. Washington, D.C.: Public Affairs Division, U.S. Coast Guard, 1976.
10. _____. *Surfboats, Rockets, and Carronades*. Washington, D.C.: GPO, 1976.
11. Bergaust, Erik, and William O. Foss. *Coast Guard in Action*. New York: Putnam's, 1962.
12. Berry, Erick. *You Have To Go Out!: The Story of the U.S. Coast Guard*. New York: David McKay Company, 1964.
13. Bixby, William. *Track of the Bear*. New York: David McKay Company, 1965.
14. Bloomfield, Howard V. L. *The Compact History of the United States Coast Guard*. New York: Hawthorn Books, 1966.
15. Boucher, Jack E. *Atlantic City's Historic Absecon Lighthouse*. Somers Point, N.J.: The Atlantic County Historical Society, 1964.
16. Bragaw, Louis K. *Managing a Federal Agency: The Hidden Stimulus*.

Baltimore, Md.: John Hopkins University Press, 1980.

17. *Brief Sketch of the Naval History of the United States Coast Guard with Citations of Various Statutes defining its Military Status from 1790 to 1922.* Washington, D.C.: Press of Byron S. Adams, n.d.

18. Brown, Riley. *The Story of the Coast Guard: Men, Wind, and Sea.* Garden City, N.Y.: Blue Ribbon Books, 1943.

19. Burroughs, Polly. *The Great Ice Ship Bear: Eighty-Nine Years in Polar Seas.* New York: Van Nostrand, 1970.

20. Bursey, Lt. Comdr. Jack, USCGR. *Antarctic Night: One Man's Story of 28,224 Hours at the Bottom of the World.* New York: Rand McNally 1957.

21. Cantwell, 1st Lt. J. C., RCS. *Report of the Operations of the U.S. Revenue Steamer* Nunivak *on the Yukon River Station, Alaska, 1899–1901.* Washington: GPO, 1902.

22. Capron, Capt. Walter C., USCG (Ret.). *The U.S. Coast Guard.* New York: Franklin Watts, 1965.

23. Carr, Roland T. *To Sea in Haste.* Washington, D.C.: Acropolis Books, 1975.

24. Carse, Robert. *Keepers of the Lights: A History of American Lighthouses.* New York: Charles Scribner's Sons, 1968.

25. _____. *Rum Row.* New York: Rinehart & Company, 1959.

26. Chaffee, Allen. *Heroes of the Shoals.* New York: Henry Bolt and Company, 1935.

27. Chapelle, Howard I. *The History of American Sailing Ships.* New York: Bonanza Books, 1935.

28. Charles, Roland W. *Troopships of World War II.* Washington, D.C.: The Army Transportation Association, 1947.

29. Cipra, David L. *Lighthouses & Lightships of the Northern Gulf of Mexico.* Washington, D.C.: Department of Transportation, 1976.

30. Colby, C. B. *Coast Guard Academy: Cadets, Training and Equipment.* New York: Coward-McCann, 1965.

31. _____. *Danger Fighters: Men and Ships of the U.S. Coast Guard.* New York: Coward-McCann, 1953.

32. Collins, Francis A. *Sentinels along our Coast.* New York: Century, 1922.

33. Conway, John S. *The United States Lighthouse Service, 1923.* Washington, D.C.: GPO, 1923.

34. Crump, Irving. *Our United States Coast Guard Academy.* New York: Dodd, Mead, 1961.

35. Dalton, J. W. *The Life Savers of Cape Cod.* Boston: The Barta Press, Printers, 1902.

36. David, Evan J. *Our Coast Guard: High Adventure with the Watchers of our Shores.* New York: Appleton-Century, 1937.

37. De Gast, Robert. *The Lighthouses of the Chesapeake.* Baltimore, Md.: John Hopkins University Press, 1973.

38. Dobbins, David Porter. *The Dobbins Life-Boat Illustrated.* Buffalo, N.Y.: Art-Printing Works of Matthews, Northrop & Co., Office of the "Buffalo Morning Express," 1886.

39. Ebasco Services Incorporated. *Study of United States Coast Guard.* New York: Ebasco Services Incorporated, January 1948.

40. Ehrhardt, John B. *Joseph Francis (1801–1893): Shipbuilder: Father of the*

U.S. Life-Saving Service. Princeton, N.J.: Princeton University Press, 1950.

41. Eldridge, F. R. *"They Have To Go Out": An Historical Sketch of the U.S. Coast Guard*. Washington, D.C.: GPO, 1947–53.

42. Engeman, Jack. *The Coast Guard Academy: The Life of a Cadet*. New York: Lothrop, Lee & Shepard, 1957.

43. Evans, Capt. Stephen H. USCG. *The United States Coast Guard, 1790–1915: A Definitive History (With a Postscript: 1915–1949)*. Annapolis, Md.: U.S. Naval Institute Press, 1949.

44. Fenton, Chief Gunner's Mate John H. USCGR(T). *The Battle of Boston Harbor: A Wartime History of Flotilla 1-412, Winthrop, Massachusetts*. N.p.: Privately printed by John H. Fenton, 1946.

45. _____. Floherty, John J. *Search and Rescue at Sea*. New York: J. B. Lippincott, 1953.

46. _____. *Sentries of the Sea*. New York: J. B. Lippincott, 1938.

47. _____. *Sons of the Hurricane*. New York: J. B. Lippincott, 1938.

48. *White Terror: Adventures with the Ice Patrol*. New York: J. B. Lippincott, 1947.

49. Forbes, R. B. *Life-Boats, Projectiles, and Other Means for Saving Life*. Boston: Wm. Parsons Lunt, 1872.

50. *Francis' Metallic Life-Boat Company*. New York: William C. Bryant & Co., Printers, 1852.

51. Fraser, Chelsea. *Heroes of the Sea*. New York: Thomas Y. Crowell, 1924.

52. Furer, Rear Adm. Julius Augustus, USN (Ret.). *Administration of the Navy Department in World War II*. Washington, D.C.: GPO, 1959.

53. Gibbs, James A., Jr. *Sentinels of the North Pacific: The Story of Pacific Coast Lighthouses and Lightships*. Portland, Oregon: Binfords & Mort, Publishers, 1955.

54. _____. *Tillamook Light*. Portland, Oreg.: Binfords & Mort, 1953.

55. _____. *West Coast Lighthouses: A Pictorial History of the Guiding Lights of the Sea*. Seattle, Wash.: Superior Publishing Company, 1974.

56. Glunt, Ruth R. *Lighthouses and Legends of the Hudson*. Monroe, N.Y.: Library Research Associates, 1975.

57. Greene, Maj. Robert E., USA. *Black Defenders of America: A Pictorial History*. Chicago: Johnson Publishing Company, 1971.

58. Gummere, Lt John F., USCGR(T). *The History of the Philadelphia Regiment: Volunteer Port Security Force*. Philadelphia, Penn.: Press of International Printing Company, 1946.

59. Gurney, Gene, and Brian Sheehan. *Educational Guide to U.S. Service & Maritime Academies*. New York: Von Nostrand, 1978.

60. Gurney, Gene. *United States Coast Guard: A Pictorial History*. New York: Crown, 1973.

61. Healy, Capt. M. A., USRM. *Report of the Cruise of the Revenue Marine Steamer Corwin in the Arctic Ocean in the Year 1884*. Washington, D.C.: GPO, 1889.

62. _____. *Report of the Cruise of the Revenue Marine Steamer* Corwin *in the Arctic Ocean in the Year 1885*. Washington, D.C.: GPO, 1887.

63. Hill, Weldon. *Onionhead*. New York: David McKay Company, 1957.

64. Holdcamper, Forrest *Preliminary Inventory of the Field Records of the*

Lighthouse Service (Record Group 26). Washington, D.C.: Office of Civil Archives, The National Archives, June 1964.

65. _____. *Preliminary Inventory of the Records of the United States Coast Guard (Record Group 26)*. Washington, D.C.: Office of Civil Archives, The National Archives, September 1963.

66. Holland, Francis Ross, Jr. *America's Lighthouses: Their Illustrated History since 1716*. Brattleboro, Vt.: The Stephan Greene Press, 1972.

67. _____. *A History of the Bodie Island Light Station*. Washington, Division of History, National Park Service, U.S. Department of the Interior, 1 February 1967.

68. _____. *A History of the Cape Hatteras Light Station, Cape Hatteras National Seashore, N. Car.* Washington, D.C.: Office of Archeology and Historic Preservation, Division of History, National Park Service, U.S. Department of the Interior, 30 September 1968.

69. _____. *The Old Point Loma Lighthouse, San Diego*. San Diego, Calif.: Cabrillo Historical Association, 1978.

70. Hooper, Capt. C. L., USRM. *Report of the Cruise of the U.S. Revenue-Steamer* Corwin *in the Arctic Ocean*. Washington, D.C.: GPO, 1883.

71. _____. *Report of the Cruise of the U.S. Revenue-Steamer* Thomas Corwin, *in the Arctic Ocean, 1881*. Washington, D.C.: G.P.O., 1884.

72. Howe, M. A. de Wolfe. *The Humane Society of the Commonwealth of Massachusetts: An Historical Review, 1785–1916*. Boston: Riverside Press, 1918.

73. Hughes, Joseph Henry, Jr. *The Making of a Coast Guard Officer: A Covenant with Honor*. New York: Philosophical Library, 1966.

74. Hughes, Riley. *Our Coast Guard Academy: A History and Guide*. New York: Devin-Adair, 1944.

75. Huntoon, Emery. *Intercept and Board*. Portland, Oreg.: Binford & Mort, 1975.

76. Ingraham, Reg. *First Fleet: The Story of the U.S. Coast Guard at War*. New York: Bobbs-Merrill, 1944.

77. Jackson, Sheldon. *Twelfth Annual Report on Introduction of Domestic Reindeer into Alaska with Map and Illustrations*. Washington, D.C.: GPO, 1889.

78. Johnson, Arnold Burges. *The Modern Lighthouse Service*. Washington, D.C.: GPO, 1903.

79. Johnson, Rear Adm. Harvey. USCG. *The United States Coast Guard— Some Adventures*. Princeton, N.J.: Princeton University Press, 1941.

80. Jonas, Carl. *Beachhead on the Wind*. Boston: Little, Brown, 1945.

81. Kaplan, H. R. *Coast Guard in Vietnam*. Washington, D.C.: Public Information Division, U.S. Coast Guard, 1967.

82. Kaplan, H. R., and Lt. Cmdr. Adrian L. Lonsdale, USCG. *Voyager Beware*. New York: Rand McNally, 1966.

83. Kaplan, H. R., and Lt. Cmdr. James F. Hunt, USCG. *This Is the Coast Guard*. Cambridge, Md.: Cornell Maritime Press, 1972.

84. Kern, Florence. *Captain William Cooke Pease: U.S. Coast Guard Pioneer*. Bethesda, Md.: Alised Enterprises, 1982.

85. _____. *Hopley Yeaton's U.S. Revenue Cutter* Scammel. Washington, D.C.: Alised Enterprises, 1975.

86. _____. *James Montgomery's U.S. Revenue Cutter* General Greene, *1791–1797*. Washington, D.C.: Alised Enterprises, 1977.
87. _____. *John Foster William's U.S. Revenue Cutter* Massachusetts, *1791–1792*. Washington, D.C.: Alised Enterprises, 1976.
88. _____. *John Howell's U.S. Revenue Cutter* Eagle, *1793–1799*. Washington, D.C.: Alised Enterprises, 1978.
89. _____. *Jonathan Maltbie's U.S. Revenue Cutter* Argus. Washington, D.C.: Alised Enterprises, 1976.
90. _____. *Richard Taylor's U.S. Revenue Cutter* Virginia. Washington, D.C.: Alised Enterprises, 1977.
91. _____. *Robert Cochran's U.S. Revenue Cutter* South Carolina, *1793–1798*. Washington, D.C.: Alised Enterprises, 1978.
92. _____. *Simon Gross's U.S. Revenue Cutter* Active, *1791–1798*. Washington, D.C.: Alised Enterprises, 1977.
93. _____. *The United States Revenue Cutter* Vigilant. Washington, D.C.: Alised Enterprises, 1976.
94. _____. *William Cooke's U.S. Revenue Cutter* Diligence, *1792–1794*. Washington, D.C.: Alised Enterprises, 1979.
95. Kerr, Ens. Evor Samuel, Jr., USCG. *The United States Coast Guard: Its Ships, Duties, Stations*. New York: Robert W. Kelly, 1935.
96. Kimball, Sumner I. *Joshua James: Life-Saver*. Boston: American Unitarian Association, 1909.
97. _____. *Organization and Methods of the United States Lifesaving Service*. Washington, D.C.: G.P.O., 1899.
98. King, Irving H. *George Washington's Coast Guard: Origins of the U.S. Revenue Cutter Service, 1789–1801*. Annapolis, Md.: U.S. Naval Institute Press, 1979.
99. Law, Rev. William Hainstock. *"The Life Savers in the Great Lakes": Incidents and Experiences among the Life Savers in Lake Huron and Lake Superior (known as District II)*. Detroit, Mich.: Winn & Hammond, 1902.
100. Lee, Henry. *How Dry We Were: Prohibition Revisited*. Englewood Cliffs, N.J.: Prentice-Hall, 1963.
101. Lombard, Asa Cobb Paine. *East of Cape Cod*. New Bedford, Mass.: Reynolds-De Walt Printing, 1976.
102. Lovell, John P. *Neither Athens nor Sparta?: The American Service Academies in Transition*. Bloomington: Indiana University Press, 1979.
103. Lyle, David Alexander. *Report on Life-Saving Ordnance and Appurtenances*. Washington, D.C.: GPO, 1878.
104. Lyne, Lt. Mary C., and Kay Arthur, USCGR(W). *Three Years behind the Mast: The Story of The United States Coast Guard SPARS*. N.p.: no publisher, n.d.
105. MacGregor, Morris J., Jr. *Integration of the Armed Forces, 1940–1965*. Washington, D.C.: GPO, 1981.
106. McGowan, Capt. Gordon. *The Skipper and the Eagle*. New York: Van Nostrand, 1960.
107. Manning, Gordon P. *Life in the Colchester Reef Lighthouse*. Shelburne, Vt.: The Shelburne Museum, 1958.
108. Mason, Lt. Theodorus B. M., USN. *The Preservation of Life at Sea: A Paper Read before the American Geographical Society, February 27, 1879*.

New York: The American Geographical Society, 1879.

109. Mayo, Robert. *A Synopsis of the Commercial and Revenue System of the United States, as Developed by Instructions and Decisions of the Treasury Department for the Administration of the Revenue Laws: Accompanied with a Supplement of Historical and Tabular Illustrations of the Origin, Organization, and Practical Operations of the Treasury Department and Its various Bureaus in Fulfillment of that System; in Eight Chapters, with an Appendix.* Washington, D.C.: J. & G. S. Gideon, 1847

110. _____. *The Treasury Department and Its various Fiscal Bureaus, their Origin, Organization, and Practical Operations, Illustrated; being a Supplement to the Synopsis of Treasury Instructions for the Administration of the Revenue Laws Affecting the Commercial and Revenue System of the United States; in Fourteen Chapters.* Washington, D.C.: Wm. Q. Force, 1847.

111. Mellor, William B., Jr. *Sank Same.* New York: Howell, Soskin, 1944.

112. Mercey, Cmdr. Arch A., USCGR, and Chief Specialist Lee Grove, USCGR, eds. *Sea, Surf and Hell: The U.S. Coast Guard in World War II.* Englewood Cliffs, N.J.: Prentice-Hall, 1945.

113. Miller, Max. *Fog and Men on Bering Sea.* New York: Dutton, 1936.

114. Morrison, John H. *History of American Steam Navigation.* New York: Stephen Daye Press, 1958.

115. Morison, Samuel E. *History of United States Naval Operations in World War II.* 15 vols. Boston: Little, Brown, 1947–1962.

116. Moscow, Alvin. *Collision Course: The* Andrea Doria *and the* Stockholm. New York: Putnam's, 1959.

117. Muir, John. *The Cruise of the* Corwin: *Journal of the Arctic Expedition of 1881 in Search of De Long and the* Jeannette. New York: Houghton Mifflin, 1917.

118. Nalty, Bernard C., Dennis L. Noble, and Truman R. Strobridge. *Wrecks, Rescues & Investigations: Selected Documents of the U.S. Coast Guard and its Predecessors.* Wilmington, Del.: Scholarly Resources, 1978.

119. Nalty, Bernard C., and Morris J. MacGregor. *Blacks in the United States Armed Forces: Basic Documents* Vol. 10. Wilmington, Del.: Scholarly Resources, 1977.

120. Nalty, Bernard C., and Truman R. Strobridge. "The U.S. Coast Guard: Midwife at the Birth of the Airplane." *Aerospace Historian* 22 (Fall 1975): 139–42.

121. Nalty, Bernard C., and Truman R. Strobridge. "The OL-5 and the Beginnings of Coast Guard Aviation." *Journal of the American Aviation Historical Society* 21 (Fall 1974): 200–203.

122. Naval Historical Foundation. *The Incredible Alaska Overland Rescue.* Washington, D.C.: Naval Historical Foundation, 1 January 1968.

123. Nelson, Stewart B. *Oceanographic Ships Fore and Aft.* Washington, D.C.: Office of the Oceanographer of the Navy, 1971.

124. Noble, Chief Marine Science Technician Dennis L., USCG. *Recollections of Vice Admiral J. E. Stika, U.S. Coast Guard, Retired, On the Revenue Cutter Service and Bering Sea Patrol.* Washington, D.C.: Public Affairs Division, U.S. Coast Guard, 1975.

125. Noble, Dennis L., and T. Michael O'Brien. *Sentinels of the Rocks: From*

"Graveyard Coast" to National Lakeshore. Marquette: Northern Michigan University Press, 1979.
126. Noble, Chief Marine Science Technician Dennis L., USCG. *United States Livesaving Service Annotated Bibliography*. Washington, D.C.: Public Affairs Division, U.S. Coast Guard, 1975.
127. Norton, William L. *Eagle Ventures*. New York: M. Evans, 1970.
128. O'Brien, T. Michael. *Guardians of the Eighth Sea: A History of the U.S. Coast Guard on the Great Lakes*. Cleveland, Ohio: Ninth Coast Guard District, 1967.
129. O'Connor, William D. *Heroes of the Storm*. Boston: Houghton Mifflin, 1904.
130. Office of Statewide Cultural Programs, Alaska. *Aids to Navigation in Alaskan History*. Anchorage, Alaska: Office of Statewide Cultural Programs, Alaska Division of Parks, Department of Natural Resources, 1974.
131. Perry, Glen. *Watchmen of the Sea*. New York: Charles Scribner's Sons, 1938.
132. Petrow, Richard. *Across the Top of Russia*. New York: David McKay Company, 1967.
133. Philadelphia Board of Trade. *Report of a Special Committee of the Philadelphia Board of Trade in relation to the Life-Saving Stations upon the Coast*. Philadelphia, Pa.: King & Baird, Printers, 1860.
134. Pine, Vice Adm. James, USCG. *The Sea and its Lore*. Princeton, N.J.: Princeton University Press, 1947.
135. Pocock, Arthur. *Red Flannels and Green Ice*. New York: Random House, 1949.
136. Pond, James L. *History of Lifesaving Appliances, and Military and Naval Constructions, Invented and Manufactured by Joseph Francis, With Sketches and Incidents of his Business Life in the United States and Europe*. New York: E. D. Slater, 1885.
137. *Proceedings of the United States Naval Institute*, 1874–.
138. Putnam, George R. *Lighthouses and Lightships of the United States*. Boston: Houghton Mifflin, 1917.
139. _____. *Sentinel of the Coasts: The Log of a Lighthouse Engineer*. New York: W. W. Norton, 1937.
140. Randell, Capt. Jack, as told to Meigs O. Frost. *I'm Alone*. Indianapolis, Ind.: Bobbs-Merrill, 1930.
141. Rankin, Robert H., and H. R. Kaplan. *Immortal Bear: The Stoutest Polar Ship*. New York: Putnam's, 1970.
142. Ranson, Lt. Comdr. M. A. USCG (Ret.), and Eloise Katherine Engle. *Sea of the Bear: Journal of a Voyage to Alaska and the Arctic, 1921*. Annapolis, Md.: U.S. Naval Institute Press, 1964.
143. Rapaport, Stella F. *The Bear: Ship of Many Lives*. New York: Dodd, Mead, 1962.
144. Ratigan, William. *Great Lakes Shipwrecks & Survivals*. Grand Rapids, Mich.: Wm. B. Eerdmans, 1960.
145. Rattray, Jeannette Edwards. *Perils of the Port of New York*. New York: Dodd, Mead, 1973.
146. _____. *Ship Ashore!: A Record of Maritime Disasters off Montauk and Eastern Long Island, 1640–1955*. New York: Coward-McCann, 1955.

147. Rawlings, Charles. *We Saw the Battle of the Atlantic: Diana, of Periscope Lane, Torpedo Junction, Hatteras Way*. New York: Pickwick Ltd., 1942.
148. Reynolds, George Richard. *The United States Coast Guard in the Northwest, 1854–1900*. M.A. thesis, University of Washington, 1968.
149. Ricketts, Noble G., and Parker D. Trask. *The "Marion" Expedition to Davis Strait and Baffin Bay under Direction of the United States Coast Guard, 1928, Scientific Results, Part 1: The Bathymetry and Sediments of Davis Strait*. Washington, D.C.: GPO, 1932.
150. Riesenberg, Felix, Jr. *Sea War: The Story of the U.S. Merchant Marine in World War II*. New York: Rinehart & Company, 1956.
151. Roscoe, Theodore. *United States Destroyer Operations in World War II*. Annapolis, Md.: U.S. Naval Institute Press, 1953.
152. Ruksenas, Algis. *Day of Shame: The Truth about the Murderous Happenings aboard the Cutter* Vigilant *during the Russian-American Confrontation off Martha's Vineyard*. New York: David McKay Company, 1973.
153. Rydell, Capt. Carl. *On Pacific Frontiers: A Story of Life at Sea and in the Outlying Possessions of the United States*. Chicago: World, 1924.
154. Samuels, Captain S. *From the Forecastle to the Cabin*. New York: Harper & Brothers, 1887.
155. Schenia, Robert L. *U.S. Coast Guard Cutters & Craft of World War II*. Annapolis, Md.: U.S. Naval Institute Press, 1982.
156. Shanks, Ralph C., Jr., and Janette Thompson Shanks. *Lighthouses and Lifeboats on the Redwood Coast*. San Anselmo, Calif.: Costano Books, 1978.
157. _____. *Lighthouses of San Francisco Bay*. San Anselmo, Calif.: Costano Books, 1976.
158. Shepard, Birse. *Lore of the Wreckers*. Boston: Beacon Press, 1961.
159. Short, Lloyd M. *The Bureau of Navigation: Its History, Activities and Organization*. Baltimore, Md.: John Hopkins University Press, 1923.
160. _____. *Steamboat-Inspection Service: Its History, Activities and Organization*. New York: Appleton-Century, 1922.
161. Shubow, Leo. *Iceberg Dead Ahead!* Boston: Bruce Humphries, 1959.
162. Smith, Darrell Hevenor, and Fred Wilbur Powell. *The Coast Guard: Its History, Activities and Organization*. Washington, D.C.: Brookings Institution, 1929.
163. Smith, Edward H., Floyd M. Soule, and Olav Mosby. *The* Marion *and* General Greene *Expeditions to Davis Strait and Labrador Sea under Direction of the United States Coast Guard 1928-1931-1933-1934, 1935, Scientific Results, Part 2: Physical Oceanography*. Washington, D.C.: GPO, 1937.
164. Smith, Edward H. *The Marion Expedition to Davis Strait and Baffin Bay under Direction of the United States Coast Guard 1928, Scientific Results, Part 3: Arctic Ice, with Especial Reference to its Distribution to the North Atlantic Ocean*. Washington, D.C.: GPO, 1931.
165. Smith Capt. Cmdt. Horatio Davis, USRCS. *Early History of the United States Revenue Marine Service (or United States Revenue Cutter Service), 1789–1849*. Edited by Rear Adm. Elliot Snow, USN. (Ret.). Washington, D.C.: Naval Historical Foundation, 1932.

166. Snow, Edward Rowe. *Famous Lighthouses of America*. New York: Dodd, Mead, 1955.
167. _____. *Famous New England Lighthouses*. Boston: The Yankee Publishing Company, 1945.
168. _____. *Great Gales and Dire Disasters*. New York: Dodd, Mead, 1952.
169. _____. *The Story of Minot's Light*. Boston: The Yankee Publishing Company, 1940.
170. Spectre, Peter H. *Auxiliary Patrols*. Annapolis, Md.: U.S. Naval Institute Press, 1970.
171. Sterling, Robert Thayer. *Lighthouses of the Maine Coast and the Men Who Keep Them*. Brattleboro, Vt.: Stephen Daye Press, 1935.
172. Stick, David. *Graveyard of the Atlantic: Shipwrecks of the North Carolina Coast*. Chapel Hill: University of North Carolina Press, 1952.
173. _____. *The Outer Banks of North Carolina, 1584–1958*. Chapel Hill: University of North Carolina Press, 1958.
174. Strobridge, Truman R. *Chronology of Aids to Navigation and the Old Lighthouse Service, 1716–1939*. Washington, D.C.: Public Affairs Division, U.S. Coast Guard, 1974.
175. _____. *The United States Coast Guard and the Civil War: The U.S. Revenue Marine, Its Cutters, and Semper Paratus*. Washington: Public Affairs Division, U.S. Coast Guard, 1972.
176. _____. *United States Coast Guard Annotated Bibliography, 1972*. Washington, D.C.: GPO, 1972.
177. Talbot, Frederick A. *Lightships and Lighthouses*. London: William Heinemann, 1913.
178. Thomas, Capt. Charles W., USCG. *Ice Is Where You Find It*. New York: Bobbs-Merrill, 1951.
179. Thompson, Lt. Lawrence, USNR, *The Navy Hunts the CGR 3070*. New York: Doubleday, 1944.
180. Townsend, Linda, and Dupree Davenport. *The History of Blacks in the Coast Guard from 1790*. Washington, D.C.: Public Affairs Division, U.S. Coast Guard, 1977.
181. Tulich, Lt. Eugene N., USCG. *The United States Coast Guard in South East Asia During the Vietnam Conflict*. Washington, D.C.: Public Affairs Division, U.S. Coast Guard, 1975.
182. US Bureau of Lighthouses. *Annual Report*. Washington, D.C.: GPO, 1910–1939.
183. _____. *Light List*. Washington, D.C.: GPO, 1910–1939.
184. U.S. Bureau of Marine Inspection and Navigation. *Annual Report*. Washington, D.C.: GPO, 1936–1942.
185. U.S. Bureau of Navigation. *Annual Report*. Washington, D.C.: GPO, 1884–1931.
186. U.S. Bureau of Navigation and Steamboat Inspection. *Annual Report*. Washington, D.C.: GPO, 1932–1935.
187. U.S. Coast Guard. *The Accomplishments of Ten Coast Guard Cutters Transferred to the United Kingdom*. Washington, D.C.: Research and Statistics Section, Operations Division, U.S. Coast Guard, 1941.
188. _____. *Air Search and Rescue: 63 Years of Aerial Lifesaving; A Pictorial History, 1915–1978*. Washington, D.C.: Public Affairs Division, U.S.

Coast Guard, 1978.

189. _____. *Annual Report*. Washington, D.C.: GPO, 1915–.

190. _____. *Bering Sea Patrol*. Washington, D.C.: Research and Statistics Section, Operations Division, U.S. Coast Guard, 1942.

191. _____. *Captains of the Ports*. Washington, D.C.: Statistical Division, U.S. Coast Guard, 1943.

192. _____. *Coast Guard History*. Washington, D.C.: GPO, 1958.

193. _____. *Coast Guard History*. Washington, D.C.: GPO, 1982.

194. U.S. Coast Guard. *The Coast Guard at War*. 30 monogrpahs. Washington, D.C.: Statistical Division and Historical Section, Public Information Division, U.S. Coast Guard, 30 June 1944–1 January 1954.

I   *Introduction*, 30 June 1944

II   *Greenland Patrol*, 15 July 1945.

III   *Alaska*, 15 February 1946.

IV   LORAN. 2 vol. Volume 1, 1 May 1946; volume 2, 1 August 1946.

V   *Transports and Escorts*. 2 vols. Volume 1, 1 March 1949; volume 2, 1 May 1949.

VI   *The Pacific Landings*, 15 March 1946.

VII   *Weather Patrol*, 1 June 1949.

VIII   *Lost Cutters*, 1 July 1947.

IX   *North African Landings*, 1 July 1946.

X   *Sicily-Italy Landings*, 1 July 1946.

XI   *Landings in France*, 1 September 1946.

XII   *Intelligence*, 1 January 1949.

XIII   *Marine Inspection*. 2 vols. Volume 1, 31 July 1944; volume 2, 1 April 1951.

XIV   *Assistance*. 2 vols. Volume 1, 30 October 1944; volume 2, 1 January 1947.

XV   *Aids to Navigation*, 1 July 1949.

XVI   *Communications*. 2 vols. Volume 1, 1 August 1947; volume 2, 1 August 1947.

XVII   *Beach Patrol*, 15 May 1945.

XVIII *Port Security*, 1 September 1949.

XIX   *Auxiliary*, 1 May 1948.

XX   *Temporary Reserve*, 1 January 1948.

XXI   *Aviation*, 15 December 1945.

XXII   *Women's Reserve*, 15 April 1946.

XXIII *Public Relations*, 1 January 1950.

XXIV *Finance*, 1 January 1954.

XXV   *Personnel*, 1 May 1950.

XXVI *Medical*, 1 December 1950.

XXVII *Legal*, 1 September 1951.

XXVIII *Naval Engineering*, 1 September 1951.

XXIX *Civil Engineering*, 1 November 1951.

XXX   *Communications Engineering*. 1 June 1948.

195. _____. *The Engineer's Digest*. April 1933–.

196. _____. *Deeds of Valor from the Annals of the United States Coast Guard*. Washington, D.C.: GPO, 1943.

197. _____. *Historically Famous Lighthouses*. Washington, D.C.: GPO, 1957.
198. _____. *International Ice patrol*. Washington, D.C.: GPO, 1956.
199. _____. *Light List*. Washington, D.C.: GPO, 1940–.
200. _____. *Operations of the Coast Guard in Time of War*. Washington, D.C.: U.S. Coast Guard, 1940.
201. _____. *Participation in International Affairs*. Washington, D.C.: U.S. Coast Guard, 1974.
202. _____. *Register of Officers and Cadets*. Washington, D.C.: GPO, 1915–.
203. _____. *Register of Reserve Officers*. Washington, D.C.: GPO, 1950–
204. _____. *Records of Movements, Vessels of the United States Coast Guard, 1790–December 31, 1933*. 2 vols. Washington, D.C.: U.S. Coast Guard, (1935).
205. _____. *Roles and Misions Study Report*. Washington, D.C.: Department of Transportation, March 1982.
206. _____. *Ships, Planes and Stations: United States Coast Guard*. Washington, D.C.: U.S. Coast Guard, 1979.
207. _____. *Sinking of the Hamilton*. Washington, D.C.: Research and Statistical Section, U.S. Coast Guard, 1942.
208. _____. *Some Unusual Incidents in Coast Guard History*. Washington, D.C.: Historical Section, Public Information Division, U.S. Coast Guard, 1950.
209. _____. *The Story of Coast Guard Aviation*. Washington, D.C.: GPO, 1964.
210. _____. *Summary of Merchant Marine Personnel Casualties, World War II*. Washington, D.C.: GPO, 1950.
211. _____. *United States Coast Guard Annotated Bibliography*. Washington, D.C.: GPO, 1982.
212. _____. *United States Coast Guard Bibliography*. Washington, D.C.: GPO, 1950.
213. _____. *United States Coast Guard Book of Valor: A Fact Book on Medals and Decorations*. Washington, D.C.: Public Relations Division, U.S. Coast Guard, 25 May 1945.
214. _____. *United States Coast Guard Combat and Overseas Operations*. Washington, D.C.: Public Relations Division, U.S. Coast Guard, May 1945.
215. _____. *The U.S. Coast Guard: Its Missions and Objectives*. Washington, D.C.: GPO, 1977.
216. _____. *U.S. Coast Guard Roll of Honor, April 6, 1917–November 30, 1918*. Washington, D.C.: GPO, 1919.
217. _____. *Weathermen of the Sea: Ocean Station Vessels*. Washington, D.C.: GPO, 1957.
218. U.S. Coast Guard Academy Alumni Association. *Bulletin*. January–March 1917, March 1939–.
219. *U.S. Coast Guard Magazine*. November 1927–June 1957.
220. U.S. Congress. Senate. *Reports of Agents, Officers, and Persons, Acting under the Authority of the Secretary of the Treasury, in Relation to the Condition of Seal Life on the Rookeries of the Pribilof Islands, and to Pelagic Sealing in Bering Sea and the North Pacific Ocean, in the Years 1893–1895*. Washington, D.C.: GPO, 1896.

221. _____. Committee on Commerce, Science, and Transportation. *The U.S. Coast Guard.* 97th Cong. 2d Sess. Washington, D.C.: GPO, 1 March 1982.
222. U.S. Department of Transportation. *Annual Report.* Washington, D.C.: GPO, 1967–.
223. U.S. Lifesaving Service. *Annual Report.* Washington, GPO, 1877–1914.
224. U.S. Lighthouse Board. *Annual Report.* Washington, D.C.: GPO, 1852–1909.
225. _____. *Laws of the United States relating to the Establishment, Support, and Management of the Lighthouses, Lightvessels, Monuments, Beacons, Spindles, Buoys, and Public Piers of the United States, from August 7, 1789, to March 3, 1855.* Washington, D.C.: A.O.P. Nicholson, Public Printer, 1855.
226. _____. U.S. Lighthouse Board. *Laws relating to the Acquisition of Title to Land required for Lighthouse Purposes, Cession of Jurisdiction, and Protection of Buoys, Beacons, Etc.* Washington, D.C.: GPO, 1975.
227. U.S. Lighthouse Establishment. *Compilation of Public Documents and Extracts from Reports and Papers relating to Lighthouses, Lightvessels, and Illuminating Apparatus, and to Beacons, Buoys and Fog Signals, 1789 to 1871.* Washington, D.C.: GPO, 1871.
228. U.S. Naval History Division. *Dictionary of American Naval Fighting Ships.* Several Volumes. Washington, D.C.: GPO, 1958–.
229. U.S. Navy Department. *Annual Report.* Washington, D.C.: GPO, 1798–.
230. _____. *Official Records of the Union and Confederate Navies in the War of the Rebellion.* Washington, D.C.: GPO, 1894–1922. Series 1: 27 vols. Series 2: 3 vols.
231. U.S. Revenue Cutter Service. *Annual Report.* Washington, D.C.: GPO, 1892–1914.
232. _____. *The United States Revenue Cutter Service in the War With Spain, 1898.* Washington, D.C.: GPO, 1899.
233. U.S. Revenue Marine Service. *Annual Report.* Washington, D.C.: GPO, 1844–1891.
234. U.S. Steamboat Inspection Service. *Annual Report.* Washington, D.C.: GPO, 1852–1931.
235. U.S. Treasury Department. *Annual Report.* Washington, D.C.: GPO, 1789–1967.
236. _____. *Report of the Cruise of the U.S. Revenue Cutter* Bear *and the Overland Expedition for the Relief of the Whalers in the Arctic Ocean, from November 27, 1897, to September 13, 1899.* Washington, D.C.: GPO, 1899.
237. _____. *Study of Roles and Missions of the U.S. Coast Guard: Report to the Secretary, U.S. Treasury Department.* 7 vols. Washington, D.C.: U.S. Treasury Department, June 1962.
238. U.S. War Department. *The War of the Rebellion: A Compilation of the Official Records of the Union and Confederate Armies.* Washington, D.C.: GPO, 1880–1901. 128 vols.
239. Vent, Myron H. *South Manitou Island: From Pioneer Settlement to Park.* Springfield, Va.: The Goodway Press, 1972.
240. Villiers, Alan. *Sailing Eagle: The Story of the Coast Guard's Square-Rigger.* New York: Charles Scribner's Sons, 1955.

241. Walton, William. *Scratch One Hearse*. New York: Time Inc., (1944).
242. Waters, Harold. *Adventure Unlimited: My Twenty Years of Experience in the United States Coast Guard*. Englewood Cliffs, N.J.: Prentice-Hall, 1955.
243. _____. *Christ over the Seven Seas*. Wilkes-Barre, Pa.: Dimension Books, 1967.
244. Waters, Harold, and Aubrey Wisberg. *Patrol Boat 999*. New York: Chilton, 1959.
245. Waters, Harold. *Smugglers of Spirits: Prohibition and the Coast Guard Patrol*. New York: Hastings House, 1971.
246. Waters, Capt. John M., Jr., USCG. *Bloody Winter*. New York: Van Nostrand, 1967.
247. _____. *Rescue at Sea*. New York: Van Nostrand, 1966.
248. Wead, Frank. *Gales, Ice, and Men: A Biography of the Steam Barkentine Bear*. New York: Dodd, Mead 1937.
249. Wechter, Nell Wise. *The Mighty Midgetts of Chicamacomic*. Manto, N.C.: Times Printing Co., 1974.
250. Weiss, George. *The Lighthouse Service: Its History, Activities and Organization*. Baltimore, Md.: John Hopkins University Press, 1926.
251. White, Leonard D. *The Republican Era: 1869–1901*. New York: Macmillan, 1958.
252. Whiting, John D. *Storm Fighters: True Stories of the Coast Guard*. Indianapolis, Ind.: Bobbs-Merrill, 1927.
253. Whitney, Dudley. *The Lighthouse*. Boston: New York Graphic Society, 1975.
254. Willard, Capt. Benjamin J. *Captain Ben's Book: A Record of the Things which Happened to Capt. Benjamin J. Willard, Pilot and Stevedore, during some Sixty Years on Sea and Land, as Related by Himself*. Portland, Maine: Lakeside Press, Engravers, Printers, and Binders, 1895.
255. Willoughby, Lt. (j.g.) Malcolm F., USCGR(T). *The Coast Guard's TRs: First Naval District*. Boston: Charles E. Lauriat Company, 1945.
256. Willoughby, Cmdr. Malcolm F., USCGR(T). *Lighthouses of New England*. Boston: T. O. Metcalf, 1929.
257. _____. *Rum War at Sea*. Washington, D.C.: GPO, 1964.
258. _____. *The U.S. Coast Guard in World War II*. Annapolis, Md.: U.S. Naval Institute, 1957.
259. Willoughby, W. F. *The Reorganization of the Administrative Branch of the National Government*. Baltimore, Md.: John Hopkins University Press, 1923.
260. Wilson, Sloan. *Ice Brothers*. New York: Arbor House, 1979.
261. _____. *Voyage To Somewhere*. New York: A. A. Wyn, 1946.
262. _____. *What Shall We Wear to This Party? The Man in the Gray Flannel Suit Twenty Years Before & After*. New York: Arbor House, 1976.
263. Wyman, Walter. *A Cruise on the U.S. Practice Ship S. P. Chase; being the first Impressions of a Surgeon at Sea, and Experiences on a Sailing Vessel of the Revenue Cutter Service on a Voyage to Spain and the Azores Islands*. New York: Grafton Press, 1910.

ARCHIVES, LIBRARIES, AND A MUSEUM.

264. Library of Congress, Washington, D.C . 20540.
265. Library, Department of Transportation, Room 2200, 400 Seventh St., S.W., Washington, D.C. 20590.
266. Library, U.S. Coast Guard Academy, New London, Connecticut 06320.
267. Manuscript Division, Room 1010, James Madison Memorial Building Library of Congress, Washington, D.C. 20540.
268. National Archives and Records Service, General Service Administration, Washington, D.C. 20408.
269. Navy Department Library, Building 44, Washington Navy Yard, Washington, D.C. 20374.
270. U.S. Coast Guard Museum, U.S. Coast Guard Academy, New London, Connecticut 06320.

XXIII

THE UNITED STATES ARMY CORPS OF ENGINEERS

Dale E. Floyd

The Continental Army first commissioned engineer officers in 1775 and organized a Corps of Engineers in 1779. Following the American Revolution, the new government drastically reduced the army and disbanded the engineers, but in 1794, Congress, threatened by the possibility of a new war, created a Corps of Artillerists and Engineers (69, 369). In 1802, a new statute split the artillery and engineers and formed a new Corps of Engineers that has served the army and the country since then.

GENERAL HISTORIES. At the present time, no good general history of the Corps of Engineers exists. A short and unscholarly 1953 Engineer School textbook is the only work that approaches general history (352). The Public Affairs Office, Corps of Engineers, has released a very brief but useful history (346). Various authors and agencies, including Abbot (1), Burr (47), Casey (55), Craighill (75), Crump (76), Dupree (97), Gordon (127), Heap (150), Itschner (172), Jewett (175), Starr (309), Sturgis (318), the Corps of Engineers (340, 344), the Engineer School (351), the Engineer Museum (358), and the Treasury Department (364), have published works that contain bits and pieces of corps general history. The American Public Works Association published in 1976 a general history of public works (17), while an engineer officer, William Black, had compiled a guide and register to them in 1895 (35).

GENERAL HISTORICAL BIBLIOGRAPHIES. The Engineer Historical Division has recently published a general historical bibliography of the Corps of Engineers (85). No other similar bibliographies exist, but the "Science and Technology in the Nineteenth Century" and "Science and Technology in the Twentieth Century" sections in the original *Guide to Sources of American Military History* and the first supplement do include many pertinent citations. Hoy and Robinson have compiled an excellent bibliography on public works (166), and the Engineer School published a list of its publications through 1910 (353). Other useful bibliographies pertaining to specific subjects are cited elsewhere in this essay.

ORGANIZATION. Due to its many military and civil works operations throughout the United States, the Corps of Engineers has established numerous field offices. To manage all of these activities, the Corps of Engineers established divisions, comprising a number of districts. For example, the North Atlantic Division, with its offices in New York City, administers the operations of the Baltimore, Capital Area, New York, Norfolk, and Philadelphia districts and reports to the Office of the Chief of Engineers in Washington, D.C. Additional commands manage overseas activities. Laboratories, such as the Waterways Experiment Station in Vicksburg, Mississippi, and the Cold Regions Research and Engineering Laboratory in Hanover, New Hampshire, perform research and development to support the various Corps of Engineers activities. Many of these offices have published histories of their activities, listed at the end of this bibliography (414–466).

BIOGRAPHICAL WORKS. Sound biographical works dealing with army engineer officers are few. Joseph G. Swift's *Memoirs* (323), the limited multi-volume publication of Sylvanus Thayer's correspondence (329), and the recent studies of Stephen Long (255, 407), Hiram Chittenden (87), Dennis Hart Mahan (131), and William Ludlow (215), however, are exceptions. George W. Goethals (33), Sylvanus Thayer (185), William L. Sibert (60), Andrew A. Humphreys (170), John Sanders (243), John W. Gunnison (245), George H. Bergy (311), George W. Whistler (368), William McRee (231), Alden Partridge (383), and other engineer officers are the subjects of mediocre biographies. Historians have written biographies, some excellent and others not, of engineer officers who gained notoriety by commanding armies in the Civil War, including P.G.T. Beauregard (396), Robert E. Lee (119), George B. McClellan (247), Henry W. Halleck (15), George G. Meade (62, 230), Gouverneur K. Warren (112, 328), Isaac I. Stevens (284, 310), John C. Fremont (251), William S. Rosecrans (195), and James B. McPherson (392). Engineer officers who gained renown in other ways, such as Henry M. Robert (305) and Alexander Macomb (283), have also received biographical treatment. Weigley wrote an exemplary biography of Montgomery C. Meigs (384), an engineer officer who became quartermaster general of the army.

Articles and pamphlets chronicle the careers of army engineers Joseph G. Totten (22), U. S. Grant III (293), William H. Chase (84), Amiel Weeks Whipple (314), William Ludlow (213), George Washington Cullum (78), George W. Whistler (11), Richard L. Hoxie (41), Charles Gratiot (174), Decius Wadsworth (271), and Simon M. Levy (292). The Engineer Historical Division has published the transcripts of oral history interviews with former engineer general officers Frederick J. Clarke (61) and William E. Potter (264).

Biographical works dealing with noncommissioned officers and enlisted men are practically nonexistent. Eugene McAndrew's short article on Sgt. Maj. Frederick Gerber (214) is one of the few. Biographical works pertaining to engineer commissioned and noncommissioned officers and enlisted men who served in specific wars are cited elsewhere in this essay.

Civilian Corps employees have also received scant biographical attention. Some civilians who accompanied engineer exploration parties have merited biographies (394). Bernard R. Green, an important civilian employee, is the subject of a biographical article (334).

EDUCATION. With the creation of the Corps of Engineers in 1802, Congress established its headquarters at West Point, New York, and charged it with the administration of a new U.S. Army Military Academy. McDonald has discussed the relationship between the engineers and the Military Academy (221), and Denton's dissertation adequately covers the founding of the school (82). Since its establishment, the U.S. Military Academy has taught both military and civil engineering to the cadets. Couper (71) and Griess (131) have written biographies of two of the engineering professors. The Corps of Engineers ran the academy, the first engineer school in the country, until 1866, when Congress transferred control to the army at large. Ambrose (14), Fleming (113), and Forman (116) have published general histories of the U.S. Military Academy.

In 1865, the army engineers established a post at Fort Totten, Willet's Point, New York Harbor, where, during the next year, they created an institution that evolved into the Engineer School of Application. Abbot (2, 4) and Alperstein (13) discuss the Fort Totten years. In 1901, the engineers moved to Washington Barracks in Washington, D.C., the present site of Fort McNair. During and immediately after World War I, the corps transferred the school and other facilities to Camp Humphreys, now Fort Belvoir, Virginia, where they still reside. Dorst (89) and LeMon (204) have written articles on the history of Fort Belvoir, and Dunne (96) discussed the Engineer School.

MILITARY. The Corps of Engineers is a major command in the U.S. Army, and its earliest tasks were military in nature. Davis and Jones have edited a collection of previously published articles dealing mostly with the engineers' military mission (80). A former West Point engineering professor's manual outlines the various army engineers' military duties (237). These duties, over the years, fall into four main categories – combat engineering, coast defense, construction, and research and development.

COMBAT ENGINEERING. In combat, the engineers' main responsibilities are to facilitate their army's and allies' movements and retard those of the enemy. Burgess (46) and Casey (54) have discussed the engineers' role in combat, and Elliott (101), Ellison (103), Haseman (144), Ladd (193), Lourie (211), Schull (300), Stanley (308), and Stratton and Hathway (315) have written about specific aspects. But at times, like any other soldier, engineers must serve as infantry, as Dziuban had explained (98).

Combat engineering in America's wars has changed and evolved over the years. In the American Revolution, engineers placed and removed obstacles, erected field fortifications, and experimented with underwater mines and submarines. Walker edited a documentary publication on army engineers in the war (378), and Heavey (151) and Ollivier (258) published short histories. Guthorn discussed engineer mapping in the American Revolution (135), Harte addressed river obstructions (142), Johnston described underwater operations (181), and Palmer wrote about the fortifications at West Point (260). Haskett (145) and Walker (377) have chronicled the engineer operations in the battle of Yorktown, and Hume discussed the engineers' association with the Society of the Cincinnati (169). Stephen Rochefontaine (49), Louis Le Begue du Portail (50), Richard Gridley (102), Robert Erskine (157), and David Bushnell (371) are the subjects of biographical works. Jeduthan Baldwin (20), Joseph Plumb Martin (226), and John Trumbull (337) wrote autobiographies.

In addition to the engineer duties in the Revolutionary War already outlined engineer officers in the War of 1812 constructed and directed the defense of frontier forts as detailed by Douglass (91), Everest (106), and Wood (493). Howell Tatum's Journal addresses various War of 1812 engineer duties (327). Cullum's (77) and Walkers's (373) publications provide a more general treatment of the engineers in the war.

Army engineers did not play a great part in the 19th-century Indian and other conflicts in the West. Engineer officers did, however, perform reconnaissances, prepare maps, and, in a few instances, accompany military expeditions, as Ludlow's journal (213) indicates. Seville's narrative (302) recounts one of a few instances, the Utah Expedition, when engineer troops served in frontier campaigns.

The Mexican War engineers mainly performed mapping, reconnaissance, and intelligence work. P.G.T. Beauregard (30), Henry W. Benham (32), George B. McClellan (218), Gustavus W. Smith (306), and Theodore Talbot (325) have provided firsthand accounts of Mexican War engineer operations. Robinson (288), Swan et al. (322), and Willing (398) have published general accounts of the engineers in this war, and Spencer discussed a failure—rubber pontoons (307).

Union engineers, both regular army and volunteer, laid hundreds of pontoon bridges and constructed extensive field fortifications in the Civil War. Participants Barnard (24) and Thompson (331) have chronicled engineer operations in the Peninsular Campaign and of the Regular Army Battalion, respectively. Owen's letters and diary provide insight into the life of a Civil War engineer (259). Lord (210) and McDonough and Bond (222) discuss the use of pontoons; Muntz (246), Nettesheim (250), and Rhoads (282) have addressed the mapping, reconnaissance, and intelligence operations; and Coggins (64) and Thienel (330) have provided general treatments of the Union engineers. The Confederate engineers' major task was the construction of permanent and temporary fortifications, which Bright (42) and Guinn (133) have detailed. McDonald edited the journal of Jedediah Hotchkiss (165), a cartographer, and Nichols has written a sound history of Confederate engineers (253).

The tropical areas where the American troops fought during the Spanish-American War and the Philippine insurrection demanded numerous engineer reconnaissances, the clearing and construction of roads and railroads, and the building of wharves and docks to aid the landing of troops and supplies. Caples (53), Chibas (57), Rees (273), and Van Ornum and Bellinger (365) have discussed these operations. John Clifford Brown (43) and David DuBose Gaillard (348) are the few subjects of biographical works. "The Engineer in the Moro Campaign" (105) and Drennon's article (93) recount engineer counterinsurgency operations. Leach (200) and Wooten (409) have written histories of the engineer battalions that served in these conflicts.

The Mexican Punitive Expedition, 1916–17, required good roads for the passage of the army's new motor-driven vehicles, as Graves (129) and O'Connor (257) note.

In World War I, the army's engineers, among other duties, constructed railroads, camps, and field fortifications, and provided camouflage. Graves has discussed war construction in general (128), Felton railroad operations (107), and Kirby map reproduction in France (189). St. Gaudens (295) and Tracy (336) have chronicled camouflage work, and Collins (66), Parsons (261), and Tomlin (335) the various engineer troop operations. Autobiographical works by engineer officers Charles G. Dawes (81), a future vice president of the United States, and Carroll J. Swan (321) are available, and Miller has provided a biography of Edward E.

Hartwick (236). The Engineer School published a brief record of the service of Regular Army Corps officers (355), Schley wrote one of the few general accounts of engineer work in the war (296), and the AEF chief engineer provided a highly useful report of operations (339).

World War II engineer troops performed a greater number of tasks than ever before. In the beginning, coast defense (67, 186, 290, 297) and other construction (111) and camouflage activities (65, 111) in the United States consumed a great amount of their energy. Later, engineers were involved in amphibian (152, 393), beach (103), bridging (281), road building (18, 196, 219, 268), and runway construction (300, 315) operations overseas.

The biography of Leif Sverdrup (117), and the journal of an enlisted man, Henry Giles (124), illustrate the varied engineer duties. The multivolume *Engineers of the Southwest Pacific* minutely chronicles the engineer operations in one theater (361). Dod discussed the engineer's war against Japan (86), and the ETO Chief Engineer described operations in Europe (347). Bowman addressed war construction (38, 39), and Bass outlined the work at engineer depots (28). A Manhattan Project engineer recounted the development of the atomic bomb (132), and Timothy (333) and Zarish (413) discussed bridging operations. Janice Giles wrote a detailed unit history (125), Walker provided an account of the war work of the Great Lakes Division (372) and Reybold generally detailed engineer operations during the war (279, 280).

The post-World War II conflicts in Korea, Vietnam, and elsewhere have demanded more and more sophisticated engineer construction, reconnaissance, and mapping skills. For Korean War operations, see Martin (227), Strong (316), and Westover (391). The Center of Military History, Department of the Army, has published *Base Development in South Vietnam, 1965-1970* (95) and *U.S. Army Engineers, 1965-1970* (263) in its Vietnam Studies series, and other authors have discussed engineer operations in the Vietnam conflict (6, 146, 187, 395). The Engineer School publication, *The Army Engineer in Vietnam*, provides useful information that is hard to find elsewhere (350). Cameron talks of engineer operations in the Dominican Republic, 1965 (52), and Hayes generally recounts the army engineers' role in the cold war (148).

COAST DEFENSE. Until 1948, when the Corps of Engineers completed the last coastal and harbor fortifications, it had the primary responsibility for coast defense. Before the missile age, the United States, surrounded by water on three sides, considered adequate coast and harbor defense a primary deterrent to enemy invasion. Starting in the American Revolution, the army engineers erected numerous seacoast fortifications to prevent enemy vessels from attacking the country's major ports and naval installations and landing troops. These fortifications varied from crude temporary batteries to sophisticated masonry and concrete structures. At various times, boards of officers and civilians met to discuss and determine the architecture, location, and number of these fortifications (238, 269, 272, 349). Kirchner (190), Lewis (207), and Robinson (286) have provided general histories of United States coastal fortifications, Floyd has compiled a historical bibliography of United States coast defense (114), and Dibble has outlined the use of slaves to build forts (83). Arthur (19), Wade (369–370), Wesley (389), and others (99) have discussed early seacoast fortifications. Hinds addressed the effectiveness of Civil War coastal forts (160), Browning studied 19th-century coastal defense policy (44), and Kirchner and Lewis (191) briefly outlined 20th-century defenses. In 1851, Totten wrote a highly useful state-of-the-art report on coastal defense (275). Allen (12), Lee (202), Robinson (287), Roe (291); Wade (370), Winslow (401), and Young (411) discussed seacoast fortification construction, and Barnes (25), Hanft (141), Kingman (188), Lattimore (198), Lessem and Mackenzie (206), and Weinert and Arthur (385) have provided histories of specific forts.

Besides planning and overseeing the construction of these structures, army engineers built wharves and railroads at the sites to aid the movement of weapons, ammunition, troops, and supplies. They also erected fire-control towers, mining casemates, power plants, and other ancillary structures and facilities at the forts and camouflaged coast defense sites (186, 290). In addition, the Corps of Engineers, between 1866 and 1901, experimented with and developed submarine mines (3, 4), and placed them in American ports and harbors during the Spanish-American War.

MILITARY CONSTRUCTION. Prior to World War II, the engineers performed various army construction missions varying from fortifications to bridges (234), road (72, 234, 249, 262), and railroads. Then, just before the United Sates entry into World War II, the War Department, in two different actions, transferred army installation and airfield construction and maintenance responsibilities to the Corps of Engineers (29, 111). Today, it plans, builds, and maintains thousands of structures and facilities at army and air force installations in the United States and around the globe (225). Other defense construction (134), such as missile silos (387), are also its responsibility. At times, army engineers plan and construct military facilities for other countries under foreign assistance programs (326, 400), such as the two Israeli airfields they recently completed in accordance with the Camp David agreement. Tulley wrote a brief overview of the military construction program (338).

RESEARCH AND DEVELOPMENT. The Corps of Engineers has continually sought new and better equipment and weapons (65). Various engineer officers, therefore, have visited foreign countries, particularly in the 19th century, to gather information and observe wartime operations (109, 115, 229). Over the years, army engineers have developed and invented materiel, including submarine and land mines (3, 5), temporary bridging equipment (281), and searchlights (138, 171, 192). During part of the 20th century an Engineer Board on equipment determined materiel requirements (224). Today, various engineer laboratories, with the assistance of other army commands and contractors, accomplish research and development for the corps. With the rapid development of science and technology in this century, Corps of Engineers' research and development has been an important adjunct to the combat engineering mission.

ENGINEER TROOPS. Although engineer troops served in the American Revolution and War of 1812, the War Department did not create a regular army engineer unit until the Mexican War. This first company, with four new ones established during the Civil War, formed a battalion. Eventually the army created mutiple battalions, then regiments, and higher commands for service in subsequent wars. Dornbusch's bibliography lists histories of these various units (88). The Engineer School published a history of engineer troops (412) and listed their various stations over the years (354). Warner (800) discussed the first battalion of engineers, Drake-Wilkes explained the troops' history and traditions (92), and Buzzaird (48), Harts (143), Laframboise (194), McCarthy (217), and Vogel (367) detailed the evolution of engineer insignia. Lenney wrote a blistering attack of the closed ranks for engineer soliders (205).

CIVIL WORKS. In 1816, a board of army and navy officers began considering the requirements of adequate defense of the United States. During its deliberations, which spanned many years, the board decided that the country's defense depended on a navy, a regular army and militia, fortifications, and interior communications by land and water (179, 238). The army engineers' unique skills and experience, in a country devoid of engineer schools except for the Military Academy, made them the likely candidates to provide adequate interior communications by land and water.

Army engineers had conducted some river and harbor surveys and done some civil works construction before, but congressional legislation in 1824 (177) and numerous subsequent acts officially assigned such tasks to them. Before the Civil War, engineers had planned and overseen the construction of roads, railroads, and canals; surveyed many rivers and harbors and removed snags from them; erected jetties; and studied sedimentation problems at the mouths of waterways (197, 244). Hill's *Roads, Rails, and Waterways* (159) and articles by Kanarek (183) and Nichols (254) discuss this work.

Following the Civil War, the improvement of rivers and harbors became a major Corps of Engineers' mission. The Progressive Era saw an even greater expansion of these functions, as Hays describes in *Conservation and the Gospel of Efficiency* (149). In the 20th century, Congress has passed a great number of acts giving the army engineers more and more civil works responsibilities. The corps' role in civil works has diversified and now includes, besides navigation improvement and development, flood control, hydropower development, coastal engineering, and water supply and natural resources management.

Black (34) and Lee (201) have attempted to explain the role of the army engineer in civil works and its relation to the military mission. Wall has discussed civil works program modernization (379), Findley has addressed project planning (110), and Frazier has recounted the development of one invention resulting from civil works (118). The Engineer School Library compiled a bibliography of civil work in 1951 (356). Holt (163) and Morgan (241) wrote narrative histories of the corps' civil works activities, but the former is somewhat outdated and the latter is a controversial, uncomplimentary account. Today, the Corps of Engineers' civil works program includes the following responsibilities—navigation development and maintenance, flood control, hydropower, water supply, coastal engineering, and natural resources management.

NAVIGATION DEVELOPMENT AND MAINTENANCE. To insure the use of the nation's waterways for the transportation of various types of raw materials, products, and military supplies and troops in an emergency (137), army engineers have dredged rivers, streams, and harbors throughout the country. A never-ending task, dredging removes from the waterways sediment that would otherwise obstruct the passage of vessels, and widens and deepens them to statutory depths (16, 343). The Corps of Engineers has also erected dams (58, 59, 122, 235), locks, and levees, and constructed canals to maintain the flow of water for transportation.

Holmes (161–162), Lippincott (208), and Maass (223) have written histories of United States and Corps of Engineers' water resources programs. Ferejohn (108) and Pross (267) have discussed the history of river and harbor legislation, Sewell (303) and Stewart (312) have addressed waterway development, the Hulls have outlined policy development (168), and Reuss and Walker have recounted the story of water projects finance (278). Gribble (130) and Itschner (173) discussed the Corps of Engineers' water management mission, and Robins explained its river and harbor functions (285). The chief of engineers has published a collection of laws pertaining to the civil works program (359), and the Corps of Engineers periodically releases the multivolume *Water Resources Development by the U.S. Army Corps of Engineers* (345). A history of the Corps of Engineers' Board of Engineers for Rivers and Harbors is the subject of a recent study by Waugh and Hourigan (381) while Walker has outlined the corps' canal-building efforts (374). *The Military Engineer* carried a bibliography on the "Regulation and Stabilization of Rivers" in 1929 (274), and the National Waterways Roundtable published conference papers on the history and evolution of U.S. waterways and ports (248). The Propeller Club released a study on river and harbor improvement initiation, authorization, and completion (266), and Hook penned a curious study on the preservation of harbor cultural resources (164). Many writers, including Corthell (70), Drumm (94), Elliott (101), Galloway (123), Lane and Williams (197), Lowrey (212), Moore (240), Mosby (244), and the Engineer School Library (357), have addressed corps work on the Mississippi River. Blust (36) and Borger (37) chose the Great Lakes, and Johnson discussed improvement and development on the Tennessee and Cumberland rivers (176).

FLOOD CONTROL. Floods have continually caused millions of dollars' of damage and vast loss of life (167, 319). Due to their earlier navigation improvement and development responsibilities and congressional authorization, the army engineers have constantly restricted rivers and streams to decrease damage from flooding. Following the passage of congressional acts in 1917 and 1936, they built flood-control dams, reservoirs, levees, and floodwalls – structural solutions – to minimize flood damage. These methods, however, displaced people and even communities, causing undue hardships (7, 27, 182, 216, 242, 390). Today, the Corps of Engineers considers nonstructural flood control remedies, such as zoning and floodplain easements in uninhabited areas (156). This permits the use of the land for recreation activities when dry and provides more cost-effective protection of life and property during floods. Cass (56) and Reuss (276) have written valuable articles on the history of flood control in the Missouri and Mississippi river basins, respectively. Hellman published a bibliography on flood control in 1928 (154).

HYDROPOWER DEVELOPMENT. To help meet the energy need of the country and provide electricity at reasonable prices, the Corps of Engineers has constructed numerous hydroelectric power plants on rivers such as the Niagara, Tennessee, and Columbia. Other government agencies have taken over the operation of most of these plants after completion. Roby (289) and Walker (376) have discussed Corps of Engineers' activities in the construction of hydroelectric power plants.

COASTAL ENGINEERING. Sand and beach erosion cause the loss of hundreds of acres of real estate every year. The Corps of Engineers has attempted to retard this erosion by the erection of jetties and other water barriers. It has also constructed breakwalls and jetties to protect coastal communities from the ravages of hurricanes and tidal waves. Hedeman has discussed the corps' role in coastal engineering (153), the Moores have addressed beach-erosion control (239), and Haferkorn has compiled a bibliography on breakwaters (136). Histories of the Corps of Engineers' Committee on Tidal Hydraulics (209) and the Beach Erosion Board (522) are also available.

WATER SUPPLY MANAGEMENT. The Corps of Engineers has, through its waterway improvement and flood control work, created numerous reservoirs. When possible, it allows municipal and commercial use of water in these reservoirs and rivers and streams. Recent legislation has also made the corps responsible for minimizing the pollution of American rivers and streams. Alberts recounted the army engineers' water supply operations in New Mexico (8).

NATURAL RESOURCES MANAGEMENT. Starting with its early explorations of the West, the army engineers have been concerned with the natural resources of the country. In the latter half of the 19th century, they explored and maintained government land and parks (21, 184). With the expansion of its civil works mission, the Corps of Engineers became the administrator of larger and larger amounts of real estate, which included wildlife (399), mineral resources, historical and archaeological sites, and recreation areas (366) such as floodplain parks and reservoir marinas. New statutes have also given the army engineers various environmental regulatory functions (74, 156, 265, 313, 386, 404). The Corps of Engineers employs numerous naturalists, archaeologists, anthropologists, and recreation specialists to develop and maintain these lands for the benefit and enjoyment of all.

CRITICISM. Over the years, many individuals and organizations have criticized the role of the Corps of Engineers, a military institution, in civil works. Some have advocated the creation of a new government engineering agency to perform these functions, and the debate on this subject continues today. Articles by Hammond (140) and Wisner (402) discuss the history of this sentiment.

Groups and individuals have also attacked the engineers for failing to consider environmental and ecological factors in planning civil works projects. Douglas (90), Heuvelmans (158), Mazmanian and Nineaber (228), Morgan (241), and Nienaber (256) are only a few of the many who wrote critical books and articles. Some of this criticism was valid, and the Corps took steps to remedy the situation. It created an Environmental Advisory Board (277), in 1970, to study such problems and advise the chief of engineers. This board and other measures have forced the Corps of Engineers to confront its problems and have made it a more environmentally aware agency. Today, the corps has hundreds of employees who monitor and administer environmental policy.

OTHER MISSIONS AND DUTIES. The Corps of Engineers performs other missions which are not specifically military or civil works functions. These duties include disaster and emergency relief, construction for other agencies and governments, exploration and mapping, and nuclear research.

DISASTER AND EMERGENCY RELIEF. Since the 1880s, the Army Corps of Engineers has performed disaster and emergency relief operations in response to floods, hurricanes, earthquakes, volcanic eruptions, fires, and other calamities. Boyle (40), Burgess (45), and Cooling (68) have provided general accounts of this mission. These operations involve attempts to minimize the destruction and subsequent clean-up. In such infamous disasters as the Johnstown flood (178), the San Francisco earthquake, and the Baltimore fire, the army engineers helped to reduce the loss of life and property and hastened recovery. Walker wrote a concise history of the corps' more recent disaster and emergency relief operations in response to tropical storm Agnes in 1972 (375).

CONSTRUCTION FOR OTHER AGENCIES AND GOVERNMENTS. The country has often assigned special construction projects to army engineers. In the first half of the 19th century, engineer officers planned and oversaw the erection of numerous lighthouses (10, 23, 155), marine hospitals (405, 406), and customs houses (203). They also directed the construction of many buildings and facilities in the nation's capital, such as the Capitol dome; the Washington Monument (382); the State, War and Navy Building (now the Old Executive Office Building) (362); the Library of Congress; and the Washington Aqueduct (342). From 1867 to 1925, the Corps of Engineers administered the Office of Public Buildings in Washington, D.C. Cowdrey's *A City for the Nation* (73) recounts the various army engineer construction projects in the District of Columbia. Recently, the army engineers have constructed buildings, launch pads, and other facilities for NASA (63), and post offices (270).

In some instances, certain engineer officers have overseen construction projects that the Corps of Engineers did not specifically administer. Perhaps the best-known example is George Washington Goethals' supervision of the Panama Canal construction (220).

Army engineers have also erected buildings and built roads and other facilities in foreign countries. Following World War II, the Corps of Engineers performed a lot of this construction as part of the war-recovery program. At present, the corps does some of this work on a contract basis with such countries as Saudi Arabia.

EXPLORATION AND MAPPING. The Army engineers explored, surveyed, and mapped newly acquired territories in the 19th century (26, 120, 255, 304, 320, 408), which Goetzmann's *Army Exploration in the American West* (126), Schubert's *Vanguard of Expansion* (299), and articles by Stunkel (317) and Symons (324) recount. The engineers also conducted boundary surveys between the United States and Canada, and the United States and Mexico. Early exploration and survey of transcontinental railroad routes was another duty (9). These activities resulted in maps (101, 139, 193, 397) and reports (104, 252, 363) that settlers among others, used to guide them into the new territories. During wars, combat engineers have explored occupied areas and provided maps of use to the populace long after the departure of troops. In recent years, the corps has assisted in the exploration of space and the mapping of the moon and other heavenly bodies (63, 147). The Engineer Topographic Laboratories (425, 426) direct much of the Corps' mapping operations today.

NUCLEAR RESEARCH. The Corps of Engineers constructed the facilities for the development of the atomic bomb, and an engineer officer, Leslie Groves, directed the project (132). Since then, army engineers, along with other agencies and organizations, have experimented with atomic fission to discover other uses for nuclear energy. For instance, the engineers conducted experiments with nuclear excavation to aid large construction projects (448). Also, at Camp Century, in Greenland, the army engineers conducted polar regions research in "a city under the ice" which sported nuclear reactors to furnish heat and electricity (79).

THE CORPS OF TOPOGRAPHICAL ENGINEERS. During the American Revolution and War of 1812, topographical engineers performed reconnaissance, surveying, and mapping work for the army. Following the latter war, the government decided to retain some of them in the service. In 1818, the War Department established a Topographical Bureau, under the chief of engineers' command, and, in 1838, a separate Corps of Topographical Engineers. These "topogs" were mainly surveyors, explorers, and cartographers. In the period before the Civil War, they accomplished most of the engineer civil works and explorations and also surveyed sites for military fortifications. During the Mexican War, they reconnoitered enemy positions and drew maps which aided the army's movements. The exigencies of the Civil War necessitated their incorporation into the Corps of Engineers, but today's army engineers still perform the topogs' former duties. Beers (31) and Ryan (294) have written histories of the Topographical Engineers, and Friis (121), Goetzmann (126), and Schubert (299) described some of their operations. Schubert's article discusses the topogs many reports and maps (298).

MISCELLANEOUS. Charles Merdinger (232) published a number of interesting articles in *The Military Engineer* on the history of civil engineering and its use by the military that the Society of Military Engineers collected and released in book form. Calhoun's *The American Civil Engineer* (51), Layton's *The Revolt of the Engineers* (199), and Merritt's *Engineering in American Society, 1850–1875* (233) recount the history of the engineering profession, including military engineering and civil works. Scott's *A Dictionary of Civil Engineering* is a valuable reference work for basic terms (301).

JOURNALS AND PERIODICALS. The earliest periodical published for military engineers was *Professional Memoirs, Corps of Engineers, U.S. Army*, which appeared between 1909 and 1920. With the founding of the Society of American Military Engineers, that organization began the publication of *The Military Engineer*, in 1920, which replaced *Professional Memoirs*. The Engineer School has published *The Engineer* since 1971. These are the only periodicals that often include articles relating to military engineering subjects, and all of them have also published some on civil works.

Between 1969 and 1983, the Corps of Engineers' Water Resources Support Center at Fort Belvoir issued *Water Spectrum*, which included numerous historical civil-works articles. In recent years, with the great interest in ecology and the enviornment, many new journals have begun publication and include articles relating to Corps of Engineers' activities. *Water Resources Bulletin, Journal of Soil and Water Conservation, Environmental Review, Ecology Law Review, Forest History, World Dredging and Marine Construction, Shore and Beach, Waterways*

Journal, *Ecology Law Quarterly*, *Conservation News*, and *Coastal Zone Management Journal* are only some of these new journals. The American Society of Civil Engineers has recently begun publication of a number of journals that deal with such subjects as construction, hydraulics, and waterways and harbors, and contain many pertinent articles.

The American Society of Civil Engineers long-running publications, *The Proceedings* and *The Transactions*, have included numerous articles on both military and civil works topics. *The Scientific American*, *Civil Engineering*, and *Engineering News-Record* have also carried relevant military and civil works articles. The American Public Works Association *Reporter* publishes pertinent articles on various aspects of the Corps of Engineers' activities.

UNPUBLISHED SOURCES. The Records of the Office of the Chief of Engineers, Record Group 77, are among the holdings of the National Archives and Records Service (180). Pre-World War I headquarters records of the Corps of Engineers, including those of the Corps of Topographical Engineers, are in the National Archives Building, in Washington, D.C. The Modern Military Field Branch, at the Washington National Records Center, in Suitland, Maryland, has custody of the accessioned headquarters records from World War I on. The National Archives' Special Archives Division has many Corps of Engineers' maps, plans, drawings, photographs, and films.

Generally, the National Archives and Records Service regional archives house the records of the nearby districts, divisions, and laboratories. Thus, the Seattle, Walla Walla, Alaska, and Portland District and North Pacific Division records are in the Seattle Records Center Regional Archives. The various records centers also store non-accessioned records, those not yet transferred to National Archives custody, for different agencies, including the Corps of Engineers. The various Corps of Engineers' field offices often maintain custody of large amounts of recent records, and some not so recent, for current business.

Other records relating to Corps of Engineers' activities are among the archives of various other military and civilian agencies in the National Archives. The topic of research will determine what other agency records should be consulted.

The Engineer Historical Division, Humphreys Engineer Center, Fort Belvoir, Virginia, maintains various personal papers collections, typescripts of oral history interviews, photographs, and other related research materials. The U.S. Military Academy Library, at West Point, New York, and the U.S. Army Military History Institute, at Carlisle Barracks, Pennsylvania, also have important unpublished materials pertaining to the Corps of Engineers.

Various manuscript repositories in the United States have personal papers of Corps of Engineers officers, noncommissioned officers, enlisted men, and civilian employees. The manuscript division of the Library of Congress has a great number including those of George B. McClellan, Cyrus B. Comstock, Henry Wager Halleck, George Washington Goethals, Orlando M. Poe, and Henry M. Robert. Harvard University has the Henry L. Abbot papers, those of Henry W. Benham are at the Rutherford B. Hayes Library, Jonathan Williams's correspondence is at Indiana University, and the University of North Carolina maintains the Harley B. Ferguson papers.

RESEARCH OPPORTUNITIES. Except in a few cases, historians have generally neglected Corps of Engineers history. Jonathan Williams, Joseph G. Totten, John J. Abert, John G. Foster, William M. Black, Henry L. Abbot, William P. Craighill, Patrick M. Mason, Cyrus B. Comstock, William H. Emory, Orlando M. Poe, and Thomas L. Casey, Sr., are only some of the army engineer officers who deserve scholarly biographical treatment. Some military topics that warrant study are the army engineers in the War of 1812, the Mexican War, the Spanish-American War, World War I, and the Korean War. The development of field fortifications, camouflage, and military bridging are also worthy subjects. In civil works, the possibilities abound, including the development of dam or levee construction, hydraulic and coastal engineering, and water-supply policy. Engineer construction of lighthouses and military reservation structures and facilities await thorough study. Finally, the engineer noncommissioned officer and enlisted man and their training are obvious topics for historical research.

BIBLIOGRAPHY

1. Abbott, Henry Lorcum. "The Corps of Engineers." *Journal of the Military Service Institution of the United States* (15 March 1894), 413–27.
2. _____. *Early Days of the Engineer School of Application, Engineer School Occasional Paper no. 14.* Washington, D.C.: Engineer School of Application, 1904.
3. _____. *Report upon Experiments and Investigations to Develop a System of Submarine Mines for Defending the Harbors of the United States Professional Paper of the Corps of Engineers no. 23.* Washington, D.C.: GPO, 1881.
4. _____. "The School of Sub-Marine Mining at Willet's Point." *Journal of the Military Service Institution of the United States* (1 April 1880), 203–24.
5. Abbott, Jackson M., and Logen Cassedy. "Land Mines: Past and Present." *The Military Engineer* 54 (September–October 1962): 367–68.
6. Ade, Louis P. "Army Engineers in Vietnam." *Army Information Digest* 21 (January 1966): 52–57.
7. Adler, Steven P., and Edmund F. Hansen, Jr. *Hill Reestablishment: Retroactive Community Study of a Relocated New England Town.* Fort Belvoir, Va.: Army Engineer Institute for Water Resources, 1978.
8. Alberts, Don E. "The Corps of Engineers and New Mexico's Water." *New Mexico Historical Review* 51 (April 1976): 93–108.
9. Albright, George L. *Official Explorations for Pacific Railroads.* Berkeley: University of California Press, 1921.
10. Alexander, Barton S. "Minot's Ledge Lighthouse." *Transactions of the American Society of Civil Engineers* 8 (April 1879): 83–94.
11. Allan, Carlisle. "George W. Whistler, Military Engineer." *The Military Engineer* 29 (May–June 1937: 177–80.
12. Allen, Richard Saunders. "19th Century American Fortifications: Training Ground for Engineers. . . ." *Consulting Engineer* 19 (November 1962): 114–19.
13. Alperstein, David M. "Fort Totten at Willet's Point." *Periodical* 11 (Summer 1977): 18–26.
14. Ambrose, Stephen E. *Duty, Honor, Country: A History of West Point.*

Baltimore, Md.: Johns Hopkins University Press, 1966.
15. _____. *Halleck: Lincoln's Chief of Staff.* Baton Rouge: Louisiana State University Press, 1962.
16. American Dredging Company. *Four Times Panama: A Century of Dredging the American Way, 1867–1967.* Philadelphia, Pa.: American Dredging Company, 1967.
17. American Public Works Association. *History of Public Works in the United States, 1776–1976.* Edited by Ellis L. Armstrong et al. Chicago: American Public Works Association. 1976.
18. Anders, Leslie. *The Ledo Road: General Joseph W. Stillwell's Highway to China.* Norman: University of Oklahoma Press, 1965.
19. Arthur, Robert. "Early Coast Fortification." *The Military Engineer* 53 (July–August 1961): 279–81.
20. Baldwin, Jeduthan. *The Revolutionary Journal of Colonel Jeduthan Baldwin, 1775–1778.* Edited by Thomas W. Baldwin. Bangor, Maine: Printed for the Du Burians, 1906.
21. Baldwin, Kenneth H. *Enchanted Enclosure: The Army Engineers and Yellowstone National Park. A Documentary History.* Washington, D.C.: GPO, 1976.
22. Barnard, John Gross. *Eulogy on the Late Brevet Major General Joseph G. Totten, Chief Engineer, United States Army.* New York: D. Van Nostrand, 1866.
23. _____. "Lighthouse Engineering as Displayed at the Centennial Exhibition." *Transactions of the Amercian Society of Civil Engineers* 8 (March 1879): 55–82.
24. Barnard, John Gross, and William F. Barry. *Report of the Engineer and Artillery Operations of the Army of the Potomac from Its Organization to the Close of the Peninsular Campaign.* New York: D. Van Nostrand, 1863.
25. Barnes, Frank. *Fort Sumter National Monument, South Carolina.* Washington, D.C.: GPO, 1952.
26. Bartlett, Richard A. *Great Surveys of the American West.* Norman: University of Oklahoma Press, 1962.
27. Baskin, John. *New Burlington: The Life and Death of an American Village.* New York: N. N. Norton, 1977.
28. Bass, George Q. "Operations of Overseas Engineer Depots." *The Military Engineer* 38 (March 1946): 87–91.
29. Beardslee, Clarence G. "Development of Army Camp Planning." *Civil Engineering* 12 (September 1942): 489–92.
30. Beauregard, Pierre G. T. *With Beauregard in Mexico; Mexican War Reminiscences.* Edited by T. Harry Williams. Baton Rouge: Louisiana State University Press, 1956.
31. Beers, Henry P. "A History of the U.S. Topographical Engineers, 1813–1863." *The Military Engineer* 34 (June 1942): 287–91; (July 1942): 348–52.
32. Benham, Henry Washington. "Recollections of Mexico and Buena Vista." *Old and New* 3 (June 1871): 644–56; 4 (July 1871): 45–58.
33. Bishop, Joseph Bucklin, and Farnham. *Goethals, Genius of the Panama Canal: A Biography.* New York: Harper & Brothers, 1930.
34. Black, William Murray. "The Relation between Civil and Military

Engineering." In *J. E. Alfred Lectures on Engineering Practice, 1917-18*. Baltimore, Md.: Johns Hopkins University Press, 1918, 39-78.

35. _____. *The United States Public Works: Guide and Register*. New York: John Wiley and Sons, 1895.

36. Blust, Frank A. "The U.S. Lake Survey, 1841-1974." *Inland Seas* 32 (Summer 1976): 91-104.

37. Borger, Henry E., Jr. "The Role of the Army Engineers in the Westward Movement in the Lake Huron-Michigan Basin before the Civil War." Unpublished Ph.D. diss., Columbia University, 1954.

38. Bowman, Waldo G. *American Military Engineering in Europe, from Normandy to the Rhine*. New York: McGraw-Hill, 1945.

39. _____. *Bulldozers Come First: The Story of U.S. War Construction in Foreign Lands*. New York: McGraw-Hill, 1944.

40. Boyle, F. M. "The Army in Disaster Relief." *Army Information Digest* 9 (April 1954): 46-52.

41. Brennan, Roland M. "Brigadier General Richard L. Hoxie, United States Army, 1861-1930." *Records of the Columbia Historical Society of Washington, D.C.* 57-59 (1961): 87-95.

42. Bright, Samuel R., Jr. "Confederate Coast Defense." Unpublished Ph.D. diss., Duke University, 1961.

43. Brown, John Clifford. *Diary of a Soldier in the Philippines*. Portland, Maine: Privately printed, 1901.

44. Browning, Robert S. "Shielding the Republic: American Coastal Defense Policy in the Nineteenth Century." Unpublished Ph.D. diss., University of Wisconsin, 1981.

45. Burgess, Carter L. "The Armed Forces in Disaster Relief." *The Annals of the American Academy of Political and Social Sciences* 309 (January 1957): 71-79.

46. Burgess, Harry. *Duties of Engineer Troops in a General Engagement of a Mixed Force, Engineer School Occasional Paper no. 32*. Washington, D.C.: Press of the Engineer School, 1908.

47. Burr, Edward. *Historical Sketch of the Corps of Engineers, U.S. Army, Engineer School Occasional Paper no. 71*. Washington, D.C.: GPO, 1939.

48. Buzzaird, Raleigh B. "Insignia of the Corps of Engineers." *The Military Engineer* 42 (March-April 1950): 101-5.

49. _____. "Washington's Last Chief Engineer, Etienne Bechet, Sieur de Rochefontaine." *The Military Engineer* 45 (March-April 1953): 118-22.

50. _____. "Washington's Most Brilliant Engineer." *The Military Engineer* 41 (September-October 1949): 358-65.

51. Calhoun, Daniel H. *The American Civil Engineer: Origins and Conflicts*. Cambridge, Mass.: M.I.T. Press, 1960.

52. Cameron, H. F., Jr. "Combat Engineers in the Dominican Republic, 1965." *The Military Engineer* 58 (January-February 1966): 30-33.

53. Caples, W. G. *The Construction of the Calamba-Batangas Road, Luzon, P.I., Engineer School Occasional Paper no. 5*. Washington, D.C.: Press of the Engineer School of Application, 1903.

54. Casey, Hugh J. "Military Engineers in War." *The Military Engineer* 35 (February 1943): 57-62.

55. Casey, Thomas Lincoln. *Letter from the Chief of Engineers to the Secretary*

of War, containing a Historical Sketch of the Corps of Engineers and Remarks upon Its Organization and Duties. Washington, D.C.: GPO, 1876.

56. Cass, Edward C. "Flood Control and the Corps of Engineers in the Missouri Valley, 1902–1973." *Nebraska History* 63 (Spring 1982): 108–22.

57. Chibas, Eduardo J. "The Work of the Engineers in the Santiago Campaign." *Journal of the United States Artillery* 10 (September–October 1898): 145–53.

58. Clark, Alvan W. *American Literature on Dams: A Bibliography.* Fort Belvoir, Va.: Engineer School, 1948.

59. _____. *Dams: A Bibliography of Books, Periodicals, and Society Publications appearing from January 1924 through March 1936.* Fort Belvoir, Va.: Engineer School, 1936.

60. Clark, Edward B. *William L. Sibert, the Army Engineer.* Philadelphia, Pa.: Dorrance & Company, 1930.

61. Clarke, Frederick J. *Engineer Memoirs: Lieutenant General Frederick J. Clarke.* An Oral History Interview Conducted by Albert E. Cowdrey and the American Public Works Association. Washington, D.C.: Historical Division, U.S. Army Corps of Engineers, 1980.

62. Cleaves, Freeman. *Meade of Gettysburg.* Norman: University of Oklahoma Press, 1960.

63. Clema, Joe A. "Army Engineers in the Space Program." *The Military Engineer* 55 (September–October 1963): 319–20.

64. Coggins, Jack. "The Engineers Played a Key Role in Both Armies." *Civil War Times Illustrated* 3 (January 1965): 40–47.

65. Coll, Blanche D., Jean E. Keith, and Herbert H. Rosenthal. *The Corps of Engineers: Troops and Equipment.* Washington, D.C.: GPO, 1958.

66. Collins, Francis B. *The Fighting Engineers; The Minute Men of Our Industrial Army.* New York: Century Company, 1918.

67. Conn, Stetson, Rose C. Engelman, and Byron Fairchild. *Guarding the United States and Its Outposts.* Washington, D.C.: GPO, 1964.

68. Cooling, Benjamin Franklin. "The Army and Flood and Disaster Relief." In *The United States Army in Peacetime: Essays in Honor of the Bicentennial, 1775–1975,* edited by Robin Higham and Carol Brandt, Manhattan, Kans.: Military Affairs / Aerospace Historian Publishing, 1975, 61–81.

69. "Corps of Artillerists and Engineers." *Journal of the United States Artillery* 29 (January–February 1908): 83–85.

70. Corthell, Elmer L. *A History of the Jetties at the Mouth of the Mississippi River.* New York: John Wiley and Sons, 1881.

71. Couper, William. *Claudius Crozet. Solider-Scholar-Educator-Engineer, 1789–1864.* Charlottesville, Va.: Historical Publishing Company, 1936.

72. Cosby, Spencer. "The Work of the Army in the Construction and Maintenance of Roads." *Professional Memoirs, Corps of Engineers, U.S. Army* 6 (July–August 1914): 539–48.

73. Cowdrey, Albert E. *A City for the Nation: The Army Engineers and the Building of Washington, D.C., 1790–1967.* Washington, D.C.: GPO, 1978.

74. _____. "Pioneering Environmental Law: The Army Corps of Engineers and the Refuse Act." *Pacific Historical Review* 44 (August 1975): 331–49.

75. Craighill, William P. "Corps of Engineers, United States Army." *Trans-*

actions of the American Society of Civil Engineers 38 (December 1897): 429–35.

76. Crump, Irving. *Our Army Engineers*. New York: Dodd, Mead, 1954.

77. Cullum, George W. *Campaigns of the War of 1812–15 against Great Britain, Sketched and Criticized, with Brief Biographies of the American Engineers*. New York: James Millier, Publisher, 1879.

78. Danford, Robert M. "Brevet Major General George W. Cullum: A Biographical Sketch." *Assembly* 18 (Summer 1959): 19–23.

79. Daugherty, Charles Michael. *City under the Ice: The Story of Camp Century*. New York: Macmillan, 1963.

80. Davis, Franklin M., and Thomas T. Jones, eds. *The U.S. Army Engineers—Fighting Elite*. New York: Franklin Watts, 1967.

81. Dawes, Charles G. *A Journal of the Great War*. 2 vols. Boston: Houghton Mifflin, 1921.

82. Denton, Edgar, III. "The Formative Years of the United States Military Academy, 1775–1833." Unpublished Ph.D. diss., Syracuse University, 1964.

83. Dibble, Ernest F. "Slave Rentals to the Military: Pensacola and the Gulf Coast." *Civil War History* 23 (June 1977): 101–13.

84. _____. *William H. Chase: Gulf Coast Fort Builder*. Wilmington, Del.: The Gulf Coast Collection, n.d.

85. Dillon, Marian, and Dale E. Floyd. *The U.S. Army Corps of Engineers: A Selective Bibliography*. Washington, D.C.: GPO, 1985.

86. Dod, Karl C. *The Corps of Engineers: The War against Japan*. Washington, D.C.: GPO, 1966.

87. Dodds, Gordon B. *Hiram Martin Chittenden: His Pubic Career*. Lexington: University Press of Kentucky, 1973.

88. Dornbusch, Charles E. *Histories, Personal Narratives, United States Army: A Checklist*. Cornwallville, N.Y.: Hope Farm Press, 1967.

89. Dorst, James A. "Ft. Humphreys and Historical Belvoir." *The Military Engineer* 15 (July–August 1923): 332–37.

90. Douglas, William O. "The Public Be Damned." *Playboy* 16 (July 1969): 143, 182–88.

91. Douglass, David Bates. "An Original Narrative of the Niagara Campaign of 1814." *Niagara Frontier* 11 (Spring 1964): 1–35.

92. Drake-Wilkes, L. P. "United States Army: History and Traditions of the Corps of Engineers." *Canadian Army Journal* 4 (January 1953): 57–73.

93. Drennon, Clarence B., III. "Engineers in Counterinsurgency—1899." *The Military Engineer* 58 (May–June 1966): 176–78.

94. Drumm, Stella. "Letters of Robert E. Lee to Henry Kayser, 1838–1846." *Glimpses of the Past* 3 (January–February 1936) 1–43.

95. Dunn, Carroll H. *Base Development in South Vietnam, 1965–1970*. Washington, D.C.: GPO, 1972.

96. Dunne, David M. "The Engineer School—Past and Present." *The Military Engineer* 41 (November–December 1949): 411–16.

97. Dupree, A. Hunter. *Science in the Federal Government: A History of Policies and Activities to 1940*. Cambridge, Mass.: Harvard University Press, 1957.

98. Dziuban, Stanley W. "When Engineers Fight as Infantry." *Army* 13

(September 1962): 68–72.

99. "Early Coast Fortification." *The Coast Artillery Journal* 70 (February 1929): 134–44.

100. Elliott, Dabney O. *The Improvement of the Lower Mississippi River for Flood Control and Navigation*. Prepared under the direction of T. H. Jackson. 3 vols. Vicksburg, Miss.: U.S. Waterways Experiment Station, 1932.

101. _____. "Military Maps and Their Reproduction." *The Military Engineer* 21 (May–June 1929): 249–55.

102. Ellis, Robert R. "Richard Gridley, First Chief Engineer of the Army." *The Military Engineer* 39 (May–October) 1963.

103. Ellision, Marvin. "Combat Engineers in Beach Operations." *Military Review* 25 (July 1945): 34–38.

104. Emory, William H. *Lieutenant Emory Reports*. Edited by Ross Calvin. Albuquerque: University of New Mexico Press, 1951.

105. "The Engineer in the Moro Campaign." *Engineering Magazine* 24 (November 1902): 259–62.

106. Everest, Allan S. "Alexander Macomb at Plattsburgh, 1814." *New York History* 44 (October 1963): 307–35.

107. Felton, Samuel M. "Military Railroads in the World War." *The Military Engineer* 17 (March–April 1925): 111–18.

108. Ferejohn, John A. *Pork Barrel Politics: Rivers and Harbors Legislation, 1947–1968*. Stanford, Calif.: Stanford University Press, 1974.

109. Ferguson, Harley B. *Report on the Engineer Equipment of the Allied Troops serving with the China Relief Expedition, 1900–1901, Professional Paper of the Corps of Engineers no. 30*. Washington, D.C.: GPO, 1901.

110. Findley, Roger W. "The Planning of a Corps of Engineers Reservoir Project: Law, Economics and Politics." *Ecology Law Review* 3 (Winter 1973): 1–106.

111. Fine, Lenore, and Jesse A. Remington. *The Corps of Engineers: Construction in the United States*. Washington, D.C.: GPO, 1972.

112. Flanagan, Vincent J. "Life of Gouverneur Kemble Warren." Unpublished Ph.D. diss., City University of New York, 1969.

113. Fleming, Thomas J. *West Point: The Men and Times of the United States Military Academy*. New York: William Morrow, 1969.

114. Floyd, Dale E. *United States Coast Defense, 1775–1950: A Bibliography*. Washington, D.C.: GPO, 1985.

115. "U.S. Army Officers in Europe, 1815–1861." In *Proceedings of the Citadel Conference on War and Diplomacy 1977*, edited by David H. White and John W. Gordon, Charleston, S.C.: The Citadel, 1979, 26–30.

116. Forman, Sidney. *West Point: A History of the United States Military Academy*. New York: Columbia University Press, 1950.

117. Franzwa, Gregory M., and William J. Ely. *Leif Sverdrup—"Engineer Soldier at His Best"*. Gerald, Mo.: The Patrice Press, 1980.

118. Frazier, Arthur H. "Daniel Farrand Henry's Cup Type 'Telegraphic' River Current Meter." *Technology and Culture* 5 (Fall 1964): 541–65.

119. Freeman, Douglas Southall. *R. E. Lee, A Biography*. 4 vols. New York: Charles Scribner's Sons, 1934–35.

120. Fremont, John Charles. *Memoirs of May Life*. Chicago: Belford, Clarke

& Company, 1887.

121. Friis, Herman R. "Highlights of the Geographical and Cartographical Contributions of Graduates of the U.S. Military Academy with a Specialization as Topographical Engineers prior to 1860." In Association of American Geographers, New York-New Jersey Division, *Proceedings of Annual Meeting 1967* (1 April 1968): 10–29.

122. Galloway, Gerald E., Jr. "Dam Building in the Army?" *Military Review* 55 (February 1975): 72–81.

123. _____. *Ex Post Evaluation of the Regional Water Resources Development: The Case of the Yazoo-Mississippi Delta*. Fort Belvoir, VA.: Institute for Water Resources, U.S. Army Corps of Engineers, 1980.

124. Giles, Henry. *The G.I. Journal of Sergeant Giles*. Boston: Houghton Mifflin, 1965.

125. Giles, Janice Holt. *The Damned Engineers*. Boston: Houghton Mifflin, 1979.

126. Goetzmann, William H. *Army Exploration in the American West, 1803–1863*. New Haven, Conn.: Yale University Press, 1959.

127. Gordon, Roy. "Engineering for People: 200 Years of Army Public Works." *The Military Engineer* 68 (May–June 1976): 180–85.

128. Graves, Ernest. *Construction in War: Lessons Taught by the World War, 1917–1919, Engineer School Occasional Paper no. 64*. Washington, D.C.: GPO, 1919.

129. _____ "Road Work on the Punitive Expedition into Mexico." *Professional Memoirs, Corps of Engineers, U.S. Army* 9 (November –December 1917): 657–81.

130. Gribble, W. C., Jr. Perspective on the Army Engineers Water Management Mission." *Water Spectrum* 6 no. 3 (1974): 1–9.

131. Griess, Thomas Everett. "Dennis Hart Mahan: West Point Professor and Advocate of Military Professionalism, 1830–1871." Unpublished Ph.D. diss., Duke University, 1969.

132. Groves, Leslie R. *Now It Can Be Told: The Story of the Manhattan Project*. New York: Harper & Brothers, 1962.

133. Guinn, Gilbert S. "Coastal Defense of the Confederate Atlantic Seaboard States." Unpublished Ph.D. diss. University of South Carolina, 1973.

134. Gurney, Gene. *The Pentagon*. New York: Crown, 1964.

135. Guthorn, Peter J. *American Maps and Mapmakers of the Revolution*. Monmouth Beach, N.J.: Philip Freneau Press, 1966.

136. Haferkorn, Henry E. *Breakwaters: A Bibliography*. Washington, D.C.: Engineer Reproduction Plant, 1932.

137. _____. "The Military Value of Interior Waterways" [Bibliography]. *Professional Memoirs, Corps of Engineers, U.S. Army* 8 (November–December 1916): 790–94.

138. _____. "Searchlights: A Short Annotated Bibliography of their Design and their Use in Peace and War." *Professional Memoirs, Corps of Engineers, U.S. Army* 8 (January–February 1916). 118–28; (March–April 1916): 250–63.

139. Hall, William C. "Military Maps." *The Military Engineer* 46 (November–December 1954: 431.

140. Hammond, A. J. 'Federal Department of Public Works? History of the

Movement." *Civil Engineering* 8 (March 1938): 155–59.

141. Hanft, Marshall. *Fort Stevens: Oregon's Defender at the River of the West.* Salem: Oregon State Parks and Recreation Branch, 1980.

142. Harte, Charles Rufus. *The River Obstructions of the Revolutionary War.* Hartford, Conn.: Society of Civil Engineers, 1946.

143. Harts, William W. "Origin of the Engineer Insignia." *The Military Engineer* 22 (September–October 1930): 405.

144. Haseman, L. L. "Engineers' Role in Counterinsurgency." *The Military Engineer* 55 (November–December 1963): 393–95.

145. Haskett, James N. "Military Engineers at Yorktown, 1781." *The Military Engineer* 48 (May–June 1976): 175–79.

146. Hayes, Thomas J. III, "Army Engineers in Vietnam." *The Military Engineer* 58 (January–February 1966): 8–9.

147. _____. "Army Engineers Map the Moon." *Army Information Digest* 20 (January 1965): 12–18.

148. _____. "Engineers in the Cold War." *The Military Engineer* 57 (July–August 1965): 243–44.

149. Hays, Samuel P. *Conservation and the Gospel of Efficiency: The Progressive Conservation Movement, 1890–1920.* Cambridge, Mass.: Harvard University Press, 1959.

150. Heap, David Porter. *The Engineer Department, U.S. Army, at the International Exhibition, 1876.* Washington, D.C.: GPO, 1884.

151. Heavey, William F. "The Corps in the Days of the Revolution." *The Military Engineer* 31 (November–December 1939: 410–15.

152. _____. *Down Ramp! The Story of Army Amphibian Engineers.* Washington, D.C.: Infantry Journal Press, 1947.

153. Hedeman, William N. Jr. "The Role of the Corps of Engineers in Protecting the Coastal Zone." *Environmental Comment* 20 (April 1975): 2–4.

154. Hellman, Florence S. *Bibliography on Flood Control.* Washington, D.C.: GPO, 1928.

155. Herbert, Neal F. "Development and Engineering of Aids to Navigation." *The Military Engineer* 69 (July–August 1977): 235–39; (September–October 1977): 326–30.

156. Hertzler, R. A. "Corps of Engineers' Experience relating to Flood-Plain Regulation." In *Papers on Flood Problems*, edited by Gilbert Fite, Chicago: University of Chicago Press, 1961.

157. Heusser, Albert H. *George Washington's Map Maker: A Biography of Robert Erskine.* Edited by Hubert G. Schmidt. New Brunswick, N.J.: Rutgers University Press, 1966.

158. Heuvelmans, Martin. *The River Killers.* Harrisburg, A.: Stackpole Books, 1974.

159. Hill, Forest G. *Roads, Rails, and Waterways: The Army Engineers and Early Transportation.* Norman: University of Oklahoma Press, 1957.

160. Hinds, James R. "Stone Walls and Iron Guns: Effectiveness of Civil War Forts." *Periodical* 12 (January 1981): 36–47.

161. Holmes, Beatrice Hort. *A History of Federal Water Resources Programs, 1800–1960.* Washington, D.C.: GPO, 1972.

162. _____. *History of Federal Water Resources Programs and Policies, 1961–1970.* Washington, D.C.: GPO, 1979.

163. Holt, W. Stull. *The Office of the Chief of Engineers of the Army: Its Non-Military History, Activities, and Organization*. Baltimore, Md.: Johns Hopkins University Press, 1923.

164. Hook, Simeon M. "The Army Corps of Engineers' Role in Preserving Harbor Cultural Resources." *Sea History* 7 (Spring 1977): 24.

165. Hotchkiss, Jedediah. *Make Me A Map of the Valley: The Civil War Journal of Stonewall Jackson's Topographer*. Edited by Archie P. McDonald. Dallas, Tex.: Southern Methodist University Press, 1973.

166. Hoy, Suellen M., and Michael C. Robinson. *Public Works History in the United States: A Guide to the Literature*. Nashville, Tenn.: The American Association for State and Local History, 1982.

167. Hoyt, William G., and Walter B. Langbein. *Floods*. Princeton, N.J.: Princeton University Press, 1955.

168. Hull, William J. and Robert W. *The Origin and Development of the Waterways Policy of the United States*. Washington, D.C.: National Waterways Conference, 1967.

169. Hume, Edgar Erskine. "The Society of the Cincinnati and the Corps of Engineers." *The Military Engineer* 25 (November–December 1933): 468–73.

170. Humphreys, Henry H. *Andrew Atkinson Humphreys, a Biography*. Philadelphia, Pa.: John C. Winston Company, 1924.

171. Ickes, Harry E. "The Development of the 60-Inch Antiaircraft Searchlight by the United States Army." Unpublished Ph.d. diss., University of Pittsburgh, 1951.

172. Itschner, Emerson C. *The Army Engineers' Contribution to American Defense and Advancement*. New York: Newcomen Society in North America, 1959.

173. _____. "The Corps of Engineers in Water Resource Development." *The Military Engineer* 46 (May–June 1954): 169–72.

174. Jenks, William L. "Fort Gratiot and Its Builder, Gen. Charles Gratiot, 1786–1855." *Michigan History Magazine*, 4, January 1920, 141–55.

175. Jewett, Henry C. "History of the Corps of Engineers to 1915." *The Military Engineer* 14 (September–October 1922): 304–06.

176. Johnson, Leland R. "Army Engineers on the Cumberland and Tennessee, 1824–1854." *Tennessee Historical Quarterly* 31 (Summer 1972): 149–69.

177. _____. "19th Century Engineering: Part I: The Contest of 1824; Part II; The Contract of 1824." *The Military Engineer* 65 (May–June 1973): 166–71; (July–August 1973): 252–57.

178. _____. "19th Century Engineering: The Johnstown Disaster." *The Military Engineer* 66 (January–February 1974): 42–45.

179. _____. "Waterways: The Fourth Pillar of Defense." *The Military Engineer* 72 (November–December 1980): 404–8.

180. Johnson, Maizie H., and Elizabeth Bethel. *Preliminary Inventory of the Textual Records of the Chief of Engineers, Record Group 77*. Two parts, each with a supplement. Washington, D.C.: The National Archives and Records Service, 1965-67.

181. Johnston, Henry P. "Sergeant Lee's Experiences with Bushnell's Submarine Torpedo in 1776." *The Magazine of American History* 29 (March 1893): 262–66.

182. Johnston, Richard W. "Caught Standing in the Way of Progress." *Sports Illustrated* 43 (24 November 1975): 50–62.

183. Kanarek, Harold K. "The U.S. Army Corps of Engineers and Early Internal Improvements in Maryland." *Maryland Historical Magazine* 72 (Spring 1977): 99–109).

184. Kelley, Francis X. "Early Preservation of Pleasuring Grounds." *Water Spectrum* 4 (Fall 1972): 37–41.

185. Kershner, James William. "Sylvanus Thayer: A Biography." Unpublished Ph.D. diss., West Virginia University, 1976.

186. Ketchum, Ralph E. "Camouflage School for Harbor Defense." *The Coast Artillery Journal* 85 (January–February 1942): 41–43.

187. Kiernan, Joseph M. "Combat Engineers in the Iron Triangle." *Army* 17 (June 1967): 42–45.

188. Kingman, John J. "The Genesis of Fort Drum, Manila Bay." *The Military Engineer* 37 (March 1945): 128–30.

189. Kirby, W. W. "Army Map Reproduction in France." *The Military Engineer* 15 (July–August 1923): 295–300.

190. Kirchner, David P. "American Harbor Defense Forts." *United States Naval Institute Proceedings* 84 (August 1958): 93–101.

191. Kirchner, David P., and Emanuel Raymond Lewis. "American Harbor Defenses: The Final Era." *United States Naval Institute Proceedings* 94 (January 1968): 84–98.

192. Kohloss, F. H. "The Development of Military Searchlights." *The Military Engineer* 22 (July–August 1930): 364–69.

193. Ladd, J. G. "The Development of Army Mapping." *Army Information Digest* 7 (July 1952): 47–49.

194. Laframboise, Leon W. *History of the Combat Support Branches: Branch Service Insignia.* Steelville, Mo.: Watson Publishing Company, 1977.

195. Lamers, William M. *The Edge of Glory: A Biography of General William S. Rosecrans, U.S.A.* New York: Harcourt Brace and World, 1961.

196. Lane, Albert L. "The Alcan Highway, Road Location and Construction Methods." *The Military Engineer* 34 (October 1942): 493–99.

197. Lane, T. A., and E. J. Williams, Jr. "River Hydraulics in 1861." *Journal of the Waterways and Harbors Division, Proceedings of the American Society of Civil Engineers* 88 (August 1962): 1–12.

198. Lattimore, Ralston B. *Fort Pulaski National Monument, Georgia.* Washington, D.C.: GPO, 1954.

199. Layton, Edwin, T., Jr. *The Revolt of the Engineers: Social Engineering and the American Engineering Profession.* Cleveland, Ohio: Press of Case Western Reserve University, 1971.

200. Leach, Smith S. *Historical Sketch of the First Battalion of Engineers during Its Tour Abroad, Engineer School Occasional Paper no. 7.* Washington, D.C.: Press of the Engineer School of Application, 1903.

201. Lee, John C. H. "United States Military Engineers in Peacetime Civil Works." *The Royal Engineers Journal* 48 (June 1944): 89–99.

202. Lee, Robert E. "Lieutenant Lee Reports to Captain Andrew Talcott on Fort Calhoun's Construction on the Rip Raps." Edited by George Green Shackleford. *Virginia Magazine of History and Biography* 60 (July 1952): 458–87.

203. Lehman, Donald J. *Lucky Landmark: A Study of a Design and Its Survival: The Galveston Customhouse, Post Office, and Courthouse of 1861.* Washington, D.C.: GPO, 1973.

204. LeMon, Warren. "Belvoir—Home of the Engineers." *Army Information Digest* 29 (August 1965): 49-53.

205. Lenney, John J., *Caste System in the American Army: A Study of Engineers and Their West Point System.* New York: Greenberg, 1949.

206. Lessem, Harold I., and George C. Mackenzie. *Fort McHenry National Monument and Historic Shrine, Maryland.* Washington, D.C.: GPO, 1954.

207. Lewis, Emanuel Raymond. *Seacoast Fortifications of the United States: An Introductory History.* Washington, D.C.: Smithsonian Institution Press, 1970.

208. Lippincott, Isaac. "A History of River Improvement." *Journal of Political Economy* 22 (July 1914): 630-60.

209. Lockett, John B. *History of the Corps of Engineers Committee on Tidal Hydraulics (January 1949 to June 1971).* Vicksburg, Miss.: U.S. Army Corps of Engineers, 1972.

210. Lord, Francis A. "Pontoons, How and Where They Were Used." *Civil War Times Illustrated* 2 (October 1963): 28-29.

211. Lourie, George E. "Development of Military Railway Service." *Military Review* 26 (September 1946): 26-33.

212. Lowrey, Walter M. "Navigational Problems at the Mouth of the Mississippi River, 1698-1880." Unpublished Ph.D. diss., Vanderbilt University, 1956.

213. Ludlow, William. "An Army Engineer's Journal of Custer's Black Hills Expedition, July 2, 1874–August 23, 1874." Edited by Eugene McAndrews. *Journal of the West* 13 (January 1974): 78-85.

214. McAndrews, Eugene V. "Sergeant Major Frederick Gerber: Engineer Legend." *The Military Engineer* 63 (July–August 1971): 240-41.

215. _____. "William Ludlow: Engineer, Governor, Soldier." Unpublished Ph.D. diss., Kansas State University, 1973.

216. McBride, Stewart Dill. "The Town That Took On the Corps of Engineers." *Reader's Digest* 112 (February 1978): 191-96.

217. McCarthy, S. A. "The Insignia of the Corps of Engineers." *The Military Engineer* 37 (July 1945): 268-71.

218. McClellan, George B. *Mexican War Diary.* Edited by William S. Myers. Princeton, N.J.: Princeton University Press, 1917.

219. McCloskey, Joseph F. "Military Roads in Combat Areas: The Development of Equipment and Techiques by the Corps of Engineers, United States Army, during World War II." Unpublished Ph.d. diss., University of Pittsburgh, 1948.

220. McCullough, David G. *The Path between the Seas: The Creation of the Panama Canal, 1870-1914.* New York: Simon & Schuster, 1977.

221. McDonald, Archie P. "West Point and the Engineers." *The Military Engineer* 57 (May–June 1965): 187-89.

222. McDonough, M. J., and P. S. Bond. "Use and Development of the Pontoon Equipage in the United States Army with Special Reference to the Civil War." *Professional Memoirs, Corps of Engineers, U.S. Army* 6 (November–December 1914): 692-758.

223. Maass, Arthur. *Muddy Waters: The Army Engineers and the Nation's Rivers.*

Cambridge, Mass.: Harvard University Press, 1951.

224. Marshall, J. C. "The Engineer Board." *The Military Engineer* 25 (July–August 1933): 317–18.

225. Marshall, Mortimer M., Jr. "From Barracks to Dormitories." *The Military Engineer* 64 (November–December 1974): 343–46.

226. Martin, Joseph Plumb. *Private Yankee Doodle*. Edited by George F. Scheer. Boston: Little, Brown, 1962.

227. Martin, Paul G. "Road Work in Korea." *The Military Engineer* 47 (September–October 1955): 380–81.

228. Mazmanian, Daniel A., and Jeanne Nienaber. *Can Organizations Change: Environmental Protection, Citizen Participation, and the Corps of Engineers*. Washington, D.C.: Brookings Institution, 1979.

229. Mazzeno, Laurence W. "Major Richard Delafield and the U.S. Military Mission to the Crimean War." *Joint Perspectives* 1 (Winter 1981): 72–83.

230. Meade, George Gordon. *Life and Letters of George Gordon Meade, Major General, United States Army*. Edited by George G. Meade. 2 vols. New York: Charles Scribner's Sons, 1913.

231. *Memoir of Colonel William McRee, USE*. Wilmington, N.C.: N.p., 1834.

232. Merdinger, Charles J. *Civil Engineering through the Ages*. Washington, D.C.: Society of American Military Engineers, 1963.

233. Merritt, Raymond H. *Engineering in American Society, 1850–1875*. Lexington: University Press of Kentucky, 1969.

234. Michie, Peter S. "American Military Roads and Bridges." *Journal of the Military Service Institution of the United States* 15 (July 1894): 675–86.

235. Miles, Samuel H. "The National Dam Inspection Program." *The Military Engineer* 70 (September–October 1978): 326–29.

236. Miller, Gordon K. *A Biographical Sketch of Major Edward E. Hartwick together with a Compilation of Major Hartwick's Letters and Diaries Written during the Spanish-American and World Wars*. Detroit: N.p., 1921.

237. Mitchell, William A. *Army Engineering*. 2d ed. Washington, D.C.: Society of American Military Engineers, 1938.

238. Moore, Jamie W. *The Fortifications Board, 1816–1828, and the Definitions of National Security*. Charleston, S.C.: The Citadel, 1981.

239. Moore, Jamie W. and Dorothy P. "The Corps of Engineers and Beach Erosion Control, 1930–1982." *Shore and Beach* 51 (January 1983): 13–17.

240. Moore, Norman R. *Improvement of the Lower Mississippi River and Tributaries, 1931–1972*. Vicksburg: Mississippi River Commission, 1972.

241. Morgan, Arthur E. *Dams and Other Disasters: A Century of the Army Corps of Engineers of Civil Works*. Boston, Mass.: Porter Sargent, 1971.

242. Morgan, W. C. "A Study of the Social and Economic Effects of Keystone Reservoir on the Community of Mannford, Oklahoma." Unpublished M.A. thesis, Oklahoma State University, 1970.

243. Morton, James St. Clair *Memoir of the Life and Services of Captain and Brevet Major John Sanders, of the Corps of Engineers, U.S. Army*. Pittsburgh, Pa.: W. S. Haen, 1861.

244. Mosby, L. W. "First Step in Big River Hydraulics." *The Military Engineer* 53 (July–August 1961): 262–63.

245. Mumey, Nolie. *John Williams Gunnison (1812–1853), The Last of the Western Explorers*. Denver, Colo.: Artcraft Press, 1955.

246. Muntz, A. Philip. "Union Mapping in the American Civil War." *Imago Mundi* 17 (1963): 90–94.
247. Myers, William Starr. *A Study of Personality: General George Brinton McClellan*. New York: Appleton-Century, 1934.
248. National Waterways Roundtable, Norfolk, Virginia, April 22–24, 1980. *National Waterways Roundtable Papers and Proceedings on the History and Evolution of U.S. Waterways and Ports*. Fort Belvoir, Va.: Institute for Water Resources, 1981.
249. Nelson, Harold L. "Military Roads for War and Peace, 1791–1836." *Military Affairs* 19 (Spring 1955): 1–14.
250. Nettesheim, Daniel D. "Topographical Intelligence and the American Civil War." Unpublished M.A. thesis, U.S. Army Command and General Staff College, 1978.
251. Nevins, Allan. *Fremont: Pathmarker of the West*. 2 vols. New York: Appleton-Century, 1939.
252. *The New American State Papers: Explorations and Surveys*. Edited by Thomas C. Cochran. 15 vols. Wilmington, Del.: Scholarly Resources, 1972.
253. Nichols, James L. *Confederate Engineers*. Tuscaloosa, Ala.: Confederate Publishing Company, 1957.
254. Nichols, Roger L. "Army Contributions to River Transportation, 1818–1825." *Military Affairs* 33 (April 1959): 242–49.
255. Nichols, Roger L., and Patrick L. Halley. *Stephen Long and American Frontier Exploration*. Newark: University of Delaware Press, 1980.
256. Nienaber, Jeanne. *Bureaucracy, Policy, and Change: The Impact of Environmentalism in the Corps of Engineers*. Fort Belvoir, Va.: Institute for Water Resources, 1975.
257. O'Connor, James A. "Road Work in Mexico with the Punitive Expedition." *Professional Memoirs, Corps of Engineers, U.S. Army* 9 (May–June 1917): 326–46.
258. Ollivier, Francois G. "The Engineer Corps of the Revolution." *The Military Engineer* 15 (September–October 1923): 411–16.
259. Owen, Thomas J. *"Dear Friends at Home": The Letters and Diary of Thomas James Owen, Fiftieth New York Volunteer Engineer Regiment, during the Civil War*. Edited and with an introduction by Dale E. Floyd. Washington, D.C.: GPO, 1985.
260. Palmer, Dave Richard. *The River and the Rock: The History of Fortress West Point, 1775–1783*. Westport, Conn.: Greenwood Press, 1969.
261. Parsons, William B. *The American Engineers in France*. New York: D. Appleton, 1920.
262. Patrick, Mason M. "Notes on Road Building in Cuba." *Professional Memoirs, Corps of Engineers, U.S. Army* 2 (July–September 1910): 263–84.
263. Ploger, Robert R. *U.S. Army Engineers, 1965–1970*. Washingotn, D.C.: GPO, 1974.
264. Potter, William E. *Engineer Memoirs: Major General William E. Potter, USA, Ret. An oral history interview conducted by Martin Reuss*. Washington, D.C.: Historical Division, U.S. Army Corps of Engineers, 1983.

265. Power, Garrett. "The Fox in the Chicken Coop: The Regulatory Program of the U.S. Army Corps of Engineers." *Virginia Law Review* 63, no. 4 (1977): 503–59.

266. Propeller Club of the United States. *River and Harbor Improvements: How They Are Initiated, Authorized, and Completed.* New York: Press of Joseph D. McGuire, 1938.

267. Pross, Edward L. "A History of Rivers and Harbors Appropriation Bills, 1866–1933." Unpublished Ph.D. Diss., Ohio State University, 1938.

268. Quattlebaum, Charles A. *Military Highways.* N.p., 1944.

269. Ranson, Edward. "The Endicott Board of 1885–1886 and the Coast Defenses." *Military Affairs* 31 (Summer 1967), 74–84.

270. Rebh, George A. "Postal Construction and the Price of Postage Stamps," *The Military Engineer* 64 (July–August 1972): 262–65.

271. Reed, C. Wingate. "Decius Wadsworth: First Chief of Ordnance, U.S. Army 1812–1821." *Army Ordnance* 24 (May–June 1943): 527–30; (July–August 1943): 113–16.

272. Reed, Rowena A. "The Endicott Board–Vision and Reality." *Periodical* 11 (Summer 1979): 3–17.

273. Rees, Thomas H. "The Engineer Battalion of the Fifth Army Corps." *Journal of the Military Service Institution of the United States* 24 (January 1899): 74–84.

274. "Regulation and Stabilization of Rivers Bibliography." *The Military Engineer* 21 (March–April 1929): 165–68.

275. *Report of General J. G. Totten, Chief Engineer, on the Subject of National Defenses.* Washington, D.C.: A. Boyd Hamilton, 1851.

276. Reuss, Martin. "The Army Corps of Engineers and Flood-Control Politics on the Lower Mississippi." *Louisiana History* 23 (Spring 1982): 131–48.

277. _____. *Shaping Environmental Awareness: The United States Army Corps of Engineers Environmental Advisory Board, 1970–1980.* Washington, D.C.: GPO, 1983.

278. Reuss, Martin, and Paul K. Walker. *Financing Water Resources Development: A Brief History.* Washington, D.C.: GPO, 1983.

279. Reybold, Eugene. "Engineers in World War II." *The Military Engineer* 38 (January 1946): 24–29.

280. _____. "The Role of American Engineers in World War II." *The Military Engineer* 37 (February 1945): 39–42.

281. Reynolds, Carroll F. "The Development of the Military Floating Bridge by the United States Army." Unpublished Ph.D. diss., University of Pittsburgh, 1950.

282. Rhoads, James B. "Civil War Maps and Mapping." *The Military Engineer* 49 (January–February 1957): 38–43.

283. Richards, George H. *Memoir of Alexander Macomb, the Major General Commanding the Army of the United States.* New York: M'Elrath, Bangs and Company, 1833.

284. Richards, Kent D. *Isaac I. Stevens: Young Man in a Hurry.* Provo, Utah: Brigham Young University Press, 1979.

285. Robins, Thomas M. "The River and Harbor Functions of the Corps of Engineers." *The Military Engineer* 32 (September–October 1940): 325–31.

286. Robinson, Willard B. *American Forts: Architectural Form and Function.*

Urbana: University of Illinois Press, 1977.

287. _____. "Military Architecture at Mobile Bay." *Society of Architectural Historians' Journal* 30 (May 1971): 119–39.

288. Robinson, William M., Jr. "The Engineer Soldiers in the Mexican War." *The Military Engineer* 24 (January–February 1932): 1–8.

289. Roby, Harrison G. "Government Hydro Power Plant Construction Takes Important Place in Works of Corps of Engineers, U.S. Army." *Civil Engineering* 19 (November 1949): 770–73.

290. Rodyenko, Peter. "Protective Concealment for Fixed Coast Defenses." *The Coast Artillery Journal* 84 (November–December 1941): 599–602.

291. Roe, Charles H. "The Building of Fort Delaware." *The Military Engineer* 21 (July–August 1929): 350–54.

292. Rosenwaike, Ira. "Simon M. Levy: West Point Graduate." *American Jewish Historical Quarterly* 61 (September 1971): 69–73.

293. Rubincam, Milton. "Major General U. S. Grant, 3d, 1881–1968." *Records of the Columbia Historical Society of Washington, D.C.* 66–68 (1966–1968): 369–408.

294. Ryan, Gary D. "War Department Topographical Bureau, 1831–1863: An Administrative History." Unpublished Ph.D. diss., American University, 1968.

295. St. Gaudens, Homer. "Camouflage Service in the A.E.F." *The Military Engineer* 17 (May–June 1925): 220–25.

296. Schley, Julian A. "Some Notes on the World War." *The Military Engineer* 21 (January–February 1929): 55–68.

297. Schroder, Walter K. *Defenses of Narragansett Bay in World War II.* Providence: Rhode Island Bicentennial Foundation, 1980.

298. Schubert, Frank N. "Legacy of the Topographical Engineers: Textual and Cartographic Records of Western Exploration, 1819–1860." *Government Publications Review* 7A (1980): 111–16.

299. _____. *Vanguard of Expansion: Army Engineers in the Trans-Mississippi West, 1819–1879.* Washington, D.C.: GPO, 1980.

300. Schull, H. W., Jr. "Runway Construction in War." *The Military Engineer* 34 (October 1942): 473–77.

301. Scott, John S. *A Dictionary of Civil Engineering.* Harmondsworth, Middlesex, England: Penquin Books, 1958.

302. Seville, William P. *Narrative of the March of Co. A, Engineers, from Fort Levenworth Kansas, to Fort Bridger, Utah, and Return, May 6 to October 3, 1858, Engineer School Occasional Paper no. 48.* Edited by John W. N. Schulz. Washington, D.C.: Press of the Engineer School, 1912.

303. Sewell, Richard J. "Cross Florida Barge Canal, 1927–1968." *Florida Historical Quarterly* 46 (April 1968): 369–83.

304. Sherwood, Morgan B. *Exploration of Alaska, 1865–1900.* New Haven, Conn.: Yale University Press, 1965.

305. Smedley, Ralph C. *The Great Peacemaker.* Los Angeles: Borden, 1955.

306. Smith, Gustavus W. *Company "A," Corps of Engineers, USA, 1846–1848, in the Mexican War.* Willet's Point, N.Y.: Battalion Press, 1896.

307. Spencer, Ivor D. "Rubber Pontoon Bridges in 1846." *The Military Engineer* 37 (January 1945): 24–27.

308. Stanley, A. T. "Barriers – Past, Present, Future." *The Military Engineer*

66 (May–June 1974): 167–68.

309. Starr, John T. "The Army Engineers–Pioneers in American Transportation." *Highway Magazine* 49 (May–June 1958): 92–95.

310. Stevens, Hazard. *The Life of Isaac Ingalls Stevens.* 2 vols. Boston: Houghton Mifflin, 1900.

311. Stewart, George R. *John Phoenix, Esq., The Veritable Squibob: A Life of George H. Derby, USA.* New York: Henry Holt, 1937.

312. Stewart, William H., Jr. "The Tennessee Tombigbee Waterway: A Case Study in the Politics of Water Transportation." Unpublished Ph.D. diss., University of Alabama, 1968.

313. Stine, Jeffrey K. "Regulating Wetlands in the 1970s: U.S. Army Corps of Engineers and the Environmental Organizations." *Journal of Forest History* 27 (April 1983): 60–75.

314. Stoddard, Francis R. "Amiel Weeks Whipple."*The Chronicles of Oklahoma* 28 (Autumn 1950): 226–30.

315. Stratton, James H., and Gail A. Hathaway. "Military Airfields: A Symposium." *Transactions of the American Society of Civil Engineers* 110 (1945): 669–848.

316. Strong, Paschal N. "Army Engineers in Korea." *The Military Engineer* 44 (November–December 1952): 405–10.

317. Stunkel, Kenneth R. "Military Scientists of the American West." *Army* 13 (May 1963): 50–58.

318. Sturgis, Samuel D., Jr. "The Dual Role of the Army Engineer." *The Military Engineer* 46 (July–August 1954): 271–72.

319. _____. "Floods." *The Annals of the American Academy of Political and Social Science* 309 (January 1957): 15–22.

320. Sultan, Dan I. "The Nicaragua Canal Survey." *The Coast Artillery Journal* 74 (January 1931): 28–32.

321. Swan, Carroll J. *My Company.* Boston: Houghton Mifflin, 1918.

322. Swan, Guy C., III, Kenneth S. McGraw, Edward K. Wood, Ronald Walters, and John Burchstead. "Scott's Engineers." *Military Review* 63 (March 1983): 61–69.

323. Swift, Joseph Gardner. *Memoirs.* Edited by Harrison Ellery. Worcester, Mass.: F. S. Blanchard & Company, 1890.

324. Symons, Thomas W. "The Army and the Exploration of the West." *Journal of the Military Service Institution of the United States* 4 (September 1883): 205–49.

325. Talbot, Theodore. *Soldier in the West: Letters of Theodore Talbot during His Service in California, Mexico, and Oregon, 1845–53.* Norman: University of Oklahoma Press, 1972.

326. Tarbox, Robert M. "Military Construction in the Middle East." *The Military Engineer* 46 (January–February 1954): 17–19.

327. Tatum, Howell. *Major Howell Tatum's Journal while Acting Topographical Engineer (1814) to General Jackson.* Edited by John Spencer Bassett. Northampton, Mass.: Department of History of Smith College, 1922.

328. Taylor, Emerson Gifford. *Gouverneur Kemble Warren: The Life and Letters of an American Soldier, 1830–1882.* Boston: Houghton Mifflin, 1932.

329. Thayer, Sylvanus. *The West Point Thayer Papers, 1808–1872.* Edited by Cindy Adams. 11 vols. West Point, N.Y.: Association of Graduates, 1965.

330. Thienel, Phillip M. "Engineers in the Union Army, 1861–1865." *The Military Engineer* 47 (January–February 1955): 36–41; (March–April 1955): 110–15.

331. Thompson, Gilbert. *The Engineer Battalion in the Civil War: A Contribution to the History of the United States Engineers, Engineer School Occasional Paper no. 44.* Washington, D.C.: Press of the Engineer School, 1910.

332. Thompson, Paul W. *What the Citizen Should Know about the Army Engineers.* New York: W. W. Norton, 1942.

333. Timothy, Patrick Henry. *The Rhine Crossing: Twelfth Army Group Engineer Operations.* Fort Belvoir, Va.: Engineer School, 1946.

334. Tittman, O. H., et al. "Memoir of Bernard Richardson Green." *Transactions of the American Society of Civil Engineers* 80 (1916): 2151–56.

335. Tomlin, Robert K. *American Engineers behind the Battle Lines of France.* New York: McGraw-Hill, 1918.

336. Tracy, Evarts. "Memoranda on the Camouflage Service of the United States Army." *Professional Memoirs, Corps of Engineers, United States Army and Engineer Department at Large* 9 (March–April 1919): 175–84.

337. Trumbull, John. *Autobiography, Reminiscences and Letters of John Trumbull, 1756–1841.* New York: Wiley & Putnam, 1841.

338. Tulley, David H. "The Military Construction Program." *The Military Engineer* 46 (November–December 1954): 403–8.

339. U.S. American Expeditionary Force, Chief Engineer. *Historical Report of the Chief Engineer including All Operations of the Engineer Department, American Expeditionary Force, 1917–1919.* Washington, D.C.: GPO, 1919.

340. U.S. Army, Corps of Engineers. *Annual Reports of the Chief of Engineers, U.S. Army.* Washington, D.C.: GPO, 1866–.

341. _____. *Final Report on Removing the Wreck of the Battleship "Maine" from the Harbor of Havana, Cuba, House Document no. 480.* 63d Congress, 2d Session. Washington, D.C.: GPO, 1914.

342. _____. *History of the Washington Aqueduct.* Written by Philip O. Macqueen. Washington, D.C.: Washington District, Corps of Engineers, 1953.

343. _____. *The Hopper Dredge: Its History, Development and Operation.* Prepared by the Office of the Chief of Engineers under the direction of the Hopper Dredge Board. Washington, D.C.: GPO, 1954.

344. _____. *Index to the Reports of the Chief of Engineers, U.S. Army, 1866–1917.* 3 vols. Washington, D.C.: GPO, 1915–1921.

345. _____. *Water Resources Development by the U.S. Army Corps of Engineers.* 50 vols. Washington, D.C.: U.S. Army Engineer Divisons, 1979.

346. _____, Public Affairs Office. *The Corps in Perspective.* Rev. ed. Washington, D.C.: GPO, 1984.

347. U.S. Army, European Theater of Operations. *Final Report of the Chief Engineer, European Theater of Operations, 1942–1945.* 2 vols. Paris: Hervé et Fils, 1945.

348. U.S. Army, Third Engineers, Volunteer, comp. *David DuBose Gaillard, A Memorial.* St. Louis, Mo.: Third United States Volunteer Engineers, 1916.

349. U.S. Board on Fortifications or Other Defenses. *Report of the Board on Fortifications or Other Defenses Appointed by the President of the United States under the Provisions of the Act of Congress Approved March 3, 1885---, House Executive Document no. 49.* 49th Congress, 1st Session, 2 vols. Washington, D.C.: GPO, 1886.

350. U.S. Engineer School. *The Army Engineer in Vietnam.* Rev. Ed. Fort Belvoir, VA.: Engineer School, 1968.

351. _____. *Historical Papers Relating to the Corps of Engineers and to Engineer Troops in U.S. Army, Engineer School Occasional Paper no. 16.* Washington, D.C.: Press of the Engineer School, 1904.

352. _____. *History and Traditions of the Corps of Engineers, Engineer School ROTC Text ST25-1.* Fort Belvoir, Va.: Engineer School, 1953.

353. _____. *List of Publications Printed by the Battalion Press, Willet's Point, New York Harbor, and by the Engineer School Press, Washington Barracks, D.C., Engineer School Occasional Paper no. 43.* Washington, D.C.: Press of the Engineer School, 1910.

354. _____. *Stations of Engineer Units, Regular Army, 1846–1937*, Engineer School Occasional Paper no. 70. Washington, D.C.: GPO, 1938.

355. _____, *World War Service of Officers and Former Officers of the Corps of Engineers, Regular Army. Engineer School Occasional Papers no. 68.* Compiled by the office of the Chief of Engineers. Washington, D.C.: GPO, 1938.

356. _____, Library. *Civil Work: A Selected List.* 2d ed. Fort Belvoir, Va.: Engineer School, 1951.

357. _____, Library. *The Mississippi River and Valley: Bibliography Mostly Non-Technical.* Compiled by Henry E. Haferkorn. Fort Humphreys, Va.: Engineer School, 1931.

358. _____, Museum. *Geneses of the Corps of Engineers.* Fort Belvoir, Va.: Engineer Museum, 1953.

359. U.S. Laws Statutes, etc. *Laws of the United States Relating to the Improvements of Rivers and Harbors.* Compiled in the Office of the Chief of Engineers. 4 vols. Washington, D.C.: GPO, 1940–68.

360. U.S. National Coast Defense Board. *Report of the National Coast Defense Board---on the Coast Defenses of the Untied States and the Insular Possessions, Senate Document no. 248.* 9th Congress, 1st Session. Washington, D.C.: GPO, 1906.

361. U.S. Office of the Chief of Engineers, General Headquarters, Army Forces, Pacific. *Engineers of the Southwest Pacific, 1941–1945.* 8 vols. Washington, D.C.: GPO, 1947-.

362. U.S. Public Building Service. *Executive Office Building.* Rev. ed. Washington, D.C.: GPO, 1970.

363. U.S. Superintendent of Documents. *Reports of Explorations Printed in the Documents of the United States.* Compiled by Adelaide R. Hasse. Washington, D.C.: GPO, 1899.

364. U.S. Treasury Department. *Statement of Appropriations and Expenditures for Public Building, Rivers and Harbors, Forts, Arsenals, Armories and Other Public Works from March 4 1789, to June 30, 1882, Senate Executive Document no. 196.* 47th Congress, 1st Session. Washington, D.C.: GPO, 1882.

365. Van Ornum, John L., and Lyle F. Bellinger. "Work of the Third Regiment, U.S. Volunteer Engineers in Cuba." *Engineering News and American Railway Journal* 41 (22 June, 1899): 400–401.
366. Verburg, Edwin Arnold. "The U.S. Army Corps of Engineers Recreation Development Program: A Comparative Perspective of Equity Related to Policies and Program Outcome." Unpublished Ph.D. diss., George Washington University, 1975.
367. Vogel, Herbert D. "Engineer Buttons and Castle." *The Military Engineer* 33 (March–April 1941): 103–4.
368. Vose, George L. *A Sketch of the Life and Works of George W. Whistler, Civil Engineer.* Boston: Lee and Shepard, 1887.
369. Wade, Arthur P. "Artillerists and Engineers: The Beginnings of American Seacoast Fortifications, 1794–1815." Unpublished Ph.D. diss., Kansas State University, 1977.
370. "The Defenses of Portsmouth Harbor, 1794–1821: The First and Second Systems of Seacoast Fortification." *Historical New Hampshire* (Spring 1978): 25–51.
371. Wagner, Frederick. *Submarine Fighter of the American Revolution: The Story of David Bushnell.* New York: Dodd, Mead, 1963.
372. Walker, Alden D., ed. *GLD [Great Lakes Division] in World War II.* Chicago: U.S. Army Corps of Engineers, 1946.
373. Walker, Charles E. "The Other Good Guys: Army Engineers in the War of 1812." *The Military Engineer* 70 (May–June 1978): 178–83.
374. Walker, Paul K. "Building American Canals." Water Spectrum 12 (Winter 1979–80): 18–25; (Summer 1980): 12–23.
375. _____. *The Corps Responds: A History of the Susquehanna Engineer District and Tropical Storm Agnes.* Baltimore, Md.: U.S. Army Engineer District, Baltimore Corps of Engineers, 1976.
376. _____. "Developing Hydropower: The Role of the Corps of Engineers, 1900–1980." In *Waterpower '81: An International Conference on Hydropower, Conference Proceedings.* Washington, D.C.: GPO, 1981.
377. _____. "An Engineering Victory: The Siege of Yorktown, 1781." *The Military Engineer* 73 (September–October 1981): 334–37.
378. _____. *Engineers of Independence: A Documentary History of the Army Engineers in the American Revolution, 1775–1783.* Washington, D.C.: GPO, 1981.
379. Wall, John Furman. "The Civil Works of the United States Army Corps of Engineers: Program Modernization." 2 vols. Unpublished Ph.D. diss., Cornell University, 1973.
380. Warner, Henry. "The Battalion of Engineers, United States Army." *United Service* n.s. 15 (May 1896): 420–26.
381. Waugh, Richard G., and Judith M. Hourigan. *A History of the Board of Engineers for Rivers and Harbors.* Fort Belvoir, Va.: Board of Engineers for Rivers and Harbors, 1980.
382. Weart, D. L. "Erection of the Washington Monument." *The Military Engineer* 15 (March –April 1923): 99–102.
383. Webb, Lester A. *Captain Alden Partridge and the United States Military Academy, 1806–1833.* Northport, Ala.: American Southern, 1965.
384. Weigley, Russell F. *Quartermaster General of the Union Army: A*

Biography of M. C. Meigs. New York: Columbia University Press, 1959.

385. Weinert, Richard P., Jr., and Robert Arthur. *Defender of the Chesapeake: The Story of Fort Monroe*. Annapolis, Md.: Leeward Publications, 1978.

386. Weller, Steven. "Public Policy as Law in Action: The Implementation of the National Environmental Act of 1969 by the U.S. Army Corps of Engineers." Unpublished Ph.D. diss., Cornell University, 1979.

387. Welling, Alvin C. "Constructing Missile Bases." *Army Information Digest* 16 (April 1961): 40–47.

388. Werner, Robert R., and John F. Wall. "The Army Corps of Engineers and NEPA." *The Military Engineer* 66 (March-April 1974): 111–13.

389. Wesley, Edgar B. "The Beginnings of Coast Fortifications." *The Coast Artillery Journal* 67 (October 1927): 281–90.

390. West, Austin Ward, Jr. "A Diachronic Analysis of the Forced Relocation of Rexford, Montana, by the Libbey Dam." Unpublished M.A. thesis, University of Idaho, 1979.

391. Westover, John G. *Combat Support in Korea: The United States Army in the Korean Conflict*. Washington, D.C.: Combat Forces Press, 1955.

392. Whaley, Elizabeth J. *Forgotten Hero: General James B. McPherson, The Biography of a Civil War General*. New York: Exposition Press, 1955.

393. Whitman, Robert P. "Two Years in the Pacific Area." *Radford Review* 2 (November 1948): 23–26.

394. Wilkens, Thurman. *Clarence King: A Biography*. New York: Macmillan, 1958.

395. Willar, William R., Jr. "Combat Engineers in Vietnam: The First Year." *The Engineer* 1 (Fall 1971): 23–25.

396. Williams, Thomas Harry. *P.G.T. Beauregard: Napoleon in Gray*. Baton Rouge: Louisiana State University Press, 1954.

397. Williams, Tom. "The Army's Map Makers." *Soldiers* 37 (August 1982): 44–47.

398. Willing, Wildurr. "The Engineers and the Mexican War." *Professional Memoirs, Corps of Engineers, U.S. Army* 7 (May–June 1915): 333–56.

399. Wilson, Drake. "Endangered Species and the U.S. Army Corps of Engineers." *Frontiers* 41 (Summer 1977): 37–38.

400. Wilson, W. K. "Overseas Military Construction." *The Military Engineer* 50 (September–October 1958): 329–31.

401. Winslow, Eben E. *Notes on Seacoast Fortification Construction, Engineer School Occasional Paper no. 61*. Washington, D.C.: GPO, 1920.

402. Wisner, George Y. "Worthless Government Engineering: A Rejoinder." *Engineering Magazine* 2 (March 1892): 743–52.

403. Wood, Eleazer D. *Journal of the Northwestern Campaign of 1812-1813 under Major-General William H. Harrison*. Annotated and indexed by Robert B. Boehm and Randall L. Buchman. Defiance, Ohio: The Defiance College Press, 1975.

404. Wood, Lance D., and John R. Hill, Jr. "Wetlands Protection: The Regulatory Role of the U.S. Army Corps of Engineers." *Coastal Zone Management Journal* 4, no. 4 (1978): 371–407.

405. Wood, Richard G. "Construction of the Louisville and Paducah Marine Hospitals." *Register of the Kentucky Historical Society* 56 (January 1858): 27–32.

406. _____. "The Marine Hospital at Napoleon." *Arkansas Historical Quarterly* 14 (Spring 1955): 38–42.
407. _____. *Stephen Harriman Long, 1784–1864: Army Engineer, Explorer, Inventor.* Glendale, Calif.: Arthur H. Clark Company, 1966.
408. Woodman, Lyman L. "Captain Raymond Explores the Yukon." *Water Spectrum* 7 (Summer 1975): 1–10.
409. Wooten, William P. *The Provisional Battalion of Engineers in the Philippines, Engineer, School Occasional Paper no. 42.* Washington, D.C.: Press of the Engineer School, 1910.
410. "Yesterday [The Engineer Museum]." *Engineer* 1 (Spring 1971): 14–17.
411. Young, Rogers W. "The Construction of Fort Pulaski." *Georgia Historical Quarterly* 20 (March 1936): 41–51.
412. Youngberg, G. A. *History of Engineer Troops in the United States Army, 1775–1901, Engineer School Occasional Paper no. 37.* Washington, D.C.: Press of the Engineer School, 1910.
413. Zarish, Joseph M. *The Collapse of the Remagen Bridge.* New York: Vantage Press, 1967.

FIELD OPERATING ACTIVITIES HISTORIES
414. Alaska District. *History of the Alaska District, U.S. Army Corps of Engineers, 1946–1974.* By William A. Jacobs and Lyman L. Woodman. Alaska: U.S. Army Corps of Engineers, 1976.
415. Albuquerque District. *The First Thirty-Six Years: A History of the Albuquerque District, 1935–1971.* By Nathan J. Sewell. Albuquerque, N. Mex.: U.S. Army Corps of Engineers, 1973.
416. Baltimore District. *The Mid-Atlantic Engineers: A History of the Baltimore District of the U.S. Army Corps of Engineers, 1794–1974.* By Harold K. Kanarek. Baltimore, Md.: U.S. Army Corps of Engineers, 1978.
417. Buffalo District. *Engineers for the Public Good: A History of the Buffalo District, U.S. Army Corps of Engineers.* By Nuala Drescher. Buffalo, N.Y.: U.S. Army Corps of Engineers, 1982.
418. Canaveral District. *History of the Canaveral District, 1950– 1971.* Atlanta, Ga.: U.S. Army Corps of Engineers, 1971.
419. California Debris Commission. *The California Debris Commission: A History.* By Joseph J. Hagwood, Jr. San Francisco: U.S. Army Corps of Engineers, 1981.
420. Charleston District. *The Lowcountry Engineers: Military Missions and Economic Development in the Charleston District, U.S. Army Corps of Engineers.* By Jamie W. Moore. Washington, D.C.: GPO, 1982.
421. Chicago District. *Those Army Engineers: A History of the Chicago District, U.S. Army Corps of Engineers.* By John W. Larson. Washington, D.C.: GPO, 1980.
422. Coastal Engineer Research Center. *The History of the Beach Erosion Board, U.S. Army Corps of Engineers, 1930–1963.* By Mary-Louise Quinn. Fort Belvoir, Va.: Coastal Engineering Research Center, 1977.
423. Construction Engineering Research Laboratory. *A History of the Construction Engineering Research Laboratory, 1968–1974.* By Gary A. Stellar. Champaign, Ill.: U.S. Army Corps of Engineers, 1975.

424. Detroit District. *Essayons: A History of the Detroit District, U.S. Army Corps of Engineers.* By John W. Larson. Washington, D.C.: GPO, 1981.
425. Engineer Topographic Laboratories. *History of the U.S. Army Engineer Topographic Laboratories, 1920-1970.* By John T. Pennington. Fort Belvoir, Va.: U.S. Army Engineer Topographic Laboratories, 1973.
426. _____. *ETL History Update, 1968-1978.* By Edward C. Ezell. Fort Belvoir, Va.: U.S. Army Engineer Topographic Laboratories, 1979.
427. Far East District. *History of the United States Army Engineer District, Far East, 1957-1975.* By Earl Whitmore. Seoul, Korea: U.S. Army Corps of Engineers, 1976.
428. Fort Worth District. *Rivers, Rockets and Readiness: Army Engineers in the Sunbelt.* By D. Clayton Brown. Washington, D.C.: GPO, 1979.
429. Galveston District. *Custodians of the Coast: History of the United States Army Engineers at Galveston.* By Lynn M. Alperin. Galveston, Tex.: U.S. Army Corps of Engineers, 1977.
430. Honolulu District. *History of the Honolulu Engineer District, 1905-1965.* By Ellen van Hoften. Honolulu: U.S. Army Corps of Engineers, 1970.
431. Huntington District. *Men, Mountains and Rivers: An Illustrated History of the Huntington District, U.S. Army Corps of Engineers, 1754-1974.* By Leland R. Johnson. Washington, D.C.: GPO, 1977.
432. Huntsville Division. *A History of the Huntsville Division, 15 October 1967-31 December 1976.* By James H. Kitchens. Huntsville, Ala.: U.S. Army Corps of Engineers, 1978.
433. Jacksonville District. *Sun, Sand, and Water: A History of the Jacksonville District, U.S. Army Corps of Engineers, 1821-1975.* By George E. Buker. Jacksonville, Fla.: U.S. Army Corps of Engineers, 1981.
434. Kansas City District. *Taming the Mighty Missouri: A History of the Kansas City District, Corps of Engineers, 1901-1971.* By Robert L. Branyan. Kansas City, Mo.: U.S. Army Corps of Engineers, 1974.
435. Little Rock District. *A History of the Little Rock District, U.S. Army Corps of Engineers, 1881-1979.* By Floyd M. Clay. Little Rock, Ark.: U.S. Army Corps of Engineers, 1971.
436. Los Angeles District. *A History of the Los Angeles District, U.S. Army Corps of Engineers, 1898-1965.* By Anthony F. Turhollow. Los Angeles: U.S. Army Corps of Engineers, 1975.
437. Louisville District. *The Falls City Engineers: A History of the Louisville District, Corps of Engineers, United States Army.* By Leland R. Johnson. Louisville, Ky.: U.S. Army Corps of Engineers, 1975.
438. Memphis District. *Army Engineers in Memphis District: A Documentary Chronicle.* Edited and with an introduction by Martin Reuss. Memphis, Tenn.: Memphis District, United Sates Army Corps of Engineers, 1982.
439. _____. *A Century of the Mississippi: A History of the Memphis District, U.S. Army Corps of Engineers.* By Floyd M. Clay. Memphis, Tenn.: U.S. Army Corps of Engineers, 1976.
440. Mississippi River Commission. *Improvements of the Lower Mississippi River and Tributaries, 1931-1972.* By Norman R. Moore. Vicksburg, Miss.: U.S. Army Corps of Engineers, 1972.
441. Mobile District. *A History of the Mobile District, 1815-1971.* By Virgil S. Davis. Mobile, Ala.: U.S. Army Corps of Engineers, 1975.

442. Nashville District. *Engineers on the Twin Rivers: A History of Nashville District, Corps of Engineers, United States Army.* By Leland R. Johnson. Nashville, Tenn.: U.S. Army Corps of Engineers, 1978.

443. New England Divison. *Army Engineers in New England: The Military and Civil Work of the Corps of Engineers in New England, 1775-1975,* By Aubrey Parkman. Waltham, Mass.: U.S. Army Corps of Engineers, 1978.

444. New Orleans District. *Lands End.* By Albert E. Cowdrey. New Orleans, La.: U.S. Army Corps of Engineers, 1977.

445. New York District. *Cradle of the Corps: A History of the New York District, U.S. Army Corps of Engineers, 1775-1975.* By Marion J. Klawonn. New York: U.S. Army Corps of Engineers, 1977.

446. North Atlantic Division. *The North Atlantic Engineers: A History of the North Atlantic Division and Its Predecessors in the U.S. Army Corps of Engineers, 1775-1975.* By John Whiteclay Chambers II. New York: U.S. Army Corps of Engineers, 1980.

447. North Pacific Division. *The History of the North Pacific Division, U.S. Army Corps of Engineers, 1888-1965.* By Roy W. Scheufele. Portland, Oreg.: U.S. Army Corps of Engineers, 1969.

448. Nuclear Cratering Group. *History of the U.S. Army Engineer Nuclear Cratering Group.* By Bernard C. Hughes. Livermore, Calif.: U.S. Army Corps of Engineers, 1969.

449. Pacific Ocean Division. *History of the Pacific Ocean Division, Corps of Engineers, 1957-1967.* By Ellen van Hoften. Honolulu: U.S. Army Corps of Engineers, 1972.

450. Philadelphia District. *The District: A History of the Philadelphia District, U.S. Army Corps of Engineers 1866-1971.* By Frank E. Snyder and Brain H. Guss. Philadelphia, Pa.: U.S. Army Corps of Engineers, 1974.

451. Pittsburgh District. *The Headwaters District: A History of the Pittsburgh District, U.S. Army Corps of Engineers.* By Leland R. Johnson. Pittsburgh, Pa.: U.S. Army Corps of Engineers, 1979.

452. Portland District. *The History of the Portland District, Corps of Engineers 1871-1969.* By Henry R. Richmond. Portland, Maine: U.S. Army Corps of Engineers, 1970.

453. Rock Island District. *A History of the Rock Island District, Corps of Engineers.* By Ronald Tweet. Rock Island, Ill.: U.S. Army Corps of Engineers, 1975.

454. Sacramento District. *Commitment to Excellence: A History of the Sacramento District, U.S. Army Corps of Engineers, 1929-1973.* By Joseph Jerimiah Hagwood, Jr. Sacramento, Calif.: U.S. Army Corps of Engineers, 1976.

455. St. Louis District. *River Engineers of the Middle Mississippi.* By Frederick J. Dobney. Washington, D.C.: GPO, 1978.

456. St. Paul District. *Creativity, Conflict, & Controversy: A History of the St. Paul District, U.S. Army Corps of Engineers.* By Raymond H. Merritt. Washington, D.C.: GPO, 1979.

457. San Francisco District. *Engineers at the Golden Gate.* By Joseph Jerimiah Hagwood, Jr. San Francisco, Calif.: U.S. Army Corps of Engineers, 1981.

458. Savannah District. *History of the Savannah District, 1829-1968.* By Mary L. Granger. Savannah, Ga.: U.S. Army Corps of Engineers, 1968.

459. Seattle District. *History of the Seattle District, 1896–1968.* By Sherman Green. Seattle, Wash.: U.S. Army Corps of Engineers, 1969.

460. Susquehanna District. *The Corps Responds: A History of the Susquehanna Engineer District and Tropical Storm Agnes.* By Paul K. Walker. Baltimore, Md.: U.S. Army Corps of Engineers, 1976.

461. Tulsa District. *The Dawning, A New Day for the Southwest: A History of the Tulsa District, Corps of Engineers, 1939–1971.* By William A. Settle, Jr. Tulsa, Okla.: U.S. Army Corps of Engineers, 1975.

462. Vicksburg District. *Of Men & Rivers: The Story of the Vicksburg District.* By Gary B. Mills. Washington, D.C.: GPO, 1978.

463. Walla Walla District. *A History of the Walla Walla District, 1948–1970.* By Howard Preston. Walla Walla, Wash.: U.S. Army Corps of Engineers, 1974.

464. _____. *Walla Walla District History, Part II, 1970–1975.* By Howard Preston. Walla Walla, Wash.: U.S. Army Corps of Engineers, n.d.

465. Waterways Experiment Station. *History of the Waterways Experiment Station.* Edited by Joseph B. Tiffany. Vicksburg, Miss.: U.S. Army Corps of Engineers, 1968.

466. Waterways Experiment Station. *A History of the Waterways Experiment Station, 1929–1979.* By Gordon A. Cotton. Vicksburg, Miss.: U.S. Army Corps of Engineers, 1979.